Perception and Cognition at Century's End

Handbook of Perception and Cognition

2nd Edition

Series Editors
Edward C. Carterette
and **Morton P. Friedman**

Perception and Cognition at Century's End

Edited by
Julian Hochberg

Department of Psychology
Columbia University
New York, New York

Academic Press

San Diego   London   Boston
New York   Sydney   Tokyo   Toronto

This book is printed on acid-free paper. ∞

Academic Press
a division of Harcourt Brace & Company
525 B Street, Suite 1900, San Diego, California 92101-4495, USA
http://www.apnet.com

Academic Press Limited
24-28 Oval Road, London NW1 7DX, UK
http://www.hbuk.co.uk/ap/

Library of Congress Catalog Card Number: 98-84439

International Standard Book Number: 0-12-301160-4

PRINTED IN THE UNITED STATES OF AMERICA
98 99 00 01 02 03 EB 9 8 7 6 5 4 3 2 1

Contents

Roots and Persisting Issues

1 *A Context for the Second Half of the Century:*
One View

Julian Hochberg

The Informed Present:
Where We Are and How We Got There
A. Outside to Inside: Approaches Concerned Chiefly with Measurable Variables of Stimulus Information and Their Cognitive Consequences (Chapters 4–10)
B. Approaches Concerned with the Individual's Past and Present Cognitive Abilities (Chapters 11–14)

6   *Pictures and Their Special Status in Perceptual and Cognitive Inquiry*

James E. Cutting and Manfredo Massironi

7   *The Internalization of Perceptual Processing Constraints*

Dennis R. Proffitt and Mary K. Kaiser

8 *A Century of Human Information-Processing Theory:*
    Vision, Attention, and Memory

Barbara Anne Dosher and George Sperling

11 *Nature, Nurture, and Development*

Elizabeth S. Spelke

12 *Language and Action: Current Challenges*

Charles E. Wright and Barbara Landau

13 *Concepts and Categorization*

Douglas L. Medin and John D. Coley

14 *Imagery, Visualization, and Thinking*

P. N. Johnson-Laird

Contributors

John D. Coley (403)
Department of Psychology
Northwestern University
Evanston, Illinois 60208

James E. Cutting (69, 137)
Department of Psychology
Cornell University
Ithaca, New York 14853

Barbara Anne Dosher (199)
Department of Cognitive Sciences
and Institute of Mathematical Behavioral
   Science
University of California
Irvine, California 92697

Barbara J. Gillam (95)
Department of Psychology
University of New South Wales
Kensington
New South Wales 2052
Australia

Julian Hochberg (3, 253)
Department of Psychology
Columbia University
New York, New York 10027

P. N. Johnson-Laird (441)
Department of Psychology
Princeton University
Princeton, New Jersey 08544

Mary K. Kaiser (169)
NASA–Ames Research Center
Moffett Field, California 94035

Barbara Landau (373)
Department of Psychology
University of Delaware
Newark, Delaware 19716

George Mandler (45)
Center for Human Information Processing
University of California, San Diego
La Jolla, California 92093
and University College
London WC1E 6BT
United Kingdom

Manfredo Massironi (137)
Istituto di Psicologia
Università di Verona
37129 Verona
Italy

Douglas L. Medin (403)
Department of Psychology
Northwestern University
Evanston, Illinois 60208

Ken Nakayama (307)
Department of Psychology
Harvard University
Cambridge, Massachusetts 02138

Dennis R. Proffitt (169)
Department of Psychology
University of Virginia
Charlottesville, Virginia 22903

Mark Rollins (23)
Department of Philosophy
Philosophy–Neuroscience–Psychology
   Program

Washington University
St. Louis, Missouri 63130

Elizabeth S. Spelke (333)
Department of Psychology
Massachusetts Institute of Technology
Cambridge, Massachusetts 02139

George Sperling (199)
Departments of Cognitive Sciences and
   Psychobiology
and Institute of Mathematical Behavioral
   Science
University of California
Irvine, California 92697

Charles E. Wright (373)
Department of Cognitive Sciences
University of California
Irvine, California 92697

Foreword

The problem of perception and cognition is in understanding how the organism transforms, organizes, stores, and uses information arising from the world in sense data or memory. With this definition of perception and cognition in mind, this handbook is designed to bring together the essential aspects of this very large, diverse, and scattered literature and to give a précis of the state of knowledge in every area of perception and cognition. The work is aimed at the psychologist and the cognitive scientist in particular, and at the natural scientist in general. Topics are covered in comprehensive surveys in which fundamental facts and concepts are presented, and important leads to journals and monographs of the specialized literature are provided. Perception and cognition are considered in the widest sense. Therefore, the work treats a wide range of experimental and theoretical work.

The *Handbook of Perception and Cognition* should serve as a basic source and reference work for those in the arts or sciences, indeed for all who are interested in human perception, action, and cognition.

Edward C. Carterette and Morton P. Friedman

Preface

Addressing major themes in the psychology of perception and cognition, this volume attempts to give the past relevance as a context for the present and to make the state of present concerns more substantial and less accidental by setting them responsibly in that context. It is intended to help bring faculty up to date in areas that are not their specialty and to provide a resource for general graduate courses and very advanced undergraduate seminars.

Although many of the chapters in this volume overlap somewhat so that they can be read independent of each other, they form a hierarchical pattern that encompasses most, but not all, major fields of current concern. In all chapters, what history is given is written not by historians but by researchers who are engaged in current issues and who, in each case, address at least the second half of this century.

Part I (Chapters 1–3) deals with early roots and philosophical context. Part II (the remainder of the volume) addresses where we are now and how we got here, reviewing major continuing concerns in their historical context over the past several decades.

In part I, Chapter 1 (Hochberg) relates the *first* half-century and its context from the viewpoint of one who learned the field while the period was ending, providing a brief prelude to the rest of the volume. Chapter 2 (Rollins) surveys how philosophers have analyzed and elaborated recent cognitive science, with mental representation as his central focus. In Chapter 3, Mandler discusses how philosophers and cognitive psychologists have used conceptions of consciousness and mind since the cognitive revolution of the 1950s made such terms permissable.

Part IIA (Chapters 4–10) is concerned chiefly with how measurable variables of sensory stimulus information support correct and incorrect perception and knowledge about the environment of objects, surfaces, and events.

In Chapter 4, Cutting addresses the implementations and antecedents of the concept *information* in the study of perception and cognition, within three major frameworks (personal experience, mathematical constraints, and biological expediency). Chapter 5 (Gillam) provides a review of illusions, in which attributes of the world are incorrectly perceived, and of the explanations previously and currently offered. Chapter 6 (Cutting & Massironi) discusses how pictures, particularly those built of lines, differ drastically from the objects and scenes that they successfully represent, thereby providing experiments in perception and cognition.

The next four chapters in this section are more concerned with the *processes* that underlie perceptual and cognitive phenomena. Chapter 7 (Proffitt & Kaiser) discusses why it is often held that the physical constraints normal to the perceptual ecology are internalized by the perceiver and what processes are proposed for that purpose. In Chapter 8, Dosher and Sperling point out how process-oriented theories, quite accurate in their quantitative account of experimental data, mark the end of the century, and they provide explicit examples of a wide range of such processes critically important to the fields of vision, attention, and memory. Chapter 9 (Hochberg) first describes the Gestaltists' proposal to replace classical pointwise sensory analysis with an account of unified configuration-determined physiological processes, using arguments based largely on apparent motion and a host of pictorial phenomena, and then surveys how differently such organizational phenomena now appear in view of current knowledge about eye and brain and current studies of attention, recognition, and imaging. Chapter 10 (Nakayama), in order to discuss how the brain as a physical object might provide us with perceptual experience, reviews the major developments in neuroscience and related efforts, assessing limitations and prospects in each field of endeavor.

The chapters in part IIB (Chapters 11–14) are increasingly concerned with topics more cognitive than perceptual. (Although historically the term perception refers to a subset of cognition, the latter now usually implies postperceptual processes.)

In Chapter 11, Spelke tracks the empirical progress made in the study of cognitive development, focusing first on one strongly perceptual topic (space perception), then on a borderline topic (object perception and representation), and finally on one clearly cognitive topic (number), and argues that there are multiple different systems of representation or knowledge in each case. In Chapter 12, Wright and Landau examine what has become of the problem of temporal integration in skilled action sequences, linguistic and otherwise, as raised by Lashley and by Chomsky in the 1950s against the then-prevalent S-R chains, and find that neither a connectionist nor a symbolic (schema-based) approach has successfully replaced the other. Chapter 13 (Medin & Coley) is concerned with concepts and categorization, central to cognitive activities, and with past, present, and probable future research and theories; these have undergone several successive and major changes in the last few decades and are undergoing more. Finally, in Chapter 14, Johnson-Laird reviews writings and research on imagery, on rule-based versus model-based reasoning, and on the theoretical and experimental distinction between mental models and images in reasoning, thereby offering "a rehabilitation of imagery in the face of the skeptics, but a limitation on imagery in the face of its more ardent adherents."

Various aspects of images or internal representations are discussed at length in Chapters 2, 4, 9, and 14, but there is no chapter devoted to that topic alone. Memory and signal detection are found only in Chapter 8, and decision theory is not presented in this volume.

I thank James Cutting for his early assistance in designing and assembling this volume, and all of the contributors for their efforts to conform to what was necessarily a contingent design.

Roots and Persisting Issues

A Context for the Second Half of the Century

One View

Julian Hochberg

I. PURPOSES AND SUBSTANCE OF THIS VOLUME

A. Goals

The purpose of this volume is to describe several major fields of perceptual and cognitive psychology over the past five decades, and where they now stand. These chapters cannot, of course, cover all subdisciplines, but we have tried to include those that retain contact with earlier questions and that remain active at the century's end. The present chapter describes major premises and promises on which the psychology of perception and cognition had been based at midcentury and served as the context for the second half-century.

B. Perception and Cognition in Scientific Psychology

As late as 1950, mainstream experimental psychology seemed about to take its place within a single continuous fabric of science, using the same fundamental units of measurement and an operationalist account that would run seamlessly from the subatomic to the behavioral (e.g., Brunswik, 1955; Feigel, 1949). If that approach were really viable, most new research would relate to that overall matrix of knowledge. In reality, however, the unification evaporated around midcentury, and many popular and intensely pursued lines of inquiry have since faded.

In the last few years, although some scars still show from earlier battles, and some irredentist agendas remain dimly visible, I believe a new unity of discourse, and

Perception and Cognition at Century's End

hence of purpose, is in sight. Much has changed (including the definitions of the words *perception* and *cognition;* see pp. 11ff), so a context for the transition period may be particularly useful.

II. AN HISTORICAL CONTEXT

The disciplined discussion of cognition was originally embedded in philosophy, and the fields retain mutual interests (see Rollins, Mandler, this volume). The present chapter only touches on those aspects of cognitive theory in the history of philosophy that are most relevant to this volume.

Taken broadly enough, the present context can be discerned in the distant past. Thus, Socrates got his listener (Cornford, 1957) to agree that depth is not seen but inferred. More extensively and effectively, Aristotle laid out much of the framework within which psychology is still considered.[1]

Issues of current concern continued to appear over the intervening centuries, mostly in the context of art and medicine, but modern discussion of perception and cognition emerged in the middle of the 17th century, as it did in most sciences.

A. The Early Modern Context

1. Descartes's Two Lines

As a part of the major intellectual activity in the 17th and 18th centuries, and in line with the search for God's laws through studying nature, Descartes (1650/1931) accounted for the apparently sentient behavior of animals without mind or soul by means of the reflex arc, one basis of robotics: This was a continuous sequence of physical causes and effect, from physical stimulus energies through inward-directed (sensory) nerves, to a central connecting network and then outward-directed (motor) nerves ending in a muscular event.

As part of the response to challenges to canon law, to rapidly changing economies, and to the growing effects of the printing press, came a strong concern as to what we can know and how we can know that it is true. To Descartes (1664/1824), ideas were not part of the physical machinery of the reflex arc, but were the privilege of the human mind or soul, which interacts with that machine. We can know that an idea is true if we can derive it rigorously from a fundamental idea, one that cannot be argued, is itself innate, provided by God, and therefore necessarily true. This epistemological prescription was countered by the empiricist assertion (Hobbes, 1651/1994) that all knowledge is based on and must be tested against sensory experience. The contrast between approaches epitomized by Descartes and Hobbes set the opposed poles of the continuing debate.

---

[1] Although he did miss out on the idea of the brain as the organ of the mind, he defined the mind's functions as cognition, conation, and affection. He catalogued the senses and stated the laws of associative memory, much as they have survived over the centuries. He also recorded in detail the acceptable steps of deductive logical thinking.

Most of psychology three centuries later, around 1950, lay close to a combination of Descartes's reflex machine and a strongly Hobbesian rejection of his epistemological prescription. We consider them in order.

2. Fleshing Out the Cartesian Machine

Descartes outlined a physically continuous causal sequence of the input–output arc between physical stimulus and physical response. The input–output distinction became much firmer when Bell (1811/1948) and Magendie (1822) separated sensory input (or afferent) nerves from motor output (or efferent) nerves. But that itself does not account for the different kinds of sensation we can receive, nor for the different kinds of things we can perceive. That account was developed by Johannes Müller and by his student Hermann von Helmholtz and provided a substantial account of the sensory system by the mid-1800s.

a. Subdividing Sensory Input: Specific Nerve Energies and Specific Fiber Energies in the Modular Analysis of the World

In Johannes Müller's (1838) *law of specific nerve energies*, each class or *modality* of sensory experience (vision, hearing, touch, etc.) reflects the activity of a different and specific class of sensory nerves and their specialized receptors. Helmholtz, his student, undertook as the next step an analytic science that accounts for every sensory difference we can experience *within* each modality (Helmholtz, 1860/1924; 1863/1885). In vision, following Young (1802), he modeled all colors as resulting from the activities of only three kinds of retinal receptors. A visual nerve provides a visual sensation even when it is activated by other causes (Hobbes, 1651/1974; Müller, 1838); a visual nerve *fiber* that provides a sensation of "red" when activated by light of 640 nm (i.e., a "red" light) provides the same sensation when activated by any other wavelength, by an electrical pulse, and so on. Only by affecting at least one nerve fiber differently can two stimuli be sensed as different. And all sensory experience reduces to the combined contributions of the active nerve fibers. Thus, three kinds of wavelength receptors (cones) by their combinations provide all experienced colors (e.g., properly mixed, a light that evokes a red sensation and one that evokes a green sensation provide an experience of yellow; adding a "blue sensation," gives us white or any other color, depending on the mixture).[2]

---

[2] In vision, Newton (1704) had shown that daylight could be divided into a mix of different components (now wavelengths), each with its own color. Also shown was that a subset of those components, if properly chosen and balanced, could by themselves appear white or any other color. These demonstrations practically demanded the trichromatic theory proposed by Young (1802) (although not uniformly cheered throughout Europe: see Goethe, 1810/1970), which was quantitatively modeled by Helmholtz (1859). This proposal reduced all vision to the responses of three classes of cone cells (plus the chromatically undifferentiated rods), each like a separate sensory modality in that it would provide the same sensory experience regardless of what stimulus occasioned its activity. In *audition*, Galileo (1638/1948) had identified the physical basis of pitch as vibratory frequency; in the 1800s Fourier had developed the mathematics of reducing all waveforms to spectra of sine waves. Ohm (1843) held that

The goal was to account for all possible sensory experiences in terms of physical cause and effect (in neural events), and by the turn of the century that goal seemed within reach for the major senses (see Titchener, 1896, for a tally), initiating what became a related group of advanced and specialized sensory sciences.

i. Quantitative measures of sensory experience and response In sensory *psychophysics,* sophisticated quantitative methods for measuring detection and incremental thresholds were used to map the sensory system; to formulate equations for the amount of stimulus change needed to make a just noticeable difference (notably, the constant proportion law; Weber, 1846); and to make and test models of how the magnitude of sensory experience (loudness, brightness, etc.) varies with physical stimulus levels (Fechner, 1860/1912; for reviews written while these were the predominant research methods, see Guilford, 1936, and Woodworth, 1938).

The threshold-based Fechnerian scales were challenged in the 1940s by more direct scaling measures, in which subjects matched numbers to the magnitude experienced with each level of stimulation (Stevens, 1946), yielding surprisingly consistent power functions, and a procedure still in use (e.g., Baird & Noma, 1978; Marks, 1974). More recent methods model the decision entailed in the detection process (Luce, 1959; Tanner & Swets, 1954; see also Luce & Krumhansl, 1988).

Because many threshold-based methods required neither a description of the experience, nor indeed any assumptions about consciousness,[3] they were pursued virtually unhampered by the fashions of Introspectionism (section II.A.5) and Behaviorism (section III.C) that afflicted the first half of the 20th century.

ii. Two early and lasting caveats about the proposed sensory analysis There are two very serious and apparently different problems with relating these substantial bodies of sensory science to any account of perception or cognition.

First, as J. Clerk Maxwell (1861) noted, when the perception of yellow is obtained by supposedly combining sensations of red and green, self-observation utterly fails to reveal those components in conscious experience. In Hering's (1878/1964) color theory, and as explicitly mapped in the Hurvich and Jameson (1957) judgment-based testing and reframing of it (and in subsequent single-cell recording: DeValois & Jacobs, 1968), this is no surprise: a different analytic unit in the sensory chain (an opponent-process cell) is activated by the combined action of the relevant cones. That is, we cannot explain the appearance of combined inputs by explaining the separate experiences that obtain when each individual receptor is stimulated. This tells us that *the construction of perceptual experience does not proceed on the stage of consciousness.*

---

each component frequency could be discerned within any mixture or chord, and Helmholtz (1863) formulated the place theory of pitch, in which each discernible pair of frequencies revealed the different peak sensitivities of a pair of receptors in the basilar membrane.

[3] Indeed, many sensory scientists found acceptable only those tasks in which the observer must detect whether two stimuli differ. It is often thought that such data seem to need no assumptions about what is subjectively experienced and can in principle be obtained as well from animals and machines as from humans.

Second, these putative input channels of sensory analysis simply do not explain or even address our perceptions of the world—objects, surfaces, people, and events. Such synthesis requires a totally different class of explanation, for which one is referred upstream in the Cartesian arc and which I discuss next as the central associative processes.

b. Synthesis through Association

To the Hobbesian empiricist, all ideas are either sense data or are associative combinations of such simple ideas (memories of sense data) as they co-occurred in the past.

Thus, one can have no idea of a colorless cat, because our visual idea of any individual cat must be composed of local sense data, necessarily of some color (Berkeley, 1710/1957). (This question of the relationship between explicit sensory imagery and ideational content, in memory and thought, is still with us; see chapters 2, 3, 9, 13, 14, this volume). And since each point in vision can offer only a sensation of color and no information about distance, our ideas about spatial structure and distances in the world cannot possibly be *simple* sensory ideas: they can only consist of patterns of depth-free visual sensations that arouse memories of vision-free kinesthetic or bodily sensations (e.g., reaching and touching, focusing and converging our eyes, etc.) (Berkeley, 1709/1993). Such patterns (later called *depth cues*) are effective because they are produced by, and learned from, the 3D layout of our habitual environment.

Our present understanding of the information actually offered and used is discussed in chapter 4 (Cutting, this volume). Pictures and their depth cues, as catalogued by Leonardo da Vinci in the 1500s (see White, 1967), have always played a critical role in formulating perceptual theory (Hochberg, 1996), with Berkeley long anticipated in this regard by Peckham in 1504 and Alhazen in 1572 (discussed by White, 1967); pictures' current contribution is discussed by Cutting & Massironi, this volume), while their importance to issues of visual organization is discussed by Hochberg, this volume.

For many today, Berkeley's (1709/1993) New Theory of Vision remains unshakable doctrine after almost 300 years, embedded in its more inclusive context of sensory analysis and associative synthesis.

3. Analysis and Synthesis in Cognition

Because of the world's regularities, or ecological contingencies, the simplest elements of sensory stimulation normally occur in clusters. Through Aristotle's laws of association, such as Contiguity, Similarity, and Contrast, the memories (or memory images) of those clusters are recalled together, forming more complex ideas. Associative learning is therefore the engine by which mental content arises, providing the synthesis of the elements into which the sensory system has analyzed any given situation.

At the level of armchair (preexperimental) psychology, the major task was to analyze each idea of interest into its simplest components, and then explain how those had become associated. The methods used were, in descending order of rigor, those of logic, plausibility, and introspection: *logic,* as in Berkeley's geometry; *plausibility,* as in Mr. Molyneux's famous "experiment," cited by Locke (1690/1979) and Berkeley (1709/1993), which argued that a man born blind would, if newly given sight, not be able to recognize and distinguish by eye a cube and sphere that had become familiar through touch alone[4]; *introspection,* with which Locke explicitly examined what we know and how we think. Of these methods, introspection was later made the official tool of the Titchnerian school of experimental psychology (see section III.A.5), was subsequently "outlawed" during the Behaviorist decades (section III.C), and has finally returned less explicitly and more cautiously in present studies of recognition and imagery.

James Mill (1829/1967), at what was probably the high point of associationist armchair psychology, presented three strong tenets that are still with us: (a) distinguishing successive from simultaneous association: the former was then invoked as the motor of mental process, later served as the basis of behavior via serial conditioning, and is now central to such notions as phase sequences, priming, and so on. (b) taking association by similarity (and by contrast) to be derived, not fundamental, principles of association and therefore of thought: thus, similarity consists of the shared elements that two complex ideas have in common (see Medin & Coley, this volume). (c) arguing that ideas that have been frequently associated in daily life become indiscernible to consciousness within the compound ideas they form.

This last point means, once again, that self-observation cannot directly supply a causal analysis of conscious content. It did not have to: Armchair analysis was soon to be anchored in experiments, as association was recruited to serve in synthesizing cognitive functions from sensory input within a unified science.

B. The Unified Associationist Experimental Undertaking: Theory and Research

It was the empiricist story as outlined in section II.A.2b that made possible the Helmholtzian proposal that the r, g, and b sensory responses are sufficient to account for all purely visual experience. The objects of cognition are not solely visual, nor are they simple; the component ideas are much simpler than anything we see and think about. Even 2D space (and simple shape) is learned by associating *local signs* on the retina with the effects of the eye movements (Lotze, 1852/1965); thus kinesthetic sensations (and/or what we would now call motor readinesses) underlie what seems introspectively to be a seamless visual space (cf. Berkeley, section III.A.3).

---

[4] This experiment was not in fact performed as such until the 20th century (e.g., von Senden, 1960), with results that are essentially uninterpretable because we now know that unused neural structures deteriorate and become unusable (Riesen, 1961).

Much the same approach was shared by most major experimental psychologists (e.g., Wundt, 1896/1907), as experimental psychology became a scientific enterprise with its own distinct academic status and laboratories.

Its major fields of study in cognitive psychology were sensation, perception, memory through associations, imagination, and thinking. All but sensation were, as we have seen, considered to depend on associative processes. These were sited in the midsection of the Cartesian machine, the brain. As we entered the present century, and until very recently,[5] the major conceptual tools available for the study of such brain processes were those of behavioral research.

III. THE FIRST HALF OF THIS CENTURY

A. Major Behavioral Research Tools

The first half-century had most of its tools in place from previous decades. Excellent and comprehensive discussions by Woodworth (1938) and Osgood (1953) bracket that period.

1. Psychophysical Methods

These methods were readily adapted to study perception and cognition (see section II.A.2.a.i).

2. Memory Methods and Other Learning Measures

Ebbinghaus (1885/1964) had developed objective procedures that yielded orderly curves from subjects' acquisition and retention of nonsense material, words, and patterns. By midcentury these and a growing variety of other methods (the simultaneous or successive pairing of stimuli as in the method of paired associates [Calkins, 1896] and conditioning [Pavlov, 1923/1927], and in discrimination learning [Köhler, 1918/1938]) comprised a major part of experimental research.

The other three tools have had a much more erratic history.

3. Reaction Times as Measures of Cognitive Processes

As detailed and referenced by Woodworth (1938, pp. 298–310), in 1850 Helmholtz had used reaction time to measure the speed of neural propagation as a result of path length, and later attempts were made by Donders in 1868 and Wundt in 1880 to use varying subtraction methods to measure the time required by some specific cognitive function. However, the subtraction method was discarded after experiments from Külpe's laboratory in 1905 showed that its results were determined during the before period, while the subject prepared for the stimulus, and did not

---

[5] This delay occurred mostly because instrumentation was lacking, but probably also because earlier views of specialized brain functions, as in Broca's area role in speech, yielded to Lashley's demonstration of equipotentiality (Lashley, 1929).

measure on-line processing time. Particularly surprising given its current omnipresence, reaction time virtually disappeared as a theory-oriented topic during the second third of this century. Something similar happened in the study of imagery, as we see next.

4. Measuring Mental Representations: Tests of Imagery, Thinking, and Knowledge

It was thought that thought consists of ideas or images left by previous sense data, and that the images left by sensations were generally taken to be like sensations, only weaker (an opinion still skirted today: see Hochberg, this volume section IV). Methods to test such cognitive content were developed by Fechner and by Galton, and the classic demonstration that viewers could mistake a weak and barely superthreshold picture for their own image (Perky, 1910) seemed a promising fact. Perhaps due to the demonstrations of *imageless thought* (see below), and the resulting threat to classical theory, imagery research largely disappeared between the mid-1930s and the 1960s, and then, like much else in cognitive psychology, it underwent an astonishing reversal of fortune, and is now a major concern in many areas of cognitive psychology (see chaps. 9, 13, 14). Introspection, however, which was abandoned at the same time, has never officially recovered.

5. Experimental Introspection

In addition to the foregoing array of behavioral tools, the experimental psychology as promulgated by Wundt at Leipzig, and even more so by his student Titchener at Cornell, relied on highly trained introspection with more standardized controls and rigorous discipline than that on which previous armchair psychology had rested.[6] This introspection-centered approach was abandoned after a set of experiments in the 1920s (described in section III.B.4.a) both questioned the components on which the classical theory rested, and revealed an inability of observers in two laboratories (Würzburg and Cornell), both trained in the same method in the same laboratory (Leipzig), to provide the same results. Thoroughly shunned during the subsequent Behaviorist era (discussed in section III.C), experimental introspection has not returned as a serious research tool. Self-observations are now generally treated as data to be explained (and to be treated with caution), and not as a direct window on mental events.

The loss of introspection as a tool did not otherwise significantly affect the associationist–empiricist approach, components of which have survived almost intact through the 1950s, and still have their theoretical supporters.

---

[6] Trained introspection rested on the attempt, under controlled conditions, to observe one's experiences while avoiding the stimulus error. That "error" consisted in not separating the sensations experienced when perceiving some object or event from the context of associations that provide the object's unanalyzed perceptual meaning.

B. Classical Theory and Its Status in the First Half of This Century: All Cognition Explained, All Its Workings Hidden

1. Perception beyond Sensations: Constancies and Illusions Reflect Invariant Ecological Contingencies and Express Unconscious Inference

The analysis of sensory input into elementary *independent* responses to the local stimulation was challenged in many ways early in this century. In such *perceptual constancies* as lightness constancy, and in such *sensory illusions* as brightness contrast, the retinal stimulation in a given local region bears little relationship to the perceived local attributes. Discrepancies between the measured sensory array, and the corresponding perceived attribute, are the rule rather than the exception in our normal perceptions of size, color, shape, and so on.

To Helmholtz, this is because we perceive just that distal situation (objects' reflectance, physical size, etc.) as would be most likely, under normal viewing conditions, to have provided the same sensory response (local brightness, retinal extent, etc.) that the present proximal stimulus pattern produced. It is the distal properties of the world, not the proximal stimulation of sensory receptor organs, with which perception is concerned. The perceptual constancies are *achieved* when the seeing conditions are correctly discounted; illusions occur when conditions are incorrectly discounted (e.g., Tolman & Brunswik, 1935; see Gillam, this volume).

Because neither that process nor the individual sensory responses on which it is putatively based are normally available to introspection, Helmholtz's theory rests on *unconscious inferences from nonnoticed sensations*. We see things, and perhaps think about them, but the processes and components on which they are based are hidden from self-observation.

2. Disentangling the Hidden Cognitive Processes

At least five critical issues are raised by this and related inference-based theories.

a. On Sensory Independence

Because the sensation provided by each specific nerve fiber cannot be discerned or noticed in a normal context, we have to assume that it is then the same as when it alone is observed alone—that, as Helmholtz explicitly assumed, each element is independent of its neighbors' stimulation and response. Such independence was vigorously challenged since the late 1800s (Hering, 1878/1964; Mach, 1896/1959) and has since been directly refuted (see Hochberg; Nakayama, this volume). Without that assumption, we cannot guess what the unconscious-inference process has to start with, or even that it is needed.[7]

---

[7] For example, Hering, Mach, and even Helmholtz had noted that the *ratio* of adjacent retinal luminances is invariant for object and surround of constant reflectances, even under changing illumination. Any neural responses made to retinal luminance ratios would usually correspond directly to objects' reflectances, perhaps accounting for at least part of the phenomena of lightness constancy and brightness contrast.

b. On Nurture versus Nature

It is only an assumption (albeit an old one) that the perception of distal properties (size, depth, etc.) must be learned. That was refuted when depth perception was demonstrated in dark-reared chicks by Thorndyke (1899) and has been well supported since with other animals (Gibson & Walk, 1960). Berkeley's logic was therefore not enough. Without actual research, we cannot know what is innate and what must be acquired. How the ability to perceive objects, layouts, and events is in fact acquired in infancy is reviewed in chapter 11 (Spelke, this volume).

c. On Differentiation versus Association

Even when we are sure that some cognitive ability is learned, that learning might consist of *learning by differentiation* rather than by association (e.g., in various forms, as proposed by Bartlett, 1932; E. J. Gibson, 1940; Tolman, 1932, 1941). That is, the response (or sensitivity) to some informative aspect of the stimulus information becomes more precise with repetition, and is not merely a stronger connection between individual elements. Such learning might well capture aspects of the viewer's proximal sensory environment that vary with the invariant properties of distal objects and events (see footnote 7), making unconscious inference an unnecessary construct (as noted later by Gibson & Gibson, 1955).

d. On the Likelihood Principle

The principle that our ideas about the world reflect *ecological contingencies* remains popular today (see Hochberg, section III, this volume). It is almost invulnerable: of course, our perceptions must *in general* agree with reality whether that agreement be learned individually or through evolution of the species. Perfect agreement, where it occurs, is therefore not diagnostic, and Helmholtz argued for that reason that *disagreements* with the ecology—illusions and other anomalies—are good places to find clues about the underlying cognitive processes (see Gillam, this volume). Approaches to how information about the world might be internalized are addressed by Proffitt and Kaiser, and by Spelke, in this volume, and limitations are discussed by Cutting and by Hochberg, both in this volume.

e. On Mental Causation: Inference and Consequent Ideas

To say that the perception of an object's size or color is inferred from its perceived distance or illumination and from its retinal extent or luminance, respectively, is to take one mental event as the cause of another. Unlike the Cartesian sensory arc, there were no physiological mechanisms whose characteristics determine the outcome and allow one to attribute such thought processes to observable neurophysiological events. There are various ways to bypass the problem in the case of the perception of physical objects (see footnote 7), but such mental causation (that is attributing one idea to the occurrence or action of preceding ideas) also remains a characteristic of imagination, thought, and problem solving in general. If we are told that perception is just like reasoning or logic, we need to know what those are like, in scientific terms, for the assertion to be meaningful.

3. Cognition beyond Perception

What I will call the Helmholtzean approach probably lasted as long as it did because it provided a purpose within which to study the "hard" sensory sciences.[8] It also may have lasted because its associationist commitments, beyond sensory studies, were superficially compatible with the branch of cognitive studies that clustered around research on learning and memory from the mid-1920s to the early 1960s, and which derived from the same empiricist position.

When considered more closely, however, the traditional empiricist theory of cognition (within which Helmholtz's theory took its place) was much less mechanistic and reactive than either the sensory sciences, or the associative learning studies, that guided most experiments in the first half of this century.

4. Cognition in a New Light: Imageless Thought, Attributes without Sensations, and the Central Role of Attention

a. Ideas and Percepts, Mental Representations, and Testing Expectations

To Helmholtz, as to J. S. Mill (1865), an idea of some object is our structured expectation of what will be sensed as a result of some action; for example, what will be seen when that object is looked at from another viewpoint. That expectation implies a mental representation of the object. The object's presence provides a permanent possibility of such sensation, thus making the object "real" to the perceiver. This means that in effect a percept is confirmed as such by testing an expectation, implicating both a motive and an action in the perceptual process. The motive is implicitly to attend with an expectation of *what* will be sensed *where*. The action is testing that expectation. Both the sensations (or simplest of ideas) and the mechanics of associations between them are now by this formulation very far down the causal ladder in any account of an idea.

Research aimed at the nature of ideas and thought was clearly needed to give them any given scientific meaning. The two lines of research from Würzburg (mentioned previously and described in this section) were so intended. In one paradigm, viewers shown a very brief display of different colors and shapes are then instructed to report one attribute; they then miss the other or conflate the two attributes in what is now termed an *illusory conjunction* (see Hochberg, this volume) (Chapman, 1932; Külpe, 1904). It is not the sensory input with its fixed attributes but the task

---

[8] In fact, much of the vast amount of sensory science done before the 1950s has lost most of its relevance and justification. What the simple independent-channel and specific-fiber machine on which the classical enterprise rested has come to look like, and the consequences of nonindependence for cognitive theory, is discussed by Hochberg and by Nakayama, in this volume.

(*Aufgabe*) that determines mental content. Moreover, shape and content are not inseparable (despite Berkeley's colorless cat, section II.A.2.b).[9]

The second paradigm showed that at least some thought proceeds with no discernable images: Observers who had been trained in the introspective method solved simple problems or thought about instructed topics and then reported on what had been observed during the process. The experimenters in Würzburg could observe no images mediating between question and answer (Ach, 1905/1951; Watt, 1905). Whether and how imagery contributes to thinking is today a vigorous research topic (see Johnson-Laird, this volume). At the time, the imageless-thought experiments were a watershed because eventually they showed that sensations were not the components of cognition. More importantly, they unleashed an unresolvable conflict of observations between Cornell and Würzburg, though both sets of observers were trained in introspection in the same laboratory (Wundt's at Leipzig). That unresolvability condemned the method and eased the way for the Behaviorist revolution (discussed next) with its dramatic change in attitude.

C. Mechanistic Association in Human Learning and Animal Behavior: A Narrowed State for Cognition

J. B. Watson's Behaviorist manifesto (1913) pronounced the scientific study of consciousness, and the notion itself, unscientific.[10] The objective memory methods remained acceptable within the Behaviorist antimentalist ideology that dominated most of experimental psychology from the 1930s to the early 1960s. But much was not, including imagery, concept-formation [like the schemata Bartlett (1932) argued for as central to the learning of meaningful sequences], and the schemas-plus-correction that seem called for in object or concept learning (Woodworth, 1938) and thinking.

1. Behaviorist Explanation and Research

Pavlov's (1923/1927) extremely influential studies of animal conditioning furnished Watson with the elements and a model of how to study and explain learning without invoking the association of ideas. A substantial body of experimental psychologists attempted to explain all behavior, and all psychological issues, only

---

[9] The attentional instruction works even if given *after* the exposure (Lawrence & Coles, 1954), implicating the memory rather than the sensation (see chap. 9, section IV.A.4, this volume). Prior to these findings, introspectionists had treated attention as merely another sensory attribute; it gains a causal status from this line of research and is now a central field of cognitive research (See Dosher & Sperling, and Hochberg, in this volume.) In response to those findings, Titchener tried taking attributes rather than sensations as the fundamental units of sensory analysis (an attempt recently revived: see chap. 9, section IV.A.2, this volume). In response to the imageless thought findings, he argued that much of thought consisted of kinesthetic imagery (as did Woodworth, 1915).

[10] Attempts at explicit and purely physical accounts of behavior extend at least from Descartes (1650/1931) for animals, and extended to humans by La Mettrie (1748/1960) and Loeb (1912).

in terms of S's (physical stimuli) and Rs (physical responses). Behavior was usually taken to consist of conditioned S–R sequences, with internal muscle responses asserted to act as S's for subsequent Rs. A rat's knowledge of a maze, for example, consists only of a sequence of motor acts associated to each other and to external stimuli at each choice point. (For Thorndyke, 1913, satisfaction [reward] and annoyance [punishment] strengthened or weakened the S–R connection; for Hull, 1935, drive reduction played that role.) But there were serious gaps at both ends of the account.

The central problem of perception was inobtrusively sidestepped insofar as behaviorist studies generally did not specify the proximal stimuli and sensory excitations with which any causal account (S–R or otherwise) would in principle begin. Instead, the account baldly started with distal attributes of the objects in the world to which the subjects had to respond. The entire question of whether and how well the distal stimulus is retrieved by the organism was simply (and unjustifiably) set aside.

At the other end of the explanatory chain, as we see next, major behaviorist theorists posited a proliferation of unobservable internal stimuli provided by internal and unobservable responses.

2. Observable and Unobservable Responses versus Cognitive Maps and Other Constructs

Even animals can readily display cognitive abilities that do not yield to analyses into observable S's and Rs, as Tolman and his colleagues showed in a much-contested series of experiments (see Hilgard, 1956, pp. 191–215, for a score card). In *place learning,* the animal goes to the correct location through a different set of movements (e.g., a short-cut or detour), as though following a *cognitive map* (Tolman, 1948) and not merely unrolling associated S–R sequences. In *latent learning,* they have evidently learned something not previously practiced or reinforced (e.g., the site of water on the path to food).

These challenges came from what E. C. Tolman called *molar behaviorism,* termed Cognitivism for the remainder of this discussion. From this standpoint, although observable behavior provides the only scientifically acceptable data, it is taken as the expression of operationally definable but unobservable cognitive processes.[11]

Some Behaviorists met such challenges by positing unobservable internal responses: (for example, *habit-family hierarchies of alternative movements* (Hull, 1934), cortical *fractional antedating goal responses* (Hull, 1931; cf. Seward, 1947), and summated

---

[11] To molar behaviorists, the organism's actions are driven by goals and signs (*sign gestalten*) within a cognitive map of its environment (Tolman, 1932, 1948). These hypothetical constructs, themselves unobservable but helpful in modeling observable behavior, are somewhat similar to Lewin's *field theory* approach to human behavior (Lewin, 1936), which described human memories and actions through constructs like valences (the attractive or repulsive properties of perceived objects) and the vectors they occasion within a hypothetical life space or behavioral environment.

gradients of response and of nonresponse to any potential goal object (Spence, 1937). But these explanations were buried as deeply as were mentalistic constructs like cognitive maps or inferred thought processes. Others avoided such issues, working at the laws of reinforcement that shape or train the occurrence of existing behaviors (most notably, Skinner, 1950).

3. Thinking as Silent Speech, Speech as S–R Behavioral Chains, and the End of the Behaviorist Hegemony

As with animals, even more so with humans, whose behaviors notably include problem solving, planned speech, and other examples of thinking. Watson (e.g., 1919), among others,[12] had equated thought with covert S–R sequences in which the vocal apparatus engages, without audible sound, and with covert eye movement sequences that occur as if the object of thought were really present.

Even if this were accepted completely, it could not explain thought unless we spelled out the relationship, as yet unknown, between such hidden activities as the content of covert speech, or private eye movements, and problem solving. Furthermore, speech itself is not reducible to an S–R chain reflex of verbal behavior.[13] And still further, as Lashley (1951) argued forcefully and influentially, skilled behaviors like typing or playing the piano, and presumably fluent speech as well, are too rapid for each act to arise in response to the preceding one. Instead, the behavior must follow an unfolding plan. (See Wright & Landau, this volume, for the present state of knowledge on skilled purposeful behavior.)

Both approaches, therefore, and not only the cognitivist one, are saddled with unobservable explanatory mechanisms. In both, those mechanisms needed explicit modeling, preferably in internal (physiological) terms, because those might one day be brought under observation (cf. Krech, 1950; Tolman, 1949). The Behaviorist approaches had an advantage in that they retained the flavor of referring, eventually, to the internal physical events in Descartes's machine (section II.A.1 and 2), whereas the Cognitivist approaches had to find some way of accounting for the goals, maps, mental representations, and hypotheses that they attributed to both animals and people.

The differences, which at times were rancorous, faded from ones of ideology into ones of theory. Those theoretical differences reflected in large part the recognition by the Cognitivists of an alternative to the entire classical approach that was offered by Gestalt theory, as noted next.

---

[12] The "motor theory of consciousness" received physiological support from Max (1937) and Jacobson (1932). Brain imaging research today comes closest to their inquiries. For how language constrains thought, see Whorf (1941).

[13] Skinner undertook instead to bring speech into the domain of emitted operant behaviors in 1948 (Skinner, 1957) and was vigorously attacked by Chomsky (1959), who said that speakers generate and understand unlimited numbers of new sentences they had never spoken before, and use underlying linguistic structures not reducible to the S–R sequences themselves.

D. The Gestalt Alternative

Behaviorist theories and the classical tradition shared two related features: independent elements, for analysis (responses and ideas, respectively); simultaneous and successive association, for synthesis. Gestalt psychology was from a different tradition in which the effect of a configuration of components (a *Gestalt*) is not simply the sum of the effects that those components have when presented separately. (Thus, the whole is other than the sum of its parts.) This approach used different research methods, focused on different phenomena and problems, and tried to make different functional divisions between cognition, feelings, and action.

In the 1930s, when Hitler's regime ruled Germany, several major Gestalt psychologists came to a United States that was largely dominated by Behaviorism. Gestalt theory rested heavily on demonstrations appealing to the observer's perceptions (a form of nonanalytic introspection that references philosophical phenomenology). This small group of refugees thus rejected both the methodological injunctions and the elementaristic, associationist assumptions of Behaviorism—assumptions that seemed to be synonymous with scientific method in their new country. They had little direct effect on the body of sensory research performed in this country, but their strong critiques and striking demonstrations clearly strengthened the hand of molar behaviorism and helped revive the study of perception, imagination, and thinking.

Little more than a decade later, the technology released by the end of World War II began to revolutionize the nature of research and the kinds of models that could be attributed to a sentient organism. The Gestaltists' rejection of the classical approach has since been strikingly vindicated, but the alternatives are now very different. Reviews of the theory itself, and of its consequences for the current concerns of perception and related research areas, are given in chapter 9, this volume. The fact is that most of the distinctions between opposing approaches to perception and cognition have become obsolete in consequence of changing technologies over the last half-century.

IV. MASSIVE CHANGES AT THE HALF-CENTURY

The next years saw sweeping changes in the context within which cognitive research proceeds. The greatest changes have been in the technology available to research; access to computers allows simulations to be used where no explicit mathematical modeling of any precision would otherwise have been practical; and above all in the enormous increase in the support for research related to the cognitive abilities of humans and for the design of machines to replace humans in performing cognitive tasks.[14]

---

[14] This was of course a quite general transformation. Initially supported by grants from the armed forces, the amount of research done through government funding grew enormously in the decades after the U.S.S.R. lofted *Sputnik* in 1957. Grants were no longer merely convenient devices to aid faculty

Studies of cognitive processes, and of mental representation, are no longer a small and isolated corner within psychology, as they were at midcentury: They extend well beyond psychology within the interdisciplinary field of Cognitive Science, and many areas of research closed down in the 1930s and 1940s are now more active than ever.

The chapters in this volume address a wide sample of the areas in cognitive psychology that have been restored to modern activity, each presented with a view of where it now stands within the context of its history over this past half-century.

References

Ach, N. (1951). Determining tendencies and awareness. In D. Rapaport (Ed.), *Organization and pathology of thought* (pp. 15–38). New York: Columbia University Press. (Originally published 1905)

Baird, J. C., & Noma, E. (1978). *Fundamentals of scaling and psychophysics.* New York: Wiley.

Bartlett, F. C. (1932). *Remembering.* Cambridge, UK: Cambridge University Press.

Bell, C. (1948). *Idea of a new anatomy of the brain.* In W. Dennis (Ed.), *Readings in the history of psychology* (pp. 113–124) Appleton-Century-Crofts. Original work published 1811.

Berkeley, G. (1993). *An essay towards a new theory of vision* (computer file). Pittsboro, NC: Intelex. ss:http://cc.columbia,edu/textarchive/BerEssa. (Original work published 1709)

Berkeley, G. (1957). *A treatise concerning the principles of human knowledge.* Indianapolis: Bobbs-Merrill. (Original work published 1710)

Brunswik, E. (1955). Historical and thematic relations of psychology to other sciences. *Scientific Monthly, 83,* 151–161.

Calkins, M. W. (1896). Association: An essay analytic and experimental. *The Psychological Review Monograph Supplements i,* no. 2.

Chapman, D. W. (1932). Relative effects of determinate and indeterminate *Aufgaben. American Journal of Psychology, 44,* 163–174.

Chomsky, N. (1959). A review of B. F. Skinner's *Verbal Behavior. Language, 35,* 26–58.

Cornford, F. M. (1957). *Theatetus: Plato's theory of knowledge.* Indianapolis: Bobbs-Merrill.

Descartes, R. (1931). *Les passions de l'Ame.* In E. S. Haldane & G. R. T. Ross (Trans.), *The philosophical works of Descartes* (pp. 332–351). Cambridge, UK: University Press. (Original work published 1650)

Descartes, R. (1824). *L'homme.* In V. Cousin (Ed.), *Oeuvre de Descartes, IV* (pp. 349–363). Paris: Levrault. (Original work published 1664)

DeValois, R., & Jacobs, G. (1968). Primate color vision. *Science, 162,* 5.

Ebbinghaus, E. H. (1964). *Memory: A contribution to experimental psychology* (H. A. Ruger & C. E. Bussenius, Trans.). New York: Dover (Original work published 1885)

Fechner, G. T. (1912). *Elemente der Psychophysik,* I. (H. S. Langfeld, Trans.). In B. Rand (Ed.), *Classical psychologists* (pp. 562–572). Boston: Houghton-Mifflin. (Original work published 1860)

Feigel, H. (1949). Some remarks on the meaning of scientific explanation. In H. Feigel & W. Sellars (Eds.), *Readings in philosophical analysis* (pp. 510–514). New York: Appleton.

Galileo, G. (1948). Mathematical discourses concerning two new sciences relating mechanics and local motion. In W. Dennis (Ed.), *Readings in the history of psychology* (pp. 17–24). New York: Appleton-Century-Crofts. (Original work published 1638)

---

research, which had long been a necessary component in academic advancement and survival; they have become an essential part of the academic salary, necessary too for the support of graduate students, and an essential component of general university financing. Publications (necessarily of what is or *seems* new) increased even more enormously, and the Citation Index became a competitive arena of concern to all. All of this makes the long view both a drag on the individual researcher and a vital necessity for the discipline.

Gibson, E. J. (1940). A systematic application of the concepts of generalization and differentiation to verbal learning. *Psychological Review, 47,* 196–229.

Gibson, E. J., & Walk, R. (1960). The "visual cliff." *Scientific American, 202,* 64–71.

Gibson, J. J., & Gibson, E. J. (1955). Perceptual learning: Differentiation or enrichment? *Psychological Review, 62,* 32–41.

Goethe, J. W. (1970). *Theory of colours* (C. L. Eastlake, Trans.). Cambridge, MA: MIT Press. (Original work published 1810)

Guilford, J. P. (1936). *Psychometric methods.* New York: McGraw-Hill.

von Helmholtz, H. L. F. (1924). *Handbuch der physiologischen Optick, vol.II.* In (J. P. C. Southall, Trans.) *Helmholtz' treatise on physiological optics, vol.II* Rochester, NY: Optical Society of America. (Original work published 1860)

von Helmholtz, H. L. F. (1959). *On the sensation of tone.* A. J. Ellis (Trans.). New York: Dover. (Original work published 1863)

Hering, E. (1964). *Outlines of a theory of the light sense.* L. M. Hurvich & D. Jameson (Trans.). Cambridge, MA: Harvard University Press. (Original work published 1878)

Hilgard, E. R. (1956). *Theories of learning* (2nd ed.). New York: Appleton-Century-Crofts.

Hobbes, T. (1994). *Human nature.* Bristol, UK: Thoemmes Press. (Original work published 1650)

Hobbes, T. (1974) *Leviathan.* Baltimore: Penguin Classics. (Original work published 1651)

Hochberg, J. (1996). The perception of pictures and pictorial art. In M. P. Friedman & E. C. Carterette (Eds.), *Cognitive ecology* (pp. 151–203). San Diego, CA: Academic Press.

Hull, C. L. (1931). Goal attraction and directing ideas conceived as habit phenomena. *Psychological Review, 38,* 487–506.

Hull, C. L. (1934). The concept of habit-family hierarchy and maze learning. *Psychological Review, 41,* 33–54.

Hull, C. L. (1935). The conflicting psychologies of learning—a way out. *Psychological Review, 42,* 491–516.

Hurvich, L., & Jameson, D. (1957). An opponent-process theory of color vision. *Psychological Review, 64,* 384–404.

Jacobson, E. (1932). Electrophysiology of mental activities. *American Journal of Psychology, 44,* 677–694.

Köhler, W. (1938). *Nachweis einfacher Structurfunktionen bein Schimpansen und beim Haushuhn.* [Simple structural functions in the chimpanzee and in the chicken] In W. D. Ellis (Ed.) *A source book of gestalt psychology* (pp. 217–227). New York: Harcourt, Brace. (Original work published 1918)

Krech, D. (1950). Dynamic systems, psychological fields, and hypothetical constructs. *Psychological Review, 57,* 283–290.

Külpe, O. (1904). Versuche über Abstraktion. *Bericht über den Ie Kongresz fur Experimentale Psychologie,* 56–58.

La Mettrie, J. O. de (1960). *L'homme machine.* In A. Vartanian (Ed.), *L'homme machine: a study in the origins of an idea* (p. 266). Princeton, NJ: Princeton University Press. (Original work published 1748)

Lashley, K. S. (1929). *Brain mechanisms and intelligence: A quantitative study of injuries to the brain.* Chicago: University of Chicago Press.

Lashley, K. S. (1951). The problem of serial order in behavior. In L. A. Jeffress (Ed.), *Cerebral mechanisms in behavior: The Hixon symposium* (pp. 112–146). New York: Wiley.

Lawrence, D. H., & Coles, G. R. (1954). Accuracy of recognition with alternatives before and after the stimulus. *Journal of Experimental Psychology, 47,* 208–214.

Lewin, K. (1936). *Principles of topological psychology.* (F. Heider & G. M. Heider, Trans.). New York: McGraw-Hill.

Locke, J. (1979). *An essay concerning human understanding* (P. H. Nidditch (Ed.), New York: Oxford University Press. (Original work published 1690)

Loeb, J. (1912). *The mechanistic conception of life.* Chicago: University of Chicago Press.

Lotze, R. H. (1965). *Medical psychology, or Physiology of the soul* (D. Cantor, Trans.). In R. J. Herrnstein & E. G. Boring (Eds.), *A source book in the history of psychology* (pp. 135–140). Cambridge, MA: Harvard University Press. (Original work published 1852)

Luce, R. D. (1959). *Individual choice behavior.* New York: Wiley.

Luce, R. D., & Krumhansl, C. L. (1988). Measurement, scaling, and psychophysics. In R. Atkinson, R. Herrnstein, G. Lindzey, & R. Luce (Eds.), *Stevens' handbook of experimental psychology* (pp. 3–74). New York: Wiley.

Mach, E. (1959). *The analysis of sensations.* New York: Dover. (Original work published 1896)

Magendie, F. (1822). *Expériences sur les fonctions des racines des nerfs rachidiens. Journal de physiologie expérimentale et pathologique, 2,* 276–279.

Marks, L. E. (1974). *Sensory processes: The new psychophysics.* New York: Academic Press.

Max, L. W. (1937). An experimental study of the motor theory of consciousness: IV. Action–current responses in the deaf during awakening, kinesthetic imagery, and abstract thinking. *Journal of Comparative Psychology, 24,* 301–344.

Maxwell, J. C. (1861). On colour vision. In W. D. Niven (Ed.), *The scientific papers of James Clark Maxwell* (pp. 267–279). London: Cambridge University Press.

Mill, J. (1967). *Analysis of the phenomena of the human mind.* NY: A. M. Kelley. (Original work published 1829)

Mill, J. S. (1865). *An examination of Sir William Hamilton's Philosophy.* London: Longmans, Green & Co.

Müller, J. (1838). *Handbuch der physiologie des Menschen, V.* Coblenz. (W. Baly, Trans.). [*Elements of physiology vol. 11*]. London: Taylor & Walton.

Newton, I. (1704). *Optiks.* London: Smith & Walford.

Ohm, G. S. (1843). *Über die Definition des Tones, nebst daran geknüpfter Theorie der Sirene und öhnlicher tonbildener Vorrichttungen. Annals of Physical Chemistry, 135,* 497–565.

Osgood, C. E. (1953). *Method and theory in experimental psychology.* New York: Oxford.

Pavlov, I. P. (1927). *Conditioned reflexes* (G. V. Anrep, Trans.). London: Oxford University Press. (Original work published 1923)

Perky, C. W. (1910). An experimental study of imagination. *American Journal of Psychology, 21,* 422–452.

Riesen, A. H. (1961). Studying perceptual development using the technique of sensory deprivation. *Journal of Nervous and Mental Disease, 132,* 21–25.

von Senden, M. (1960). *Space and sight.* (P. Heath, Trans.). London: Methuen.

Seward, J. P. (1947). A theoretical derivation of latent learning. *Psychological Review, 54,* 83–98.

Skinner, B. F. (1950). Are theories of learning necessary? *Psychological Review, 57,* 193–216.

Skinner, B. F. (1957). *Verbal behavior.* New York: Appleton-Century-Crofts.

Spence, K. W. (1937). The differential response in animals to stimuli varying within a single dimension. *Psychological Review, 44,* 430–444.

Stevens, S. S. (1946). On the theory of scales of measurement. *Science, 103,* 677–680.

Tanner, W. P. Jr., & Swets, J. A. (1954). A decision-making theory of visual detection. *Psychological Review, 61,* 401–409.

Thorndyke, E. (1899). The instinctive reactions of young chicks. *Psychological Review, 6,* 282–291.

Thorndyke, E. (1913). *The psychology of learning.* New York: Teachers College.

Titchener, E. B. (1896). *An outline of psychology.* New York: Macmillan.

Tolman, E. C. (1932). *Purposive behavior in animals and men.* New York: Appleton.

Tolman, E. C. (1941). Discrimination vs. learning in the schematic sowbug. *Psychological Review, 46,* 318–382.

Tolman, E. C. (1948). Cognitive maps in rats and men. *Psychological Review, 55,* 189–208.

Tolman E. C. (1949). Discussion. *Journal of Personality, 18,* 48–50.

Tolman, E. C., & Brunswik, E. (1935). The organism and the causal texture of the environment. *Psychological Review, 42,* 43–77.

Watt, H. J. (1905). Experimentelle Beiträge zur einer Theoire des Denkens. *Archiv. für die gesamte psychologie, 4,* 289–436.

Watson, J. B. (1913). Psychology as the behaviorist views it. *Psychological Review, 20,* 158–177.

Watson, J. B. (1919). *Psychology from the standpoint of a behaviorist.* Philadelphia, PA: Lippincott.

Weber, E. H. (1846). (B. Haupt, Trans.). In R. J. Herrnstein & E. G. Boring (Eds.), *Sourcebook in the history of psychology,* Selection no. 10 (pp. 34–39). Cambridge, MA: Harvard University Press.

White, J. (1967). *The birth and rebirth of pictorial space.* Boston: Boston Book and Art Shop.

Whorf, B. L. (1941). The relation of habitual thought and behavior to language. In L. Spier, A. L. Hallowell, & S. S. Newman (Eds.), *Language, culture and personality: essays in memory of Edward Safir* (pp. 75–93). Menatha, WI: Sapir Memorial Public Fund.

Woodworth, R. S. (1915). A revision of imageless thought. *Psychological Review, 22,* 1–27.

Woodworth, R. S. (1938). *Experimental psychology.* New York: Holt.

Wundt, W. (1907). *Outlines of psychology.* (C. H. Judd, Trans.). Leipzig: Kroner. (Original work published 1896)

Young, T. (1802). On the theory of light and colours. *Philosophical Transactions of the Royal Society of London, 92,* 12–48.

CHAPTER 2

Philosophy, Perception, and Cognitive Science

Mark Rollins

I. INTRODUCTION

"The owl of Minerva flies at dusk," Hegel famously declared, referring to the historical role of philosophy in the development of civilization. But the owl also flies at dawn. The past half century has seen the dawn of cognitive science. And it is generally said that philosophy has somehow figured in it. The aim of this essay is to indicate something of the nature of that role. One useful way to understand the relation of philosophy to cognitive science is to treat the latter as having roots in the former; in particular, in ancient questions about the nature of knowledge and the mind's relation to the body or brain. However, philosophical interests in these questions have also evolved with the dynamic interaction among disciplines evident in the last 50 years. It is true that, to some extent, philosophy always elaborates a fixed set of positions on a small range of fundamental questions, but the real interest in the field lies in the particular details of those elaborations. What philosophy has gained from cognitive science are new empirical perspectives on its traditional concerns, new ways of posing philosophical questions, and—on a more fine-grained level of investigation—new problems. Cognitive science has derived from philosophy broad conceptual frameworks and methodological proposals aimed at integrating empirical results. In recent years these efforts have been based on an ever closer scrutiny of the ideas and concepts used in scientific theories. To understand the current tenor of philosophy and cognitive science, this dynamic must be kept in mind.

Perception and Cognition at Century's End

A number of persistent issues in philosophy have taken new directions with the rise of cognitive science; for example, the mind–body relation, intentionality, and consciousness. But at the center of these controversies stand questions about the nature and necessity of representation in perception and cognition. I shall focus on those questions.

II. METHODOLOGY AND THE MIND–BODY PROBLEM

The three dominant views of the mind–body relation are Functionalism, Identity Theory, and what I shall call Neobehaviorism. According to the Functionalist, mental abilities are essentially causal powers: the capacity to produce a certain output given the right sort of input. These powers cannot be identical to neurological structures or properties because the same causal capacity or function can be implemented by many, very different types of structure or physical property. By contrast, the Identity theorist treats each bona fide type of mental function as identical to a type of physical structure or process in the brain.[1] Both Functionalism and Identity theory accept the psychological reality of mental states, in particular, mental representational states. In this they differ from Neobehaviorism, a position implicit in the work of Dennett [1987].[2] According to the latter, mental representations (e.g., beliefs) can be construed as functional states of the brain, but such states are only useful fictions. They are posited by cognitive science to make predictions, but they have a status similar to other scientific abstractions, such as *center of gravity* or *equator*. They help us conceptualize other real phenomena, but they do not themselves exist in the same sense as the phenomena so conceived. This is, in part, a point about how science works.

In fact, each of these views has consequences for our understanding of cognitive science. For instance, Functionalism implies the "autonomy of psychology." According to that thesis, psychology can formulate its laws without regard to the neurological substrate on which the function depends. The result is a *theory-dualism,* because psychological theories of perception and cognition are supposed to be irreducible to biological theories of brain processes and structures.[3] By contrast, Identity theory allows for reduction, but that possibility rests on a theory of meaning (for psychological terms) that the Functionalist rejects. Because similar mental functions are multiply realizable in quite different types of brains, any reduction will have to be species-specific. If Identity theory is true, *pain* or *belief* or *mental representation* must mean different things when applied to cats or cockatiels than when used to describe humans.

Recent research on perception has played an important role in the mind–body debates. For example, it is well known that Marr's (1982) theory of vision exem-

---

[1] Hence it is a "type–type physicalism."

[2] Harman (1989, p. 834) calls this view "complex behaviorism."

[3] The term *theory dualism* is P. S. Churchland and Sejnowski's (1989). Reprinted in Lycan (1990, p. 228).

plifies three *levels of explanation,* which he argued are required for an adequate account: (a) the computational level, in which the real-world tasks and goals of the visual system are identified; (b) the algorithm level, where the operations required to perform the tasks are specified; and (c) the level of implementation which is, for humans and other animals, the domain of neuroscience. This trilevel theory of explanation is a natural elaboration of the more fundamental distinction between functions and structures on which the Functionalist philosophy of mind rests. Thus the success of Marr's theory can be taken to show the value of the Functionalism, arguably the most influential theory during the rise of cognitive science since 1950.

However, in recent years, Marr's way of distinguishing among levels of explanation has been rejected by a number of philosophers and scientists (P. S. Churchland, Ramachandran, & Sejnowski, 1994, p. 248; Kosslyn, 1994, pp. 33–38). They appeal to connectionist computational models on the one hand, and to empirical evidence on the other. Specifically, the reliance on patterns of connectivity in a network to encode information makes the connectionist computational model somewhat more biologically realistic than Marr's classical type, and the model has other properties that seem brainlike as well.[4] Thus, connectionist models blur the distinction between computational function and implementational structure. Add to that the observation that a similar blurring is a common practice in neuroscience, where many more than three levels of description are found anyway, and the result is that Functionalism loses substantial ground.

Neobehaviorism stands ready to take its place. Despite the blurring of structure–function boundaries in the actual practice of cognitive science, the Neobehaviorist can argue for the legitimacy of an *idealized* definition of mental functions that is precise and unambiguous, on the grounds that such a description is highly useful. What is crucial is that the functions be decomposable into more and more elementary ones. This ensures that the functions can be performed by a physical device like the brain and underwrites the possibility of a systematic account. The result is a view of levels of explanation that is similar to Marr's. Indeed, Dennett (1987) has developed his own trilevel model of explanation, in which the bottom and middle levels are essentially Marr's, whereas the top level—the *intentional stance*—goes beyond Marr by allowing explanation in terms of beliefs and other propositional attitudes that are common in our ordinary descriptions of ourselves. To be sure, Dennett doubts that explanation in terms of beliefs and desires can ever rise above the level of rough-and-ready generalizations. Nonetheless, he thinks such generalizations do have a fair amount of predictive value, and on his scale of utility, other psychological constructs fare much worse. For instance, he has frequently criticized the inclusion of mental images and qualia (in anything like their traditional, folk psychological forms) in cognitive theory as misleading and unhelpful (Dennett, 1981, pp. 174–189; 1991, chs. 4, 10, and 12; cf. Rollins, 1989).

---

[4] Like the "graceful degradation" of functions that results from trauma.

However, this instrumentalistic conception of cognitive science has not been widely embraced.[5] It makes the acceptability of psychological theory too relativistic, dependent largely on the predominant interpretive practice. Moreover, Neobehavioristic skepticism about images and qualia appears to have been undercut empirically. Although the relevant scientific theories are controversial, both constructs have figured in recent accounts of perception and perceptual awareness. For instance, by employing a variety of techniques to study the visual system in the brain, Stephen Kosslyn (1994) now claims to have shown decisively that perceptual processes sometimes require augmentation by imagery. Further, reductionists who rely on the current generation of connectionist models sometimes claim to have a potentially adequate account of qualia as physiological phenomena (e.g., P. M. Churchland, 1990, pp. 146–149). Moreover, they claim that Functionalists and Neobehaviorists working in the Marr tradition tend to overemphasize language-like representations and propositional attitudes (P. M. Churchland, 1990).

Thus metaphysical issues about the relation between mind and body have spawned questions about the nature of explanation in cognitive science and about the status of mental representations. Indeed, perhaps the most pressing question that cognitive science must now confront is this: What is the nature of representation in perception and cognition? To answer this question, it is necessary to consider some theories of representational form and content.

III. COMPUTATION AND REPRESENTATION

Old debates about the mind–body relation took new turns with the rise of artificial intelligence. Indeed, the publication of Turing's article, "Computing Machinery and Intelligence," exactly at midcentury, was an important landmark in the recent history of cognitive science (1950). In particular, the possibility of symbol manipulation by a physical device seemed to open the door to an understanding of representation in the brain. When a well-defined notion of information processing as computation became available, it served to define a class of brain functions that are specifically pertinent to intelligence, perception, and thought; the concept of a functional state or brain function became more concrete. But then two controversies naturally arose: (a) one about the very idea that cognitive and perceptual functions are computational functions; and (b) the other about the possibility of attributing genuine meaning to strings of internal symbols, linking them to the external world. In effect, the first problem concerns the *form* that mental representation takes; the second concerns its *content*. I shall consider the first issue here and take up the problem of content in section IV.

With regard to form, perhaps the most basic question to ask about computational theories of the mind is this: *Are* cognitive and perceptual functions actually

---

[5] For example, Kitcher (1988) argues that, contrary to Dennett's skeptical view, the success of Marr's agenda points the way to a rigorous science that includes beliefs and desires.

computational functions or, instead, are they more like biological, organic functions? Is the mind really an automaton, or is it rather a kind of animal, identical to, or coexisting symbiotically with, the brain and body? Against the classical computer model, there have been two lines of attack.

First, John Searle has rejected the idea that the mind is in any sense a formal system and has attributed intentionality to the causal properties of the brain instead. Searle's well-known analogy to a Chinese room (1984, pp. 31–38), in which a native English speaker simply matches printed Chinese symbols according to rules, with no knowledge of their referents, is intended to show the implausibility of a computer model of language understanding, and thus, of computer models generally (where the models are taken literally, as in "strong" artificial intelligence). The argument has been very widely discussed, but on the whole it seems not to have won many converts. One problem is that Searle's positive alternative theory of intentionality is not entirely clear. His rejection of the feasibility of any combination of parallel processing, brain simulation, and robotics—so long as it is driven by a formally described program—seems tantamount to a claim that computational properties inevitably supervene on causal properties of the wrong sort. What remains to be seen is what the right sort of causal properties are supposed to be.

As a second line of attack, other philosophers have denied the opposition between mind-as-computer and mind-as-brain on the basis of connectionism as a biologically realistic model of computation (Churchland & Churchland, 1990). The precise nature and status of representation in a connectionist machine is controversial, but the representations are standardly said to be *nonsymbolic*. As occurrent states, they are identified with activation patterns in a network of highly interconnected nodes (e.g., neurons) where the character of a pattern is due to both the nature of the input and the strengths or weights of the connections. The latter also constitute relatively stable mental dispositions; thus the weightings can be construed as a means of storing information in memory. A connectionist machine trained to recognize objects of a certain sort can be said to partition into distinct regions a multidimensional space that is defined by input units. The partitioned regions then function as *prototypes* for categorizing the inputs. In this case, relations among representations are closer to associations among regions of similarity than to logical inferences using descriptions; more precisely, they consist in vector transformations.

The virtues and vices of connectionism have been subjected to close scrutiny in recent years (Fodor & Pylyshyn, 1988; Pinker & Prince, 1988; Smolensky, 1988). Notoriously, critics have argued that the subsymbolic representations employed by connectionist models fail to capture two central features of human cognition: its productivity and systematicity. As with language, thought exhibits semantic compositionality: The meaning of a complex expression is a function of the meaning of its parts. This allows us to generate seemingly endless new thoughts and to understand novel constructions in virtue of our knowledge of rules governing relations among parts of speech. But because connectionist processes lack any obvious syntactical grounding for semantic composition, it is hard to see how they provide for productivity and systematicity. Advocates reply that connectionist models can *simulate* the use of symbols when necessary, and that it is not obvious that thought and perception are always entirely systematic anyway. Thus it is unclear how telling the presence or absence of these features should be taken to be.

This debate about representation and connectionism converges naturally with the question of whether there must be a universal *language of thought*. Fodor (1975) argues that perception, like concept acquisition and considered action, requires hypothesis formation and testing. And, he claims, the fact that hypotheses express propositions means that all these forms of intelligence depend on a language-like medium; in perception in particular, information is encoded in structural descriptions like those that can be employed by a digital computer. Pylyshyn (1986) has argued that something like a language-based format for representation is required for any good computational model of cognition. However, this view has been challenged as implausible for animals and prelinguistic children, who can perceive but lack linguistic abilities. And, indeed, some connectionists claim that the language-of-thought thesis is generally incredible. They argue that even for adult humans, information processing and storage, in all its forms, rests on subsymbolic representation in neural pattern activations. This illustrates how the issue of computational architecture can play a central role in philosophical debates.

However, although the issue of computational architecture is clearly an important one, it is only one question among many about perception and cognition. Answering it can hardly be seen as decisive for all the others. Connectionism makes possible a wider range of options with regard to the nature and necessity of representation in perception and cognition. And it does cast doubt on a language-based account like Fodor's, in which propositional attitudes play the central representational role. Many theorists have also proposed hybrid models of various types, and features originally associated with classical computation and descriptive representation have been appropriated by connectionists. Rather than lobbying for or against one or another type of computational architecture in general terms, a more useful approach is to consider evidence and arguments with regard to each of several proposed properties (e.g., of perceptual systems), and then to determine the viability of one computational model or the other for producing the property in question. Computer simulations can, of course, play a role in both identifying the relevant capacities and arguing for how they are most likely implemented.

This way of proceeding is exemplified by recent work on vision. Again, Marr's theory provides a starting place. That theory makes certain commitments that link it naturally to a classical computational approach: Vision is explained in terms of a series of distinct processing stages, where earlier stages are independent of later ones and must be complete before the later ones can begin. Information is represented in structural descriptions that comprise more and more complete constructions, culminating in a fully three-dimensional, object-centered representation appropriate for matching to perceptual categories stored in long-term memory. And the system is *modularized;* no top-down effects of extraneous background knowledge or beliefs are allowed to penetrate the perceptual processes as such, which are highly domain specific (i.e., they are activated only by certain well-defined types of stimuli).

Philosophers have taken such commitments to be important. For one thing, the attribution of modularity to the visual system reflects an engineering approach to the study of vision that many philosophers think will allow cognitive science more generally to succeed, while retaining the mental representations that are distinctive of common sense psychology (Burge, 1986; Kitcher, 1988). In particular, Marr argues that identifying the built-in assumptions that constrain the visual system can lead to the discovery of particular algorithms, which can be proved mathematically to give uniquely accurate results. For example, given assumptions like the *continuity* of surfaces, it is possible to describe a formula for computing stereoscopic depth (Marr & Poggio, 1976). Or, if the *rigidity* of objects is assumed, their shapes can be computed from motion information about only four coplanar points. For another thing, a Marr-style approach is held to have epistemological implications. Although Fodor has claimed that the modularity thesis does not imply a foundationalist theory of knowledge, he nonetheless clearly thinks that it provides a bulwark against epistemic relativism. More recently, in Irving Biederman's (1987) model of object Recognition-by-Components (RBC), Marr's generalized cylinders and axis relations are replaced by "geons" (geometrical ions) as the primitive components of visual objects. Geons are identified by curvature, symmetries, and segmentation points defined by concavities in contour. Biederman argues that the relations among geons are such that, in general, three of them will suffice to specify any object. This *principle of geon recovery* has been said to show the epistemic reliability or accuracy of the visual system (i.e., how it supports the production of true beliefs) (Goldman, 1993, p. 106).

However, the point is that not all of the philosophically relevant features of Marr's or Biederman's RBC accounts are wedded to classical computationalism. For instance, Biederman's theory includes parallel processing to enhance the speed and power of the system and to explain why complex objects do not require more time to recognize than simple ones (cf. Goldman, 1993, p. 108). And aspects of Biederman's model have been included in some recent treatments of perception that are fundamentally nonclassical (i.e., that employ a connectionist, neural network model and allow substantial cognitive penetration even in early stages of visual information processing) (e.g., Kosslyn, 1994), pp. 108–111). Such adaptations also reject a pure language of thought; nonetheless, they posit a central role for descriptions in the interpretation of analog processes. To be sure, these theories deviate from the classical assumption of strictly defined stages, in favor of a more *cooperative* model of computation. But the real issues in that regard do not have to do simply with classical versus connectionist architecture. Rather, they concern whether such hybrid models can explain the details of our success at object recognition; whether visual components are in fact stored in memory; whether object-centered representations are required at all, rather than viewer-centered ones; whether there is evidence for supplementary attentional mechanisms, and so on.

Nonetheless, it is clear that there are competing styles of theorizing about perception, which often do cluster about one or the other computational model. And comparing those styles, I believe, opens a window onto the current state of the philosophy–science dynamic. In order to indicate the tenor of the alternative styles of theorizing, I shall contrast two ways of imposing constraints on the scope of representation. One way is Marr's: Attributing certain built-in assumptions to a modularized visual system in which there are distinct stages of processing, which makes it possible to prove the effectiveness of some algorithm in computing the desired result. In this case, the constraints and assumptions typically support the production of veridical representations. But the other way is to propose constraints that work to limit the reliance on representation, in the face of evidence that, for many tasks, it may not be required. In the section that follows, I consider these alternative approaches at greater length.

A. Restricting Representation

The idea that modularity and hardwired assumptions are built into the visual system is, to some extent, motivated by design considerations. Such features are conducive to survival because they make possible the sort of fast, automatic, and accurate responses that are often called for by real-world perceptual tasks. Moreover, according to Marr, modularity facilitates continuous and incremental improvements in the system over the course of evolution, because it allows design flaws to be corrected one at a time, without having to revise the entire system. But the plausibility of the modularity thesis and of specific constraints and assumptions must ultimately rest on empirical evidence; and there is, in that regard, considerable controversy. For example, the discovery of numerous pathways that descend from higher regions of the visual cortex to lower ones (and beyond), or of cells capable of responding to multiple types of information suggest bases in the brain for cognitive penetration and domain overlap in what might otherwise be thought to be modules (Van Essen, Anderson, & Felleman, 1992). In addition, there is strong evidence for the context dependence of perceptual tasks; for instance, the facilitation of letter recognition by the location of the letter in a word (i.e., the word superiority effect) (McClelland & Rumelhart, 1981). However, the most basic point in favor of modularity is simply the fact that we are able to quickly make determinate, correct judgments in the face of a highly indeterminate world. How else are we to explain that fact? The modularity thesis amounts to a limitation on the uses of representation. Perceptual inferences can only be drawn in certain ways, based upon a limited range of knowledge, and the relevant inferences are mandatory when the input is of the right sort. If this is not the basis for the reliability and automaticity of the visual system in performing certain tasks, what is?

The alternative goes by several names; for the sake of convenience, I shall refer to it as the Heuristic Design Principle (HDP). In the literature on perception, the various forms of HDP reflect a growing dissatisfaction with the traditional opposition between *direct* and *indirect* theories. To show that this opposition is misleading, these new accounts treat the perceived world as informationally rich rather than impoverished and claim that much of the information is available through repeated sampling. But they hold that internal processes and representations are required nonetheless.

Consider, for example, a view that P. S. Churchland, Ramachandran, and Sejnowski (1994) call the *Interactive Theory of Vision*. Negatively, this view can be described simply as a rejection of the theory of "Pure vision," a classically computational, Marr-style, stage-dependent, modular account, the defining feature of which is that it treats vision as culminating in an elaborate, highly specific and detailed, three-dimensional representation of a scene. On the Interactive theory, perception requires only representations of "visual semiworlds," representations that are partial or incomplete. The theory is called 'interactive' because vision is affected by other sensory modalities and by the motor control system. It is this collaboration that lets partial representations suffice.

Indeed, in defending a related view that he calls the *Utilitarian Theory of Perception*, Ramachandran claims that such short-cuts and make-do devices are quite pervasive: Perception is for him a "bag of tricks" (1990), a nonoptimal collection of strategies in which cooperation among various abilities relieves the system of the need to construct complete sense representations. The guiding principle is one of economy: "(T)he human visual system will do as little processing as it can get away with for the job at hand. . ." (Ramachandran, 1990, p. 349). Thus, it discards much available information along the way.

For instance, in regard to a phenomenon he calls "motion capture," Ramachandran (1990) argues that the visual system need not solve the correspondence problem in lining up images of a moving object point-for-point. When a leopard is seen as leaping from tree to tree, it is not necessary for the visual system to compute the trajectory of each and every spot on its body (for instance, using an algorithm like that proposed by Ullman). Instead, detailed spot information is disregarded, and the spots are carried along with the information that is processed about the leopard's moving shape. In this case, the perceptual strategy is part of the dynamic design of the brain and exploits a feature of the perceiver's environment; namely, that in it, spots normally don't normally jump off of moving surfaces. This is an assumption on which the strategy depends, but it is an "ecologically specific" one rather than a general, ideal rule, and it need not itself be explicitly represented. Perceptual success is thus a contingent function of relations between the organism and its environment. However, this version of HDP is also distinct from Gibson's ecological theory because it makes perception depend on substantial internal processing that often results in at least partial representations.

A third example of the HDP approach comes from Kosslyn (1994). In keeping with a general *Principle of Opportunistic Processing,* Kosslyn argues that there are four different ways the perceiver might identify an object's components and the arrangement among them: Visual components can be identified either by matching to part representations stored in visual memory or by attending to each location on the object at which parts appear and "drawing" a representation in the visual buffer. Then the organization among parts can be defined either by a precise specification of their locations in a coordinate system, or by a description if their categorical spatial relations (e.g., above, below). How any given object is recognized will depend on how these four parameters are combined. Construed in this way, perceptual strategies need not be common design features of the visual systems of all perceivers; they can be the basis for individual differences.

Thus, determinate perceptual responses are delivered, not by the operation of an ideal algorithm, but as a result of perceptual skill or expertise that derives from highly trained habits. It's worth noting that, if perceptual habits are sufficiently deeply entrenched, they may produce effects that closely resemble the effects of modularity; *virtual modularity,* one might call it. Fodor (1983) has argued that one of the advantages of modularity is that it allows the perceiver to do more than one task at a time; the visual counterpart of walking and chewing gum without falling down. The reason is that modules have dedicated resources and therefore do not have to compete for memory, processing resources, and so on. But there is now evidence that suggests that the "automatizing" of nonmodular perceptual functions may give the same result by freeing up neurocomputational resources that were previously required to learn to do a new perceptual task. Exactly how this might be done by the brain is still a matter of speculation. However, brain imaging techniques show that areas of the brain active during training on a given task often become inactive after the task has been learned, and various plausible neural mechanisms for revising the brain's circuitry, by reweighting synaptic connections, have been proposed (Posner & Raichle, 1994; Anderson & Van Essen, 1987; Kosslyn, 1994). Automatizing is yet another economical strategy.

In sum, then, HDP limits the reliance on representation in perception in six ways:

1. In so far as training does create virtual modules and special purpose domains, it produces the same sort of independence from effects of extraneous background knowledge that modules do.
2. As with behavioral habits, perceptual habits require less effort, energy, attention, fewer resources, and especially less need to consult rules stored in memory for forming explicit, complete representations, than nonhabitual perception does. The situation here is analogous to learning to use a typewriter or play the piano.
3. When groups of abilities or subsystems are used together to perform a task, the representations that occur in each one of the cooperating units can be of a different sort than would otherwise be required; for instance, they will often be coarsely coded spatial properties that overlap.
4. Such habits and heuristics may *replace* propositional attitudes. They are themselves more like contentless control functions than intentional states.
5. The interaction of perceptual and motor systems, in particular, underwrites

the possibility of sampling and resampling information in the environment. In light of that, it is argued, there is no need to represent all of the information in memory.

6. On these accounts, perceptual change need not always depend on inductive learning, by which the perceiver acquires new concepts. Instead, perceptual change can be produced through training in the use of already available resources.[6]

Although the HDP approach clearly opens up new lines of thought about perception and tells us something about the nature of representation, two important cautionary notes are in order. First, one should not exaggerate the extent to which mental representation becomes unnecessary if HDP is correct. It is simply a mistake to think that degraded or impoverished stimuli can be overcome in every case merely by continued sampling. Indeed, in many cases, the whole point of positing representation has been that such resampling is precluded.[7] Second, even if the representations in question are only partial, their content must somehow be individuated. A theory of partial mental content must still be given. I turn next to a consideration of three possible accounts.

---

[6] P. S. Churchland et al. (1994) note similarities between their view of *Interactive vision*, Ballard's (1991) discussion of *animate vision*, and various treatments of *active vision* in Blake and Yuille (1992). Recently, James Cutting (1986) has advocated a theory of *directed vision* which has some of the characteristics of an HDP approach. But there are important differences among these new accounts. For instance, according to Cutting, multiple sources of information *over*specify objects or events. There is neither impoverishment requiring internal constructions nor a one-to-one correspondence between environmental properties and detected stimuli, as Gibson maintains. This claim has been criticized by Gilden (1991), who links his own view to Ramachandran's (1990). According to Gilden, the redundant information that Cutting describes is not actually used by perceivers, even though it is available. Instead, they rely on heuristics for accessing only the information required for the task at hand. However, Cutting, too, argues that perceptual systems may use different sources of information at different times, even for the same type of task (p. 248). And although he prefers to speak of representation as external rather than internal, the issue of representational content or meaning is still relevant and remains to be addressed (p. 252). Some of the theories of content I discuss allow representation to be a *relation* between the perceiver and the external world in ways that seem compatible with directed vision (cf. also Schwartz, 1996, and P. S. Churchland et al., 1994, p. 51). Thus, construed broadly, HDP can include a variety of accounts. Which version of HDP is correct is a question beyond the scope of this paper. My point is that it is not compatible with everything: Specifically, it excludes the theories of Fodor, Marr (in part), and, as I shall argue, Dretske, and Millikan. If HDP is right, then these theories, as theories of perceptual content individuation, must be wrong.

[7] This may be because the object is simply removed from sight. Or it may have to do with the nature of the object. For instance, representational paintings pose some notorious problems for an ecological theory of perception. Because the point-of-view they contain is fixed, one cannot move through them, so to speak, getting a more elaborate sample. A reliance on stored representations in such cases may be required. See also Hochberg, 1980, p. 52 for an argument that the impossibility of overcoming static depth cues by motion parallax is not limited to pictures; and Hochberg (1972, p. 69) for a defense of "mental maps" in guiding attention.

IV. THEORIES OF CONTENT

Earlier, I considered the influence of computational models (as employed in cognitive neuroscience) on the problem of the basic nature or form of mental representation. But that question merely lays the foundation for the second and more central issue of representation: Insofar as the brain *is* a symbol manipulator, is cognitive science limited to explaining cognitive and perceptual abilities in terms of the purely syntactical, formal properties of the symbols, or can it attribute semantic properties—truth, meaning, reference—to them as well? Alternatively, if the visual system is best understood in connectionist terms, in what way might the contents of its nonsymbolic representations be identified? Even if we replace truth with veridicality, reference with denotation, and meaning with extension or use, we must still explain what makes one representation different from another; what makes them be "about" different things. For instance, if stable perceptual prototypes are required for the categorization of visual input, and such prototypes are essentially partitions in connectionist weight space, then on what basis can we identify any partition's domain (i.e., the conditions under which it gets activated)?

On the face of it, the answer may seem obvious. By careful and controlled testing, we can discover the external features that produce activity in the relevant detector mechanisms and treat those features as the content of basic representations. In effect, we might try to individuate perceptual content in terms of the typical causal covariance between internal states and external objects or events. The most rigorous and systematic philosophical account of this sort is found in Dretske's (1981) attempt to express the relevant covariance in information theoretic terms. Ignoring the more technical aspects of information theory here, we can summarize Dretske's basic view like this: Internal states are reliable indicators of their external factors, in so far as the indicators covary with external conditions in a lawlike way. To be lawlike, the covariance must be counterfactual supporting: A **p**-detector is one that would be activated, ceteris paribus, if a **p** were present in the visual array. This theory seems to fit the practice of cognitive neuroscience well; witness the purported discovery of line and bar detector cells in the visual cortex by Hubel and Wiesel.

However, there are certain notorious problems with this theory as it stands. Generally, the problems have to do with a causal indeterminacy of two sorts. One kind of indeterminacy derives from the inevitable presence of extended causal chains. Any putative cause of a psychological state will itself have a cause that could be said to be the relevant cause of the state in question. The issue then is, where in the chain is the salient covariant factor to be located? Which one is to be identified as the content of the representation, the cause that the representation is 'about'? Dretske has argued that this question can be answered empirically, by appeal to the perceptual constancies. The right way to describe the causal factors in perception is determined by the type of features—shape, size, color, etc.—that in fact remain constant under changes in viewing conditions.

But this leaves the second sort of indeterminacy untouched. This type of indeterminacy is especially important, because it raises an even more fundamental worry about *misrepresentation* that any theory of content must confront. Of course, empirically we know that perceptual errors are commonplace. But the very concept of representation would also seem to carry with it the possibility of making mistakes. Whatever can be true must also be potentially false. But if the content of a representation is specified in terms of whatever activates the relevant detector mechanism, then it seems that representation can never go astray. Content will always match cause.

This is true, by the way, even if we define content in terms of the typical or most frequent type of cause, rather than the actual one in a particular case. For instance: The deer hunter who occasionally shoots a cow cannot be said to have misperceived on the causal account. Supposing that he sometimes shoots at deer, too, the most typical cause of his perceptual state should be disjunctively described as a *cow-or-deer*, whenever the target before him is one or the other; because that disjunction describes best what appears most often in the hunter's visual field. But once the door is open to disjunctive causes in this way, the possibility of error can always be precluded by invoking a suitable disjunction. No matter what causes my perceptual experience, *x,* that thing then becomes a candidate for inclusion in the disjunction that describes the content of that experience. What I see, whether I shoot at cows or deer or *x*'s, is always some instance of a *cow-or-deer-or-x* type of thing. Hence, I can never misperceive at all on the causal account. This is the disjunction problem.

Dretske's attempt to deal with this problem involves an appeal to teleology. Going beyond causal covariance alone, he tries to block error-excluding disjunctions by appealing to the *needs and goals* of the perceiving organism, taken as a member of its species. For example, like the hunter who shoots at cows-or-deer, a fly-eating frog that snaps at BBs might be said to snap at *flies-or-BBs*. Except that ecological considerations strongly suggest that what the frog sees (mistakenly when it snaps at BBs) are flies; because flies are what it needs to eat in order to survive. The teleological theory of content thus entails a shift in the level of analysis: from the typical causes of an individual's perceptual response to the conditions for the evolution of perceptual states in the species. Perceptual content for a particular perceiver is determined, not by what usually causes that perceiver to respond, but by what led to the relevant response capacity becoming part of his species' phenotype. Having identified a **p**-detector mechanism as such (by invoking some plausible evolutionary history), we can then ascribe **p**-contents to the perceive whenever we believe the relevant mechanism is active, regardless of what actually activates it.

In its most purely teleological form (separated from any essential dependence on information theory or individual causal covariance), such an account has been developed by Ruth Millikan (1984). In her Adaptational Role Theory, categories or perceptual content are defined in terms of "proper functions" and "normal conditions." The proper function of a perceptual mechanism is to indicate a state of affairs that obtains under normal conditions. Those are the conditions in which the species acquired the mechanism; that is, in which the fact that mechanism indicated the relevant state of affairs aided survival. In Millikan's example, a bee's dance means "there is nectar over there" because it was the presence of nectar in a certain direction that supported the selection of the dance capacity. For perceptual content, normal conditions will be those that make it veridical. If the state in question is a belief, normal conditions will be those that make it true; for example, the fact that it is raining for the belief that "it's raining." Note, however, that the role of truth or veridicality conditions in determining the content of mental representations has nothing to do with the fact that they cause the representation to occur. A correspondence between the representation and what it represents is merely the condition under which the perceiver should be able to use the representation to achieve its ends and fulfill its needs. Thus, there is room for mistakes. The bee's dance might occur when there is no nectar; but that does not change its biological function nor, therefore, its meaning. Similarly in perception: What in fact activates the **p**-detector on any particular occasion might be something other than **p**.

How the teleological account avoids the disjunction problem can be illustrated in the following way. Suppose that floating specks of dust are sometimes eaten by evolving frogs. We might say that, under normal conditions, whenever the frog eats either a real fly or a bit of dust, what it perceives and represents to itself is actually an instance of *fly-or-dust*. That is the most typical cause of its perceptual behavior, now described under normal conditions. But Millikan denies that, even under normal conditions, what determine content are typical *causes*. Instead, what matter are typical *uses* of information: what the frog does with what it sees. In this case, it uses the visual information to get nourishment. Thus teleological considerations rule out nonnutritious 'dust' as any part of the description of what the frog perceives.

Of course, the frog may not see flies as such, either. What does a frog know about flies anyway? Perceptual content for the frog is presumably something fairly basic; *small, dark, moving object,* perhaps. The problem with that description is that it includes specks of dust and BB's, too, so disjunction begins to loom large again. Yet teleology can still help, even at this coarser level of description. The frog does not *need* to see small, dark, moving objects. What the frog does need to find is food; so if the description of its perceptual content must be kept basic, then *food* is the better term. Of course, that concept will comprise its own disjunction (e.g., *flies-or-moths-or-mosquitoes*). But disjunctive contents on the teleological account simply do not proliferate as they do for causal theories. There are limits to what can actually constitute food. Therefore, a dust-eating frog will misrepresent its prey. *Fly-or-mosquito-or-**dust*** is ruled out as a description of its perceptual content, because dust cannot function as food.

However, it is precisely here, I think, that serious problems with teleological accounts begin to appear. First, if the frog knows nothing about flies, why should it know anything about food? *Food* is our concept, not the frog's. Invoking it to describe the animal's perceptual content amounts to an act of teleological interpretation. But such interpretations can vary considerably, so there may be no determinate way to identify content. The problem at the root of this indeterminacy is that needs cannot be identified in isolation.

For example, the needs of an organism can include not just a target item like food, but also an effective way to get it. What the organism needs is the ability to use its resources efficiently when it seeks nourishment, to enhance its overall chance of survival. Thus, to avoid overequipping the frog with unnecessarily sophisticated perceptual abilities, a generic food detector will suffice; something that picks up *flies-or-moths-or-mosquitoes,* but cannot tell one from the other.[8] But if that is the case (i.e., if nature economizes in selecting visual mechanisms that do not waste resources), then why should nature not just give the frog a *fly-or-moth-or-mosquito-or-dust (-or-BB)* detector, as long as dust specks are harmless and BB's are rare in the evolving frog's ecological niche? Granted, such a costs-and-benefits analysis will bottom out somewhere; not every item the frog eats can be added to the disjunction. But the point is that, given the possibility of such alternative interpretations, it is unlikely that a definitive evolutionary story can ever be told about the normal conditions under which a brain structure or perceptual mechanism has evolved. This is surely even more true when we move from frogs to the more complex case of humans. The individuation of perceptual content by adaptational roles thus comes to rest on preferred interpretations. Once we recognize that needs cannot be defined atomistically, individuating content in terms of them becomes an almost hermeneutic affair. Teleological accounts open the door to creeping antirealism.

Of course, one way to restrict teleological interpretations of content, so that a definitive one can be given, is to assume that perceptual systems have been *optimally designed.* This is an idealization that is reflected in Millikan's appeal to normal conditions (cf. Cummins, 1989). Assumptions of optimality are very much in the tradition of Marr's engineering approach to the visual system; so there is some precedent in the study of vision. But this sort of adaptationism in evolutionary biology is methodologically suspect (cf. Gould & Lewontin, 1978; cf. Dennett, 1987). And empirically, the evidence for HDP suggests that the assumption of optimality is a mistake. Even if one preferred description of visual content could be singled out on the grounds that having detector mechanisms for it would maximize efficiency, there is no reason to believe that natural selection must achieve it. Evolution is simply not that well-oiled. Visual detectors, both ours and the frogs', may be considerably less than the best.

The third approach to mental content individuation is Conceptual Role Semantics (CRS). On this account, defended in various versions by Block (1986), Harman (1982), Johnson-Laird (1977), and Miller and Johnson-Laird (1976), mental contents are determined holistically by the relations into which their bearers enter with other content-bearing states. On the classical model of symbolic representation and computation, the relevant relations are mostly conceptual and inferential. A certain belief, for instance, is the belief that it is by virtue of how it gets used in conjunction with other beliefs, desires, intentions, and so on, typically in drawing inferences, often in practical syllogisms that culminate in action. These relations depend on a conceptual framework in which various conceptual roles are essentially interdefined.

---

[8] Dennett (1991) has defended teleological costs-and-benefits analysis of this sort.

On the face of it, CRS may seem to be solipsistic; by individuating mental representations in terms of their relations to one another, such accounts appear to rely wholly on internal factors, breaking the bond with the external world that seems so obviously to be perception's goal. But that is not really the case. First, the point of appealing to internal relations is to explain intentionality (i.e., how mental states can be about things). To think that, on CRS, all mental representations are actually about other mental representations is to confuse the cause of intentionality with the "aboutness" that is its effect. Second, CRS comes in different varieties, some of which have well-defined externalist dimensions. For example, on a *two-factor* account, CRS is combined with a causal-referential factor, so that the referent of a mental representation is determined by its causal relations to external states of affairs, while its meaning or sense of characterization of those states of affairs is determined by its conceptual role (Block, 1986). Furthermore, according to the so-called *long-armed* version of CRS, the relevant conceptual roles themselves need not stop at the boundary of the skin. Conceptual and other functional roles are, in the first instance, causal roles; they are causal powers identified computationally in terms of typical inputs and outputs (Harman, 1982). The assumption of CRS is that representational/computational functions map onto the causal powers of the brain, so that a certain kind of causal process will also constitute a computational process. But it is perfectly consistent with this approach to expand the scope of the functional system to include causal interactions between the body and the world, so that descriptions of the functions within the system make essential reference to external affairs.[9]

Nonetheless, other problems remain. One major worry about CRS is that it embodies a deep circularity that threatens explanation. If each type of content is identified with reference to the others, then there can never be a starting point for content identification. Whatever the relata are that define the relevant functional roles, those relata will themselves be identified by their relations to other relata; yet those (second tier) relata will be likewise identified in terms of other (third tier) relata; and so on. Moreover, CRS implies that there can be indefinitely variable fine-grained differences in perceptual content across perceivers, thus thwarting psychological generalization. Taken together, these concerns constitute a *content instability problem*: Meanings or contents cannot be identified without some fixed points of reference.

However, it is important to be clear about what the problem is. First, it is necessary to distinguish between the *individuation* and the *attribution* of content. The former is an ontological matter regarding the properties by which contentful states are set apart from noncontentful ones, and one type of content is said to differ from another. The latter is an epistemological problem regarding how we know when to ascribe the content so individuated, in order to explain behavior. Content instabil-

---

[9] In this case, external causal factors will have a different status than on the causal covariance theory. They will contribute to a set of relations in a system; it is those interrelations that determine content, rather than the external causes taken alone.

ity is primarily an attribution problem. As a familiar practice in science, the inter-definition of the terms and functions posited by a theory is not objectionable. If scientific theories tell us how the world really is, then holistic individuation per se is not ontologically suspicious. Neither are relational properties, even higher order ones, much cause for alarm. To be sure, there are some special worries when the items in question are intentional contents and meanings. Conceptual role semantics makes individuation conditions for mental contents into *similarity* (rather than identity) conditions (cf. Block, 1986, p. 629). Thus semantic holism implies that representations differ by degrees. But ontologically speaking, degreed representations are really no odder than other degreed states, like temperature or baldness. If we can speak of degrees of belief (as many philosophers are inclined to do), then we can legitimately speak of degrees of perceptual content.

But here the problem becomes clear: Unlike the case with degrees of temperature, ascribing degrees of belief and other mental states is a special challenge. For we have nothing comparable to a mental thermometer by which to measure the similarity of a perceiver's representation to some standard. This problem is of particular concern when CRS is extended to perceptual contents, which provide the observational basis for other, higher-order relations among concepts and beliefs. We ought to be able to say clearly what people *see,* at least, if we are to have any hope of saying what they believe.[10]

Nonetheless, I shall now try to show that CRS is the most plausible theory of content for the limited representations posited by HDP. Moreover, I believe that HDP points the way to overcome the content instability problem: Rather than making the vision scientist's life harder, the discovery of various forms of perceptual strategy can actually help ground attributions of content for CRS.[11]

V. PERCEPTUAL STRATEGIES AND MENTAL CONTENT

There are two reasons for appealing to CRS in light of the evidence I have discussed. The first is simply that strategic plasticity and CRS often go hand-in-hand. Indeed, the latter is sometimes said to be the basis for the former, so evidence for

---

[10] This problem has led some philosophers, who are friendly to CRS, to argue that meaning holism for mental states must stop where perception begins. For them, in order to protect against instability, perceptual content must be thoroughly *nonconceptual* (Crane, 1993; Peacocke, 1993). Without concepts, content need not be specified in terms of unstable conceptual roles. I agree that perception is not concept dependent at every stage of processing or for every task, but it seems obvious that perception cannot be wholly concept-free. In any case, holistic individuation is not limited to concepts. Thus, there may be a *functional* role semantics (FRS) for perceptual functions that do not depend on concepts. For instance, as an alternative to concepts, Peacocke proposes spatial representations that he calls "scenarios." As he notes, these bear comparison to mental images. But as I have previously argued elsewhere, FRS is the most plausible theory of image content (Rollins, 1989; cf. Block, 1986, p. 662, who argues that it is the *only* plausible account). If so, then another solution to holistic content instability, something other than the mere exclusion of concepts, is required.

[11] For a more extended argument, see Rollins (forthcoming).

one is evidence for the other. Of course, perceptual plasticity does not require content holism.[12] But in the cases I have cited, the two ideas are in fact mutually reinforcing. The second reason for recent theories of perception to prefer CRS is that the other two theories of content are simply not very plausible in conjunction with a hybrid account. Both Dretske and Millikan have in fact suggested connections between Gibson's views and theirs. Thus, we might think that it is one of their theories of content, and not CRS, that works best with ecological considerations in mind. But that, I suggest, would be a mistake.

The concept of information does play an important role for both Dretske and Gibson. On Dretske's (1981) information-theoretic view, there is a stage of analog processing in early vision that is noncognitive and nonconceptual that provides a form of information that is the same, even for perceivers who hold different concepts, beliefs, or theories.[13] Through these early processes, we see objects rather than facts; and "our sense perception of objects is itself direct and unmediated" (1990, p. 136). However, Dretske has himself cautioned against confusing this sort of direct realism about the *objects* of perception with Gibson's direct realism about perceptual *processes*. As Dretske notes, one can hold the former view while still positing internal representations (so long as it is not the representations themselves that are said to be directly perceived). Thus Dretske deviates from Gibson in two ways: by allowing internal representations (albeit nonconceptual ones) to mediate early vision; and by making later vision ("cognitive perception"—1990, p. 142) depend on concepts and beliefs. In any case, this sort of stage-dependent analysis of perception as partly ecological (early on) and partly constructivist (later in the processing stream) does not really provide a new alternative. It amounts to restricting the scope of representation in just the way that the modularity thesis does.[14] Thus it may fall under the weight of empirical evidence. A theory of perception that limits internal representations by acknowledging the direct accessibility of external information should not be a reliable indicator theory.

Likewise, ecology does not entail teleology. It might be thought that appealing to basic, need-driven content, (e.g., food instead of flies) amounts to a kind of coarse coding. Thus the teleological approach would seem consistent with the idea that the visual system can get by with undetailed and incomplete representations in a certain sense. But the rationale for coarse coding in the two cases is really quite different. On the Adaptationist account, coarse coding is due to an optimal design engineering by nature. But according to HDP, it reflects the need for a suboptimal *making-do*. To be sure, using available resources for a variety of jobs *is* a kind of efficiency. However, it is an efficiency of use, not of design.

---

[12] A causal–teleological theory that makes perception dependent at every stage on inference, with full access to background knowledge, would also do the trick.

[13] See Turvey et al. (1981) for a related discussion of the nature of perceptual laws in Dretske's sense as the basis for a Gibsonian account of intentionality in perception.

[14] As Dretske himself notes (1990, pp. 140–141).

Millikan (1995) has recently suggested that Gibsonian affordances, taken as opportunities for action, are really perceived by way of what she calls "pushmi-pullyu representations." Unlike beliefs, such representations have both a descriptive and a directive function: They represent both what is the case and what is to be done. Perceptual representations of this sort are states of the organism that vary directly according to certain differences in the distal environment (p. 151). At the same time, they represent possible ways of moving within that environment. The idea of direct variation here is similar to Dretske's, but for Millikan, such representations are not unconceptualized, and they only have content by being the objects of attitudes (albeit not beliefs).

Millikan's idea is interesting, but, like Dretske's, it hardly seems to integrate the direct and indirect elements of perception. Rather, it simply analyzes apparent directness in terms of representations of a certain sort. Moreover, adding this new category of representation may be unnecessary and hence unmotivated. Opportunities for action can also be afforded by the interactive relation between perceptual and motor systems, in a way that is more compatible with CRS. Thus, again apart from philosophical problems intrinsic to the teleological approach, I doubt that it can provide an account of perceptual content that is motivated by HDP.

Whether CRS can provide such an account depends, in part, on how it handles the instability of content attribution. I have suggested that acknowledging strategic perceptual plasticity can help in that regard. That claim turns on the fact that strategies can be identified independently of the inferences and computations that would ordinarily be said to make up conceptual roles. The reason is that this allows a better articulation or elaboration of the conditions under which a particular perceptual representation is likely to be used. The problem of content attribution arises, I think, when we try to ascribe content on the basis of the very functional relations by which it is individuated. The appeal to perceptual strategy provides an alternative. Although perceptual strategies may presuppose the possession of certain types of representation, they do not themselves constitute the representations that are presupposed.

To see that this is so, consider that the semantic properties of complex representations constructed from more basic concepts depend on the truth functional, logically implicational, and evidential relations that are required for inference. When one speaks of the conceptual roles that define concepts, one usually has these relations in mind. But this is not true when concepts are deployed for strategic purposes. In this case, the use of concepts or other representations is governed as much by a concern for speed, efficiency, or power, as by the pursuit of truth. Therefore, using perceptual categories and concepts strategically need not be what defines those categories and concepts, and knowing something about perceptual strategies gives us additional information, a different vantage point, from which to ascribe content.

And here an interesting point emerges. I have argued that the theories of content advocated by Dretske and Millikan do not fit well with strategically limited uses of representation. That is, they do not serve to individuate the contents in question.

Nonetheless, both can be said to have identified important aspects of content *attribution*, if a role for strategies is factored into the account; for strategies are linked to them in especially strong ways. Indeed, much of the evidence for how the perceiver deploys his resources on a task will come from the very causal and evolutionary considerations put forth by Dretske and Millikan for indicator and adaptational role semantics. Yet now these considerations serve not to individuate content, but as a basis for attributing strategic uses of it. This makes sense: Speed, power, and efficiency of response will aid survival, and strategies for achieving them are activated (rather than individuated) by external causal conditions. Having identified a perceptual task, a plausible next step in explanation is to determine the way the perceiver is likely to perform the task, by taking account of the environmental conditions, the needs and interests of the perceiver, and any special abilities he may possess. This evidence works to ground attributions of perceptual content by providing more and different types of support for the inference to the best explanation in which content ascription consists. Because the relevant factors include aspects of motor and attentional control, and because strategies are not themselves combinatorial in the logical and semantic sense that marks mental representation and inference, strategic diversity is limited in a way that, say, belief formation is not. This allows for a kind of *convergence* on content from two directions: one deriving from explicitly intentional, prior belief and other content attributions, and the other from the evidence for probable perceptual strategies.

One final reason for thinking that perceptual strategies are a distinct and important complement to the conceptual or functional roles by which representations are individuated is that it explains how perceptual experience and abilities can change without any change in concepts or perceptual categories. Paul M. Churchland (1989) has argued in this vein that the world can be perceived in new ways when preexisting concepts or perceptual prototypes are redeployed to cover new cases (cf. Rollins, 1993). This can happen, he suggests, when perceivers learn to recognize different objects in ambiguous figures. Such perceptual shifts, which are often the result of redirected attention, are analogous to the growth of scientific understanding that results from extending old concepts to new domains (as in the most familiar example, when light was construed as wave-like). In such a case, there is theoretical development without any new additions to the conceptual repertoire. Likewise, Churchland suggests, perceptual understanding of a scene is affected by redeploying available representations rather than adding new categories or types.

The problem is that this idea does not clearly sit well with the strong conceptual holism that Churchland and other advocates of CRS embrace. What is needed is some principled way to segregate the changes in functional relations among representations that are not constitutive of them. The solution is to say that the controlled redeployment of concepts or other representations need not result in the production of higher-order representations. Thus significant changes in perceptual experience and ability do not always depend on a further elaboration of a scene. This amounts to construing the redeployment of representational resources as a strategy in precisely the sense that HDP suggests. In this way, I believe, a viable semantics for limited representations can be achieved.

VI. CONCLUSION

If Hegel is right about philosophy, then we should expect its recent flourishing (in a more naturalistic guise) to correspond to the death of *something*. Perhaps not civilization as we know it, but at least a cluster of old-fashioned oppositions: between mentalism and nonmentalism, representation and behavioral dynamics, indirect and direct theories of perception. Recent research in cognitive psychology and neuroscience has produced a wealth of curiously similar results about the surprising effects of short-term perceptual plasticity. These, it would seem, are results in search of a theory. Perhaps, armed with a theory of perceptual content that is compatible with the evidence, philosophy can now help in the development of an overarching frame.

References

Anderson, C., & Van Essen, D. (1987). Shifter circuits: A computational strategy for dynamic aspects of visual processing. *Proceedings of the National Academy of Science, 84,* 6297–6301.

Ballard, D. (1991). Animate vision. *Artificial Intelligence, 48,* 57–86.

Biederman, I. (1987). Recognition by components. *Psychological Review, 94,* 115–147.

Blake, A., & Yuille, A. (Eds.) (1992). *Active vision.* Cambridge, MA: MIT Press.

Block, N. (1986). Advertisement for a semantics for psychology. In P. A. French, T. E. Uehling, & H. K. Wettstein (Eds.), *Midwest studies in philosophy, Vol. 10* (pp. 615–678). Minneapolis: University of Minnesota Press.

Burge, T. (1986). Individualism and psychology. *Philosophical Review, 95,* 3–45.

Churchland, P. M. (1990). *Matter and consciousness.* Cambridge, MA: MIT Press.

Churchland, P. M. (Ed.). (1989). *A neurocomputational perspective.* Cambridge, MA: MIT Press.

Churchland, P. S. (1986). *Neurophilosophy.* Cambridge, MA: MIT Press.

Churchland, P. S., & Churchland, P. M. (1990). Could a machine think? *Scientific American,* January, pp. 32–37.

Churchland, P. S., Ramachandran, V. S., & Sejnowski, T. J. (1994). A critique of pure vision. In C. Koch & J. David (Eds.), *Large scale neuronal theories of the brain* (pp. 23–60). Cambridge, MA: MIT Press.

Churchland, P. S., & Sejnowski, T. J. (1989). Neural representation and neural computation. In L. Nadel, L. A. Cooper, P. Culicover, & R. Harnish (Eds.), *Neural connections, mental computation* (pp. 15–48). Cambridge, MA: MIT Press.

Cummins, R. (1989). *Meaning and mental representation.* Cambridge, MA: MIT Press.

Cutting, J. (1986). *Perception with an eye for motion.* Cambridge, MA: MIT Press.

Dennett, D. (1991). *Consciousness explained.* Boston: Little, Brown.

Dennett, D. (1987). *The intentional stance.* Cambridge, MA: MIT Press.

Dennett, D. (1981). *Brainstorms.* Cambridge, MA: MIT Press.

Dretske, F. (1990). Seeing, believing, and knowing. In D. Osherson, S. Kosslyn, & J. Hollerback (Eds.), *Visual cognition and action* (pp. 129–148). Cambridge, MA: MIT Press.

Dretske, F. (1986). Misrepresentation. In R. Bogdan (Ed.), *Belief* (pp. 17–36). Cambridge, UK: Oxford University Press.

Dretske, F. (1981). *Knowing and the flow of information.* Cambridge, MA: MIT Press.

Fodor, J. A. (1990). *A theory of content and other essays.* Cambridge, MA: MIT Press.

Fodor, J. A. (1983). *The modularity of mind.* Cambridge, MA: MIT Press.

Fodor, J. A. (1975). *The language of thought*. New York: Crowell.

Fodor, J. A., & Pylyshn, Z. W. (1988). Connectionism and cognitive architecture. *Cognition, 28,* 3–71.

Gilden, D. L. (1991). On the origins of dynamical awareness. *Psychological Review, 98,* 554–568.

Goldman, A. (1993). Epistemic folkways and scientific epistemology. In Alvin Goldman (Ed.), *Readings in philosophy and cognitive science* (pp. 95–118). Cambridge, MA: MIT Press.

Gould, S. J., & Lewontin, R. (1978). The Spandrels of San Marco and the panglossian of paradigm: A critique of the adaptationist programme. *Proceedings of the Royal Society of London, 205,* 581–598.

Harman, G. (1982). Conceptual role semantics. *Notre Dame Journal of Formal Logic, 23,* 242–256.

Harman, G. (1989). Some philosophical issues in cognitive science. In M. Posner (Ed.), *Foundations of Cognitive Science* (pp. 831–848). MIT Press.

Hochberg, J. (1972). The representation of things and people. In M. Mandlebaum (Ed.), *Art, Perception, and Reality* (pp. 47–94). Baltimore: Johns Hopkins University Press.

Hochberg, J. (1980). Pictorial functions and perceptual structures. In M. Hagen (Ed.), *The Perceptions of Pictures Vol. II* (pp. 97–93). Academic Press.

Johnson-Laird, P. (1977). Procedural semantics. *Cognition, 5,* 189–214.

Kitcher, P. (1988). Marr's computational theory of vision. *Philosophy of Science,* March, 1–24.

Kosslyn, P. (1994). *Image and brain*. Cambridge, MA: MIT Press.

Lycan, W. (1990). *Mind and Cognition*. Cambridge, MA: Blackwell Publishers.

Marr, D. (1982). *Vision*. San Francisco: Freeman.

Marr, D., & Poggio, T. (1976). Co-operative computation of stereo disparity. *Science 194:* 283–287.

McClelland, J., & Rumelhart, D. (1981). An interactive activation model of context effects in letter perception. *Psychological Review, 88,* 375–407.

Miller, G., & Johnson-Laird, P. (1976). *Language and perception*. Cambridge, MA: MIT Press.

Millikan, R. (1995). Pushimi-pullyu representations. In L. May, M. Friedman, & A. Clark (Eds.), *Mind and morals* (pp. 145–161). Cambridge, MA: MIT Press.

Millikan R. (1984). *Language, thought, and other biological categories*. Cambridge, MA: MIT Press.

Peacocke, C. (1993). Scenarios, concepts, and perception. In T. Crane (Ed.), *The contents of experience* (pp. 105–135). Cambridge: Cambridge University Press.

Pinker, S., & Prince, A. (1988). On language and communication. *Cognition, 28,* 73–93.

Posner, M., & Raichle, M. (1994). *Images of mind*. New York: Freeman.

Pylyshyn, Z. (1986). *Computation and cognition*. Cambridge, MA: MIT Press.

Ramachandran, V. S. (1990). Interactions between motion, depth, color, and form: The utilitarian theory of perception. In C. Blakemore (Ed.), *Vision: Coding and efficiency* (pp. 346–360). Cambridge, UK: Cambridge University Press.

Rollins, M. (forthcoming). *Minding the brain: The perceptual encoding of mental content*. Cambridge, MA: MIT Press.

Rollins, M. (1993). Deep plasticity: A general encoding approach. *Philosophy of Science, 61,* 39–59.

Rollins, M. (1989). *Mental imagery: On the limits of cognitive science*. New Haven, CT: Yale University Press.

Schwartz, R. (1996). Directed perception. *Philosophical Psychology, 9,* 81–91.

Searle, J. (1984). *Minds, brains, and science*. Cambridge, MA: Harvard University Press.

Smolensky, P. (1988). On the proper treatment of connectionism. *Behavioral and Brain Sciences, 11,* 1–74.

Turing, A. (1950). Computing machinery and intelligence. *Mind, LIX,* 236.

Turvey, M. T., Shaw, R. E., Reed, E. S., & Mace, W. M. (1981). Ecological laws of perceiving and acting. *Cognition, 9,* 237–304.

Van Essen, D., Anderson, C., & Felleman. (1992). Information processing in the primate visual system. *Science, 255,* 419–423.

CHAPTER 3

Consciousness and Mind as Philosophical Problems and Psychological Issues

George Mandler

I. MIND AND CONSCIOUSNESS: CENTRAL ISSUES

In 1953, E. G. Boring, the intrepid chronicler of who did what and when in psychology's history, reviewed the history of introspection and its implications for the study of consciousness. He deplored the lack of distinction and of conceptual clarity of mind and consciousness, and in the spirit of the times—just before the so-called cognitive revolution that signalled a return to a prebehaviorist psychology—he concluded that operationism had successfully fused the dichotomies of matter and mind, conscious and unconscious by showing that "human consciousness is an inferrèd construct . . . [and] . . . literally immediate observation . . . does not exist (Boring, 1953, p. 187)." With the rejection of operationism and of behaviorism, contemporary philosophy and psychology have since then tackled the question of mind and consciousness anew—with what results? There is no real answer to that question, and I shall restrict myself to a selective review of the current state of the art and some of its precursors. The enterprise will involve asking what the referent of mind might be, how to deal with enduring questions about consciousness, sketching philosophical and psychological approaches to consciousness, and then returning to a view of mind within the context of psychological functionalism. I conclude with an overview of psychology's recent revived interest in conscious and unconscious processing modes, and with selected views on the mind–body issue.

The philosophy of mind and consciousness, fairly recently awakened from a place-holding slumber, currently abounds with conjectures and speculations. I cannot do

Perception and Cognition at Century's End
Copyright © 1998 by George Mandler.

justice to the full range of opinions expressed, but I will sketch a few positions relevant to a psychology of consciousness. Just the sheer number and variety of labels for different and contradictory positions in philosophy are enough to deter one from trying to summarize "contemporary" philosophy. Here is a sample: Eliminative materialism, analytic functionalism, analytic behaviorism, homuncular functionalism, direct realism, commonsense relationism, and many more (see also Rollins, chap. 2, this volume).[1]

It might be useful if philosophers could agree on some basic propositions (even testable ones?) so that the rest of us could derive some benefit from their labors. At least psychology has over the years adopted central tendencies that, even though usually wrong, permitted the identification of a dominant mainstream of thought. Undaunted, I start with an attempt to define the domain of a philosophy of mind.

II. WHAT IS A PHILOSOPHY OF MIND ABOUT?

There are two major problems confronting an attempt to delimit a philosophy of mind. First, some philosophers are not at all sure that it would be possible to arrive at any understanding of mind, whatever it is. And second, there is no agreement whether "mind" refers to the contents of consciousness or whether something else or more is implied.

Thomas Nagel is an excellent example of a philosopher who, though implicitly claiming otherwise, denies the possibility of understanding the mind, without quite telling us what this "mind" might be. It is described as a "general feature of the world" like matter (1986, p. 19) that cannot be understood by any physical reduction and which also is beyond any evolutionary explanation. Nagel assures us that "something else" must be going on, and he is sure that whatever it may be, it is taking us to a "truer and more detached" understanding of the world (p. 79). Whereas I do not wish to advertise any great advance in contemporary psychology, it is difficult to follow someone who on the one hand refuses to examine current psychological knowledge and on the other hand insists that "the methods needed to understand ourselves do not yet exist" (p. 10). Nagel contends that "the world may be inconceivable to *our* minds" (p. 10). Humans are by no means omniscient, but one cannot truly claim to know or to prejudge what knowledge is or is not attainable. There surely are aspects of the world that are currently inconceivable, and others that were so centuries ago, but many of the latter are not now and the former may not be in the future.

There seems to be no public agreement as to the referent for the ubiquitous term *mind,* and dictionaries are not particularly helpful. For example, Webster's is quite catholic in admitting "the complex of elements in an individual that feels, perceives, thinks, wills, and esp. reasons" AND "the conscious mental events and capabilities in an organism" AND "the organized conscious and unconscious adaptive mental

---

[1] For an accessible, though biased, review of the current scene, see Searle (1995).

activity of an organism." Philosophers rarely tell us which of these minds they have in mind. One wonders how obscure these deliberations must appear to a French or German reader who has no exact equivalent for our "mind" and must rely on *esprit, Sinn, Seele, Geist,* or *Psyche.* Apart from the public display of disunity, it is likely that most philosophers would agree to a use of "mind" as a quasi-theoretical entity that is causally involved in mental events, including consciousness. I will return to the conflict between seeing "mind" as representing the contents (and sometimes functions) of consciousness compared with using "mind" as a summary term for the various mechanisms that we assign to conscious and unconscious processes. First, some considerations of the questions that puzzle us about consciousness.

III. THE PUZZLE OF CONSCIOUSNESS

Philosophers and others are often fascinated by the puzzle of the subjective mind, the "irreducibly subjective character of conscious mental processes" (Nagel, 1986, p. 7). It is undoubtedly the case that contents are interpretatively subjective (i.e., that their meaning is a function of the conscious person's unique semantics), and that the experience is restricted to the subject. However, both common experience and scientific history tell us that just because direct experience is not available to us, this does not mean that we cannot profitably use indirect methods, both simple and complex, to make sense of those hidden events. Having done so fruitfully in areas as diverse as nuclear physics, paleobiology, and psychopathology, there is no reason why we cannot do the same with consciousness. In the absence of direct access, sophisticated theory is available here as it has been in other areas. There is nothing magical about consciousness that might prevent us from developing a useful and predictive theory about it.

The basic problem that philosophers have created was starkly presented by Descartes and his assertion of the infallibility of the conscious world, which was not to be doubted. The external, physical world, on the other hand, was not definitively ascertainable within the Cartesian theatre (cf. Dennett, 1991; Lycan, 1987). That position was seriously undermined by the logical positivists who made the verification of scientific assertions a cornerstone of their position. Their verificationism led to the insistence on a shared protocol language about public events. Such an elevation of public consensus about the physical world questioned the apparent dominant position of the inner theatre and gave valuable support to the behaviorism of the early 20th century. The behaviorists, for their own reason and history, ruled the inner world out of court. Watson, arguably a man of limited vision and talent, simply declared consciousness of no scientific value or interest. More sophisticated behaviorists, such as B. F. Skinner—the major creative mind of the movement—easily admitted the existence of private events but because of the lack of verifiability and the absence of specific links to external events Skinner denied them any causal significance, a position shared by many philosophers and psychologists for often different reasons. On the other hand, Skinner would not have any truck with mentalism (e.g., 1964), and some philosophers (e.g., Lycan, 1987, p. 132) seem puzzled that Skinner admitted the inner events but declined to consider them mental. Once again we are faced with the sometime identification of consciousness with mind, though we rarely encounter an unequivocal definition of the latter.

Is it possible to establish consciousness as a well-defined and circumscribed theoretical entity? People assert the unquestionable experience of feelings, attitudes, thoughts, images, ideas, beliefs, and other contents of consciousness, but these contents are not accessible to anyone else. Thus, it is not possible to build a phenomenal psychology that is shared (*pace* phenomenological research). Nevertheless, a theory of phenomenal experience may be shared. Once private consciousness is expressed in words, gestures, or in any way externalized, it becomes necessarily a transformation of the private experience, and these external data become the data for the construction of a theory about the underlying consciousness. Events and objects in consciousness can never be available to the theoretician without having been restructured, reinterpreted, and appropriately modified. Can the perennial problem of private datum and public inference be stated concisely in order to indicate the possible extent and solution of the problem?

There are two related phenomena that seriously affect our knowledge of private consciousness. First, the nature of the interrogation biases the reported content of consciousness. More basically, the act of examination itself may affect the conscious contents available to the experiencing individual. For example, the conscious act of interrogating one's consciousness must occupy some part of the limited capacity of consciousness. Or, as Kant (1798/1978) already noted, we tend to import content into consciousness during introspection instead of just observing what is there. As a result, the available, initial content is altered. We are faced with what has been implicated as the uncertainty principle of psychology: "The particular difficulty that the questioner may influence the answer recalls the uncertainty principle in physics, which limits the knowledge we can gain about any individual particle" (Adrian, 1966).

The second problem to be faced is the fact that the contents of consciousness are not simply reproducible by some one-to-one mapping onto verbal report. Even if these contents were always couched in language (which they are not), some theory of transmission would be required. As a result, we are faced, on the one hand, with the individual's awareness of the conscious state and, on the other, with the psychologist's theoretical inference about those contents, on the basis of whatever data are available. Both sorts of knowledge may be used in the construction of a psychology of cognition, although it may be impossible with current knowledge and techniques to determine, in any exact sense, the relation between the personal and the public representation of consciousness.

In brief, then, private experiences are important aspects of the fully functioning mental system, and it is possible to get transformed reports about those events. It should be possible to develop appropriate theories that connect the contents of consciousness, their transformations, their report, and other mental functions. However, it is not possible to build a theory that makes precise predictions about private experience, since the outcome of those predictions cannot be properly evaluated by the psychologist-observer. What one can and must do is to develop theories about consciousness that allow us to evaluate its function and the consequences and relations among states of consciousness and other cognitive and behavioral events. It is this theoretical approach to consciousness that seems to be aversive for philosophers, many of whom seem to want to know what consciousness *really* is. This attitude might also explain why there is so little philosophical interest in the functions of consciousness. A more potent reason may be the search for the *essential* functions of consciousness (i.e., those that could not conceivably be performed by other mechanisms, such as the unconscious). Such a test tends to undermine most postulations of conscious functions.[2]

This position does admit the development of theories, by individuals, about themselves. To the individual, one's experience *is* a datum, and consequently personal theories about one's own structures are, within limits, testable by direct experience. These individual, personal theories of the self are both pervasive and significant in explaining human action, but they cannot, without peril, be generalized to others or to the species as a whole (Mandler & Mandler, 1974).

IV. PHILOSOPHICAL POSITIONS

Having happily accepted one or another form of Cartesian dualism for nearly 300 years,[3] anglophone philosophy briefly partook of behaviorist escapades in the first half of the 20th century wile wrestling with the purified attitudes of logical positivism. Things changed radically around 1960 with the advent of the currently favored way of dealing with the mind—functionalism (see Putnam, 1960). At its simplest, philosophical functionalism depends on sensory inputs and observable behaviors linked by a set of causal relations to describe (in various ways) the "how" of consciousness and mind. At this point we need to distinguish among three of the several uses of the concept of functionalism.

In *philosophical functionalism* the important focus is how information functions; how it is used. The physical implementation is not central and varies from interpreter to interpreter. At its best, this kind of functionalism attempts to arrive at testable hypotheses about mental and cerebral organization. *Linguistic functionalism* defines a position in contrast to extreme nativism. Linguistic functionalism asserts that the factors and variables that shape language are a function of the way language is used (i.e., the way people use and adapt language). *Psychological functionalism* is a term that has

---

[2] Psychologists face a similar problem when approaching questions of animal consciousness (e.g., Griffin, 1984), which tend to be rejected because nonconscious mechanisms are considered to be equally able to perform functions assigned to consciousness.

[3] While this was the central tendency, the opposition had an honorable history dating back to Hobbes and Spinoza.

not been frequently used since its predominance at the turn of the century in the work of Angell, Carr, Dewey, and others. It addresses the question about the (usually adaptive) function of various mental and behavioral mechanisms—what they are and why and how their function contributes to mental/cognitive organization and function.

Partly in reaction against the identity theory of mind and brain (e.g., Smart, 1959), philosophical functionalism was part of the general change in the cognitive and social sciences that took place in the late 1950s and early 1960s.[4] Lycan, in defending a strong version of functionalism as "honest-to-goodness natural teleology," is interested in the various components as they serve (weakly teleologically) the supervening current operation or function of a system (1987, p. 44). He invokes a hierarchical system for all complex phenomena with any level of the hierarchy being unpacked into many lower levels of lesser complexity, thus avoiding the problem of a simple homuncular regression (see also Dennett, 1978). The general concern—here and elsewhere—is with mechanisms: how does the system/mind/organism manage relations between inputs and outputs, and how does it achieve a particular state? Van Gulick (1980) similarly uses functionalism to define psychological (conscious) states within a network of perceptual conditions and organism behaviors. He concludes that such a functional approach permits us to think about content in a naturalistic way and to discern continuities that fit the facts about content. I stress this approach because it focuses on the distinction between philosophical and psychological functionalism. Approaching that difference, Sober (1985) made a distinction between the dominant machine functionalism and teleological functionalism. In contrast to the "how" questions of machine functionalism, the teleological variety asks also what the functions of particular system/organs/processes are. It is this sense of functionalism which, as I shall discuss below, asks the kind of questions that psychologists prefer, and which treat various positions as ostensibly fallible theories about consciousness (or the mind). I should add that I do not believe that this kind of psychological functionalism falls under the rubric of functional analyses and their problems (see Cummins, 1975). Rather than say, for example, that consciousness has the function of making unconscious material available for further processing, I prefer to approach a sense of function as in, How does consciousness function (operate) in and contribute to an information-processing system?

Many of the philosophers' concerns center on the status of common sense, everyday folk psychology (FP). There appears to be some underlying notion that FP characterizes the psychology that most psychologists do. When philosophers reject FP they reject it frequently on grounds similar to those used by psychologists, except that psychologists rarely bother to document their rejection. On the other hand, the employment by psychologists of such theoretical notions as schemas, (unconscious) organizations and strategies, mental and/or neural activation, and so forth, as well as the absence in most current psychological theories of such beloved

---

[4] See G. Mandler (1996) for a discussion of these changes situated in their social context.

folk-theoretical terms as belief, attitude, and will, clearly differentiate FP and psychological psychology. One can even argue that a consequential theory of cognitive processes does not involve intentionality (however defined) but rather that intentional states are one of the phenomena to be explicated and understood by a psychological theory. When rejecting FP, philosophers rarely use an appropriate and convenient psychological theory to contrast with it, but prefer to strike out on their own. For example, Paul Churchland demonstrated that the (much maligned) FP is in fact a theory about the mind and then claimed to show how, as a theory, it is false. He undermined his own position by advocating a replacement of natural language theory by one that expresses brain states directly—eliminative materialism (P. M. Churchland, 1981). That is an equally fallible theory with little evidence to support it, and it has the additional handicap of depending on the brain theories of the moment to describe what it is that the brain does; being even less plausible than folk psychology, it is unlikely to replace it.

V. PSYCHOLOGISTS AND CONSCIOUSNESS

Psychologists have displayed two different attitudes to mind and consciousness: In the aftermath of behaviorism they tended to shy away from considerations of consciousness as if behaviorist dicta were still in force, but they were willing to assign one or another processing function to consciousness; on the other hand, they have talked about mind as a repository of mental mechanisms rather than of consciousness. I shall start with a discussion of the first aspect.

An excellent summary of the history of the recent revival of consciousness has been presented by Shallice (1991), and for an extensive discussion of the issues involved in psychological approaches to consciousness see Mandler (1985a, Ch. 3). I shall confine myself here to the highlights of the revival. Ulric Neisser (1963), the early chronicler of cognitive psychology, had tried to come to terms with consciousness in the psychoanalytic context, but tended to avoid it later in his book that defined the new cognitive psychology (Neisser, 1967). By 1970, consciousness started to become respectable and useful in human information-processing systems, to accommodate serial processing (Atkinson & Shiffrin, 1968), to account for attention in choice and rehearsal (Posner & Boies, 1971; Posner & Keele, 1970), and to select and set goals for action systems (Shallice, 1972). In 1973 Posner and Klein (1973) discussed the functions of consciousness in terms of a direct contact between consciousness and the limited capacity characteristics of mental operations. They note several reasons why the operations of consciousness are closely related to "operations that require access to the limited capacity system (p. 34)" and that these operations are cross-modal (i.e., not tied to any particularly modality). More recent is Baars's (1983) proposal that consciousness is a system that distributes and organizes global information. Most of these accounts considered the workings of the information-processing system and then assigned consciousness to one or another function of that system. In other words, they were functionalists in the psychological sense. In 1975 I presented a defense of the importance of consciousness in which I insisted that consciousness must be taken into account in any full description of the cognitive human system, and listed a variety of functions that might be assigned to it.

An important step in the understanding of consciousness and its functions was undertaken by Marcel (1983). Marcel sees consciousness as a constructive process in which the phenomenal experience is a specific construction to which previously activated schemas have contributed. He relates his position to the rejection of the identity assumption, which postulates that conscious states are merely another state of a preconscious structure. The identity position characterizes practically all current views of consciousness, which postulate that some preconscious state "breaks through," "reaches," "is admitted," "crosses a threshold," or "enters" into consciousness. In other words, conscious states are just unconscious ones in conscious clothing. A constructivist position states, in contrast, that most conscious states are constructed out of preconscious structures in response to the requirements of the moment. We can be conscious only of experiences that are constructed out of activated schemas. We are not conscious of the process of activation or the schemas and their constituent part themselves. A constructed conscious experience depends on the activated schemas, and the resulting phenomenal experience is "an attempt to make sense of as much data as possible at the highest or most functionally useful level possible" (Marcel, 1983). A similar interpretation of consciousness was advanced by John (in Thatcher & John, 1977, pp. 294–304). He noted that in consciousness "information about multiple individual modalities of sensation and perception is combined into a unified multidimensional representation" (i.e., that "consciousness itself is a representational system"). However, despite these various forays, there is no consistent psychological theory in which consciousness plays an integral part.

I cannot close this section on the various views of consciousness without discussing at least briefly those philosophers and psychologists who have either dismissed the relevance of consciousness to a theory of mind and behavior or who have espoused positions too new or too far removed from the mainstream of thought to be evaluated critically at this time.

VI. VIEWS APART FROM THE MAINSTREAM

Two classes of opinion on mind and consciousness deviate from the mainstream positions outlined here. One group—the deniers—asserts the causal inertness or functional irrelevance of consciousness, the other—the innovators—invokes a novel view of the central nervous system in order to account for conscious phenomena.

The major players in the denial groups are those who cannot conceive any possible functional significance in consciousness. They at least discuss (and dismiss) the possibility that consciousness has some important mental functions, in contrast to those (philosophers in particular) who do not even consider such functionality. Typical of the deniers are Patricia S. Churchland (1983), Jackendoff (1987), and Thagard (1986)[5] who are classical epiphenomenalists (i.e., are willing to allow the phenomenon of consciousness but deny it any functional significance; see also Rollins, chap. 2, this volume for discussion). An interesting position is held by Gregory (1981), who denies consciousness any functional significance because it occurs *after* the event to which consciousness is relevant.[6]

Among the innovators, several recent attempts have made relatively little contact with either philosophy or with phenomenal consciousness directly. The two most visible have been Penrose's and Edelman's accounts. Penrose (1994), who ambitiously wishes to involve some future quantum theory with a causal account of consciousness, is the most creative and challenging of the various contemplators of consciousness. However, I believe his argument that brains and minds are not computers is overwrought and tilts at windmills that have currently only a few hot winds at their service; most of us know that minds are not digital computers, and Penrose's positive arguments about some future quantum-theoretical account is generally devoid of current evidence and ignores psychological insights and evidence about differences between conscious and unconscious processes. Edelman (e.g., 1989) actually presents a more innovative theory of cognition and memory than a theory of consciousness. The latter is brought in as a result of perceptual categorization and its relation to memory—a sort of feedback or reentrant mechanism that "creates" consciousness. Edelman is persuasive and makes important arguments, but it is not quite clear why—after he has built an ambitious and complex machinery of mind—he also needs consciousness.

One other position on consciousness should be mentioned that is implied in several philosophical disquisitions. It is related to questions about the status of scientific laws in general and physical ones in particular. These speculations raise questions that current knowledge is incapable of answering. They are of the order of Why is the world the way it is and not otherwise? or Why are physical laws as they are? Similarly, it may be the nature of animal (or specifically mammalian or human) brains or minds that the concomitant of brain activity is conscious experience and that is just the way these animal brains are constituted. To ask why they are that way or what aspects of them *produce* consciousness is not a sensible question at the present time, any more than it is to ask why general relativity holds—rather than some other aspect of the physical world. Such a view avoids worrying about *qualia* and related speculations about their interindividual generality. *Qualia* would be given aspects of the world to be accepted and not to be explained.

VII. MIND AS MECHANISM

I have previously noted the point of view that mind and consciousness are coextensive. I now wish to consider another position that sees mind as the sum total of

---

[5] Thagard is an unusual epiphenomenalist because he denies consciousness any significance in "cognitive" functions but allows it as possible in social or pedagogic contexts.

[6] I have considered this particular problem in the section on the feedback function of consciousness below, which shows one way in which consciousness affects subsequent events.

mechanisms that we ascribe to people (or even to nonhuman animals) in order to make their behavior understandable and coherent. Such a position sees mind and consciousness as independent, though related, concepts (see, for example, Mandler, 1985a, passim); it is implicitly present in many psychological discussions of mind and has been at times explicitly defined. For example, some 45 years ago, Karl Deutsch suggested that "*Mind* might be provisionally defined as any self-sustaining physical process which includes the seven operations of abstracting, communicating, storing, subdividing, recalling, recombining and reapplying items of information" (Deutsch, 1951, p. 216).

Such an approach to mind as a collection of mechanisms is also implied by some philosophers, even though they are preoccupied with the mental functions of consciousness. For example, Searle (1992) notes that "most of the mental phenomena in [a] person's existence are not present to consciousness" and "most of our mental life at any given point is unconscious" (p. 18). He then, however, maintains that our access to unconscious mental states is derived solely from conscious mental states. Not only does such a view signal a return to an initial *tabula rasa* that only becomes populated by the individual's experiences, but it also denies any kind of acquisition of skills or knowledge without conscious participation or any kind of preexperientially given structures.

A view of mind as *mere* mechanism may seem like some sort of Rylean behaviorism. Ryle noted, for example, that "[t]o find that most people have minds . . . is simply to find that they are able and prone to do certain sorts of things" (1949, p. 61). Ryle then rejects any "occult" agency behind these acts, but he is unwilling to consider a *theoretical* set of mechanisms (a *mind?*) by which we try to understand the observed working of the individual. One might note that the insistence on going from the observed to the postulated and vice versa is a characteristic of psychological thinking and theorizing that may sound behavioristic but is in fact no different from what any science does.

And finally, if mind is the repository of perceptual, cognitive, behavioral mechanisms then it can also be argued to be the function that is performed by the brain (see also below). If "mind is what the brain does," then similar relations can be seen in the form and function of other human organs (Mandler, 1985a). A related sentiment is echoed in Lycan's statement that "the mystery of the mental is no more a mystery than the heart, the kidney, the carburetor or the pocket calculator" (1987, p. 44).

VIII. PSYCHOLOGICAL ISSUES: FUNCTIONALISM AND EMPIRICAL RESULTS—WHAT IS THE FUNCTION OF CONSCIOUSNESS?

There have been relatively few positions on what it is that consciousness does for cognition/mind/information processing. For most psychologists the functions of consciousness have been of relatively recent interest. Frequently, some psychological process is said to be equivalent to consciousness, such as attention or short-term memory or a way station between short-term and long-term memory. I shall return to the psychological function of consciousness shortly. But first, how about the philosophers?

In keeping with the variety of positions espoused by philosophers, there are a number of different views on the functions of consciousness. These positions roughly divide into four categories: First, there are those who deny consciousness any important role in generating actions or thoughts (e.g., P. S. Churchland, 1983; see Rollins, chap. 2, this volume for further discussion); then there are those who assign consciousness some ineluctable character and function, which suggests that it cannot be studied scientifically (e.g., McGinn, 1991; Nagel, 1986); third, there are the philosophical functionalists, interested in how (but not really why) consciousness works (e.g., Lycan, 1987); and finally a group who sometimes consider the why tangentially but primarily advance suggestions as to the structure and function of consciousness within the larger picture of human action and thought (e.g., Searle, 1992; Van Gulick, 1988).

The notion that somehow thought and action are initiated by conscious contents tends to be held by some philosophers, but I believe this assignment of causal agency to consciousness is in part due to the confusion of notions of mind and consciousness. For psychologists, mind rather than consciousness is given causal agency, particularly to the extent that a cognitive psychology of mind uses the concept of mind as standing in for the sum of psychological processes. As I have noted above, it seems to be used in that sense in some philosophical writing.

Consider as an example Searle's (1992) connection principle, which insists that functioning unconscious states can be admitted only when they are potential conscious contents (i.e., that all unconscious intentional states are in principle accessible to consciousness). Searle's unconscious states are *not* theoretical entities (as they are in most psychological theories) but postulated neurophysiological processes, some of which are accessible to consciousness and others (unintentional ones) that are inaccessible. This insistence on potential accessibility to consciousness creates such counterfactual assertions as the notion that the "grammars of particular languages . . . obviously contain a large number of rules that are accessible to consciousness" (Searle, 1992, p. 242). This is surely news to anybody who reflects on the fact that without instructions people cannot bring grammatical rules to consciousness, and surely my 3-year-old granddaughter would be hard put to do so, not to mention the arguments over what these grammatical rules are.

Dennett (1991) tackles consciousness from a classical position of scientism—the insistence that subjective phenomena cannot be handled by the third-person attitudes of traditional science. This has an advantage—also used by Ryle—of not having to deal with the problem of the subjective qualities of consciousness, but rather to treat them as subjective fictions that have no causal import. Dennett's book is a rich source of speculations, and his arguments are generally important, despite the fact that he is wedded to the computer metaphor, including the postulation of a virtual implementation of mental life to substitute for the rejected subjective experiences (see also Mandler, 1993).

A somewhat different position is taken by Flanagan (1992, 1997) who advocates what he calls the *natural method,* which combines evidence from three areas—phenomenology, psychology/cognitive science, and neuroscience. The goal is to understand "what consciousness is, how it works, and what, if anything, it is good for" (Flanagan, 1997). Flanagan is more concerned than most philosophers with the function of consciousness within general mental functioning, noting, for example, that our conception of consciousness will depend on our notion of a science of the mind in general.

IX. PSYCHOLOGICAL FUNCTIONALISM AND CONSCIOUSNESS

I summarize here a proposal about the functions of consciousness that should also serve as a challenge to others to improve or change it. It deals with some relatively simple characteristics that—as a first step—describe some of the ways in which consciousness affects action and thought.[7] I stress four points: (a) the constructive nature of consciousness; (b) the limited capacity of consciousness; (c) the serial nature of consciousness; and (d) the feedback function of consciousness.

Given the recent insights into the parallel and distributed nature of (unconscious) mental processing, our conceptions of the human mind (broadly interpreted) needed a mechanism to handle the problem of choice and priorities. Specifically, we are faced with a bottleneck created by the multitude of possible thoughts and actions of comparable "strengths" competing for expression contrasted with the need for a unique choice of acts for effective action in the environment. I suggest that this problem is handled by the buffering function of consciousness that imposes *limited capacity* and *seriality* on mental contents. Conscious and unconscious processes are—in major ways—contrasted by their differences in seriality and capacity. The unconscious is where the action is, where all possible thoughts and acts may be activated without much regard to order or number; conscious thought and action impose considered and limited serial action. Conscious processes are serial and limited in capacity to some five contemporaneous items or chunks, whereas unconscious processes operate in parallel and are—for all practical purposes—"unlimited" in capacity. Seriality is phenomenally obvious and experimentally pervasive, whereas limited capacity requires more analysis but is experimentally demonstrable in perception, conceptual thought, memory, and so on.[8] Given the assumption that current conscious contents are constructed out of available activated structures and current demands, then under different demands the same underlying structures should

---

[7] For a more extended discussion of these points, see G. Mandler (1993, 1997).

[8] The notion that our conscious contents only represent a part of all the information relevant to a particular percept, with the rest being unconsciously given, was asserted by Kant (1798/1978) in his discussion of representations (ideas) of which we are not conscious.

give rise to different conscious representations (see Mandler, 1992). The relatively slow, serial, capacity-limited nature of conscious contents also makes possible the juxtaposition of previously unrelated mental events and the creation of novel concatenations. The fourth assumption, the feedback assumption, asserts the causal utility of conscious events, as well as their effect on subsequent activations of consciously represented events. The feedback assumption states that repetition priming (i.e., the additional activation of underlying representations when words or acts are repeated) also applies to conscious representations. Alternatives, choices, or competing hypotheses that have been represented in consciousness will receive additional activation and thus be enhanced. Given the capacity limitation of consciousness combined with the selection of conscious states relevant to current concerns, very few preconscious candidates for actions and thoughts will achieve this additional, consciousness-mediated activation. What structures are most likely to be available for such additional activation? It will be those preconscious structures that have been selected as most responsive to current demands and intentions. Whatever structures are used for a current conscious construction will receive additional activation. In contrast, alternatives that were candidates for conscious thought or action but were not selected will be relegated to a relatively lower probability of additional activation and therefore will be less likely to be accessed on subsequent occasions. The evidence for this general effect is derived from current research showing that the sheer frequency of activation affects subsequent accessibility for thought and action, whether in the area of perceptual priming, recognition memory, preserved amnesic functions, or decision making (for a summary of some of these phenomena, see Mandler, 1989). The proposal extends such activations to internally generated events as well and, in particular, to the momentary states of consciousness constructed to satisfy internal and external demands. Thus, just as reading a sentence produces activation of the underlying schemas, so does (conscious) thinking of that sentence or its gist activate these structures. In the former case, what is activated depends on what the world presents to us; in the latter the activation is determined and limited by the conscious construction. Note that in order for the feedback function to make sense, we must assume that the "adaptive" function of construction that selects appropriate mental contents is operating. This hypothesis of selective and limited activation of situationally relevant structures requires no homunculus-like function for consciousness in which some independent agency selects and directs thoughts and actions that have been made available in consciousness.[9]

X. CONSCIOUSNESS AND EMPIRICAL PSYCHOLOGY

It is characteristic of modern psychology that much of its concern with problems of consciousness during the past 15 to 20 years has taken place in an arena removed

---

[9] For further elaboration of these notions, see G. Mandler (1992, 1997).

from the philosophical and theoretical discussions I have reviewed above. And it may also be relevant that the common observation that much of what we remember or perceive is done without any conscious effort did not receive any serious consistent attention until recently. Psychologists' lack of attention to the real world occurred despite the fact that the midwife of experimental work on memory, Hermann Ebbinghaus, discussed memories that are involuntary (i.e., other than produced by deliberate searches) over 100 years ago.[10]

This distinction between deliberate, conscious access to memories (or thoughts and actions) and the nondeliberate, automatic coming-to-mind of such mental contents has been prominent in recent work in cognitive psychology. However, it is not quite clear whether psychologists working on these phenomena are always willing to see them in the light of the workings of human consciousness.

Although most of the work with conscious and unconscious phenomena has been in the area of memory, research on lexical decision, priming, and spreading activation makes distinctions among memory and other cognitive categories rather tenuous. Much of this work has been discussed under the distinction between implicit and explicit processes—the distinction between effortful deliberate memorial recovery and indirect automatic memorial recovery (see Schacter, 1987, for a history and review).

There has been an increasing tendency in recent years to assign different kinds of memorial functions to different, sometimes independent, systems. The number of such distinctions among systems is large, but I believe that they share one common characteristic. They refer to access to knowledge that is in the one case achieved automatically (without conscious search), and in the other case achieved by the intervention of conscious, usually deliberate, search processes. During the earlier period of concern with these distinctions, the difference was referred to as one between automatic and controlled (i.e., conscious) processes (e.g., Shiffrin & Schneider, 1977).

In discussions of the distinction between memories that are brought to mind deliberately (consciously searching) and nondeliberate ones (unconscious/automatic), a number of apparent dichotomies have been proposed, as summarized in the following list:

Immediate	Mediated
Uncontrolled	Controlled
No capacity demand	Capacity demanding
Direct access	Indirect access
Involuntary	Voluntary

These various characteristics have been invoked to support the following three quasi-theoretical systems that make use of the general distinction between conscious and unconscious access:

[10] For a discussion of Ebbinghaus' insights into the range of memory phenomena that were ignored by psychologists for nearly a century see Mandler (1985b).

PROCEDURAL	DECLARATIVE
SEMANTIC	EPISODIC
IMPLICIT	EXPLICIT

The first five sets of attributes describe characteristics of the two poles of the various automatic-nonautomatic distinctions. Among other characteristics, all of these distinctions refer to the use or nonuse of conscious processes to store or retrieve information. I am specifically referring to the conscious or unconscious processes whereby information is accessed; the final product is in most cases, of course, a conscious content. The second column of the list describes aspects of access to information or action that involve consciousness. Conscious intervention involves relatively slow processes, mediated or controlled, and which are demanding of conscious capacity and have the phenomenal appearance of being voluntary. The same kinds of characteristics have been ascribed to the three "systems" in the second list.

As far as the distinction between procedural and declarative knowledge is concerned, "procedural" knowledge is generally considered to be a system that runs off without conscious intervention (cf. Cohen & Squire, 1980) in contrast to conscious declarative knowledge. The distinction is generally coextensive with the more traditional distinction between knowing how and knowing that, which was introduced by Ryle (1946, also chap. 2 in Ryle, 1949), who also argued that knowing that presupposes knowing how. Jean Mandler (1984) has noted that in the infant the original acquisition of skills (knowledge) is procedural and probably remains procedural (i.e., unconscious). Just like children, adults acquire some skills procedurally (i.e., without conscious access to the components of the skill), though secondary structures that address or help construct the procedures may be invoked, as in the case of learning to play tennis or ride a bicycle. We frequently know "that" we know "how" and may even know "how" we know "that." Whatever the utility of the procedural/declarative distinction, it seems obvious that the intervention of consciousness is an alternative way of describing one of its primary features.

The contemporary distinction between a semantic and an episodic system originated with the French philosopher Henri Bergson, who postulated two kinds of memory: one kind is automatic and acts as a habit, the other is "pure" memory, which records all the events of daily life; all conscious states are registered in the order in which they occur. Conscious recalling uses the pure memory and its images (Bergson, 1896). Contemporary use describes semantic knowledge as abstract and general; it is also unitized (i.e., highly integrated), and often represents the kind of qualitatively different structure that may be ascribed, for example, to expert knowledge. Episodic knowledge, on the other hand, is described as concrete, personal, and dated; it may or may not be subject to qualitative integration. Recently, there has been some argument about the episodic/semantic distinction and its use in psychological theory and experiments (Tulving, 1986). Some episodic autobiographic knowledge seems to have automatic characteristics, and some general semantic knowledge requires contextual retrieval. In terms of the automatic/controlled dimension, the distinction between automatic knowing and deliberate remembering does not easily map into the distinction between semantic and episodic information. The distinction between semantic/general and episodic/autobiographic knowledge has obvious heuristic value, but little in the way of principled theoretical utility. Whereas automatic and nonmediated access describes much of semantic knowledge, and conscious access much of episodic knowledge, the distinction between the two systems is far from clear. Apart from experimental critiques of the distinction (cf. Tulving, 1986), at the phenomenal level it seems unclear why my (semantic) knowledge of the azalea outside my window is systematically different from the similar (episodic) azalea I saw yesterday and of which I am reminded.

In summary, the dichotomies advocated and the systems proclaimed may map fuzzily into one common characteristic, the use of consciousness in achieving access to information. There are of course a number of other distinctions that these dichotomies describe—my only concern here is their common characteristic. The use and intervention of conscious processes is the result of specific tasks, demands, and intentions. It is surely consistent with the constructive nature of consciousness that it is the semantic/meaningful and declarative content that is captured in conscious states rather than syntax or procedure; it is the former that make claims to immediate relevance and importance.

There has been some argument as to the reality of the implicit/explicit distinction: for example, whether new knowledge may be acquired implicitly or whether declarative knowledge can only be acquired consciously (see, for example, Reber, 1997, for the yea-sayers and Shanks, Green, & Kolodny, 1994, for the naysayers). Whatever theoretical stance one wishes to adopt, we still need to deal with the phenomena of information apparently unconsciously encoded and the dissociations observed when material is, for example, processed semantically (deeply) or only formally (superficially), or when amnesic patients are able to generate problem solutions automatically that they cannot produce consciously (Craik & Tulving, 1975; Graf, Squire, & Mandler, 1984).

I prefer to think of implicit and explicit processes primarily as a function of different aspects of a single representational system. Within such a system sheer presentation and activation of mental contents—their integration—produces availability and "implicit" utilization, but elaboration and conscious participation is required for "explicit" uses that relate such contents to other mental events and contents (cf. G. Mandler, 1989).

How are these various systems to be seen in terms of the functions of consciousness described in previous sections? Clearly, conscious memories are limited and serially represented, but they can also be said to be only those aspects of the outer or inner world that are relevant to the current concerns of the individual, that are in the attentional spatio-temporal field (cf. Kahneman & Treisman, 1984; Hochberg, chap. 9, this volume). Seriality prevents confusion among competing memories, and limited capacity makes possible decision processes extending over limited and manageable domains.

An understanding of the role of consciousness in memorial functions also restructures the current confusion among various versions of short term, working, primary, and scratch pad memories (Mandler, 1985a, Ch. 4). Consciousness is the common end point of all of these memorial varieties. William James used the term *primary memory* to refer to the current contents of consciousness that are immediately present and need no "retrieval." Given the limitation of conscious capacity, one would expect all such contents to be limited to some five to seven units, the limits usually imposed on "short-term" memories. Thus, one of the components of short-term memory involves current conscious contents. Instead of postulating an additional short-term memory system or "box," degree of activation may define quickly accessible memorial contents. Assuming a rather steep initial decay of activation, material that has been presented or processed during preceding seconds can be quickly and efficiently brought into conscious constructions. Rehearsal may either maintain material within current conscious constructions or keep activation very high so that the material can be quickly brought into consciousness. In addition there are mental contents that are kept at relatively high levels of activation. These are "state-of-the-world" memories that contain information of who and where we are, what we are doing, and what our currently effective goals and plans are. Finally, the executive functions of short-term memory (if any) are subsumed under the serial and prospective functions of consciousness described above. This kind of approach eliminates the need for different short and long-term systems and brings short-term and long-term phenomena into a common theoretical framework.

XI. YES, VIRGINIA, THERE IS A BRAIN: THE MIND–BODY DISTINCTION[11]

There is, strictly speaking, no mind–body *problem;* dealing with so-called minds is not incompatible with a modern materialism. Mind is what the brain does; just as energy conservation is what a liver does. There are specific functions associated with large operational units such as organs, organisms, and machines, and these functions (and their associated concepts) cannot without loss of meaning be reduced to the constituent processes of the larger units. The speed of a car, the conserving function of the liver, and the notion of a noun phrase are not reducible to internal-combustion engines, liver cells, or neurons. Emergence is a label that has often been applied to these new properties of larger assemblies. Similarly, Searle (1992) notes that consciousness is an emergent feature of neurons just as solidity and liquidity are emergent features of molecules, and he also argues that consciousness might be distributed over large portions of the brain (see also Crick, 1994).

Just as philosophers have advanced a multitude of interpretations of mind and consciousness, so have neurophysiologists and neuropsychologists proposed many

[11] For the young in body, the title goes back to an editorial in the *New York Sun* in 1897 in reply to an inquiry by a young reader. The editor reassured her: Yes, Virginia, there is a Santa Claus.

different suggestions for the physical location or realization of consciousness. Kinsbourne (1997) has summarized some of the various localizations that have been proposed. These range from Descartes' pineal gland to Baars (1983; Baars, Fehling, LaPolla, & McGovern, 1997) specialized work space and there are many others in between. Following an extensive review of conscious functions and possible structures, Kinsbourne concludes that consciousness is a function of complex brains, in keeping with Sherrington's (1993, p. 22) assertion that there is no microscopical, physical, or chemical clue to consciousness, only greater complexity. This conclusion is consistent with the psychological arguments about the need for some such function as consciousness when information-processing brains become large and very complex. The argument about consciousness as an emergent function of brains needs also to be placed in the context of reductionist arguments. Most current commentators are materialists, and as materialists they subscribe to the first part of what Weinberg has called *grand reductionism,* that is, "the view that all of nature is the way it is . . . because of simple universal laws, to which in some sense all other scientific laws may in some sense be reduced" (Weinberg, 1995, p. 39). The claim of reduction contained in the second half does not follow, and it actually only refers to a subset of materialist dogma—physicalism. In any case, complex emergent functions need their own laws and principles which cannot without loss of meaning be reduced to the "universal laws" (see, for example, Putnam, 1980).

Finally, the notion that consciousness may be a function of brain complexity and increasing processing demands leads to a cognate position on the possible evolution of consciousness. One can suggest that consciousness will arise in complex brains to reflect the difficulties of dealing with parallel complexity and contemporaneity. Thus, consciousness is not an all-or-none phenomenon, but rather will arise in limited areas of information processing, such that mammals other than humans might be conscious of some limited, information-loaded aspects of their cognitive processes, that infants may at first have rather limited conscious capacities when there are fewer processing demands,[12] and that adults with special skills and cognitive subsystems (as for example, pianists, mathematicians, or jugglers) will have special consciousnesses related to those areas of thought and action.

XII. CODA

Have we come very far from Boring's concerns of some 50 years ago? I would say not, except that we have begun to think about the problem more creatively rather than dismissing it as a pseudo-problem. We now have manifold ideas and a plethora of hypotheses about consciousness. Some of these will survive, but all contribute to an active interest in a phenomenon too long left to mere speculation. Some 50 years hence we might have a better understanding of how and why consciousness functions.

---

[12] But see J. M. Mandler (1997) for a different view.

Acknowledgments

I am grateful to Celia Heyes, Kimberly Jameson, Patricia Kitcher, and Jean Mandler who commented on earlier drafts of this chapter. Their comments prevented many missteps; the remaining speculative essay and any errors of omission and commission are all mine.

References

Adrian, E. D. (1966). Consciousness. In J. C. Eccles (Ed.), *Brain and conscious experience*. New York: Springer.

Atkinson, R. C., & Shiffrin, R. M. (1968). Human memory: A proposed system and its control processes. In K. W. Spence & J. T. Spence (Eds.), *The psychology of learning and motivation*. New York: Academic Press.

Baars, B. J. (1983). Conscious contents provide the nervous system with coherent global information. In R. J. Davidson, G. E. Schwartz, & D. Shapiro (Eds.), *Consciousness and self-regulation*. New York: Plenum.

Baars, B. J., Fehling, M. R., LaPolla, M., & McGovern, K. (1997). Consciousness creates access: Conscious goal images recruit unconscious action routines, but goal competition serves to "liberate" such routines, causing predictable slips. In J. D. Cohen & J. W. Schooler (Eds.), *Scientific approaches to consciousness*. Hillsdale, NJ: Lawrence Erlbaum Associates.

Bergson, H. (1896). *Matière et mémoire: essai sur la relation du corps a l'esprit*. Paris: F. Alcan.

Boring, E. G. (1953). A history of introspection. *Psychological Bulletin, 50,* 169–189.

Churchland, P. M. (1981). Eliminative materialism and the propositional attitude. *Journal of Philosophy, 78,* 67–90.

Churchland, P. S. (1983). Consciousness: The transmutation of a concept. *Pacific Philosophical Quarterly, 64,* 80–93.

Cohen, N. J., & Squire, L. R. (1980). Preserved learning and retention of pattern analyzing skill in amnesia: Dissociation of knowing how and knowing that. *Science, 210,* 207–209.

Craik, F. I. M., & Tulving, E. (1975). Depth of processing and the retention of words in episodic memory. *Journal of Experimental Psychology: General, 104,* 268–294.

Crick, F. (1994). *The astonishing hypothesis: the scientific search for the soul*. New York: Touchstone/Simon and Schuster.

Cummins, R. (1975). Functional analysis. *Journal of Philosophy, 72,* 741–765.

Dennett, D. C. (1978). *Brainstorms*. Montgomery, VT: Bradford Books.

Dennett, D. C. (1991). *Consciousness explained*. Boston: Little, Brown & Company.

Deutsch, K. W. (1951). Mechanism, teleology, and mind. *Philosophy and Phenomenological Research, 12,* 185–223.

Edelman, G. (1989). *The remembered present: A biological theory of consciousness*. New York: Basic Books.

Flanagan, O. (1992). *Consciousness reconsidered*. Cambridge, MA: MIT Press.

Flanagan, O. (1997). Prospects for a unified theory of consciousness or, What dreams are made of. In J. D. Cohen & J. W. Schooler (Eds.), *Scientific approaches to consciousness*. Hillsdale, NJ: Lawrence Erlbaum Associates.

Graf, P., Squire, L. R., & Mandler, G. (1984). The information that amnesic patients do not forget. *Journal of Experimental Psychology: Learning, Memory, and Cognition, 10,* 164–178.

Gregory, R. L. (1981). *Mind in science*. New York: Cambridge University Press.

Griffin, D. R. (1984). *Animal thinking*. Cambridge, MA: Harvard University Press.

Jackendoff, R. (1987). *Consciousness and the computational mind*. Cambridge, MA: MIT Press.

Kahneman, D., & Treisman, A. (1984). Changing views of attention and automaticity. In R. Parasuraman & D. R. Davies (Eds.), *Varieties of attention* (pp. 29–61). New York: Academic Press.

Kant, I. (1978). *Anthropology from a pragmatic point of view* (V. L. Dowdell, Trans.). Carbondale, IL: Southern Illinois University Press. (Original work published 1798)

Kinsbourne, M. (1997). What qualifies a representation for a role in consciousness? In J. D. Cohen & J. W. Schooler (Eds.), *Scientific approaches to consciousness*. Hillsdale, NJ: Lawrence Erlbaum Associates.

Lycan, W. G. (1987). *Consciousness*. Cambridge, MA: MIT Press.

Mandler, G. (1975). Consciousness: Respectable, useful, and probably necessary. In R. Solso (Ed.), *Information processing and cognition: The Loyola symposium* (pp. 229–254). Hillsdale, NJ: Lawrence Erlbaum Associates.

Mandler, G. (1985a). *Cognitive psychology: An essay in cognitive science*. Hillsdale, NJ: Lawrence Erlbaum Associates.

Mandler, G. (1985b). From association to structure. *Journal of Experimental Psychology: Learning, Memory, and Cognition, 11*, 464–468.

Mandler, G. (1989). Memory: Conscious and unconscious. In P. R. Solomon, G. R. Goethals, C. M. Kelley, & B. R. Stephens (Eds.), *Memory: Interdisciplinary approaches* (pp. 84–106). New York: Springer Verlag.

Mandler, G. (1992). Toward a theory of consciousness. In H.-G. Geissler, S. W. Link, & J. T. Townsend (Eds.), *Cognition, information processing, and psychophysics: Basic issues* (pp. 43–65). Hillsdale, NJ: Lawrence Erlbaum Associates.

Mandler, G. (1993). Review of Dennett's "Consciousness explained". *Philosophical Psychology, 6*, 335–339.

Mandler, G. (1996). The situation of psychology: Landmarks and choicepoints. *American Journal of Psychology, 109*, 1–35.

Mandler, G. (1997). Consciousness redux. In J. C. Cohen & J. W. Schooler (Eds.), *Scientific approaches to consciousness*. Hillsdale, NJ: Lawrence Erlbaum Associates.

Mandler, J. M. (1984). Representation and recall in infancy. In M. Moscovitch (Ed.), *Infant memory* (pp. 75–101). New York: Plenum.

Mandler, J. M. (1997). Representation. In D. Kuhn & R. S. Siegler (Eds.), *Cognition, perception, and language* (Vol. 2, of W. Damon (Ed.) Handbook of child psychology). New York: Wiley.

Mandler, J. M., & Mandler, G. (1974). Good guys vs. bad guys: The subject-object dichotomy. *Journal of Humanistic Psychology, 14*, 63–87.

Marcel, A. J. (1983). Conscious and unconscious perception: An approach to the relations between phenomenal experience and perceptual processes. *Cognitive Psychology, 15*, 238–300.

McGinn, C. (1991). *The problem of consciousness*. Oxford: Basil Blackwell.

Nagel, T. (1986). *The view from nowhere*. New York: Oxford University Press.

Neisser, U. (1963). The multiplicity of thought. *British Journal of Psychology, 54*, 1–14.

Neisser, U. (1967). *Cognitive psychology*. New York: Appleton-Century-Crofts.

Penrose, R. (1994). *Shadows of the mind: A search for the missing science of consciousness*. New York: Oxford University Press.

Posner, M. I., & Boies, S. J. (1971). Components of attention. *Psychological Review, 78*, 391–408.

Posner, M. I., & Keele, S. W. (1970, September). *Time and space as measures of mental operations*. Paper presented at the 78th American Psychological Association Annual Convention, Miami Beach, FL.

Posner, M. I., & Klein, R. M. (1973). On the functions of consciousness. In S. Kornblum (Ed.), *Attention and performance IV* (pp. 21–36). New York: Academic Press.

Putnam, H. (1960). Minds and machines. In S. Hook (Ed.), *Dimensions of mind*. New York: Collier Books.

Putnam, H. (1980). Philosophy and our mental life. In N. Block (Ed.), *Readings in the philosophy of psychology* (Vol. 1). Cambridge, MA: Harvard University Press.

Reber, A. (1997). How to differentiate implicit and explicit modes of acquisition. In J. D. Cohen & J. W. Schooler (Eds.), *Scientific approaches to consciousness*. Hillsdale, NJ: Lawrence Erlbaum Associates.

Ryle, G. (1946). Knowing how and knowing that. *Proceedings of the Aristotelian Society, 46*, 1–16.

Ryle, G. (1949). *The concept of mind*. London: Hutchinson's University Library.

Schacter, D. L. (1987). Implicit memory: History and current status. *Journal of Experimental Psychology: Learning, Memory, and Cognition, 13*, 501–518.

Searle, J. R. (1992). *The rediscovery of the mind*. Cambridge, MA: MIT Press.

Searle, J. R. (1995). The mystery of consciousness: I. and II. *The New York Review of Books, 62* (Nos. 17 & 18), 60–66, 54–61.

Shallice, T. (1972). Dual functions of consciousness. *Psychological Review, 79,* 383–393.

Shallice, T. (1991). The revival of consciousness in cognitive science. In W. Kessen, A. Ortony, & F. Craik (Eds.), *Memories, thoughts, emotions: Essays in honor of George Mandler* (pp. 213–226). Hillsdale, NJ: Lawrence Erlbaum Associates.

Shanks, D. R., Green, R. E., & Kolodny, J. A. (1994). A critical examination of the evidence for unconscious (implicit) learning. In C. Umiltà & M. Moscovitch (Eds.), *Attention and Performance XV: Conscious and nonconscious information processing* (pp. 837–860). Cambridge, MA: MIT Press.

Sherrington, C. S. (1933). *The brain and its mechanism.* Cambridge, UK: Cambridge University Press.

Shiffrin, R. M., & Schneider, W. (1977). Controlled and automatic human information processing: II. Perceptual learning, automatic attending, and a general theory. *Psychological Review, 84,* 127–190.

Skinner, B. F. (1964). Behaviorism at fifty. In T. W. Wann (Ed.), *Behaviorism and phenomenology* (pp. 79–97). Chicago: University of Chicago Press.

Smart, J. J. C. (1959). Sensations and brain processes. *Philosophical Review, 68,* 141–156.

Sober, E. (1985). Panglossian functionalism and the philosophy of mind. *Synthese, 64,* 165–193.

Thagard, P. (1986). Parallel computation and the mind-body problem. *Cognitive Science, 10,* 301–318.

Thatcher, R. W., & John, E. R. (1977). *Foundations of cognitive processes.* Hillsdale, NJ: Lawrence Erlbaum Associates.

Tulving, E. (1986). What kind of a hypothesis is the distinction between episodic and semantic memory? *Journal of Experimental Psychology: Learning, Memory, and Cognition, 12,* 307–311.

Van Gulick, R. (1980). Functionalism, information and content. *Nature and System, 2,* 139–162.

Van Gulick, R. (1988). Consciousness, intrinsic intentionality, and self-understanding machines. In A. M. E. Bisiach (Ed.), *Consciousness in contemporary science* (pp. 78–100). Oxford, UK: Clarendon Press/Oxford University Press.

Weinberg, S. (1995). Reductionism redux. *The New York Review of Books, 62* (No. 15), 39–42.

The Informed Present: Where We Are and How We Got There

A. Outside to Inside: Approaches Concerned Chiefly with Measurable Variables of Stimulus Information and Their Cognitive Consequences
(Chapters 4–10)

B. Approaches Concerned with the Individual's Past and Present Cognitive Abilities
(Chapters 11–14)

CHAPTER 4

Information from the World around Us

James E. Cutting

A note on the word 'information': In the cognitive sciences use of the word seems . . .
equivocating. . .[I]t moves between information-theory references of high-technical color . . .
and quite vernacular senses not far from gained or given 'knowledge,'
of the world or whatever it may be.

—Baxandall (1995, p. 164)

We perceive *objects* and *events.* Objects are the furniture and clutter in the world around us. They include both artifacts, such as books, chairs, and roads; and natural kinds, such as rocks, trees, and lakes. They can even be nested, including natural objects in artifacts, such as trees in pictures. Events are things that happen over time and, as relevant to perception, they involve either the motion of, or change in, objects over time, or they result from our own movement with respect to objects. On what basis do we perceive objects and events? In psychology, cognitive science, and related fields, the answer in the late 20th century is: We perceive objects and events on the basis of *information.*

It has become difficult to imagine a science of perception or cognition without the concept of information. Information pervades our theories to such a degree that one should wonder how we could do without it. Indeed, the etymology of the term is sufficiently felicitous that no one in our time should pass easily over it: To inform someone means to take a *form* (perhaps of an object) and instill it with*in* something or someone (perhaps even the mind of a perceiver).[1] From such a definition it is a short step to the notion that we perceive the objects and events around us on the basis of information, and that we can act upon and generally know about our world because of information as well. In large part, perception can be said to be the process of *in-forming* the mind.

Nevertheless, our idea of information often baffles scholars in other fields.

[1] The *Oxford English Dictionary* gives "shape" as the major meaning of the Latinate root *form,* and the first meaning of the prefix *in-* (*in*—pref[2]) as "in, within, internal."

Indeed, it sometimes appears to them—and sometimes to us—as an unexamined buzzword used perhaps, as Baxandall suggested, in an attempt to bridge the scientific and the everyday. Moreover, we may often forget that information played no role in the theories of James (1890), Titchener (1906), Bartlett (1932), Koffka (1935), Woodworth (1938), Gibson (1950), or any other psychological theorist before the second half of this century. The reason, of course, is straightforward: Information theory was developed in the field of engineering by Shannon and Weaver (1949), and it was their work that gave the term its scientific meaning.

Briefly, within an information-theoretic framework, information is a numerical measurement of the a priori likelihood of an event or occurrence. In particular, it is a transformation (the base-two logarithm) of the number of items in the set to which a particular item of interest belongs assuming equal likelihood of their occurrence. This type of information is measured in *bits,* or the number of binary choices statistically necessary to determine exactly the item under consideration. The usual situation considered is one of transmission; thus, it can to be said that information was *transmitted* in bits. As an example, consider drawing a playing card from a standard deck. If someone draws a single card and announces that it is a spade, that statement implies a set size of four possibilities, and has excluded three of them. It has transmitted the $\log_2(4)$, or 2 bits of information. If one learns instead that it is a jack, one is dealing with a set size of thirteen, and has excluded twelve. Thus, the $\log_2(13)$, of 3.7 bits of information have been transmitted. In this manner, being told the card is a jack provides more information than being told it is a spade.[2] Notice that traditionally one speaks only about the amount of information; in this view information by itself has neither content nor meaning (but see MacKay, 1969).

At midcentury, information theory had rapid impact on our discipline. It was quickly applied to language, memory, perception, and action (Attneave, 1954; Broadbent, 1958; Cherry, 1957; Garner, 1962; Miller, 1951; Quastler, 1955). But, too useful to be confined to a particular calculation, the meanings for the term speciated. For example, frustrated with its lack of attention to meaning, Gibson (1966) discussed the bases of perception in terms of "information about," specifically eschewing information theory. More importantly, however, the information-processing approach to cognitive psychology was born (e.g., Haber, 1969; Lindsay & Norman, 1972; Neisser, 1967), where the time course of the perception of something (typically briefly presented letters or text) was analyzed and plotted, but sel-

---

[2] Despite the powerful applications of information theory to electronics and computer technology, there are problems in its application to psychology. One concerns a priori knowledge; one may not know about cards or games. Garner (1962) solved this through the notion of uncertainty, information should be measured against a knowledge base. Thus, if one knows it is a jack and is told it is a jack, there is no information transmission. With respect to perception, major problems include the fact that the objects of the world do not often come in set sizes of known number (a dog comes from a set of how many animals), and that they often belong to multiple sets (a dog is both an animal and a pet, and there are more kinds of the former than the latter); and that the source of information may be lying (the card is really a deuce, not a jack). See Cutting (1986) for further discussion.

dom was the information itself measured in any particular way. The proliferation of meanings for the term information has continued and at the end of the 20th century our current notions of it often have little to do with the original ideas of Shannon and Weaver (see also Cutting, 1987, for a review).

I take the flowering of the term information as evidence, not necessarily of loose thinking among psychologists, but of scientific necessity. That is, the implications of the term information have been so important that it was appropriated by our discipline in new ways as an attempt to solve the critical problems in perception and cognition. Why is the term information so indispensable? What are its historical antecedents? Where exactly is it located? These are the questions this chapter will attempt to address.

At base, I claim we use the term information to solve a certain aspect of a central problem in the history of philosophy—the mind–body problem. More precisely, we wish to account for transformation from the physical stuff of the world into neural, and particularly mental, stuff within the perceiver and knower. Quite literally, we assume that information is the medium that allows an object or event to be registered by the senses and, as a product of exploration and attention, registered in the mind of the perceiver.

I will also claim that, historically, psychology in general, and visual perception in particular, has broached three frameworks in which this transformation is accomplished—through appeals to personal experience with the world, to mathematical constraints that may structure the world, and to biological expediency as creatures evolved in the world. There is no inherent reason why an assembly of all three should not serve perceivers (as well as researchers), but they begin with different assumptions and are thus partly incompatible. I will present them exclusively, and as they were broached. My approach will also condense several otherwise historically separable lines of thought, and this process will necessarily make some strange bedfellows along the way. Nonetheless, I think its result can best represent the kinds of thought the psychology of this century has had about the concept of information. As would be expected, part of it also bears relatively close relation to the exposition by Proffitt and Kaiser (chap. 7, this volume) on internalization of external constraints; Information is external to the perceiver and brings evidence of the outside world into the mind of the perceiver.

I. FRAMEWORK 1: EXPERIENCE IN AN UNRULY WORLD

> We see, and cannot help seeing, what we have learnt to infer. (J. S. Mill, 1889, p. 226)

North American psychology inherited much from the British philosophical tradition of empiricism from the 17th through the 19th centuries. More particularly, from John Mill (1829), John Stuart Mill (1848), and their antecedents (see, for example, Pastore, 1971), we received the idea that the laws of association, based on the law of contiguity, govern all of what we now call perception and cognition. That is, as individuals we are exposed to many co-occurrences of objects and events around us; from this exposure we covertly built up a large store of them; and we use the covariance matrix to guide our percepts, thoughts, and actions. Thus, the information in this context can be generally associated with the idea of "knowledge" as Baxandall (1995) noted above; the physical aspects of the objects and events themselves are typically only vague, referential ghosts.

This experiential build-up process is thought to be generally reflexive and unconscious; and, as implied by the quote of J. S. Mill above, it leads to percepts that we would now call automatic (Shiffrin & Schneider, 1977) and cognitively impenetrable (Pylyshyn, 1989). In this view, habits tie the world together and information lies in mere and shear frequency; it is tallied, as in Morton's (1969) logogen model of word recognition, with each occurrence and co-occurrence of things we perceive.

Throughout the historical period including Hume and Berkeley, the Mills and Russell, and then in this century Brunswik, the psychology of mind developed the idea that through the associations collected over the long haul of personal experience we build up the skill to interpret the world around us. In this view, for example, each of us generally sees and understands the world in the same way because we share an overwhelming number of similar experiences with it; someone raised in a completely different environment would likely perceive our world in quite a different way (Helmholtz, 1878/1971). The central problem that associationism tried to face and solve, at least with respect to perception, was the initially near-hopeless, "blooming, buzzing confusion" (James, 1890, Vol. 1, p. 488) of the world around us. How are we to make sense of the world? The associationistic answer came through the power of experience and memory within the organism. The frequency information presented by the world itself was a tangle of probability and, thus, was incompletely untrustworthy.

A. From Local Signs to Cues

From a German tradition, and particularly from Lotze (e.g., Boring, 1942; Pastore, 1971), we inherited the idea of local signs, small bits of clusters or arrangements of experienced pattern that lie in what we now call the visual array and help knit it together so we can infer what is to be seen. This idea is rather far from our idea of information but it is antecedent to another, more closely related term—*cue*. Faithful to its 16th-century etymology representing marginal notes in theater documentation (*q,* for *quando,* Latin meaning "when"), a cue was a prompt for action provided to a knowledgeable actor.[3] That is, a cue could be effective only if one already knew the play to be acted. Both James (1890) and Titchener (1906) used the term cue in this way, as a prompt for action. Later, Woodworth (1938) and oth-

---

[3] *The Shorter Oxford English Dictionary* gives this as the etymology of the word "cue;" the *Oxford English Dictionary* gives it as well, but suggests further that it is unproved.

ers changed its meaning and applied it to perception. Thus, cue was now a prompt for how to perceive. Cues were applied most particularly to the perception of depth and what we now might call layout. Indeed, lists of "cues to depth" can be found in most contemporary textbooks in perception and in introductory psychology, and they are a legacy of associationism from the early part of this century.

Meanwhile, outside of many important aspects of this tradition, Koffka (1935) provided a new perceptual framework—that of proximal and distal stimuli—which entered into common discourse. This distinction helped psychologists locate the place of these cues (see also Hochberg, chap. 1, this volume). With respect to visual perception it could then be said that we perceive distal objects and events (those that generally lay beyond arm's reach) on the basis of proximal cues, aspects of those objects and events that we would now say are projected to the eye of the observer. Thus, cues would now begin to have a status different from the objects and events to which they were related, yet also exist in the world, external to the observer.

Finally, with Brunswik (1956), cues came to have their most articulated definition. A cue was a visual pattern or set of visual relations about which we have accumulated much experience. When dealing with a set of objects, that personal history suggests to each of us that each proximal depth cue is associated with a particular distal arrangement of objects. Moreover, that association occurs with some probability, called *cue validity*, which perceivers have registered over their lifetime. In this view, for mathematical reasons if not experiential ones, that probability is always greater than zero and always less than unity; cue validity, then, dictates the surety with which, for example, the layout of the objects in depth can be discerned. The work of Massaro (1987) is the clearest contemporary extension of this idea, and the central aspects of his program have been couched in terms of Bayes theorem (Massaro & Freedman, 1990).

B. An Assessment and a Metatheory

The two great strengths of an experiential approach are that it is open (a) to all cognitive and perceptual experience, and (b) through all sensory modalities. Moreover, applications in music (Krumhansl, 1990), auditory perception (Saffran, Aslin, & Newport, 1996), word perception (Morton, 1969), and letter perception (Estes, 1976) have shown it to have considerable merit. Nevertheless, as with any approach, it has its weaknesses. For example, more narrowly in any Bayesian approach, if an individual is to perceive a particular object or event he or she must have a reasonably good prior assessment of its possible occurrence.[4] More broadly in any experiential approach if the perceiver is to make any sense of the world, he or she must similarly draw on previous experiences.

---

[4] It is not by accident that a priori knowledge plagues both an information-theoretic approach and a Bayesian approach to perception. Both try to solve the problem of information through probability, and probability cannot be assessed without some fore-knowledge of what will occur and when.

Leaving aside the problems of initial knowledge (Chomsky, 1959) and the contextualization of the covariance matrix of cue validities (Hochberg, 1965), the Bayesian approach in particular, and the associationistic approach in general, also make it difficult to account for learning to perceive new objects. In Piagetian terms (e.g., Piaget, 1978) the theory handles assimilation well—of fitting new exemplars of objects into old categories—but it does not handle accommodation well—the comprehension and establishment of new categories of objects and events based on what we see (see also Medin & Coley, chap 13, this volume). The Bayesian/cue-validity approach also makes for potential evolutionary mischief. To quote the title of Gibson's (1957) critique of Brunswik (1956), one would then seem to face "survival in a world of probable objects." Probabilities too far from unity could lead to death.

It should be little surprise that this general framework, as applied to perception, is most generally associated with the metatheoretical view *indirect perception* (Ayer, 1956; Gibson, 1979), although not all who would espouse this metatheory would also rely so heavily on either associationism or Bayes's theorem. Nevertheless, this framework and this metatheory both rely as little as possible on discussions of stimulus properties. In this view, external information is relatively weak and nonspecific; the mapping of sources of information back to the events and objects that generated them is many-to-many, a tangle of context-dependent relations. Since the sense data from the stimuli in the world are thus viewed as incompletely trustworthy, the approach relies heavily on the computational power of a knowledgeable perceiver. At the end of the 20th century one might also state that proponents of this view emphasize top-down processes.

II. FRAMEWORK 2: MATHEMATICS AND NATURAL LAW IN A WELL-ORDERED WORLD

> [O]rdinary sense perception could . . . not fulfill its task—that of building up an objective world—if it were not able to comprehend the isolated sense data under certain group concepts and . . . the "invariants" in reference to this group. (Cassirer, 1945, p. 288)

The second framework is quite different, and stems from Galileo's *mathesis universalis* (e.g., Pylyshyn, 1972). Galileo, and scores of philosophers and scientists since, believed that the book of nature was written in the language of mathematics. In particular, twentieth-century mathematicians (Kline, 1959, 1980) and physicists (Einstein, 1921; Feynman, 1965; Wigner, 1959) have often expressed awe and pride in the fact that mathematics seems to be such an appropriate tool to measure and describe nature. From accurate measurement and description, it is assumed, comes understanding and theory. Not surprisingly, then, many theorists have attempted to use math to ply their way into understanding human nature and the mind. Results are not always successful (see admonitions by Uttal, 1990), but there are many sustaining ideas in this notion that make it a central pillar among approaches to perception.

The basic assumption of this framework is quite different than that of associationism. The world is not seen to be chaotic; instead the world, and particularly the visual world, is well ordered, and that order is reflected in the mathematics applied to it. The basic task of the researcher is to follow the appropriate natural law (e.g., Kugler & Turvey, 1987) and discover the appropriate mathematics, and then to apply them usefully to perceptual and cognitive issues. The problem for the perceiver is much less difficult; natural law is followed because there is no alternative, and mathematics is used because that is the way perceptual systems work. The natural law and mathematics are deeply ingrained in the nervous system, and their rules constrain and guide perception and cognition. Thus, information from the world presents itself in a language of mathematics, and the perceptual system uses that language to discern properties and identities of the objects and events. Perceivers, then, generally perceive the same sorts of things, not because they share the same history, but because they all follow the same natural laws, expressible in mathematical relations.

A. Geometry

Historically, the first type of mathematics applied to perception was geometry. Literally meaning "earth-measure," geometry is the basis of surveying and has been used for more than two millennia to describe, and impose structure on, the layout of the world around us. Euclid's Elements are more often studied, but his Optics (Burton, 1945) is more pertinent to vision and cognitive science. Having laid out geometry in his Elements, his Optics is a set of theorems and proofs about vision and about how we perceive the layout of the world. Classical optics then developed slowly over many centuries, and scrutiny of original works in translation and of analyses from different disciplines yields the same result: The optics of Alhazen (Lindberg, 1976), Grosseteste (Ronchi, 1957), Descartes (1637/1971), Leonardo (Richter, 1883), and Smith (1738), followed the pattern of Euclid. Thus, despite the claims of Gibson (1966, 1979) and others, this tradition embraces the view that optics is about the visual perception of layout (Ronchi, 1970). To be sure, the geometry of Euclid, and later of projective geometry (e.g., Nicod, 1930), is largely one of transparency where objects do not appear to occlude other objects. Nonetheless, the beginning of a perceptual theory can be found in Euclid.

As an informal proof of the centrality of visual perception to optics consider the following sketch of an analysis. In the Burton (1945) translation of his optics, Euclid presents more than 60 proofs about physical relations and phenomena in the world with respect to vision. His proofs contain 58 diagrams, and in 55 of them one point within the diagram is the eye of the perceiver, and angles are measured with respect to this point. Similarly, Richter's (1883) compilation of Leonardo's notebooks on linear perspective (which includes several of Euclid's proofs) includes 53 drawings, 46 of which include the eye or a point that could represent the eye. So too, most of optics texts from the medieval period to Smith (1738) equate optics and vision, and use diagrams similar to those of Euclid and Leonardo. Only with Newton

(1730/1952; Dover edition) was the centrality of vision to optics offset. In only 9 of his 57 diagrams does the eye appear, and in these often only gratuitously. Thus, Newton removed the eye from optics, and perhaps with it mathematical approaches to vision from the mainstream scientific thought.[5]

B. Projective Geometry

Euclid's Optics (Burton, 1945) is about how geometrical shapes project to the eye of the perceiver. As a mathematical discipline, however, projective geometry did not mature until the 19th century (e.g., Kline, 1959). Nonetheless, aspects of projections dominated practical applications of mathematics in mapmaking (e.g., Snyder, 1993), in Renaissance painting and architecture (see La Gournerie, 1859; Olmer, 1943). The appeal of projective geometry to the study of vision, if not to the other sensory modalities, is straightforward. One of the classic entrées into the study of visual perception is the conundrum of ambiguity in a two-dimensional image (retinal or pictorial) as it represents a particular three-dimensional object. That is, although the projection from the 3D object to the 2D image is well ordered and mathematically certain, the attempt at reverse projection (sometimes called *inverse optics*) from the 2D image back to the 3D object is not. More information or more restrictions are needed. For example, if the object were in motion and one assumes that it is known to be rigid, then multiple images of it or its moving image would dictate the presence of a single, unambiguous object, and inverse optics can be carried out. This fact became the basis of the enterprise called structure-from-motion (e.g., Ullman, 1979).

Fortunately, visual perception appears to follow some aspects of projective geometry. Perhaps the clearest proponent of this view has been Johansson (e.g., Johansson, von Hofsten, & Jansson, 1980) who, with Gibson (1950, p. 153n), proposed that a particular theorem from projective geometry—that of the cross-ratio—would be useful to perceivers. There then accrued evidence for its occasional, but not universal use (Cutting, 1986; Niall, 1992; Niall & Macnamara, 1990; Simpson, 1986). A serious problem with this approach emerged at about the same time as its initial corroborations: The assumption of rigidity is often invalid. Perceivers often see things as nonrigid when they are rigid even when a rigid interpretation is possible (Braunstein & Andersen, 1984; Hochberg, 1987; Norman & Todd, 1993; see also Hochberg, chap. 9, this volume). This renders the perceptual achievement of structure-from-motion much more difficult to understand.

C. Group Theory and Invariance

In a French tradition—from Poincaré (1905) through Casirer (1944, 1945) to Piaget (1970)—a differently styled approach to perception and cognition began, based in

---

[5] Newton's text should have been called *Dioptrics,* rather than *Optics,* because it deals largely with lenses.

group theory and the systematization of geometries in Felix Klein's Erlanger Program (e.g., Klein, 1908). In North America psychologists were slow to appreciate the power of this approach, but Gibson (1950, 1960) began it with a discussion of *invariants*. Later, he (Gibson, 1965, 1979; see also Michaels & Carello, 1981; Wagemans, Van Gool, & Lamote, 1996) would embrace invariants as they are revealed through *transformations,* thus opening a door to group theory that he would never step through.

Group theory, invariants, and transformations go together roughly like this: The shape of rigid objects remains invariant (unchanging) under at least six transformations (ways of invoking a change). Three of these transformations are translations of that object in space (in Cartesian coordinates along x, y, z) and the other three are rotations (again in x, y, z). These six transformations and their combinations form a mathematical group (see also Proffitt & Kaiser, chap, 7, this volume). Groups of transformations exist only when the members follow particular set of rules: closure, association, identity, and inversion (e.g., Bell, 1945). Any transformation of an object along one or more of these six dimensions, often called the Galilean group, leaves the object unchanged in shape.

With some elaboration, such as allowing for transformations under changes in illumination, Gibson tried to make this approach into theory of visual perception. From outside his particular perspective, years of study of structure-from-motion began (see Braunstein, 1976, and Ullman, 1983, for reviews). Other psychologists, also outside of Gibson's direct influence, began to consider not the invariants, but the groups of transformations themselves (e.g., Carlton & Shepard, 1990; Garner, 1970; Hoffman, 1966; Leyton, 1992; Palmer, 1991) as keys to understanding perception.

D. An Assessment and a Metatheory

The great strengths of any mathematical approach are its clarity, its precision, and its power through the use of deductive inference. The Piagetian idea of assimilation is little problem since the mathematics of one set of stimuli or one task will be quite different than another; and accommodation would likely to driven by different mathematical solutions in the presence of different stimuli. To be sure, the issue of similarity (e.g., Goodman, 1972; Medin & Coley, chap. 13, this volume) plagues the mathematical approach to the same degree as the associationistic approach.

One of the major drawbacks of most mathematical approaches to perception is that their utility seems almost exclusively confined to vision. Projective geometry has essentially no application elsewhere; geometry, although it might play some role in taste through stereochemistry (Amoore, 1970; but see Schiffman, 1974), seems largely visual; and even group theory, the most abstract of mathematics, has its clearest application in vision (but see Balzano, 1980).[6]

---

[6] There are many other approaches to perception which might be called mathematical. Many of these have their bases in statistics (see Cutting, 1987), particularly the statistics of form. These include those by Field (1987), Julesz and Bergen (1983), Lord and Wilson (1984), Pentland (1983), Uttal (1983, 1985), and Zusne (1970). These do not fit neatly into the three approaches discussed here.

Although it does not exhaust the metatheoretical possibilities in a mathematical framework for perception, Gibson's version of a basis for perception came to be known as *direct perception* (Gibson, 1979; Michaels & Carello, 1981). Gibson (1979) rejected the central idea of cues from associationism—that the world presents itself in a confused, disorganized manner. Instead, without direct appeal to group theory, Gibson was convinced that invariants revealed themselves under object motion, observer movements, and change of illumination. A small army of researchers then set out to find invariants and other higher-order relations; many were found, but it now appears that invariants of the kind that Gibson proposed are too few for perception to proceed on their basis alone (see Cutting, 1993). Although the basis of direct perception is debated (Michaels & Beek, 1996; Oudejans, 1991; Pittenger, 1990; Stoffregen, 1990), several agree (Burton & Turvey, 1990; Cutting, 1986, 1991), that the theory generally proceeds on the assumption that there is a one-to-one mapping between a source of information in the world (typically an invariant) and the object associated with it. In the late 20th century one would generally say that almost all such mathematical approaches to perception are based on bottom-up processes.

III. FRAMEWORK 3: BIOLOGY IN AN EXPEDIENT WORLD

One could argue that . . . the visual system often *cheats,* i.e., uses rules of thumb, short-cuts, and clever sleights-of-hand that were acquired by trial and error through millions of years of natural selection. (Ramachandran, 1985, p. 101)

A third major framework for the notion of information in perception is nascent, and at the end of the 20th century it remains relatively ill formed. The central idea is both a theoretical one and a methodological one: Perception has evolved to solve particular tasks at particular times. To study each task separately is the ideal, and when one does so it is sometimes said—rather oddly—that one has a *computational theory* (after Marr, 1982). More precisely, this means that one has some idea of what is important to the organism, some idea of how which situations and tasks are important to it, and some faith that this task can be meaningfully studied separately from other tasks.

More deeply, the idea is that, over the long haul of evolution, biology has been both adventitious and conservative. To meet the requirements of new species radiating out into different niches, evolution has molded new tissues and functions out of old ones, but also changed them minimally as needed. Thus, just as the bones of the inner ear were molded out of material from the jaw (e.g., Gould, 1983); neurological tissue devoted to one task may have been modified and incorporated into use for another. Such a process would not make a well-designed machine, but it would emphatically make a well-adapted one. Moreover, if perceivers generally perceive the same sorts of things, it is not because of personal history or natural law, but because they share the same biological underpinnings. This approach generally proceeds on two fronts—through appeals to ontegeny, or comparisons across the development of individuals (see Spelke, chap. 11, this volume), and through appeals to phylogeny, or comparisons across species. It is the latter that I will focus on.

A. Tricks and Modules

The most extreme form of this biological approach was given by Ramachandran (1985) as suggested above—that perception proceeds merely from a "bag of tricks." Unfortunately, to promote this idea is to promote only half the story; one must also attempt to understand why the "tricks" are as we find them. The idea fosters first the suggestion of *modules* (Fodor, 1983; Marr, 1982), isolable subsystems within the brain that act more or less independently; and second, a piecemeal modularity of visual systems on a large scale such that every perceptual task may be different, involving different and generally noninteracting neural tissue. An indefinitely large number of relatively isolated visual modules may turn out to be the case, but at present I regard this as unlikely.

A more parsimonious approach is to start globally, and to limit the number of modules to a small number until converging evidence can be found that firmly segregates each, both in terms of perceptual phenomena and neurological locus. One such approach suggests there are at least two visual systems, one for perceptual tasks involved with action, and the other for those involved with cognition and categorization (see Milner & Goodale, 1995).[7] The future truth of the degree of modularity of the visual system seems likely to lie somewhere between two systems proposed by Milner and Goodale (1995), and the very large number as would be suggested by Ramachandran (1985).

If perception and cognition have followed the route of biological expediency, then major claims of the other two frameworks are weakened: Neither the force of personal experience nor the cleanliness of a single type of mathematics seem likely to rule all of perception and cognition. On one hand, the time scale of personal experience will pale in the face of the time scale of evolution and, on the other, mathematics may be too structured and rigorous in the face of a rubric for change no more constraining than utility. At best, then, personal experience and mathematics would have different, more particular, and separable roles to play within each task and within each module. Thus, from the point of view of biological expediency, information could be measured in terms of frequency, of geometric relations, or of any other form that a sensory system could capitalize upon (chemical valences, spectral profiles, temperature, spatiotemporal patterning, and so forth). From my point of view, aspects of projective geometry still seems likely to work best for vision, but again, what these aspects may turn out to be is as yet undetermined.

---

[7] The recent history of neuroscience can be painted as one of opposing pairs of proposed systems. For two influential predecessors to Milner and Goodale, see Schneider (1969) and Ungerleider and Mishkin (1982).

In addition, in a biological approach human beings become very much part of the fabric of all life, complex and simple. By extension, one might expect that neither the many-to-many nor the one-to-one relations between information and objects proposed by indirect and direct perception, respectively, would generally hold. On the one hand, the computational power needed to untangle the many-to-many relations between information and objects seems daunting. Species with simpler nervous systems might not be able to survive. Since we evolved from simpler species, many-to-many relations are not likely to have been those with which we started, and thus perhaps they do not hold for us now. On the other hand, the rigid uniformity of one-to-one relations between information and objects would seem to inhibit evolution. Over the course of evolution, newly redesigned sensory systems might find it difficult to exploit the complex of regularities to be found in the world, if there were not different ways to perceive the same objects and events. Moreover, since newly redesigned systems often retain older capabilities, it would then be surprising if different information were not used in different tasks with the same objects and events (see Hochberg, chap. 9, this volume, for further discussion).

B. An Assessment and a Metatheory

The great strength of the biological approach lies in its pragmatics; necessity, contingency, and happenstance—rather than logic or math—drive the evolution of cognitive and perceptual processes. Even associations, which are largely context blind, are less pragmatic; what works in this framework is what rules. Piagetian notions of assimilation and accommodation are accomplished by whatever means necessary, and thus loom less important in this approach. The great weakness of this approach, however, is the inverse of pragmatics. One must worry about Kiplingesque just-so stories as explanations for the states of affairs that one finds in perception and cognition; pure teleology is unhelpful.

Although not exhaustive of the possibilities, one metatheoretical solution to this problem, which I have called *directed perception* (Cutting, 1986, 1991, 1992; see also Cutting & Massironi, chap. 6, this volume), is to suppose that the relationship between information and objects/events is many-to-one. Because each source of information is proposed to map back to a single object/event or its property, each source of information can specify to some degree what is to be perceived; however, because more than a single source of information may be associated with each object/event, species are free to move from reliance on one to a reliance on another; and if many information sources are used different individuals within a species are free to weight their use of various sources to different degrees. Finally, a process could be viewed as both bottom-up and top-down; see Proffitt (1993) for an elaboration of a biological approach to perception that embraces such constraints in both directions.

IV. MULTIPLE SOURCES OF INFORMATION AND THE PROBLEMS THEY PRESENT

> The education of our space-perception consists largely of two processes—reducing the various sense-feelings to a common measure and adding them together into the single all-including space of the real world. (James, 1890, Vol. 2., pp. 268–269)

A. On the Abundance of Information

Regardless of which of these three frameworks one follows, or which of the three metatheories loosely allied to them one espouses, any perceptual theorist must face several issues: First, does he or she acknowledge the existence of multiple sources of information in the world for a given object or event? Those influenced by an experiential framework or by indirect perception on the one hand, and those influenced by a biological framework or by directed perception on the other, will all generally embrace such multiplicity. Although those influenced by group-theoretic frameworks may be relatively neutral to this idea, those influenced by direct perception do not typically embrace the idea of multiple sources of information (but see Michaels & Beek, 1996; Oudejans, 1991).

The latter road, espousing a one-to-one relation between information and the object or event to which it refers, may be a difficult one to follow. Following Gibson (1979) perceptual variables are often parsed in terms of those that are lower order and higher order. On the one hand, lower-order variables are ones typically closer to traditional psychophysics—wavelength, extent, intensity—and acknowledged by all researchers to be manifold. On the other, higher-order variables thought to be used by the perceptual system are certain efficacious combinations of the lower-order variables. The problem is that in the face of potential multiplicity of lower-order information sources, each of which seem correlated with certain perceptions, one must search for a higher-order combination that, by itself, is both sufficient to sustain perception and is not overly correlated with the lower-order variables (Burton & Turvey, 1990; Michaels & de Vries, 1998).[8] Unfortunately, the potential combinatorics of adding, multiplying, or dividing even a modest number of lower-order variables can make the search difficult. Moreover, as noted above when discussing invariants, the search for higher-order variables that are demonstrably used by the perceiver has been slow and laborious. This search has turned up some important examples. However, if Gibson were correct in his insistence the perception used these alone, one might have thought they would have been easier to find (Cutting, 1993).

---

[8] There are other distinctions in the ecological community besides higher- and lower-order information. One is the extrinsic–intrinsic distinction proposed by Warren (1984). Extrinsic information is measured in standard physical units (time, mass, extent); intrinsic information converts these measures relevant to the organism. Measures of objects in the world in terms of the eye-height of the observer is one standard for intrinsic measurement.

B. On the Use of Abundant Information

Accepting the potential for the existence of multiple sources of information for any given perceptual situation, the second issue is, How do perceptual systems deal with this multiplicity? Various schemes of integration and selection have been proposed. To be concrete so that these schemes can be easily discussed, consider the situation depicted in the upper part of Figure 1. Imagine that this is not a picture, but a real display seen with one eye.

Here, somewhat ironically since this example is taken from Gibson (1950, 1979), two traditional sources of information are provided for judgments of the relative depth, or the layout with respect to the observer, of the two vertically oriented panels: Relative size and height in the visual field (sometimes called height in the picture plane, or angular elevation). Both sources appear to work in concert to make Panel A appear closer than Panel B. That is, because both panels are depicted to have the same shape one might assume that, in the depicted world, they are objects of the same physical size; that is, since the projection of Panel A is larger than that of Panel B, Panel A must be closer. In addition, because the base of Panel A is lower in the picture than that of Panel B, again it must be the closer.

How might these two sources contribute to the perception of layout? In an

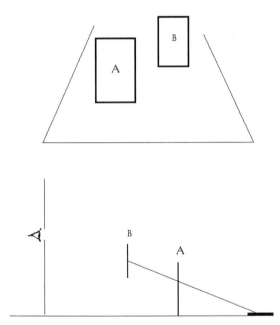

FIGURE 1   A "cue-conflict" situation adapted from Gibson (1950, p. 179; Gibson, 1979, p. 158). In the upper part of the figure, (A) appears to be closer to the reader than (B) because of differences in relative size and height in the visual field. But the lower part of the figure shows that this is not true, as would be revealed with the addition of binocular disparities.

experiment using these two and other sources, both in isolation and in combination, Künnapas (1968) found that judgments of distance were greater and less variable the more sources of information that were present in the stimulus. That is, as it might be in this case, the more sources that are present the greater and more consistent the judged distance between the panels. Both effects are important, the former contributing to the impression of greater perceived extent in the world and the latter contributing to the stability of that percept.

How should we understand these effects? There are several possibilities, and the scheme I will promote here is an elaboration of those of Bülthoff and Mallot (1988) and Massaro (1987). In general two classes of information use exist, which I will call selection and integration (see also Cutting, 1986; Cutting, Bruno, Brady, & Moore, 1992).

C. Styles of Selection

1. Satisficing

The most pragmatic style of selection can be called *satisficing,* a decision-making term from Simon (1955). That is, an observer can simply search for adequate information in the stimulus, stop when it is found, and thus ignore any other source that may be present. Satisficing, from "satisfies," is generally quick and meets the demands of a search task—information is found and acted upon. It contrasts with *optimizing,* which is a slow search process and, in this context, would entail exhaustive search for all sources of information and the subsequent use of all of them. In using a satisficing strategy, one may find different sources of information on different trials but performance is always about the same and adequate to the demands of the task. No particular commitments to the roles of consciousness and attention are made here; consciousness and attention could either be present or absent. In the case shown in the upper part of Figure 1, satisficing would occur if observers sometimes used height in the visual field to judge which panel were further away, sometimes used relative size, but never used both.

Cutting, Flückiger, Baumberger, and Gerndt (1996) presented evidence for a satisficing strategy in a wayfinding task, where observers judged the direction of their heading with respect to their gaze in a situation of simulated pursuit fixation during forward locomotion. Three sources of information were manipulated factorially. These were the displacement direction of the largest object in the field of view, the inward displacement of any object toward the fovea, and the outward deceleration of any object. Performance was the same (about 80%) when one, two, or three sources were present—regardless of which ones they were—and performance was at chance (50%) when no information was present.

2. Suppression

A second selection strategy is similar, but more consistent than satisficing. Given the presence of two sources of information, the observer might consistently select one source and base his or her judgment on that source alone, suppressing the other. Again, no commitment to consciousness or attention is made. In the context of the upper part of Figure 1, a suppressive result would occur if observers always based a relative-distance judgment on relative size when both size and height were present, but they used height when it was present alone.

Evidence for suppressive selection, like satisficing, can occur when the judgment for the two sources combined is no different than for one of them in isolation. It can also occur in other psychophysical situations where the two sources are manipulated orthogonally, and performance is found to vary only with one. For example, Cutting (1986, Experiments 7 & 8) showed that, in a task where observers judged the rigidity of moving objects, subjects used the cross-ratio (an invariant from projective geometry, discussed earlier) when that object rotated, but used a yoked set of flow vectors when it translated. In that latter case, the cross-ratio was present and could have been used during every trial, but observers' results suggested that they suppressed the cross-ratio in favor of the yoked flow vectors.

The stimulus arrangement shown in upper part of Figure 1 two sources of information are present and both yield the same depth order. Within traditional terminology, this might be called a *cue-consistent* display. Other stimulus arrangements might have both, or more, sources present, but with each or a combination yielding different depth orders. Such have been called *cue-conflict* displays (see Woodworth, 1938).

3. Veto

A particularly vigorous example of selection occurs when one source of information simply overrules another in a cue-conflict situation, which Bülthoff and Mallot (1988) called veto. An example of this is suggested in the lower part of Figure 1, also from Gibson (1950, 1979). The juxtaposition of the two sections of the figure suggests that the base of the smaller-appearing, higher panel in fact does not abut the surface of support but, by an unseen system of support, is levitated above it. Most importantly, if a third source of information, binocular disparities, is added by allowing the viewer to see the display with two eyes then the disparity information will veto the effectiveness of height in the visual field and relative size. Why? How?

In one account (Cutting & Vishton, 1995), disparities will reveal that the base of Panel B is not at the same depth as the portion of the surface of support projected just beneath it. Thus, one of the assumptions of height in the visual field—gravity, or that the bases of both objects lay on the surface of support (see Cutting & Vishton, 1995)—is proven incorrect and, thus, the source is invalidated. Disparities will then also be likely to show that Panel B is in fact closer than Panel A, and that an assumption underlying the use of relative size, that the depicted objects are the same physical size, is also invalidated. In this manner, veto is an example of selection working at the level of the assumptions underlying each information source. Other examples have been found in the literature, with binocular disparity information vetoing relative motion (Turner, Braunstein, & Andersen, 1997).

D. Styles of Integration

1. Accumulation

The alternative to selection is integration, where the perceiver uses two or more information sources in concert. The most straightforward type of integration is accumulation, of which there are several types. Here, and most easily, judgments for the two-source stimulus must be greater than those for stimuli with either source alone. Accumulations of information can be additive, as suggested by the quote of James above, or subadditive—although much depends on assumptions about the nature of the underlying scale that observers use (Cutting et al., 1992; Massaro & Cohen, 1993).

If, in the presence of two consistent sources of information, the relative-depth judgment is equal to the sum of the judgments of each source separately, then additivity can be said to occur; if, on the other hand, relative depth judgments are less for the combined-source case, the subadditivity can be said to occur. Cutting et al. (1992) found that in judgments of exocentric depth, relative size and height in the visual field were combined subadditively, but that pairwise combinations of relative size and occlusion, relative size and motion parallax, and occlusion and motion parallax, were all combined additively (see also Wanger, Ferwerda, & Greenberg, 1992). In situations of conflicting ordinal information, evidence of integration—additive or subadditive—would be that the two-source stimulus yields judgments less than the absolute value of the largest of the two one-source stimuli.

2. Cooperation

Another type of integration occurs when the combination of two consistent sources yields a judgment greater than either one-source stimulus alone. This may be called superadditivity or, more likely, cooperation. The latter term is sometimes used much more broadly to indicate many more possible interactions, and even additivity.

Perhaps the best example of cooperation was demonstrated by Tittle, Perotti, and Norman (1997); they found that the combination of stereo and motion information supported depth judgments better than the summation of the separate probabilities from stereo and motion information alone. It is particularly interesting that stereo information seems to veto motion information in source-conflicted situations (Turner, Braunstein, & Andersen, 1997) but cooperate with it in source-consistent situations; the former result supports the idea of the modularity of the two systems, whereas the latter result supports some degree of their integrality.

3. Disambiguation

Finally, a third type of integration occurs with the disambiguation of one source of information by another. The best developed presentation of this idea can be found in the work of Landy, Maloney, Johnston, and Young (1995). These authors claim that the kinetic depth information (Wallach & O'Connell, 1953; see also, Proffitt, Rock, Hecht, & Schubert, 1992) yields information about local ordinal depth but without information about the sign of depth. Thus, one might know that three parts of an object occur at egocentric distances in either the orders A, B, C, or C, B, A; but rejecting other possibilities. The back projection from a relatively distant point-light source of a bent coat hanger on a rotating turntable, for example, will reveal the hanger's 3D structure up to the possibility of reflection (this despite the fact that only one of the possibilities will be a completely rigid interpretation). The addition of stereo information, however, will disambiguate the sign of depth order, and only one of the interpretations will generally be seen.[9] Once the information has been disambiguated, then processes of accumulation or cooperation can come into play.

V. INFORMATION AND WHAT IT REPRESENTS

> [T]urns of the head are also registered by vision. They are specified by what I have called the *sweeping* of the field of view over the ambient array. (Gibson, 1979, p. 118)

As suggested in the introduction, I claim that we use the term information to help solve one aspect of the Cartesian problem of two worlds, the physical and the mental. If the concept of information is to do any theoretical work it must help us bridge this gap: Information presents to the perceiver a "digestible" form of the object or event that it represents. How do we suppose it does this?

From a general associationistic framework and from one of indirect perception, information can only *suggest* what object or event might be present; the observer must do some work (usually "mental" work, often called "computation") to discern what is to be perceived, and even then can never be quite sure. From most mathematical frameworks and from direct perception, information is said to *specify* the object or event that is present. Many biological approaches make no particular commitment here, but directed perception chooses the idea of specification over suggestion. Much mischief can be involved in the idea of specification (see Oudejans, 1991; Massaro & Cohen, 1993; Schwartz, 1996), but in many cases the specification of a percept by information can be written as a deductive syllogism (Cutting, 1991; see also Richards, Rubin, & Hoffman, 1982). That is, given certain assumptions (axioms), a definitive conclusion can be drawn.

Consider again the example shown in the upper part of Figure 1, with two sources of information—height in the visual field and relative size—and consider height first. Given the assumptions outlined by Cutting and Vishton (1995) that (a) the panels and the ground plane are opaque; that (b) gravity is present, allowing the bases of the upright panels to lie on the ground (and no "accidental," hidden supports are present); that (c) the observer's eye is above the surface of support; and that

---

[9] One can also argue that the kinetic depth effect does not yield information about depth but instead yields information about shape (Cutting & Vishton, 1995; Cutting, 1997).

(d) the panels are not too distant with respect to eye height, it can be deductively concluded that Panel A is in front of Panel B. The amount of distance between the panels is not specified; thus, the deduction is valid only as an ordinal judgment. Nonetheless, under these assumptions, height in the visual field *specifies* ordinal depth, which panel is in front of the other.[10]

Consider next relative size. Assuming that (a) the two panels represent objects of the same physical size, and that (b) they are not too near, one could proceed by noticing that Panel A is about 1.5 times bigger than Panel B. One could then deduce that Panel B is about 1.5 times farther away than Panel A. In this manner, relative size can *specify* (at least within measurement error) the ratio of relative distances of the panels from the observer. Notice first that this is not absolute information—the panels could be 1 and 1.5 m away, or 20 and 30 m away—but the information has the potential of specifying depth relations beyond mere ordinality.

Whether the visual system uses information beyond ordinality is unclear. On the one hand, Landy et al. (1995) have assumed that sources of information using different scales are used by the visual system—ordinal, ratio, absolute, and even the unsigned depth of the kinetic depth effect. On the other hand, Cutting and Vishton (1995; Cutting, 1997) have assumed that all sources degenerate to ordinal scales. The former approach has the advantage of coming closer to a metric representation of space; the latter has the advantage of scale convergence (Birnbaum, 1983)—"reducing the various sense-feelings to a common measure" as suggested above by James (1890, pp. 268–269)—where different information can be more easily integrated. Through multiple constraints within ordinality, one can also begin to build up a near metric representation of depth. Cutting and Vishton (1995) have discussed this in an analogy to nonmetric multidimensional scaling (e.g., Shepard, 1980).

VI. SUMMARY: WORKING AMONG THREE FRAMEWORKS

As suggested in the introduction, there is no particular reason why information could not serve the perceiver from the points of view of all three frameworks. Nonetheless, research cannot easily proceed considering all three simultaneously. One must be wary of simple amalgams of approaches with different underlying assumptions (Henle, 1957); such admixtures tend not to be principled, and thus they lose logical and theoretical force.

Consider some antinomies that inhibit simple concatenation of frameworks. The associationistic approach generally assumes that cues are probabilistically related to the objects they represent (with the probability greater than 0.0 and less than 1.0); aspects of the mathematical and biological approaches generally assume

---

[10] It should escape no one that writing the process of perception as a deduction seems quite close to the notion of unconscious inference (e.g., Helmholtz, 1878). There are differences, however, between inductive inference (which is basically guesswork) and deductive inference (which is sure and upon which mathematics is based; see Skyrms, 1975). The issue, then, is where the premises from the inference come from (see Cutting, 1991).

that information specifies what it represents (with the probability 1.0). The associationistic approach is generally unconcerned with assumptions, and can be modeled by inductive inference; mathematical and biological approaches, when pushed, generally lay out assumptions and follow a line of deductive inference from them. Associationistic and mathematical approaches, on the other hand, are rarely modular and rarely interested in neurophysiology; biological approaches are almost always modular and always look to actual or plausible neural structures. And the associationistic and biological approaches have ample room for individual differences; a mathematical approach usually does not. Yet despite these differences, there is much to recommend each approach.

The strength of an associationistic approach is that personal history and all sensory modalities are considered. Such approaches are also quite sympathetic with the recent development of simulated neural networks (e.g., Anderson, 1995), and they play most sympathetically with cognition and perception as they might work together. On the other hand, the general weakness of the approach is that it fails to take seriously the structure of the stimulus. Both mathematical and biological approaches tend to do this.

The strength of any mathematical approach is its deductive rigor, and the ease with which it can apply to vision and a few other domains, such as music. This rigor affords a power of deductive inference generally unavailable in associationistic or biological approaches. Mathematical approaches typically make little commitment to modularity, personal history, or evolutionary history, but their great potential weakness was foreshadowed by Cassirer (1944, p. 11): "The precision of mathematical concepts rests upon their being confined to a definite sphere. They cannot, without logical prejudice, be extended beyond that sphere into other domains." In other words, mathematical approaches are likely to retain their power only in relatively narrow domains.

The strength of a biological approach is in its pragmatics, and its emphases on task specificity, evolutionary continuity, and the radiation of species into new niches requiring new developments in perceptual systems. It makes little commitment to personal history (except as it can emphasize flexibility), and its emphasis on contingency is distinctly noncausal. The weakness of the approach lies in its difficulty in dealing, in an instructive way, with uniquely human faculties—such as language and reading—and in knowing when one has pushed it too far. The biological approach can account for adaptation and findings structures and phenomena as we see them; it also allows for neutral evolution, where genetic drift and truly random factors may be at the root of structures and phenomena.

What is most gratifying about all three approaches to perception, however, is that—at least to some degree or another—they all appear to work. Advances in our understanding can be gained through pursuit of any of the three. Thus, as the sciences of perception and cognition continue to mature into the next century, we are likely to find ourselves fascinated, coerced, and even cajoled by developments made within each.

Acknowledgments

Supported in part by a National Science Foundation Grant SBR-9212786. I thank Nan E. Karwan for her comments.

References

Amoore, J. E. (1970). *The molecular basis of odor.* Springfield, IL: Thomas.

Anderson, J. A. (1995). *An introduction to neural networks.* Cambridge, MA: MIT Press.

Attneave, F. (1954). Some information aspects of visual perception. *Psychological Review, 61,* 183–193.

Ayer, A. J. (1956). *The problem of knowledge.* London: Macmillan.

Balzano, G. J. (1980). The group-theoretic description of 12-fold and microtonal pitch systems. *Computer Music Journal, 4,* 66–84.

Bartlett, F. (1932). *Remembering.* Cambridge, UK: Cambridge University Press.

Baxandall, M. (1995). *Shadows and enlightenment.* New Haven, CT: Yale University Press.

Bell, E. T. (1945). *The development of mathematics.* New York: McGraw-Hill.

Birnbaum, M. (1983). Scale convergence as a principle for the study of perception. In H. Geissler (Ed.), *Modern issues in perception* (pp. 319–335). Amsterdam: North-Holland.

Boring, E. G. (1942). *Sensation and perception in the history of experimental psychology.* New York: Appleton-Century-Crofts.

Braunstein, M. (1976). *Depth perception through motion.* New York: Academic Press.

Braunstein, M., & Andersen, G. (1984). A counterexample to the rigidity assumption in the visual perception of structure from motion. *Perception, 13,* 213–217.

Broadbent, D. E. (1958). *Perception and communication.* New York: Pergamon.

Brunswik, E. (1956). *Perception and the representative design of psychological experiments.* Berkeley: University of California Press.

Bülthoff, H., & Mallot, H. A. (1988). Interpreting depth modules: Stereo and shading. *Journal of the Optical Society of America, A, 5,* 1749–1758.

Burton, G., & Turvey, M. T. (1990). Perceiving lengths of rods that are held but not wielded. *Ecological Psychology, 2,* 295–324.

Burton, H. (1945). The optics of Euclid. *Journal of the Optical Society of America, 35,* 357–372.

Carlton, E., & Shepard, R. N. (1990). Psychologically simple motions as geodesic paths: I. Asymmetric objects. *Journal of Mathematical Psychology, 34,* 127–188.

Cassirer, E. (1944). The concept of group and the theory of perception. *Philosophy and Phenomenological Research, 5,* 1–35.

Cassirer, E. (1945). Reflections on the concept of group and the theory of perception. In D. Varene (Ed.), *Symbol, myth, and culture* (pp. 271–297). New Haven, CT: Yale University Press.

Cherry, C. (1957). *On human communication.* New York: Wiley.

Chomsky, N. (1959). A review of B. F. Skinner's *Verbal Behavior. Language, 3,* 26–58.

Cutting, J. E. (1986). *Perception with an eye for motion.* Cambridge, MA: The MIT Press.

Cutting, J. E. (1987). Perception and information. *Annual Review of Psychology, 38,* 61–90.

Cutting, J. E. (1991). Why our stimuli look as they do. In G. Lockhead & J. R. Pomerantz (Eds.), *Information and structure: Essays in honor of Wendell R. Garner* (pp. 41–52). Washington, DC: American Psychological Association.

Cutting, J. E. (1992). Four ways to reject directed perception. *Ecological Psychology, 3,* 25–34.

Cutting, J. E. (1993). Perceptual artifacts and phenomena: The role of Gibson in the 20th century. In S. Masin (Ed.), *Foundations of perceptual theory* (pp. 231–260). Amsterdam: Elsevier Science.

Cutting, J. E. (1997). How the eye measures reality and virtual reality. *Behavior Research Methods, Instruments, and Computers, 29,* 27–36.

Cutting, J. E., Bruno, N., Brady, N., & Moore, C. (1992). Selectivity, scope, and simplicity of models: A lesson from fitting judgments of perceived depth. *Journal of Experimental Psychology: General, 121,* 364–381.

Cutting, J. E., Flückiger, M., Baumberger, B., & Gerndt, J. D. (1996). Local heading information and layout from full-cue simulated pursuit-fixation displays. *Investigative Ophthalmology & Visual Science, 37,* S455.

Cutting, J. E., & Vishton, P. M. (1995). Perceiving layout and knowing distances: The integration, relative potency, and contextual use of different information about depth. In W. Epstein & S. Rogers (Eds.), *Perception of space and motion* (pp. 231–260). San Diego: Academic Press.

Descartes, R. (1971). Dioptics. In E. Anscomb & P. T. Geach (Eds. and Trans.), *Philosophical writings.* Indianapolis, IN: Bobbs-Merrill. (Original work published 1637.)

Einstein, A. (1921). Geometry and experience. In A. Einstein (Ed.), *Sidelights on relativity* (pp. 27–56). New York: Dover.

Estes, W. K. (1976). The cognitive role of probability learning. *Psychological Review, 83,* 37–64.

Feynman, R. (1965). *The character of physical law.* Cambridge, MA: MIT Press.

Field, D. J. (1987). Relations between the statistics of natural images and the response properties of cortical cells. *Journal of the Optical Society of America, A, 4,* 2379–2394.

Fodor, J. A. (1983). *Modularity of mind.* Cambridge, MA: MIT Press.

Garner, W. R. (1962). *Uncertainty and structure as psychological concepts.* New York: Wiley.

Garner, W. R. (1970). Good patterns have few alternatives. *American Psychologist, 58,* 34–42.

Gibson, J. J. (1950). *Perception of the visual world.* Boston: Houghton Mifflin.

Gibson, J. J. (1957). Survival in a world of probable objects. *Contemporary Psychology, 2,* 33–35.

Gibson, J. J. (1960). The information contained in light. *Acta Psychologica, 17,* 23–30.

Gibson, J. J. (1965). Constancy and invariance in perception. In G. Kepes (Ed.), *The nature and art of motion* (pp. 60–70). New York: Brazilier.

Gibson, J. J. (1966). *The senses considered as perceptual systems.* Boston: Houghton Mifflin.

Gibson, J. J. (1979). *The ecological approach to visual perception.* Boston: Houghton Mifflin.

Goodman, N. (1972). Seven strictures on similarity. In N. Goodman (Ed.), *Problems and projects* (pp. 437–446). Indianapolis, IN: Hackett.

Gould, S. J. (1983). Quick lives and quirky changes. In S. J. Gould (Ed.), *Hen's teeth and horse's toes* (pp. 56–65). New York: Norton.

Haber, R. N. (Ed.). (1969). *Information-processing approaches to visual perception.* New York: Holt.

Helmholtz, H. von (1971). The facts of perception. In R. Kahl (Ed. & Trans.), *Selected writings of Hermann von Helmholtz* (pp. 366–407). Middletown, CT: Wesleyan University Press. (Original work published 1878.)

Henle, M. (1957). Some problems of eclecticism. *Psychological Review, 64,* 296–305.

Hochberg, J. (1965). Representative sampling and the purposes of perception research: Pictures of the world and the world of pictures. In K. R. Hammond (Ed.), *The psychology of Egon Brunswik* (pp. 361–391). New York: Holt, Rinehart, & Winston.

Hochberg, J. (1987). Machines should not see as people do, but must know how people see. *Computer Vision, Graphics, and Image Processing, 37,* 221–237.

Hoffman, W. C. (1966). The Lie algebra of visual perception. *Journal of Mathematical Psychology, 3,* 65–98.

James, W. (1890). *Principles of psychology* (2 vol.). New York: Henry Holt & Company.

Johannsson, G., von Hofsten, C., & Jansson, G. (1980). Event perception. *Annual Review of Psychology, 31,* 27–66.

Julesz, B., & Bergen, J. R. (1983). Textons, the fundamental elements in preattentive attention. *Bell Systems Technical Journal, 62,* 1619–1645.

Klein, F. (1908). *Elementary mathematics from an advanced standpoint.* New York: Macmillan.

Kline, M. (1959). *Mathematics and the physical world.* New York: Dover.

Kline, M. (1980). *Mathematics: The loss of certainty.* New York: Oxford.

Koffka, K. (1935). *Principles of Gestalt psychology.* New York: Harcourt.

Krumhansl, C. L. (1990). *Cognitive foundations of musical pitch.* New York: Oxford University Press.

Kugler, P. N., & Turvey, M. T. (1987). *Information, natural law, and the self-assembly of rhythmic movement.* Hillsdale, NJ: Erlbaum.

Künnapas, T. (1968). Distance perception as a function of available visual cues. *Journal of Experimental Psychology, 77,* 523–529.

La Gournerie, J. de (1859). *Traité de perspective linéaire contenant les tracés pour les tableaux, plans et courbes, les bas-reliefs et les décorations théatrales, avec une théorie des effets de perspective.* Paris: Dalmont et Dunod.

Landy, M. S., Maloney, L. T., Johnston, E. B., & Young, M. J. (1995). Measurement and modeling of depth cue combination. *Vision Research, 35,* 389–412.

Leyton, M. (1992). *Symmetry, causality, mind.* Cambridge, MA: MIT Press.

Lindberg, D. C. (1976). *Theories of vision from al-Kindi to Kepler.* Chicago: University of Chicago Press.

Lindsay, P. H., & Norman, D. A. (1972). *Human information processing.* New York: Academic Press.

Lord, E. A., & Wilson, C. B. (1984). *The mathematical description of shape and form.* Chichester, UK: Ellis Horwood.

MacKay, D. M. (1969). *Information, mechanism, and meaning.* Cambridge, MA. MIT Press.

Marr, D. (1982). *Vision.* San Francisco: Freeman.

Massaro, D. W. (1987). *Speech perception by ear and by eye: A paradigm for psychological research.* Hillsdale, NJ: Erlbaum.

Massaro, D. W., & Cohen, M. (1993). The paradigm and the fuzzy logical model of perception are alive and well. *Journal of Experimental Psychology: General, 122,* 115–124.

Massaro, D. W., & Friedman, D. (1990). Model of information integration given multiple sources of information. *Psychological Review, 97,* 225–252.

Michaels, C. F., & Beek, P. (1996). The state of ecological psychology. *Ecological Psychology, 7,* 259–278.

Michaels, C. F., & Carello, C. (1981). *Direct perception.* Englewood Cliffs, NJ: Appleton-Century-Crofts.

Michaels, C. F., & de Vries, M. M. (in press). Higher-order and lower-order variables in the visual perception of relative pulling force. *Journal of Experimental Psychology: Human Perception and Performance.*

Mill, J. (1829). *Analysis of the phenomena of the human mind* (Vol. 1, 2nd ed.). London: Longmans, Green, Reader, & Dyer.

Mill, J. S. (1848). *System of logic* (8th ed.). London: Longmans, Green.

Mill, J. S. (1889). *An examination of Sir William Hamilton's philosophy* (6th ed.). London: Longmans, Green, Reader, & Dyer.

Miller, G. A. (1951). *Language and communication.* New York: McGraw-Hill.

Milner, A. D., & Goodale, M. (1995). *The visual brain in action.* Oxford: Oxford University Press.

Morton, J. (1969). Interaction of information in word recognition. *Psychological Review, 76,* 165–178.

Neisser, U. (1967). *Cognitive psychology.* Englewood Cliffs, NJ: Appleton-Century-Crofts.

Newton, I. (1952). *Opticks* (4th ed.). New York: Dover. (Original work published 1730.)

Niall, K. (1992). Projective invariance and the kinetic depth effect. *Acta Psychologica, 81,* 127–168.

Niall, K., & Macnamara, J. (1990). Projective invariance and picture perception. *Perception, 19,* 637–660.

Nicod, J. (1930). *Foundations of geometry and induction.* New York: Harcourt, Brace and Company.

Norman, J. F., & Todd, J. T. (1993). The perceptual analysis of structure from motion for rotating objects undergoing affine stretching transformations. *Perception & Psychophysics, 53,* 279–291.

Olmer, P. (1943). *Perspective artistique. Vol 1: Principes et méthodes.* Paris: Plon.

Oudejans, R. R. D. (1991). *The specificity debate.* Unpublished Masters thesis, Vrije Universiteit of Amsterdam.

Palmer, S. E. (1991). Goodness, Gestalt, groups, and Garner: Local symmetry subgroups as a theory of figural goodness. In G. Lockhead & J. Pomerantz (Eds.), *Perception of structure: Essays in honor of Wendell R. Garner* (pp. 23–40). Washington, DC: American Psychological Association.

Pastore, N. (1971). *Selective history of theories of visual perception, 1650–1950.* New York: Oxford University Press.

Pentland, A. P. (1983). Fractal-based description of natural scenes. *IEEE Pattern Analysis and Machine Intelligence, 6,* 661–674.

Piaget, J. (1978). *Behavior and evolution.* New York: Pantheon.

Piaget, J. (1970). *Structuralism.* New York: Basic Books.

Pittenger, J. (1990). Multiple sources of information: Threat or menace? *International Society for Ecological Society Newsletter, 4*(2), 4–6.

Poincaré, H. (1905). *Science and hypothesis.* (G. B. Halstead, Trans.). New York: Dover.

Proffitt, D. R. (1993). A hierarchical approach to perception. In S. C. Masin (Ed.), *Foundations of perceptual theory* (pp. 75–111). Amsterdam: Elsevier Scientific.

Proffitt, D. R., Rock, I., Hecht, H., & Schubert, J. (1992). Stereokinetic effect and its relation to the kinetic depth effect. *Journal of Experimental Psychology: Human Perception and Performance, 18,* 3–21.

Pylyshyn, Z. (1972). Competence and psychological reality. *American Psychologist, 27,* 546–552.

Pylyshyn, Z. (1989). Computing in cognitive science. In M. I. Posner (Ed.), *Foundations of cognitive science* (pp. 52–91). Cambridge, MA: MIT Press.

Quastler, H. (Ed.). (1955). *Information theory in psychology: Problems and methods.* Glencoe, IL: Free Press.

Ramachandran, V. S. (1985). Guest editorial. *Perception, 14,* 97–103.

Richards, W. A., Rubin, J. M., & Hoffman, D. D. (1982). Equation counting and the interpretation of sensory data. *Perception, 11,* 557–576.

Richter, J. P. (Ed. & Trans.). (1883). *The notebooks of Leonardo da Vinci.* New York: Dover.

Ronchi, V. (1957). *Optics: The science of vision.* (E. Rosen, Trans.). New York: New York University Press.

Ronchi, V. (1970). *The nature of light.* London: Heinemann.

Saffran, J. R., Aslin, R. N., & Newport, E. L. (1996). Statistical learning by 8-month-old infants. *Science, 274,* 1926–1928.

Schiffman, S. S. (1974). Physiochemical correlates of olfactory quality. *Science, 185,* 112–117.

Schneider, G. E. (1969). Two visual systems: Brain mechanisms for localization and discrimination are dissociated by tectal and cortical lesions. *Science, 163,* 896–902.

Schwartz, R. (1996). Directed perception. *Philosophical Psychology, 9,* 81–91.

Shannon, C. E., & Weaver, W. (1949). *The mathematical theory of communication.* Urbana, IL: The University of Illinois Press.

Shepard, R. N. (1980). Multidimensional scaling, tree-fitting, and clustering. *Science, 210,* 390–398.

Shiffrin, R. M., & Schneider, W. (1977). Controlled and automatic human information processing: II. Perceptual learning, automatic attending, and a general theory. *Psychological Review, 84,* 127–190.

Simon, H. A. (1955). A behavioral model of rational choice. *Quarterly Journal of Economics, 69,* 99–118.

Simpson, W. A. (1986). The cross-ratio and the perception of motion and structure. In N. I. Badler & J. Tsotsos (Eds.), *Motion: Representation and perception* (pp. 125–129). New York: North-Holland.

Skyrms, B. (1975). *Choice and chance* (2nd ed.). Belmont, CA: Wadsworth.

Smith, R. (1738). *A compleat system of optics,* 2 vols. Cambridge, UK: Cornelius Crownfield.

Snyder, J. P. (1993). *Flattening the earth: 2000 years of map projections.* Chicago: University of Chicago Press.

Stoffregen, T. (1990). Multiple sources of information: For what? *International Society for Ecological Psychology Newsletter, 4*(2), 5–8.

Titchener, E. B. (1906). *An outline of psychology.* New York: Macmillan.

Tittle, J. S., Perotti, V. J., & Norman, J. F. (1997). The integration of binocular stereopsis and structure-from-motion in the discrimination of noisy surfaces. *Journal of Experimental Psychology: Human Perception and Performance, 23,* 1035–1049.

Turner, J., Braunstein, M. L., & Andersen, G. J. (1997). Relationship between binocular disparity and motion parallax in surface detection. *Perception & Psychophysics, 59,* 370–380.

Ullman, S. (1979). *The interpretation of visual motion.* Cambridge, MA: The MIT Press.

Ullman, S. (1983). Recent computational studies in the interpretation of structure from motion. In J. Beck, G. Hope, & A. Rosenfeld (Eds.), *Human and machine vision* (pp. 459–480). New York: Academic Press.

Ungerleider, L. G., & Mishkin, M. (1982). Two cortical visual systems. In D. J. Ingle, M. A. Goodale, & R. J. W. Mansfield (Eds.), *Analysis of visual behavior* (pp. 549–586). Cambridge, MA: MIT Press.

Uttal, W. R. (1983). *Visual detection of form.* Hillsdale, NJ: Erlbaum.

Uttal, W. R. (1985). *The detection of nonplanar surfaces in visual space.* Hillsdale, NJ: Erlbaum.

Uttal, W. R. (1990). On some two-way barriers between models and mechanisms. *Perception & Psychophysics, 48,* 188–203.

Wagemans, J., Van Gool, L., & Lamote, C. (1996). The visual system's measurement of invariants need not itself be invariant. *Psychological Science, 7,* 232–236.

Wallach, H., & O'Connell, D. N. (1953). The kinetic depth effect. *Journal of Experimental Psychology, 45,* 205–217.

Wanger, L. R., Ferwerda, J. A., & Greenberg, D. P. (1992, May). Perceiving the spatial relationships in computer-generated images. *IEEE Computer Graphics, 12,* 44–59.

Warren, W. H. (1984). Perceiving affordances: Visual guidance of stair climbing. *Journal of Experimental Psychology: Human Perception and Performance, 10,* 683–703.

Wigner, E. P. (1959). The unreasonable effectiveness of mathematics in the natural sciences. In E. P. Wigner (Ed.), *Symmetries and reflections* (pp. 222–237). Woodbridge, CT: Ox Bow Press.

Woodworth, R. S. (1938). *Experimental psychology.* New York: Holt.

Zusne, L. (1970). *Visual perception of form.* New York: Academic Press.

CHAPTER 5

Illusions at Century's End

Barbara Gillam

The term *illusion* typically refers to a discrepancy between perceived reality and objective or physical reality. The term illusion, however, is not always applied to such a discrepancy. Pictures, for example, deliberately foster an impression of three-dimensional (3-D) space at odds with their physical flatness, yet this 3-D impression is not considered an illusion. The origin of the impression in mimicry of the stimulus conditions produced by the 3-D world is obvious. The effect is not mysterious. The definition of illusion must therefore be expanded to exclude those cases where perception is obviously in line with represented reality. Not everyone would agree, but I would put "subjective" or "illusory" contours into the same category as pictures (see Figure 1). Despite the absence of a luminance boundary where they are seen, subjective contours obviously arise because they mimic the form relations normally associated with an occluding surface boundary. Therefore, although there may be controversy about the mechanisms underlying them, they lack the mystery associated with illusions. Defining illusions the way I have means of course that different examples do not necessarily have anything in common either in function or mechanism.

In this chapter discussion will be restricted to the *geometrical-optical illusions* that have preoccupied students of perception for about 130 years. These are simple line drawings in which one or another perceived metric property is markedly erroneous. I shall not attempt to be exhaustive even with respect to these (for a detailed catalogue see Coren & Girgus, 1978; Robinson, 1972) but will concentrate on the most celebrated: the Müller-Lyer, the Zöllner, the Poggendorff, the Ponzo, and some variants of these (see Figure 2).

Perception and Cognition at Century's End

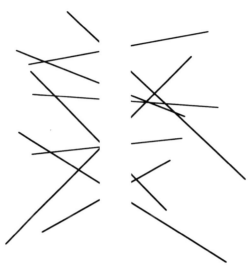

FIGURE 1   Subjective contours are perceived along collinear terminations (Gillam, 1987). Such orderly terminations in disordered lines are very likely to be due to an occluder.

Geometrical-optical illusions have attracted an enduring interest for several reasons. First, they arise from extremely simple stimuli that apparently seem to pose little problem for the visual system, which has a highly sophisticated apparatus able to decipher inputs that are apparently much more complex than the classical illusion figures. Second, they embody very large errors (for example, about 25% size enhancements). This is important to bear in mind in evaluating the significance of the innumerable studies of illusions reported in the literature. Major theoretical importance is often claimed for effects that, although statistically significant, are very small compared to the full illusion.

Are we any nearer to explaining illusions at the end of this century than at the end of the last? Much of the history of illusion research during the 20th century has been very similar to its history during the 19th. As will be clear in what follows, in many cases the wheel has been reinvented and often with methodology that is no better than was used last century. Unfortunately, much modern illusion research is quite poor experimentally; often collected in mass sessions using pencil and paper. (In this report, however, I shall concentrate on studies that are methodologically sound.) The prominent theories now are similar to those of old. Many are closer to restatements of the problem than to explanations. Findings are reified into processes. Examples are assimilation or confluxion (Auerbach, 1894; Müller-Lyer, 1889) and contrast (Heymans, 1896). "The confluxion effect consists in the magnitude of the part partaking in the magnitude of the whole; and the contrast effect consists in the exaggeration of the difference between the magnitude of the part and the magnitude of the whole" (Lewis, 1909, p. 40; see also Virsu, 1967). More elaborate pro-

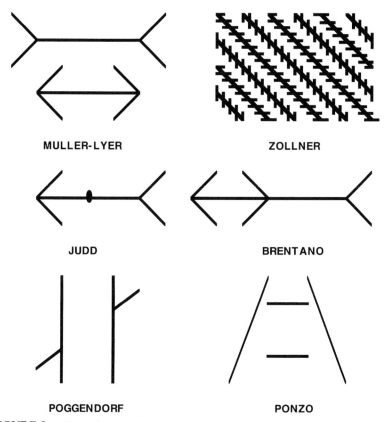

FIGURE 2   Illusion figures (Gillam, 1980). [Reprinted by courtesy of the artist, Jerome Kuhl.]

cesses postulated in recent years, such as integrative fields (Pressey & Pressey, 1992), cognitive mistracking (Hotopf, 1981; Weintraub, 1993), and axis compromise (Day & Halford, 1994) are ad hoc in the sense that outside the illusions they are trying to explain there is little evidence for the effects claimed by the postulated processes. There were also theories like this in the 19th century. Wundt (1898), for example, proposed eye movement tendencies as an explanation for the Müller-Lyer illusion. Such theories, although not satisfactory explanations, can be heuristically useful and have produced some data that do constrain theory.

Other investigators have held that an understanding of illusions requires consideration of their possible relationship to the processes of normal vision. This view, in both the 19th and 20th centuries, has led to attempts to explain illusions as fragmentary aspects of the normal decoding of the two-dimensional (2-D) representation of 3-D scenes (Filehne, 1898; Gillam, 1971, 1980; Green & Hoyle, 1963; Gregory, 1963, 1968; Kristof, 1961; Redding & Hawley, 1993; Tausch, 1954; Thiéry, 1896; Warren & Bashford, 1977). There is no more agreement about the validity of this approach now than there was 100 years ago. Yet we do know a great deal more about how the 3-D world is perceived. It should be possible to say something more definitive about illusions in relation to the geometry of projection and its decoding. In recent years other functions of vision, such as orientation constancy (Day, 1972), amodal completion (Cleary, 1966; Zanuttini, 1976), and solving aperture problems (Mather, O'Halloran, Antis, 1991) have also been proposed as explanations of particular illusions, but these ideas are not broadly developed.

In one area of vision research there has been enormous recent progress. At the end of the 20th century we have a far greater knowledge than was available a century ago of how the visual system functions physiologically. Helmholtz (1866) postulated retinal blur as an explanation of certain illusions. Little was known then of the brain mechanisms underlying vision. This century has seen many of the new discoveries of visual physiology and the psychophysics of early visual processes applied to illusions. Have illusions finally been explained this way? Can they be?

Another recent advance has been the discovery of modularity in the visual system (Goodale & Milner, 1992; Livingstone & Hubel, 1986; Zeki, 1993). Many representations of the visual input, postulated as having different purposes, are found in the visual cortex. How do illusions fit into current views of visual representation?

In this chapter I shall attempt to analyze the issues raised above and to answer the question, Where do illusions stand in relation to theories of perception in the late 20th century? Readers may not agree with the conclusions, but I hope at least to raise the issues with clarity.

I. WHY ILLUSIONS ARE CONSIDERED THEORETICALLY DIAGNOSTIC

The major geometrical-optical illusions, such as the Müller-Lyer and the Poggendorff, are considered diagnostic to a number of theoretical positions in perception. The main reason why they have this status is because most theories of visual perception try to explain how the visual system achieves veridical perception of the environment, but veridical perception does not discriminate among such theories. They must be tested by devising stripped-down stimuli that will elicit unrealistic percepts predicted by the theory in question but not by others. Illusions are accidentally discovered, unrealistic responses to minimal stimuli that seem like ready-made tests of visual theory. Because they are errors, it would seem that they can only be explained by the quirks of the visual system itself. It is not surprising that they have been seized upon by a variety of theorists as evidence for particular visual processes. In this chapter the concentration will be on theories for which illusions are considered diagnostic but that have content outside the illusion domain. Little attention will be paid to theories that have been devised in an ad hoc manner to explain illusions alone. This distinction is not an absolute one of course, as most visual theories have some added content or assumptions when applied to illusions.

II. THEORIES OF PERCEPTUAL REPRESENTATION

There are two main issues of representation for which illusions are considered diagnostic.

A. Is Perception Euclidean?

In recent years there has been considerable discussion of the kind of representation or representations vision creates of the world. A particular preoccupation has been whether or not there is a Euclidean representation. Even to speak of a representation from which perceptual attributes are somehow read is to introduce the old problem of what homunculus does the reading. The question of whether or not perception is Euclidean can, however, be posed with less philosophical baggage. To what degree are different spatial judgments transitive, in that one judgment can be predicted from another according to a Euclidean metric? This is an important question in understanding the way perception arises from sensory input. It is related to the question of percept–percept couplings (Hochberg, 1981) whose existence does not imply a homunculus reading off an internal 3-D representation of external space but may imply a perceptual organization in which the redundancies and the transitivities of real-world properties, resulting from its Euclidean structure, are incorporated. Illusions have a particularly important role in deciding such issues. When perception accurately reflects external reality it is not possible to tell whether judgments are transitive because (a) they are each *independently* responsive to the input from the environment or (b) because they reflect contingencies in the way perception is organized. In illusion figures, on the other hand, if an error occurs in one domain (e.g., size) there is no reason for it to occur in another domain (e.g., position) unless the responses are linked by an underlying common metric (not necessarily Euclidean). It is therefore particularly interesting to see if judgments of different properties of illusion figures are transitive. When responses to illusion figures are probed, it is found that the visual system is not Euclidean in any general way nor do different judgments necessarily share a common metric. It is an empirical matter to tease out which responses are transitive and which are not. This has implications for perceptual theory, as will be shown. Illusions are in fact a powerful tool for investigating the particularities of how space is encoded visually.

B. Do Perception and Action Use the Same Perceptual Representation?

Another question of representation does not concern the transitivities of perceptual properties with one another, but the relationship between perceived properties and motor actions regarding the same stimuli. Goodale and Milner (1992) have argued that the same object may be represented differently in those parts of the brain that control perceived space and action space, respectively. The argument largely derives from observations of patients. Those with brain damage in the posterior parietal area often exhibit difficulty carrying out appropriate actions (such as grasping) with respect to objects, yet they are able to recognize them. Patients who have damage in the inferior temporal area, however, can often accurately reach for and grasp objects but have difficulty recognizing them. Illusions also have importance in relation to this question. Because illusions are errors presumed to be caused by properties of the putative perceptual system (the one responsible for conscious perception and recognition), it is possible that they will not be exhibited by the putative system governing motor responses. This, if true, might provide a useful converging operation, using non-brain-damaged people, with respect to the presumed independence of these two systems, which has largely been based on patient data.

There is some confusion in the illusion literature regarding which of these two different issues of perceptual representation is being addressed by particular experimental observations. It is hoped that what follows will clarify this issue.

The first question, that of transitivity, will be addressed by considering in some detail the question of the relationship between size and position in the Müller-Lyer illusion. Transitivity between these two judgments has been taken for granted until recently, and many theories have attributed the Müller-Lyer illusion to a shift in the perceived position of the apices. These theories include those proposed by Morgan, Hole, and Glennerster (1990) and Gillam (1978), although for entirely different theoretical reasons; Morgan's theory is physiological, whereas Gillam's is functional.

If the distance between the two endpoints of a line is perceptually enlarged or diminished by adding fins or arrowheads, it is obvious that in a perceptually Euclidean world the positions of each of these points must appear to be shifted laterally either apart or together, respectively. This question was not specifically investigated until recently, although implicit recognition of the possible independence of these judgments may be inferred from the fact that when the illusion is measured by matching the arrowhead figure with the fin figure, the one is rarely placed directly under the other. It is as if this would make the judgment too easy because instead of making a size match subjects could align apex positions.

Position is usually investigated using a reaching response. However, a failure to find errors in reaching that are equivalent to the size errors found in the Müller-Lyer illusion could be due to *either* an intransitivity between position and the size within the perceptual system or else to a dissociation between the perceptual and motor systems of vision of the type proposed by Goodale and Milner (1992). The data on reaching are contradictory, but can be summarized and interpreted as follows: Those studies where free viewing was used have shown little or no error in reaching. Presumably this is because subjects look at the apex and reach to where they are looking. This applies to the first experiment by Mack, Heuer, Villardi, and Chambers (1985) as well as a recent experiment by Post and Welch (1996). When fixation (on the center of the figure) is used (Cook & Gillam, 1996) or subjects reach to a *remembered* apex location (Mack et al., 1985, Experiment 2) significant errors are found, although less than expected on the basis of the size illusion. Cook and Gillam's results are shown in Table 1. These observations might be taken as indicating that position is misperceived along with size and that this influences motor responses.

TABLE 1   Showing the Percent Illusion (Judgment) and
Percent Error in Reaching (Reach) for Fin
and Arrow Head Müller–Lyer Figures[a]

Figure	Reach	Reach control	Judgment
Fins	−4.7★	−11.3★★	−7.0★★
	(5.4)	(5.0)	(5.5)
Arrow	5.9★★	14.6★★	16.2★★
	(3.8)	(5.3)	(5.9)

[a]The reach control was a plain line stimulus with an added length of 10%.

★Comparison with zero, $p < 0.05$.

★★Comparison with zero, $p < 0.01$.

Other data, however, are not consistent with the idea that position is misperceived in the Müller-Lyer figure. Gillam and Chambers (1985) had subjects move
a dot on a computer screen laterally until it appeared underneath each of the apices
of a horizontally oriented Müller-Lyer figure. Separate measurements were taken
for the arrowhead figure, the fin figure, and a plain line control of the same length.
Subjects were very accurate at this task, and the authors concluded that the size illusion is not based on misperception of position and that size and position judgments
do not depend on a common metric. Morgan et al. (1990) questioned this conclusion, arguing that Gillam and Chambers's subjects may have been judging orientation rather than position, because the task involved placing the dot so that it formed
a vertical implicit line with the apex in each case. (It should be noted that this would
still mean an intransitivity between orientation and position.)

Gillam and Blackburn (1996) conducted another experiment to eliminate this
possibility. Subjects were shown two fin version Müller-Lyer figures one above the
other. In some trials the lower figure was vertically aligned with the upper figure,

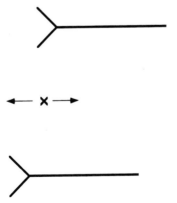

FIGURE 3   An example of the stimulus arrangements used in Gillam and Blackburn's (1996)
experiment (see text).

TABLE 2   Comparison of Size Illusion and Position Illusion for Fins Figure (see Figure 3)[a]

Method	Stimulus	Location of lower figure	Mean error (mm)
Size	Fins	Left	13.16 (1.37)
		Right	11.27 (0.86)
Alignment	Fins	Left	1.58 (0.93)
		Center	1.27 (0.92)
		Right	1.40 (1.06)
Alignment	Line	Left	−1.32 (0.69)
		Center	−0.82 (0.55)
		Right	−1.17 (0.83)

[a]Size was measured by adjustment of the size of a plain line comparator. Position was measured by moving a dot to appear aligned with either the left or right apices of the upper and lower figures (both with fins).

whereas in other trials it was laterally displaced either left or right relative to the upper (see Figure 3). Subjects were required to laterally move a dot placed between the two horizontal figures until it was in line with either both the two left apices or (on other trials) both the two right apices. Subjects were accurate in this task, showing no sign of the error that would be predicted if the apex positions were displaced in a manner consistent with the size error (see Table 2). Clearly, in this case the judgment could not be based on reproducing a particular orientation; both figures have the same fins and therefore displacements of position should not influence orientation, yet the setting of the dot will be displaced if the positions are seen incorrectly. Wenderorth (1983) used a similar method to tease apart orientation from position judgments in a different context. It may be concluded that the Müller-Lyer size illusion is not the result of a displacement in the perceived position of the endpoints of the shaft. Why then do reaching responses sometimes show an illusion? Do eye movements also show it? It is interesting that although many studies have shown that eye movements to the Müller-Lyer figures are displaced from the apices in the direction of the appendages (Festinger, White, & Allyn, 1968), when subjects are carefully instructed to fixate the apex they are able to do so (Wong, 1981). The displacements often found seem to reflect attempts to pick up optimum information rather than misperception of position. It can be concluded that under specific instructions to be accurate, eye movements are not directed to positions consistent with the size effect, whereas hand movements tend to be. This is not as surprising as it might at first appear. The visual information required for hand and eye movements are not the same. To reach the two sides of an object at different distances from the observer the hand will have to move laterally the same amount at each distance. In other words, the hand needs information about distal size. The eye has different requirements. To fixate the two sides of the same object the eye will have to move less when the object is farther away. Eye movements have to intersect not the physical object but its angular projection and may therefore be guided by a different signal from hand movements. Hochberg (1981) suggested that eye movements must be guided by the "visual field" in Gibson's terms not the "visual world." Studies in which subjects reach to where they are looking are not subject to illusion because they do not require a judgment about the object at all. When this strategy is prevented, a displacement of position does occur in reaching.

To summarize, it seems that size and position are not transitive and do not reflect a common metric. The position of the apices of the Müller-Lyer illusion are not shifted apart relative to other objects in the visual field, as would be predicted from the size effect. The position signal may be important in guiding eye movements, which also show little distortion. Hand movements, on the other hand, which normally require distal size information, do show some of the errors predicted by the size judgments. There is no evidence from illusion studies that perception and action are based on distinct representations.

The situation is somewhat more complicated than this however. There are several phenomena that do suggest an apparent position effect in the Müller-Lyer figure as a whole, even while local positions are not shifted. In the Morinaga paradox (Figure 4a) the Müller-Lyer components appear displaced relative to one another in the opposite direction from the displacement predicted by the size effect. This displacement does not, however, seem to result from the individual displacements of the apices so much as from the organization of the fins across the two figures into a unit. They form trapezia that have been shown in other contexts to produce apparent displacements (Day & Halford, 1994; Gillam, 1973). Displacement is also apparent in the double Judd figure (Figure 4b). The right component seems displaced upwards relative to the left component (Stuart, Day, & Dickinson, 1984), and indeed Benussi (1912) reported apparent up and down motion if these two figures

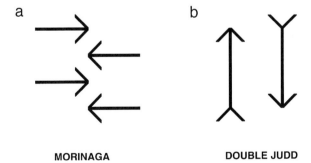

MORINAGA   **DOUBLE JUDD**

FIGURE 4   (a) Morinaga paradox. The apices are vertically aligned. They appear displaced in directions opposite to those predicted from the Müller-Lyer illusion. (b) Double Judd figure. The left figure appears higher than the right figure.

are presented in fast alternation at the same retinal location. Again this appears to be an effect involving one entire figure relative to the other, rather than local shifts in position of the apices. It is as if there are asymmetric size effects within the two figures that lead to an apparent global position shift. Globally, whole objects can appear to be shifted relative to each other while each local component appears to be in the correct position relative to unbiased local points.

III. PHYSIOLOGICAL THEORIES

Physiological theories attempt to explain illusions by showing that the retinal or cortical image of the "test" component of a figure, (e.g., the shaft of the Müller-Lyer figure) is altered by the context or "inducing" component of a figure, (e.g., the arrowheads and fins of the Müller-Lyer figure). Early theories based on retinal processes, such as blur, are now discredited for a number of reasons, the most obvious being the survival of illusions in the purely binocular (cyclopean) images produced by fusing random-dot stereograms (Julesz, 1971). Modern physiological theories postulate cortical processes instead (see Wenderoth, 1992). These theories tend to be of two main types. It has long been held that many illusions, such as the Zöllner, Hering, and Poggendorff (see Figure 2) can be explained by the expansion of acute angles (Hering, 1861). This century, following physiological discoveries it was proposed that this expansion arises from partial inhibition of the response of cortical detectors to a line of a particular orientation in the presence of neighboring lines of a slightly different orientation, resulting in a shift of the test line's peak response away from the orientation of the inducing line or lines (Blakemore, Carpenter, & Georgeson, 1970; Burns & Pritchard, 1971; Wallace, 1975; White, 1975). This theory is speculative with respect to mechanisms (see Morgan, 1995) and also has some problems dealing with data. The Zöllner illusion is present even when the test lines are replaced by gaps in the inducing lines thus eliminating acute angles (Earle & Maskell, 1995; Hill, 1971; Pierce, 1901) (see Figure 5). The Poggendorff illusion is clearly not primarily attributable to lateral inhibition because it is greatly diminished when the entire configuration is rotated so that the transversals are vertical or horizontal (Day & Dickinson, 1976; Leibowitz & Toffey, 1966; Weintraub & Krantz, 1971) (see Figure 6a). The degree of illusion is also much reduced or even reversed when the figure is amputated so that only the acute angles remain (Figure 6b) (Day, 1973; Weintraub & Krantz, 1971). The illusion appears to be almost entirely attributable to the obtuse angle components.[1,2] Weintraub and Tong (1974),

---

[1] Pierce (1901) and Wenderoth and Johnson (1982) have questioned the relevance of amputated versions of illusions since they are essentially different figures. However if a theory of illusions rests on an image distortion of a component of the figure then it is surely reasonable to isolate that component to see if the putative effect exists.

[2] Small degrees of orientation shift as a function of orientation context have been observed physiologically and psychophysically but only for small line separations and small angular differences (Morgan, 1995).

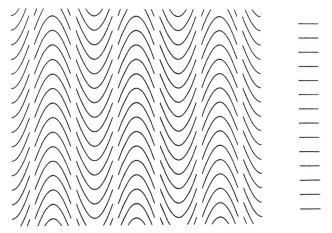

FIGURE 5   The Zollner Illusion with no explicit test lines. [From Earle & Maskell, 1995, *Perception, 24(12)*, 1397–1406, Fig. 6. Pion, London.]

Hotopf and Ollerearnshaw (1972), and Day and Dickinson (1976) have all shown that the perceived orientation of an oblique line transversal in the Poggendorff illusion is little different from the orientation of the same oblique line on its own. Also, unlike the Zöllner illusion, the Poggendorff disappears if the transversals cut across the parallels. Although most of these observations have been known since last century (Judd, 1899) the notion that the Poggendorff illusion is attributable to the expansion of acute angles is persistent (e.g., Spillman & Ehrenstein, 1995).

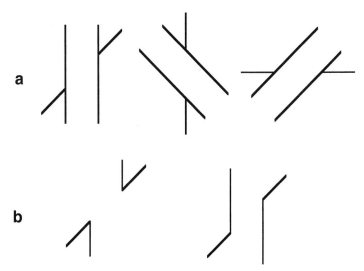

FIGURE 6   Poggendorff Illusion variants. The illusion is much reduced when the figure is rotated. There is little illusion for the acute angle components and almost full illusion for the obtuse angle components.

A second class of physiological theory is based on the concept of low-pass filtering of the image. This idea began with Ginsberg (1979), who proposed that size judgments are based on the responses of cortical low spatial frequency channels that effectively blur the shaft and appendages (although he did not specify how length is computed from such low-pass images). Morgan and Casco (1990) have applied a similar theory to the Zöllner illusion. They note, following Judd (1899), that this illusion is accompanied by a separation illusion and assert that an adequate theory will explain both the orientation and separation illusions (lateral inhibition only attempted to account for orientation). They propose that both effects are the result of convolving the image with a DOG (difference of gaussians) filter, which has the effect of blurring the intersection of the lines and making both the separation and the relative orientation indeterminate. They claim that in the face of this indeterminacy the visual system defaults to an orthogonal solution, since the orthogonal orientation between two parallel lines has a special ecological significance (it signals whether a given separation can be passed through by an object such as a hand). A possibility that Morgan and Casco do not allow for, however, is that the spacing illusion (see Figure 7a) is not an *underestimation* of the length of the horizontal line bounded by obliques but an *overestimation* of the horizontal line bounded by vertical lines. Observation of both figures relative to a plain line (Figure 7a) indicates that the spacing illusion is largely, if not entirely, owing to the latter effect. This H illusion has previously been reported by Restle and Decker (1977) and Adam and Bateman (1980); it also exists in partial form as the divided line illusion (see Figure 7b). It could be related to the occlusion implications of T junctions. Given these considerations, the Morgan and Casco theory must be judged solely as an explanation of the orientation effect of the Zöllner illusion. The main problem with this

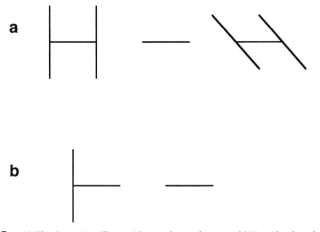

FIGURE 7   (a) The Separation Illusion (the crossbar in the vertical H is wider than the crossbar in the oblique H). It is usually assumed that the latter is misperceived. Adding a control reveals that the error is largely in perceiving the width of the vertical H. (b) The Divided Line Illusion. The horizontal lines are the same length.

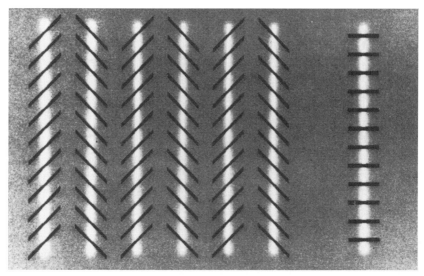

FIGURE 8   The Zollner Illusion with reversed luminance polarity. [From Earle & Maskell, 1995, *Perception, 24(12),* 1397–1406, Fig. 3. Pion, London.]

or any low-pass theory applied to the Zöllner illusion (as Morgan himself has recently pointed out; Morgan, Medford, & Newsome, 1995) is that it cannot account for the survival of the illusion when luminance polarity is reversed (Earle & Maskell, 1995; see Figure 8).

Also, this theory must, like lateral inhibition theory, accommodate the persistence of the illusion when the test lines are replaced by gaps. It is difficult to see how the blurring process would occur under these conditions. Another problem is that in order to explain Zöllner effect, which is a global tilt, Morgan and Casco propose that the local shifts in orientation at each intersection influence the total line orientation via "collector units." This notion is analogous to the global orientation effect produced by local orientations in the Twisted Cord illusion (Figure 9). However, in the Twisted Cord illusion the local orientations are still visible while influencing the global orientation. In the Zöllner figure the postulated local orientation shifts cannot be seen. Only a global effect is observed. The illusion does not appear to be based on a local effect at all (Morgan et al., 1995; Parlangeli & Roncato, 1995; see Figure 10).

In general it can be concluded that neither lateral inhibition nor low-pass theories can explain illusions such as the Zöllner and the Poggendorff as first-order (luminance-based) processes. A different theory of the Zöllner illusion was proposed by Tyler and Nakayama (1984), who confirmed Pierce (1901) in showing that a similar tilt illusion, although possibly of smaller magnitude than the full Zöllner, occurs with no intersections (see Figure 11). They show that the orientation of the entire column of lines is assimilated slightly to the orientation of the components for small

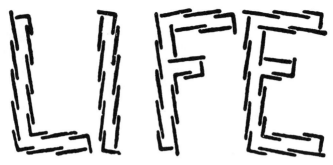

FIGURE 9   The Twisted Cord Illusion.

angles and shows a (greater) repulsion from that orientation at larger angles. They speculate that there is facilitation between (a) receptive fields responsive to small orientations and those responsive to large orientations at small angular differences and (b) inhibition between the same channels at larger angular differences. This is, however, little more than a restatement of the findings couched in physiological terms.

Morgan et al. (1990) have proposed a physiological account of the Müller-Lyer illusion along the following lines: objects composed of several different parts are located at the centroid of the individually measured positions of those parts. This is achieved by units with large overlapping receptive fields that have input from lower-order units (which are eclectic with respect to preferred contrast polarity, color, orientation, etc.) distributed over the receptive field. Thus position is coded only in a relatively coarse manner, averaging over object parts. The judged distance between

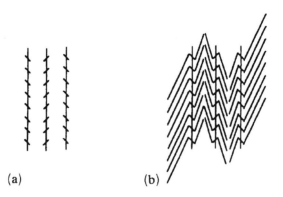

(a)   **(b)**

FIGURE 10   Showing that the Zollner Illusion is nonlocal. The direction of apparent slant in the parallels is determined by the more remote lines. The illusion reverses direction from (a) to (b), though the intersecting lines are identical in the two cases. [From Parlangeli & Roncato, 1995, *Perception 24(5),* 501–512, Fig. 1. Pion, London.]

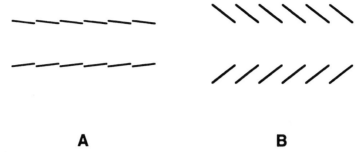

A **B**

FIGURE 11 Zollner-type figures from Tyler and Nakayama (1984). In (A) a small effect of assimilation of the orientation of the inner ends of each set of lines to the lines themselves is found. In (B) the effect is a larger one of contrast (the usual Zollner effect). [Reprinted by permission of Lawrence Erlbaum Associates.]

the ends of the shaft in the Müller-Lyer illusion will then be influenced by the positional shift of the ends of the shafts toward the centroid of neighboring details.

"The benefit is the high efficiency of locating objects composed of parts; the cost is the inability to make veridical judgments of the positions of parts of objects with respect to parts of other objects" (Morgan & Glennerster, 1991, p. 2083). I have already shown, however, that attributing the Müller-Lyer illusion to distortions in the perceived positions of the apices is untenable. It may be possible for Ginsberg's theory, which is not explicitly based on position, to get around this problem by arguing that size but not position is based on low-pass spatial filtering. However, attempts to test low-pass theories of the Müller-Lyer illusion directly by eliminating low spatial frequency components in the image (Carlson, Moeller, & Anderson, 1984), while not entirely successful in doing so (Garcia-Perez, 1991), nevertheless strongly indicate that the Müller-Lyer illusion is not carried by these channels, at least in first-order images. The fact that reversing the contrast of Müller-Lyer fins and arrowheads relative to the shafts (Morgan & Glennerster, 1991) does not destroy the illusion also argues against this view, as does the elegant finding of Morgan et al. (1990) that adding Müller-Lyer appendages to a line introduces a bias in the size judgment but does not influence precision.

Even if image theories did not have such a range of problems in accounting for illusions in their own terms, there is beyond that a conceptual difficulty with most of them. It is difficult to see why the *perception* of angular magnitude, for instance, would not be calibrated to take account of whatever cortical representation two adjacent lines produce. Surely the way angles or lines are cortically represented is irrelevant so long as this representation gives rise to appropriate perception of the external world. Likewise, it is difficult to see why low spatial frequency information would be selectively used as the basis for size judgments when it is so inaccurate. The essential difficulty is that many physiological theories still have embedded within them the notion that it is the *image* that is seen rather than the world, so that all a theory of illusions has to do is to propose a mechanism of image distortion with no consideration as to why perception would reflect such a distortion.

IV. FUNCTIONAL THEORIES

There have always been those who argue that the major illusions are of such a magnitude that it is highly likely that they are responses that serve a useful function in normal vision, although they constitute errors in the perception of line drawings. Such a view can involve merely a suggestion of function associated with an essentially physiological theory, or function can be the major focus of the theory. Although, as Marr (1982) pointed out, a full understanding of perception requires a knowledge of function, algorithm, and mechanism, there are a number of areas of perception where we know a great deal about what the system is doing and how it is doing it in a formal sense without knowing much if anything about the physiological mechanisms. Perceptual organization and the perception of spatial layout are examples.

As already indicated, some modern physiological and computational approaches to illusions do consider function. Morgan and colleagues consider that illusions reflect the fact that the visual system is no better than it needs to be. "What we call illusions arise when the visual system is asked to perform some task for which it is ill-adapted" (Morgan et al., 1990, p. 800). They regard perception of position as subserving reaching and grasping and believe that for this purpose it is sufficient to locate objects consisting of a number of parts at the centroid of those parts. Similarly, they consider that contour separation has significance mainly for the act of passing objects between the contours. Perception of contour separation will be biased towards the orthogonal because it is the best indicator of this function. (Although as Mather et al., 1991, point out, the orthogonal will only be a good indication of whether an aperture can be passed through if both sides of it are in the same depth plane). It is interesting that Morgan et al. do not subscribe to the Goodale and Milner view that the representations serving perceptual judgment and motor performance are different. They propose instead that a single representation serves both functions but is only accurate enough to meet the needs of motor performance. They assume that recognition and object comparison, for example, which depend on perceptual properties, would not be disadvantaged by large errors in judging distal size. This is, in my view, highly questionable. Nevertheless, the notion that perception is cruder than it appears to be is an interesting idea that deserves further investigation (see also Cavanagh, 1995).

It is curious that physiological theories that do consider function have been silent with respect to the most obvious and popular functional theory. The visual system is certainly ill-adapted to purely 2-D perception.

The best known and oldest functional view of illusions is that they are biases in responding to a 2-D array but that serve 3-D scene perception. Vision, according to this view, is not for the viewing of line drawings but for the perception of scenes, and it is to scene perception we need to turn to begin to understand illusions. This theory keeps surfacing because it promises not only to account for the presence of errors in the perception of line drawings but also for the *absence* of such errors in normal veridical perception (errors that most other illusion theories must propose as the by-products of the processes they postulate to explain illusions). The advantage of showing that illusory "distortion" serves veridical scene perception is that it avoids invoking mechanisms that seem to have no other purpose than to cause the visual system to make mistakes. This advantage is usually overlooked. It is, however, very important because it gives scene-based theories an a priori probability that more ad hoc theories do not possess. Because scene-based theories are much better developed than other functional theories and have survived in one form or another for 100 years despite enormous criticism, considerable attention will be given to them here.

The first step in considering the view that illusions serve scene perception is to see whether the line arrangements that give rise to illusions occur in the pictures of scenes and, if so, to examine the role such line arrangements have in scene perception. Figure 12 shows a scene containing the Müller-Lyer, the Judd, the Poggendorff, and the Ponzo configurations. The front of the rug is identical in length to the lower edge of the back wall (regular Müller-Lyer). The picture rail is collinear with the base board (Poggendorff), and the two dogs are the same size (Ponzo). Figure 13 shows two ground planes incorporating versions of the Zöllner configuration as well as the Sander configuration (which is shown in its usual form for comparison). The two vertical lines in Figure 13b are physically parallel (Zöllner). The oblique lines are the same length (Sander).

It is obvious that in all these cases the way perceived properties (such as orientations and extents) deviate from the projective properties of the picture correspond *both* to the designated illusion *and* to the objective properties these configurations represent in a scene. Illusory responses could therefore be deviations from image properties and relationships in the direction of the scene properties and relationships that would normally give rise to that image. The similarity of illusory responses and the scene implications of images has been known since the 19th century, and it provides a compelling basis for seriously considering the view that illusions are not so much error as adaptive responses in normal viewing. The major obstacle to such a view is the absence of any awareness of a 3-D scene in looking at isolated illusion figures. In most cases they appear entirely 2-D, and it is supposed that they elicit entirely 2-D processing. But does such processing exist? The real world is very difficult to see in projective terms. Try asking someone viewing a real room whether a base board is projectively collinear with a moulding. The judgment is quite impossible. Gillam (1980) points out that pictures fall phenomenologically between illusion diagrams and real scenes in that they can be seen both according to the objective reality they represent and also according to their projective (2-D) properties. In

FIGURE 12   A scene containing the Müller-Lyer, Ponzo, and Poggendorff Illusions (see text).

viewing Figure 12 for example, people can report both the relative sizes of the extents represented or the relative sizes of the extents on the picture plane.

Judgments of projective relationships in pictures are, however, highly inaccurate and biased in the direction of the scene properties the configuration represents. Sedgwick and Nicholls (1993) have recently been investigating the "cross-talk" in perception between the perception of projective and objective properties. The really critical question for scene theories of illusions is whether the cross-talk from objective to projective properties occurs *regardless* of conscious awareness of any objective (scene) significance of the configuration. Illusion figures could be regarded as one extreme on a continuum of phenomenological awareness of the scene implications of a particular configuration, with real scenes at the other end of the continuum and pictures in between? Sanford (1898) quotes Thiéry as saying,

> It is no more necessary that the perspective factor should be conscious in order that it may influence the final form of perception than that the partial tones in a note on a violin should be consciously recognised before it can be distinguished from a note on the same pitch on a flute. (p. 222)

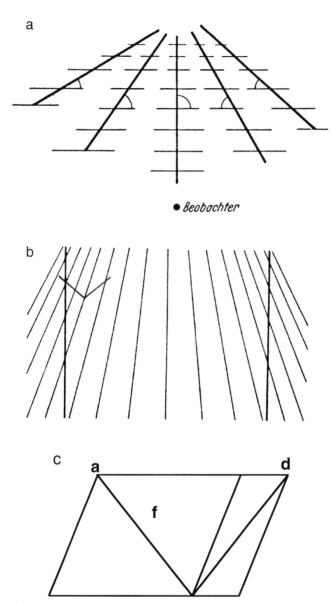

FIGURE 13   (a) and (b) are ground planes containing versions of the Zollner configuration; (b) also contains a form of the Sander Illusion (shown as an illusion figure in [c]). (a) from Tausch (1954). *Psychologische Forschung, 24,* 299–348. Copyright © 1954 Springer-Verlag; (b & c) from Kristof (1961).

A. Criticisms of Primary Constancy Scaling

There are two ways in which scene-appropriate scaling of the 2-D array could occur for illusion figures:

1. If depth is "registered" unconsciously
2. If scaling is directly triggered by image features without the mediation of "apparent" or "unconscious" depth.

What evidence is there outside the illusion domain for each of these processes?

A great deal of the literature on size and shape constancy assumes the validity of the size–distance (or shape–slant) invariance hypothesis. The size–distance invariance hypothesis or the notion that perceived size is necessarily the product of a calculation using retinal size and perceived distance has, however, been refuted over and over again (Epstein, Park, & Casey, 1961; Kilpatrick & Ittelson, 1953; Sedgwick, 1986). Its simplicity unfortunately ensures that it always survives to triumph over the empirical evidence. It seems so self-evident that even when the data show little relationship between perceived size and perceived distance in specific instances, it is assumed that subjects must be making a calculation using a "registered distance" different from the one perceived and reported. I have argued strongly against this approach in another volume of this series (Gillam, 1995) and the arguments will not be repeated here. Suffice it to say that the construct of "registered distance" is ad hoc and also unnecessary. Observations in which size and distance do not have an invariant relationship are much better explained by assuming that image features can directly scale size and other properties. There is no logical reason to assume that distance is more primary than size. Gibson gives a number of examples of direct size scaling. The horizon ratio (Rogers, 1995; Sedgwick, 1973) is an example. Examples also exist outside the pictorial domain, such as the zooming of size in response to decreased convergence (for a discussion see Gillam, 1995).

Both unconscious depth and direct ("primary") constancy scaling have been proposed as the basis of illusions. Gregory (1968), who made explicit the distinction between primary constancy scaling (unmediated) and secondary constancy scaling (mediated by apparent depth), has perhaps caused confusion by the statement that in illusion figures "depth is not seen because it is countermanded by the competing depth information of a visible background" (p. 289). He conducted an experiment to illustrate that when the background is removed the depth response is released. This experiment and its interpretation seem to have fostered the idea that primary constancy scaling is just like secondary constancy scaling but with *unconsciously registered* depth, although this does not seem to be Gregory's view in his other writings. As a result, despite the fact that it is completely unnecessary to assume that primary scaling is mediated by any kind of depth response, most of the many critics of a scene-based approach to illusions restrict themselves to attacking the notion that illusions are caused by unconscious depth. Almost none of Gregory's critics have identified primary constancy scaling with Gibson's (1966) direct size scaling, which is the most reasonable interpretation of it.

FIGURE 14   Gregory's famous real-scene Müller-Lyer Illusion. [From Gregory, R. L. (1970). *The Intelligent Eye*. London: Weidenfeld and Nicolson, by permission of Oxford University Press.]

The major criticisms of Gregory's theory in the literature are listed below. They all refer to the Müller-Lyer illusion, which was his prime example (see Figure 14), and they all assume that primary constancy scaling involves unconscious registration of a depth difference between the figure with fins and the figure with arrowheads.

1. The effect of angle cannot be explained by attributing the illusion to the greater typical distance of shafts with outgoing fins, because the further away a corner is the flatter its corners should appear to be (Gauld, 1975; Hotopf, 1966).
2. They do not explain the Brentano form of the illusion (Fisher, 1968) nor the Judd form (Morgan, 1969, 1995), because differences in shaft distance for the fin and arrowhead cases, registered unconsciously or not, do not apply to these figures. (For these forms see Figure 2.)
3. They do not explain the absence of an illusion of width associated with the illusion of length because a scaling due to implicit distance should cause both (Predebon, 1981; Waite & Massaro, 1970) (Figure 15).

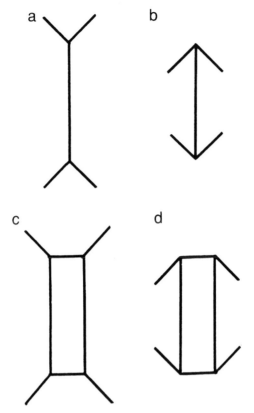

FIGURE 15   Showing that the Müller–Lyer Illusion only occurs for length not width. [From Predebon, 1981, *American Journal of Psychology, 94(1),* 159–172. Copyright 1981 by the Board of Trustees of the University of Illinois. Used with permission of the University of Illinois Press.]

4. The illusion is only found for parts of the shaft near the tips, whereas depth should affect the whole line (Morinaga, 1941; Morgan, 1969).
5. Obtuse and acute angles are ambiguous with respect to whether they represent near or far corners (Georgeson & Blakemore, 1973).
6. The illusion occurs for amputated versions of the figures which reduce the resemblance of the components to far and near corners (Day & Dickinson, 1976).
7. The illusion is not reversed when the fins are made to reverse depth stereoscopically (Georgeson & Blakemore, 1973; Massaro & Anderson, 1970).
8. "A theory which appeals to the idea of automatic compensation for unconsciously perceived depth is in obvious danger of being irrefutable" (Humphrey & Morgan, 1965, p. 744.

Even without these criticisms the notion that the Müller-Lyer illusion is due to perceiving (unconsciously) a line bounded by fins as "far" lacks sense. Far relative to what? It is obvious that the illusion does not depend on comparing the fin form with the arrowhead form but is present for either of these compared with a plain line. Clearly in the perspective view of a scene, lines bounded by obtuse angles can represent many distances, as can lines bounded by acute angles. This version of scene-based theories, which we consider to be a straw man, will be rejected with no further discussion, and only the much more plausible direct scaling version will be examined. If the unconsciously registered depth idea is abandoned, and illusions are attributed to direct size scaling by context as it occurs in normal 3-D perception, then the theory of primary constancy scaling is no more irrefutable than any other. Refutations must show either that illusory distortions are not in the correct direction to produce veridical perception when applied to the same configurations in 3-D scenes, or that illusions are influenced by parameters that would not promote accurate scene perception with respect to the property in question. Criticisms that do pose difficulties for direct scaling theory will be considered later.

B. Relational Theories and Contrast

So-called contrast illusions are perhaps the most obviously compatible with direct theories of size perception. These include the Titchener circles (Figure 16) and the Ponzo illusion (Figure 2). These can be considered examples of Gibson's (1966) idea that apparent size is given by the relationship between the size of an object in the optic array and the size of the grain of the surrounding elements, a view also expressed in Rock and Ebenholtz's (1959) relational theory of size perception. The identification of many size contrast effects with scene-relevant processing is hardly controversial and does not rule out theories proposing physiological mechanisms. Indeed illusions can be regarded as diagnostic of the way direct size scaling works. Figure 17a shows a version of the conventional Ponzo illusion along with a version in which the test lines are each rotated 90 degrees. There is no illusion in the second case (Humphrey & Morgan, 1965). Unconscious depth theorists consider this a refutation of primary scaling, but Gillam (1973) suggested on the basis of these observations that direct size scaling (unlike secondary constancy scaling in which

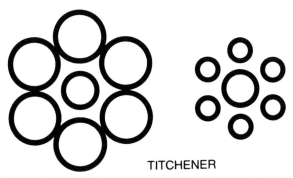

FIGURE 16   Titchener Circles showing size contrast (also known as the Ebbinghaus illusion).

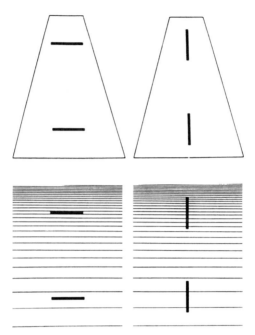

FIGURE 17   (a) Showing that the Ponzo Illusion only occurs when lines are placed along the compressed dimension. (b) Showing that when the dimension of compression is reversed, the previously equal lines now show the illusion (Gillam, 1980). [Reprinted by courtesy of the artist, Jerome Kuhl.]

size is based on apparent depth) only works for dimensions in which a scale is present in the background. She predicted that the effect shown in the Ponzo figure would reverse for a texture gradient that provides a scale along the vertical and not the horizontal dimension. This was confirmed (see Figure 17b, supporting the view that direct scaling is restricted to the dimension where a scale is provided. This argument also applies to the Müller-Lyer figure shown in Figure 15.

The orientation contrast represented by the Zöllner illusion and other illusions of orientation contrast can also be regarded as serving the purposes of scene perception. Individual lines superimposed on a background of differently oriented lines tend to be seen as shifted to an apparent orientation that is more orthogonal to the background lines (see Figure 13). It should be noted that the Zöllner illusion cannot be explained via unconscious depth, as suggested by Figure 18. If this were the basis of the illusion, the orientation of the test lines at the cusp between different inducing orientations should be affected as well as the test lines in the middle of each set of inducing orientations. This does not occur. As in the case of size contrast, the direct scaling process for orientation seems to be a response to the relationship between the test element and its immediate context, rather than an interpretation of the scene as a whole. A functional approach to the Zöllner illusion does not have difficulty with the direction of contrast polarity nor with the continuing

FIGURE 18   The Zollner Illusion in a real scene (from Filehne, 1898).

presence of the illusion when aligned gaps replace contours. If the effect is regarded as a scaling of line orientation by prevailing background orientation, not a local expansion of acute angles, it becomes unnecessary to postulate a collector mechanism for the overall orientation shift.

C. Assimilation Illusions—The Müller-Lyer and Its Variants

Assimilation illusions are the most controversial theoretically. The Müller-Lyer is the star of the illusion world, and resistance to a scene-based explanation of it has been fierce over many years. Having rejected as a straw man the version of this theory targeted by most of the criticisms, I shall outline what I believe, in light of the data, is the only possible scene-based account of the Müller-Lyer illusion.

Perhaps the most important fact about the Müller-Lyer illusion is that it is a local effect. Lines bounded by obtuse angles are enlarged; lines bounded by acute angles are diminished (Day & Dickinson, 1976; Tausch, 1962). Restle and Decker (1977) showed that it is the angle near the intersection with the shaft that is critical. Tausch showed that the size illusion increases linearly with the number of angles impinging on a line (see Figure 19). The illusion is therefore not the result of the resemblance of each component to a corner. The usual version with eight angles in all is an example of an effect that has "evolved to be conspicuous" (Morgan & Casco, 1990). It is a superstimulus for the scaling of size by angles. Therefore, to explain the illusion as the by-product of normal perspective processing the focus must shift to examining the role of obtuse and acute angles in the perspective views of 3-D

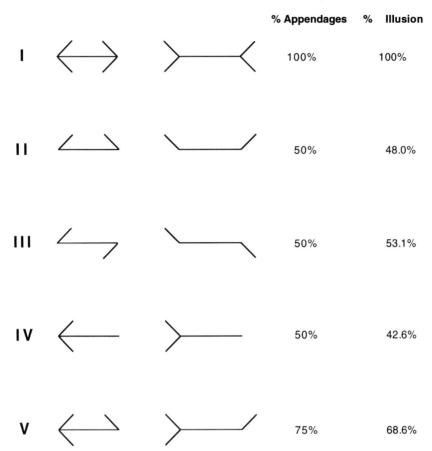

FIGURE 19   Results of an experiment by Tausch (1962) showing the percent illusion as compared with the percentage of appendages present in the Müller-Lyer figures, compared to the complete figure.

scenes and the way they must be decoded in order to achieve veridical perception. It can be demonstrated that the obtuse angle and acute angle induced size scaling effects that make up the Müller-Lyer and similar illusions are indeed appropriate decoding responses to perspective projections of rectilinear arrangements in the environment.

Consider Figure 20. The rectangle in the center incorporates a conventional Müller-Lyer configuration with the obtuse-angle-bounded line small and the acute-angle-bounded line large. It is easy to see how enhancement of the first and diminution of the second would result in perception of a more rectilinear figure in line with the properties of the scene. Gillam (1978) suggested that there may be a greater tendency to enhance the obtuse-angle-bounded line to match the acute-angle-bounded one (the smaller to the larger) rather than the other way around. This would account for the well-known asymmetry in the illusion magnitude for the two forms (Heymans, 1896). Furthermore, the stronger the tendency for this to

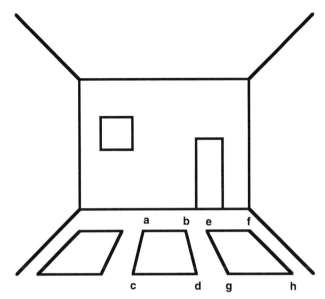

FIGURE 20   The Müller-Lyer (a b c d) and Judd (e f g h) figures in a scene (see text).

occur, the larger the obtuse-angle illusion would be and the smaller the acute-angle illusion. This would account for the finding that the two forms are negatively correlated (Adam & Bateman, 1983; Christie, 1969; Smith, 1906) and perhaps for other differences between the two forms (Sekuler & Erlebacher, 1971). In the case just considered, the acute angles are near and the obtuse angles far in the scene. Consider however the projection of the rectangle on the right in Figure 20, where the entire figure is to the right of the vanishing point, and acute angles and obtuse angles are not consistently near or far in the scene. On the right side of the figure, the acute angle is too far to the right, whereas the obtuse angle is too far to the left in the projection relative to the rectangular shape it depicts in the scene. On the left of the figure the opposite is the case. The tendency to diminish the parts of horizontal lines close to the acute angles and enhance the parts of horizontal lines close to obtuse angles (as can be demonstrated to occur in the Judd form of the Müller-Lyer [see Figure 2]) will lead to a more rectilinear perception of the object.

The important point here is that it is not only depth that influences whether the corner of an object in a scene will project as an obtuse or acute angle. This is also determined by the relationship of the object to the vanishing point of the optic array. The further to the left (or right) the figure is in relation to the observer's viewpoint (which defines the vanishing point), the more deviant the projection will be from the distal object in the manner described. An equivalent analysis can be applied to receding figures above or below the vanishing point. It is obvious then that an adequate decoding process for perspective transformations of angles cannot be based solely on depth relations within the figure.

The fact that the size scaling associated with acute and obtuse angles is a local effect is not incompatible with what is known generally about the way perspective works. Hochberg (1968) has shown that perspective depth cues act locally in the Penrose impossible figures. Given that size scaling by angle attachments is local, then both the Judd and Brentano versions of the Müller–Lyer figure (see Figure 2) can be understood as cumulations of local effects.

De Lucia and Hochberg (1991) produced some variants of the Müller–Lyer illusion, for they consider it difficult for perspective-based theories to account. In one case they arranged 3-D objects in such a way as to form the 2-D Müller–Lyer illusion and showed that the illusion still holds (Figure 21a). Embedding illusions in real scenes (Lucas & Fisher, 1969) goes back a long way (see Figure 21b). While their existence is not compatible with unconscious depth theories, it is consistent with the view that size scaling by angle is automatic and does not depend on interpretation. Primary scaling is based on the decoding of arrays that are typical perspective projections and will make errors when objects are arranged in atypical ways (for example, so that acute angles do not represent right angles).

It is interesting in this connection to examine whether the Müller–Lyer illusion persists when the shaft is placed stereoscopically away from the fins in depth. This situation is shown in Figure 22. It appears that the illusion under these conditions is diminished but not entirely eliminated. This question needs to be investigated quantitatively.

A second demonstration of De Lucia and Hochberg (1991) involves a version of illusion using right angles (see Figure 23).

This figure supports previous observations that the illusion still occurs when a line that is only implicit forms implicit obtuse and acute angles with the bounding contours. This was also shown by Mountjoy (1966), who found that the illusion of the Müller–Lyer shaft is accompanied by an opposite illusion of the fin tips. The postulated size scaling therefore cannot be based on the physical presence of acute and obtuse angles. Figure 23b shows that configurations like the one produced by De Lucia and Hochberg occur in representations of a scene and that the type of scaling they report promotes veridicality. The acute angles are typically formed by vertical and horizontal lines and the (implicit) diagonal of a frontal plane object (ab). On the other hand, the obtuse angles are formed by vertical and horizontal lines and a diagonal between objects separated obliquely (ac). The latter is very likely to be a foreshortened space in the optic array, and therefore expanding it is the correct decoding. There is no obvious scene-based reason for the diagonal of a square to be perceptually shrunken. It is difficult to tell whether it is however, because oblique comparison dots may themselves be treated as perspective projections of receding horizontal lines and perceptually expanded. The general difficulty of trying to decide just which component of a figure is seen "correctly" arises again in connection with the Poggendorff illusion.

Another interesting aspect of Figure 23b is that the rectangles at different depths look noncollinear. It is as if the scaling is figure specific. This may partly account for the fact that the Müller–Lyer illusion does not increase indefinitely with fin length (Heymans, 1896; Restle & Decker, 1977), which Krueger (1972) points out

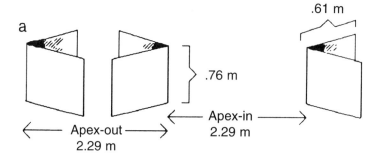

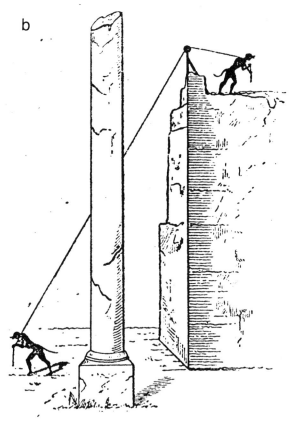

FIGURE 21 (a) The Müller-Lyer Illusion using real objects (from DeLucia & Hochberg, 1991, *Perception and Psychophysics, 50*(6), 547–554, reprinted by permission of Psychonomic Society, Inc.). (b) Poggendorff Illusion in a real scene (Filehne, 1898).

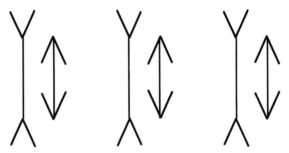

FIGURE 22   (a) The Müller–Lyer Illusion when the shaft and fins are separated stereoscopically.

is difficult for scene-based theories to explain. Warren and Bashford (1977) and Redding and Hawley (1993) have made the point that the scaling of length by angle may be better regarded as a process concerned with object perception rather than a process for decoding entire scenes (see Figure 24).

One valid criticism of scene-based theories of the Müller-Lyer illusion is that the illusion occurs with appendages to the shafts that do not resemble perspective features (Day, 1972). Examples are shown in Figure 25.

This raises the possibility that the Müller-Lyer illusion is just an example of a general tendency for the size of parts of a figure to be influenced by the size of the whole. Brigell, Uhlarik, and Goldhorn, (1977) and Day (1977) have proposed theories reminiscent of 19th century assimilation theories, in which parts and whole stimulate common size detectors, resulting in a size bias of the part in the direction of the size of the whole (the opposite of Tyler and Nakayama's [1984] theory of the Zöllner illusion, where the orientation of the whole is influenced by the orientation of the parts). What evidence is there for this assertion? What function would such a process serve? It is certainly the case that circular and even square appendages to a line influence its apparent size. These effects, however, cannot be explained by a simple assimilation process. The size effect depends strongly on what the appendage is (see Figure 25). Several investigators have shown that adding small lines of the same orientation to a horizontal line has only a small effect on its apparent length (Day, 1977). On the other hand, the addition of boxes (the Baldwin illusion) has at its optimum about half to two-thirds of the effect of adding fins covering the same horizontal extent and shows similar decline as the ratio of appendage length to shaft length increases (Brigell et al., 1977). Open boxes that more closely resemble the Müller-Lyer have, however, only about a quarter of the effect of equivalent fins (Tausch, 1954). It is therefore not good enough simply to call all these effects "assimilation," especially because assimilation clearly does not occur much at all for those very figures where the whole and the parts most resemble each other and would be expected to stimulate common detectors most adequately, namely the appendages that add extra line lengths onto the shaft. Another factor that should be considered in relation to assimilation theory is that the Müller-Lyer illusion is markedly reduced with even a very small displacement of the fins/arrowheads from the shaft (Worrall & Firth, 1974).

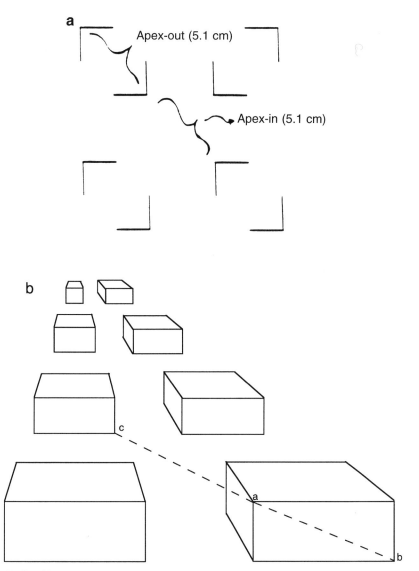

FIGURE 23   (a) DeLucia and Hochberg's (1991) figure showing that the Müller-Lyer illusion occurs without oblique lines (apex-in appears longer than apex-out). (b) DeLucia and Hochberg's configuration embedded in a scene (ac appears longer than ab). (From DeLucia & Hochberg, 1991, *Perception and Psychophysics, 50*(6), 547–554, reprinted by permission of Psychonomic Society, Inc.)

It should be noted that the situation where a line (or more exactly an edge) has obtuse- or acute-angle attachments, the strongest effect, is ubiquitous in viewing the carpentered world in which we live. Extents with other additions such as boxes also occur, the boxes representing occluding surfaces. Appendages such as circles are uncommon and may simulate these other effects.

FIGURE 24   A photograph of a wire cube and some amputated versions of it, showing Müller-Lyer type configurations. [From Warren & Bashford, 1977, *Perception, 6(6),* 615–626, Fig. U. Pion, London.]

Scene-based theory accounts for the size invariance of the Müller-Lyer illusion with distance and has no difficulty with the lack of effect of introducing opposite polarity for shafts and fins. It also accounts for the decrement in the illusion found where the figure is scanned (see Coren & Girgus, 1978, and Gillam, 1980, for a discussion). It is a problem for such theories that there is a haptic analogue to the Müller-Lyer (Over, 1967; Suzuki & Arashida, 1992), but this difficulty is confounded by the fact that the haptic modality has a lack of resolution of vertices that does not occur for the visual Müller-Lyer and also that the Brentano form is often used, which introduces artifacts for the haptic version (Gillam, 1978). The possibility that visual imagery plays a role in haptic illusion has also been raised (Frisby & Davies, 1971).

Recently Nijhawan (1995) has shown that illusions occur in binocular 3-D con-

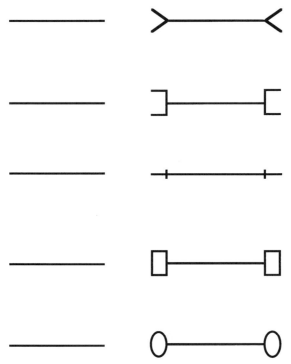

FIGURE 25   The arrowhead form of the Müller-Lyer Illusion compared with the illusion caused by various other appendages (see text).

figurations of acute and obtuse angles like the Müller-Lyer but which produce *reti-nal images* in which the fins/arrowheads are at right angles to the shafts, and con-versely that such illusions are absent or reversed despite the fact that the retinal image contains the conventional configuration. He claims that "primary constancy scaling" cannot predict these results because it is based on the retinal image. This is not, how-ever, correct for binocular vision, which he uses. Perspective processing and there-fore primary constancy scaling is based on "paradigm" object or scene representa-tions (Gregory & Harris, 1975) in which oblique lines represent horizontal lines, obtuse and acute angles represent right angles, and converging lines represent paral-lel lines. In binocular vision there is direct (binocular not retinal) information about shape and angle, which may be responded to as paradigm objects in contradiction of stereo depth relationships (Gillam, 1967; Gillam, Cook, & Blackburn, 1996).

To summarize discussion of the Müller-Lyer illusion, scene-based theories are appealing because the essential Müller-Lyer configuration, a straight edge ending in an acute or obtuse angle, is one of the major features of a perspective view, and scal-ing of the kind which the illusion exemplifies is an appropriate decoding of it. Indeed, it is part of what the visual system *needs* to do to respond adequately to per-spective views. The main problem with this account is that other appendages also produce size illusions to varying degrees. These could, however, be regarded as crudely simulating perspective features or as having an entirely different cause (for example, in simulating occlusion).

The Poggendorff illusion (see Figure 2) is as large as the Müller-Lyer and has attracted almost as much attention. Image-based theories have failed for reasons already given. I have proposed (Gillam, 1971, 1980) that the 2-D illusion in this case also reflects automatic processing appropriate to such line arrangements if regarded as projections of 3-D scenes. Figure 12 illustrates that for a 3-D scene, the degree of alignment in the picture plane is an accidental result of the observer's viewpoint. Oblique lines are typically the perspective view of receding horizontal lines. Con-figurations of such lines that are collinear in 3-D space (Figure 27b) and those that are not (Figure 27a) may both project collinear images. The visual system must depend on context to elicit a response appropriate to the actual physical arrangement. Specif-ically, figures to which oblique lines are attached may be important indicators of whether the region between their inner ends represents a continuum from one to the other in 3-D space (Figure 27b) or an interruption of the recession in the form of an interposed plane (in the case of Figure 27a a frontal plane). In the latter, but not the former, case the height difference between the inner ends of the lines in the pic-ture plane actually represents a height difference between parallel lines in the scene. As in the case of the Müller-Lyer illusion, this effect of context on perceived height can be direct. It need not depend on perceived depth. It has been shown in support of this view, that if all components of a Poggendorff figure converge to a single van-ishing point, the illusion is reduced by over half (see Figure 27b) (Gillam, 1971).

Most modern theories of the Poggendorff illusion make no reference to 3-D pro-cessing. They explain the illusion by postulating various kinds of distortion specific to the Poggendorff figure of which the noncollinearity is a consequence. The fol-

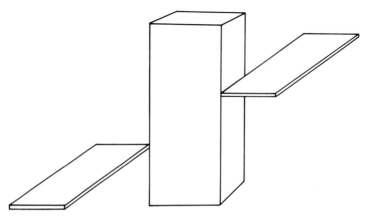

FIGURE 26   The Poggendorff configuration arising from horizontal planes at different heights. [From "Introduction to Perception" by Rock, 1975. Reprinted by permission of Prentice-Hall, Inc., Upper Saddle River, NJ.]

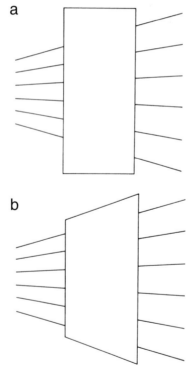

FIGURE 27   (a) Showing multiple Poggendorff illusions when a frontal plane interrupts a set of transversals. The Poggendorff illusion is very much diminished if the parallels define a plane that is collinear with the transversals in 3-D space (b).

lowing analysis of exactly what aspects of the figure are distorted will serve to evaluate both these claims and the 3-D theory of the illusion. Reference in this discussion will be made to previous research and also to Figure 28, in which the classical
Poggendorff figure has two additions: (a) an oblique line parallel to the transversals
but placed between the parallel lines; notice that it appears parallel to the transversals but *not* to the implicit oblique extent between them; (b) two dots placed on the
parallel lines and parallel to the transversals; notice the dots do *not* appear parallel to
the transversals but *do* appear parallel to the implicit oblique extent between them.

The major illusion-specific distortions postulated to account for the illusion are
as follows:

1. The illusion could in theory be explained by acute angle expansion. This
   possibility has already been rejected in the course of discussing physiological theories. Note, however, that the independent oblique line in Figure 28
   has the same apparent slope as the transversals.
2. If the separation between the parallels were seen as too narrow, the illusion
   would be explained. However, evidence does not support such a misperception (Pierce, 1901; Day, Stecher, & Parker, 1992; Wilson and Pressey,
   1976). One version of this idea, namely that a Müller-Lyer type effect
   shrinks the implicit oblique extent between the transversals (Greist-Bousquet & Schiffman, 1981) is also refuted by this evidence.
3. An alternative Müller-Lyer type illusion might exist in which there is
   expansion of extents on the parallels on the obtuse-angle side of the transversals and diminution of extents on the acute-angle side. This possibility is
   refuted however by Figure 28, in which it can be seen that there is no difference between the apparent distances between the left transversal and the
   dot on the left and the right transversal and the dot on the right.
4. Is the illusion caused by a *general* elongation of extents within the parallel
   lines? This possibility is refuted by the fact that the oblique line between
   the parallels in Figure 28 is not seen as elongated. It has the same apparent

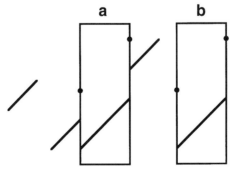

FIGURE 28   (a) A Poggendorff configuration with the addition of (i) an inner oblique parallel to
the transversals, and (ii) dots on the parallels forming an implicit oblique parallel to the transversals. For
significance see text. (b) The same configuration without the transversals (see text).

slope as the transversals and not the steeper slope of the implicit line joining their inner ends.

5. We are left with the fact that the slope of the implicit line joining the inner
   ends of the transversals is perceived as steeper than the transversals themselves. Evidence for this comes from studies by Pierce (1901), Day and
   Dickinson (1976), and Weintraub and Tong (1974). The effect is a large
   one, accounting for more than half of the displacement illusion. This slope
   effect has been attributed to "cognitive mistracking" by Weintraub and
   Tong (1974). However, the fact that the greater slope of the implicit extent
   between the transversals is shared by the extent between the dots means
   that it is not caused by the transversals at all and cannot be due to cognitive
   mistracking. The dots do not have transversals attached. These observations
   can, however, be explained in terms of the scene analysis presented earlier.
   The slope of the transversals, which represent horizontal lines, should be
   seen as less steep than the slope of an equivalent extent on the frontal
   plane. The inner ends of the transversals and the dot pair in Figure 28a
   have the same apparent slope because they are placed on the parallels that
   represent a frontal plane. The steeper slope is not shared by the inner
   oblique. In fact, a large size illusion, similar to the Poggendorff, exists for
   the distances between the dots and the ends of the inner oblique (see Figure 28b). The extent on the right looks much greater than the one on the
   left although they are the same. The observations on Figure 28a and 28b
   require quantitative confirmation but seem rather strong.

Unfortunately, the situation is more complex than I have indicated. If Figure 28
is turned 90 degrees, the relative slopes do not change. This means that the slopes
of the dots and of the extent between the parallels defined by the ends of the transversals are less than the slope of the transversals themselves. In other words, the transversals now appear more vertical and the slope between the parallels more horizontal. To explain this as scene-based processing requires an entire assumption, that
in a left–right context, rather than an up–down context, the transversals may be
processed as oblique lines representing horizontal lines orthogonal to the frontal
plane (as in Figure 13b) and therefore more vertical than their representation. This
example shows the complexity of trying to pin down the 3-D significance of
sketchy 2-D drawings, which are inherently ambiguous.

There are a number of other facts relating to the Poggendorff illusion that are
consistent with a scene-processing view. Most of these are discussed in Gillam
(1971) and will not be repeated here. However there are some new observations
that support this approach.

The illusion is interestingly diminished if random texture is placed between the
parallels (Masini, Costa, Ferraro, & De Marco, 1994 [see Figure 29]). In this case it
is easy to see the transversals not as attached to the plane of the parallels (and therefore processed as at different heights), but as passing in front of the parallels and cam-
ouflaged by them. This can also occur for a completely black figure with some effort.

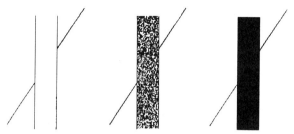

FIGURE 29   A figure from Masini et al. (1994, *Perception and Psychophysics, 55*(5), 505–512, reprinted by permission of Psychonomic Society, Inc.). The transversals appear collinear and joined by a subjective contour. This seems to involve the "capture" of components of the texture by the transversals. This does not occur so strongly for the black figure and not at all for the white figure.

In both cases the illusion disappears and is replaced by a subjective contour across the figure, although Masini et al. do not mention this.

The Poggendorff illusion also appears to be much diminished if the transversals are stereoscopically separated from the parallels, particularly when the transversals are in front (see Figure 30); although this also requires further quantification.

V. CONCLUSION

What is the significance of illusions? Do they deserve the attention they have received? I have argued that illusions do offer important indicators concerning the way in which the brain achieves an accurate perception of the external world. In particular, they are

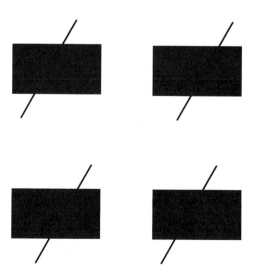

FIGURE 30   Poggendorff configuration in which the transversals are separated stereoscopically from the parallels.

manifestations of automatic, noncognitive responses to typical perspective features in scene-relevant ways. On the other hand, I would agree with Morgan (1995) to some extent that certain particularly famous illusions may simply be coincidental aggregations of properties that survive as an aggregate because of the massive effect they produce, rather than because of the paramount importance of that particular combination of properties in real-world vision. If that is the case, it is important to find the component processes themselves. This applies particularly perhaps to the Müller-Lyer illusion. In that case analysis of the literature reveals that the basic effect is a local one of angles, that empty extents as well as lines are scaled, that the size effect is not derived from a change of position, although a global apparent position shift may result. We know that there is a similar effect when lines or boxes are placed at the ends of lines, although it is not so large as the effect of angles. Given all the research on the Müller-Lyer illusion, however, it is remarkable that so little effort has been devoted to a general analysis of size scaling effects and the stimuli that produce them, and that should surely be the direction of future research. The Poggendorff and Ponzo illusions appear simpler in the sense that they are probably not aggregates of a number of local processes but relatively pure examples of a contextual effect on collinearity/size, respectively. This does not mean that they are completely understood.

The unfortunate tradition in this domain has been to postulate processes that do little more than describe the effect itself and to collect enormous numbers of unrelated minor facts often with very poor methodology. It is to be hoped that future illusion research will be driven by trying to relate the particular phenomenon to more general perceptual processes.

References

Adam, J., & Bateman, L. (1980). Control stimuli in investigations of the acute-angled and obtuse-angled Müller-Lyer illusions. *Perception, 9*(4), 467–474.

Adam, J., & Bateman, L. (1983). A correlational analysis of symmetry between the arrowhead and featherhead Müller-Lyer illusions. *Perception, 12*(2), 119–129.

Auerbach, F. (1894). Erklärung der Brentano'schen optischen Tauschung. *Zeitschrift für Psychologie, 7,* 152–160.

Benussi, V. (1912). Stroboskopische Scheinbewegungen und geometrischoptische Gestalttaüschungen. *Archiv für der Gesamte Psychologie, 24,* 31–62.

Blakemore, C., Carpenter, R. H. S., & Georgeson, M. A. (1970). Lateral inhibition between orientation detectors in the human visual system. *Nature, 228,* 37–39.

Brigell, M., Uhlarik, J., & Goldhorn, P. (1977). Contextual influence on judgments of linear extent. *Journal of Experimental Psychology: Human Perception and Performance, 3*(1), 105–118.

Burns, B. D., & Pritchard, R. (1971). Geometrical illusions and the response of neurones in the cat's visual cortex to angle patterns. *Journal of Physiology, 213,* 599–616.

Carlson, C. R., Moeller, J. R., & Anderson, C. H. (1984). Visual illusions without low spatial frequencies. *Vision Research, 24*(10), 1407–13.

Cavanagh, P. (1995). Vision is getting easier every day, *Perception, 24*(11), 1227–1232.

Christie, B. A. (1969). A contaminating factor in the measurement of geometric illusions. *Psychonomic Science, 17,* 69–70.

Cleary, A. (1966). A binocular parallax theory of the geometric illusions. *Psychonomic Science 5*(6), 241–242.

Cook, M. L., & Gillam, B. (1996). Errors in reaching in the Müller-Lyer illusion. Unpublished manuscript.

Coren, S., & Girgus, J. S. (1978). *Seeing is deceiving: The psychology of visual illusions.* Hillsdale: Erlbaum.

Day, R. H. (1972). Visual spatial illusions: A general explanation. *Science, 175,* 1335–1340.

Day, R. H. (1973). The Poggendorff illusion with obtuse and acute angles. *Perception and Psychophysics, 14*(3), 590–596.

Day, R. H., & Dickinson, R. G. (1976). The components of the Poggendorff illusion. *British Journal of Psychology, 67*(4), 537–552.

Day, R. H., & Dickinson, R. G. (1976). Apparent length of the arms of acute and obtuse angles, and the components of the Müller-Lyer Illusion. *Australian Journal of Psychology, 28*(3), 137–148.

Day, R. H. (1977). Perceptual assimilation as a basis for one class of components in geometrical visual illusions. In R. H. D. & G. V. Stanley (Eds.), *Studies in perception* (pp. 142–164). Perth: University of Western Australia Press.

Day, R. H., Stecher, E. J., & Parker, A. L. (1992). The Poggendorff illusion and apparent interparallel extents. *Perception, 21*(5), 599–610.

Day, R. H., & Halford, A. L. P. (1994). On apparent misalignment of collinear edges and boundaries. *Perception and Psychophysics, 56*(5), 517–524.

DeLucia, P. R., & Hochberg, J. (1991). Geometrical illusions in solid objects under ordinary viewing conditions. *Perception and Psychophysics, 50*(6), 547–554.

Earle, D. C., & Maskell, S. J. (1995). Spatial filtering and the Zöllner-Judd geometrical illusion: further studies. *Perception, 24*(12), 1397–1406.

Epstein, W., Park, J., & Casey, A. (1961). The current status of the size-distance hypotheses. *Psychological Bulletin, 58*(6), 491–514.

Festinger, L., White, C. W., & Allyn, M. R. (1968). Eye movements and decrement in the Müller-Lyer illusion. *Perception and Psychophysics, 3*(5B), 376–382.

Filehne, W. (1898). Die geometrisch-optischen Taüschungen als Nachwirkungen der in körperlichen Sehen erworbenen Erfahrung. *Zeitschrift für Psychologie, 17,* 15–61.

Fisher, G. H. (1968). An experimental and theoretical appraisal of the inappropriate size-depth theories of illusions. *British Journal of Psychology, 59*(4), 373–383.

Frisby, J. P., & Davies, I. R. L. (1971). Is the haptic Müller-Lyer a visual phenomenon? *Nature, 231,* 463–465.

Garcia-Perez, M. (1991). Visual phenomena without low spatial frequencies: A closer look [letter] *Vision Research, 31*(9), 1647–1653.

Gauld, A. (1975). A note on inappropriate constancy-scaling and the Müller-Lyer illusion. *British Journal of Psychology, 66*(3), 307–309.

Georgeson, M. A., & Blakemore, C. (1973). Apparent depth and the Müller-Lyer illusion. *Perception, 2*(2), 225–234.

Gibson, J. J. (1966). *The senses considered as perceptual systems.* Boston: Houghton-Mifflin.

Gillam, B. J. (1967). Changes in the direction of induced aniseikonic slant as a function of distance. *Vision Research, 7,* 777–783.

Gillam, B. J. (1971). A depth processing theory of the Poggendorff illusion. *Perception and Psychophysics, 10*(4A), 211–216.

Gillam, B. J. (1973). The nature of size scaling in the Ponzo and related illusions. *Perception and Psychophysics, 14*(2), 353–357.

Gillam, B. J. (1978). A constancy-scaling theory of the Müller-Lyer illusion. In J. P. Sutcliffe (Ed.), *Conceptual analysis and method in psychology: Essays in Honor of W. M. O'Neil* (pp. 57–70). Sydney: Sydney University Press.

Gillam, B. J. (1980). Geometrical illusions. *Scientific American, 242*(1), 102–111.

Gillam, B. J. (1987). Perceptual grouping and subjective contours. In S. Petry and G. Meyer (Eds.), *The perception of illusory contours.* (pp. 268–273). New York: Springer-Verlag.

Gillam, B. J. (1995). The perception of spatial layout from static optical information. In W. E. & S. Rogers. (Ed.), *Perception of space and motion* (pp. 23–67). New York: Academic Press.

Gillam, B. J., & Blackburn, S. G. (1996). Showing that position is not misperceived in the Müller-Lyer illusion. Unpublished manuscript.

Gillam, B. J., & Chambers, D. (1985). Size and position are incongruous: Measurements on the Müller-Lyer figure. *Perception and Psychophysics, 37*(6), 549–556.

Gillam, B. J., Cook, M. L., & Blackburn, S. G. (1996). Conflict between stereo and perspective in resolving the slant of cyclopean trapezoids. *Perception, 25,* 41.

Ginsburg, A. P. (1979). Visual perception based on spatial filtering constrained by biological data. *Proceedings of the International Conference on Cybernetics and Society.* (IEEE Catalog No. 79CH1424-1SMC).

Goodale, M. A., & Milner, A. D. (1992). Separate visual pathways for perception and action. *Trends in Neuroscience, 15*(1), 20–25.

Green, R. T., & Hoyle, E. M. (1963). The Poggendorff illusion as a constancy phenomenon. *Nature, 200,* 611–612.

Gregory, R. L. (1963). Distortion of visual space as inappropriate constancy scaling. *Nature, 199,* 678–680.

Gregory, R. L. (1968). Perceptual illusions and brain models. *Proceedings of the Royal Society, B, 71,* 279–296.

Gregory, R. L. (1970). *The intelligent eye.* London: Weidenfeld and Nicolson.

Gregory, R. L., & Harris, J. P. (1975). Illusion-destruction by appropriate scaling. *Perception, 4*(2), 203–220.

Greist-Bousquet, S., & Schiffman, H. R. (1981). The role of structural components in the Müller-Lyer illusion. *Perception and Psychophysics, 30*(5), 505–511.

Helmholtz, H. von (1866). *Handbuch der physiologischen Optik.* Leipzig: Voss. Translated by Southall, J. (1962). New York: Dover.

Hering, E. (1861). *Beitrage zur Physiologie. I. Vom Ortssinne der Netzhaut.* Leipzig.

Heymans, G. (1896). Quantitative Untersuchungen uber das "optische Paradoxen." *Zeitschrift fur Psychologie, 9,* 221–255.

Hill, A. L. (1971). On the enlargement of acute angles. *Perceptual and Motor Skills, 33,* 1238.

Hochberg, J. (1968). In the mind's eye. In R. Haber (Ed.), *Contemporary theory and research in visual perception.* New York: Holt, Rinehart & Winston.

Hochberg, J. (1981). On cognition in perception: Perceptual coupling and unconscious inference. *Cognition, 10*(1–3), 127–134.

Hotopf, W. H. N. (1966). The size-constancy theory of visual illusions. *British Journal of Psychology, 57*(3), 307–318.

Hotopf, W. H. N., & Ollerearnshaw, C. (1972). The regression to right angles tendency and the Poggendorff illusion II. *British Journal of Psychology, 63*(3), 369–379.

Hotopf, W. H. (1981). Mistracking in alignment illusions. *Journal of Experimental Psychology: Human Perception and Performance, 7*(6), 1211–1246.

Humphrey, N. K., & Morgan, M. J. (1965). Constancy and the geometric illusions. *Nature, 206,* 744–746.

Judd, C. H. (1899). A study of geometrical illusions. *The Psychological Review, 6*(3), 241–261.

Judd, C. H. (1905). The Müller-Lyer illusion. *Psychological Review Monograph Supplement, 29,* 55–82.

Julesz, B. (1971). *Foundations of cyclopean perception.* Chicago: University of Chicago Press.

Kilpatrick, F. P., & Ittelson, W. (1953). The size-distance invariance hypothesis. *Psychological Review, 60*(4), 223–231.

Kristof, W. (1961). Uber die Einordnung geometrisch-optischer Taüschungen in die Gesetzmassigkeiten der visuellen Wahrnehmung. *Part I. Archiv für die gesante Psychologie, 113,* 1–48.

Krueger, L. E. (1972). Gregory's theory of illusions: Some disconfirming evidence in the case of the Müller-Lyer illusion. *Psychological Review, 79*(6), 538–539.

Leibowitz, H., & Toffey, S. (1966). The effect of rotation and tilt on the magnitude of the Poggendorff illusion. *Vision Research, 6*(1), 101–103.

Lewis, E. O. (1909). Confluxion and contrast effects in the Müller-Lyer illusion. *British Journal of Psychology, 3,* 21–41.

Livingstone, M. S., & Hubel, D. H. (1987). Psychophysical evidence for separate channels for the perception of form, color, movement, and depth. *The Journal of Neuroscience, 7*(11), 3416–3468.

Lucas, A., & Fisher, G. H. (1969). Illusions in concrete situations. II. Experimental studies of the Poggendorff illusion. *Ergonomics, 12*(3), 395–402.

Mack, A., Heuer, F., Villardi, K., & Chambers, D. (1985). The dissociation of position and extent in Müller-Lyer figures. *Perception and Psychophysics, 37*(4), 335–344.

Marr, D. (1982). *Vision: A computational investigation into the human representation and processing of visual information.* San Francisco: WH Freeman & Co.

Masini, R., Costa, T., Ferraro, M., & De Marco, A. (1994). Modifications of the Poggendorff effect as a function of random dot textures between the transversals. *Perception and Psychophysics, 55*(5), 505–512.

Massaro, D. W., & Anderson, N. H. (1970). A test of a perspective theory of geometrical illusions. *American Journal of Psychology, 83*(4), 567–575.

Mather, G., O'Halloran, A., & Anstis, S. (1991). The spacing illusion: A spatial aperture problem? *Perception, 20*(3), 387–392.

Morgan, M. J. (1995). Visual illusions. In V. Bruce (Ed.), *Unsolved mysteries of the mind* (pp. 29–57). New Jersey: Erlbaum.

Morgan, M. J. (1969). Estimates of length in a modified Müller-Lyer figure. *American Journal of Psychology, 82*, 380–384.

Morgan, M. J., & Casco, C. (1990). Spatial filtering and spatial primitives in early vision: An explanation of the Zöllner-Judd class of geometrical illusion. *Proceedings of the Royal Society of London B: Biological Sciences, 242*(1303), 1–10.

Morgan, M. J., & Glennerster, A. (1991). Efficiency of locating centres of dot-clusters by human observers. *Vision Research, 31*(12), 2075–2083.

Morgan, M. J., Hole, G. J., & Glennerster, A. (1990). Biases and sensitivities in geometrical illusions. *Vision Research, 30*(11), 1793–1810.

Morgan, M. J., Medford, A., & Newsome, P. (1995). The orthogonal orientation shift and spatial filtering. *Perception, 24*(5), 513–524.

Morinaga (1941). Quoted in T. Oyama. Japanese studies of the so-called geometrical-optical illusions. *Psychologia, 1960, 3,* 7–20.

Mountjoy, P. T. (1966). New illusory effect of the Müller-Lyer figure. *Journal of Experimental Psychology, 71*(1), 119–123.

Müller-Lyer, F. C. (1889). Optische Urteilstaüschungen. *Archiv für Anatomie und Physiologie, Physiologische Abteilung, 2*(suppl.), 263–270.

Nijhawan, R. (1995). 'Reversed' illusion with three-dimensional Müller-Lyer shapes. *Perception, 24*(11), 1281–1296.

Over, R. (1967). Haptic judgment of the Müller-Lyer illusion by subjects of different ages. *Psychonomic Science, 9*(6), 365–366.

Parlangeli, O., & Roncato, S. (1995). The global figural characteristics in the Zöllner illusion. *Perception, 24*(5), 501–512.

Pierce, A. H. (1901). *Studies in auditory and visual perception.* New York: Longmans Green.

Post, R. B., & Welch, R. B. (1996). Is there dissociation of perceptual and motor responses to figural illusions? *Perception, 25*(5), 569–582.

Predebon, J. (1981). Length judgments in modified Müller-Lyer figures. *American Journal of Psychology, 94*(1), 159–172.

Pressey, A., & Pressey, C. A. (1992). Attentive fields are related to focal and contextual features: A study of Müller-Lyer distortions. *Perception and Psychophysics, 51*(5), 423–436.

Redding, G. M., & Hawley, E. (1993). Length illusion in fractional Müller-Lyer stimuli: An object-perception approach. *Perception, 22,* 819–828.

Restle, F., & Decker, J. (1977). Size of the Müller-Lyer illusion as a function of its dimensions: Theory and data: *Perception and Psychophysics, 21*(6), 489–503.

Robinson, J. O. (1972). *The psychology of visual illusion.* London: Hutchinson.

Rock, I. (1975). *An introduction to perception.* New York: Macmillan.

Rock, I., & Ebenholtz, S. (1959). The relational determination of perceived size. *Psychological Review, 66,* 387–401.

Rogers, S. (1995). Perceiving pictorial space. In W. Epstein & Rogers, S. (Ed.), *Perception of space and motion* (pp. 119–163). New York: Academic Press.

Sanford, E. C. (1898). *A course in experimental psychology. Part I: Sensation and perception.* London: Heath.

Sedgwick, H. A. (1973). The visible horizon: A potential source of visual information for the perception of size and distance (Doctoral dissertation, Cornell University, 1973). *Dissertation Abstracts International, 34,* 1301B–1302B.

Sedgwick, H. A. (1986). Space perception. In K. Boff & J. Thomas (Ed.), *Handbook of perception and human performance* (pp. 1–57). New York: Wiley.

Sedgwick, H. A., & Nicholls, A. L. (1993). Interaction between surface and depth in the Ponzo illusion. *Investigative Ophthalmology and Visual Science, 34*(4), 1184.

Sekuler, R., & Erlebacher, A. (1971). The two illusions of Müller-Lyer: Confusion theory reexamined. *American Journal of Psychology, 84*(4), 477–486.

Smith, W. G. (1906). A study of some correlations of the Müller-Lyer visual illusions and allied phenomena. *British Journal of Psychology, 2,* 16–51.

Spillman, L., & Ehrenstein, W. H. (1995). From neuron to Gestalt: Mechanisms of visual perception. In R. Greger (Ed.), *Comprehensive human physiology* (pp. 1–32). Berlin: Springer-Verlag.

Stuart, G. W., Day, R. H., & Dickinson, R. G. (1984). Müller-Lyer: Illusion of size or position? *Quarterly Journal of Experimental Psychology [a], 36*(4), 663–672.

Suzuki, K., & Arashida, R. (1992). Geometrical haptic illusions revisited: Haptic illusions compared with visual illusions. *Perception & Psychophysics, 52*(3), 329–335.

Tausch, R. (1954). Optische Taüschungen als artifizielle Effekte der Gestaltungs-prozesse von Grössen und Formenkonstanz in der natürlichen Raumwahrnehmung. *Psychologische Forschung, 24,* 299–348.

Tausch, R. (1962). Empirische Untersuchungen im Hinblick auf ganzheits und gestalt-psychologische Wahrnehmungser-erklärungen. *Zeitschrift für Psychologie, 166,* 26–61.

Thiéry, A. (1896). Uber geometrisch-optischen Taüschungen. *Philosophische Studien, 12,* 67–126.

Tyler, C. W., & Nakayama, K. (1984). Size interactions in the perception of orientation. In L. S. & B. R. Wootten (Ed.), *Sensory experience, adaptation and perception* (pp. 529–546). New Jersey: Lawrence Erlbaum Associates.

Virsu, V. (1967). Geometric illusions. I. Effects of figure type, instruction, and pre- and intertrial training on magnitude and decrement of illusion. *Scandinavian Journal of Psychology, 8*(3), 161–171.

Waite, H., & Massaro, D. W. (1970). Test of Gregory's constancy scaling explanation of the Müller-Lyer illusion. *Nature, 227*(259), 733–734.

Wallace, G. K. (1975). The effect of contrast on the Zöllner illusion. *Vision Research, 15*(963), 963–966.

Warren, R. M., & Bashford, J. A. (1977). Müller-Lyer illusions: Their origin in processes facilitating object recognition. *Perception, 6*(6), 615–626.

Weintraub, D. J., & Krantz, D. H. (1971). The Poggendorff illusion: Amputations, rotations, and other perturbations. *Perceptions and Psychophysics, 10,* 257–264.

Weintraub, D. J., & Tong, L. (1974). Assessing Poggendorff effects via collinearity, perpendicularity, parallelism, and Oppel (distance) experiments. *Perception and Psychophysics, 16*(2), 213–221.

Weintraub, D. J. (1993). The logic of misperceived distance (or location) theories of the Poggendorff illusion. *Perception & Psychophysics, 53*(2), 231–238.

Wenderoth, P., & Johnson, M. (1982). Visual illusions with acute and obtuse angles: Configurational effects and observer strategies. *Perception and Psychophysics, 31*(3), 243–250.

Wenderoth, P. (1983). Identical stimuli are judged differently in the orientation and position domains. *Perception and Psychophysics, 33*(4), 399–402.

Wenderoth, P. (1992). Perceptual illusions. *Australian Journal of Psychology, 44*(3), 147–151.

White, K. G. (1975). Orientation effects on contour interaction in the Zöllner illusion. *Perception and Psychophysics, 17*(4), 387–392.

Wilson, A. E., & Pressey, A. W. (1976). The role of apparent distance in the Poggendorff illusion. *Perception and Psychophysics, 20*(4), 309–316.

Wong, E. (1981). *Information used by the occulomotor system in saccadic programming and the relationship of perceptual and saccadic responses.* Unpublished Doctoral Dissertation, New School for Social Research.

Worrall, N., & Firth, D. (1974). The components of the standard and reverse Müller-Lyer illusions. *Quarterly Journal of Experimental Psychology, 26,* 342–354.

Wundt, W. (1898). Die geometrisch-optischen Taüschungen. *Abhandlung der mathphys. der sachs. Ges. d. Wiss., 24*(53), 53–178.

Zanuttini, L. (1976). A new explanation for the Poggendorff illusion. *Perception and Psychophysics, 20*(1), 29–32.

Zeki, S. (1993). *A vision of the brain.* Oxford: Blackwell Scientific Publications.

CHAPTER 6

Pictures and Their Special Status in Perceptual and Cognitive Inquiry

James E. Cutting
Manfredo Massironi

On December 18, 1994, in the Ardennes in the south of France, three explorers discovered a cave with elaborate wall paintings, now estimated to be 30,000 years old.[1] These are more than twice as old as those in the more celebrated caves of Niaux, discovered no later than the 17th century; of Altamira, discovered in the 19th; and of Lascaux, discovered in the mid-20th (see Chauvet, Brunel Deschamps, & Hillaire, 1995; Clottes, 1995; Lorblanchet, 1995; Ruspoli, 1986). Indeed, in what is now known as the Grotte Chauvet are works that may date to the time that *homo sapiens sapiens* appeared in Europe (Laboratoire de Préhistoire du Musée de l'Homme, 1982; Nougier, 1969; Wymer, 1982). What is most compelling about these paintings is that, given the migratory nature of our species and the unlikely survival of any such works, they are just about as old as they can be. They show more than 300 portrayals of animals, including bison, deer, elephants, horses, hyenas, ibexes, lions, oxen, rhinoceroses, a panther and an owl, many apparently depicted in motion and some never found in cave paintings before. They are etched or colored in black, yellow, or red; most are drawn with considerable grace and tech-

---

[1] There is quite some controversy over dating of the Chauvet paintings. From a report of carbon dating, a relatively early indication in the press was that they were 30,000 years old (*"Les peintures de la grotte Chauvet datent de 30 000 ans avant notre ère"* Le Monde, Juin 4/5, 1995). Noting potential problems with this method, Clottes (1996) suggested that they were only about 20,000 years old. Lorblanchet (1995), however, met these criticisms and disputed the use of any criteria other than carbon dating. Whichever dating is correct, however, the Chauvet paintings are the oldest known, large collection of images.

nique. With Mithen (1996, p. 156) we note: "Although this is the very first art known to humankind, there is nothing primitive about it."

Clearly, pictures have been with us a long time and, with the Chauvet discoveries, much longer than previously thought. Pictures can no longer be seen as an artifact of the development of a particular culture. They now seem likely to be a defining characteristic of our species. The antiquity and ubiquity of pictures suggests the ability to understand pictures is deeply embedded in the human mind, even the genome. The Chauvet discoveries promote reconsideration of many questions. What is the relation between a picture and the aspects of the world it represents? What is it about our mental makeup that makes pictures an excellent medium in which to communicate to others about the world around us? In some pictures, how is it that a few lines come to stand for the objects and desires of the artist? In this chapter we intend to outline answers to these questions. Our approach is broad and interdisciplinary (see also Hochberg, 1996); for focused discussions of perceived space see Sedgwick (1986) and Cutting and Vishton (1995), and for discussions of pictorial space see Goldstein (1979, 1987), Rogers (1995), and Hagen (1986).

I. PICTURES AND THE WORLD

A. Cognition and Fortuitous Pictures

> If you look at walls that are stained or made of different kinds of stones and imagine some kind of scene, you begin to see . . . picturesque views of mountains, rivers, rocks, trees, plains, broad valleys, and hills of different shapes. You can also find in them battles and rapidly moving figures, strange faces and costumes. (Leonardo, in Baltrušaitis, 1989, p. 61)

Here, as an exercise for students, Leonardo da Vinci appealed to a cognitive capacity within humans to interpret natural patterns and to reorganize them in novel ways (see also Chastel, 1952; Holt, 1957). Such stains, or more simply clouds in the sky, can be called *unintended pictures;* no artist created them but they are the result of natural processes. The idea in this perceptual exercise is that one can and should "go beyond the information given" (Bruner, 1973) in these patterned visual surfaces and mentally elaborate, confabulate, and simply see new things.[2] The roots of pictorial art may be similar. Soon after their appearance in Europe, paleo-artists began to modify the rock surfaces of caves with their own markings. For example, in the Altamira cave one finds a bison head that was created by painting eyes on a rock protuberance (Nougier, 1969), and similar works appear at Lascaux and Chauvet. Such acts transform a rock surface into a picture/sculpture; the paleo-artist used the *accidental* properties of the layout of a surface and elaborated them with a graphic act.

---

[2] Indeed, even James Gibson (1979, p. 282) who otherwise did not ordinally deal with such matters, stated that "a Rorschach blot is a picture of sorts containing information not only for bleeding hearts and dancing bears but for dozens of other events" as well. See also Gibson (1956).

The major questions for this inquiry, then, are two: First, is this elaborative ability a part of our normal process of picture perception? Although representing very different perspectives, Arnheim (1974), Gombrich (1972), Sartre (1948), and Wollheim (1968) have all said yes; and we would generally agree, but only for some pictures and then only in some ways. (Later in this chapter we will discuss the interpretation of lines and line drawings that, to us, unequivocally invoke aspects of cognition). Second, is picture perception like our visual perception of the world around us? Costall (1990), Gibson (1979), Hagen (1986), and others have all said no, and again we would generally agree. Pictures typically have a dual character; the optical array does not. That is, pictures are both objects themselves and thus they typically depict, or *represent* other objects as well. This duality is most often carried by "conflicting cues" (e.g., Woodworth, 1938), which are not particularly common in the real world. Before discussing pictures further, however, we need to place pictures in a larger cognitive and perceptual context.

B. Pictures and Metatheory

Pictures have cast a remarkable enchantment over the way we have come to think about vision, and not within psychology alone. The eye–camera analogy . . . has not only been very influential in its own right, but has also helped conceal a further, and highly persuasive, assumption: that our "normal" mode of experiencing our surroundings—the posture we adopt to the world—is that of a *spectator* looking at a picture. (Costall, 1990, p. 273)

With this indictment, Costall captured what could be a major problem in cognitive and vision science: If the projections of the world to our eyes are not like pictures, then we in our discipline may be in deep trouble. Almost all of our visual perception and cognition experiments over a century have used pictures as stimuli, and yet we almost always use their results as evidence of how we perceive in the natural world (see also Cutting, 1991b). Ittelson (1996) has called this the *pictorial assumption*. Our view is that the situation is not so bleak as Costall or Ittelson would suggest, but with them we agree that a proper understanding of the relation of pictures to the visual world is central to visual science.

The role of picture perception in the study of visual perception and cognition raises an important issue. Much of the history of interest in perception has been a debate between two classes of metatheory, one that emphasizes an elaborative (cognitive, "top-down") component to perception and another that emphasizes the adequacy of the information in the to-be-perceived objects and events, and thus the general lack of need for cognitive component (and hence is "bottom-up"). The former is represented, in different ways, by the views of Plato (Cornford, 1957), Leonardo (Richter, 1883), Berkeley (1709), Mill (1842), Helmholtz (1867/1925), Russell (1914), the Gestalt psychologists (e.g., Koffka, 1935), and others (e.g., Hochberg, 1968; Rock, 1983); that is, innate ideas, learned associations, unconscious inference, and principles of perceptual organization all emphasized what is not literally present in the stimulus. On the other hand and in modern terms, the views of Epicurus (C. Bailey, 1928), S. Bailey (1855), and Gibson (1966, 1979) emphasized what is present in the stimulus.

Despite centuries of debate, however, we see no particular conflict inherent in these theories as they have been applied in the 20th century; they simply apply to different domains to differing degrees. We believe the first class of theories—those endorsing elaborative processes that have by tradition come to be called theories of *indirect perception* (e.g., Ayer, 1956; Rock, 1997)—apply to many kinds of pictures, particularly line drawings. We believe the second class of theories—those endorsing stimulus properties and, since the time of John Locke, called *direct perception*—applies most easily to everyday situations (see Cutting, 1986, for an historical review). Theorists in support of the role of inference (or induction) in perception typically use, or refer to, "impoverished displays" (line drawings of various kinds) to show a role of cognition in perception, and from Gibson they would have received no quarrel. Gibson (1979) regarded picture perception as an instance of indirect perception. Those against a role for inference in perception have tended to use, or to refer to, more naturalistic displays, and ideally to natural environments, to show that cognition need not play such a role (see Cutting, 1991b).

The continuing fascination, of course, is that this bifurcation between the perception of pictures and the perception of the visual world is not nearly so neat as we have first drawn it; there are exceptions and gradations between. Moreover, a history of pictures can be interpreted, in part, as one of applying, through technological means, the wherewithal to make images that increasingly approximate three-dimensional worlds that we can easily understand and envision. The development of linear perspective (e.g., Kubovy, 1986; White, 1957), then photography (e.g., Scharf, 1968), then cinema (e.g., Toulet, 1988), and then the promise of computer-generated virtual reality (e.g., Ellis, Kaiser, & Grunwald, 1991) would seem to attest to this. Moreover, there are two corollaries to this progression. First, all of these technological advances make pictures less and less like a decorated surface and more and more like a world within which we can act, and all should, in principle, make their perception more and more "direct." Second, to discover the role of cognition in picture perception one might best look to the oldest kinds of pictures humankind has produced, rather than the newest.[3]

But the everyday world, of course, is not always as replete with information as some might have us believe. On and just under the surfaces of oceans and lakes, in deserts, polar regions, and rain forests, and almost everywhere at night (without artificial lighting, e.g., Schivelbusch, 1988), the layout of the world is not always sufficiently patterned and comprehensible for objects and events to be easily seen. All of these situations make the real world less and less like a place within which mean-

---

[3] This is not to imply a temporal imperative, but instead to remove the discussion from a close reliance on photography and Renaissance art.

ingful action can take place on the basis of usable information and more and more like an information-poor void. Again, there are two corollaries. First, by our argument, all of these should make perception more and more "indirect." Second, the information still available in impoverished natural environments might be most like that found in pictures.

The overall idea, then, is that if there is sufficient information in the array (natural or pictorial) to specify to the observer what would ordinarily be needed for daily action and recognition, then no overtly inferential, cognitive process is deemed necessary; if, on the other hand, the information is somehow deficient, then inference and cognition stand ready and may, seamlessly, play a role. When, how, and if cognition plays such a role, of course, is still much researched and debated. There is, however, another entry in this short list of metatheoretical positions—*directed perception* (Cutting, 1986, 1991a)—and we will use its central tenet to set the stage for our further discussion. First, however, let us set up the contrasts.

Indirect perception has been characterized as a many-to-many mapping between the information available to the senses and the events or objects in the world. This potentially unruly mapping has given rise to the emphasis on "cues" as probabilistic sources of information (Brunswik, 1956; Cutting, chap. 4, this volume; Gibson, 1957; Hochberg, chap. 1, this volume). The idea is that, as a perceiver, one wanders through the world as a Bayesian algorist, computing the surety of what one sees based on stores of matrices representing the covariation of "cues" with objects and events (see Massaro, 1987; Massaro & Friedman, 1990). To us, such a view seems computationally cumbersome and unlikely (see also Hochberg, 1966).

Direct perception, on the other hand, has been characterized as the one-to-one mapping between information and events or objects, hence the emphasis on invariants and the surety of information (e.g., Burton & Turvey, 1990). The idea here is that one wanders through the world as an actor and collector of information, with perceptual systems exactly fitting the requisites of the ecological niche (see Cutting, 1991a). To us, such a view seems biologically implausible because it implies preadaptation of perceptual systems to ecological niches, and thus would make evolution difficult, if not impossible.

Directed perception, in contrast to both, is characterized by the many-to-one mapping between information and events or object properties. That is, more than one source can specify a particular aspect of the object or event to be perceived.[4] This idea emphasizes that the world is typically a plenum of adequate information (reducing cognitive demands), and the observer wanders through it selecting or combining information as it is useful and as it matches the capacities of the perceptual system (allowing evolution to occur). This metatheoretical viewpoint will

---

[4] Clearly, there is much potential mischief in the idea of specification (Schwartz, 1996). Cutting and Vishton (1995) suggest that the traditional "cues," or sources of information, about depth specify only ordinality, and then only when their assumptions are valid.

be important in our discussion to follow because, with a picture or a sculpture, an artist can select, enhance, or exaggerate one class of information sources from the world and use them in an artwork, letting other sources lie idle and unused (see also Massironi, 1982, chapter 2).

II. PICTURES, REPRESENTATION, AND COMMUNICATION

To encompass cave paintings, photographs, sketches, and caricatures, Gibson (1971, p. 31) defined a picture as "a surface so treated that a delimited optic array to a point of observation is made available that contains the same kind of information that is found in the ambient optic arrays of an ordinary environment." Thus, a picture is a *surrogate* for ordinary visual perception, and the contents of the picture are surrogates for objects in the real world (see also Gibson, 1954; Hochberg, 1962).[5] The picture brings things into view that might otherwise be at great distance, in time or space, or it even imports them from imagination.

This definition would seem to be appropriate to many kinds of pictures and, with the technological extension of motion, to cinema and television as well. Such a view is not particularly comfortable with modern or abstract art of many kinds (see Gibson, 1979, p. 268), and it promotes a boundary between pictures and sculpture that seems awkward. One of the attractions of this definition, however, is that it is quite clear and concrete. Moreover, it makes an assumption prevalent in most all approaches to pictures, which we also endorse—most pictures are *representations*. Although Gibson was not comfortable with the idea of representations (e.g., Gibson, 1979, p. 279; Cutting, 1985), it dominates his and most other approaches to pictures.

A. Representation, Pictures, and Sculpture

A picture can only light upon some aspect of reality; the rest it must consign to the shadows. No picture, however fond of its subject, can embrace all of its aspects. . . . So realism is no simple matter, each picture makes a highly intricate choice of features, playing upon some, ignoring others. (Schier, 1986, pp. 162–163)

Discussions of representations are at the core of late 20th-century cognitive psychology; in fact, it is difficult to imagine a cognitive psychology that did not have representations as a foundation (see, for example, Epstein, 1993; Hochberg, chap. 1, this volume; Johnson-Laird, chap. 12, this volume; Rumelhart & Norman, 1988). Representations are typically couched as mental entities bearing some rela-

---

[5] Some theorists have tried to drive a wedge between issues of surrogation and representation (e.g., Schwartz, 1997). From our perspective there is none; both take the elements within pictures to stand for something else in another world.

tion to the world outside. Pictures, however, are different; they are physical entities whose contents typically bear some relation to this same world (see also Hagen,
1979, 1980; Willats, 1997). What is this relation? We believe that five things must
be considered:

a. The *representing medium*. This includes the physical nature of the surface(s) and
the choices made in altering them. For photographs, paintings, and engravings such
a surface is typically planar and two-dimensional, but these are textured in different
ways; for a sculpture the surface typically has local two-dimensionality, but wraps
around in three dimensions. Consideration must also be given to the markings on
the surface(s), the lines, brush strokes, pixels, etchings, or moldings.

b. *The depicting array*. This concerns the composition of the elements in (a)—the
particular arrangement of lines, brush strokes, pixels, and so on, for a picture and
the surface arrangements in a sculpture.

c. *The depicted array*. This contains a selection of aspects of the modeled world
(that is, a selection from the possibilities of (d) below). Concretely, this could be a
landscape, a collection of flowers, a face, or even a set of ideas; but equally it can
focus on the light at a given time on the landscape, the particular riot of color in
the flowers, or the expression in the face that the artist wishes to model. Typically,
any talk about the depicted array is simply a description of the scene without reference to larger aspects of culture.

d. *A depicted world,* "real" or imaginary, only a small part of which is depicted in
the picture. This world traditionally has had considerable cultural significance and
history, and these provide a background context for how the picture was to be seen
when it was composed.

e. The concern with the *mapping,* or correspondence, between (b) the depicting array and (c) the depicted array.

This scheme is adapted from Palmer (1978, in press), who discussed representations
in general, but when adapted to our purposes the system works reasonably well. For
pictures and sculptures, the success of (e)—the mapping from (b) to (c)—is measured in our recognition that a particular piece of art is an artifact that stands in
place of a landscape, a collection of flowers, a face, or even an idea. We claim this
mapping, or surrogation, is not culturally relative (e.g., Hochberg & Brooks, 1962;
Hochberg, 1995, 1996), it is not dependent on photographic assumptions, and it is
also not the basis for aesthetic judgment.

1. Six Examples

To be concrete about representation in pictures and sculpture, let us consider six
cases—a photograph, an engraving, a painting, two sculptures, and then a final paint-

ing. Traditionally, the first four would be called examples of "representational" art, the last two would not.

a. Sam Shere's Explosion of the Hindenberg

For example, this piece, in the collection of the Museum of Modern Art, New York, is (a) a black-and-white photograph that is (b) a surface with a particular pattern of light intensities that mimic (c) the explosion of a large dirigible against a metal tower, representing (d) the event of the *Hindenberg's* destruction in Lakehurst, New Jersey, in 1937. What makes the picture a representation, according to our account, is the relationship between what is seen in the patterns on the photograph and what might be imagined about, or have been seen during, the actual burning of a dirigible. When the picture is reproduced, as in a book (e.g., Newhall, 1964), the picture of the picture is no less a representation, or mapping between (b) the pattern of light intensities and (c) the explosion of a large airship. Even a bad photocopy of the photograph remains a representation to the degree that the scene is still discernible. If it were discovered that somehow the picture did not actually depict the explosion of the *Hindenberg,* but perhaps of some other dirigible at some other time, this would not detract from it as a representation. Thus, the truth of the situation—which is part of the relation between (c) and (d), and sometimes called denotative reference—is not at issue in our scheme, although it can be very relevant other contexts (see Goodman, 1968; Mitchell, 1992; Schier, 1986).

b. Albrecht Dürer's St. Jerome in His Study

This piece, in the collection of the Metropolitan Museum of Art, New York, is (a) a two-dimensional black-and-white surface, (b) engraved to look like (c) an old man in a rather lavish study with a lion, wolf, skull, and other objects near his side, (d) denoting St. Jerome and the iconographic symbols associated with him. For a complete understanding of the picture it is important to know the iconography of the image (Panofsky, 1955; see also, for example, Ivins, 1969; Mitchell, 1995)—another part of the relation between (c) and (d)—but this knowledge is not pertinent to the discussion of representation as we define it. As before, any photographic reproduction of this work for any purpose (e.g., Carlbom & Paciorek, 1978) is no less a representation than the original, as long as the quality of the reproduction allows retention of the perceived relations of (b) to (c).

c. Leonardo's Mona Lisa (La Joconde)

This piece, in the Louvre, is (a) a two-dimensional varicolored, painted canvas, (b) composed to look like (c) a lady with an enigmatic expression of repose on a balcony in front of a surreal landscape, who was, according to the traditional account, (d) the wife of Francesco del Giocondo. Because the painted surface looks like a woman with an interesting expression, it is a successful representation—the mapping (b) to (c)—but this tells us nothing of cultural or historical significance (see, for example, Baxandall, 1985). That the painting may be, in the late 20th century, the most famous painting in Western culture,[6] that is, it has been parodied by Duchamp, Warhol (see Solso, 1994), Monneret, and others, or that the image of the woman was almost certainly never meant to be considered a portrait of Giocondo's wife (Turner, 1993) does not add or detract from it as a representation as we define it. Again, a photograph (or even a bad photocopy of a photograph) of *Mona Lisa* is as good a representation as is the original so long as the image is recognizable as a woman on a balcony in front of a landscape; it still reveals the relationship between (b) and (c).

d. Michelangelo's David

This piece, in the Academy in Florence is (a) a three-dimensional arrangement of dappled marble surfaces, (b) sculpted into the complex shape of (c) a muscular young man with outsized hands, carrying a sling over his shoulder, in a pose of reflection, denoting (d) the mythical character who defeated Goliath. Because of the perceptually close relationship between (b) the sculpted shape and (c) a young man, regardless of one's vantage point, the mapping is apt. That the story of David and Goliath is a myth is not relevant here. Similarly, that the piece of work is beautiful and justly renowned has to do with many things not necessarily a part of (b) and (c). Moreover, and what makes the discussion of the sculpture relevant to pictures, a photograph of the artwork preserves the basic relationship of (b) to (c), except that the viewpoint is now constrained. Clearly, however, there are canonical views (Palmer, Rosch, & Chase, 1981); a picture of *David* from the front seems likely to be a better representation *of the artwork* than one from the side or back.

e. Henry Moore's Two Forms

Consider a traditionally less "representational" example, in the Museum of Modern Art, New York. It is (a) a set of varnished, wooden block surfaces, (b) carved into two objects; the first a small, roundish one and the second a gourd-like one with a hole in it with its concave surface facing the first, suggesting (c) a relationship; "the smaller of the two units is compact and self-sufficient . . . although straining noticeably towards its partner . . . [t]he larger seems wholly engaged in its leaning over the smaller, dominating it, holding it down, protecting, encompassing, receiving it" (Arnheim, 1974, p. 272), and denoting (d) an infant and mother. The fact that Moore's sculpture does not physically look like an infant and mother does not, in our view, detract from it as a representation. The shapes suggest a set of relations between the two objects. A photograph of the sculpture does the same, although again it constrains the viewpoint. Notice here that, unlike the cases above, the depicted array is not a physical space; instead, it is a set of relations, even of ideas triggered by Moore's abstract title. Thus, in our view, pictorial representation can

---

[6] The results of a poll published in the September 24, 1995, London Sunday Times (The Culture, Section 10, p. 29) found that Michelangelo's Sistine Chapel ceiling was thought to be the most famous painting by 20% of the *Times* readership; Leonardo's Mona Lisa ranked second with 17%.

easily diverge from realism, both in art and in science (as in the case of graphs, discussed below). The import here is that most discussions of representation would not easily admit Moore's work.

f. Peter Joseph's Dark Ochre Color with Red Border

Our notion of representation, however, is not unbounded. For completion's sake, consider this piece in the Lisson Gallery, London. This late-20th century work is (a) a two-dimensional canvas (b) painted in two colors, with a large central rectangular patch of ochre (a dark yellow) and red border around it. The painting does not particularly suggest anything other than what it is, and we would claim it represents nothing in particular. Thus, it is "nonrepresentational," both in our terms and in traditional descriptions of certain classes of modern art. A photograph of the work may be a representation of the work (see, for example, Denvir et al., 1989), but there remains no depicted array allowing a mapping of the work to anything else.

2. Fidelity: The Attempt to Quantify the Mapping

With these examples in mind, the scheme outlined above is intended to clarify certain aspects of the nature of representation. The power of the concept, however, is in (e) the mapping of the relationship between the two arrays, (b) and (c), which we claim is based on recognition. Other theorists have tried to quantify this relation in a more rigorous way. The idea that such a quantification is possible across all the various kinds of pictures is, we think, based broadly on assumptions of "progress" in the arts, and particularly on photography and the idea of photorealism (e.g., Friedhoff & Benzon, 1991). Such schemes assume that a picture is best considered as a frozen optical array (the projection of the real world to a particular station point); that is, that the depiction is physically and measurably similar to the depicted array.

Initially, for example, Gibson (1954, 1960) was concerned with the *fidelity,* or optical similarity, of the picture to the world it represented, and he held out promise for measuring degrees of fidelity between the two. This view is essentially Pirenne's (1970, 1975) as well. In principle, and in the parlance of the late 20th century, one could compare the image, point-for-point in a photograph or pixel-by-pixel in a video image, with corresponding regions in the optical array, and achieve a measure of similarity between the two. There are, however, several kinds of problems. For example, most pictures most of the time are not looked at from the point of composition that would make them best mimic an optical array of a real world. This creates few problems perceptually (Goldstein, 1979, 1987; Halloran, 1989, 1993), but in a reconstruction of the depicted space behind the picture plane it creates projective distortions in planes parallel to the picture plane and affine distortions in planes orthogonal to it (Cutting, 1987, 1988). Moreover, walking in front of a picture creates continuous distortions of this kind, which appear to be of little perceptual consequence (Wallach, 1987).

In addition, the idea of fidelity suggests a progressive scale: A 140-mm film image of a landscape would typically have better fidelity than a 35-mm film image of it, which in turn would typically have better fidelity than a video image of it, than a detailed line drawing of it, and so forth. Such a progression makes a certain amount of sense, and one could indeed quantify such relations. Nonetheless, it sets up at least three other problems when one considers pictures in general.

First, and most simply, any principled comparison between the composition of a picture (the depiction) and the world (the depicted) needs a real world. Thus, despite the fact that most Renaissance and Baroque paintings are constructed in rigorous perspective, the paintings are of fictitious, idealized environments, so no fidelity computation could in principle be made. At most, they could only "look" real, and hence we are back to similarity by recognition, not similarity by physical measurement.

Second, and more insidiously, the fidelity assumption leads further to the idea that the photograph of a landscape has more fidelity than a painting of it by Constable, which might have more fidelity than an engraving by Piranesi, and so forth. These comparisons make little sense because the media and the intents of the artists have shifted. We would probably all agree that Piranesi's 18th-century engraving of the Roman Forum was very faithful to what one would see in the Roman Forum, even today (see Levit, 1976). Any concrete measure of the engraving's fidelity, however, would entail the comparison of lines in a picture with the projection of "lines" from the real environment. These latter lines, however, are often fictions. Despite the influence of Marr (1982), in a computer analysis of images any filtering or thresholding technique which produces lines from a naturalistic scene will produce many lines one had not wanted and will omit many lines one would have wished to see (Willats, 1990; but see also Hayes & Ross, 1995). The abstraction of the environment to an array of lines assumes a relationship between (a) the medium of engraving and (c) the Roman Forum that is not part of the mapping between (b) the composition of the lines and (c) the Roman Forum. Thus, if one were still concerned with measuring fidelity, one must use different metrics for photographs than for engravings and other line-based images.

Third and most importantly, the idea of fidelity generally ignores the selection processes in composing a pictured scene. Consider some choices of various artistic schools. It can be said that many Renaissance artists were fascinated by the geometric properties of architectural environments and how they could be used to create the impression of the layout of a space. It can be said that many Baroque artists were fascinated with object shape and textures and how light and shadow played upon surfaces. It can be said that many Impressionists were fascinated with ambient light itself, and it can be said that the Italian Futurists were fascinated with motion and how it interacted with form or could be stripped from it. Following the central tenet of directed perception, the natural world is a plenum of information and the artist may only use some of it in a depiction. Thus, to suggest that some artistic images have greater fidelity than others is to flirt with unwarranted glosses over history, culture, and artistic intent.

3. Retreat from Fidelity

Gibson (1966, 1979), for one, later realized that fidelity was not the answer to the understanding of the utility of pictures. His rationale centered on a concern with portrait caricatures, which were poor in fidelity (however it be measured) but which nonetheless were recognizable and understandable, sometimes more so that line drawings of a face they were intended to represent (Brennan, 1985; Rhodes, Brennan, & Carey, 1987; see also Gombrich, 1963; Hochberg, 1972; Perkins, 1975). From our perspective, Gibson's concern divides two ways—first the difference between line drawings and photographs, and second the difference between exaggeration and veridical proportioning. The first will be addressed in a later section on the functions of lines, and the second concerns communication, addressed in the next section.

Gibson (1971, 1973) next proposed that the mapping was not at the level of lines, pencils of light, or pixels, but at the level of something more abstract—*information,* even *invariants.* He felt that the information in the depicting and depicted arrays must be the same. We think such an approach loses the strikingness of the concept of fidelity but, with the exception of the discussion of invariants (Cutting, 1993; Topper, 1977, 1979; but see Costall, 1990; and Hagen, 1986), it is probably closer to the truth. Nonetheless, it passes off any explanatory power of fidelity to the concept of information, a topic of another chapter (Cutting, chap. 4, this volume).

At present, then, we suggest the best way to address the mapping function in pictorial representation is a pragmatic one: One should simply appeal to the psychology of recognition. The contents of a picture (the depiction) resemble what is depicted not solely in terms of information, but to the degree "there is an overlap between the recognitional abilities triggered by" the picture and the depicted (Schier, 1986, p. 187). Such an appeal forces the realization that in any theory of picture perception the perceiver, not some objective measurement, determines whether or not a picture depicts as the artist had intended.

B. Communication

Communication is essentially a social affair. Man has evolved a host of different systems of communication which render his social life possible. (Cherry, 1957, p. 3)

1. Sharing

To communicate means, among other things, *to share* and there is an important sense in which this is what pictures do best; the artist, among other things, shares with the viewer some of his or her intents. Pictures—like utterances in language—are composed to communicate intents; they are often, but not always, composed to represent objects and events. Thus, even traditionally defined, nonrepresentational pictures are intended to communicate, and communication is thus a broader purpose of pictures than is representation.

2. Selecting

To communicate also implies to select. This 20th-century idea comes from Shannon and Weaver (1949). They proposed a rigorous, albeit somewhat counterintuitive, mathematical definition: Communication is based on information; information occurs through the selection of one entity from a set of entities; and information is measured in the size of the set from which the selection occurs.[7] Artists select their medium for a particular work; they select the style with which they will compose their work; they select what they wish to portray (even if it is to portray nothing); and they select which world or domain they wish to represent. Selections and choices delimit possibilities, and they emphasize intent.

3. Constrained by Purpose

The artist, however, is not all powerful in his or her ability to make the selection process successfully communicate. Some representations are inherently better than others to communicate particular ideas about the same object or event. For example, a rendering of a room in perspective might nicely illustrate its contents and their general spatial relations, but if the aim of the picture is to have another person construct that room, a multiview orthographic projection would be better (e.g., Carlbom & Paciorek, 1978). Thus, communication is sharing by selection as *constrained* for a particular *purpose;* the choices of what to communicate are not wholly independent of how to communicate it (Massironi, 1989); there are important reasons why recipes, musical scores, and architectural plans look different.

If the aim of scientific research is to broaden and continuously redefine the limits of nature and its contents, it can be said that the aim of an artistic research is to broaden and continuously redefine the limits of communication and its contents. However, the artist alone is not charged with discovering new methods and establishing new rules for the communication of new contents; scientists are so charged as well. When new contents arise and need to be transmitted and when old methods do not suffice, a new way to represent them is found. This fact is perhaps no clearer than in a special kind of picture drawn by scientists for other scientists and students—the graph.

4. The Example of Illustrations, Charts, and Graphs

Illustrative drawings, more broadly, have always been a part of geometric presentations in mathematics. For example, Euclid's *Optics* (from the third century B.C.) contains many graphical constructions (Burton, 1945). These represent two-dimen-

---

[7] When dealing with finite sets, this idea has great appeal and application. The problem with this idea in many applications, however, is that the size of set one is dealing with is generally unknown. If there is an animal present and you declare it to be a tiger, how many possible animals have you selected from? Has the same information been relayed if we declare it a house cat? See Cutting (1986) for more criticisms, see also Dretske (1981) for a lengthy defense of this and related issues, and see Cutting (chap. 4, this volume).

sional geometric space. In addition, charts and maps have been a part of nearly every culture known (e.g., Harvey, 1980; Snyder, 1993). These, too, represent two-dimensional space. In most scientific illustrations, however, graphs or diagrams use a paper's space more abstractly. To anticipate later discussion, the functions in graphs plotting the data are *objects*, when more than one is present they are typically *textured* differently, and the axes framing the plotted space are *edges*.

The graph is an unusual prototype in the domain of pictures: (a) It is unequivocally representational (it represents data); (b) it is nonrealistic (it stands for no possible optical array); (c) it is conventional (one needs to know some rules to understand it properly; most pictures do not require this); and (d) it communicates effectively (it can show a trend embedded in hundreds, even thousands, of data points). In the late 20th century roughly about 10% of scientific journal space seems to devoted to graphs (Cleveland, 1984), although disciplines and subdisciplines vary widely in how often graphs are deployed.[8]

The first scientific graphs, with x and y axes and plots of data, seem to have appeared with the works of Johann Heinrich Lambert and William Playfair in the 18th century (see, for example, Tufte, 1983). Important conceptual advances in graphing were made by Marey (1878) and by Tukey (1970), and overviews and explorations can be found in Bertin (1967), Cleveland (1985), Kosslyn (1994), Schmid (1983), and Tufte (1983, 1990).[9] Each of these latter works makes suggestions about how to construct graphs, and perhaps most interestingly, although they are written by scientists, there is very little direct evidence in support of many of their specific claims. Tufte (1983), for example, deplored pie charts, but Spence (1990) found them to communicate most efficiently of all graphical forms.

More importantly in our context, Tufte (1983, chap. 4) also made a suggestion directly relevant to pictorial communication. That is, he proposed a data–ink ratio for measuring the utility of graphs; the more data that could be displayed with the least amount of ink, the better the graph communicated. The idea is that, in a graph or figure, scientists share condensations of their data, where each visible data point excludes (or selects from) other possibilities, constrained by the presentational space and perceptual capacities of the reader. Too many functions are visually confusing; too few are wasteful; dense maps are best. As attractive as, and as closely tied to information theory as, the data–ink idea is, it seems largely an aesthetic appeal; ease of reading a graph does not seem correlated with data and ink. As with pictures more generally, communication by graphs seems a craft, not a science. Culture, education, and history all matter in reading graphs, much more so than in perceiving pictures more generally. Graphs follow conventions and, despite the claims of Good-

[8] Perhaps the quintessence of refrainment from using images is Staudt (1847), a treatise on projective geometry without any figures.

[9] Bertin's (1967) is perhaps the most striking and comprehensive, suggesting that shape, orientation, texture, color, luminance (value in his terms), and size are the primitive graphical elements; almost four decades later such a list sounds remarkably like a list of neurophysiological channels in vision (e.g., Spillman & Werner, 1990).

man (1968) and others, the grip of conventions is not large on how pictures, in general, are to be perceived.

As suggested by our choice of graphs, we believe that most theoretical approaches to pictures are fraught with at least two difficulties. First, they are often too enamored of photographs, a technological johnny-come-lately in the domain of pictures. Second, at least within psychology, theorists have also been too enamored of the relationship of figure to ground, a distinction attributed to Rubin (1915). With Kennedy (1974), we feel this distinction has been often overplayed and overinterpreted (see also Hochberg, 1995; Hochberg, chap. 1, this volume). Instead, in the pictorial medium that is the oldest to our species, the communicating elements are *lines,* and it is in understanding line drawings that cognition appears to play its clearest role.

III. THE BASIC PICTORIAL ELEMENTS

Whether one drags a finger across the sand, a burnt stick across a wall, or a pencil across a sheet of paper, the result is the same; one has drawn a line, a marking of more length than width. Lines are part of the root elements of pictures; they are abstract, they are surrogates, they have power to represent, and most importantly they communicate form and depth. They are only a part of the root elements because their perceptual and cognitive impact does not accrue from their isolation; their impact depends on their juxtaposition to two vacant, adjacent pictorial areas along their flanks. We will call each such area a region. Both lines and regions are often part of depicted objects, and regions are often part of the background. More importantly, it is the relation between lines and regions that creates objects and layout within a picture.

We claim the various line–region combinations exist in four basic forms. They create pictorial objects, edges of objects, cracks within or between objects, and texture. Interestingly and importantly, these four line–region types are present in the oldest yet-discovered cave paintings (see Chauvet et al., 1995). Thus, no development, no sequence of discovery, no process of pictorial understanding appears to mark their use. For these reasons, these four types of line–region appear to be good candidates as primitives for pictures—and of course they are in good use today by artists (e.g., Hirschfeld, 1970; Levine, 1976; Steinberg, 1966, 1982) and by children (e.g., Gardner, 1980; Kellogg & O'Dell, 1967; van Sommers, 1984; Willats, 1997).

A. Taxonomy of Pictorial Lines

> Intricacy of form, therefore, I shall define to be that peculiarity in the lines, which compose it, that *leads the eye a wanton kind of chase,* [italics in original] and from the pleasure that it gives the mind, entitles it to the name of beautiful. (Hogarth, 1753, p. 25)

1. Lines as Edges

Perhaps most important pictorial elements are the lines that produce a segregation across regions, and this was Rubin's (1915) fundamental insight. That is, the presence of a line can make the region on one of its sides fundamentally different than that on the other (see also Hochberg, 1972). This type of line is an *edge*. The line-as-edge pictorially creates an object by representing its contour, and it dictates that the one region is closer to the observer in depicted space than the other. The line typically belongs to the object region, making its border; it does not belong to the background region.[10] Leeuwenberg's (1971; Leeuwenberg & Boselie, 1988) structural information theory made this relation formally explicit. Such lines often do not have free terminals, but either abut or join other edge lines, or curve eventually making a convex shape. When they do have free terminals they typically run in pairs into the central region of a larger convex shape, representing the contour of a part protruding from a larger object (see Koenderink & van Doorn, 1982). The perceived object lies generally within the convexity of the line, and the line denotes the object's self-occluding contour or shape, as seen from the perspective of the viewer.

Edge lines would seem to constitute the bulk of all large traces in line drawings, and they are also the grist for a plethora of visual illusions. Many cases of multistability are predicated on the reversal of polarity in depth of the two regions around lines-as-edges, and many cases of impossible figures are predicated on different assignments of depth to regions along the same line (cf. Figure 11 in Hochberg, chap. 9, this volume). Edge lines form the basis of the Rubin's (1915) faces–goblet illusion (which was commonly invoked with real goblets in the Victorian era with the profiles of Victoria and Albert on opposite sides; see also Hoffman & Richards, 1984, for an earlier attribution); they play in Ratoosh's (1949) figure of ambiguous interposition; they beguile in central regions of Schuster's (1964) devil's pitchfork; and they delight in many more. See Figures 1a–1d, and see also Kanizsa (1979), Robinson (1972), Rock (1984), Shepard (1990), and Gillam (chap. 5, this volume).

2. Lines as Objects

Some pictorial lines represent long, thin *objects*—trees, branches, or twigs; the horns or legs of animals; the fingers of a hand, or eyebrows; television antennae; and as suggested above, functions on a graph. An early television antenna is suggested in Figure 1e.[11] Such lines cut through a background but in an important sense do not segment it; the region on one side of the line is to be interpreted as made of the same stuff as the region on the other, be it atmosphere, ground, another object, or

---

[10] This claim is different from Leonardo's (Richter, 1883, p. 29), who suggested that an edge line did not belong to the object and, although of infinite thinness, lay between the object and the background.

[11] These lines have also been generalized to create entities that are not really objects at all, rays of light, or even motion. For example, Gombrich (1972, p. 229) noted: "There is hardly a picture narrative in which speed is not conveniently rendered by a few strokes which act like negative arrows showing where the object has been a moment before." It may be that Töpffer invented this technique in the mid-19th century (Groensteen & Peters, 1994), and these lines, symbolically or otherwise (Rosenblum, Saldaña, & Carello, 1993), act as emblems denoting motion. See also McCloud (1993) for an illuminating discussion of such lines in contemporary comics.

Edge Lines (and some figural reversals)

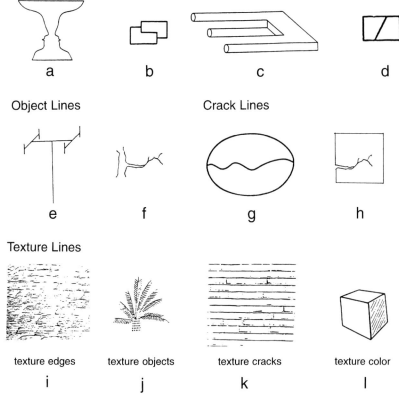

a	b	c	d

Object Lines   Crack Lines

e	f	g	h

Texture Lines

texture edges	texture objects	texture cracks	texture color
i	j	k	l

FIGURE 1   A taxonomy of lines. Edge lines separate the regions on either side and assign them different ordinal depth. Four figures that play with this relationship are shown: (a) the faces/goblet illusion, after Rubin (1915); (b) an ambiguous occlusion figure, after Ratoosh (1949); (c) the devil's pitchfork, after Schuster (1964); and (d) a rectangle/window, after Koffka (1935). Second are shown some object lines: (e) is a mid-20th century version of a television antenna; and (f) shows the twigs at the end of a tree branch. Third are figures with crack lines: (g) is the mouth of a clam, after Kennedy (1974); and (h) is a crack in a block. Note that (f) and (h) are exact reciprocals—switching from an object-line to an edge-line interpretation. Finally, four texture line types are shown: (i) texture edges and color in cobblestones, after de Margerie (1994); (j) texture objects, after Steinberg (1966); (k) texture cracks, after Brodatz (1966); and (l) texture color, indicating shadow.

graphical space. Moreover, such a line represents an object in front of the two regions; that is, the layout of the picture is such that whatever is on either side of such a line is farther from the observer than is the object depicted by the line itself. Lines-as-objects typically terminate freely at one or both ends, with the surrounding regions often, but not always, wrapping around the point(s) of termination.

When an object represented by a line gets sufficiently large, the line-as-object bifurcates and becomes two opposed lines-as-edges, as suggested in the tree branch of Figure 1f.

3. Lines as Cracks

Some lines represent a rupture in a continuous surface, drawn as an edge shared between two similar objects, or parts of an object. Following Kennedy (1974), we will call these *cracks*. Some such lines are drawn to represent, for example, the small gap between elevator doors; or, on a face, a mouth (the shared edge between the upper and lower lips), a shut eye, or a crease in a forehead. A clam's mouth is suggested in Figure 1g. When cracks get sufficiently large, the line representing it bifurcates and, as with object lines, becomes two lines-as-edges, as suggested in the lower right panel. Except in portraits and other drawings involving animals and people, however, single lines-as-cracks appear to be relatively rare in pictures. Perhaps this is because, when they exist outside of faces, they are often relatively unimportant. See Stevens (1974) for a discussion of the structure of natural cracks.

Just as there can be ambiguity with edge lines, there can be ambiguity between objects lines and crack lines. Koffka's (1935, p. 153) example of a rectangle and line, shown in Figure 1d, is a case in point. The figure can be seen many ways; for example, as a rectangular figure with a diagonal cut through it (leaving a crack), or a rectangular window with a diagonal wire (an object) crossing behind it. Notice that, here, as the object and crack interpretations interchange, so typically does the polarity of the edge line around the rectangle. Compare also with Figures 1f and 1h.

4. Lines as Texture, as Mass

Finally, perhaps the second most important type of line is typically quite short and drawn in groups, repeating the same stroke successively or repeating it with some patterned deviation. These are *texture*. Such lines are usually close to one another, with correspondingly smaller flanking regions. Indeed, these lines are often as much as, or more than, an order of magnitude closer together than nontexture lines, and thus their regions are correspondingly smaller, even nonexistent. Texture lines tend to cover a surface, even overlap it, which is often defined by an edge line. On the larger scale of the picture the small regions between lines, together with the lines themselves, both become aspects of the texture of a surface. Hair, grass, waves, cobblestones, cloth, glass, and shadows are often drawn with such lines and their impression creates a sense of smoothness or roughness, softness or hardness, blockiness, transparency, or opacity. In the traditional art literature these are called *mass* (e.g., Speed, 1913; see also Baxandall, 1995), and Hayes and Ross (1995) have suggested ways in which they are processed differently by the visual system than the other types of lines. A few examples of texture are shown in Figures 1i–1l. Closer inspection reveals these textural elements subdivide, and some have the same general properties as the first three classes of lines only at a smaller scale, giving the structure of many pictures a fractal-like quality.

a. Texture-Lines-as-Edges

These depict small objects nested within a larger object. Examples include depictions of cobblestones in a street (Figure 1i), the patternings in tree bark on a trunk, or waves on a large body of water. Each such edge has a near side and a far side, but in a drawing or painting seldom is there any attempt to draw all cobbles, all bits of bark, or all waves. What is drawn are only a few emblematic strokes. Gombrich (1979) called this the etcetera principle, and it is applicable to texture of all types.

b. Texture-Lines-as-Objects

These appear on larger objects. Examples include palm fronds (Figure 1j), ripples on a pond, hairs on a head, fur on a pelt, and grass on a lawn. In such cases each line represents a single small object. Moreover, at a particular local pictorial depth around the stroke each such texture line appears against a pair of regions of slightly greater depth.

c. Texture-Lines-as-Cracks

These may or may not create small objects, but they always make patterns on a larger object. The mortar lines between bricks are created by texture lines (Figure 1k) and designate small objects within a larger one, but the tessellated cracks in the dried mud of a lake bed do not inherently create smaller objects; they are simply texture patterns on a large objects. But in each case what lies unseen inside the crack is at a slightly greater depth.

d. Texture-Lines-as-Color

These typically represent shadow or different shades of lightness (e.g., Figure 1l). Thus, they are surrogates for achromatic color. At a normal viewing distance from the picture, dark lines and tightly spaced light regions tend to assimilate and approach a gray. No depth relations are implied, except perhaps as inferred by a light source. For examples and discussion, see Baxandall (1995), Cavanagh and Leclerc (1989), Hayes and Ross (1995), and Wade (1995).

5. Overview

Logically, these line types create many spatial, scalar, and segmental possibilities. First, the layout of the surface of the picture can mimic spatial properties of an optical array. That is, what is on the left of the picture is to the left of the viewer's central visual field, what is on the right is on the right, what is near the top of the picture is above the level of the viewer's eye, and what is at its bottom is below it, and everything else ordinally in between. Such relations were axioms in Euclid's optics (Burton, 1945), and we will return to this idea. Second, global differences between large and small are often denoted by the difference between lines depicting objects and their edges (whose regions are relatively large) and lines depicting texture (whose regions are relatively small). Moreover, in architectural drawings and in engravings, intermediate scale differences can also be carried by variations in line width, with larger lines binding more important aspects of the picture, intermediate lines binding intermediate-size objects, and smaller ones associated with texture. And finally, most of these lines are used to segment objects and parts of objects in depth. Let us develop this latter idea in more detail.

B. From Phenomenology to Structure: How Lines Create Local Pictorial Depth

> We stick to the convention that a wall or a piece of paper is flat, and curiously enough, we still go on, as we have done since time immemorial, producing illusions of space. (Escher, 1967, p. 15)

Locally, lines and regions appear to depict as many as, but no more than, two implicit distances from the observer, which we will call *depth A* (the nearer) and *depth B* (the farther). Thus, the specified local depth around a line is always ordinal (see also Hochberg, 1995); that is, one can never know (and we would claim one shouldn't be expected to know) how much distance is between depth A and depth B, only that the first is portrayed to be closer to the observer. Moreover, given the plethora of possible perceptual ambiguities of relative depths around lines in line drawings, depth assignment appears to be done cognitively. Locally, edge lines, objects lines, and crack lines can all appear identical; their ability to trigger recognition appears part and parcel of their ability to assign depth structure.

1. Local Depth Discontinuity from Lines-as-Edges

Figure 2a again shows part of Rubin's figure but superimposed on the right side are the depth relations for a line-as-edge when seen as a face; the line itself is at depth A and is attached to the region to the left, which is also at depth A. Thus, the line belongs to a depicted object. The other region, to its right, is at depth B and belongs to the background. The left side of the figure is reversed, for the goblet interpretation. We will code such configurations [aAb] or [bAa] as one runs across the region/line/region configuration, where a capital letter indicates the local depth of a line and a lower-case letter the local depth of the associated region. Many things enhance the interpretation of such lines as edges and the determination of which region is nearer, such as curvature (objects tend to be seen within the convex side of the line; see Attneave, 1954; Hoffman & Richards, 1984). Relations among shape curvatures can also suggest three-dimensional form (see Koenderink & van Doorn, 1976; Koenderink, 1990; Richards et al., 1986, 1987).

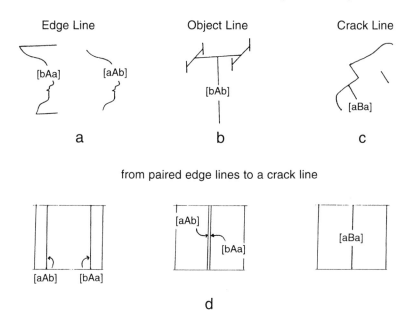

FIGURE 2   Ordinal depth relations implied by three types of lines. Lines are coded by capital letters; regions by lower-case letters; and depth by ordinal position in the alphabet. In (a) the reversible edge
lines in Rubin faces/goblet shows an edge of [bAa] for the left-hand edge in the goblet interpretation
and [aAb] in the face interpretation. In (b) the object line seen as an antenna shows depth relations of
[bAb]. In (c) the crack line of the mouth in the upturned, sleepy face is interpreted as [aBa]. The process
of how paired edge lines can become a crack line is suggested in sequences in (d), for elevator doors.

2. Local Depth Discontinuity from Lines-as-Objects

Figure 2b shows the schematic depth relations for a set of object lines, representing
an antenna. The lines are at depth A and the two adjacent regions are both at depth
B. We will code such configurations [bAb] for the depth relations running across
region, line, and region. Such lines-as-objects are always part of the nearest local
depth to be seen and the line-as-object is itself different than, and in front of, the
regions on both sides, which are at the farther local depth. According to our analysis, because only a two-valued ordinal depth pattern is possible, both sides of the
background must be generally at the same depth. A more conservative version of
this idea, however, can be seen in the consideration of slanted surfaces, particularly
of a ground plane. In Figure 3, there is a schematic tree and a horizon line behind
it. One can assume that the ground plane as it is represented on either side of the
tree is behind the tree, but the ground plane below the trunk (where the line ter-
minates) is in front. The relation of this terminal to the horizon is the only information available about the slant of the ground surface. We will return to this figure
later in applying rewrite rules to depth order.

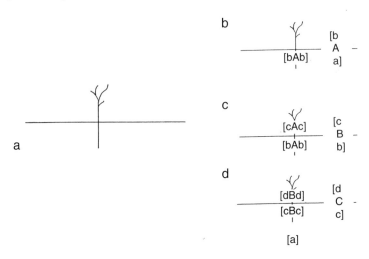

FIGURE 3   A tree in front of a horizon, and several stages of rewriting depth rules to build up depth.

3. Local Depth Discontinuity from Lines-as-Cracks

In Figure 2c is a schematic face with a mouth marked by a sideways T. Since the near vertical line is interpreted as the edge of the profiled face, then the horizontal branch is a crack representing the mouth. Such line–region configurations will be coded [aBa], the opposite local depth polarity to lines-as-objects. This is the only case where the line represents something at more distance than the neighboring regions, so let us offer proof of this relation. Consider the drawings in Figure 2d, representing the closing of elevator doors. As the doors close, the two door edges (reading left to right) are represented as [aAb] and [bAa], respectively. Notice that the line edges themselves belong to the doors. But when the gap between the door is too small to represent with two lines, the representation changes. The line now belongs to the gap that disappeared, and represents the spatial arrangement of [aBa]. Thus, [aAb] + [bAa] → [aBa].

4. Local Depth Continuity and Lines-as-Texture

At a global level (that is, with respect to the whole picture) small texture lines do not really segregate their regions; both lines and regions are part of the same entity (the texture elements) and are at the same general depth and create mass (e.g., Speed, 1913). Thus, although texture edges, texture objects, and texture cracks denote particular depth relations at a local scale, at the level of the whole picture we propose that all texture should be notated as [aAa]; suggesting that texture is interpreted as markings on a surface (Ittelson, 1996), generally as shadow, or as color.

C. Toward a Grammar of Multiple Lines and Regions: A Sketch of How Pictorial Depth Is Built Up

> The information in a line drawing is evidently carried by the connections of the lines, not by lines as such. (Gibson, 1979, p. 288)

From the local depth relations inherent in lines, and from a few constraints concerning the lines themselves, we can begin to formulate a grammar of pictorial lines and regions. Lines can end in three ways: they can terminate freely, join another line end, or abut a line flank. For the latter two cases let us establish some nomenclature: Lines typically meet at places we will call *junctions.* In general there are three types of junctions: (a) *joins,* which are of two types: the first occur where the end of one line meets the end of another (although sometimes there is a small gap), which we will call an L-junction (although the two lines, of course, need not meet at right angles—indeed, any angle will do). The second occur where one line meets at the ends of two or more, which we will call a Y-junction. Next there are (b) *abutments,* where the termination of one line is generally against the flank of another, which we will call a T-junction; and (c) *intersections,* where two or more lines cross, which we will call an X-junction. Anderson and Julesz (1995) partly developed a similar system.

1. Joins or L- and Y-Junctions

L-junctions have strict interpretation. Each line must be the same type; other combinations, we claim, would be agrammatical and lead to illusions of depth. Thus, an edge line can only meet another edge line with the same polarity ([aAb] or [bAa]), an object line can only meet another object line, and a crack line can only meet another crack. Y-junctions are even more restrictive; line elements are generally all objects or all cracks, and no mixtures or edges are allowed. Edge lines are generally excluded due to the unlikely co-occurrence of a bend in the edge (or contour) of one object and the intersection of the edge of an occluded object behind it. This is a version of what is sometimes called Helmholtz's rule (see Hochberg, 1971) or more generally a nonaccidental property (see Witkin & Tenenbaum, 1983).

2. Abutments or T-Junctions

These come in several kinds. The line elements could be homogenous: a T-junction could be made of object lines, as in Figure 2, or of crack lines. They could also be made of edge lines. For example, if one interpreted Koffka's rectangle in Figure 1d as a rectangular window with the edge of an object partly seen (with open background on the other side), then there are three ordinal depths—the window edge, the object edge, and the background. On the other hand, the line elements could be inhomogeneous. Consider again Koffka's rectangle. If one sees a wire behind the window, the object line (wire) abuts the edge line and is at a different (farther) distance. Abutments of the shaft at a nearer distance would imply an accidental property, and are typically avoided in pictorial representations (but see Hochberg, 1995).

3. Intersections or X-Junctions

These come in two types, again homogeneous and inhomogeneous. Homogeneous intersections occur when all four lines are objects or cracks, and thus they are no different than Y-junctions. Inhomogeneous intersections are more interesting, where an object line can cross an edge.

4. An Example of Building Depth

Consider the example of a tree crossing the horizon line in Figure 3a. Notice from Figure 3d that at least four relative depths can be built up: The ground in front of the terminal of the trunk is closest to the observer (depth A); the trunk is next (depth B); then ground behind the trunk (depth C); and finally the sky beyond the horizon (depth D). By our scheme, this is done in three ways, applying recursive rewrites of the spatial rules above.

a. Pass 1

Figure 3b is dominated by an X-junction. The whole line system, then, could represent a more or less X-shaped object, a mostly X-shaped crack, or an object and an edge. If the latter is entertained, the vertically oriented set of lines may be recognized as tree-like. Thus, this line and the regions around it are assigned depths of [bAb]. The horizontal line is an edge line; again reading upwards, it is assigned [aAb]. At the intersection, then, there is an inconsistency of depths. The horizon edge must be behind the object tree. (In X-junctions, edges are always behind objects, never the reverse, because edges belong to objects that are not usually transparent).

b. Pass 2

As shown in Figure 3c, these initial assignments must be then rectified. Given ordinal depths A and B, we can now assign further ordinal depths C, D, and so on. The object/tree line below the horizon remains [bAb]; the edge/horizon line becomes [bBc]; and the object/tree line above the horizon becomes [cAc]. Thus ordinal consistency is almost restored.

c. Pass 3

As suggested earlier, the space beyond the terminal of an object line is not necessarily at the same depth as the regions on either side of it. Thus, given that a horizon has been recognized, height in the visual field is now appropriate to the interpretation of the image, and the space below the terminal of the object/tree will be seen as closest to the observer (the ground occluding the roots of the tree). Thus, that space is now [a], the object/tree line below the horizon is [cBc], the edge/horizon line becomes [cCd], and the object/tree line above the horizon becomes [dBd].

We make no claim that this explicit order of recursion is a psychological instantiation of what actually happens. Nonetheless, we suggest that ordinal depth in a line drawing can be built up by lines and their intersections. We claim further that cognition, not perception, governs the assignment of depth and depth order through application of rules about lines and regions, and through recognition of objects that result from them.

D. A Note on the Problems and Successes of Linear Perspective

The eye can never be a true judge for determining with exactitude how near one object is to another . . . except by means of . . . the standard and guide of perspective. (Leonardo, in Richter, 1883, p. 53)

Linear perspective, perhaps because at the end of the 20th century it seems to be the major predecessor to photorealism, has played a dominate role in discussions of picture perception. We believe that linear perspective is important but not fundamental to pictures. It is the fruit of a particular culture and requires much training to employ well. Its import here, however, is that linear perspective, along with its allied projections (see Carlbom & Paciorek, 1978; Hagen, 1986), create new pictorial elements—rectilinear surfaces. As suggested by Leonardo da Vinci, these play a powerful role in extending the interpretation of picture beyond the mere ordinality of lines. In our view, this power comes at a price.

Conflicts of depth arise in some of these projective representations—the Necker cube, Mach's folded sheet, and Schröder's staircase are but a few (see, for example, Robinson, 1972, p. 175; Gillson, 1996), as suggested in Figure 4. In each of these cases, the rectilinearity of surfaces has tried to replace lines as information about depth and shape. The result, for us, is that edge lines no longer can dictate which region is closer to the observer; many edges do not have either a near or a far side, and multistability results. This problem also plays itself out in the agrammatical figures of Escher (1967), based in part on Penrose and Penrose (1958).

The benefit of linear perspective, of course, is that with the use of projections of parallel lines one can build up a much richer representation of the geometric layout of a given space. To be sure, that space must be architectural, because parallel lines are exceedingly rare in nature, but the effect is powerful and robust (Kubovy, 1986).

Linear perspective is a system. It is a systematic combination of at least five "pictorial cues," or sources of information, some of which have been in use since the first pictures. For example, the Chauvet paintings show the use of both occlusion (near objects interpose and clip the contours of farther objects) and height in the visual field information (near objects attached to the ground are lower in the visual field than are farther objects of the same size). Evidence for the use of relative size (closer objects are depicted as larger than farther objects of the size physical size) existed in pre-Renaissance art and in traditional Japanese and Chinese art. Relative density (more objects or textures placed within areas representing more distance

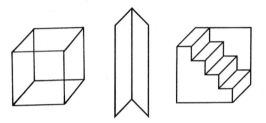

FIGURE 4   (a) The Necker cube, (b) Mach's folded card, and (c) Schröder staircase. We claim depth ambiguity occurs, in part, because the regions astride edge lines cannot be assigned ordinal depths.

regions) and aerial perspective (distant objects taking on the color of the atmosphere) arose in Renaissance times. A rigorous use of linear perspective incorporates all of these while copiously using linear, parallel lines. These lines are extremely effective in reducing noise in the assessment of the five sources of information.

We began this essay noting that pictures have a dual character—they are objects and they typically depict objects. We now believe that different information carries this dual quality. Cutting and Vishton (1995), for example, noted that picture perception is normally done at close range, and the other sources of information for depth—accommodation, convergence, and the lack of binocular disparities and motion perspective—all dictate that a picture is a flat surface. The traditional pictorial sources—occlusion, relative size, relative density, height in the visual field, and perhaps aerial perspective—indicate that a scene is depicted. Thus, pictures are a natural testing ground for the notion of "conflicting cues" (e.g., Woodworth, 1938), but the conflict is resolved by treating the picture either as an object, or as a depiction.

IV. SUMMARY

Pictures are ubiquitous in most cultures and times. Not surprisingly, then, they have exercised considerable influence on psychological theory over the course of this century. In particular, they have been used to shape and guide the forms of perceptual and cognitive theory. Those emphasizing cognitive influences on perception have generally chosen to illustrate their points with pictures that are simple line drawings (e.g., Rock, 1983); those emphasizing the relative independence of perception from cognition have, when using pictures at all, used pictures as rich in information as possible (e.g., Gibson, 1950, 1979). Any thorough investigation of pictures reveals it to be an extremely broad class, offering much to any theory.

From our perspective, pictures are a means of representation and communication. They, themselves, are typically two-dimensional objects crafted in such a way that the markings on their surface usually stand for (represent) something else, displaced in time and space. The information in the picture typically copies, mimics, or accentuates what might be available to the eye in a given situation at a given time.

Pictures allow an artist/draftsperson/photographer to share his or her ideas by selecting them from the indefinitely large number of things to represent. This selection is constrained by the purpose of the artist and the means of communication.

Because so much has been written, much of it quite excellent, about psychological aspects of photography (e.g., Pirenne, 1970; Scharf, 1968; see also Adams, 1980) and art (e.g., Gombrich, 1972; Hagen, 1986), particularly linear perspective (e.g., Kubovy, 1986)—all of which emphasize latter-day developments in the history of pictures—we have chosen to concentrate on primitive elements in pictures that have been with our species for at least 300 centuries. These elements are lines, considered in conjunction with their bordering regions. These lines appear to come in four kinds; they can represent edges of objects, objects themselves, cracks in objects, or texture on objects. Moreover, no process of development seems to mark their use; they can be found in the oldest art known (Chauvet et al., 1995; Lorblanchet, 1995). Each of these lines can be used to build up ordinal depth in a picture and in doing so seem unequivocally to invoke cognition in their perception. Later developments in pictures, particularly linear perspective and photography because of their richness of perceptual information, would seem to make the role of cognition less apparent, if not less important.

But most importantly, we claim that to understand the perception and cognition of everyday environments, one should also consider the perception and cognition of pictures. This is not simply because many psychological experiments use pictures as surrogates for everyday environments, but because, although we did evolve to look at natural environments, we emphatically did not evolve to look at pictures. Thus, pictures, insofar as they work, rely on preexisting capacities. They can be used as experiments, often naturalistic experiments, in discovering how we perceive and know what we see.

Acknowledgments

Supported in part by National Science Foundation Grants ASC-9523483 and SBR-9212786, and a John Simon Guggenheim Memorial Fellowship to J. Cutting during 1993–1994. We thank Nan E. Karwan and Michael Kubovy for fruitful ideas and discussion.

References

Adams, A. (1980). *The camera.* Boston: Little Brown.
Anderson, B. L., & Julesz, B. (1995). A theoretical analysis of illusory contour formation in stereopsis. *Psychological Review, 102,* 705–743.
Arnheim, R. (1974). *Visual thinking* (revised ed.). Berkeley, CA: University of California Press.
Attneave, F. (1954). Some informational aspects of visual perception. *Psychological Review, 61,* 183–193.
Ayer, A. J. (1956). *The problem of knowledge.* London: Macmillan.
Bailey, C. (1928). *The Greek atomists and Epicurus.* Oxford, UK: Oxford University Press.
Bailey, S. (1855). *Letters on the philosophy of the human mind* (Vol. 1). London: Longman, Brown, Green, and Longmans.

Baltrušaitis, J. (1989). *Aberrations: An essay on the legend of forms.* (R. Miller, Trans.). Cambridge, MA: MIT Press.

Baxandall, M. (1985). *Patterns of intention.* New Haven, CT: Yale University Press.

Baxandall, M. (1995). *Shadows and enlightenment.* New York: Oxford University Press.

Berkeley, G. (1709). *An essay toward a new theory of vision.* London: J. M. Dent.

Bertin, J. (1967). *Sémiologie graphique.* Paris: Editions Gauthier-Villars.

Brennan, S. (1985). The caricature generator. *Leonardo, 18,* 170–178.

Brodatz, P. (1966). *Textures.* New York: Dover.

Bruner, J. (1973) *Beyond the information given.* J. M. Anglin (Ed.), New York: W. W. Norton.

Brunswik, E. (1956). *Perception and the representative design of psychological experiments.* Berkeley, CA: University of California Press.

Burton, G., & Turvey, M. T. (1990). Perceiving the lengths of rods that are held but not wielded. *Ecological Psychology, 2,* 295–324.

Burton, H. E. (Trans.) (1945). The optics of Euclid. *Journal of the Optical Society of America, 35,* 357–372.

Carlbom, I., & Paciorek, J. (1978). Planar geometric projections and viewing transformations. *Computing Surveys, 10,* 465–502.

Cavanagh, P., & Leclerc, Y. G. (1989). Shape from shadows. *Journal of Experimental Psychology: Human Perception and Performance, 15,* 3–27.

Chastel, A. (1952). *Léonard da Vinci par lui-même.* Paris: Nagel.

Chauvet, J.-M., Brunel Deschamps, E., & Hillaire, C. (1995). *La grotte Chauvet à Vallon-Pont-d'Arc.* Paris: Seuil.

Cherry, C. (1957). *On human communication.* Cambridge, MA: MIT Press.

Cleveland, W. S. (1984). Graphs in scientific publications. *The American Statistician, 38,* 261–269.

Cleveland, W. S. (1985). *The elements of graphing data.* Monterey, CA: Wadsworth.

Clottes, J. (1995). *Les cavernes di Niaux.* Paris: Seuil.

Clottes, J. (1996). Le grotte ornate del Paleolitico. *Le Scienze: editione italiana di Scientific American, 329*(1), 62–68.

Cornford, F. M. (Ed. & Trans.). (1957). *Plato's Theaetetus.* Indianapolis, IN: Bobbs-Merrill.

Costall, A. P. (1990). Seeing through pictures. *Word & Image, 6,* 273–277.

Cutting, J. E. (1985). Gibson, representation, and belief. *Contemporary Psychology, 30,* 186–188.

Cutting, J. E. (1986). *Perception with an eye for motion.* Cambridge, MA: MIT Press.

Cutting, J. E. (1987). Rigidity in cinema seen from the front row, side aisle. *Journal of Experimental Psychology: Human Perception and Performance, 13,* 323–334.

Cutting, J. E. (1988). Affine distortions of pictorial space: Some predictions for Goldstein (1987) that La Gournerie (1859) might have made. *Journal of Experimental Psychology: Human Perception and Performance, 14,* 305–311.

Cutting, J. E. (1991a). Four ways to reject directed perception. *Ecological Psychology, 3,* 25–34.

Cutting, J. E. (1991b). Why our stimuli look as they do. In G. Lockhead & J. R. Pomerantz (Eds.), *The perception of structure: Essays in honor of Wendell R. Garner* (pp. 41–52). Washington, DC: American Psychological Association.

Cutting, J. E. (1993). Perceptual artifacts and phenomena: Gibson's role in the 20th century. In S. Masin (Ed.), *Foundations of perceptual theory* (pp. 231–260). Amsterdam: Elsevier Science.

Cutting, J. E., & Vishton, P. M. (1995). Perceiving layout and knowing distances: The integration, relative potency, and contextual use of different information about depth. In W. Epstein & S. Rogers (Eds.), *Perception of space and motion* (pp. 69–117). San Diego, CA: Academic Press.

Denvir, B., Mackintosh, A., Nash, J. M., Ades, D., Everitt, A., Wilson, S., & Livingstone, M. (1989). *Histoire de l'art moderne.* Paris: Flammarion.

Dretske, F. (1981). *Knowledge and the flow of information.* Cambridge, MA: MIT Press.

Epstein, W. (1993). The representational framework in perceptual theory. *Perception & Psychophysics, 53,* 704–709.

Escher, M. C. (1967). *The graphic work of M. C. Escher* (J. E. Brigham, Trans.). New York: Ballantine Books.

Ellis, S., Kaiser, M. K., & Grunwald, A. J. (1991). *Pictorial communication in virtual and real environment.* London: Taylor & Francis.

Friedhoff, R. M., & Benzon, W. (1991). *The second computer revolution: Visualization.* New York: Freeman.

Gardner, H. (1980). *Artful scribbles.* New York: Basic Books.

Gibson, J. J. (1950). *Perception of the visual world.* Boston: Houghton Mifflin.

Gibson, J. J., (1954). A theory of pictorial perception. *Audio-Visual Communication Review, 1,* 3–23.

Gibson, J. J. (1956). The non-projective aspects of the Rorschach experiment: IV. The Rorschach blots considered as pictures. *Journal of Social Psychology, 44,* 203–206.

Gibson, J. J. (1957). Survival in a world of probable objects. *Contemporary Psychology, 2,* 33–35.

Gibson, J. J. (1960). Pictures, perspective, and perception. *Daedalus, 89,* 216–227.

Gibson, J. J. (1966). *The senses considered as perceptual systems.* Boston: Houghton Mifflin.

Gibson, J. J. (1971). The information available in pictures. *Leonardo, 4,* 27–35.

Gibson, J. J. (1973). On the concept of formless invariants. *Leonardo, 6,* 43–45.

Gibson, J. J. (1979). *The ecological approach to visual perception.* Boston: Houghton Mifflin.

Gillson, G. (1996). *Spatial ambiguity.* Brooklyn: Rhombic Press.

Goldstein, E. B. (1979). Rotation of objects in pictures viewed at an angle: Evidence for different properties of two types of pictorial space. *Journal of Experimental Psychology: Human Perception and Performance, 5,* 78–87.

Goldstein, E. B. (1987). Spatial layout, orientation relative to the observer, and perceived rotation in pictures viewed at an angle. *Journal of Experimental Psychology: Human Perception and Performance, 14,* 256–266.

Gombrich, E. H. (1963). The cartoonist's armoury. In E. H. Gombrich (Ed.), *Mediations on a hobby horse* (pp. 127–142). London: Phaidon Press.

Gombrich, E. H. (1972). *Art and illusion.* (2nd ed.). Princeton, NJ: Princeton University Press.

Gombrich, E. H. (1979). *The sense of order.* London: Phaidon Press.

Goodman, N. (1968). *The languages of art.* Indianapolis, IN: Bobbs-Merrill.

Groensteen, T., & Peeters, B. (1994). *L'invention de la bande dessinée.* Paris: Hermann.

Hagen, M. (1979). A new theory of the psychology of representational art. In C. F. Nodine & D. F. Fisher (Eds.), *Perception and pictorial representation* (pp. 196–212). New York: Praeger.

Hagen, M. (1980). Generative theory: A perceptual theory of pictorial representation. In M. Hagen (Ed.), *The perception of pictures* (Vol. 2, pp. 3–46). New York: Academic Press.

Hagen, M. (1986). *Varieties of realism.* Cambridge, UK: Cambridge University Press.

Halloran, T. O. (1989). Picture perception is array-specific: Viewing angle versus apparent orientation. *Perception & Psychophysics, 45,* 467–482.

Halloran, T. O. (1993). The frame turns also: Factors in differential rotation in pictures. *Perception & Psychophysics, 54,* 496–508.

Harvey, P. D. A. (1980). *The history of topographical maps: Symbols, pictures, and surveys.* London: Thames & Hudson.

Hayes, A., & Ross, J. (1995). Lines of sight. In R. Gregory, J. Harris, P. Heard, & D. Rose (Eds.), *The artful eye* (pp. 339–352). Oxford: Oxford University Press.

Helmholtz, H. von (1925). *Handbook of physiological optics (Vol. 3).* J. P. Southall (Trans.). Menasha, WI: Optical Society of America. [Originally published in 1867].

Hirschfeld, A. (1970). *The world of Hirschfeld.* New York: H. N. Abrams.

Hochberg, J. (1962). The psychophysics of pictorial perception. *Audio-Visual Communication Review, 10,* 22–54.

Hochberg, J. (1966). Representative sampling and the purposes of perceptual research: Pictures of the world, and the world of pictures. In K. R. Hammond (Ed.), *The psychology of Egon Brunswik* (pp. 361–381). New York: Holt, Rinehart, and Winston.

Hochberg, J. (1971). Perception. In J. W. Kling & L. A. Riggs (Eds.), *Handbook of experimental psychology* (3rd ed., pp. 396–550). New York: Holt, Rinehart, and Winston.

Hochberg, J. (1972). The representation of things and people. In E. H. Gombrich, J. Hochberg, & M. Black (Eds.), *Art, perception, and reality* (pp. 47–94). Baltimore, MD: Johns Hopkins Press.

Hochberg, J. (1995). The construction of pictorial meaning. In T. A. Sebeok & D. J. Umiker-Sebeok (Eds.), *Advances in visual semiotics* (pp. 111–162). Amsterdam: Mouton de Gruyter.

Hochberg, J. (1996). The perception of pictures and pictorial art. In M. P. Friedman & E. C. Carterette (Eds.), *Cognitive ecology* (pp. 151–203). San Diego, CA: Academic Press.

Hochberg, J., & Brooks, V. (1962). Pictorial recognition as an unlearned ability: A study of one child's performance. *American Journal of Psychology, 75,* 337–354.

Hoffman, D. D., & Richards, W. R. (1985). Parts of recognition. *Cognition, 18,* 65–96.

Hogarth, W. (1973). *Analysis of beauty.* New York: Garland Publishing. (Original work published 1753)

Holt, E. B. G. (1957). *A documentary history of art.* Garden City, NY: Doubleday.

Ittelson, W. H. (1996). Visual perception of markings. *Psychonomic Bulletin & Review, 3,* 171–187.

Ivins, W. M. (1969). *Prints and visual communication.* New York: Da Capo Press.

Kanizsa, G. (1979). *Organization in vision.* New York: Praeger.

Kennedy, J. (1974). *A psychology of picture perception.* San Francisco: Jossey-Bass.

Koenderink, J. (1990). *Solid shape.* Cambridge, MA: MIT Press.

Koenderink, J., & van Doorn, A. J. (1976). The singularities of visual mapping. *Biological Cybernetics, 24,* 51–59.

Koenderink, J., & van Doorn, A. J. (1982). The shape of smooth objects and the way contours end. *Perception, 11,* 129–137.

Koffka, K. (1935). *Principles of Gestalt psychology.* New York: Harcourt.

Kellogg, R., & O'Dell, S. (1967). *The psychology of children's art.* New York: Random House.

Kosslyn, S. M. (1994). *Elements of graph design.* New York: Freeman.

Kubovy, M. (1986). *The psychology of perspective and Renaissance art.* Cambridge, UK: Cambridge University Press.

Laboratoire de Préhistoire du Musée de l'Homme. (1982). *Les premiers habitants de l'Europe.* Paris: Musée d'Histoire Naturelle.

Leeuwenberg, E. (1971). A perceptual coding language for visual and auditory form. *American Journal of Psychology, 84,* 307–347.

Leeuwenberg, E., & Boselie, F. (1988). Against the likelihood principle in visual form perception. *Psychological Review, 95,* 485–491.

Levine, D. (1976). *Artists, authors, and others: Drawings.* Washington, DC: Smithsonian Institution Press.

Levit, H. (1976). *Views of Rome, then and now.* New York: Dover.

Lorblanchet, M. (1995). *Les grottes ornées de la prehistoire: Nouveaux regards.* Paris: Editions Errance.

Marey, E. J. (1978). *La méthode graphique dans les sciences expérimentales et particulièrement en physiologie et médecine.* Paris: G. Masson.

Margerie, A. de (Ed.). (1994). *Gustave Caillebotte, 1848–1894.* Paris: Réunion des Musées Nationaux.

Marr, D. (1982). *Vision.* San Francisco: Freeman.

Massaro, D. W. (1987). *Speech perception by ear and by eye: A paradigm for psychological research.* Hillsdale, NJ: Erlbaum Associates.

Massaro, D. W., & Friedman, D. (1990). Models of integration given multiple sources of information. *Psychological Review, 97,* 224–252.

Massironi, M. (1982). *Vedere con il disegno.* Padova: Franco Muzzi & C. Editore.

Massironi, M. (1989). *Commuicari per immagini.* Milan: Il Mulino.

McCloud, S. (1993). *Understanding comics.* Northampton, MA: Kitchen Sink Press.

Mill, J. S. (1842). Bailey on Berkeley's theory of vision. In J. S. Mill (1874), *Dissertations and discussions* (Vol. 2, pp. 162–191). New York: Holt.

Mitchell, W. J. (1992). *The reconfigured eye: Visual truth in a post-photographic era.* Cambridge, MA: MIT Press.

Mitchell, W. J. T. (1995). *Picture theory.* Chicago: University of Chicago Press.

Mithen, S. (1996). *The prehistory of the mind.* London: Thames & Hudson.

Newhall, B. (1964). *The history of photography.* New York: The Museum of Modern Art.

Nougier, L. R. (1969). *Art préhistorique.* Paris: Librarie Générale Française.

Palmer, S. E. (1978). Fundamental aspects of cognitive representation. In E. Rosch & B. B. Lloyd (Eds.), *Cognition and categorization* (pp. 259–303). Hillsdale, NJ: Erlbaum Associates.

Palmer, S. E. (in press). *Visual science.* Cambridge, MA: MIT Press.

Palmer, S. E., Rosch, E., & Chase, P. (1981). Canonical perspective and the representation of objects. In J. Long & A. Baddeley (Eds.), *Attention and performance 9* (pp. 135–151). Hillsdale, NJ: Erlbaum.

Panofsky, E. (1955). *The life and art of Albrecht Dürer.* Princeton, NJ: Princeton University Press.

Penrose, L. S., & Penrose, R. (1958). Impossible objects: A special type of illusion. *British Journal of Psychology, 49,* 31–33.

Perkins, D. (1975). A definition of caricature and caricature and recognition. *Studies in the Anthropology of Visual Communication, 2,* 1–23.

Pirenne, M. H. (1970). *Optics, painting, & photography.* Cambridge, UK: Cambridge University Press.

Pirenne, M. H. (1975). Vision and art. In E. C. Carterrette & M. P. Friedman (Eds.), *Handbook of perception: V. Seeing* (pp. 434–490). New York: Academic Press.

Ratoosh, P. (1949). On interposition as a cue for the perception of distance. *Proceedings of the National Academy of Sciences, Washington, 35,* 257–259.

Rhodes, G., Brennan, S., & Carey, S. (1987). Identification and ratings of caricatures: Implications for mental representations of faces. *Cognitive Psychology, 19,* 473–497.

Richards, W. A., Dawson, B., & Whittington, D. (1986). Encoding contour shape by curvature extrema. *Journal of the Optical Society of America, A, 3,* 1483–1489.

Richards, W. A., Koenderink, J., & Hoffman, D. D. (1987). Inferring three-dimensional shapes from two-dimensional silhouettes. *Journal of the Optical Society of America, A, 4,* 1168–1175.

Richter, J. P. (Ed. & Trans.). (1883). *The literary works of Leonardo da Vinci.* London: Samson, Low, Marston, Searle, & Rivington. Reprinted as *The notebooks of Leonardo da Vinci.* New York: Dover, 1970.

Robinson, J. O. (1972). *The psychology of visual illusion.* London: Hutchinson University Library.

Rock, I. (1983). *The logic of perception.* Cambridge, MA: MIT Press.

Rock, I. (1984). *Perception.* New York: Scientific American.

Rock, I. (1997). *Indirect perception.* Cambridge, MA: MIT Press.

Rogers, S. (1995). Perceiving pictorial space. In W. Epstein & S. Rogers (Eds.), *Perception of space and motion* (pp. 119–163). San Diego, CA: Academic Press.

Rosenblum, L. D., Saldaña, H. M., & Carello, C. (1993). Dynamic constraints on pictorial action lines. *Journal of Experimental Psychology: Human Perception and Performance, 19,* 381–396.

Rubin, E. (1915). *Synsoplevede figurer.* Copenhagen: Gyldendals.

Rumelhart, D., & Norman, D. (1988). Representation in memory. In R. C. Atkinson, R. J. Herrnstein, G. Lindzey, & R. D. Luce (Eds.), *Steven's handbook of experimental psychology* (Vol. 2, pp. 511–587). New York: Wiley.

Ruspoli, M. (1986). *Lascaux.* Paris: Bordas.

Russell, B. (1914). *Our knowledge of the external world.* Chicago: Open Court.

Sartre, J.-P. (1948). *L'imagination.* Paris: Presses Universitaires de France.

Scharf, A. (1968). *Art and photography.* London: Penguin.

Schier, F. (1986). *Deeper into pictures.* Cambridge, UK: Cambridge University Press.

Schivelbusch, W. (1988). *Disenchanted night.* Berkeley: University of California Press.

Schmid, C. F. (1983). *Statistical graphics.* New York: Wiley.

Schuster, D. H. (1964). A new ambiguous figure. *American Journal of Psychology, 77,* 673.

Schwartz, R. (1996). Directed perception. *Philosophical Psychology, 9,* 81–91.

Schwartz, R. (1997). Pictures, puzzles, and paradigms. *Philosophia Scientiae, 2,* 107–115.

Sedgwick, H. (1986). Space perception. In K. R. Boff, L. Kaufman, & J. P. Thomas (Eds.), *Handbook of perception and human poerformance* (Vol. 1, Chap. 21, pp. 1–57). New York: Wiley.

Shannon, C. E., & Weaver, W. (1949). *The mathematical theory of communication.* Urbana, IL: The University of Illinois Press.

Shepard, R. N. (1990). *Mind sights.* New York: Freeman.

Snyder, J. P. (1993). *Flattening the earth: 2000 years of map projections.* Chicago: University of Chicago Press.

Solso, R. L. (1994). *Cognition and the visual arts.* Cambridge, MA: MIT Press.

Sommers, P. van (1984). *Drawing and cognition.* New York: Cambridge University Press.

Spence, I. (1990). Visual psychophysics of simple graphical elements. *Journal of Experimental Psychology: Human Perception and Performance, 16,* 683–692.

Speed, H. (1913). *The practice and science of drawing.* London: Seeley, Service, & Company.

Spillman, L., & Werner, J. S. (1990). *Visual perception: The neurophysiological foundations.* San Diego: Academic Press.

Staudt, K. G. C. von (1847). *Geometrie der lage.* Nürnburg: Fr. Horn.

Steinberg, S. (1966). *Le masque.* Paris: Maeght Editeur.

Steinberg, S. (1982). *Still life and architecture.* New York: The Pace Gallery.

Stevens, P. S. (1974). *Patterns in nature.* Boston: Little, Brown.

Topper, D. R. (1977). On interpreting pictorial art: Reflections on J. J. Gibson's invariant hypothesis. *Leonardo, 10,* 195–300.

Topper, D. R. (1979). Further reflections on J. J. Gibson's hypothesis of picture perception. *Leonardo, 12,* 135–136.

Toulet, E. (1988). *Cinématographie, invention du siècle.* Paris: Découvertes Gallimard.

Tufte, E. R. (1983). *The visual display of quantitative information.* Cheshire, CT: Graphics Press.

Tufte, E. R. (1990). *Envisioning information.* Cheshire, CT: Graphics Press.

Tukey, J. W. (1970). *Exploratory data analysis.* Reading, MA: Addison-Wesley.

Turner, A. R. (1993). *Inventing Leonardo.* New York: Knopf.

Wade, N. (1995). *Psychologists in word and image.* Cambridge, MA: MIT Press.

Wallach, H. (1987). Perceiving a stable environment when one moves. *Annual Review of Psychology, 38,* 1–27.

White, J. (1957). *The birth and rebirth of pictorial space.* London: Faber & Faber.

Willats, J. (1990). The draughtsman's contract: How an artist creates an image. In H. Barlow, C. Blakemore, & M. Weston-Smith (Eds.), *Images and understanding* (pp. 235–256). Cambridge, UK: Cambridge University Press.

Willats, J. (1997). *Art and representation.* Princeton: Princeton University Press.

Witkin, A. P., & Tenenbaum, J. M. (1983). On the role of structure in vision. In J. Beck, B. Hope, & A. Rosenfeld (Eds.), *Human and machine vision* (pp. 481–543). New York: Academic Press.

Wollheim, R. (1968). *Art and its objects.* New York: Harper & Row.

Woodworth, R. S. (1938). *Experimental psychology.* New York: Holt.

Wymer, J. J. (1982). *The paleolithic age.* New York: St. Martin's Press.

CHAPTER 7

The Internalization of Perceptual Processing Constraints

Dennis R. Proffitt
Mary K. Kaiser

I. INTRODUCTION

Most discussions of perception begin with the observation that there is more to perception than can be accounted for by an analysis of the optical information upon which it is based. An example of this insufficiency of proximal information is the inverse projection problem. Determining the shape of a retinal projection is a well-posed problem given that the form, size, distance, and orientation of the object relative to the eye is known. On the other hand, if the shape of the projection is known, then determining the form, size, distance, and orientation of the projected object is an ill-posed problem that cannot be solved without the employment of constraints inherent to the perceptual system (Poggio, Torre, & Koch, 1985). This is the inverse projection problem.

In everyday perception, the ambiguity of optical information is rarely recognized. People perceive a definite visual world even though that world is not uniquely specified by the available optical information. This implies that the perceptual system introduces constraints in the processing of proximal information. These constraints are internal to the system, meaning that they are brought to the occasion of perception by the perceiver as opposed to being detected in the currently available optical information.

In this chapter, we provide an organized survey of the wide variety of internalization proposals by sorting them into four distinct classes, each defined by the nature of the constraints subject to internalization. Our treatment is far from exhaustive, since a truly comprehensive account would include just about every-thing in the field of perceptual research. Also, all of the accounts that we survey have problems and detractors, but a critical analysis is beyond the scope of this chap-ter. Rather, we have attempted to survey the kinds of proposals that have been made and to exemplify each with a discussion of research that clearly embodies the inter-nalization notion under consideration.

II. THE VARIETIES OF INTERNALIZATION PROPOSALS

Four distinct kinds of perceptual processing constraints can be identified: *statistical regularities, geometrical optics, universal laws of organization,* and *group concepts.* Within particular accounts, constraints of more than one kind are sometimes proposed. Moreover, constraints of one sort often imply constraints of another.

A. Internalization of Statistical Regularities

Although there are an infinite number of distal objects, having different configura-tions and being at different observer-relative distances, that could yield identical retinal projections, not all of these objects are equally likely to occur. Thus, a use-ful perceptual strategy would be for the perceptual system to internalize the prob-ability of occurrence for the various objects that it encounters. In this manner, the perceptual system would interpret an image as the most likely distal object consis-tent with the prevailing stimulation. This is a very old and lasting idea. For exam-ple, Helmholtz (1894/1971) proposed that perceptions are constrained by regular-ities that have been derived from experience and imprinted into memory:

> Among the most universal and exceptionless of these are combinations of observed phe-nomena resulting from laws of nature, which require either their simultaneous occur-rence or their uniform sequence in a specific period of time. While simultaneous occur-rences or particular sequences which are the result of lawless accident will, to be sure, be repeated occasionally, they will not be repeated without exception. (p. 503)

Today, the internalization of experienced regularities is exemplified in the work on parallel distributed processing (PDP) models. (See McClelland and Rumelhart, 1986, for a superb introduction to this area.) PDP models consist of processing units analogous to neurons. There are input units, output units, and typically some number of layers of intermediary units called hidden units. The input units are connected to the hidden units in a one-to-many fashion (often exhaustively), and the hidden units are connected to the output units in a similar one-to-many way (see also Hochberg, chap. 9, this volume). Like neurons, the units can be either excitatory or inhibitory, and they pass some proportion of their level of activity on to postsynaptic units; the proportion is determined by a weight. There are numerous other important parameters in the structure and functioning of these models; however, this sketch will suffice for our purposes. A stimulus consists of vectors across the input units that affect their activation level. This activation propagates throughout the network, resulting in some pattern of activation for the output units.

A PDP network can detect and classify regularities in its stimulus inputs as the result of a learning process that typically requires supervised training. Following the presentation of each stimulus, the values of the output units are compared with their desired values and an error-correction procedure takes place in which synaptic weights are adjusted toward desired values, typically as the result of a process termed "back-propagation." This feedback of error-correction information is the least plausible aspect of these networks as models of actual nervous system functioning (Crick, 1989).

In pattern-associating PDP networks, the output values that should be associated with a given input must be known a priori by the system; otherwise error-correction cannot occur. Similarly, many accounts of perceptual learning require that the distal state of affairs must be known by some means other than the information currently available within a modality. For example, as discussed by Hochberg (chap. 1, this volume) Berkeley (1709/1963) proposed that visual information could never provide the necessary conditions for perceiving extent or depth. Rather, he argued, purposive actions provide sensations of extent that, over time, become associated with visual awareness. In modern terms, kinesthetic information provides information about actual depth, information that can be used to train the visual network to respond appropriately to the depth information latent in its visual inputs.

The notion of supervised learning can be used to distinguish between two classes of internalization approaches. Those in the first class are like Berkeley's account in that they entail supervised learning about relationships between proximal information and the distal events that cause them. Those in the second class internalize statistical regularities without supervision. This latter class deals not with discovering regularities between inputs and distal events but rather with extracting regularities between different dimensions within sensory inputs.

1. Perceiving the Most Probable Object Consistent with Proximal Stimulation

Following the Berkeley–Helmholtz tradition, many accounts suggest that the perceptual system learns about the predictive probabilities relating stimulus information to distal events. Within this class of theories there is a common thread—the aforementioned need for supervised learning—but there are also important distinctions. Some theories propose that the perceptual system acquires knowledge of object properties that can, in turn, be used to delimit perceptual interpretations. Other accounts stress that stimulus variables may become predictive of distal relationships. Finally, a third type of account appeals to the likelihood that the object is not being observed from an unlikely vantage point. The first sort of proposal results in top-down processing, whereas the second two function in a more bottom-up manner.

a. Knowledge about Objects

The most familiar examples of perceptions seemingly based upon object knowledge are to be found in the Ames demonstrations (Ittelson, 1968). For example, in the distorted room demonstration, the observer views a nonrectangular room from a specific point of observation. The room was fabricated so as to project to this vantage point an image that is consistent with rectangularity. An observer in this situation perceives a rectangular room. Ames proposed that, in general, perceptions are based upon a multiplicity of visual cues that are weighted by their past prognostic reliability. Some of these cues, such as binocular disparity, are clearly bottom-up in nature, whereas others exert top-down influences. In the case of the distorted room, he suggested that the surface corresponding to the floor is perceived as a floor. Floors are known to be horizontal, and thus, this floor is perceived to be so when in fact it is not.

Note here the requirement for supervised training. Because every image of a horizontal surface is ambiguous as to whether it is, indeed, horizontal, the discovery that floors are almost always horizontal must be based upon information other than singular images. Multiple views of floors can specify their orientation. This information, obtained over time, could be used to train the perceptual system to construe singular images of floors as being horizontal. Note also that, in this example, the perceiver's probability knowledge influences perception in a top-down manner: The surface is first categorized and then probabilistic knowledge about the category is retrieved and used.

Another demonstration brings this point home. Ames had constructed two rectangular rooms, one with normal siding and the other with leaves affixed densely over all of its walls, floor, and ceiling. The leaves gave this latter room a very odd and unfamiliar appearance. Viewers observed each of these rooms wearing aniseikonic glasses that distorted the retinal projection. When observing the normal room while wearing the glasses, observers reported that it looked rectangular. The cues specifying its "room-ness" were dominant. On the other hand, when viewing the leaf room while wearing the distorting glasses, viewers reported its configuration not to be rectangular, but rather to be consistent with the distorted projection. In this case, the perceptual system placed a greater weight on the binocular cues specifying a nonrectangular configuration.

b. Image Features Having Probabilistic Relationships to Object Relationships

Probabilistic knowledge could be acquired and used to delimit perceptual interpretations in a more bottom-up fashion. Kubovy (1986) argued that the Ames distorted room demonstration could be explained without reference to familiarity. He noted that all of the surfaces in an Ames distorted room meet at edges that projected fork or arrow junctions consistent with Perkins's laws. Perkins's laws were discovered independently by Perkins (1972, 1973) and Shepard (1981). The first of Perkins's two laws states that a fork junction (a shape like the letter Y) is perceived to be the projection of the vertex of a rectangular solid if and only if each of the three angles forming the Y-configuration is greater than 90 degrees. The second law states that an arrow junction is perceived to be the vertex of a rectangular solid if and only if each of the small interior angles is less than 90 degrees and together sum to more than 90 degrees. These laws will correctly detect rectangularity if the object is, in fact, rectangular and is not viewed too peripherally (Kubovy, 1986). Returning to the Ames distorted room demonstration, Kubovy suggested that it need not be identified as a room prior to the evocation of a rectangularity assumption. Rather, the detection of fork and arrow junctions consistent with Perkins's laws will spontaneously evoke a perception of rectangularity. To demonstrate the plausibility of his position, Kubovy provided a drawing of an unfamiliar object that conforms to Perkins's laws and is perceived to be rectangular.

That Perkins's laws are deeply internalized is further supported by a remarkable set of studies by Enns and Rensink (1991) (see chap. 9, Hochberg, this volume). In a visual search task, they presented either fork or arrow junctions. Target and distractors were identical except that the target was oriented at a 180-degree angle relative to the array of distractors. When the junctions obeyed Perkins's laws, search occurred preattentively, whereas configurations that violated Perkins's laws required slower, more effortful search. Similarly, when the junctions occurred in depictions of simple polyhedra, search times were again strongly influenced by whether the configuration obeyed Perkins's law.

Note again that an internalization of Perkins's laws would require supervised learning, either for the individual or for the species. A junction consistent with Perkins's laws is ambiguous with respect to the orientation of surfaces that could have produced it. The ecological reliability of Perkins's laws depends upon the overwhelming prevalence of rectangularity in our artificial world, a notion that seems to us to be exactly what Brunswik (1956) had in mind in his ecological account of perception. Learning that, on most occasions, junctions consistent with Perkins's laws are projections of rectangular objects requires a discovery of rectangularity by some other means. Again, seeing multiple perspectives of the object could serve as the informational basis for supervision.

c. Generic Sampling

The classical proposal that the perceptual system assumes that a given view is not an improbable accident, variously called generic sampling (cf. Nakayama & Shimojo, 1992), the coincidence-explanation principle (Rock, 1983), and nonaccidental properties (Binford, 1971; Lowe, 1985), remains widely popular today (Hochberg, 1972; Hoffman & Richards, 1985; Kanade & Kender, 1983); see Hochberg (chap. 9, this volume). When looking at a drawing of a circle, for example, one perceives it to be a two-dimensional (2-D) configuration and not the circular surface of a cylinder viewed from a unique vantage point normal to the surface. Almost all perspectives on a cylinder will show its sides as well as one of its circular surfaces. Only when viewed from a small number of special points of view would a cylinder project a simple circle or rectangle. The principle of generic views states that the perceptual system assumes that its current vantage point is not an accidental one. Returning to the Ames distorted room demonstration, the experimental vantage point is truly unique in that it is the only one that would result in the perception of a rectangular room. All other points of view show the room to be distorted. By the generic sampling principle, the rectangular perception is due to the assumption that the vantage point is not accidental. This approach requires the perceptual system to undergo some degree of supervised training so as to become familiar with what object properties are to be anticipated when generic sampling occurs. It should be noted that Anderson and Julesz (1995) have pointed out that, for a given image, the principle of generic sampling may make different predictions depending upon the size scale at which the evaluation is made. That is, the application of the generic sampling principle to global features may result in a different perceptual interpretation relative to one that analyzes the image at a smaller size scale.

2. Extracting Statistical Properties Inherent in Sensory Inputs

Another perceptual learning process requires no supervision and entails an acquisition of statistical regularities across perceptual dimensions as these regularities occur over time. The two exemplars of this class are associative learning and perceptual adaptation. Both of these types of learning make use of quasi-Hebbian learning mechanisms.

As discussed at greater length by Hochberg (chap. 9, this volume) Hebb (1949) proposed a basic learning principle by which changes in synaptic weights occurred as a consequence of both pre- and postsynaptic neural firing rates. Consider the pair of neurons depicted in Figure 1A. The essence of Hebb's rule is that the weight determining the proportion of neuron **A**'s activity that is added to that of neuron **B** is instantaneously increased in proportion to the product of both **A** and **B**'s activity level. In other words, the magnitude of **A**'s influence on **B** increases in proportion to the likelihood that they tend to be active at the same time. This basic mechanism has been refined to account for the attenuation of weights due to habituation (Horn, 1985) and for the magnitude of current weightings (Levy & Desmond, 1985). Unlike supervised learning mechanisms such as back propagation, Hebbian learning mechanisms have a high degree of neural plausibility (Levy, Colbert, & Desmond, 1990; Levy & Desmond, 1985).

a. Associative Learning

In classical conditioning, separate stimuli come to be associated as a result of their repeated co-occurrence over some time frame. This affords the organism with an opportunity to internalize probabilities about the covariation of events in its environment. Figure 1B shows a simple neural arrangement capable of this sort of associative learning. Hawkins, Abrams, Carew, and Kandel (1983) provided evidence that this sort of arrangement is found in *Aplysia;* Gluck and Thompson (1987) developed a sophisticated treatment of the relevant modeling issues. To the neural arrangement in Figure 1A is added a third neuron, **F,** in Figure 1B called a presynaptic facilitation mechanism by Kandel and Tauc (1965). Learning is proposed to occur via a Hebbian-like mechanism in which the weight of **A** on **B** changes as a function of the product of the activities of **A** and **F,** minus the activity of **A**. In other words, the influence of **A** on **B** increases whenever both **A** and **F** are active and decreases when **A** but not **F** is active. In the context of classical conditioning,

A

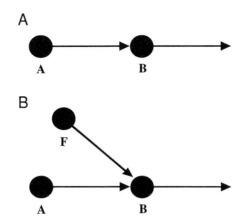

B

FIGURE 1   Simple neural connections. In (A), Neuron **A** has an excitatory synapse with Neuron **B**. In (B), both Neurons **A** and **F** have an excitatory influence on Neuron **B**.

think of **A** as receiving information about the presence of a conditioned stimulus (CS), **F** as indicating the presence of an unconditioned stimulus (UCS), and **B** as influencing the relevant conditioned response (CR). Over repeating pairings of the UCS with the CS, the influence of **A** on **B** will grow in a manner consistent with classical conditioning. Thus, if there is a statistical regularity in the co-occurrence of two stimuli, then this probability can be internalized through the change in the appropriate synaptic weights.

It could be argued that classical conditioning is not a good instance of perceptual learning because the learning may be on the motor side of the sensorimotor process. We have two responses to this objection. The first response is that the distinction between sensory and motor processes is one that is becoming increasingly difficult to make. Visual pathways segregate in early vision in a manner that reflects the motor functions that they subserve (Milner & Goodale, 1995). Second, classical conditioning can be used to explain purely visual aftereffects, such as the McCollough effect.[1] At the microscopic level, however, the analogy of classical conditioning to associative learning in the cerebral cortex is tenuous. The primary site of

[1] The McCollough effect is an orientation-specific color aftereffect (McCollough, 1965). One way to evoke this aftereffect is to present a pattern containing red horizontal and green vertical stripes. After staring at this pattern for a minute or so, the observer inspects a similar pattern in which all of the stripes are white. The aftereffect that is experienced is that the horizontal and vertical stripes now appear tinged with the complement of the previously presented color: white horizontal stripes appear pale green and vertical ones appear pink. Siegal and Allan (1992; Siegal, Allan, & Eissenberg, 1992) proposed that this aftereffect is an instance of classical conditioning: the UCS is color, the CS is orientation, and the CR is color adaptation. Although various specifics of their proposal have been called into question (e.g., by Dodwell & Humphrey, 1993; Durgin & Proffitt, 1996; Skowbo, 1984), this general class of theories remains one of the candidate explanations for this phenomenon.

synaptic modification in simple classical conditioning is at the cerebellum Purkinje cell (Krupa & Thompson, 1995). Moreover, the modification rules operating at this site seem to differ from those seen in the cerebral cortex. (Compare Ito, 1989, with Levy, Colbert, & Desmond, 1990).

b. Adaptation

Phenomena like aftereffects are also amenable to explanations in terms of adaptation. There are also accounts that stress mechanisms of recalibration and error-correction (e.g., Bedford, 1993, 1995; Dodwell & Humphrey, 1990, 1993; Held, 1980); however, these will not be discussed because they require some form of supervised learning. Rather, we think that there is a great deal to be gained in pursuing unsupervised mechanisms, and in this regard, we find the proposals of Helson (1964) and Barlow (1990; Barlow & Földiák, 1989) to be especially promising.

Aftereffects are often thought of as entailing fatigue, and once this notion is raised, the phenomena lose much of their interest-grabbing power. Helson (1964), on the other hand, emphasized the information enhancement functions of adaptation. Neural response may diminish as a result of prolonged exposure; however, this need not implicate fatigue; rather, it may imply a growth of inhibition or the possibility of active processes that weaken or remove excitation. Moreover, unlike error-correction mechanisms that assume some homeostatic state, Helson proposed that adaptation served the function of establishing a reference point from which departures from the expected could more easily be detected.

Barlow (1990; Barlow & Földiák, 1989) presented an elegant model of contingent adaptation that makes use of simple inhibitory networks to remove the correlation between physical stimuli so as to enhance the detection of uncorrelated events. Durgin (1996; Durgin & Proffitt, 1996) has applied this model to the phenomenon of color contingent aftereffects of texture density. The functional virtue of such adaptive mechanisms is that they enhance the perceptual system's sensitivity to departures from its prior associative experience.

Returning to the Helmholtzian notion of internalizing statistical regularities, Barlow and Földiák (1989) showed how their model of inhibitory decorrelation can achieve much of what Helmholtz had in mind. Helmholtz suggested that we see the most probable object or event consistent with the prevailing stimulation. Barlow and Földiák provided a familiar example. If a stereogram is viewed while translating the head back-and-forth, then the nearer objects will appear to move in the same direction as the observer. An inferential explanation of this phenomenon goes as follows: Normally, when stationary objects are viewed in depth by a moving observer, motion parallax occurs. In the stereogram situation, this motion parallax is absent. In order to reconcile this conflict, the perceptual system derives an interpretation in which the objects within the scene move in a manner that would nullify their motion parallax and thereby bring the stereo and motion parallax information into concordance. Barlow and Földiák's model accounts for this phenomenon by postulating that some population of neurons sensitive to stereo depth and others sensitive to motion parallax are connected by mutually inhibitory connections so as to nullify their covariance. When the stereogram is observed, the inhibition emanating from the stereo neurons causes an imbalance in the motion-detection neurons, such that the scene is interpreted as motion in the opposite direction from a stationary scene evoking canonical parallax. Barlow and Földiák (1989) were careful to note that their explanation is highly speculative; however, with elegant simplicity, it shows how the internalization of statistical structure could be achieved without supervision or unconscious inferences.

B. Internalization of Geometrical Optics

A large body of research in psychophysics is motivated by a knowledge that certain stimulus variables could, in principle, provide information about environmental properties. The "in principle" argument stems from a geometrical analysis of the stimulus in terms of what an ideal observer in possession of the relevant capabilities could derive from it. Assuming observers are found to be sensitive to the stimulus variables and that they appear to extract the relevant environmental properties from them, the question then turns to the nature of underlying perceptual processes and the degree to which they implement the geometrical rules that were employed in the ideal-observer analysis. Consider, for example, the absolute distance information provided by a single point of light in a binocular viewing situation. Because a point source is being used, binocular parallax and size cues have been eliminated; however, convergence information could be useful. Descartes (1637/1956) described how convergence could indicate distance through an application of "natural geometry." Clearly, if the vergence angle and the distance between the eyes is known, then the distance to the object could be computed; moreover, we know that convergence information alone is quite effective in evoking absolute distance perceptions for distances within a meter (Foley, 1985). Does this imply that the perceptual system possesses an internalized geometry, and if so, what form does it take? (See also Cutting, chap. 4, this volume).

Our development of this issue will focus on two concerns. First, unlike convergence, almost all perceptual information is subject to the inverse projection problem regardless of whether the interpretive system is in possession of the relevant geometrical competence. In order to use an internalized geometry, the system must make use of a priori constraints that make basic assumptions about the effective environment. The first part of this section will examine the different ways in which internalized geometries have been construed, and the second will discuss proposals of a priori constraints.

1. Internalized Geometries

Modern theories that employ internalized geometries typically trace their origins back to Helmholtz (1867/1925), although the notion that the perceptual system performs geometrical computations is far older. For example, the 11th-century physicist, Ibn al-Haytham (Alhazen), concluded that, "We judge the size of an object by comparison of its visual angle with its distance" (Reimann, 1902, p. 3; translated from German by Kaufman & Rock, 1989). A well-known exemplar of this notion is a demonstration reported by Emmert (1881). An observer first forms an afterimage by looking at a bright light and then looks at near and far surfaces. The afterimage will appear to be localized on whatever surface is being inspected, and thus will appear to be located at different observer-relative distances. Note that the visual angle of the afterimage remains constant, whereas its apparent distance varies as the observer looks about. Emmert observed that the apparent size of the afterimage was larger when looking at far surfaces as opposed to nearer ones. From this observation he formulated what has become known as *Emmert's Law*, which states that the perceived size of an afterimage is proportional to its apparent distance. Emmert's Law is a special case of the size–distance invariance hypothesis, which states that an image subtending a constant visual angle will increase in perceived size as perceived distance increases (Gogel & Mertz, 1989; Weintraub & Gardner, 1970).

Two important generalizations are implied by the size–distance invariance hypothesis. First, the perceptual rules that relate perceived size and distance apply to psychological variables; that is, the prescribed invariance is between perceived variables, not physical ones. The second generalization is that the perceptual system follows rules that resemble the geometry of central projection. Both of these generalizations are inherent to many psychological accounts of internalized geometry; however, other accounts—especially those that derive from computational accounts of vision—apply internalized geometries to optical as opposed to psychological variables. Epstein (1995) noted that, in the former theories, the perceptual system is *rule following,* meaning that once perceived variables such as distance are derived, the perceptual system follows geometrical rules to derive additional perceptual variables, such as apparent size. Computational theories, on the other hand, were characterized by Epstein as *rule instantiating.* These accounts appeal to optical as opposed to perceived variables and employ algorithms that obey geometrical laws without implying that the perceptual system has access to a general system of geometrical principles. Theories of the first sort will be discussed first.

a. Internalized Geometries Applied to Perceived Variables

An important and elegant account in this area is Gogel's (1990, 1993) theory of "phenomenal geometry." Gogel argued that the perception of location and change of location depend upon three psychological variables—perceived distance, perceived direction, and perceived self-motion—combined within the appropriate equations prescribed by Euclidean geometry. Consider an example. When an observer moves back and forth relative to a stationary object, the object ought to appear stationary; however, sometimes it appears to move as the observer moves. An example of this concomitant motion is observed when an observer moves his or her head while examining a stereogram. As discussed in an earlier section on adaptation, in such a situation the nearer objects appear to move in the same direction as the observer. Gogel's (1990, 1993) phenomenal geometry specifies perceived concomitant motion, W', with the following equation:

$$W' = K' - D' \, tan(\phi'/2),$$

where K' is the perceived lateral distance moved by the observer's head, D' is the perceived distance to the target, and ϕ' is the perceived angular displacement of the target. If all of the perceived variables are equivalent to their distal counterparts, then no concomitant motion will be seen when a stationary target is viewed by a moving observer. In the case of the illusory motion seen when a moving observer views a stereogram, the perceived distances are not correct because every object in the scene is actually at the same distance. Disparity information, however, causes the perceived distance of some objects to be nearer than others, and thus, D' is smaller than the actual distance, D. The above equation predicts the perceived motion as a necessary outcome of misperceiving distance.

The most thorough presentation of this sort of approach is found in Rock's (1983) *Logic of Perception;* in its concluding chapter, he posed the question, "What are the principles about the behavior of light that have been internalized and that are relevant for perception?" (1983, p. 325). He concluded that the perceptual system has internalized at least four different kinds of principles. The first consists of the laws of central projection, including (a) the relationship between visual angle, distance, and size, (b) the laws of perspective foreshortening, (c) linear perspective, and (d) those principles required to derive 3-D structure from moving objects, as in the kinetic depth effect. The second sort consists of internalized rules concerned with the optical consequences of self-motions. Within this class are principles for extracting form and distance from motion parallax and binocular disparities. The third class deals with the perceptual implications for perceiving occlusion and transparency. Finally, the fourth kind of rules refers to reflectance and illumination laws that constrain the perception of surface lightness and brightness.

Rock argued that geometrical laws determined the form of perceptual experience and that the laws of physics, apart from those that relate to optical projection, are not internalized by the visual system:

> That an object can appear to be suspended in midair or to rise against the pull of gravity or to penetrate an impenetrable surface or to suddenly move without any observable cause may surprise us or puzzle us or amuse or delight us as seemingly magical because we do know about gravity and mechanics even without formal education, but none of these violations of the laws of physics is relevant for visual perception. (1983, p. 325)

Interestingly, even very young infants are surprised when one object appears to pass through another impenetrable one (Baillargeon, 1986; Spelke, Breinlinger, Macomber, & Jacobson, 1992); however, they are not surprised to see an object seemingly suspended in midair (Spelke et al., 1992). Consistent with Rock's position, Spelke et al. assigned the presence or absence of knowledge about physical laws to the domain of cognition as opposed to constraints on perceptual experience (see also Spelke, chap. 11, this volume).

Accounts that apply internalized geometry to perceived variables encounter difficulties when assessments of relevant phenomenal variables are made and it is found that their combination does not predict the perceptual outcome in a reasonable manner. The best example of this is the moon illusion (see Hershenson, 1989; and see Gillam, chap. 5, this volume, for accounts of other illusions).

The moon appears larger when near the horizon than when viewed overhead. Paradoxically, it also appears nearer when viewed near the horizon. This seems to violate the size–distance invariance hypothesis. The moon subtends the same visual angle regardless of its elevation in the sky; however, because it appears nearer at the horizon, it ought to also appear smaller. The most influential account of the moon illusion is Kauffman and Rock's (1962, 1989) "further-bigger-nearer" theory. By this account, the moon's distance is perceptually registered to be farther away when near the horizon than when overhead. *Registered distance* is a preconscious specification of distance that is used by the perceptual system to compute size. Because the moon is registered to be more distant at the horizon, by the size–distance invariance hypothesis, it must be larger. Perceived size is then employed to determine perceived distance, and again employing the size–distance invariance hypothesis, because the moon is larger at the horizon it is perceived to be nearer. In other words, registered distance is used to compute apparent size which, in turn, is used to compute apparent distance. The size–distance–invariance hypothesis is preserved; however, this account departs radically from its predecessors by applying internalized geometry to variables that are not consciously perceived.

b. Internalized Geometries Applied to Optical Variables

Rather than appealing to perceived variables, there is a greater tendency today to analyze a scene into optical variables that can be geometrically related to distal properties of the scene. Consider the example of time to contact (TTC). If an observer is on a collision course with an object, then TTC can be approximately determined by the following equation, first put forth by an astrophysicist (Hoyle, 1957) in a science fiction novel and later developed by Lee (1974, 1976):

$$\text{TTC} = \theta \ / \ \delta\theta/\delta\tau$$

where θ is the current angular extent (in radians) of the object, and $\delta\theta/\delta\tau$ is its rate of expansion. Here, it is assumed that the object is approaching the observer with a constant velocity. Empirical studies have shown that, when presented with the relevant information, people can make reasonably accurate relative and absolute TTC judgments (McLeod & Ross, 1983; Schiff & Detwiler, 1979; Schiff & Oldak, 1990; Simpson, 1988; Todd, 1981). Notice that the TTC formulation is based upon optical variables as opposed to perceived variables.

In general, computational analyses attempt to specify how optical variables could be extracted and related through the appropriate geometrical equations so as to specify environmental properties. In this vein, a considerable amount of effort has been directed at problems such as stereo vision, the computation of optical flow, extracting 3-D structure from patterns of projected motion, and the specification of shape from shading. Consider, for example, the structure-from-motion problem. The first analyses were developed by Ullman (1979, 1983), who showed how three different views of four noncoplanar points would suffice as the minimal conditions for deriving structure from motion. Bennett and Hoffman (1986; Hoffman & Bennett, 1985, 1986) developed and extended this approach. Other strategies to derive 3-D structure from motion have been developed by Koenderink (1986; Koenderink & van Doorn, 1986), Longuet-Higgins and Prazdny (1984), Bennett, Hoffman, Nicola, and Prakash (1989), and Huang and Lee (1989) to name but a few. Todd (1995) provides an excellent survey of this literature.

2. A Priori Constraints

A virtue of computational approaches is the precision with which perceptual problems are explicated. A consequence of this explicitness is that it becomes apparent that more is needed to solve perceptual problems than an internalization of geometrical optics. Poggio, Torre, and Koch (1985) stated that the problems faced by early vision are "ill-posed" problems, meaning that the solution to the inverse projection problem does not reside entirely in the data inherent in optical variables. Poggio et al. stated, "The main idea for 'solving' ill-posed problems, that is for restoring 'well-posedness', is to restrict the class of admissible solutions by introducing suitable a priori knowledge" (p. 315). Ullman's (1979) account of extracting 3-D structure from motion is a good case in point. If objects are allowed to deform as they rotate, then extracting structure from motion becomes an ill-posed problem. Ullman constrained the solution space of this problem by incorporating a rigidity assumption into his model by which only rigid structures could be extracted.[2] Similarly, Grimson (1981) incorporated a constraint by which local surfaces are assumed to be smooth in his implementation of a depth from binocular stereo algorithm. Poggio, Torre, and Koch (1985) discussed a general regularization theory by which a priori constraints on visual processing are viewed as minimization criteria. By this account, the interpretation of the current optical information is constrained by a parameter that is minimized according to some criterion. The constraints on rigidity, local smoothness, and the generic sampling principle (Nakayama & Shimojo, 1992) are all examples of such regularization constraints. The latter constraint, generic sampling, was discussed in the section on internalizing statistical regularities and, indeed, all of these a priori constraints are consistent with the notion that the perceptual system possesses internalized knowledge about environmental regularities that are usually true. In the case of the rigidity constraint, for example, it

---

[2] With respect to human perception, it has long been known that depth and structure can be seen when objects in motion violate the rigidity principle (Braunstein & Anderson, 1986; Hochberg, 1987; von Hornbostel, 1922; see also Hochberg, chap. 9, this volume). In response to such findings, Ullman (1984) modified his rigidity constraint.

could be that causing an object to rotate also causes it to deform; however, this would be highly unlikely. Marr (1982) called such internalized regularities "natural constraints." Consistent with Marr's proposal, at the heart of all accounts entailing the internalization of geometrical optics, lies a priori knowledge about what sorts of conditions are most likely to occur in the world.

C. Internalization of Universal Laws of Organization

Because the brain is part of the physical universe, it obeys universal laws. Once this fact is recognized, the question becomes, Which, if any, of these laws is relevant to the task of understanding perception? Since the brain is made up of physical matter, it is subject to the laws of mechanics, quantum theory, relativity theory, and so forth. But what does that tell us? These physical laws prevail at levels of analysis that have little relevance for perceptual theory. When perceptual theorists look for universal laws of relevance, they are attracted to those that apply to complex systems.

The Gestalt psychologists introduced a systems approach to psychology and proposed that phenomenal experience is constrained by dynamical laws of organization that apply everywhere in the universe. These laws specify what is most simple and natural in the physical universe. Consider first the now classic soap bubble example as an instance of how physical constraints can result in symmetry (Attneave, 1982; Koehler, 1929; Koffka, 1935). A soap bubble consists of a gas surrounded by a liquid film. The law of entropy requires that the ensemble of gas molecules tends toward a state in which the individual molecules are moving in all directions with equal probability. This randomness results in equal pressure on the liquid film at all orientations, thereby producing the spherical shape of the bubble. The sphere is the most symmetrical of all 3-D forms, and thus from the random motions of the gas molecules under the constraint of the soap film emerges order.

In looking at perceptual phenomena, Koffka (1935) and Koehler (1929) saw a similar emergence of order, which they attributed to the workings of dynamical constraints. They proposed the Law of Praegnanz, which states that perceptions will be as "good" as the prevailing stimulation allows. Perceived "goodness" implied the operation of a minimum principle that promoted simple, regular, and symmetrical perceptual organizations. Psychophysical isomorphism was proposed as the mechanism by which physical constraints came to be manifested in perceptual phenomena. By this account, there is an isomorphism between the pattern of activity in the brain and the organization inherent in perception. The brain was proposed to be an undifferentiated volume conductor in which dynamical laws organized molar brain processes. This conjecture about physiological structure did not long survive critical scrutiny (Lashley, Chow, & Semmes, 1951). Although the tie to universal laws of dynamics has been dropped from most minimum principle formulations (Attneave, 1954; Garner, 1974; Hochberg & McAlister, 1953; Leeuwenberg, 1971, 1982), the notion of there being minimum principles in perceptual processing has proved to be a powerful and lasting idea (see Hochberg, chap. 9, this volume).

Universal laws have crept into discussions of perception in two ways. The first is the strong form advocated by the Gestalt psychologists: Perception directly reflects the application of universal laws within the physical medium of the brain. The second form makes a weaker claim: Perception reflects properties common to all complex systems. The latter proposal will be discussed first.

In his enormously influential essay, "The Architecture of Complexity," Simon (1962/1981) expressed skepticism in the hope of finding universal laws that are applicable to all complex systems and that are informative about their behavior.

> A number of proposals have been advanced in recent years for the development of "general systems theory" that, abstracting from properties peculiar to physical, biological, or social systems, would be applicable to all of them. We might well feel that, while the goal is laudable, systems of such diverse kinds could hardly be expected to have any nontrivial properties in common. Metaphor and analogy can be helpful, or they can be misleading. All depends on whether the similarities the metaphor captures are significant or superficial. (p. 193)

Instead of looking for universal laws, Simon suggested that it might be more useful to look for common properties that all complex systems possess. In the remainder of the essay, Simon discussed the hierarchical structure that is inherent in all natural complex systems. The essence of his argument is that all self-organizing complex systems possess hierarchical structure, because only such structures would have had time to evolve. In a world governed by entropy and accident, hierarchical structure is a necessary condition for the evolution of complexity.

Proffitt (1993) applied this notion of hierarchical structure to perception. He argued that all perceptual processes are hierarchically organized and governed by influences that operate over different time scales. For example, a photoreceptor's response to light is governed by processes operating at quite short durations as compared to those that govern the organism's goal-directed exploration of the environment. The slower exploratory activities are, however, responsible for the manner in which the photoreceptor is illuminated at any given moment, and thus, influence the receptor's pattern of activity over time. As another example, the functioning of the digestive and auditory systems seems independent when studied over short time scales; however, as Pavlov (1927) showed, their functions can become coordinated through the history of their associated activation. Digestion and audition correspond to what Simon (1962/1981) called, nearly decomposable systems, meaning that the short-run behavior of either system is approximately independent of short-run behavior of the other, whereas their long-run behavior is coordinated.

A final example of looking for common properties of complex systems is seen in Gilden, Thornton, and Mallon's (1995) investigation of people's ability to reproduce line lengths and to respond in a reaction time test. Looking only at error sequences, he found that people's spatial or temporal responses fluctuated as $1/f$ noise. $1/f$ noise fluctuates with a power density that is inversely proportional to frequency. $1/f$ noise has been observed in a wide variety of complex systems ranging from quasar emissions to traffic flow. It has been speculated that $1/f$ noise is symptomatic of hierarchically organized systems that relax following perturbations with no preferred spatial or temporal scale (Weissman, 1988). Gilden suggested that the presence of $1/f$ noise may have implications for understanding the architecture of natural complex systems, including those responsible for perception and cognition.

In Simon's, Proffitt's, and Gilden et al.'s use, hierarchical structure is viewed as a common property of complex systems, not as a universal law responsible for their emergence. The stronger claim that can be made about universal laws is that they affect perception directly through their governance of underlying brain processes. This is, of course, the Gestalt psychologists' position, and it is reemerging in the contemporary science of complex systems.

As when Simon wrote in the early 1960s, there is a move afoot to uncover universal laws for complex systems. Often called complexity theory, this attempt has borrowed heavily from dynamical systems approaches in physics with an emphasis on the role of nonlinear systems and chaos theory. Best-selling books have appeared that chronicle complexity theory's recent developments (e.g., Kauffman, 1995; Lewin, 1992). A primary pursuit within this approach is to discover the laws of formation for self-organizing complex systems. Should such laws be discovered, their implications for perceptual theory would be profound.

Currently, the connection between proposed principles—often instantiated in computer simulations—and actual phenomena is highly tenuous. Hogan (1995) noted that computer simulations of complexity principles tend to be related to actual phenomena via a reminiscence principle, meaning that the simulation exhibits properties that are reminiscent of the behavior of some system; however, the actual connection between theory and reality is mostly metaphorical.

Dynamical systems accounts have been applied in a fairly direct fashion in studies of motor systems and their development (cf. Kelso & Jeka, 1992; Smith & Thelen, 1993). For example, Clark, Truly, and Phillips (1993) argued that locomotion may be modeled as a limit-cycle system because the underlying physiology functions in a manner appropriate to this description. Within the perceptual realm, the invocation of dynamical systems theory has been mostly metaphorical.

As an example, Smith (1991) introduced a discussion of the emergence of convection rolls when a gas is heated from below as a metaphor for how the perception of structure develops over time. This dynamical systems metaphor helped to illustrate a point about the role of time in the evolution of structure; however, no claims about common underlying processes were intended. This use of metaphor is reminiscent of Simon's remarks quoted above: "Metaphor and analogy can be helpful, or they can be misleading. All depends on whether the similarities the metaphor captures are significant or superficial" (p. 193).

D. Internalization of Group Concepts

Put simply, group concepts explicitly specify how a state of affairs can change in some respects, and yet in other respects remain the same. As applied to the problems of perception, group theory specifies the constraints on perceiving constancy. Perceptual constancies (discussed at more length by Hochberg, chap. 9, this volume) entail an appreciation of constant object properties under varying conditions of proximal stimulation. So, for example, size constancy is achieved under conditions in which projected size varies with distance. Shape constancy must be gleaned from retinal projections that vary in shape with object orientation. Color constancy is the perception of a constant surface color under conditions of varying spectral illumination. Traditional accounts of perceptual constancy range from Helmholtz's (1867/1925) approach of taking into account relevant variables—perceived distance is used to compute perceived size—to Hering's (1920/1964) account, which looks for interactions among relevant variables at a more global level—perceived color depends upon surrounding colors. More general, however, than any particular account of perceptual constancy are the mathematical constraints that limit the form that any solution to the constancy problem can take. These constraints are specified by group theory.

The importance of the group concept for perceptual theory was made clear in an important paper by Cassirer (1944). He credited Helmholtz (1868/1883) with the first attempt to apply the group concept to perceptual problems, and his critique of Helmholtz's position is relevant to issues that are still prevalent today (see also Cutting, chap. 4, this volume).

Helmholtz accepted the Kantian conception of space as a transcendental form of intuition only insofar as it designated a possibility of space. The quantification of space requires definite axioms pertaining to the congruency between different parts of space, and it was Helmholtz's position that the form of this quantification derived from empirical experimentation. Helmholtz (1870/1971) provided a thought experiment in which he asked his readers to consider what knowledge of space might be had by a being that lived in a non-Euclidian world. For example, he discussed how an intelligent being living on the surface of a small sphere might construe the shortest distance between two points. In Euclidean space, the shortest distance between two points is a unique straight line. For two points on a sphere, the line that passes through them forms an arc of a great circle around the sphere, and thus, there are two lines connecting the points, only one of which is the shortest. If the two points are at opposite ends of a diameter of the sphere, then there are an infinite number of lines of equal length that connect the two points. The differences between Euclidean space and that of this sphere-world are many. For this reason, Helmholtz argued that experience with the particular form of a space is required in order to discover the appropriate axioms that are applicable to it.

Cassirer's critique of the role of experience in quantifying space relied heavily on insights from Poincaré (1913/1946), who pointed out that there are irreducible differences between the axioms of geometry and empirical observations: "We do not make experiments on ideal lines or ideal circles, we can only make them on material objects" (p. 61). Poincaré related the postulates of group theory to perceptual constancies and concluded that experience plays only a small role in the internalization of group concepts. Groups are defined by the set of operations that preserve invariance. One such operation is the inverse transformation: every invariance-preserving operation has an inverse that returns the quantity to its original state. With respect to the problem of size constancy, every displacement changes the retinal size of the object; however, every displacement can be countered by another that returns the object to a position that projects its original retinal size. What distinguishes displacement from an irreversible modification of the object can be discovered through experience. Displacing an object produces a change in retinal size that can be compensated for through another displacement of the object or the observer. Destroying a portion of the object has no correcting transformation that returns the object to its original state. Experience, thus, provides evidence that a correcting transformation does or does not exist.

Experience, however, does not provide the geometrical form for why the presence of an inverse operation specifies invariance. Group theory provides the necessary definitions. Of the relationship between experience and group concepts, Cassirer concluded, "experience proves not to be the source of concepts, but merely the occasional cause of their formation" (p. 5), and later he stated,

> Instead of following in the footsteps of geometrical empiricism, such as to search for the "facts which lie at the basis of geometry," we may raise the question whether there are any concepts and principles that are, although in different ways and different degrees of distinctness necessary conditions for both the constitution of the perceptual world and the construction of the universe of geometrical thought. It seems to me that the concept of group and the concept of invariance are such principles. Perhaps we can, by their instrumentality, bring certain mathematical and psychological problems under a common denominator—although in quite a different way than Helmholtz attempted to achieve such a synthesis. (p. 19)

As a capsule summary of Cassirer's essay, three central notions about group theory were presented. First, the perception of constancy implies group concepts of invariance. Second, such perceptions entail an appreciation of invariance-preserving transformations over and above an extraction of currently available information. Finally, the internalization of group concepts is achieved with little influence from experience.

Direct appeals to group concepts can be seen in a variety of different approaches to perception. One of the most general applications of group theory is found in Marr's (1982) definition of the descriptive level of analysis that he referred to as *computational theory* (see also Nakayama, chap. 7, this volume, for further discussion). The computational level of analysis specifies *what* is accomplished by a particular process and *why*. Marr introduced this notion with the example of a cash register. Since a cash register performs addition, a computational theory of a cash register would require a theory of addition. The group-theoretic constraints on addition entail the following (Marr, 1982; p. 22):

1. If you buy nothing, it should cost you nothing; and buying nothing and something should cost the same as buying just the something. (The rules for zero.)

2. The order in which goods are presented to the cashier should not affect the total. (Commutativity.)
3. Arranging the goods into two piles and paying for each pile separately should not affect the total amount you pay. (Associativity; the basic operation for combining prices.)
4. If you buy an item and then return it for a refund, your total expenditure should be zero. (Inverses.)

With respect to vision, Marr broke perceptual processing into a hierarchy of levels from early to advanced vision, and provided general computational theories for the processes inherent at each level.

Does this application of group concepts to perception imply that group theory is internalized by the perceptual system? To answer this question we again make use of Epstein's (1995) distinction between following rules and instantiating them. Returning to the cash register example, clearly such a machine has no internalized knowledge about group-theoretic constraints on addition; however, it has been constructed in such a way that it cannot violate these constraints. That is, the cash register instantiates group concepts through the constraints placed on its information-processing capabilities.

A similar analysis can be applied to Gibson's (1979) theory of perception. Were he alive today, we doubt that Gibson would agree with our inclusion of his theory in a chapter on internalization; however, we believe that his approach belongs in this section on the internalization of group concepts (see also Cutting, chap. 4, this volume). Gibson stated that the central problem for perception is to detect in the flux of optical flow those invariants that specify the persisting properties of the environment, and those variants that indicate ongoing changes in surface layout and the perceiver's relationship to it. For Gibson, this meant that the perceptual system must distinguish between those transformations that specify permanence and those that specify change. Consider, for example, reversible occlusion. When an object goes out of sight by passing behind another surface that is between it and the observer's vantage point, then it does so by an occlusion transformation. Detecting this transformation specifies that, although the object is out of sight, it continues to exist. This is because occlusion is reversible. Although Gibson did not write in group-theoretic terms, reversibility is a group concept. With Gibson's theory, as with Marr's, such concepts are inherent in the constraints on perceptual process but are not necessarily represented within the system in any tangible way.

Perhaps the first formal application of group concepts to specific perceptual phenomena was Hoffman's (1966) use of Lie groups to account for a number of perceptual illusions. This approach was extended by Caelli, Hoffman, and Lindman (1978) to include additional group-theoretic concepts and their application to such domains as motion perception. Foster (1975) applied group concepts to the perception of apparent motions in an influential treatment that served as a foundation for Shepard's (1984) subsequent theorizing. (We will turn to Shepard's work shortly.)

Studies of symmetry perception have a strong affinity for group-theoretic exposition since symmetry, itself, is defined by group concepts. Palmer (1982) provided a group-theoretic account for symmetry perception and for a variety of Gestalt grouping principles. Wagemans, Van Gool, and Lamote (1996) applied group concepts to general issues in perceiving invariants.

One of the most ambitious applications of group concepts to perception, cognition, and indeed, all acts of mind is found in Leyton's (1992) book, *Symmetry, causality, mind*. In essence, Leyton proposed that perception entails an appreciation for the history of objects. When, for example, one sees a squashed can, not only is the can observed, but also perceived is its transformed state that implies some process that deformed it. Leyton argued that all objects are perceived to be symmetrical if they are so, and if not, then they are perceived to have been symmetrical in the past and to have become deformed through some process that is inferred, as in the crumpled can example.

The most influential and elegant account of perception viewed as the internalization of group concepts is the work of Shepard (1984, 1994). His analysis considered three domains: (a) perceiving and imagining the position and motion of objects, (b) perceiving color constancy, and (c) generalization and categorization. We will briefly discuss only the first domain.

Shepard (1994) proposed that perceived object motions are represented in the six-dimensional manifold jointly determined by the Euclidean group of 3-D space and the symmetry group of each object. For an explication of the group-theoretic concepts entailed by this representation, see Shepard (1994; Carlton & Shepard, 1990). For our purposes, we focus on two aspects of Shepard's account. First, Shepard proposed that the representational space for perceiving object motions is constrained by geometrical, not physical, constraints. A second, related assertion is that internalized group-theoretic constraints are more general than the constraints experienced within the organism's niche. This latter proposal reaffirms Cassirer's (1944) argument that group concepts are not reducible to experienced regularities.

To exemplify both of these proposals, consider the phenomena of long-range apparent motion. When two displaced points of light are sequentially flashed with the appropriate timing, then a single point of light is perceived to move from one location to the other. Under typical viewing conditions, this light appears to move along a straight trajectory connecting the location of the two lights. That the apparent trajectory is a straight line suggested to the Gestalt psychologists that a minimization principle was operative (Koehler, 1929). Now consider what is observed when two shapes are sequentially flashed that differ not only in location but also in orientation (see Figure 2). Without constraint, any trajectory is possible, such as that shown in Figure 2A. The minimal energy path as prescribed by physics is depicted in Figure 2B, and the minimal displacement path as prescribed by kinematic geometry is depicted in Figure 2C. It has been found that curved trajectories are perceived when observers view this event (Bundesen, Larsen, & Farrell, 1983; Farrell, 1983; Foster, 1975; McBeath & Shepard, 1989; Proffitt, Gilden, Kaiser, & Whelan, 1988).

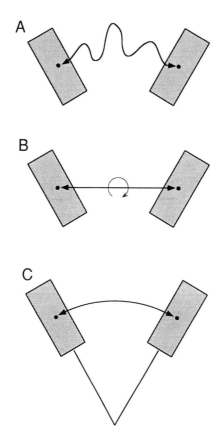

FIGURE 2   An apparent motion display in which a rectangle is sequentially flashed in two locations and at different orientation. Without constraint, the apparent motion path could take any trajectory such as that depicted in (A). (B) The least energy path: a straight trajectory for the rectangle's center and a concomitant rotation around this point. (C) The minimal path as prescribed by kinematic
geometry: a single rotation of the rectangle around a point external to the object.

When an object falls and simultaneously changes orientation, its center of mass
follows a straight trajectory parallel to gravity, while the rest of its mass rotates
around this center. This is the least energy path, and coincides with that drawn in
Figure 2B. That people do not see this path in apparent motion, but rather observe
curved paths such as in Figure 2C, implies that the constraints on the mental representation of object motions are prescribed by geometry and not physics. Kinematic geometry is the branch of mathematics that specifies what object motions are
geometrically possible, and thus includes those motions that are simplest under
physical constraints. Kinematic geometry, however, is more general than physics,
and minimal motions within this system are not constrained by dynamical proper-

ties such as mass, force, and energy. Thus, based upon these apparent motion findings and numerous other experimental phenomena, Shepard (1994) argued that geometry is more deeply internalized than physics.

In our everyday experience, we encounter object motions constrained by the laws of physics. All objects have mass and move under the application of forces. Given the omnipresence of physical constraints in our ecological niche, it is somewhat surprising that these more restrictive constraints have not been internalized. And yet, this seems to be the case. Studies indicate that our ability to perceive dynamical properties is severely limited (Gilden, 1991; Proffitt & Gilden, 1989). Thus, the evidence to date suggests that the perceptual system has internalized the geometrical concepts that define the invariance of form under motion as opposed to those that apply to the conservation laws of physics.

III. CONCLUDING REMARKS

As Poggio, Torre, and Koch (1985) noted, internalized constraints have been proposed in order to promote solutions to the ill-posed problems that are presented to the perceptual system. The precise form of an hypothesized constraint depends upon the nature of the problem under consideration. Thus, the variety of internalization proposals reflects the plethora of tasks that confront the perceptual system. A corollary to this observation is that the psychological reality of any of these proposed constraints depends upon the ecological validity of the purported ill-posed problems. That is, the rationale for proposing an internalized constraint is tied to the rationale for believing that the perceptual system actual solves problems of the specified sort.

With respect to the perceptual problems that we have presented in this chapter, we are troubled by the fact that almost all of the tasks require the perceptual system to combine optical information with internalized constraints as a means of computing a perceptual representation for some distal state of affairs. By these accounts, the goal of the computation is the perceptual representation.

From other perspectives, most notably Gibson's (1979), the goal of perception is action. (See also Milner & Goodale, 1995.) When the perceptual problem is transformed from forming representations to controlling actions, the nature of the computational problem can change dramatically.

Consider the example of an outfielder catching a baseball. By one representation of this problem, the outfielder needs to construct an accurate spatial representation of where the baseball will land and then runs to that vicinity. An alternative account proposes that the fielder can use simple visual cues to ensure success. Such cues serve as action-related "invariants" that inform the organism that its behavior is proceeding in a manner that will achieve its current goal (Gibson, 1979).

McBeath, Shaffer, and Kaiser (1995) proposed such a model. They reanalyzed the geometry of the baseball-catching situation and isolated a cue that could be used to guide intercept behavior. If the fielder moves such that the ball maintains a linear trajectory relative to environmental landmarks (say home plate and the horizon), interception is ensured (Figure 3). In McBeath et al.'s model, control is based on nulling trajectory curvature. Their empirical studies of outfielder performance found that behavior is consistent with this model. This approach provides an example of how behavior can be guided by intrinsically 2-D visual cues, without postulating a need for a 3-D spatial representation.

The point of this example is to remind the reader that accounts of perceptual process are tied to assumptions about what the perceptual system is attempting to do. Gibson (1979) argued that most theories of perception misrepresent the problems that the perceptual system must solve. From his perspective, the perceptual system did not evolve to form mental representations, but rather to guide purposive actions. The actions entailed in perceiving form and heading, as discussed by Cutting (chap. 4, this

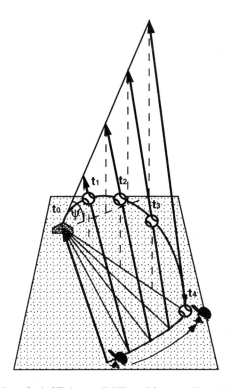

FIGURE 3   The Linear Optical Trajectory (LOT) model proposed by McBeath, Shaffer, and Kaiser (1995). The bird's-eye view shows a running path that maintains a linear optical ball trajectory from initiation (t_0) to completion (t_4). The runner moves so as to maintain a constant angle (ψ), defined by the ball, home plate, and a horizontal line emanating from home plate. Reprinted with permission from McBeath, M. D., Shaffer, D. M., & Kaiser, M. K. (1995). How baseball outfielders determine where to run to catch fly balls. *Science, 268,* 569–573. Copyright 1995 American Association for the Advancement of Science.

volume) change the picture once again. As the baseball-catching example demonstrates, the optical information of relevance and the requirements for processing constraints depends greatly on how the perceptual problem is characterized.

In summary, internalized constraints are ubiquitous in perceptual theories; the specific form that each takes depends upon the perceptual problem under consideration. Although there is a wide variety of specific proposals, internalization accounts fall into four classes. Common to all accounts is a need to supply constraints on visual processing so as to make the perceptual problem of relevance a well-posed one. Typically, internalized constraints are posited as a last resort since, if some distal state of affairs can be extracted from optical information without the need for an internalized constraint, then no constraint will be postulated. That almost all perceptual accounts rely heavily on internalized constraints attests to the difficulty found in posing perceptual problems in a manner that permits a solution based solely on proximal information. Note, however, that ill-posed problems provide two quite different opportunities. One can either search for reasonable constraints, or attempt to recast the problem. The considerable merit to be found in the internalization proposals surveyed in this chapter gives evidence to the value of the former endeavor, whereas research, such as that inspired by Gibson (1979), demonstrates that much can also be gained by the latter.

References

Anderson, B. L., & Julesz, B. (1995). A theoretical analysis of illusory contour formation in stereopsis. *Psychological Review, 102,* 705–743.

Attneave, F. (1954). Some informational aspects of visual perception. *Psychological Review, 61,* 183–193.

Attneave, F. (1982). Pragnanz and soap bubble systems: A theoretical exploration. In J. Beck (Ed.), *Organization and representation in perception* (pp. 11–29). Hillsdale, NJ: Erlbaum.

Baillargeon, R. (1986). Representing the existence and the location of hidden objects: Object permanence in 6- and 8-month old infants. *Cognition, 23,* 21–41.

Barlow, H. B. (1990). A theory about the functional role and synaptic mechanism of visual after-effects. In C. Blakemore (Ed.), *Vision: Coding and efficiency* (pp. 363–375). Cambridge, UK: Cambridge University Press.

Barlow, H. B., & Földiák, P. (1989). Adaptation and decorrelation in the cortex. In R. M. Durbin, C. Miall, & G. J. Mitchison (Eds.), *The computing neuron* (pp. 54–72). Wokingham, UK: Addison-Wesley.

Bedford, F. (1993). Perceptual learning. In D. Medin (Ed.), *The psychology of learning and motivation: Vol. 30* (pp. 1–60). San Diego, CA: Academic Press.

Bedford, F. (1995). Constraints on perceptual learning: Objects and dimensions. *Cognition, 54,* 253–297.

Bennett, B., & Hoffman, D. (1986). The computation of structure from fixed axis motion: Nonrigid structures. *Biological Cybernetics, 51,* 293–300.

Bennett, B., & Hoffman, D., Nicola, J., & Prakash, C. (1989). Structure from two orthographic views of rigid motion. *Journal of the Optical Society of America, 6,* 1052–1069.

Berkeley, G. (1963). *An essay towards a new theory of vision.* In C. M. Turbayne (Ed.), *Works on vision: George Berkeley* (pp. 19–102). Indianapolis: Boobs-Merrill. (Original work published 1709)

Brausntein, M., & Andersen, G. J. (1986). Testing the rigity assumption: A reply to Ullman. *Perception, 15,* 641–644.

Brunswik, E. (1956). *Perception and the representative design of psychology experiments* (2nd ed.), Berkeley: University of California Press.

Bundesen, C., Larsen, A., & Farrell, J. E. (1983). Visual apparent movement: Transformations of size and orientation. *Perception, 12,* 546–558.

Caelli, T., Hoffman, W. C., & Lindman, H. (1978). Subjective Lorentz transformations and the perception of motion. *Journal of the Optical Society of America, 68,* 402–411.

Carlton, E. H., & Shepard, R. N. (1990). Psychologically simple motions as geodesic paths I & II. *Journal of Mathematical Psychology, 34,* 127–228.

Cassirer, E. (1944). The concept of group and the theory of perception. *Philosophy and phenomenological research, 5,* 1–35.

Clark, J. E., Truly, T. L., & Phillips, S. J. (1993). On the development of walking as a limit-cycle system. In L. B. Smith & E. Thelen (Eds.), *A dynamics systems approach to development: Applications* (pp. 71–93). Cambridge, MA: MIT Press/Bradford Books.

Crick, F. (1989). The recent excitement about neural networks. *Nature, 337,* 129–132.

Descartes, R. (1956). *La dioptrique.* In C. Adams & P. Tannery (Eds.), *Oeuvres de Descartes: Vol. 6* (pp. 79–228). Paris: Libraire Philosophique J. Vrin. (Original work published 1637)

Dodwell, P. C., & Humphrey, G. K. (1993). What is important about McCollough effects? Reply to Allan and Siegel. *Psychological Review, 100,* 347–350.

Dodwell, P. C., & Humphrey, G. K. (1990). A functional theory of the McCollough effect. *Psychological Review, 97,* 78–89.

Durgin, F. H. (1996). Yet another contingent aftereffect: Visual aftereffect of texture density contingent on color of frame. *Perception & Psychophysics, 58,* 207–223.

Durgin, F. H., & Proffitt, D. R. (1996). Visual learning in the perception of texture: Simple and contingent aftereffects of texture density. *Spatial Vision, 9,* 423–474.

Emmert, E. (1881). Size proportions of after images. *Clinical Monthly Newsletter for Opthalmology, 19,* 443–450.

Enns, J. T., & Rensink, R. A. (1991). Preattentive recovery of three-dimensional orientation form line drawings. *Psychological Review, 98,* 335–351.

Epstein, W. (1995). The metatheoretical context. In W. Epstein & S. Rogers (Eds.), *Perception of space and motion: Handbook of perception and cognition* (2nd ed.) (pp. 1–22). San Diego: Academic Press.

Farrell, J. E. (1983). Visual transformations underlying apparent movement. *Perception & Psychophysics, 33,* 85–92.

Foley, J. M. (1985). Binocular distance perception: Egocentric distance tasks. *Journal of Experimental Psychology: Human Perception and Performance, 11,* 133–149.

Foster, D. H. (1975). Visual apparent motion of some preferred paths in the rotation group *SO(3). Biological Cybernetics, 18,* 81–89.

Garner, W. R. (1974). *The processing of information and structure.* Hillsdale, NJ: Erlbaum.

Gibson, J. J. (1979). *The ecological approach to visual perception.* Boston: Houghton Mifflin.

Gilden, D. L. (1991). On the origin of dynamical awareness. *Psychological Review, 98,* 554–568.

Gilden, D. L., Thornton, T., & Mallon, M. W. (1995). 1/f noise in human cognition. *Science, 267,* 1837–1839.

Gluck, M. A., & Thompson, R. F. (1987). Modelling the neural substrates of associative learning and memory: A computational approach. *Psychological Review, 94,* 176–191.

Gogel, W. C. (1990). A theory of phenomenal geometry and its applications. *Perception & Psychophysics, 49,* 105–123.

Gogel, W. C. (1993). The analysis of perceived space. In S. C. Masin (Ed.), *Foundations of perceptual theory* (pp. 113–182). Amsterdam: Elsevier.

Gogel, W. C., & Mertz, D. L. (1989). The contribution of heuristic processes to the moon illusion. In M. Hershenson (Ed.), *The moon illusion* (pp. 193–234). Hillsdale, NJ: Erlbaum.

Grimson, W. E. L. (1981). *From images to surfaces: A computational study of the human early vision system.* Cambridge, MA: MIT Press.

Hawkins, R. D., Abrams, T. W., Carew, T. J., & Kandel, E. R. (1983). A cellular mechanism of classical conditioning in *Aplysia:* Activity-dependent amplification of presynaptic facilitation. *Science, 219,* 400–405.

Hebb, D. (1949). *The organization of behavior.* New York: Wiley.

Held, R. (1980). The rediscovery of adaptability in the visual system: Effects of extrinsic and intrinsic chromatic dispersion. In C. S. Harris (Ed.), *Visual coding and adaptability* (pp. 69–94). Hillsdale, NJ: Erlbaum.

Helmholtz, H. von (1925). *Handbook of physiological optics:* Vol. 3. (J. P. C. Southall, Trans.). New York: Dover. (Original work published 1867)

Helmholtz, H. von (1883). Ueber die Thatsachen, die der Geometrie zum Grunde liegen. In H. von Helmholtz *Wissenschaftliche abhandlungen,* Vol. II. Leipzig: J. A. Barth. (Original work published 1868)

Helmholtz, H. von (1871). The origin and meaning of geometric axioms: I. In R. Kahl (Ed.), *Selected writings of Hermann von Helmholtz* (pp. 246–265). Middletown, CT: Wesleyan University Press. (Original work published 1894)

Helmholtz, H. von (1971). The origin and correct interpretation of our sense impressions. In R. Kahl (Ed.). *Selected writings of Hermann von Helmholtz* (pp. 501–512). Middletown, CT: Wesleyan University Press. (Original work published 1894)

Helson, H. (1964). *Adaptation-level theory: An experimental and systematic approach to behaving.* New York: Harper & Row.

Hering, E. (1964). Grundzuge der Lehre vom Lichtsinne. In L. Hurvich & D. Jameson (Trans.). *Outlines of a theory of the light sense.* Cambridge, MA: Harvard University Press.

Hershenson, M. (1989). *The moon illusion.* Hillsdale, NJ: Erlbaum.

Hochberg, J. (1972). Perception: I. Color and shape; II. Space and movement. In J. W. Kling & L. A. Riggs (Eds.), *Woodworth and Scholsberg's experimental psychology* (pp. 395–550). New York: Holt, Rinehart & Winston.

Hochberg, J. (1987). Machines should not see as people do, but must know how people see. *Computer Vision, Graphics and Image Processing, 37,* 221–237.

Hochberg, J., & McAlister, E. (1953). A quantitative approach to figural "goodness." *Journal of Experimental Psychology, 46,* 361–364.

Hoffman, D. D., & Bennett, B. M. (1985). Inferring the relative three-dimensional positions of two moving points. *Journal of the Optical Society of America A, 2,* 242–249.

Hoffman, D. D., & Bennett, B. M. (1986). The computation of structure from fixed axis motion: Rigid structures. *Biological Cybernetics, 54,* 1–13.

Hoffman, D. D., & Richards, W. A. (1985). Parts of recognition. *Cognition, 18,* 65–96.

Hoffman, W. C. (1966). The Lie algebra of visual perception. *Journal of Mathematical Psychology, 3,* 65–98.

Hogan, J. (1995). From complexity to perplexity. *Scientific American, 272*(6), 104–109.

Horn, G. (1985). *Memory, imprinting and the brain.* Oxford: Clarendon Press.

Hornbostel, E. M. von (1922). Ueber optische inversion. *Psychologische Forschung, 1,* 130–156.

Hoyle, F. (1957). *The black cloud.* London: Heineman.

Huang, T., & Lee, C. (1989). Motion and structure from orthographic projections. *IEEE Transactions on Pattern Analysis and Machine Intelligence, 11,* 536–540.

Ito, M. (1989). Long-term depression. *Annual Review of Neuroscience, 12,* 85–102.

Ittelson, W. H. (1968). *The Ames demonstrations in perception.* New York: Hafner.

Kanade, Y., & Kender, J. R. (1983). Mapping image properties into shape constraints: Skewed symmetry, affine-transformable patterns, and the shape-from-texture paradigm. In J. Beck, B. Hope, & A. Rosenfeld (Eds.), *Human and machine vision* (pp. 237–257). New York: Academic Press.

Kaufman, I., & Rock, I. (1962). The moon illusion I. *Science, 136,* 953–961.

Kaufman, I., & Rock, I. (1989). The moon illusion thirty years later. In M. Hershenson (Ed.), *The moon illusion* (pp. 193–234). Hillsdale, NJ: Erlbaum.

Kauffman, S. (1995). *At home in the universe: The search for the laws of self-organization and complexity.* New York: Oxford University Press.

Kandel, E. R., & Tauc, L. (1965). Mechanism of heterosynaptic facilitation in the giant cell of the abdominal ganglion of Aplysia depilans. *Journal of Physiology, 181,* 28–47.

Kelso, J. A. S., & Jeka, J. J. (1992). Symmetry breaking dynamics of human multilimb coordination. *Journal of Experimental Psychology: Human Perception and Performance, 18,* 645–668.

Koehler, W. (1929), *Gestalt psychology.* New York: Liveright.

Koenderink, J. J. (1986). Optical flow. *Vision Research, 26,* 161–179.

Koenderink, J. J., & van Doorn, A. J. (1986). Depth and shape from differential perspective in the presence of bending deformations. *Journal of the Optical Society of America A, 3,* 242–249.

Koffka, K. (1935). *Principles of Gestalt psychology.* New York: Harcourt Brace.

Krupa, D. J., & Thompson, R. F. (1995). Inactivation of the superior cerebellar peduncle blocks expression but not acquisition of the rabbits classically-conditioned eye-blink response. *Proceedings of the National Academy of Sciences of the United States of America, 92*(11), 5097–5101.

Kubovy, M. (1986). *The psychology of perspective and Renaissance art.* Cambridge, UK: Cambridge University Press.

Lashely, K. S., Chow, K. L., & Semmes, J. (1951). An examination of the electrical field theory of cerebral integration. *Psychological Review, 58,* 123–136.

Lee, D. N. (1974). Visual information during locomotion. In R. B. McLeod & H. Pick (Eds.), *Perception: Essays in honor of J. J. Gibson* (pp. 250–267). Ithaca, NY: Cornell University Press.

Lee, D. N. (1976). A theory of visual control of braking based on information about time-to-collision. *Perception, 5,* 437–459.

Leeuwenberg, E. L. J. (1971). A perceptual coding language for visual and auditory patterns. *American Journal of Psychology, 84,* 307–349.

Leeuwenberg, E. L. J. (1982). Metrical aspects of patterns and structural information theory. In J. Beck (Ed.), *Organization and representation in perception* (pp. 57–71). Hillsdale, NJ: Erlbaum.

Levy, W. B., Colbert, C. M., & Desmond, N. L. (1990). Elemental adaptive processes of neurons and synapses: A statistical/computational perspective. In M. A. Gluck & D. E. Rumelhart (Eds.), *Neuroscience and connectionist models* (pp. 187–235). Hillsdale, NJ: Erlbaum.

Levy, W. B., & Desmond, N. L. (1985). The rules of elemental synaptic plasticity. In W. B. Levy, J. A. Anderson, & S. Lehmkuhle, (Eds.), *Synaptic modification, neuron selectivity, and nervous system organization* (pp. 105–122). Hillsdale, NJ: Erlbaum.

Lewin, R. (1992). *Complexity: Life at the edge of chaos.* New York: Macmillan.

Leyton, M. (1992). *Symmetry, causality, mind.* Cambridge, MA: MIT Press/Bradford Book.

Longuet-Higgins, H. C., & Prazdny, K. (1984). The interpretation of a moving retinal image. *Proceedings of the Royal Society of London B, 208,* 385–397.

Marr, D. (1982). *Vision: A computational investigation into the human representation and processing of visual information.* San Francisco: Freeman.

McBeath, M. K., Shaffer, D. M., & Kaiser, M. K. (1995). How baseball outfielders determine where to run to catch fly balls. *Science, 268,* 569–573.

McBeath, M. K., & Shepard, R. N. (1989). Apparent motion between shapes differing in location and orientation: A window technique for estimating path curvature. *Perception & Psychophysics, 46,* 333–337.

McLeod, R. W., & Ross, H. E. (1983). Optic-flow and cognitive factors in time-to-collision estimates. *Perception, 12,* 417–423.

McClelland, J. L., & Rumelhart, D. E. (1986). *Parallel distributed processing: Explorations in the microstructure of cognition. Vol. II: Psychological and biological models.* Cambridge, MA: Bradford Books.

McCollough, C. (1965). Color adaptation of edge-detectors in the human visual system. *Science, 149,* 1115–1116.

Milner, A. D., & Goodale, M. A. (1995). *The visual brain in action.* Oxford: Oxford University Press.

Nakayama, K., & Shimojo, S. (1992). Experiencing and perceiving visual surfaces. *Science, 257,* 1357–1363.

Palmer, S. E. (1982). Symmetry, transformation, and the structure of perceptual systems. In J. Beck (Ed.), *Organization and representation in perception* (pp. 95–144). Hillsdale, NJ: Erlbaum.

Pavlov, I. P. (1927). *Conditioned reflexes.* New York: Oxford University Press.

Perkins, D. N. (1972). Visual discrimination between rectangular and nonrectangular parallelepipeds. *Perception & Psychophysics, 12,* 396–400.

Perkins, D. N. (1973). Compensating for distortion in viewing pictures obliquely, *Perception & Psychophysics, 14,* 13–18.

Poggio, T., Torre, V., & Koch, C. (1985). Computational vision and regularization theory. *Nature, 317,* 314–319.

Poincaré, H. (1946). *The foundations of science.* (G. B. Halsted, Trans.). New York: Science Press. (Original work published 1913)

Proffitt, D. R. (1993). A hierarchical approach to perception. In S. C. Masin (Ed.), *Foundations of perceptual theory* (pp. 75–111). Amsterdam: Elsevier.

Proffitt, D. R., & Gilden, D. L. (1989). Understanding natural dynamics. *Journal of Experimental Psychology: Human Perception & Performance, 15,* 384–393.

Proffitt, D. R., Gilden, D. L., Kaiser, M. K., & Whelan, S. M. (1988). The effect of configural orientation on perceived trajectory in apparent motion. *Perception & Psychophysics, 43,* 465–474.

Reimann, E. (1902). Die scheinbare Vergrosserung der Sonne und des Mondes am Horizont, I. *Zeitschrift fur Psychologie, 30,* 1–38.

Rock, I. (1983). *The logic of perception.* Cambridge, MA: MIT Press.

Schiff, W., & Detwiler, M. L. (1979). Information used in judging impending collision. *Perception, 8,* 647–658.

Schiff, W., & Oldak, R. (1990). Accuracy of judging time-to-arrival: Effects of modality, trajectory, and gender. *Journal of Experimental Psychology: Human Perception and Performance, 16,* 303–316.

Shepard, R. N. (1981). Psychophysical complementarity. In M. Kubovy & J. R. Pomerantz (Eds.), *Perceptual organization* (pp. 279–341). Hillsdale, NJ: Erlbaum.

Shepard, R. N. (1984). Ecological constraints on internal representation: Resonant kinematics of perceiving, imagining, thinking, and dreaming. *Psychological Review, 91,* 417–447.

Shepard, R. N. (1994). Perceptual-cognitive universals as reflections of the world. *Psychonomic Bulletin & Review, 1,* 2–28.

Siegel, S., & Allan, L. G. (1992). Pairings in learning and perception: Pavlovian conditioning and contingent aftereffects. *The Psychology of Learning and Motivation, 28,* 127–160.

Siegel, S., Allan, L. G., & Eissenberg, T. (1992). The associative basis of contingent color aftereffects. *Journal of Experimental Psychology: General, 121,* 79–94.

Simon, H. (1981). The architecture of complexity. In H. Simon (Ed.), *The sciences of the artificial* (2nd ed.) (pp. 193–229). Cambridge, MA: The MIT Press. (Original work published 1962)

Simpson, W. A. (1988). Depth discrimination from optic flow. *Perception, 17,* 497–512.

Skowbo, D. (1984). Are McCollough effects conditioned responses? *Psychological Bulletin, 96,* 215–226.

Smith, L. B., & Thelen, E. (Eds.). (1993). *A dynamics systems approach to development: Applications.* Cambridge, MA: MIT Press/Bradford Books.

Smith, L. B. (1991). Perceptual structure and developmental process. In G. R. Lockhead & J. R. Pomerantz (Eds.), *The perception of structure: Essays in honor of Wendell R. Garner.* Washington, DC: American Psychological Association.

Spelke, E. S., Breinlinger, K., Macomber, J., & Jacobson, K. (1992). Origins of knowledge. *Psychological Review, 99,* 605–632.

Todd, J. T. (1981). Visual information about moving objects. *Journal of Experimental Psychology: Human Perception and Performance, 7,* 795–810.

Todd, J. T. (1995). The visual perception of three-dimensional structure from motion. In W. Epstein & S. Rogers (Eds.), *Perception of space and motion: Handbook of perception and cognition, 2nd edition* (pp. 201–226). San Diego: Academic Press.

Ullman, S. (1979). *The interpretation of visual motion.* Cambridge, MA: MIT Press.

Ullman, S. (1983). Recent computational studies in the interpretation of structure from motion. In J. Beck & A. Rosenfeld (Eds.), *Human and machine vision* (pp. 459–480). New York: Academic Press.

Ullman, S. (1984). Maximizing rigidity: The incremental recovery of 3-D structure from rigid and non-rigid motion. *Perception, 13,* 255–274.

Wagemans, J., Van Gool, L., & Lamote, C. (1996). The visual system's measurement of invariants need not itself be invariant. *Psychological Science, 7,* 232–236.

Weintraub, D. J., & Gardner, G. T. (1970). Emmert's Laws: Size constancy vs. optical geometry. *American Journal of Psychology, 83,* 40–54.

Weissman, M. B. (1988). $1/f$ noise and other slow, nonexponential kinetics in condensed matter. *Reviews of Modern Physics, 60,* 537.

CHAPTER 8

A Century of Human Information-Processing Theory
Vision, Attention, and Memory

Barbara Anne Dosher
George Sperling

I. THE EVOLUTION OF PSYCHOLOGICAL THEORY

A. Overview

Both theories and the types of data that are considered appropriate for theories underwent major changes during the 20th century. There were some outstanding examples of careful theorizing in perception and other areas of psychology in the late 19th century, but few theories were what we would, at the end of the 20th century, call *process theories*. At the end of the 19th century, such process theories as there were, were mentalistic, speculative, and unsuccessful. At the end of the 20th century, theories have become process oriented, detailed, and accurate in their account of experimental data. Concurrently, there has been a continuing trend in the style of data collection: In the late 19th century, it was the norm to use a small range of relatively simple stimuli and to encourage the observer to make complex—frequently introspective—responses. In the domain of perception, particularly, there has been a trend toward using increasingly simple responses (e.g., merely selecting one of two intervals in a two-interval forced choice procedure), with the complexity being displaced from the response to the stimuli. The advent of computer-generated displays has accentuated this trend. In this chapter, we illustrate the development of theories with examples from the areas of visual perception, attention, and memory.

Perception and Cognition at Century's End

B. Why and Whither Theories? Utility and Expected Lifetime

Some theories have immediate practical utility, for example, Newton's laws. Newton's theory enables us to calculate the time of occurrence of eclipses, satellite orbits, and many other useful properties of objects in motion. On the other hand, a theory that relates the origin of the universe to a big bang 17 or so billion years ago has little immediate utility. Such a theory can be regarded as having infinitely deferred practical utility but some immediate aesthetic value.

Theories achieve longevity by being the best theory at a given level of complexity (Sperling, 1997). For example, Newton's laws are not valid at extremely high speeds, but they are the most accurate theory at their level of complexity and therefore seem destined for immortality. Moreover, they have both practical and aesthetic value, something which few psychological theories have achieved.

C. Theories

1. Accomplishments at the End of the Nineteenth Century

The nineteenth century produced some outstanding researchers in psychology, including the following:

1. Weber offered a simple and quite reasonable theory about the discrimination of differences (Weber's Law). A just noticeable increment or decrement was proposed to be a constant percentage (the Weber constant) of the value of the stimulus that was being incremented or decremented (Weber, 1846).
2. Fechner further developed a psychophysics of sensory discrimination and scaling, including much of what we now call signal detection theory (Fechner, 1860; see also Nakayama, chap. 7, this volume).
3. Pavlov proposed the theory of conditioning, now called Pavlovian or classical conditioning (Pavlov, 1927).
4. Helmholtz (1866/1924) elaborated Ohm's (1843) theory of acoustic perception based on Fourier analysis of sounds. He also proposed a quite detailed theory of the coordinated movements of the eyes and of corresponding points on the retinas, a comprehensive color theory based on Thomas Young's (1802) observations, and many other fine-grained theories (Helmholtz, 1924).
5. At the turn of the century, Binet developed an IQ test (Binet & Henri, 1896; Boring, 1942), and it was followed by many useful developments in test theory and statistical hypothesis testing.
6. Ebbinghaus made numerous observations about memory, including the effects of repetition, of interference, and of the consistency of measures of memory strength as indexed, for example, by recall, recognition, or savings on relearning (Ebbinghaus, 1885; 1964).

With such solid, hard-earned progress, one might have thought that psychology would be regarded as off to a marvelous start in the 19th century. Unfortunately, these theories addressed specific phenomena. Except for Pavlovian conditioning and IQ, the developments were too scientific—too technical—to be of general interest. They did not begin to address global psychological questions to which a larger public sought answers, such as "How does the mind operate?" and "What is the nature of consciousness?"

2. Mentalism

The void was eagerly filled by an entirely different kind of theorist, the mentalists. Foremost among these were Wundt and James; later, Freud and the Gestaltists worked within a similar framework. Wundt proposed that consciousness could be understood in terms of a succession of mental states or "ideas." Perceptionists of the 19th century generally took "ideas" for granted in their explanations of various phenomena of perception, but Wundt made the idea itself the central object of study. The succession from one idea to the next was determined by three kinds of influences: the current idea, the internal state of the organism, and the external stimuli. Ideas had various sensory properties that could be determined by introspection. Our graphical interpretation of the mentalists' basic model is illustrated in Figure 1.

The mentalists' theory was a departure from the formal quantitative work of their predecessors mainly in the data that were considered appropriate for modeling. In a formal sense, we would say today that their theory dealt with a particular kind of (typically verbal) behavior, introspection, which was intended to describe the subject's mental state. That is, the data that mentalism addressed were statements about the contents of consciousness, rather than actions that were directly related to solving an environmental problem.

Another characteristic of the introspectionists is that they tended to present very simple stimuli and to record very complex responses. For example, a simple patch

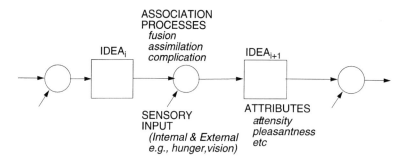

FIGURE 1   The mentalists' model. The content of consciousness is assumed to be an "idea." The succession from the current idea (designated IDEA$_i$) to the next idea (IDEA$_j$) is determined by internal and external stimuli, the IDEA$_i$ and by various, incompletely specified processes of association. An idea is defined by its attributes; some of which (such as attensity and pleasantness) received considerable attention at the time but today seem quite obscure. (Reproduced with permission of G. Sperling.)

of red might be presented, and a long response would be made concerning the uniformity of the perceived hue, its vividness, attensity, and other attributes.

Among the problems of mentalism recognized almost immediately was that not all thought processes are available to introspection. Some better known examples are the so-called "imageless thought" of Külpe's Würzburg School (Boring, 1950), and Freud's unconscious drives and suppressed ideas.

At the beginning of the 20th century, no adequate theoretical apparatus for dealing with long, complex responses (sentences or paragraphs) was available. For the remainder of the 20th century, a different approach would be much more successful. The complexity was placed in the stimulus, and the response was kept as simple and as constant as possible (the principle adhered to by the successful experimentalists cited earlier). Thus, one might vary the properties of a patch of light, its wavelength composition, exposure duration, the background, the configuration, and so on, while the only response recorded was "yes" if it was discriminable from nothing (i.e., from a null stimulus)—or "no" when it was not.

Yet another problem with the mentalists' approach was that consciousness is perhaps an incidental by-product of adaptive behavior. Suppose only evolutionarily adaptive behavior matters, and adaptive behavior occurs with or without consciousness. Many important mental operations simply precede consciousness and are therefore automatic and inaccessible; others are related to the mechanisms of introspection itself and therefore inaccessible (i.e., a camera cannot photograph its internal parts), and other mental operations are inaccessible for a myriad of other reasons.

For all these reasons, the mentalists' efforts were a dismal failure in the sense that, although the phenomena they investigated remain of interest even today, essentially nothing of value remains of their theoretical efforts.

3. Behaviorism

The mentalist approach incited two early 20th-century counter movements: the behaviorists, who initially wanted to discard verbal behavior entirely, and the "dustbowl" empiricists, who eschewed theory and hoped to solve the problems of psychology by cataloging all the useful empirical relations that might be of psychological interest.

The behaviorist era was initiated by John B. Watson and was carried through the 1950s by B. F. Skinner (Skinner, 1938; Watson, 1919). In fact, the behavioral and empirical approaches were quite similar, and are schematically represented in Figure 2. The description of psychological phenomena is represented by a collection of S_i-R_i relations, that relate a particular presented stimulus S_i to a particular observed response R_i. The behaviorists' concentrated on the observation that "reinforcement," the delivery of a favorable outcome for a particular S_i-R_i combination tended to make R_i a more likely response to future occurrences of stimulus S_i.

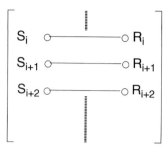

FIGURE 2   A basket of empirically observed stimulus–response (S–R) associations. Only a few associations are shown. The behaviorists, from Watson to Skinner, attempted to understand behavior by determining all the S–R associations of importance. Reinforcement (reward) following the occurrence of a particular S-R sequence was assumed to make the association of the R with S more likely when S reoccurred.
The empiricists, psychologists of the first half of the 20th century, were concerned less with learning processes than with sensory and cognitive issues; they attempted to collect all the useful relationships under
the formula: S-O-R (stimulus-organism-response). (Reproduced with permission of G. Sperling.)

To avoid state dependence—an S–O–R theory in which the response depended
on the state (e.g., hunger) of the organism, O, the behaviorists sought to incorporate the state into the stimulus. Thus, the organism works for food not because of
an internal state (hunger), but because the complete description of the stimulus
incorporates not only, say, the current visual stimulus, but also the description of the
recent history of food deprivation. This is incredibly cumbersome, and it is not surprising that the behaviorists left us with a cornucopia of observations but no sur-
viving theory.

The problem with trying to create a psychology without theory but with
merely an exhaustive enumeration of all the interesting and useful S–R relationships, or S–O–R relationships, is illustrated by a simple example. Consider a primitive computer screen. It has only 16×16 pixels and each pixel displays only one
of two possible gray levels. Suppose we wish to make a list of the stimuli produced by this incredibly impoverished display screen and to record some simple
responses that might be made to each possible stimulus. These are 2^{256} different
displays. We cannot record even one response to each display because the number
of different stimuli (2^{256}) is larger than the number of atoms in the universe. If
the brute force approach of cataloging behavior is hopeless even in this contrived
trivial environment, consider how much more futile it would be in complex natural environments.

4. The Cognitive Revolution

What has emerged in the second half of the 20th century, the post-World War II
era, is a cognitive revolution in which descriptive and process theories are integrated
with empirical work. Typically, process theories are represented as flow chart diagrams

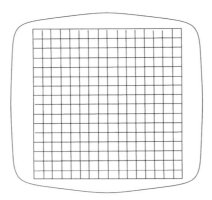

FIGURE 3   A computer display screen with 16 × 16 pixel resolution. If each pixel can display two different gray-scale values, there are 2^{256} different possible displays. (Reproduced with permission of G. Sperling.)

with boxes, which represent processes, connected by arrows, which represent the flow of information. Initially, a box represents a process that is perhaps too complex to be described precisely; subsequently the box is expanded into component boxes and arrows that define it more precisely. For example, a component that in an early theory is called simply "motion detection" and left undefined can now be expanded into three distinct motion-direction systems and five seperate motion energy computations, each of which can be further expanded into numerous subcomponents. Ideally, these more highly specified components are more closely related to biological substrates and to neural computations than the more abstract branch from which they sprang. This sequence of successive refinements in the second half of the twentieth century is strongly reminiscent of the history of atomic and nuclear physics during the earlier part of the century. Initially there were atoms, then they were divided into protons, electrons, and neutrons; then these components were described in more detail and further subdivided.

In the next sections, we illustrate the evolution of theory in the second half of the 20th century with several examples with which we have special familiarity: computational models of vision (motion perception in particular), visual attention, and serial versus parallel models of short-term recognition memory.

II. VISUAL PERCEPTION

A. Progress in Models of Perception

The straightforward formulations of perceptual relationships of Weber, Fechner, Mach, and Helmholtz at the end of the 19th century were superceded by the introspective descriptions of the mentalists. The introspective approach to perception was continued by the Gestalt school, in the sense that gestaltists were concerned with the appearance of objects (i.e., whether they exhibited "good form", or whether they grouped into one configuration or another), rather than with skilled or adaptive behavior.

A useful indicator of whether or not experiments concern adaptive behavior is whether the experiments use corrective feedback or, at least, could profitably use it. Feedback and adaptation are inextricably linked. Experiments with feedback measure capacity—the asymptotic level of performance reached with training. Experiments without feedback assess achievement—skills the subject has already acquired before entering the experiment and proclivities—how the subject prefers to respond (Sperling, Dosher, & Landy, 1990).

In the United States, the first half of the 20th century was a period marked on the whole (with a few notable exceptions) by an intense counterreaction to mentalism that discarded not only the subject matter and style of the mentalists but the also discarded any use of theory, and blindly embraced atheoretical, empirical work. Before the growth of formal psychology departments at the beginning of the 20th century, psychology had been the domain of physicists, physicians, and other scientists who brought with them powerful skills from other domains. Early 20th century psychology had developed a new domain of study, but not yet an appreciation for the crucial importance of technical advances for making new discoveries in the new domain. Finally, in the second half of the 20th century, psychophysicists returned to some of the principles of the original psychophysicists by formulating and working out detailed computational models of perception. Again the initial impetus came from nonpsychologists.

B. Physiological and Computational Models of Early Vision

A revolution in the style of perceptual observations, in the computational theory to explain them, and in the neurophysiology that underlay them occurred in the period immediately following World War II (see also Nakayama, chap. 10, this volume). In 1953, Kuffler (1953) discovered the center-surround receptive fields of cat ganglion cells. There were in two types: ON-cells fired when light fell on the center of their receptive field and ceased firing when light fell on the annular surround; OFF-cells responded similarly to reductions (rather than increases) in light. The center-surround concept was quickly generalized to limulus (Hartline, Wagner, & Ratliff, 1956) where lateral inhibition had been overlooked for more than 20 years by Hartline and his collaborators. Vision physiology was propelled forward by Hubel and Wiesel (1962, 1965, 1968), who discovered the elongated receptive fields of the simple cells in cat occipital cortex and subsequently in monkey V1. This opened the gate to a flood of single neuron studies that at century's end is still growing exponentially.

From a computational point of view, it seems likely that ON- and OFF-ganglion cells operate as a push–pull pair in which one member signals an increase in stimulation and the other a decrease (Sperling, 1970, Appendix B). The computational analog of a Kuffler ON–OFF pair of center-surround ganglion cells is a spatial-frequency bandpass filter. Such filters can also be viewed as an outgrowth of the mathematical processes of spatial interaction that had been proposed by Mach (Mach 1865; Ratliff, 1965). Here, they are incorporated into the most elementary computational model for visual processes, illustrated in Figure 4a. The basic model consists of a linear filter followed by a detector (Sperling, 1964). The reason for using linear filters is that it is quite easy to measure the input–output properties of an unknown linear filter with either sine waves or impulses. After the initial measurement, the response of the filter to any waveform whatever can be readily computed.

Among the defining properties of a linear filter is "sinewaves in, sinewaves out." Therefore, a linear filter cannot serve as a model of psychophysical performance; observers in psychophysical experiments do not output sine waves. Typically, observers report binary decisions, "yes, I see it" or "no I don't." To make a computational model of the detection performance, the linear filter(s) must be paired with

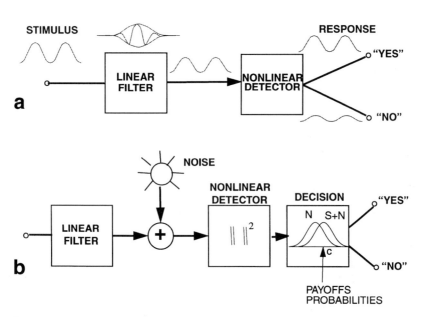

FIGURE 4   (a) A simple model for sensory thresholds and related paradigms. For determining spatial thresholds of a low-contrast stimuli, such as sine gratings or isolated bars, the linear filter typically is assumed to be a smoothed 2-D Laplacian or a Gabor function to represent a Kuffler center-surround receptive field. Subsequently, the detection component reports detection ("yes") if the filter output exceeds a threshold, otherwise, the detector reports nondetection ("no"). (b) A decision theory elaboration of the threshold model. Internal noise (N) is added to the output of the linear filter. The combined signal is processed by a nonlinear detector (typically, a device that measures energy), which outputs positive real numbers (typically, the amount of energy). The Decision box illustrates the probability density distribution of energy on trials with signal S + N and on trials without signal N. If the energy value on a particular trial exceeds a criterion (c), the Decision component outputs a "yes" (to indicate detection); otherwise it outputs "no." The numerical value of c is determined by rewards, probabilities, past outcomes, and the like. (Reproduced with permission of G. Sperling.)

a nonlinear detector that computes a decision from the output of the linear filter. In the earliest models, the decision component was a simple threshold device. When its input exceeded the threshold, it produced a positive response (e.g., the detector's output was $+1$ indicating detection); otherwise the detector output was zero.

C. Illustrations of the Power of a Linear System Model: Flicker Vision

Computational models, involving linear filtering and sinewave analysis, were introduced to vision researchers by two engineers: Otto Schade at RCA applied linear analysis to description of spatial images (1948, 1956, 1958). DeLange (1952, 1958a,b), an engineer at Phillips who conducted vision experiments privately in his basement, proposed a linear model for flicker vision. Compared to what had come before, the power of this simple model is illustrated by three examples.

1. In 1953, Carney Landis published his bibliography of flicker fusion that contained more than a thousand citations. Yet, for every new waveform that might be investigated, the only way to determine whether it would be seen as flickering or not was empirical; there was no theory. The simple model of Figure 4a, with the flicker filter as described by DeLange, made a prediction for every conceivable waveform. It is an interesting parenthetical note that Ives, a Bell Labs engineer involved in the development of television, published data (Ives, 1922a) and proposed a theory of temporal vision (Ives, 1922b) that anticipated DeLange by 30 years. Unfortunately, the vision community of the early 20th century was technically unprepared to appreciate such developments and, except for an isolated follow-up by Cobb (1934), Ives's pioneering work was overlooked.

2. The photochemical theory of Hecht (prominent in the 1950s) held that flicker vision was governed by a photochemical process in which a receptor pigment became exhausted during the light-on portion of the flicker cycle and recovered in light-off portion of the cycle. In terms of linear theory, Hecht's process was equivalent to what is called a single "RC-stage." DeLange's empirical measurements of flicker sensitivity determined the threshold modulation amplitude of a sine wave flickering field versus its temporal frequency. His graph of log threshold amplitude versus log frequency had a slope of -8 at higher temporal frequencies, which would result from 8 or more RC stages in series, not from a single RC stage. Hecht's single RC-stage theory is dramatically falsified.

3. The limit of human flicker fusion is about $60-70$ Hz or so, never significantly higher, frequently lower. Yet, a remarkable new phenomenon was reported (Brown & Forsyth, 1959) that assertedly required a revision of flicker theory. Two lights were set to flicker at frequencies too high to detect the flicker. Nevertheless, when these two invisible flickers were alternated in a combination stimulus, the previously invisible flicker became visible. Unfortunately, the authors (and the referees who accepted this article for publication in *Science*) did not understand linear filters. It

never occurred to them that this result was a simple, but counterintuitive corollary of a linear filter model, such as DeLange's (Levinson, 1959). In the mid-20th century, the study of perception was rediscovering what the 19th-century perceptionists (mostly physicists) had originally taken for granted: The analysis of perception requires the same computational tools as engineering and the hard sciences.

D. Multiple Channel and Detection Models

In the retina, Kuffler's center-surround cells occur in a great range of sizes, as do Hubel-Wiesel simple cells. The obvious extension to psychophysics was made by Campbell and Robson (1964, 1968), who discovered that when an observer stares at a grating with a particular spatial frequency, the observer becomes less sensitive to gratings of this and similar frequencies, but there is little change in sensitivity for gratings that differ in spatial frequency by a factor of more than two or three (see also Nakayama, chap. 10, this volume). This observation requires an elaboration of the simple filter model. Many spatial-frequency tuned filters, called channels, operate as visual processors. A visual stimulus is analyzed concurrently by many parallel channels, and a decision is based on the combination of their outputs. This important elaboration of the linear filter model is necessary to explain many phenomena of visual perception, from adaptation and masking, and is particularly significant for modeling object recognition.[1]

Another new development of the 1950s focused on the decision component of the filter-plus-detector models. Wald (1947, 1950) originally devised a sequential decision theory for military applications in World War II. Wald died prematurely in a plane crash; his methods were elaborated and applied to psychophysics by Tanner, Swets, and Green, where they became known as signal detection theory (SDT) (e.g., Green & Swets, 1966). The SDT model (Fig. 4b) and subsequent ideal detector models have replaced the simpler threshold model (Fig. 4a).

An enormous amount of research in visual psychophysics during the second half of the 20th century has focused on working out the properties of these extremely simple models: bandpass linear filtering (multiple channels) followed by a detector that implements a detector based on elementary signal detection theory. Signal detection theory was originally one-dimensional. When more than one channel is involved in a decision, a multidimensional theory is required—a significant complication (see Sperling & Dosher, 1986, and Graham, 1989, for reviews).

E. First-Order Perception of Motion

The 1950s saw the first computational model of visual motion perception. It was proposed by Reichardt (originally with Hassenstein, 1956) to account for insect

---

[1] Channel combination models have been extensively investigated in audition (see Sperling & Dosher, 1986, for a review), but this parallel development has been largely overlooked by vision scientists.

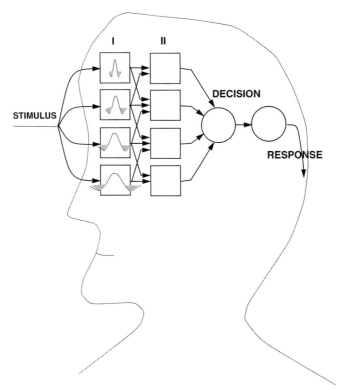

FIGURE 5   Channels. Center-surround receptive fields of ganglion cells and lateral geniculate cells occur in a wide range of sizes. Their outputs are processed in size-specific "channels" for several stages (I, II) before signals processed by receptive fields of different size combine. (Reproduced with permission of G. Sperling.)

vision (Reichardt, 1957). It, too, was an engineering model based on linear filters, although it incorporated a stage of multiplication, which is a highly nonlinear operation. The basic principle of this model is universal to visual motion models—the comparison of a visual input from one location with the time-delayed input from an adjacent location (Fig. 6). What was new was its implementation in terms of linear filters and its architecture of two subunits, tuned to opposite directions of motion, whose outputs were subtracted to form the final output.

There were at least half a dozen attempts to apply the Reichardt model to human vision, but a successful transposition was delayed by 30 years until van Santen and Sperling (1984). The problem was that human vision is not perfectly described by linear filters. There are two significant nonlinearities prior to visual motion computation—light adaptation and contrast gain control—that perturb measurements of the motion computation (see Fig. 7 and Sperling, 1989). Light adaptation usually does not vary unintentionally within a psychophysical experiment, so it has not

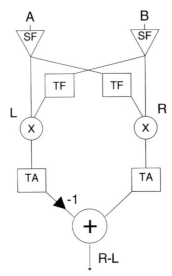

FIGURE 6   Reichardt motion model. The Reichardt model embodies one of a number of equivalent, and nearly equivalent, algorithms for motion extraction. It consists of two subunits: R responds positively to rightward movement; L responds positively to leftward movement. An input signal is extracted at two locations by spatiotemporal filters SF_1 and SF_2. When the time taken by a rightward-moving object to pass from SF_1 to SF_2 equals the delay imposed by the internal temporal delay filter (TF), the delayed and nondelayed signals arrive simultaneously at the multiplier, and thereby produce a large positive output. TA represents an optional Temporal Averaging/smoothing filter. Subtraction of the L subunit's response from the R subunit's response results in a Reichardt output that is positive for rightward movement, negative for leftward movement, and zero for nonmoving static or flickering stimuli. [Adapted from Fig. 2B in J. van Santen & G. Sperling (1984). Temporal covariance model of human motion perception. *J. Op. Soc. Am. A, 1, 5,* 453; with permission.]

been a problem for the linear-filter-plus-detector theories. But contrast gain-control mechanisms are important. The first-order motion system that detects ordinary translation (see below) begins to saturate at extremely small contrasts (4% according to Nakayama & Silverman, 1985; between 1% and 2% according to Lu & Sperling, 1997).

There is a compelling evolutionary basis for contrast gain control. Ideally, most judgments would be completely independent of stimulus contrast (e.g., judgments of motion direction or velocity) or judgments of the distance between two points. In practice, even an ideal visual system could achieve independence of contrast only when a sufficient number of photons were received (i.e., for contrasts greater than some small threshold contrast). Therefore, contrast gain control can usefully operate only above a threshold contrast. Below this threshold contrast, there is no significant contrast gain control, and only in this limited range can motion mechanisms be probed by inputs that are unperturbed by contrast gain control.

As humans routinely detect first-order motion with contrasts of 0.2% (1 part in

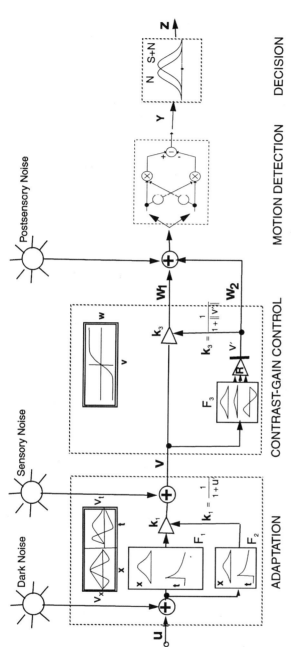

FIGURE 7 Four stages of visual processing: Adaptation, contrast gain control, motion detection, and a decision stage. The x and t, respectively, indicate spatial and temporal filters; the triangles k_i represent gain control mechanisms in which the signal on the horizontal path is divided by the signal in the vertical path, the sun symbols represent sources of random noise, and the + signs represent addition. Graphs within double outline boxes represent the aggregate characteristics of the component. Thus, V_x versus x indicates the spatial receptive field. The solid monophasic line represents the receptive field at low luminances; the lighter triphasic line represents the receptive field at high luminances. The symbol R in the triangle of the gain-control path represents rectification (absolute value computation) and the addition of rectified inputs in various different phase relations. F indicates a set of filters (receptive fields); the boldface letters, U, V, W, Y, Z, are used to designate the inputs/outputs at various stages within the system. [Adapted from Fig. 2 in G. Sperling (1989). Three stages and two systems of visual processing. *Spatial Vision, 4,* 186; with permission.]

500), there is ample dynamic range to explore the motion mechanism with very low contrast stimuli that bypass gain-control nonlinearities. For such low-contrast stimuli, it can be shown that the Reichardt model holds exactly. (See van Santen & Sperling, 1984, for three demonstrations of counterintuitive displays that demonstrate Reichardt properties of human motion perception: immunity of sine wave motion perception to an added stationary sine wave pedestal of the same spatial frequency; immunity to added homogeneous flicker if the flicker has a different temporal frequency; and motion amplitudes at adjacent locations multiply to determine motion strength).

To denote the formal similarity of dynamic motion perception to static slant perception, we note that a monocular motion stimulus is a cube in 3D space, x,y,t where x and y are spatial dimensions, and t is time. If we consider translatory motion of a simple visual stimulus (such as a tall vertical bar), then its motion is represented as a slanted line in x,t space (Watson & Ahumada, 1983). The decision as to whether there is motion to the left or right in x,t is equivalent to a decision of whether the line slants from upper left to lower right or vice versa in x,y (Fig. 8a, b).

A Hubel-Weisel simple cell is a cortical neuron that has an oriented receptive field, as illustrated in Figure 8c-f. A linear-filter mechanism that can determine line slant in x,y is the implementation of the Hubel-Weisel simple cell as an oriented bandpass filter. Even though a Hubel-Wiesel filter seems ideally suited for detecting slant, by itself, it is insufficient. Depending on where a line happens to fall on the filter, the output may be either negative, positive, or zero. Adding filters to cover many possible spatial locations, so that some, at least, will be perfectly placed, does not the solve the problem. Some are perfectly placed to have maximal positive outputs, others to have maximal negative output, and so the expected (average) output is zero. The obvious solution is not simply to add outputs, but to rectify them first, that is, to discard the sign of the filter outputs before combining them. Squaring the outputs accomplishes this with great mathematical elegance; the sum of squared outputs is called "power" or "energy." When outputs of filters with a only a particular orientation are squared and summed, the summed output is "directional power." For biological systems, perfect squaring is unnecessary; a wide range of monotonically increasing functions of the absolute value would be quite adequate.

A model for the slant detection in which the direction power is computed for competing orientations was proposed by Granlund and Knutsen (1983). Adelson and Bergen (1985), unaware of their work, proposed the equivalent model for the computation of motion direction, in which the hypothetical filters were slanted in x,t instead of as Hubel-Weisel filters) in x,y. A remarkable fact is that these differently motivated and differently constructed motion models [elaborated by Reichardt (van Santen-Sperling) and Adelson-Bergen], are computationally equivalent. Indeed, it was also shown (van Santen & Sperling, 1985), that an elaboration of the mathematically elegant Watson-Ahumada motion detection filter based on Hilbert transforms also was equivalent to the Reichardt model. From an input–output point

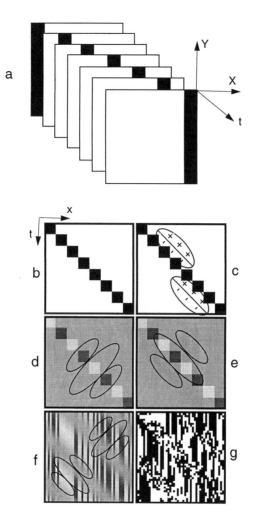

FIGURE 8 First- and second-order motion and texture stimuli. (a) Eight frames of a vertical bar that moves from left to right as a function of time (t). The last frame is shown in its entirety, the previous frames are mostly obscured. (b) An x-t cross-section of (a). (c) An x-t cross-section of (a) with Hubel-Wiesel edge filters superimposed in two different phase relationships. The filter outputs are either positive or negative depending on where they happen to fall in the stimulus. Notice also the equivalence of the problem of direction-of-motion detection in x-t with the direction-of-slant detection in x-y. (d) A "reversed phi" stimulus. A moving bar changes from white-on-gray to black-on-gray in successive frames. The Hubel-Wiesel line filter superimposed on the reversed phi stimulus illustrates it has a large output and therefore "perceives" slant from upper right to lower left, the so-called Fourier direction. Human perceive motion or slant in the Fourier direction when the stimulus is extremely small or viewed in peripheral vision, and in the nonFourier direction under normal viewing. (e) Reversed phi stimulus with a Hubel-Wiesel filter oriented in the non-Fourier direction to illustrate that its output will be approximately zero. Nevertheless, this is the direction in which humans normally perceive motion (or slant). (f,g) Drift-balanced and microbalanced stimuli for which Hubel-Wiesel receptive fields oriented at $+45°$ and $-45°$ have exactly equal expected outputs. Detection of left-to-right motion or upper-left to lower-right slant necessarily requires second-order motion or texture processing. [Adapted from Fig. 1 in C. Chubb & G. Sperling (1989). Two motion perception mechanisms revealed through distance-driven reversal of apparent motion, *Proc. NAS USA, 86*, 2986; with permission of the authors.]

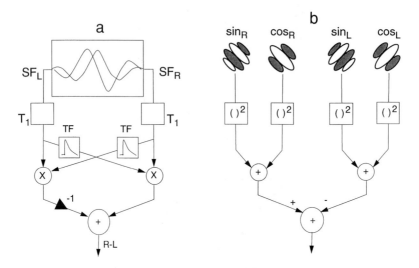

FIGURE 9   Two equivalent motion models. (a) Reichardt motion model. Spatial filters (receptive fields) are indicated as sine SF_L and cosine SF_R Gabor functions. T_1 indicates a temporal filter (incorporated into filter SF in Fig. 6), other details as in Fig. 6. (b) A directional energy detector (after Granlund & Knutsen, 1983). In the x, y (spatial) domain, it computes rightward- versus leftward-slanting orientation power. In x,y, sin_R and cos_R indicate rightward slanting Hubel-Wiesel receptive fields (spatial bandpass filters), and sin_L, cos_L are leftward-slanting receptive fields. $(\ )^2$ indicates squaring and $+$ indicates summation. Interpreting the coordinates as x,t yields a direction motion-energy detector that determines the rightward minus leftward motion power. (Reprinted with permission of G. Sperling.)

of view, these three theories of first-order motion are equivalent. Of course, which of these, if any, corresponds to the biological mechanisms that sense motion is not yet resolved.

F. Second-Order Perceptual Processes

A further development in psychophysical research has been the discovery of second-order processes of perception. In first-order visual perception, the unit on which processing is based is the amount of light reaching any small area, i.e., the units of first-order processing are photons.

In second-order perception, the units of processing are features. Typically, a visual feature is a small patch of a particular kind of texture. However, features are defined not by logical analysis of visual stimuli but by the analyses performed by second-order neural systems. We call a particular kind of visual micropattern a feature if there are (second-order) neurons that process it analogously to the way that (first-order) neurons process photons.

The study of second-order perception was an outgrowth of the advent of computer-controlled graphic displays. New display technology made it easy to create texture stimuli that were invisible to first-order processes, but which elicited analogous (second-order) perceptual responses to first-order stimuli. For example, spatial interactions, such as lateral brightness induction, Mach bands, Chevreul illusions, and the Craik-O'Brien Cornsweet illusion, can be reproduced in stimuli that have no systematic variations in luminance (Chubb, Sperling, & Solomon, 1989; Lu & Sperling, 1996a) but that vary systematically in *texture contrast* as a function of space (Figs. 10 and 11).

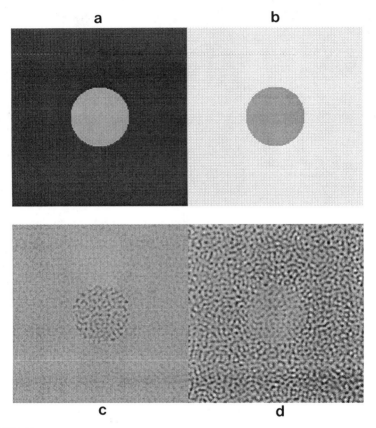

FIGURE 10   Classical lightness illusion (a,b) and the analogous second-order "contrast–contrast" illusion (c, d). The central disks in (a) and (b) have the same luminance, but the surround in (b) reflects more photons than the surround of (a). In sensory systems, active neurons tend to inhibit their neighbors, so the (more inhibited) central disk in (b) appears less bright than the (less inhibited) disk in (a). In (c) and (d), the expected luminance is the same everywhere, and the contrast of both central disks is the same. Only the surrounds differ. In second-order illusions, features take the role of photons in first-order illusions. In (d) the greater abundance of features in the surround, due to its higher contrast, makes its inner disk appear to be of lower contrast than the disk in (c). [Adapted from Fig. 1 in C. Chubb, G. Sperling, and J. Solomon (1989). Texture interactions determine perceived contrast. *Proc. NAS USA, 86,* 9632; with permission of the authors.]

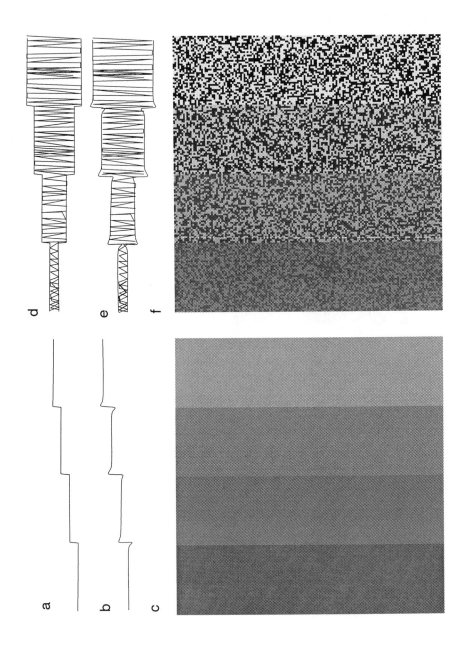

Second-order processes have been most studied in the domain of motion perception, in which parallel first- and second-order processing systems have been discovered. Both of these are primarily monocular, fast, and both approach the theoretical limits in their efficiency of utilizing stimulus information that actually reaches the retina (Geisler, 1989; Solomon & Sperling, 1994). Both first- and second-order motion systems are activated by highly specific stimulus properties (Fig. 12).

Motion is processed at higher levels by a third-order motion system. The third-order motion system is much slower and less sensitive than the first- or second-order motion system, but is indifferent to the eye of origin of successive stimuli and it has amazing versatility. The mechanism of third-order motion depends on an automatic figure–ground computation. That is, for purposes of further processing, the visual system divides the visual stimulus into areas that are marked as "figure" (which are then forwarded to shape and object recognition modules) and into parts that are unmarked—the ground upon which figures appear. The ground is not further analyzed. Classical illusions such as Rubin vases (see also Cutting & Massironi, chap. 6, this volume; Hochberg, chap. 9, this volume) result from stimuli that admit two alternative, stable figure–ground divisions that produce very differently perceived figures. The figure–ground computation is performed automatically on every visual input, whether or not the input is noisy or ambiguous. The result of figure–ground computations is recorded in a "salience field," a representation of the visual field in which salient areas (e.g., figure) are marked, and the background is unmarked.

Third-order motion is an automatic computation that records translations of marked areas. Similarly, the object recognition process takes its input only from marked locations. Attention interacts with both of these processes, third-order motion and object recognition, by determining which features are more salient and therefore more likely to be marked. All these relations are illustrated in Figure 13.

G. Development of Motion Models

The point of this exposition is not to inform the reader of the specific details of these complex processes; for these, there are reviews (Sperling, Chubb, Solomon, &

FIGURE 11 First- and second-order Chevreul illusions. In (a) and (c), the luminance increases stepwise but the brightness appears "scalloped" as in (b). That is, the bright side of the edge appears brighter than equally luminous neighboring areas and the dark side appears dimmer than equally luminous neighboring areas. In (d) and (f), contrast increases stepwise, expected luminance remaining constant throughout. The apparent contrast appears correspondingly scalloped at the contrast steps as in (e). [(a) and (b) reprinted from Fig. 1 in Z. Lu and G. Sperling (1996). Second-order illusions: Mach Bands, Chevreul, and Craik-O'Brien-Cornsweet. *Vision Research, 36, 4,* 560; (c) and (f) reprinted from Fig. 4 in Z. Lu and G. Sperling (1996). Second-order illusions: Mach Bands, Chevreul, and Craik-O'Brien-Cornsweet. *Vision Research, 36, 4,* 566; and (d) and (e) reprinted from Fig. 2 in Z. Lu and G. Sperling (1996). Second-order illusions: Mach Bands, Chevreul, and Craik-O'Brien-Cornsweet. *Vision Research, 36, 4,* 561; with kind permission from Elsevier Science Ltd, The Boulevard, Langford Lane, Kidlington OX5 1GB, UK.]

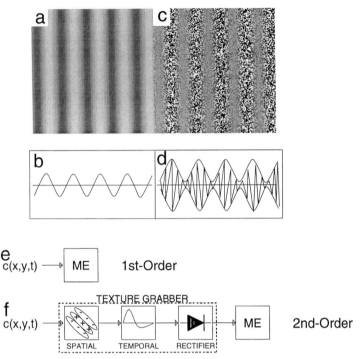

FIGURE 12 First- and second-order motion stimuli. (a) A single-frame of a first-order stimulus—a sinusoidally modulated luminance grating. (b) A graphical representation of the sinusoidal modulation of (a). (c) A single-frame of a second-order stimulus—a contrast-modulated random-texture grating. (d) A graphical representation of one horizontal line of (c). The random function represents the *carrier* texture: its envelope is the modulator. To create an impression of motion, the modulators in (b) and (d) translate horizontally from frame-to-frame. (e) A motion energy (ME) computation suffices to extract motion. (f) Second-order contrast-modulation motion is detected by first extracting the textural features (via a "texture grabber" represented by the first three boxes in [f]), and then computing ME of the features equivalently to computing the ME of photons in first-order motion. The texture grabber consists of three stages: an ordinary linear spatial filter, (SPATIAL box), a temporal bandpass filter (TEMPORAL box), and rectification (absolute value or square). [Reprinted from Fig. 2 in Z. Lu and G. Sperling (1995). The functional architecture of human visual motion perception. *Vision Research, 35, 19,* 2699; with kind permission from Elsevier Science Ltd, The Boulevard, Langford Lane, Kidlington OX5 1GB, UK.]

Lu, 1994; Lu & Sperling, 1996b) and source papers (Chubb & Sperling, 1988; Lu & Sperling, 1995a; Lu & Sperling, 1995b). Rather it is to illustrate how, during the course of a century, the study of motion has progressed from the description of the phenomenon of two flash apparent motion by Exner (1875), a relatively straightforward objective description, to the mentalism of Wertheimer and the Gestaltists (as manifest in their reliance on introspective observations, i.e., "pure objectless phi motion"), to the first computational description by Reichardt in the 1950s, and to

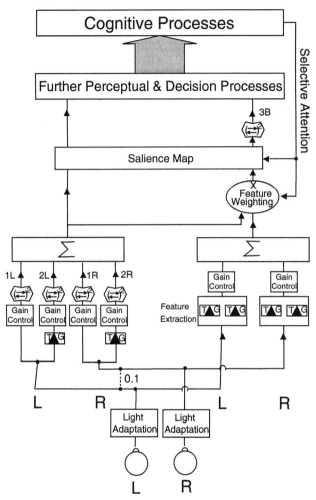

FIGURE 13   The functional architecture of the brain system that determines motion direction. The most critical components, motion energy extractors (e.g., Reichardt models $(\rightleftarrows)^2$ texture grabbers (TG) are defined in Figs. 12 and 9). Signals arriving at the left (L) and right (R) eyes are first analyzed separately for first- and second-order motion content resulting in L and R first- and second-order signals (1L, 2L, 1R, 2R); these are combined in Σ according to rules not yet fully understood. The right half of Figure 13 illustrates the combination of texture features before motion extraction, feature weighting that is modified by the state of attention, and a representation of the most significant features (figure versus ground) in a salience map. The third-order motion system, which has only about $\frac{1}{3}$ the speed and resolution and $\frac{1}{10}$ the sensitivity of the first- and second-order motion systems, takes the output of the salience maps as its input and computes third-order motion. [Reprinted from Fig. 13 in Z. Lu and G. Sperling (1995). The functional architecture of human visual motion perception. *Vision Research, 35, 19,* 2719; with kind permission from Elsevier Science Ltd, The Boulevard, Langford Lane, Kidlington OX5 1GB, UK.]

the working out of the consequences of computational models in the second half of the century.

The representation of knowledge about perception of motion direction has resulted in models of ever increasing complexity. The Reichardt model of the 1950s (Fig. 6) has nine components (boxes). The Reichard model appears five times as a component of in the motion architecture model of the 1990s (Fig. 13). A texture grabber has three components and appears six times in Figure 13. Thus 9 of the 23 components of Figure 13 expand immediately to 69 subcomponents, and the most complex components have not been expanded.

Figure 13 represents just one local spatial region. It is reproduced in every visual neighborhood, thousands of times in all. As soon as neighboring processing is considered, spatial interactions come into play. The entire motion-architecture model of Figure 13, with all its neighboring reproductions and interactions, represents just one channel—one level of resolution in a pyramid structure. The whole architecture is repeated, at least in first-order motion perception, at many different levels of resolution. A model that simultaneously incorporates both spatial relations and different levels of resolution is obviously enormously more complex and will involve many spatial and vertical processes that are not represented in the simplified architecture of Figure 13. And all this complexity arises from a model merely of the perception of motion direction; velocity is not even considered. The closing years of the 20th century have seen an explosion of computation models for more complex aspects of motion perception, such as the perception of velocity, of three-dimensional structure from two-dimensional motion, the perception of visual heading from motion flow fields, and so on. The step-by-step substantiation, elaboration, and integration of such models seems to be one important direction for the study of motion perception in the 21st century. It is a harbinger of developments to come in the study of other sensory processes, and it illuminates the enormous difference between theories of the 19th and 21st centuries.

III. VISUAL ATTENTION

A. Early Conceptions of Attention

Unlike perception, which had an extensive empirical development by the late 19th century, the study of attention largely began with the questions and observations of the mentalists near the turn of the century. Attention and its relation to consciousness was actively discussed. William James (1890) said,

> Every one knows what attention is. It is the taking possession by the mind, in clear and vivid form, of one out of what seem several simultaneously possible objects. . . . One principal object comes then into the focus of consciousness, others are temporarily suppressed. (pp. 403–404)

Unfortunately, although everyone knew what attention was, there was very little agreement about what they knew. The psychologists of the period, such as James,

Wundt, Tichener, and Ladd, who based their accounts on introspective observations, failed to agree on either the effects of attention or its mechanisms. To quote Kulpe (1895/1921):

> Every psychologist of any independence at the present time analyses and derives attention in his own way. Some reduce it to . . . sensations of muscular contraction or of strain; others regard it as an emotion, which exercises an especial influence upon the motor side of our activity. Another, psychophysical theory makes it the primary office of attention to reinforce excitation in the sensory centres; and a fourth hypothesis characterises its positive function as a process of inhibition. (p. 423)

An intriguing observation of that period that is perhaps typical of the introspective approach is described by Wilhelm Wundt in the late 1800s (translated into English, 1912/1924, pp. 19–22). Wundt asked his reader to fixate the *o* in the center of an array of letters (Fig. 14), and to maintain fixation while moving the "subjective-fixation" of attention to the *n* on the right-hand side. By introspection, the letters surrounding the *n* were "perceive[d] more clearly," whereas the letters elsewhere "seem to retreat into the darker field of consciousness." (p. 21). Wundt was aware that visual acuity falls off away from the point of fixation of the eye, and that attention, although ordinarily coordinated with eye movements, can be separated from fixation. Attention to locations in space is one major theme of this section, and the relation of attention and eye movements is considered later in the section.

B. Documenting an Effect of Attention: Response Time and Detection

Logical, practical, and theoretical difficulties arise from Wundt's observation. Visual distribution and extent of the area of visual clarity might be difficult or impossible to ascertain with introspective measures, because the evaluation of the clarity of an

```
              t  h  m
           m  v  x  w  a  s  f
        l  g  i  c  s  f  p  d  t
        z  r  a  e  n  p  r  h  v  z  l
        r  f  u  c  t  h  f  b  n  d  s
        k  h  e  p  n  o  t  v  b  s  i
        n  z  l  u  c  r  k  m  d  g  n
        d  i  n  i  w  g  e  t  v  r  f
           s  a  t  f  l  b  p  n  k
           m  d  w  c  k  t  g
              p  a  v  e  r
```

FIGURE 14   A stimulus devised by Wundt (1912/1924, p. 19) to illustrate that attention could move independent of the eye, and that the point of "subjective fixation" of attention creates an impression of perceptual clarity. The observer was asked to fixate the central *o* and attend to the letter *n* one up and four to the right, and observe the gradient of attention. [Following Wundt (1912/1924). p. 19.]

unattended location, the necessary control, would require shifting at least some attention to the unattended location—a paradox. However, introspection itself is not the problem. Introspection enters the 21st century in good health and with a firm basis under the guise of sensory scaling. As practiced in the 20th century, sensory scaling involves two methods: relating real numbers to perceived sensory quality or intensity, and judging various modes of equivalence of different sensory experiences. These are forms of introspection in which the possible range of response is extremely restricted. When some of these methods of refined introspection have been applied to attention, the results have been disappointing. Judgments of appearance seem to be remarkably indifferent to the state of attention (e.g., Prinzmetal, Amiri, Allen, Nwachuki, & Bodanske, 1995, find that reports of stimulus properties such as color are essentially the same, though perhaps less variable, for attended as compared to unattended conditions). Failing to replicate Wundt's casual introspective observation under the more rigorous conditions typical of scaling experiments is a practical problem, but it may be due to the logical paradox alluded to above.

From the point of view of evolution, the subjective qualities of perception are not the relevant consideration; what matters is whether or not responses to stimuli are competent and adaptive. Measurement of the behavioral consequences of focusing visual attention at a given location awaited the development of appropriate experimental methods for the measurement of accuracy and—after the reintroduction of reaction time (RT) measures into psychology in the 1960s—RT.

Perhaps the first serious experimental attempt to assess the consequences of distribution of attention over the visual field was by Mertens (1956). His observers fixated a central point and were asked to detect a weak flash of light that could occur in one of four positions corresponding to the corners of a square around fixation. Observers judged whether or not a flash occurred during a test trial. Mertens contrasted a focused attention condition in which the observer knew that flashes could occur in only one known location with a divided attention condition in which the observer knew that the flash could occur at any location. Merton concluded that focused attention impaired detection. Unfortunately, Mertens's conclusion was incorrect, because he considered only hits, and not false alarms (i.e., he was unaware of signal detection theory). We will return to Mertens and his conclusion after further development.

In the 1970s, Posner and his students (e.g., Posner, Nissen, & Ogden, 1978) measured the consequences of focusing attention on certain locations in visual space using RT rather than response accuracy. An illustration of his paradigm and some sample results are shown in Figure 15. Observers fixated on a central cross. The test stimulus was a flash of light that appeared on most but not all trials; the flash was either to the right or the left of fixation. Observers pressed a single key as soon as they saw any flash (go–no-go paradigm). To manipulate the distribution of attention, a left- or right-pointing cue arrow appeared prior to the light flash on some trials; the arrow indicated the likely location of the flash, and observers were

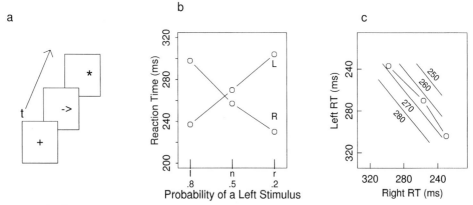

FIGURE 15   (a) An illustration of Posner, Nissen, and Odgen's (1976) paradigm for measuring the consequences for response latency of focusing attention on a location in space. (b) Sample response time (RT) data showing the costs and benefits of focal attention. R, right; L, left. (After Sperling & Dosher, 1986, Fig. 2.18a.) (c) Regraphing of the data that further illustrates the trade-off in RT data, along with utility contours. (After Fig. 2.18 in Sperling and Dosher (1986), with permission of the authors.)

expected to attend to that location. On the 80% of trials when the flash occurs in the attended location, mean RT is rather fast whereas RT on the 20% of trials when the flash occurs in the unattended location is rather slow; RTs for uncued trials are intermediate. RTs were about 240 ms for attended flashes, 300 ms for unattended flashes, and 270 ms for uncued flashes. Accuracies were generally ignored. Posner interpreted RT differences as the "costs" or "benefits" (relative to uncued performance) of attention to a location in space.

Go–no-go experiments, with their emphasis on empirical documentation of the consequences of attention, represent an advance in experimental methodology. Yet both the Mertens and the Posner et al. investigations lacked the theoretical tools necessary for unambiguous interpretation. As explained below, several alternative interpretations of these results are possible.

The experiments relate to—but do not answer—a host of questions: how quickly is attention deployed, how is attention distributed spatially, and, importantly, does attention improve clarity or sensitivity or does it change which information is selected for subsequent decision or memory? Progress on each of these questions is taken up in turn.

C. Episodes of Attention: Attention Switching

An observer's decision to focus attention on a particular location in space, either in response to a cue in an experiment such as Posner's, or to acquire new information in natural situations, initiates a new attentional episode. Attention is switched from its current state to a new focus. It is now known that the time course of a switch of visual attention is not instantaneous. It involves the opening and closing of an

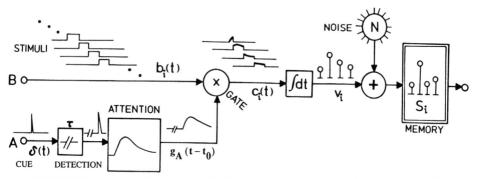

FIGURE 16   An attention-gating model. When an attention cue appears in input stream A, the attention-modulating system gates information from a second stream of visual input, B, into memory for report. In the figure, t refers to time, $\delta(t)$ and τ are processing delays, $g_A(t - t_0)$ describes the attention gate; $b_i(t)$ and $c_i(t)$ are weighted inputs; and v_i and S_i are item strengths. [From Fig. 11 in G. Sperling and E. Weichselgartner (1995). Episodic theory of the dynamics of spatial attention, *Psychological Review, 102, 3,* 524; with permission of the American Psychological Association.]

attention "gate" that selectively admits information from one part of the visual field to further processing or to memory.

The temporal characteristics of a switch of attention were treated quantitatively by Reeves and Sperling (1986). In their gating model (Fig. 16), a cue to switch attention produces, after a short delay, the opening of a gate at the cued location. Information at the newly attended location is gated into memory. The memorial representation is the basis for conscious awareness of information at the cued location.

In Reeves and Sperling's experiments, a target item occurs in one sequence of letters and, as soon as the target appears, observers must report the next item or items that appear in a second, spatially separated sequence. The delay in opening the attention gate, as well as the temporally continuous operation of the gate, can be inferred from the item(s) the observer reports from the newly attended location. These observations tell us about the temporal aspects of attention as a process that controls the flow of information into memory, an important phenomenon that is further discussed in section IV.

D. Spatial and Temporal Distribution of Attention

As a consequence of improvements in both data collection and in process models, Wundt's initial question about the spatial extent of focused attention can now be quantitatively answered within a more general "episodic" model of attention (Sperling & Weichselgartner, 1995). Spatial attention is regarded as a sequence of discrete states, quite analogous to the fixation states of the eyes in sequences of saccadic eye movements. The model allows the estimation of the spatial distribution of attention and of the time course of switching attention from one location to another.

At any given time, the observer is in a particular attentional state associated with a spatial attention function defined at each position in space, $f(x,y)$. The switch from one attentional state to another is described by a temporal transition function. Each attentional state defines an attentional episode, and a transition from one state to another demarks one episode from the next (Fig. 17). Figure 18 illustrates hypothetical distributions of attention to two different locations in space (e.g., left and right) during two attentional episodes, one before and one after a switch of attention.

The episodic model of attentional distribution and attentional switching accounts closely for many sets of attentional data. Estimated spatial attention functions

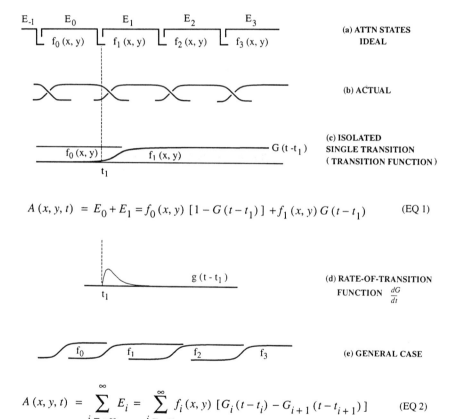

$$A(x, y, t) = E_0 + E_1 = f_0(x, y)[1 - G(t - t_1)] + f_1(x, y) G(t - t_1) \qquad \text{(EQ 1)}$$

$$A(x, y, t) = \sum_{i=-\infty}^{\infty} E_i = \sum_{i=-\infty}^{\infty} f_i(x, y)[G_i(t - t_i) - G_{i+1}(t - t_{i+1})] \qquad \text{(EQ 2)}$$

FIGURE 17   An episodic theory of attention. (a) a series of attention states, with idealized instantaneous shifts of attention between states; (b) actual attention episodes with non-instantaneous attention shifts; (c) details of a single attention transition function; (d) corresponding rate of transition function for a single transition; (e) general case of transition between episodes. [From Fig. 2 in G. Sperling and E. Weichselgartner (1995). Episodic theory of the dynamics of spatial attention. *Psychological Review, 102, 3,* 505; with permission of the American Psychological Association.]

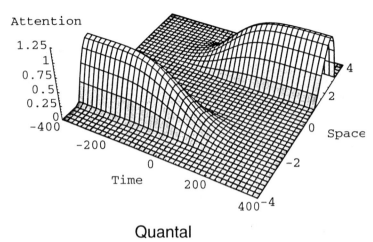

Quantal

FIGURE 18   The spatial attention functions (e.g., for a left or right location) and the temporal transition function as they shift (from left to right) in the Sperling and Weichselgartner (1995) model. The spatial attention functions are graphed as attentional weight or effectiveness as a function of the two variables time and spatial location. [From Fig. 1 in G. Sperling and E. Weichselgartner (1995). Episodic theory of the dynamics of spatial attention. *Psychological Review, 102, 3,* 504; with permission of the American Psychological Association.]

generally look similar to that depicted in Figure 18, but are of course sensitive in part to experimental manipulations and the nature of the behavioral measure. The distribution of targets over space (Sperling & Weichselgartner, 1995) and the focus required by the task (LaBerge & Brown, 1989) affect the spatial distribution of attention.

An important relationship holds between the spatial and temporal properties of attention. The spatial attention functions and temporal transition functions estimated for a wide range of experiments (e.g., Lyon, 1987; Shulman, Remington, & McLean, 1979; Tsal, 1983) are space–time separable (e.g., the functions represent "quantal" movements of attention). Attention is focused around one location and then, at the time of a switch in focus, attention is focused around the next location. Contrary to a number of early speculations (Shulman, Remington, & McLean, 1979; Tsal, 1983), moving attention from one location to the next is not accomplished in an analog manner—attention does not move through the intermediate locations (Sperling & Weichselgartner, 1995). Visual attention operates like a bank of stationary spotlights in which only one light may be turned on at a time. As one spotlight turns off, another spotlight focused at a different location turns on.

With continuing investigation, the earlier attention-gating model (Fig. 16) has evolved into much more detailed model (Fig. 19). The quantitative form of the model allows the estimation of both the spatial and temporal aspects of attention and attention shifts, and the same model with the same parameters applies to a wide variety of experimental designs and situations.

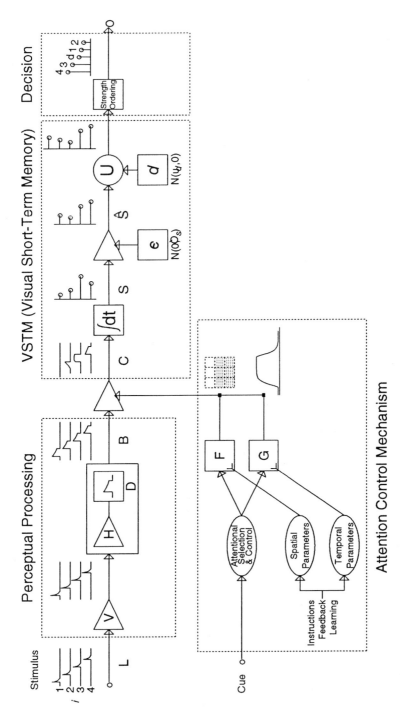

FIGURE 19 An elaborated attention–gating model specifying the details of the attention–gating function in terms of spatial and temporal parameters of attention shifts. (Reprinted with permission of G. Sperling.)

As in visual perception, the history of theorizing in spatial attention began with catalogs of phenomena and vague verbal interpretations and has progressed to well-specified models of performance applicable to a wide range of stimulus situations. Like the motion models, the attention models of Reeves and Sperling (1986) and Sperling and Weichselgartner (1995) are quantifiable, specific, and embody a complex information-processing architecture. However, like the early attempts by Mertens, Posner, and others, the attention-gating models do not distinguish between different mechanisms that may underlie the measurable changes in behavior. In particular, they do not distinguish between changes in the perceptual strength (clarity) of stimuli and changes in the criteria or thresholds for response, or the entrance into a memory store.

E. Bias versus Discrimination in Detection Accuracy and Reaction Time

James felt that attention to some objects was accompanied by the suppression of other objects—a notion of limited capacity. Hence, perceptual "clarity" was improved for attended objects and reduced for unattended ones. The strong form of the perceptual clarity claim must demonstrate attentionally manipulated changes in sensory strength, or discriminability. (There are other interpretations of the term clarity. For example, Treisman (1986) argues that the features of multifeature stimuli are bound together only in the focus of attention. See Hochberg, chap. 9, this volume, for a discussion.) Distinguishing between attentional modulation of perceptual clarity and other attentional changes requires the application of signal detection theory. As discussed above (section II), signal detection theory was introduced into psychology in the 1960s in the domain of auditory psychophysics (Green & Swets, 1966). In the SDT framework, differences in detection performance as a function of attention reflect either changes in perceptual strength (discriminability) or changes in criterion (bias), or both. Signal detection theory provides a way of estimating the strength of a stimulus in the face of changes in performance that reflect only changes in decision rules or criteria. (Additionally, the number of signal and noise sources may be an issue, see below.)

Suppose an observer is asked to respond when she sees a weak flash of light. In SDT the evidence for a light flash occurring during the trial interval is represented on a unidimensional scale of perceptual strength. The distribution of perceptual strengths (often assumed to be gaussian) is higher if the light flash actually occurred (signal) than if it did not (noise) (Fig. 20a). If the subjective evidence or strength sampled on a particular trial is above a criterion then the observer says that a flash occurred, otherwise they do not. The number of detection responses obviously depends not only on the visibility (intensity or duration) of the flash, but on the criterion (lax or strict) that the subject adopts for a response. A lax criterion may produce many "detect" responses even for a relatively weak stimulus, whereas a strict criterion may produce few "detect" responses even for a relatively stronger stimulus.

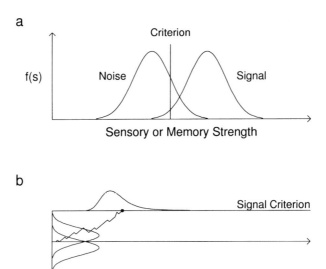

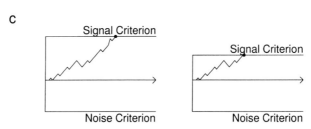

FIGURE 20   Principles of signal-detection theory account for decision structure. (a) Distributions of evidence or strength for target-present (signal) and target-absent (noise) trials, along with one possible criterion. (b) A random walk or diffusion model with similar signal-detection assumptions. Information is sampled over time, resulting in a decision whenever the cumulated information reaches either a signal or noise evidence criterion. (c) A set of random walks that can account for the costs and benefits when the observer is cued to expect a signal on the right, and changes the distance to the information boundaries accordingly; the left portion represents the long response times when a signal appears unexpectedly on the left, and the right portion the shorter response times when a signal appears on the right as expected. (With permission of B. Dosher.)

SDT is critical to the correct understanding of a number of attentional paradigms. In Mertens's flash detection experiment, attending to a single cued location was contrasted with dispersed attention where no single location was the focus. In Posner's experiment, performance with dispersed (uncued) attention was compared with performance when the target occurred in an attended or an unattended location. An SDT analysis makes clear that at least two things other than perceptual strength might account for differences between conditions: changes in criteria, or bias, and changes in sources of noise in the decision process.

F. Criterion Shifts or Bias

Attentional instructions may cause the observer to shift criteria, and this may affect performance without any changes in perceptual strength of the stimuli. In the Posner experiment, when observers are cued to expect a flash on the right, observers may simply lower their criterion for sensory evidence on the right and raise their criterion for evidence on the left. A model of response times that is related in spirit to SDT incorporates bias, and can accomodate a cost–benefit relation in response times is also illustrated in Figure 20. This form of RT model (Fig. 20b) is called either a random walk or diffusion model (Ratcliff, 1978). The trade-off between left and right RTs is nearly perfect (Fig. 15c), as well as completely consistent with a reasonable interpretation of the utility of overall performance given the trade-off in speed and the probabilities of each stimulus (see Sperling & Dosher, 1986, for a full development). In the Mertens experiment, analogously, the criterion for a flash-present response should be lower for the focused than for the dispersed attention condition in order to equate false alarm rates.

Changes in criterion or bias are attentional effects in the sense that they are behavioral changes reflecting a voluntary attentional manipulation. They change performance in the absence of changes in perceptual strength, and do not necessarily reflect the operation of a limited-capacity attentional mechanism.

G. Decision Noise

When the experimental situation is even somewhat complicated—involving either several possible very different stimuli or several locations for a simple stimulus—the multiple-channel architectures similar to those outlined for visual perception (Fig. 5) pose added sources of complication. In these situations, a second explanation for changes in performance in different attentional conditions involves *decision noise*. This is a nonperceptual explanation in that it does not assume any change in the perceptual processes themselves, but merely reflects the necessity of processing multiple sources of information. Decision noise is relevant when attention to many objects is contrasted with attention to a single object. It reflects structural changes in the decision rules with changing attentional instructions.

In the Mertens experiment, for example, the observer is dealing with only one evidence sample if the location of a signal flash is known. The sample of perceptual strength from the single known location is either from the signal or from the noise distribution. In trials where the signal location is not cued, four evidence samples are relevant, one from each of the four possible locations. The four samples are drawn either from one signal and three noise distributions or from four noise distributions (Fig. 21). The number of noise samples turns out to be critical, because it determines the number of sources of false alarms errors (saying target when there was none). Even if perceptual strength and decision criteria were identical in the two situations, an observer would exhibit more false alarm errors on unknown-a

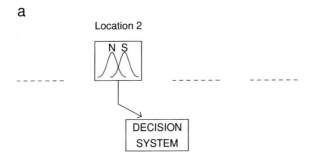

b

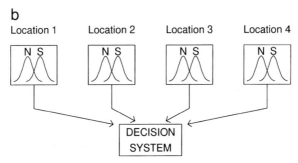

FIGURE 21   Preformance losses may reflect the decision structure in multichannel paradigms. (a) Illustrates signal detection with one known location (one channel); the stimulus may be either noise or signal on any trial. (b) Illustrates signal detection from four possible locations (four channel architecture); the stimulus may be either noise (noise in all locations) or a signal (signal in one location and noise in the remaining three) on any trial. Integrating observations from the four locations increases the sources of false alarms, producing performance deficits that reflect statistical decision loss rather than differences in the perceptual representation of the stimulus. (With permission of B. Dosher.)

location trials than on known-location trials because there are more chances to sample a high value of perceptual strength from the noise distribution from four locations than from one. Sometimes observers attempt to equate false alarm errors for the known- and unknown-location conditions; to do this they must raise their criterion on unknown-location trials. Although this may equate false alarms, it also necessarily leads to fewer correct detection responses. In either case, these decrements in performance reflect structural differences in the decision rules used in the two kinds of trials, not true differences in perceptual strength or discriminability. These decrements are called either decision noise or uncertainty loss.

In order to demonstrate that attention improves discrimination—or alternatively that spreading attention over many locations results in reduced discrimination because it is difficult to attend to too many things at once—decision or uncertainty loss must be estimated and factored out, or otherwise taken into account in the interpretation. Sperling and Dosher (1986) provide an overview of theoretical approaches to the estimation of decision loss and also describe classes of experiments that circumvent the issue of decision loss.

Often, decrements in performance associated with an increase in the number of attended locations do not exceed the loss due to decision noise (Graham, 1989; Palmer, 1994; Palmer, Ames, & Lindsay, 1993; Shaw, 1980, 1984). In some cases, a single target such as a flash is tested at one of several locations; in others, the target is shown among a certain number of distractors. In the latter case, sensory factors such as lateral masking must be eliminated or controlled. For many simple tasks, such as detection based on intensity increments, line orientation, target size, or target color, decrements in performance are almost exactly as predicted by decision noise calculations (Palmer, 1994; Palmer et al., 1993; Shaw, 1984). Certain more complex detection tasks do show discriminability differences between attended and unattended locations, presumably due to attentional capacity limitations (Downing, 1988; Shaw, 1984). The form and causes of attentional changes in perceptual discrimination in the more complex tasks are just beginning to be understood.

H. Attention Operating Characteristics

Verbal statements that attention is limited in processing capacity are traceable back to the turn of the century. These verbal statements have given way to methodological and formal developments that allow a full characterization of not just the extent to which performance on several subtasks depends on a limited capacity resource, but a precise evaluation of the nature of the trade-off between task performances.

A powerful methodological alternative to the SDT analyses of decision noise (leading to somewhat complex forms of decision or output models) involves the concurrent measurement of performance in two tasks (see Sperling & Dosher, 1986, for a full development). Concurrent measurements in two tasks that may be competing for attention evaluates the attention operating characteristic (AOC). The purpose of an AOC is to evaluate whether the two tasks can be performed together, or whether they require competing attentional capacity. Figure 22 illustrates an idealized AOC. The x-axis is performance on Task A; the y-axis is performance on Task B. Baseline conditions (solid circles) measure how well each task is done alone. If two tasks can be done simultaneously without loss, then joint performance will fall at the independence point (open circle). If the two tasks make competing demands on attention, the performance will fall below and to the left of the independence point. Joint performance should be measured under several attentional instructions (solid triangles), for example, 20–80%, 50–50%, and 80–20% Task A–Task B performance, from top-left to bottom-right. Systematic changes with instructions directly demonstrate *cognitive* attentional control over the joint performance of the two tasks.

The AOC is a powerful method for evaluating whether competing attentional resources are required for two tasks. In an early example (Figure 23a–c), Sperling and Melchner (1978) examined how observers searched for a digit among letters in

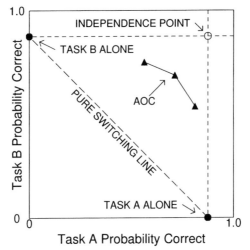

FIGURE 22   Attention operating characteristic (AOC) for the concurrent performance of two tasks. In this illustration, performance on both Task A and Task B are measured as percent correct. Baseline performance (solid circles) is measured for each task performed alone. The other marks represent performance for concurrent performance. The dashed line connecting the baseline accuracies represent the performances achievable by performing Task A on a proportion p of trials and Task B on proportion 1-p. The *ideal point* (open circle) represents no loss for task combination. Hypothetical joint performance (solid triangles) represents the outcome for joint performance of partially interfering tasks under instructions to emphasize (from left to right) Task B, give equal emphasis, and emphasize Task A. (Reprinted with permission of the authors.)

two spatially distinct parts of a long sequence of alphanumeric displays. Task A consisted in searching an outer ring of characters, while Task B consisted in searching an inner square of letters. So long as characters in the inner square and the outer ring were the same size, the two tasks could be performed with little loss (near the independence point). In contrast, if characters in the inner square were smaller and those in the outer ring larger, performance was substantially below the independence point. It is difficult to attend to two spatial scales simultaneously if both identity and location must be reported (Farrell & Pelli, 1993). And if the observer must search for a letter among digits in the inner square and a digit among letters in the outer square, performance is near the line connecting the two baseline points, indicating that observers can (probabilistically) do one or the other task but not both.

These powerful new methods have provided answers to a host of classic questions. For example, a line of related research using AOCs demonstrates that attentional selection is generally mediated by selecting a location, and that selection by physical features such as color or size is comparatively weak unless the color or size can be used to identify and then attentively select a stable set of locations (Shih & Sperling, 1996). In these studies, simply knowing in advance the color or size of a target stimulus is only beneficial when that color or size is associated with a predictable location.

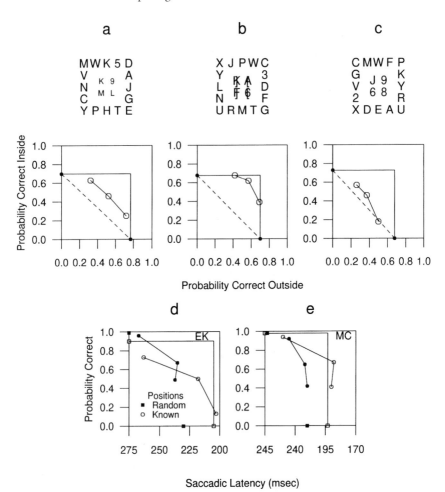

FIGURE 23   Observed AOCs for two concurrent visual search tasks and for concurrent cued report task and a cued saccade task. (a–c) Detection performance, respectively, of searching for a digit among letters in a small inner array and a large outer array; of searching for a digit among letters among a large masked inner array and a large outer array; and of searching for a letter among digits in a large inner array and of a digit among letters in a large outer array (Sperling & Melchner, 1978). Task interference is high when dealing simultaneously with small and large characters, or when the search targets and distractors are mapped oppositely in the two tasks. [Reprinted from Fig. 1 in G. Sperling and M. J. Melchner (1978). The attention operating characteristic: Examples from visual search. *Science, 202,* 316; with permission of the American Association for the Advancement of Science.] (d–e) AOCs for two subjects reporting a letter from one cued location and making a saccade to another (Kowler, Anderson, Dosher, & Blaser, 1995). Distance of the AOC from the ideal point demonstrates that letter identification and programming the target location for the saccade compete for the same resources. [Adapted from E. Kowler, E. Anderson, B. Dosher, and E. Blaser (1995). The role of attention in the programming of saccades. *Vision Research, 35, 13,* 11; with kind permission from Elsevier Science Ltd, The Boulevard, Langford Lane, Kidlington OX5 1GB, UK.]

Another example answers a number of classic questions about the extent to which movements of attention are coupled to movements of the eyes. This application of the methods also illustrates the use of two quite different task measurements to define an AOC. Using AOCs, Kowler, Anderson, Dosher, and Blaser (1995) demonstrated that looking for a target and moving the eye to a new location compete for the same visual attention resources. The two task measurements were percent correct in target identification at a cued location and aspects of saccadic performance, such as saccadic RT (msec) (Fig. 23d–e). When the target to be identified and the goal of the saccade are at different locations, there are attentional trade-offs in performance. Although attention can move independently of the eye when the eye is fixed, the eye cannot move independently of visual attention: the location of the upcoming saccade must be attended briefly (see also Remington, 1980; Hoffman & Subramaniam, 1995).

I. Neural Models of Attention

As illustrated in the previous discussion, theoretical mechanisms and empirical measurements of attention have both advanced significantly over the last several decades. A related strand of work is examining how mechanisms of attention are instantiated in the brain. There are a number of approaches to correlating behaviorally determined attention mechanisms with brain mechanisms: evaluating performance loss with brain lesions; measurement of brain activity during attentional processing; and the development of neural computational models of attention. A few brief examples illustrate the nature of current approaches.

Based largely on performance in brain-lesioned populations, Posner and colleagues (e.g., Posner & Petersen, 1990) claim several attentional subsystems: sensory orienting, signal detection, and vigilance subsystems. The orienting subsystem is thought to primarily support effects of spatial attention, such as those illustrated in Figure 15. Posner and Peterson suggest that a posterior subsystem (including parietal cortex, pulvinar and superior colliculus) mediates spatial orienting. Patients with lesions of these areas may exhibit abnormalities in patterns of movements of attention and of the eyes.

Event-related brain potentials (ERPs) provide one measure of brain activity. Hillyard and colleagues find that spatial focus of attention results in amplified or weakened responses to attended and unattended stimuli during even the first few milliseconds of ERP responses to the stimuli (Hillyard, Mangun, Woldorff, & Luck, 1995). They (Mangun & Hillyard, 1990) also find ERP correlates of attentional allocation in the later processing of more complex arrays. Observer's AOCs were measured under attentional instructions to favor the left, evaluate left and right equally, or favor the right portion of a letter array. ERP markers, especially long RT (350 ms and later) components, show amplitudes that correspond to target detection performance for left and right field letter arrays in an evoked potential AOC.

The relationship between behavioral models and neural substrates is just beginning to be elucidated. A deeper integration of biological and behavioral mechanisms is a dominant future direction.

IV. IMMEDIATE MEMORY

A. The Attentional Gate

Attention selects or gates information (regions, inputs) for subsequent processing by a variety of higher-order perceptual and cognitive processes.

Some selected inputs are further perceptually processed. Take two diverse examples: In visual search, attention may identify a subset of stimuli for subsequent evaluation (e.g., red items when searching for a red O among black Os and red Xs) (see Dosher, 1996; Wright & Main, 1996; and Hochberg, chap. 9, this volume, section IV.B). In motion perception, attentional selection may determine the perceived direction of motion of motion-ambiguous displays (Lu & Sperling, 1995a).

Primarily, however, attention gates information into memory. The strong relation between attention and immediate memory was recognized early. "We cannot deny that *an object once attended to will remain in memory,* whilst one inattentively allowed to pass will leave no traces behind" (James, 1890/1950, p. 427.) Immediate memory, memory for the order of very rapid stimuli, and even our inferences about sensory memory are partially determined by attentional gating.

B. Consciousness and Immediate Memory

In the early views of the introspecitionists, consciousness, attention, and immediate memory were intertwined (see Mandler, chap. 3, this volume). Objects that were attended were also conscious, although recently attended objects or objects at the edge of attention might fade from or fail to achieve consciousness. Objects or thoughts in primary or immediate memory were also conscious, or alternately, those items in consciousness also occupied primary memory (James, 1890/1904). In a recent related view (Cowan, 1993), short-term memory corresponds to currently or recently active long-term memory representations, and the currently active set is the focus of attention.

Based partly on introspection and partly on early attempts at experimentation, fundamental limits on information pickup were asserted by Wundt (1912/1924), Titchener (1919), and Woodworth (1921), who cite values between four and six items as the limit on the "scope," "span," or "range" of attention or consciousness. "Six simple impressions form the limit for the scope of attention" (Wundt, 1912/1924, p. 31). "The maximal range of the visual attention . . . comprises six impressions" (Titchener, 1919, p. 289). "He can tell four or five, and beyond that makes many mistakes" (Woodworth, 1921, p. 262). These values arose variously from experimental paradigms that today we would label subitization (counting or estimation of number from a single glance), sensory memory (reporting items from a briefly displayed array), and short-term or working memory (repeating items in order from a printed or spoken list).

Beginning the century with these intuitive notions of information limits and rudimentary experiments, theoretical progress has involved the recognition and isolation of functional subcomponents of attention and memory systems, and empirical progress has involved the development of paradigms and behavioral measurements. The development of models of memory structures, and of the component processes of encoding and retrieval for those structures, has paralleled the development of techniques for treating observable response accuracies and response times. These new models embody more detailed information flow diagrams, analogous to those seen for the processes in perception and attention.

C. Gating Brief Displays into Memory

When a display is presented only very briefly, attentional mechanisms may be the primary determinant of which information is encoded into short-term memory. Models of performance with brief displays distinguish perceptual processes, visual memory, and working memory structures (Fig. 19). Each structure imposes its own limits on the maintenance and report of incoming information.

Visual sensory memory, sometimes called iconic memory, is a short-lived (0.25–2 sec) representation of visual information that is eliminated by visual masking (Sperling, 1960). Experiments investigating visual sensory memory use briefly flashed displays, often several rows of letters. In uninstructed report conditions, four to five items can typically be reported. The reports represent unselective transfer in the sense that the particular items gated to working memory and report systems reflect stereotyped readout preferences—left to right, near the center. In instructed report conditions, a tone cues a particular row for report. When the instructional tone occurs, gating into working memory becomes selective. When a cue that appears *after* the offset of the brief stimulus is still useful in determining readout, there must be continued availability of information in visual sensory memory.

Accuracy of report (percent correct, or estimated number of letters available) systematically increases as a visual mask is delayed, and systematically decreases as the report cue is delayed after stimulus offset, in a regular, interactive fashion. These systematic effects are well explained by computational models that describe the clarity of the sensory memory, the elimination of sensory memory by masking, and an attentional gating mechanism that transfers information from different locations in the display depending on whether the transfer is uninstructed or instructed by the cue (Gegenfurtner & Sperling, 1993). The acquisition of information from displays with complex time functions and contrast manipulations (e.g., blank intervals, intensity manipulations, etc.) reflects similar mechanisms of availability and information gating (Busey & Loftus, 1994; Loftus & Ruthruff, 1994). As in the case of flicker fusion in perception, these models make predictions about a wide variety of display manipulations.

As in the case of flicker fusion, a good model can provide an obvious explanation for an otherwise inexplicable set of findings. For example, attentional gating sometimes produces very distinctive illusory perceptions. In an experiment by Reeves and Sperling (1986) (as described in section III), two series of briefly displayed letters or digits appeared in different locations. The observer switched attention to the target location as soon as a cue appeared in the cuing location. In some conditions, observers were asked to report the first four items seen. For rapid rates of display (<200 ms per item), temporal order is not accurately or explicitly encoded, and paradoxical and systematic misperceptions of order occur. If the first item after the cue to switch were labeled A, and the subsequent items were labeled B, C, etc., observers might report that the first four items after the cue were, in order, D, E, C, F. This does not reflect guessing about order, since the report order is stable over trials.

The attentional gate explains this sort of illusory percept, as illustrated in Figure 24. At some delay following processing of the cue to switch attention to the target location, the attention gate opens and then closes, transferring information from the sensory representation into working memory and the report system. Information transfer reflects the amount of processing allowed by the gate: items that appear while the gate is fully open are transferred to memory with higher strength, whereas those that appear while the gate is only partially open are transferred to memory with lower strength. In the absense of explicit coding for order, perceived order reflects memory strength.

In sum, performances where brief displays prevent observers from extending information acquisition naturally over time are now understood as an interaction between several systems: perceptual processes resulting in a perceptual representation, a visual (or auditory) memory, and attentional gating of information into the more durable working memory system that supports verbal report. Ther are now models for a variety of display situations, and those models are computational and detailed, accounting for large bodies of parametric data.

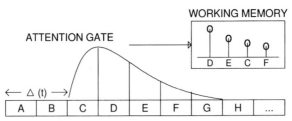

FIGURE 24   The attention gate determines the percept of stimulus order for very rapid displays where explicit order coding is deficient. A rapid sequence of items is shown along with the function for the attention gate. The area under the function determines item strength; for rapid presentation where order is not encoded explicitly, item strength determines perceived order. [Reprinted from Fig. 15 in A. Reeves and G. Sperling (1986). Attention gating in short-term visual memory. *Psychological Review, 93*, 2, 195; with permission of the American Psychological Association.]

D. Limitations of Immediate Memory

When information acquisition is not limited by brief displays, immediate memory itself limits performance. Beginning with the introspective notions of immediate or primary memory and consciousness (James, 1890/1950), ideas about short-term or working memory have shifted radically over the last several decades.

Miller's (1956) influential paper, "Magical number seven," was one of the first examples of the introduction of capacity limitations into psychological theory. That paper solidified the notion that short-term memory reflected a capacity limit on the number of items, and did not depend strongly on other properties of those items.

Miller focused on measurements of short-term memory capacity that required a serially presented set of items to be repeated immediately in the correct order, called immediate memory span. He rejected the notion that the memory span was influenced by the "information content." Information content was calculated based on an information-theoretic notion of predictability. In the information-theoretic sense, items drawn from small sets like the digits carry less information than items from very large sets, such as all English nouns. Miller claimed relatively small differences in measured span for items from these quite different materials sets. In short-term memory limits, an item was an item, so long as it corresponded to a known and labelable object. (Capacity for novel items is substantially reduced.)

This conception of short-term memory was further developed in the context of a system model (Atkinson & Shiffrin, 1968) distinguishing between sensory memory, short-term memory, and long-term memory, and proposing a set of control processes involved in transfer from one system to another. Taken together, these developments supported a conception of short-term memory as a memory system with a small number of "slots" capable of storing (or pointing to) items expressible as long-term memory codes.

E. Retrieval Limits of Immediate Memory

Task performance reflects not just representation in memory, but recovery from memory as well. Complete models of the memory system include processes of both storage and retrieval. Contemporaneous with the theoretical view that short-term memory was a system with a capacity of "seven plus or minus two" items, the question of the availability of those items became paramount. Were the items in short-term memory also in the focus of attention or consciousness? Were the items then immediately available, as suggested by introspectionist accounts, or were further limits imposed by the demands of recovery from memory?

In a ground-breaking study that reintroduced RT as a psychological measure of performance, Sternberg (1966) reasoned that accessibility of the items in short-term memory could be inferred from the time required to recognize an item. His claim was a startling one—that short-term memory was characterized by a limit in retrieval: Items were not immediately available, but rather were recognized by sequentially comparing a test item to all items held in short-term memory (Sternberg, 1966).

In his experiments, observers were shown a list of items one after the next (Fig. 25a). Each item was attended and transferred into short-term store. In response to a test item occurring 1–2 sec later, the observer pressed one key if the test item was a list member, and another if it was not. Mean response times increased linearly with the size of the memory load, or list length, for both list members and nonmembers. Critically, the added time per item was essentially identical whether the test item was a member or nonmember (Fig. 25b).

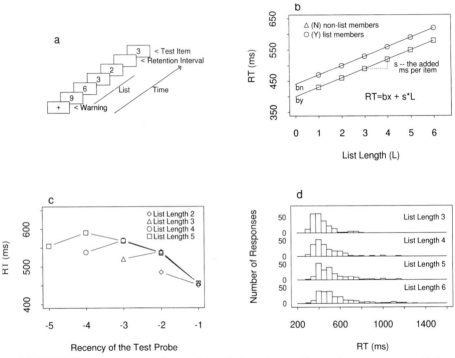

FIGURE 25   Measurement of retrieval time for items in immediate or short-term memory. (a) A paradigm from Sternberg (1966) for testing the availability of items in immediate memory. Observers decide whether the test probe is a list member or nonmember and press a response key. (b) Average response times (RT) increase approximately linearly with immediate memory load (list length) for both members and nonmembers. One view suggested that test probes were compared serially and exhaustively with each item in immediate memory. (c) Average RT for different list positions and memory loads (list lengths) strongly reflect recency. The abscissa indicates the position in the list of the test probe measured from the position of the test (the last list member is −1, the next to the last is −2, etc.). (d) RT distributions for different memory loads show that the differences are in the long tails of the distributions. The fastest times are the same and differentially reflect tests of the last list item (following Hockley, 1984). [Adapted by permission of Macmillan Reference USA, a Simon & Schuster Macmillan Company, from Figures 1 and 3 in B. Dosher and B. McElree (1992). Memory search: Retrieval processes in short term and long term recognition. *Encyclopedia of Learning and Memory* (L. R. Squire, Editor in Chief). Copyright © 1992 by Macmillan Publishing Company.]

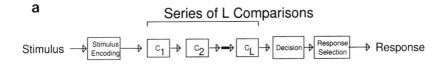

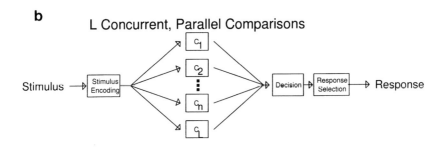

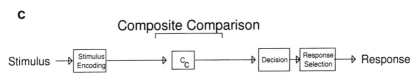

FIGURE 26 Serial and parallel retrieval mechanisms for comparing a test item with the memory representation of a list in memory. Certain parallel retrieval mechanisms can mimic serial mechanisms at the level of average response time for a list length (Townsend & Ashby, 1983). (a) a serial exhaustive comparison mechanism in which the test item is compared, in series, to each member of the memory list (Sternberg, 1966); (b) A parallel comparison mechanism in which the test item is compared at the same time with all elements in memory; (c) Recognition as direct access to a relevant memory in which all items in the list are stored in a single composite memory representation (McElree & Dosher, 1989). [Adapted by permission of Macmillan Reference USA, a Simon & Schuster Macmillan Company, from Figure 2 in B. Dosher and B. McElree (1992). Memory search: Retrieval processes in short term and long term recognition. *Encyclopedia of Learning and Memory* (L. R. Squire, Editor in Chief). Copyright © 1992 by Macmillan Publishing Company.]

Sternberg reasoned that an item was recognized as being in immediate memory by a serial and exhaustive comparison process (Fig. 26). The process was serial because each added memory item increased response time by an equal amount. The process was exhaustive because if comparisons terminated upon finding a match, then on average a list member should be found halfway through the search; this leads to a two-to-one relationship in slopes between recognition of nonmembers and members. Sternberg also argued that access of ordered information (say the item that came after the probe item in the list) also involved a sequential comparison process.

Taken together, the accuracy and the response time data suggested that short-term memory is item-limited and that items in the memory are not immediately available, but require a recovery process. The consequence of access to item information that involves serial and exhaustive processing is that adding items to short-term memory must be accompanied by increasing access times. Attractive though it may be, Sternberg's model is incorrect. The kinds of measurements needed to reject the model and the revised model of immediate memory limitations are considered next. These advances followed theoretical developments regarding the observable consequences of different processing architectures and methodological advancements allowing a more sophisticated measurement of the time course of retrieval.

F. Developing Reaction Time and Accuracy Methods

In Sternberg's method, only the size of the short-term memory load varied; the test display and the response were equivalent for all conditions. This design eliminated some of the complexities of prior attempts to interpret response times. This demonstration case was critical in the reintroduction of response time into the arsenal of empirical approaches in psychology (Sternberg, 1969).

However, accuracy and RT are not independent. They are simply two measurable aspects of the same behavior. In important theoretical advances during the 1970s and 1980s, models of response time *and* accuracy were developed, ambiguities in interpretation were documented, and elaborated response paradigms were invented (see Luce, 1986, for a review).

Townsend and Ashby (1983) articulated the equivalence, at the level of average response times, of certain parallel processing architectures—in which processes occur simultaneously—to serial processing architectures of the sort proposed by Sternberg. Distinguishing between serial and parallel architectures and their variants requires a closer examination of the data, possibly including the distributional properties of response times, the relation between response time and accuracy for responses, and the trade-off between processing time and accuracy when speed–accuracy relationships are explicitly manipulated.

G. The Revised Model of Short-Term Memory Retrieval

The initial conclusion that retrieval from immediate memory reflected a serial comparison process to items contained in the short-term memory buffer has been replaced with a revised model in which retrieval from immediate memory reflects a set of parallel comparisons with an active subset of memory items. Support for this revised model includes some clear illustrations of the development of RT and accuracy technologies.

Two sets of observations about immediate memory performance rule out serial and exhaustive comparisons as a retrieval limit: (a) RT and accuracy vary systematically with the item recency (e.g., Monsell, 1978) (Fig. 25c); and (b) the fastest responses are about the same for different memory loads (e.g., Hockley, 1984) (Fig.

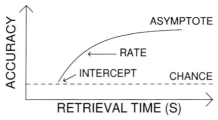

FIGURE 27   Idealized speed–accuracy trade-off functions measure the full time course of retrieval speed and limits in memory accuracy. The intercept measures the first point at which information is available, the rate of information accrual is measured by the fast-rising portion, and the asymptote measures the limits in memory accuracy. [Reprinted from Fig. 3 in B. A. Dosher (1982). Effect of sentence size and network distance on retrieval speed *JEP: Learning, Memory and Cognition, 8, 3,* 176; with permission of the American Psychological Association.]

25d). Neither observation is consistent with an exhaustive serial comparison process. The RT differences over list position or recency coexist perfectly with the approximately linear increases in average RT as a function of memory load in Figure 25b (Dosher & McElree, 1992). The linear increases reflect the decreasing average recency of items from longer lists.

Elaborated response methods allow the direct measurement of increases in accuracy with additional processing times. In one method (Dosher, 1976, 1981; Reed, 1973), observers are interrupted at various times during recognition, and accuracy is measured as a dependent variable (Fig. 27). This yields functions relating accuracy to the time spent in processing, often called speed–accuracy trade-off (SAT) functions (see also Wickelgren, 1977). SAT data allow the estimation of when the first information is beginning to be available (intercept), how quickly information accrues over time (rate), and the limit on memory accuracy (asymptote).

These powerful elaborated response methods revealed that immediate memory access reflects a parallel, direct access process of retrieval for recognition. Figure 28 shows SAT functions for different list positions for list loads of 3, 4, 5, and 6 items (Dosher & McElree, 1992; McElree & Dosher, 1989). Information begins to be available at the same time for all memory loads and list positions, and information accrues at the same rate for all memory loads and list positions, except for the most recent item. The most recent item (immediate repetition) is more immediately available. Items in the memory load differ only in ultimate accuracy of memory. More recent items are most accurately recognized, and less recent items are successively less so. That is, Sternberg felt that all items in short-term memory were represented with equal accuracy, but that they were recovered by a serial scanning process. Instead, the availability of items is different for items in different positions of the list, with the most recent items being stronger, but items are accessed via a parallel or direct-access matching process.

These results led directly to very different conclusions about how items are stored in and retrieved from short-term memory. Following Miller, the item is taken as the

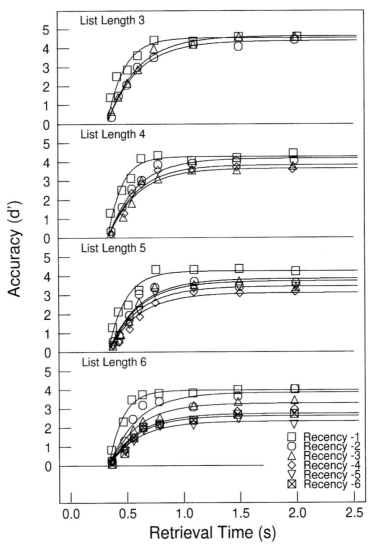

FIGURE 28   Full retrieval functions for immediate memory retrieval in recognition. (Data from McElree & Dosher, 1989). The retrieval speed is independent of memory load and list position, except that the most recent item is retrieved very quickly. Memory accuracy (ultimate availability) varies with recency. [Reprinted from Figs. 7 & 12 in B. McElree and B. A. Dosher (1989). Serial position and set size in short-term memory: The time course of recognition. *JEP: General, 118, 4,* (pp. 357 & 364); with permission of the American Psychological Association.]

unit of memory (rather than the information content carried by each item). However, unlike certain early conceptions of working memory, immediate memory in the revised model does not consist of a buffer of a certain size. Rather, items are activated or encoded as a consequence of attending those items (gating them into memory) during study. The limits in the number of items available for report reflect forgetting of items that were once attended and encoded into memory during stimulus input, but whose representations have since become weaker. The strength of the memory representations for items is decremented as new items are processed (due to specific interference) and as time passes (due to generalized processing interference).

Figure 29 shows a process model of short-term working memory and the interrelated modules of perceptual processing, attentional gating, and very short-term memory subsystems. Each of these componens, to a greater or lesser degree, can be expanded to show key subcomponents. The perceptual processing, attention gating, and the very short-term visual memory modules are shown only schematically (but

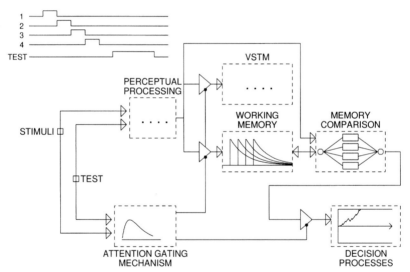

FIGURE 29   A direct access model of working memory, its dependence on attention gating, and the corresponding decision mechanism. Incoming stimulus items are shown on the upper left. Perceptual processing modules are merely sketched in; the relevant perceptual processing subcomponents depend on the task. An attention-gating process similar to that shown in Figure 19 routes stimulus information into very short-term memory (sensory memory), working memory, and the memory comparison and decision processes. Working memory consists of a set of memory traces activated at the time of study and subsequently undergoing loss of strength or activation as later items are processed or recalled. Memory comparison modules show parallel comparison operations as subcomponents. The output of the comparison module drives a decision module; this decision structure, combined with strength information from the comparison module, determines the accuracy and latency of recognition responses. (Reprinted with permission of B. Dosher.)

see earlier figures). Working memory is shown as a set of activated memory traces undergoing loss in activation or strength over time. In recognition, retrieval occurs by a parallel process of direct access or direct comparison of the test item with memory. The result of the comparison process(es) drives a decision unit with associated patterns of response times and accuracies.

The average item in a larger "memory load" is less available simply by virtue of the fact that some items in the larger loads will have been processed less recently than any item in a smaller load, and those less recent items suffer some loss. Again, this is shown as activated items in the working memory module undergoing loss. Immediate recognition paradigms largely reflect loss during the continuing process of list exposure. Limits on immediate memory measured by ordered recall or span reflect memory loss not just during the list presentation, but memory loss during rehearsal periods and during output as well (Dosher, 1994). Estimated spans depend on the stimuli (almost eight for digits, as low as three for nonsense trigrams or unlabelable visual forms), and may depend on various characteristics such as the degree of interference between stimuli (affecting forgetting rates) and the length of the articulatory code for the stimuli (Baddeley, 1986), which affects the time delays at output (Dosher & Ma, 1996).

H. The Development of Memory Models

In sum, we began the century with a set of empirically observed limits on verbal report and some fairly vague ideas about possible causes of those limits. At the end of this century, empirical and theoretical developments support a quite different and more specific understanding of a host of short-term processing limits. Various task limits are now understood to reflect limits in one of several different processing modules, including very short-term visual or auditory memory, attention gating, and working memory. The subcomponents of several of the major component modules are quite precisely known; process models support a wide class of both qualitative and quantitative predictions, only some of which have been touched on here.

V. CONCLUSIONS

This abbreviated review provided an overview of the development of experimental methodology and theory during the 20th century with examples chosen from three areas of psychology: computational models of visual motion perception, visual attention, and short-term memory systems. The developments in these areas have strong elements of similarity. In each case, the century begins with a set of base observations—some empirical, many introspective—and with some vague, often competing, verbal notions about how to characterize the corresponding mental mechanisms. In each case, a period of rapid development and refinement began after World War II and has continued to the present, resulting in relatively complex process models of those mechanisms, coupled with the introduction of elaborated empirical methods for testing and analysis. In psychology and biology, unlike classical physics, an increase in knowledge is normally accompanied by increased complexity of theory (Sperling, 1997). Simple models have been systematically replaced by more complex models. A model component called simply "memory" expands into "coding, storage, and retrieval," and each of these processes is further expanded as both the control structures and the internal structures are made explicit. In Figure 13, a component that in an earlier model might simply have been called "motion detection" is expanded into three motion-direction systems involving five separate motion–energy components and six separate texture-grabber components, each of which again expands into numerous subcomponents. It is hoped that this explosive increase in complexity will eventually bring information-processing architectures into convergence with neural-processing architectures, which are undergoing their own parallel explosive increase in complexity.

Commentaries on progress in psychology often include a quote from James or Wundt to illustrate the prescience of the early psychologists, and to implicitly suggest that we know little more now than was known in 1900. It should be abundantly clear from this review how misguided this view is. The problems of vision, attention, and memory have not been resolved, nor are they likely to be resolved in the next century. But our understanding of these problems, the data that are now available, and the kinds of theories that are under consideration are enormously different from and improved over those that were available at the end of the 19th century.

In physics, one of the fruits of improved knowledge of atomic structure was an atomic bomb. Knowledge about visual processes certainly has been helpful in the design of photographic media and video communication systems but, on the whole, improved understanding of human information processing has not yet yielded any practical fruits with the impact of an atomic bomb. The lure of practical discovery to be made in the future has diverted considerable resources to the study of human information processing. Perhaps there are great practical rewards awaiting. Perhaps the study of the mechanisms of the human mind will continue to command our attention simply because of its intrinsic interest.

Acknowledgments

The experimental and theoretical work described herein was supported by the Air Force Office of Scientific Research (AFOSR), Life Science Directorate, Visual Information Processing Program, the Office of Naval Research, Cognitive and Neural Sciences Division, and by the National Science Foundation, Memory and Cognition Program. The preparation of the manuscript was supported by the AFOSR. Sections I and II of the manuscript were written primarily by G. S.; sections III and IV primarily by B. D.

References

Adelson, E. H., & Bergen, J. R. (1985). Spatio-temporal energy models for the perception of motion. *Journal of the Optical Society of America A, 284*–299.

Atkinson, R. C., & Shiffrin, R. M. (1968). Human memory: A proposed system and its control processes. In K. W. Spence & J. T. Spence (Eds.), *The psychology of learning and motivation: II* (pp. 89–195). New York, NY: Academic Press.

Baddeley, A. (1986). *Working memory.* Oxford, UK: Clarendon Press/Oxford University Press.

Binet, A., & Henri, V. (1896). La psychologie individuelle. *L'annee Psychologie, 2,* 411–465.

Boring, E. G. (1950). *A history of experimental psychology (2nd ed.).* New York: Appleton-Century-Crofts, Inc.

Boring, E. G. (1942). *Sensation and perception in the history of experimental psychology.* New York: Appleton-Century-Crofts, Inc.

Brown, C. R., & Forsyth, D. M. (1959). Fusion contour for intermittent photic stimuli of alternating duration. *Science, 129,* 390–391.

Busey, T., & Loftus, G. (1994). Sensory and cognitive components of visual information acquisition. *Psychological Review, 101,* 446–469.

Campbell, F. W., & Robson, J. G. (1964). Application of Fourier analysis to the modulation response of the eye. *Journal of the Optical Society of America, 54,* 581.

Campbell, F. W., & Robson, J. G. (1968). Application of Fourier analysis to the visibility of gratings. *Journal of Physiology, 197,* 551–556.

Chubb, C., & Sperling, G. (1988). Drift-balanced random stimuli: A general basis for studying non-Fourier motion perception. *Journal of the Optical Society of America A: Optics and Image Science, 5,* 1986–2006.

Chubb, C., Sperling, G., & Solomon, J. A. (1989). Texture interactions determine perceived contrast. *Proceedings of the National Academy of Sciences, USA, 86,* 9631–9635.

Cobb, P. W. (1934). Some critical comments on the Ives theory of flicker. *Journal of the Optical Society of America, 24,* 91–98.

Cowan, N. (1993). Activation, attention, and short-term memory. *Memory & Cognition, 21,* 162–167.

DeLange, H. Dzn. (1958a). Research into the dynamic nature of the human fovea-cortex systems with intermittent and modulated light. I. Attenuation characteristics with white and colored light. *Journal of the Optical Society of America, 48,* 777–784.

DeLange, H. Dzn. (1958b). Research into the dynamic nature of the human fovea-cortex systems with intermittent and modulated light. II. Phase shift in brightness and delay in color perception. *Journal of the Optical Society of America, 48,* 784–789.

DeLange, H. Dzn. (1952). Relationship between critical flicker-frequency and a set of low frequency characteristics of the eye. *Journal of the Optical Society of America, 44,* 380–389.

Dosher, B. A. (1998). Models of visual search: Finding a face in the crowd. In Sternberg, S., & Scarborough, D. (Eds.), *Invitation to Cognitive Science* (Vol. 4), Boston, MA: MIT Press., in press.

Dosher, B. A. (1994). Forgetting in STM recall: Presentation rate and output time. *Proceedings of the Thirty-Fifth Annual Meeting of the Psyconomics Society.* (p. 56). Austin, TX: Psychonomic Society Publications.

Dosher, B. A. (1981). The effects of delay and interference: A speed–accuracy study. *Cognitive Psychology, 13,* 551–582.

Dosher, B. A. (1976). The retrieval of sentences from memory: A speed–accuracy study. *Cognitive Psychology, 8,* 291–310.

Dosher, B. A., & Ma, J. J. (1998). Output loss or rehearsal loop? Output time vs. pronunciation time limits in immediate recall for forgetting-matched materials. *Journal of Experimental Psychology: Learning, Memory & Cognition,* in press.

Dosher, B. A., & McElree, B. (1992). Memory search: Retrieval processes in short term and long term recognition. In L. R. Squire, et al (Eds.), *Encyclopedia of learning and memory* (pp. 398–406). New York: MacMillan.

Downing, C. J. (1988). Expectancy and visual-spatial attention: Effects on perceptual quality. *Journal of Experimental Psychology: Human Perception & Performance, 14,* 188–202.

Ebbinghaus, H. (1885). *Über das Gedächtnis (Memory)*. Leipzig: Duncker and Humblot. Transl. H. A. Ruger & C. E. Bussenius. (1964; original translation 1913).

Exner, S. (1875). Experimentelle Untersuchung der einfachsten psychischen Processe. *Archives Gesamte Physiolgie Mesch. Tiere, 11,* 403–432.

Farell, B., & Pelli, D. G. (1993). Can we attend to large and small at the same time? *Vision Research, 33,* 2757–2772.

Fechner, G. T. (1860). *Elemente der Psychophysik*. Leipzig: Breitkopf und Härtel.

Gegenfurtner, K. R. & Sperling, G. (1993). Information transfer in iconic memory experiments. *Journal of Experimental Psychology: Human Perception and Performance, 19,* 845–866.

Geisler, W. S. (1989). Sequential ideal-observer analysis of visual discriminations. *Psychological Review, 96,* 267–314.

Graham, N. (1989). *Visual pattern analyzers*. Oxford: Oxford University Press.

Granlund, G. H., & Knutsson, H. (1983). Contrast of structured and homogeneous representations. In O. J. Braddick & A. C. Sleigh (Eds.), *Physical and biological processing of images* (pp. 282–303). New York: Springer-Verlag.

Green, D. M., & Swets, J. A. (1966). *Signal detection theory and psychophysics*. New York: John Wiley.

Hartline, H. K., Wagner, H. G., & Ratliff, F. (1956). Inhibition in the eye of Limulus. *Journal of General Physiology, 39,* 651–673.

Hassenstein, B., & Reichardt, W. (1956). Systemtheoretische Analyse der Zeit-, Reihenfolgen- und Vorzeichenauswertung bei der Bewegungsperzeption des Rüsselkäfers Chlorophanus. *Z. Naturforschung, 11b,* 513–524.

Helmholtz, H. (1924). *Helmholtz's treatise on physiological optics* (3rd ed.), J. P. C. Southall, Ed. Washington, D.C.: Optical Society of America. Translation of *Handbuch der Physiologischen Optik von H. von Helmholz*. (1909). A. Gullstrand, J. von Kries, and W. Nagel, (Eds.), Manburg und Leipzig: Leopold Voss. Original work published 1866; third edition published 1909

Hillyard, S. A., Mangun, G. R., Woldorff, M. G., & Luck, S. J. (1995). Neural systems mediating selective attention. In M. S. Gazzaniga (Ed.), *The cognitive neurosciences* (pp. 665–681). Cambridge, MA: MIT Press.

Hockley, W. E. (1984). Analysis of response time distribution in the study of cognitive processes. *Journal of Experimental Psychology: Learning, Memory and Cognition, 10,* 598–615.

Hoffman, J. E., & Subramaniam, B. (1995). The role of visual attention in saccadic eye movements. *Perception and Psychophysics, 57,* 787–795.

Hubel, D. H., & Wiesel, T. N. (1968). Receptive fields and functional architecture of monkey striate cortex. *Journal of Physiology, 195,* 215–243.

Hubel, D. H., & Wiesel, T. N. (1965). Receptive fields and functional architecture in two nonstriate visual areas (18 and 19) of the cat. *Journal of Neurophysiology, 28,* 229–289.

Hubel, D. H., & Wiesel, T. N. (1962). Receptive fields, binocular interaction, and functional architecture in the cat's visual cortex. *Journal of Physiology, 160,* 106–123.

Ives, H. E. (1922a). Critical frequency relations in scotopic vision. *Journal of the Optical Society of America, 6,* 253–268.

Ives, H. E. (1922b). A theory of intermittent vision. *Journal of the Optical Society of America, 6,* 343–361.

James, W. (1950). *The principles of psychology*. New York: Henry Holt & Co. (Dover Edition). (Original work published 1890)

Kowler, E., Anderson, E., Dosher, B. A., & Blaser, E. (1995). The role of attention in the programming of saccades. *Vision Research, 35,* 1897–1916.

Kuffler, S. W. (1953). Discharge pattern and functional organization of mammalian retina. *Journal of Neurophysiology, 16,* 37–68.

Kulpe, O. (1921). *Outlines of psychology: Based upon the results of experimental investigation.* (E. B. Titchener, Trans.). London: George Allen & Unwin, Ltd. (Original work published 1895)

LaBerge, D., & Brown, V. (1989). Theory of attentional operations in shape identification. *Psychological Review, 96*, 101–124.

Landis, C. (1953). *An annotated bibliography of flicker fusion phenomena. Covering the period 1740/1952.* Armed Forces NRC Vision Committee Secretariat. Ann Arbor: University of Michigan.

Levinson, J. (1959). Fusion of complex flicker. *Science, 130*, 919–921.

Loftus, G. R., & Ruthruff, E. (1994). A theory of visual information acquisition and visual memory with special application to intensity–duration tradeoffs. *Journal of Experimental Psychology: Human Perception and Performance, 20*, 33–49.

Lu, Z-L., & Sperling, G. (1996a). Second-order illusions: Mach bands, Chevreal and Craik-O'Brien-Cornsweet. *Vision Research, 36*, 559–572.

Lu, Z-L., & Sperling, G. (1996b). The three mechanisms of human visual motion detection. *Current Directions in Psychological Science, 5*, 44–53.

Lu, Z-L., & Sperling, G. (1996c). Contrast gain control in first- and second-order motion perception. *Journal of the Optical Society of America A: Optics and Image Science, 13*, 2305–2318.

Lu, Z-L., & Sperling, G. (1995a). The functional architecture of human visual motion perception. *Vision Research, 35*, 2697–2722.

Lu, Z-L., & Sperling, G. (1995b). Attention-generated apparent motion. *Nature, 379*, 237–239.

Luce, R. D. (1986). *Response times: Their role in inferring elementary mental organization.* New York: Oxford University Press.

Lyon, D. L. (1987). How quickly can attention affect form perception? *Technical Report AFHRL-TR-87-28.* Brooks Air Force Base, TX: Air Force Human Resources Laboratory.

Mach, E. (1865). Über die Wirkung der raumlichen Vertheilung des Lichtreizes auf die Netzhaut. *I.S.-B. Akad. Wiss. Wien. math.-nat. Kl., 54*, 303–322.

Mangun, G. R., & Hillyard, S. A. (1990). Allocation of visual attention to spatial locations: Tradeoff functions for event-related brain potentials and detection performance. *Perception & Psychophysics, 47*, 532–550.

McElree, B., & Dosher, B. A. (1989). Serial position and set size in short-term memory: The time course of recognition. *Journal of Experimental Psychology: General, 118*, 346–373.

Mertens, J. J. (1956). Influence of knowledge of a target location upon the probability of observation of peripherally observable test flashes. *Journal of the Optical Society of America, 46*, 1069–1070.

Miller, G. (1956). The magical number seven, plus or minus two: Some limits on our capacity for processing information. *Psychological Review, 63*, 81–87.

Monsell, S. (1978). Recency, immediate recognition memory, and reaction time. *Cognitive Psychology, 10*, 465–501.

Nakayama, K., & Silverman, G. H. (1985). Detection and discrimination of sinusoidal grating displacements. *Journal of the Optical Society of America A, 2*, 267–274.

Ohm, G. S. (1843). Über die Definition des Tones, nebst daran geknüpfter Theorie die Sirene und ähnlicher tonbildener Vorrichtungen. *Annal. Phys. Chem., 135*, 497–565.

Palmer, J. (1994). Set-size effects in visual search: The effect of attention is independent of the stimulus for simple tasks. *Vision Research, 34*, 1703–1721.

Palmer, J., Ames, C. T., & Lindsey, D. T. (1993). Measuring the effect of attention on simple visual search. *Journal of Experimental Psychology: Human Perception and Performance, 19*, 108–130.

Pavlov, I. P. (1927). *Conditioned reflexes: An Investigation of the physiological activity of the cerebral cortex.*

Posner, M. I., Nissen, M. J., & Ogden, W. C. (1978). Attended and unattended processing modes: The role of set for spatial location. In H. I. Pick, Jr., & E. Saltzman (Eds.), *Modes of perceiving and processing information.* Hillsdale, NJ.: Erlbaum.

Posner, M. I., Petersen, S. E. (1990). The attention system of the human brain. *Annual Review of Neuroscience, 13*, 25–42.

Prinzmetal, W., Amiri, H., Allen, K., Nwachuku, I., & Bodanske, L. (1995). *The phenomenology of attention.* Proceedings of the 36th Annual Meeting of the Psychonomic Society, (p. 46). Austin, TX: Psychonomic Society Publications.

Ratliff, F. (1965). *Mach bands*. San Francisco: Holden-Day.

Ratcliff, R. (1978). A theory of memory retrieval. *Psychological Review, 85,* 59–108.

Reed, A. V. (1973). Speed–accuracy trade-off in recognition memory. *Science, 181,* 574–576.

Reeves, A., & Sperling, G. (1986). Attention gating in short term visual memory. *Psychological Review, 93,* 180–206.

Reichardt, W. (1957). Autokorrelationsauswertung als funktionsprinzip des zentralnervensystems. *Zeitschrift Naturforschung, 12b,* 447–457.

Remington, R. (1980). Attention and saccadic eye movements. *Journal of Experimental Psychology: Human Perception and Performance, 6,* 726–744.

van Santen, J. P. H., & Sperling, G. (1984). Temporal covariance model of human motion perception. *Journal of the Optical Society of America A, 1,* 451–473.

van Santen, J. P. H., & Sperling, G. (1985). Elaborated Reichardt detectors. *Journal of the Optical Society of America A, 2,* 300–321.

Schade, O. H. (1958). On the quality of color-television images and the perception of color detail. *Journal of the Society of Motion Picture Television Engineers, 67,* 801–819.

Schade, O. H. (1956). Optical and photoelectric analog of the eye. *Journal of the Optical Society of America, 46,* 721–739.

Schade, O. H. (1948). Electro-optical characteristics of television systems. I. Characteristic of vision and visual systems. *RCA Review, 9,* 5–37.

Shaw, M. L. (1984). Division of attention among spatial locations: A fundamental difference between detection of letters and detection of luminance increment. In H. Bouma & D. G. Bouwhais (Eds.), *Attention and performance X.* (pp. 109–120). Hillsdale, NJ: Erlbaum.

Shaw, M. L. (1980). Identifying attentional and decision-making components in information processing. In R. S. Nickerson (Ed.), *Attention and performance VIII* (pp. 277–296). Hillsdale, NJ: Erlbaum.

Shih, S-I., & Sperling, G. (1996). Is there feature based attentional selection in visual search? *Journal of Experimental Psychology: Perception and Psychophysics, 22,* 758–779.

Shulman, G. L., Remington, R. W., & McLean, J. P. (1979). Moving attention through visual space. *Journal of Experimental Psychology: Human Perception and Performance, 5,* 522–526.

Skinner, B. F. (1938). *The behavior of organisms: An experimental analysis.* New York: D. Appleton-Century Co.

Solomon, J. A., & Sperling, G. (1994). Full-wave and half-wave rectification in 2nd-order motion perception. *Vision Research, 34,* 2239–2257.

Sperling, G. (in press). The goal of theory in experimental psychology. In R. L. Solso (Ed.), *Mind and brain sciences in the 21st century.* Cambridge, MA: MIT Press.

Sperling, G. (1989). Three stages and two systems of visual processing. *Spatial Vision, 4* (*Prazdny Memorial Issue*), 183–207.

Sperling, G. (1970). Binocular vision: A physical and a neural theory. *American Journal of Psychology, 83,* 461–534.

Sperling, G. (1964). Linear theory and the psychophysics of flicker. *Documenta Ophthalmologica, 18,* 3–15.

Sperling, G. (1960). The information available in brief visual presentations. *Psychological Monographs, 74,* 1–29.

Sperling, G., Chubb, C., Solomon, J. A., & Lu, Z-L. (1994). Visual preprocessing: First- and second-order processes in the perception of motion and texture. In J. M. Zurada, R. J. Marks II, & C. J. Robinson (Eds.), *Computational intelligence: Imitating life* (pp. 223–236). New York: IEEE Press, The Institute of Electrical and Electronics Engineers, Inc.

Sperling, G. (1996). Five Public lectures. June 9, 1996: Western Attention Meeting, Pomona, College, Claremont, CA, "Computational Theory of Visual Attention"; University of Western Sydney, Macarthur, Campbelltown NSW 2560 Australia, July 29, 1996: University of New South Wales, Sydney, Australia, July 31, 1996: University of Western Australia, Nedlands Australia. August 1, 1996: "Atoms of the Mind: An Historical Overview of Theories of Attention"; November 22, 1996: Plenary lecture, Workshop on Short-term Storage and Processing in Human Cognition, University of Leipzig, Germany, "Mechanisms of Visual Short-Term Memory and Attention."

Sperling, G., & Dosher, B. A. (1986). Strategy and optimization in human information processing. In K.

Boff, L. Kaufman, and J. Thomas (Eds.), *Handbook of perception and performance* (*Vol. 1*, Ch. 2, pp. 2-1–2.65). New York: Wiley.

Sperling, G., Dosher, B. A., & Landy, M. S. (1990). How to study the kinetic depth effect experimentally. *Journal of Experimental Psychology: Human Perception and Performance, 16,* 445–450.

Sperling, G., & Melcher, M. J. (1978). The attention operating characteristic: Some examples from visual search. *Science, 202,* 315–318.

Sperling, G., & Weichselgartner, E. (1995). Episodic theory of the dynamics of spatial attention. *Psychological Review, 102,* 503–532.

Sternberg, S. (1969). The discovery of processing stages: Extensions of Donders' method. *Acta Psychologica, 30,* 276–315.

Sternberg, S. (1966). High speed scanning in human memory. *Science, 153,* 652–654.

Titchener, E. B. (1919). *A text-book of psychology.* New York: Macmillan Co.

Townsend, J. T., & Ashby, F. G. (1983). *Stochastic modeling of elementary psychological processes.* Cambridge, UK: Cambridge University Press.

Treisman, A. (1986). Features and objects in visual processing. *Scientific American, 255,* 114B–125.

Tsal, Y. (1983). Movements of attention across the visual field. *Journal of Experimental Psychology: Human Perception and Performance, 9,* 523–530.

Wald, A. (1950). *Statistical decision functions.* New York: Wiley.

Wald, A. (1947). *Sequential analysis.* New York: Wiley.

Watson, A. B., & Ahumada, A. J. Jr. (1983). A look at motion in the frequency domain. In J. K. Tsotsos (Ed.), *Motion: Perception and representation* (pp. 1–10). New York: Association for Computing Machinery. (Also published as NASA Technical Memorandum 84352).

Watson, J. B. (1919). *Psychology from the standpoint of a behaviorist.* Philadelphia and London: J. B. Lippincott Co.

Weber, E. H. (1846). Der tastsinn und das gemeingefühl. In R. Wagner (Ed.), *Handwörterbuch, III, ii,* 546–549.

Wickelgren, W. A. (1977). Speed–accuracy tradeoff and information processing dynamics. *Acta Psychologica, 41,* 67–85.

Woodworth, R. S. (1921). *Psychology: The study of mental life.* New York: Henry Holt, & Co.

Wright, C. E., & Main, A. M. (1996). *Selectively searching for conjunctively-defined visual targets.* Mathematical Behavioral Sciences Report MBS-96-14, University of California, Irvine.

Wundt, W. (1924). *An introduction to psychology.* (Rudolf Pintner, Trans.). London: George Allen & Unwin, Ltd. (Original work published 1912)

Young, T. (1802). On the theory of light and colors. *Philosophical Transactions, 92,* 20f.

CHAPTER 9

Gestalt Theory and Its Legacy

Organization in Eye and Brain, in Attention and Mental Representation

Julian Hochberg

I. INTRODUCTION AND OVERVIEW

This chapter first reviews some of the phenomena behind the Gestalt theorists' attempt to replace the mainstream approach to visual cognition; why the replacement itself failed to take (sections I and II); and then it reconsiders those phenomena within our present knowledge of brain structure, of successive attention, and of the contribution of mental representation (sections III, IV, and V), ending with a very different picture and prospect.

A. The Default Agenda: Atomism and Associationism

Until midcentury, mainstream psychology and physiology explained perception in terms of independent local sensory units, and of the remembered associations between them—that is, of their memory *images,* as learned from the world's contingencies. (Pejoratively, this was *atomism.*)

1. Perception = Sensations + Images

In vision, the retinal receptors were the fundamental units, each providing both an elementary sensation of color, and its *local sign* (Lotze, 1852/1965), which was a learned association based on the eye movements that would fixate that spot.[1] Each

---

[1] For early history, see Boring (1942). Such *associations* could be experimentally manipulated (e.g., by retraining the relationships between eye movements and the retinal pattern) (Helmholtz, 1866/1962), a

Perception and Cognition at Century's End

visual sensation was taken as independent (now termed *modular*); and in concert they were considered to provide only an aggregate of local, independent visual sensations—no shapes, motion, or depth.[2]

a. Binding Sensations into Perceived Shapes and Objects through Local Signs within a Behavioral Coordinate System

Through repeated simultaneous and successive associations, a frequently-encountered *proximal* pattern of stimulation provides a set of local sensations, and their memory images are bound together as a learned unit which in turn becomes associated with *distal* properties of layout, reflectance and distance. All shape and pattern perception starts therefore with such fundamental local visual sensations, each spatially tagged by its local sign (its associations with previous eye movements noted as *v* in Figure 1). The content of any perceived or imagined object is the set of sensations and images mutually associated by the object that provided them. Those associations comprise a structured mental representation. For example, Helmholtz's idea of some table (he wrote) was what he would expect to see from another viewpoint, implying that mental representations can yield information about the structure—or configuration—of the object they represent. (This line of study did not take hold for a century (Kosslyn, 1975; Shepard & Metzler, 1971), for several reasons. (see Hochberg, chap. 1, this volume; see also Woodworth, 1938, pp. 41ff.)

The objective study of mental representations of configured stimuli is now central to cognitive psychology, to brain science, and to artificial intelligence, and remains intimately involved in at least some accounts of the perceptual process (section IV). Chapters 2, 3, and 12, in this volume, are concerned to different degrees with the nature of images. As noted next, mental representations and their structure were taken as central to what we perceive, as distinct from what we sense.

2. Major Problems with This Approach and Their Solutions

Problem one is that independence is violated, as in color contrast in which one region's perceived color changes as the stimulation of its surround changes. Problem two is that we normally perceive the world's *distal* properties, and not the sensory responses to the *proximal* sensory stimulation: objects' sizes (as opposed to retinal extents), their reflectances (as opposed to their retinal luminances), their distances from the viewer, and so on. Helmholtz proposed that we draw unconsciously on what we have learned about the world's contingencies. This process of taking context into account yields the *perceptual constancies,* which received substantial research until the 1970s (see Epstein, 1977). When incorrect, we get the *illusions* chap. 8, (see Gillam, chap. 5, this volume; Coren & Girgus, 1978).

---

field in which much research was done without significantly penetrating the problem of binding "what" to "where" in object perception. For review, see Welch (1986, esp. pp. 25–27).

[2] We now know, of course, that individual retinal receptors do not serve as independent analyzers (see sect. III.B, and Nakayama, chap. 10, this volume).

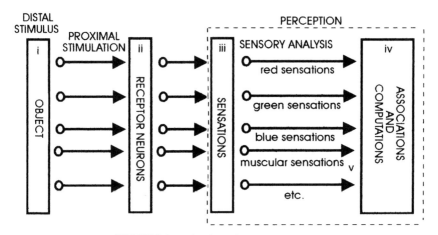

FIGURE 1   The classical opponent: Atomism.

Although the terminology has changed, the ideas are still active (section III.A.1). Helmholtz's *unconscious inference* (Hochberg, chap. 1, section III.B, this volume), placed *mental causation* at the heart of what otherwise had seemed a straightforward quantitative science of mind: The *mental representation* consulted in the course of inference contains the structure of the object and its surroundings, and the relevant physical principles. These allow the viewer to infer, for example, the object's distal size from the size of its retinal image together with its perceived distance (which is itself inferred from the depth cues). With its atomistic foundation, this approach was Gestalt theorists' prime target.

B. Gestalt Theory and Its Predecessors: Theories of Direct Global Perception

There was strong opposition to the idea of these independent punctiform sensory channels. Most notably, Hering (1861) and Mach (1896/1959) argued for specific neural interactions at the lowest levels of the sensory system, networks accounting *directly* for some perceived distal (world) properties without invoking inference or learning; Von Ehrenfels (1890) had argued that an attribute of the whole configuration, or *Gestalt quality,* was missing from the list of sensory primitives; Schumann (1904) had devised robust grouping and completion demonstrations (e.g., Figure 7A) and Rubin (1915, 1921) had detailed the *figure–ground* observations that became so central to the Gestalt position. Beyond these, a strong case had been made that motion perception is direct, and not constructed from momentary sensations of color at successive local signs (Wohlgemuth, 1911). But it was Max Wertheimer and his associates Kurt Koffka (1935), Wolfgang Köhler (1920, 1947), Wilhelm Metzger (1934), and other writers of the Berlin school who attempted *an integrated theory of perception and cognition* with such configurational phenomena as its starting point.

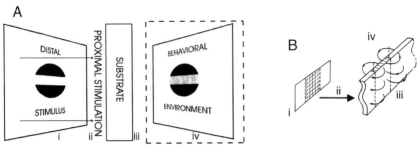

FIGURE 2   (A) The Gestalt alternative. (B) One try at the substrate.

(For a recent account from an historian's standpoint, see Asch, 1995; for contemporary critique, see Petermann, 1932; for a precursor to this section of the present chapter, see Hochberg, 1974b.)

In the Gestalt approach, our perceptions are directly determined by effects of the stimulus *configuration* upon our self-organizing nervous systems, not by the aggregate of their *local* stimulus properties. The melody remains the same when transposed into different sequences of frequencies and auditory receptors; the same visual form is perceived when transposed to totally different receptors by changing its location, size, color, orientation, and so on. The whole is not a listing of its component local sensations (or activated receptors).

Nor is unconscious inference needed to explain our perception of distal properties. In *Gestalttheorie,* organization in perception reflects that of an *isomorphic physiological substrate,* an interconnected, self-equilibrating structure. Thanks to evolution, its responses to most patterns of proximal stimulation (Figure 2Aii) correspond reasonably well to the distal structures (Figure 2Ai) of our normal ecology.

II. STARTING OVER: THE GESTALTISTS' REFORMULATION OF PSYCHOLOGY AND NEUROPHYSIOLOGY

The approach rests on configuration-dependent phenomena that are not the sum of the point-by-point effects of the stimulus pattern, nor (presumably) the results of learned associations. Instead, the perceptual phenomena reflect (are isomorphic to) the configuration-dependent processes in the underlying physiological substrate, and therefore provide our most ready method to study those processes. Correspondingly, only our understanding of the configuration-dependent processes in the substrate will explain and predict the perceptual phenomena.

The substrate should therefore be central to a Gestalt theory, but the concept was developed only in primitive attempts by Wertheimer (1912/1961, 1923/1965) to explain apparent motion, and by Köhler to explain why figures appear denser than their surrounds (Köhler, 1920), why figure and ground reverse (Köhler, 1947; Hochberg, 1950), and why contours appear to be displaced from sites previously *satiated* by other contours (Köhler & Wallach, 1944). These proposals invoked configured bioelectrical current flow between regions of neural tissue. In the example in Figure 2B, the sensory stimulus at *i* provides a region of neural activity (*ii*) to the cortex (*iii*), generating a configuration-dependent pattern of bioelectric current (*iv*); such explanations now have no neurophysiological credibility (see Hochberg, chap. 1, and Nakayama, chap. 10, this volume).

In practice, two quite different kinds of generalization were offered to summarize the horde of Gestalt demonstrations: (a) the "*laws of organization,*" general principles suggested by examining how their configurations seem to determine the appearance of various stimulus patterns; (b) versions of the *minimum principle,* which is that we perceive the simplest structure that will fit the proximal configuration.

A. Phenomena to Be Explained, Gestalt Explanations Where They Were Offered, and Some Current Research

1. Motion and Structure-through-Motion

a. Apparent Motion

To atomistic analysis (Figure 1), motion is not itself a sensation, but a succession of color sensations, with adjacent local signs. Since motion is in fact perceived between two stationary, successively stimulated spots even when the timing and separation are such that the objects themselves cannot be discerned (the *phi* phenomenon, i.e., in which there is no perceived succession of color sensations), Wertheimer (1912) argued that motion is itself directly perceived.

Through well-established microelectrode findings (Lettvin, Maturana, McCulloch, & Pitts, 1959; see chap. 8, Dosher & Sperling, this volume), we know today of a range of neural processes activated by successive stimulation, now modelled in quantitative and explicit form. At short space–time separations, the motion occurs between nearest successive contours, regardless of configuration or meaning (Burtt & Sperling, 1981; Kolers & Pomerantz, 1971; Navon, 1976; Orlansky, 1940). At greater space–time separations, however, something more like the results of inference is manifest: The motion perceived then tends to be whatever would be most likely to have resulted in the displacement.[3] In any case, when a set of bodies are in relative motion, how that motion is in fact allocated among them provides an important body of configuration-dependent phenomena, discussed next.

b. Induced Motion, Vector Analysis, and Structure-through-Motion

Perceived movements can be very different from those in *either* the retinal stimulation *or* the world. Depending on configuration, a stationary spot (Figure 3Aii)

---

[3] The question of whether or not there are two separate response systems (e.g., Anstis, 1980; Braddick, 1980; Leibowitz, 1955; Saucer, 1954), or whether the "short-range" process is perceptual and all else "cognitive" (e.g., Cavanagh, & Mather, 1989), is being outstripped by process models and research (see Dosher & Sperling, chap. 8, this volume) and depends on definitions discussed in section V.

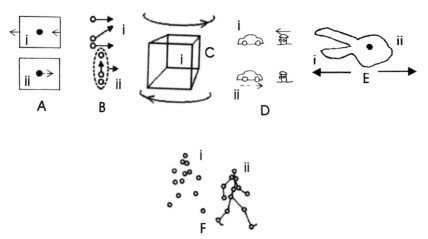

FIGURE 3   Emergent motion phenomena (arrows: direction of real or perceived movement). (A) Induced motion (Duncker); (i) real; (ii) perceived. (B) "Vector analysis" (Johansson effect); (i) real; (ii) perceived. (C) Rotating wire cube, with (i) being the rear edge, and rotating as shown above. As first reported by von Hornbostel in 1922, the cube reverses spontaneously, and then (i) is perceived as the near edge, rotating as shown below, distorting as it does so. (D) In dark surroundings, Brosgole & Whalen (1967) found that motion follows familiarity; the motion at (i) would be seen as at (ii). (E) A version of Jastrow's duck/rabbit (Jastrow, 1900). Under the right conditions, its direction of apparent motion depends on how it is construed (MacBeath et al., 1992). (F) A "dot walker," stationary (i) and moving (ii) as described by Johansson (1973).

appears to move if its surroundings move (Duncker 1929) (Figure 3Ai). Such *induced motion* is a robust phenomenon displayed whenever a moving object is kept stationary on the motion picture screen by a tracking camera (see Hochberg & Brooks, 1996a). In Figure 3B, the motion pattern (*i*) is perceived as (*ii*) (Johansson, 1950). To Johansson and his colleagues (Johansson, 1950, 1982), the phenomenon comprises a simple vector analysis (Koenderink, 1994; Restle, 1979, for an earlier use of vectors, see Brown & Voth, 1937).

In a related set of phenomena, originally termed the kinetic depth effect (KDE) and now subsumed under structure-through-motion (STM), stimulus patterns which appear two-dimensional (2-D) when stationary may spring into recognizable three dimensionality when in motion: sets of rods and wire forms (Metzger, 1934; Wallach & O'Connell, 1953), or patterns of random dots embedded in a field of similar dots, reveal themselves as a tridimensional structure only when moving (Julesz, 1971; White & Mueser, 1960). Well-developed analyses of STM have received considerable cross-disciplinary attention (e.g., Koenderink & VanDoorn, 1975; Ullman, 1979), perhaps because they are easier to embody in machinery or to simulate than the traditional account of space perception, *if* the structure (object, layout) to be perceived is itself *rigid*. Most such algorithms do therefore explicitly assume that what is being perceived is the motion of a distally rigid structure (e.g.,

Hoffman & Bennet, 1986; Johansson, 1982; Longuet-Higgins & Prazdny, 1980; Ullman, 1979)—or approximately rigid (Ullman, 1984).

Such modeling, often as rigorous as it seems, is attractive as science and as potential engineering, but it must not be taken as the whole story. Demonstrations to the effect that the coherance of the moving surfaces that the viewers perceive determines the perceived motions (He & Nakayama 1994; Nakayama & Shimojo, 1992; Yantis, 1995) argue for a different class of analysis, and there are other effects that draw on variables of familiarity and meaning that would seem to defy systematic mathematical treatment.

But first, there is the matter of the rigidity assumption. If visual perception followed a rigidity constraint, things would be relatively simple in visual cognition.

i. The organism does not follow simple and homogeneous constraints (like a rigidity constraint)   With such a rigidity constraint, only one distal layout will fit to (and be specified by) the temporal pattern of light to the eye, and explaining perception would be a much easier task (see Cutting, chap. 4, this volume; Hochberg, 1988), but humans do not follow that constraint. We readily perceive the 3D structures of *non*rigid objects (Cutting, 1982; Todd, 1982). What is more telling, *moving rigid objects,* both real and pictured, may appear to be in reversed 3D structure and therefore as grossly nonrigid (Figure 3C). Although this was known for at least 75 years (von Hornbostel, 1922), the rigidity assumption is still repeatedly invoked (Johansson, 1982, Hoffman & Bennett, 1986). Perhaps the many recent demonstrations of this point may finally force that point through (for example, see Braunstein & Andersen, 1986; Gogel & Tietz, 1992; Hochberg & Beer, 1990; Pomerantz, 1983; Schwartz & Sperling, 1983; for extended discussion, see Hochberg, 1988).

ii. Biological and other familiar motions   Familiarity and meaning, not just measurable stimulus parameters, can be demonstrated in the motions we perceive. In Figure 3D, given a stationary car or plane and a moving tree or house, within a blank field, the vehicle tends to be seen as moving (Brosgole & Whalen, 1967). When in Figure 3E, the ambiguous figure (similar to one by Jastrow, 1900) is replaced by two identical figures on each side so as to allow long-range stroboscopic motion to one or the other, it appears to move to (i) or (ii) if seen as a duck or a rabbit, respectively (McBeath, Morikawa, & Kaiser, 1992).

Most entertaining (and perhaps diagnostic of the whole set of phenomena), the human "dot figures" in Figure 3F (Johansson, 1973) are meaningless patterns when stationary (i) but when moving (ii) reveal a human in action, which even allows friends and genders to be recognized through their gait (Cutting & Proffitt, 1981). The same dot-walkers who are perceived in recognizable 3D motion when upright and moving, are merely unrecognizable, disorganized motion patterns when inverted (see Shiffrar, Lichtéy, & Chatterjee, 1997, for recent research and references). The effect of inversion assures us that it is the *previous experience of the viewer,* and not the configuration as such, mediating these phenomena.

Short-range motion is indeed a direct response, and seems as independent of past familiarites as Wertheimer argued, but it shows no effects of configuration. Longer-range motion shows effects of configuration (Figures 3A,B) but also shows the effects of familiarity for which classical theory calls.

c. Summary and Three Morals

Research on this motion-related subset of "the Gestalt phenomena" continues vigorously. Direct neural response to motion is firmly in, and independent local signs as the basis on which events are built by learned associations, is firmly out. Wertheimer and his predecessors were right in that.

On the other hand, there are three ways in which I think the Gestaltists' expectations have failed, as I will argue they fail in the other Gestalt phenomena as well: First, motion perception is not governed by a single unified field principle, but proceeds through multiple processes (see Dosher & Sperling, chap. 8, this volume, for detailed discussion of this point). Second, the most rapid and direct ("sensory") response is unaffected by the kinds of configurational phenomena that characterize the Gestaltists' concerns (identity, grouping, simplicity, etc). Third, although configuration is highly important in longer-range motions and event perception quite generally, there are clear warnings that familiarity may be just as much of a factor. Indeed, the two may be one, as will be seen in further discussions when Helmholtz reenters the picture.

2. Four Autochthonous Organizing Principles in the Perception of Objects, Layouts, and Their Pictures

Most of the Gestalt principles remain informally observed "laws of organization," called *autochthonous,* meaning that they are determined by the nature of the organism and not by familiarity or culture (of course, calling them that does not make it so; see section V). They seem to promise practical applications in the graphic arts, in visual communication, and in any part of real life in which concealment (e.g., camouflage) and its reverse (e.g., advertising and interface design) are important (see Figure 4G). Although often dismissed as hopelessly subjective (e.g., Marr, 1982), they offer the credentials toward which the most perceptually oriented neurophysiological models should strive (see sections III.B and V).

a. Figure–Ground and Grouping

Figure–ground segregation refers to the observation that where a contour partitions any visible area (Figure 4A), it seems to unanalytical but careful viewing (i.e., to "phenomenological observation") that only one region at a time has a perceived and therefore potentially recognizable shape. The other area, or ground, extends to some indefinite extent behind the figure's edge (Figures 4A–C). Which region becomes a figure seems to depend on a number of organizing principles.

In *grouping,* unconnected dots or patches may be perceived as composing larger

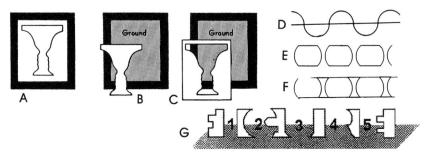

FIGURE 4   (A) An ambiguous figure–ground pattern, with alternative readings at (B) and (C). (D) *Good continuation:* Line and wave, not half-disks. (E) *Enclosedness:* Muffins, not spindles (as at F). (F) *Proximity:* Spindles, not muffins (as at E). (G) Cryptic shapes (see text and Figure 17F).

configurations (e.g., Figure 5) under similar organizing principles. Four commonly cited organizing principles are illustrated next.

b. Demonstrations of Organizing Principles

Good continuation (Figure 4D) refers to the observation that we organize our perceptions so as to preserve unbroken contours; *enclosedness* (Figure 4E), *proximity* (Figure 4F), and *similarity, uniformity* or *homogeneity* (Figures 7E,F), should be self-explanatory given the demonstrations in those figures. Figures 5A–D show similar grouping demonstrations. That these factors are autochthonous, and not the effects of associative learning or convention, was argued using examples like Figures 6A and 6B, in which shapes familiar from previous experience (after Köhler, 1929) or from explicit practice (Gottschaldt, 1926, 1929), respectively, are readily concealed by applying the law of *good continuation* or *closedness* so that they are ground, not figure. (In section V, I argue that such demonstrations are misleading.)

This all seems directly applicable to the design of pictures, diagrams, and visual interfaces quite generally. Even more appealing is the possibility that not only figure–ground segregation and grouping, but most of the perceived *distal* properties

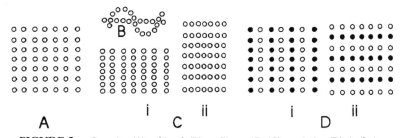

FIGURE 5   Grouping (A) unbiased; (B) see Figure 4D; (C) proximity; (D) similarity.

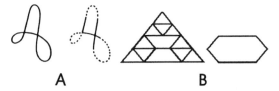

A   B

FIGURE 6   In each pair, the pattern at left conceals the form at right. (A and B are modeled after Köhler, 1929, and Gottschaldt, 1929, respectively.)

of objects in the world also emerge directly from such organization, as discussed next and in section II.A.4.

c. Beyond Figure–Ground Segregation at the Area's Edges: Subjective Contours, Completion, Interposition, Transparency, and Ordinal Depth

The depth ascribed to Figures 5A–C is clearer in the examples in Figure 7A–F, as is the continuation of one surface behind another. Schumann (1904) introduced Figure 7A, which demonstrates *subjective contours* (e.g., those bounding the white bar), *amodal* (nonsensory) *completion* (of the disk and annulus behind the bar); the term *amodal* is from Michotte, Thines, and Crabbe (1964). The transparency phenomena (Figure 7E,F) also depend on completion: Without good continuation and uniformity at work, Figure 7E would be seen as seven separate regions. (We return to Figure 7F in section V.) After recent striking examples, like those in Figures 7B and C from Kanizsa (1974, 1979) and others from Bradley, Dumais, and Petry (1976), this area is now the target of extensive research and attempted explanations. Some of the latter are Helmholtzian inference (see Hochberg, chap. 1, this volume;

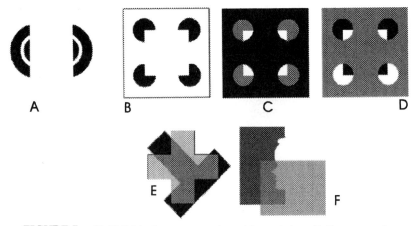

A   B   C   D

E   F

FIGURE 7   (A–D) Subjective contours and amodal completions; (E, F) transparencies.

e.g., Rock, 1977), but these are usually *post hoc;* some are phrased in terms of organization (e.g., Kanizsa, 1979; Michotte et al., 1964), but with no attempt to relate to an underlying substrate. Indeed, these phenomena, especially that discovered by Prazdny (1983), shown in Figure 7D, and the fact that subjective contours occur in patterns defined only by the movements of randomly scattered dots (Prazdny, 1986) virtually rule out the self-organizing current-flow models like Figure 2B, even if the latter were otherwise plausible physiologically.

Modern neurophysiology,[4] on the other hand, offers to account for many aspects of these phenomena in terms of known sensory and cortical analyzing units that are far more complex than the classically simple point receptors of the pre-1950s (those of Figure 1). These explanations depend on specific pattern-sensitive physiological mechanisms (as opposed to familarity-based inferences) but they do not invoke global configurations; this repeats what we saw in the case of apparent motion (section II.A.1). To know what mechanisms to look for, however, depends on the details of perceptual research, and on knowing which phenomena are manifestations of the same underlying mechanisms.

Like the figure–ground phenomenon, the completion demonstrations usually entail an obvious segregation in depth (Coren, 1972). In the traditional Helmholtzian depth cue of *interposition* (Ratoosh, 1949), at any intersection it is the region whose contour changes the least that appears the nearer (Figure 8A,B), although there are exceptions, as in Figures 8C, which I will show as important and diagnostic later (section II.A.4). More generally, interposition, and the *good continuation* of Figure 5D, as well as the extension of amodal contours (Figures 7,8B), has been subsumed as one phenomenon (Kellman & Shipley, 1991; Kellman, Yin, & Shipley, in press), subject to the caveat noted in Figure 8C.

The depth in these figures is merely ordinal or layered,[5] but more structured extensions into 3D can also emerge from flat configurations under the appropriate organizing principles, considered next.

d. Tridimensional Spatial Structure from Flat Designs on Paper:
How Pictures Flow from the Principles of Organization

The Necker Cube at right (and similar pictured objects) appear flat, as at left in Figure 9, if it would break good continuation at (i, ii) or destroy symmetry to perceive

---

[4] Recent research and theory on the specific cortical bases of the perceptual phenomena of edge completion and surface fill-in are Grossberg, 1993; Grossberg and Mignolla, 1985; Nakayama & Shimojo, 1990, 1992; Peterhans & von der Heydt, 1994.

[5] Does one "really perceive" the interrupted or occluded surface behind the other? Both yes and no, since *perceptual consequences* (Hochberg, 1956) for both assumptions can be obtained (cf. Gerbino, 1988): In Figures 7E,F, single stimulus regions appear as *two* layered surfaces whose apparent colors depend on whether and how the depth segregation is perceived, as well as on the relative local luminances (Fuchs, 1923; Heider, 1933). The degree of perceived transparency has been measured by how viewers match the regions' colors against test stimuli (Beck, Prazdny, & Ivry, 1984; Gerbino, Staltiens, Troost, & de Weert, 1990; Metelli, 1974, 1984).

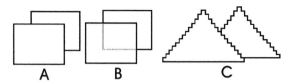

FIGURE 8   (A) interposition, and the amodal completion it implies (as in B). (C) Global configuration prevails over the local junctions unless the latter are closely attended [From Chapanis & McCleary (1953). *Journal of General Psychology, 48,* 113–132. Reprinted with permission of the Helen Dwight Reid Educational Foundation. Published by Heldref Publications, 1319 Eighteenth St. N.W., Washington, D.C. 20036-1802. Copyright © 1953.]

them as 3D (Kopfermann, 1930). The cube at right appears 3D because it would break good continuation at (i) and destroy symmetry to perceive it as flat.

Without calling on learned depth cues or unconscious inferences, therefore, the distal properties we perceive in the world might arise from the Gestalt organizing principles. The major principles do still seem to be effective summaries of diverse robust phenomena.[6] One problem however is that very many such principles have been proposed (Helson, 1926), so that they should often be in conflict (as in Figure 5D,F), and the outcome cannot then be predicted because they are mostly unquantified. These obstacles may be surmounted, as is noted in section II.A.4. But first I discuss an approach that attempted to capture the more unified assumption of a dynamic, interactive substrate, of which the individual Gestalt principles were supposedly mere aspects, not independent modular mechanisms.

3. "Simplicity" or Homogeneity as a Unifying Principle: The Global Minimum Principle, Its Predecessors, and Information-Theoretic Successors

It would be simpler, more scientifically satisfying, and more diagnostic of the nature of the physiological substrate if a main underlying principle could be formulated.

Gestalt theorists frequently invoked *Prägnanz* (that one perceives the "best" organization that could fit the stimulus pattern). Musatti offered the potentially more specific yet comprehensive proposal that we perceive just that grouping that comprises the most *homogeneous* or uniform organization (Musatti, 1931; see Woodworth, 1938, pp. 626f). Mach (1896/1959) had held that perception follows principles of economy and probability, and Koffka (1935) and Werner (1935) suggested that organization follows a *minimum principle*—that we perceive the *simplest* alternative. To be meaningful, such formulations need be more specific.

---

[6] The main Gestalt phenomena themselves appear convincing and important. They are ignored in books on "Vision," mostly because they still rest largely on "phenomenological observations" made during extensive trial and error with drawings. Here, *phenomenological* means as unbiased and full a description of direct experience as possible (cf. Koffka, 1935; Köhler, 1947). Until recently, more of what has turned out to be true of the underlying neurophysiology was based on phenomenology than vice versa (Hochberg, 1988), but that has probably changed, and in any case I think that Sperling's 1960 findings (discussed in p. 281) tell us that *we need indirect measures of direct experience.*

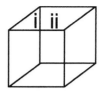

FIGURE 9   Two views of a cube. At right, Necker (1832); at left, Kopfermann (1930).

Three proposals tried to be specific (Attneave, 1954; Garner, 1962; Hochberg & MacAlister, 1953). Attneave (1954) proposed that *information theory* (Shannon & Weaver, 1949) could describe complexity in terms of the viewer's uncertainties. Some sections of a pattern are less predictable or redundant (e.g., the inflection points in Figure 10A), and serve to identify the object (Attneave, 1959). Considerable research (reviewed by Brown & Owen, 1967; Zusne, 1970) obtained subjects' judgments of the simplicity and other properties of such randomly generated nonsense forms, as introduced by Attneave and Arnoult (1956), but did not investigate the Gestalt phenomena themselves.

Closest to information theory proper, Garner (1962, 1966) held a pattern's "goodness" to depend not on its individual characteristics, but on the number of equivalent patterns in the set from which it must be differentiated (its uncertainty or entropy). How subjects rate the goodness of patterns like those in Figure 10B, and how they sort the patterns into groups, are well predicted from such measures (Garner & Clement, 1963).

Closest to the Gestalt phenomena, Hochberg and MacAlister (1953) proposed that we perceive the simplest of the alternative structures that fit a stimulus pattern, where *simplest* refers to the measures needed to specify or explicitly describe the structure. Thus, the figures in each row of Figure 10C are equally complex as 3D wire forms, but increase in their complexity as flat patterns from left to right. Various measures have been proposed, and are still in use.[7] Most of the Gestalt phenomena in Figures 3B, 4, 7, and 8A seem to invite a similar simplicity analysis.

And such analyses seemed to offer vastly more. The pictorial depth cues, on which most traditional accounts of object and space perception depend (Hochberg, chap. 1, and Cutting & Massironi, chap. 6, this volume), are susceptible to the same analysis. Compare the 3D and 2D alternative readings that fit the picture in Figure 10D (Hochberg, 1978; Hochberg & MacAlister, 1953). *The minimum principle seems ready to explain most of the visual perception—IF we can apply and verify appropriate*

---

[7] Hochberg and Brooks (1960) found weighted equations that accounted quite well for viewers' tridimensionality ratings for objects like those in Figure 10C. (E.g., $C_i = [a+d+2(c)]$, where C_i is the relative 2D complexity of each view of the 3D object, a is the number of angles, d is the number of different angles, and c is the number of continuous lines.) A variation of that approach, further minimizing redundancies among the measures, is still pursued and elaborated by Leeuwenberg and his colleagues (Boselie & Leeuwenberg, 1986; Leeuwenberg, 1971; Mens & Leeuwenberg, 1993). Such measures of simplicity are discussed in some detail by Pomerantz (1981) and by Pomerantz and Kubovy (1986). Since about 1962, I have seen no reason to pursue them (see footnote 9).

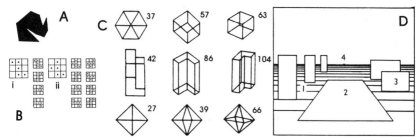

FIGURE 10   (A) An Attneave–Arnoult shape, with its informative inflection points (Attneave & Arnoult, 1956). (B) To Garner, (i) is a better shape than (ii) (and subjects judged it so) because it has fewer alternatives from which to be distinguished (the alternatives are at right, in each case; Garner & Clement, 1963). (C) Kopfermann shapes, perceived as increasingly 3D from left to right within each row (Hochberg & MacAlister, 1953): Measured 2D complexity increases within each row as shown by the numbers (see text, and footnote 7), as does perceived tridimensionality. (D) Four pictorial depth cues for which 3D readings are simpler to specify than a 2D reading: (1) Relative size (3D: 2 side lengths; 2D: 6 lengths). (2) Perspective (3D: 1 angle, 2 lengths; 2D: 2 angles, 3 lengths). (3) Interposition (3D: 1 angle, 2 lengths; 2D: 2 angles, 6 lengths). (4) horizon line (3D: 1 line length; 2D 5 line lengths). Similar results obtain with other measures.

measures. (Notice that these examples are all *global simplicity theories,* in the sense that they have no provision for partitioning the object or scene being measured.)

If perception followed a minimum principle, things would be relatively easy.

But I do not believe, for reasons discussed next, that a global simplicity theory is at all viable. And those same reasons require a wrenching revision of how we regard all of the Gestalt heritage.

4. The Gestalt Unravels: Global Simplicity Is Out, Piecemeal Contributions Are In. So How Big Is a Stimulus?

a. Complex over Simple? Impossible over Possible? Piecemeal versus Wholistic?

Although the last approach continues,[8] I for one abandoned it in 1962 (Hochberg, 1962, 1968), after brooding over the famous Penrose impossible figure (Penrose & Penrose, 1958). Figure 11D (Hochberg, 1970, 1978) focuses the problem: When a perfectly possible, consistent wire object with one occluding (covered) side *1*, is attended at intersection *2*, perceived depth at that intersection soon undergoes repeated spontaneous reversals between the alternative orientations at E (and reverses apparent direction of rotation, if it is rotating; Hochberg & Peterson, 1987; Peterson & Hochberg, 1983).

---

[8] In addition to variations on nonsense patterns like those in Figure 10Bi,iii, there have been attempts to deal with phenomena like Figure 3B (Cutting & Proffitt, 1982; Proffitt & Cutting, 1980; Restle, 1979).

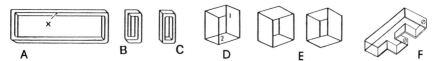

FIGURE 11   (A, B) Impossible figures, designed after Penrose and Penrose (1958) by Hochberg (1962) to vary distance between corners. Compare A, B, and C (a possible figure). (D) A wire cube with an occluding surface added at (1) (Hochberg, 1970, 1978; see also Gillam, 1979); it enters reversal when fixated at intersection (2), reversing perceived direction of rotation when it does so (Hochberg & Peterson, 1987). (E) The two alternative orientations between which reversals occur in D (although the cube at right obviously will not fit at (2), and is probably not fully perceived during reversal). (F) The number of intersections contradicted by reversal at the left intersection can be increased indefinitely (Peterson & Hochberg, 1983).

This contradicts any global minimum principle (Hochberg, 1981).[9] It puts the very notion of Gestalt psychology in question, since something less than the whole object (or whole layout) is being taken into account (Hochberg, 1982), a point for which evidence abounds well beyond this case:

A rotating object spontaneously breaks in two, replacing one rotation direction with two (Gillam, 1972). In Figure 8C, attending to the intersections between the two shapes reverses the depth, and lines change their functions in Figures 11A and 11D with changes fixation/attention. Visible stationary elements added to moving dots like those of Figure 3B are not included in their "vector analyses" if they are not attended (Hochberg & Fallon, 1976). Kanizsa (1979) and Kanizsa and Gerbino (1982) provide a variety of static figures which contradict intuitive simplicity principles (although most can be fit by the formulas of Hochberg & Brooks, 1960 and of Leeuwenberg, 1971).

Such examples show that the whole configuration is not effective at one time, and Figure 11B hints that extrafoveal distance from fixation is part of what is involved.

These examples suggest that when examining a configured object (and not just the telltale figures in 11A and 11D), attention must be directed to the next point to be inspected, must then be moved to that point, and so on, as sketched in Figure 12A. Moreover, only incomplete information about the structure is remembered from one glance to the next (that is what the "?" marks signify). When regarding a succession of aperture views (Figure 12B) intended to simulate glances without their normal persistent peripheral context, viewers could keep track of relatively simple structures (e.g., noting that the cross's right arm was skipped), but only by

---

[9] Either the whole figure at D must spontaneously reverse, thus yielding a *less* simple structure than is actually present, or the local feature must reverse independently of its context (Hochberg, 1974a), or both. Although it is true that the minimum principle is violated in this example only by the amount of one intersection (Attneave, 1981; Boselie & Leeuwenberg, 1986; Hatfield & Epstein, 1985), we can readily arrange for many more local violations (as in Figure 11F), and in any case that misses the point: The overall simplicity measure can be greatly altered by what happens at just one intersection.

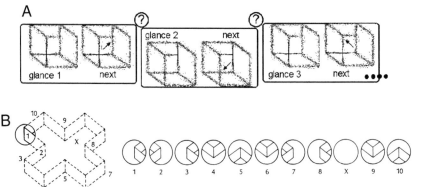

FIGURE 12   (A) What is implied about perceptual inquiry by Figures 11A and 11D. Three glances (blurred outside the center of attention), with a shift in attention to the next region, followed by a glance to that region. As the question marks indicate, the failure to note the inconsistencies in Figure 11A suggests that there is much that one doesn't remember from one glance to the next. (B) Successive presentations of central views (at right) of the corresponding corners in the cross at left as the cross moves behind the aperture [Figure from "In the Mind's Eye" by Julian Hochberg from *Contemporary Theory and Research in Visual Perception* by Ralph N. Haber, Copyright © 1968 by Holt, Rinehart, and Winston, reproduced by permission of the publisher.] Observers can in fact keep track of the views (e.g., noting which arm was skipped at *x*), but must pay specific attention—must deliberately build a mental representation to do so.

making an effort—the construction in memory was not automatic. This is a very different way of considering configurations, and we return to the issue when discussing attention and mental representation in section IV.

In any case, I think the message of such figures is clear: unless parsed according to a specified *elective strategy* (cf. Stins & van Leeuwen, 1993; van Leeuwen, 1995), the configurations remain unexplicated. We need an alternative to the minimum principle, and a less holistic way of dealing with Gestalten.

b. Alternatives That Retain Something of the Minimum Principle

In 1982, Attneave proposed a mixed system, in which higher-order analyzers (dipoles) *within* a cortical 3D (or 2 1/2 D) structural representation assigned the locations of perceived surfaces according to a finite set of principles (colinearity, orthogonality, etc.), and with mutual facilitation between similar dipoles. He still assumed (unnecessarily, I believe: cf. section V) that a self-equilibrating ("soap bubble") process combined the dipoles' output, but that the dipoles themselves might be learned (as *cell assemblies,* see sect. III.A.3.a.i), and that the *individual principles could prevail against overall simplicity.* This is very like other more recent models still being explored (e.g., p. 274). But it is no longer anything like a unified minimum principle, and it does not address the piecemeal parsing of the field of view. Indeed, Attneave (1957) quite early drew on a *schema-plus-correction* formulation, as did Hochberg (1957) and Oldfield (1954); in this conception (see p. 285), taken from Woodworth (1938), simplicity follows from resource limitations, whether or not we posit an active minimum principle as well.

On a different tack, Hatfield and Epstein (1985) and Simon (1967) have speculated that something like the minimum principle could be formulated for *local* regions. Nobody has actually tried it, to my knowledge. But even if this could be done, *we would still need some way of knowing how much of the configuration to include, and how to relate the local and global structures.*

Gestalt psychology, in the sense of a global minimum principle (whether called simplicity, praegnanz, homogeneity, etc.) reflecting a unified underlying physiological process(es) seems to me unviable and misleading. Gestalt psychology as a concern with the effects of configuration on perceptual organization, and with its possible underlying mechanisms, is stronger than it ever was.

Without a superprinciple from which to derive the individual organizing principles, we can only explicate and measure the latter, and then study how they combine.

c. Measuring the Gestalt Phenomena

Such measures are increasingly being obtained for the major Gestalt phenomena, using a variety of methods beyond phenomenological description.

These methods include (a) obtaining responses in forms suitable for quantitative scaling procedures; (b) titrating one nonmeasurable property (e.g., ordinal depth of an occluder) against a quantitative psychophysical variable (e.g., binocular disparity), or (c) titrating two measurable properties to determine relative strengths; (d) measuring what should be a consequence of some perceived state, itself nonmeasurable (e.g., as noted in the caption for Figure 11D); (e) priming some subsequent same/different response.[10] Where the determinants of alternative perceived organizations are roughly balanced in some sense, spontaneous reversals occur, and their frequencies, relative durations, and time to first reversal can all be readily measured. Such *multistability* can be found in most of the Gestalt phenomena, and in natural scenes quite generally (Zimmer, 1995).[11] To ensure that it is not just the viewer's

---

[10] As examples of such more objective or quantitative measures as noted in (a) through (e): (a) for the principle of good continuation (section II.A.2.c; for recent review, see Kellman, in press); for proximity and similarity in grouping (Beck, 1972; Hochberg & Silverstein, 1956; Kubovy, 1994; Kubovy & Wagemans, 1995); for symmetry (in its effects on completion: Sekuler, Palmer, & Flynn, 1994).

[11] The easiest measurement methods to devise are probably those based on ambiguity or *multistability* (Attneave, 1971; Mach, 1896/1959; Necker, 1832). Reversals themselves are probably stochastic (as Hock, Schoner, & Voss, 1997, have shown with multistable motion patterns), and not directly caused by "satiation" or built-up resistance to each continued figural process, as Köhler had proposed (see p. 256); but reversion rates and balance are affected by and therefore can measure adaptive figural and attitudinal factors. Reversion times between multistable alternatives are themselves stable, for a given viewer and situation, and can be modeled (Ditzinger & Haken, 1995; Haken, 1990). Having the subject indicate which of several alternatives was seen allowed Kubovy and Wagemans (1995) to measure the entropy, or degree of reduction of potential response alternatives, as a response to the entropy (structural alternatives) attributable to the stimuli. And how fast one or the other alternative can be first identified is now a widely used measure in a variety of contexts: for example, to estimate the order of global versus local processing (Hughes et al., 1996; Navon, 1977; see section IV.C), to infer which of two alternatives was seen as figure and which as ground (Driver & Baylis, 1995; see section V.B), and so on.

reports (e.g., key presses) but their percepts that are measured, multistability can often be paired with other methods, such as (a–e), above.[12]

That is, acceptably objective measures can surely be found with which to test the organizing principles, to state them quantitatively, and then to try to use these as diagnostic of the underlying visual processes. It remains to be seen whether viable combining laws can be attained. It also remains to be seen whether we can find principled bases that tell us what the effective configuration consists of in each case. More generally, without some way to identify what the effective configuration will be in any instance, we can have no predictive theory of configurational effects—no Gestalt theory, nor any other definite theory of how perception works, and of how some configuration will be perceived.

III. RESETTING THE PROBLEMS AND THEIR CONTEXT

A. Contexts of the Gestalt Phenomena in the 1950s and How They Speak to Our Present Concerns

1. Brunswik: The Gestalt Phenomena and the Likelihood Principle

Of the three major perceptual theorists of the 1950s, only Brunswik directly addressed the Gestalt principles. Egon Brunswik (1947, 1956), continuing his long-term positivist commitment, sidestepped both the sensations and the inference of Figure 1 by arguing that associative learning, and the perception based upon it, directly reflects the probabilities of ecological co-occurrence.[13] Perception thereby resembles inference in its *outcome,* being a *ratiomorphic* (Brunswik, 1955, 1956) or reasoning-like reflection of the physical likelihoods that relate proximal and distal variables. As part of this process, perceivers learn the cues as to what in the visual field belongs to the same object—thereby providing what we have described as the Gestalt laws.

Without quantitative measures of likelihood, however, the likelihood principle can offer to explain *almost every possible outcome* and so is not predictive.[14] Fully aware of this problem (which many likelihood advocates still do not grasp), Brunswik

---

[12] The very fact of reversal is sometimes taken to show that a specific structure has really been perceived. Thus, after a wire form's shadow, originaly flat-looking when stationary, was seen as tridimensional while rotating, it looked 3D even when it was stationary *as attested by its undergoing spontaneous reversals in apparent depth* (Wallach, O'Connell, & Neisser, 1953). This kind of criterion is stronger if the viewer is asked about some *perceptual consequences* that can be inferred from the stimulus only through *perceptual coupling* like size/distance, slant/shape, and so on (Hochberg, 1956; Hochberg & Peterson, 1987).

[13] This *likelihood principle* must necessarily appear to explain most perceptual phenomena (including most of the examples in section II.A.2), at least qualitatively and after the fact, and is often invoked today (Gregory, 1972, 1980; Rock, 1977, 1984, 1993; Shepard, 1984).

[14] But it is true that specific explanations, once offered, can and have been contested (cf. Parks & Rock, 1990, vs. Purghé, 1995), so it can progress.

therefore proposed that *ecological surveys* would serve to measure the *ecological validities* with which some *cue* (some aspect of proximal stimulation) and its distal referent is correlated; these measures should in turn serve to predict quantitatively the probability that viewers would in fact use that cue.

Very few such surveys have been done. That the law of proximity (Figures 4F,5C) would reflect the probability that things closer in the visual field are parts of the same object, was supported by measurements on magazine photographs reported by Brunswik and Kamiya (1953). (The obvious limitations of this procedure underscore the difficulties in making such surveys.) We may add, even without surveys, that the law of good continuation might simply reflect the fact that only by very unlikely coincidence would edges at different distances coincide within the limits of our extremely sensitive vernier acuity (Hochberg, 1972, 1988), perhaps contributing to the nature of figure–ground segregation itself (see Figures 13A,17D). Indeed, with the right premises, we can abduct many examples of the simplicity principle to support the likelihood principle: only from one of infinitely many viewpoints would an "L" and a square line up exactly, and so on (Figure 10D3).

Brunswik's ecological approach had many virtues that have not been done justice over the years. It did have several problems, two being particularly important here. First, his approach tends to dismiss the size parameters of sensitivity as "merely" mediating variables; in fact, the correct choice of units would seem a large part of what an appropriate ecological survey would determine (cf. Figure 8C). Second, it does not consider how much of the stimulus pattern to consider in deciding likelihood (the point raised by Figure 11D).

2. Gibson's Rejection of Line Drawings (and the Gestalt Demonstrations) as Nondiagnostic

Similar in some ways to Brunswik (see Burton, 1996; Hochberg, 1974a), James J. Gibson considered perception as the direct pickup of the information about the distal world,[15] information potentially available as higher-order variables in the proximal stimulation. The proximal information needed for effective behavior in the natural environment was not to be found in local stimulus properties but in the *invariances* that underlie the changing contents of proximal stimulation and in that sense *specify* (reflect) the physical structures of the distal world. Originally, Gibson (1950), took local gradients of optical texture to define the surface orientations of which objects and layouts are composed (viewers have in fact turned out to be too insensitive to such gradients for the latter to serve as the primitives of object perception; see

---

[15] That point remained constant despite several major reformulations (Reed, 1988), with landmarks provided by Gibson's books of 1950, 1966, and 1979. The existence and constancy of appropriate invariances had already been recognized but not emphasized nor pursued to the same end by Helmholtz (1881), and Hering (1861), and more recently by Koffka (1935) (see Cassirer, 1944; Cutting, 1986; Hochberg, 1974a). Gibson's effort was new and revolutionary in that he tried assiduously to work around the need for *any* perceptual process other than the pickup of such invariances.

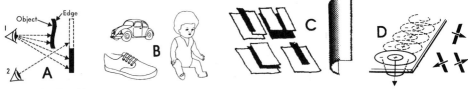

FIGURE 13   Figure–ground and outline pictures. (A) When crossing a surface's edges or occluding tangents, accommodation and convergence must change, and differential occlusion of the further surface occurs with each small change in viewpoint (whereas the nearer surface moves as a whole). The edge belongs only to the surface side; because very different eye movements are needed to reach any point on that edge from equal distances to either side (Figure 17D), shape is related but not identical to the choice of figure. (B) Outline drawings of objects recognized by a child with no prior training with pictures (see text). (C) Lines arise from various ribbons and boundaries in the world. Most important in representing objects are probably the steep Lambertian gradients provided by nonspecular surfaces (the rightmost figure). (D) Sensory analyzers for lines of a given motion and direction. (A, C and D are from Hochberg, 1978; B is from Hochberg and Brooks, 1962).

Todd & Norman, 1995). Gibson (1966) then concentrated instead on the invariances that arise from the *optic flow* that the world provides the eye of the moving observer (Gibson, 1979; Lee, 1980). That approach has proved highly appealing, and continues quite strongly today, but has not systematically addressed objects' forms or any of the Gestalt phenomena.

Because he rejected illusions and line drawings as the results of unnatural impoverishment and as *therefore nondiagnostic of the processes that underlie normal perception* (see Michaels & Carello, 1981), he ignored the Gestalt phenomena that rely so on line drawings. I believe he was clearly wrong there: Line drawings *must* surely be diagnostic of object perception in at least some ways, as witnessed by Figure 13B, a set of drawings correctly recognized by a child with virtually no prior experience with pictures, and no education in drawing recognition (Hochberg & Brooks, 1962). Graphic presentations in general and line drawings in particular have probably always been important to our species, and have certainly been a source of important phenomena (cf. Ittelson, 1996). As to what stimuli in our ecology offer the equivalent of lines, see Figure 13C, D; Cutting, chap. 4, this volume; Cutting & Vishton, 1995; Hochberg, 1962, 1980, 1996, 1997).[16] What lines' relationship to perceived shape might be is discussed in connection with Figures 13A and 17D.

But Gibson was concerned with the ways in which the world might offer information about the distal world without drawing on mental structure (e.g., see p. 254), and he stressed the idea that objects may offer or *afford* information as to the pur-

[16] Because they are so fundamentally different as physical objects from the things and states they identify, and display many of the organizational principles that provide for object perception in the physical world (see Metzger, 1953, on protective coloration), pictures are an enormous (and perhaps diagnostic) blindspot in this approach.

poses they can serve,[17] which I think can be important to an understanding of perceptual behavior itself (in section IV; cf. Figure 12A).

Like Brunswik, therefore, Gibson had no interest in neural underpinnings, or in the retinally aimed action sequences that comprise visual inquiry. For those, we turn to Donald O. Hebb.

3. Hebb's Cell-Assemblies and Phase Sequences: Parallel Processing and the Central Role of Attention in Organization

D. O. Hebb (1949) specifically undertook to reconcile *Gestalttheorie,* traditional psychology, and then-current neurophysiology. He started with the assumption that all parts of the cortex are interconnected, and with the idea of *neurobiotaxis:* that when two neurons fire simultaneously, the synaptic connection between them is strengthened so that if one is activated, the other is then more likely to be. This is now called Hebbian learning by those who design *parallel distributed processing* (PDP) models of brain function (although it is much older; see Hochberg, chap. 1, this volume).

Starting with these, Hebb offered two basic concepts for perception and cognition: (a) *cell assemblies* and (b) *phase sequences.*

a. Cell Assemblies and Connectionist (PDP) Models of Perceptual Learning

i. Cell assemblies as feature learning   In Hebb's view, one neuron cannot usually be activated by another neuron with which it synapses, firing by itself, but requires several neurons firing at once. Through neurobiotaxis, their synaptic thresholds lower when two neurons fire together. Cell assemblies thereby form, and these tend to fire as units in response to some frequently recurring simple feature of sensory stimulation (a corner, a line, a vowel, a pressure pattern); they are distributed in parallel throughout the interconnected brain. Such assemblies, and not the firing of specific receptor neurons, would be the smallest units of perceptual processing.

ii. Simulated learned (PDP, connectionist) neural networks and prewired receptive fields   With Hebb's cell assemblies in mind (and against a background of earlier mathematical modeling of neural networks (e.g., McCullough & Pitts, 1943/1965), Rosenblatt (1958) undertook the computer simulation of a network (a "perceptron") that would learn to distinguish one letter (or other shape) from another. Input

---

[17] The preeminent purposive behaviorist, Tolman (1933) built his system of guided behavior around the concepts of *sign-gestalten* (e.g., information as to manipulability) and the *means-end readinesses* that use them. To a similar point (Cutting, 1986), Gibson argued that an ecologically realistic theory of perception must deal primarily with *affordances:* the information in the light at the eye offering information as to what behavior some object *affords* (i.e., makes possible or supports). Affordances that might serve for stair climbing and detecting body-width apertures have been identified (Warren, 1984; Warren & Wang, 1987). I think it would surely be fruitful if affordance research were to address *our most frequent and fundamental behavior, visual inquiry* (Hochberg, 1997)—the directing of the highly restricted momentary gaze to those parts of the visual field that should provide the information needed for subsequent behavior, including where to glance next.

cells of a sensory layer (S) were connected in parallel and randomly with cells of an associative layer (A), which in turn connected randomly and reciprocally to cells in a response layer (R). The goal was that a specific cell in R should eventually come to respond when a specific letter fell on S. To reach this goal, the weights with which A cells contribute to the excitation or inhibition of R cells were changed throughout the network, with each wrong response.

Given the general need for pattern-recognizing computers, and its potential relevance to neurobiology, this area escalated enormously in the 1980s. Models now include an additional (hidden) level (H), and most use an external supervisor to change the weights after incorrect responses (*back propagation*), although self-supervising networks are now available (Becker & Hinton, 1992; Carpenter & Grossberg, 1987; Hinton, Dayan, Frey, & Meal, 1995).[18] Such simulations are essentially cell assemblies intended to recognize objects, not just features, with no need for phase sequences. Some of them do provide for testing top-down expectations (Carpenter & Grossberg, 1992), or for fitting a generative model to data (Hinton et al., 1995). But most present models fail to address attentive looking, or the highly specialized functions of eye and brain that we have learned about over the past two decades. These would grow naturally out of Hebb's neglected process, the phase sequence, considered next.

b. The Phase Sequence as Perceived Object or Event: Synergistic Assembly of Present Parts and Past Prospects

To Hebb, cell assemblies are not the counterpart of perceived objects (e.g., letters), but are responses to frequently encountered features, like the parts of a letter, or the corners (A, B, C) of a triangle. They normally fire only when the input from the stimulus is joined with input from other cell assemblies, whether previously or currently activated. It is from these that the *phase sequence* emerges, with these two characteristics of special concern here:

1. What the eye fixates dominates the cell assembly primed by that glance (Hebb, 1949).
2. The motor behaviors in moving from one fixation to another form one component of a new superordinate structure which emerges, with practice, as the phase sequence. When fully learned, the phase sequence can be

---

[18] For relatively introductory surveys, see Lippmann (1987) and Quinlan (1991). Connectionist nets have been used to spell out various models of learning (e.g., Seidenberg & McClelland, 1989, on language learning), memory (Metcalfe, 1994), and category formation (Gluck & Bower, 1988; Markman, 1989); to recognize pictured objects, like human faces, from different viewpoints or otherwise transformed (Ullman, 1996; Zemel & Hinton, 1991); to form figure–ground units (Kienker, Sejnowski, Hinton, & Schumacher, 1986), and to explain the kinds of multistability mentioned in footnote 11 (Amit, 1989; Haken, 1990). With perceptual phenomena as his starting point (especially Figure 7D), and incorporating specialized analyzing units into his computational neural network, Grossberg (1993, 1994) offers a plausible and inclusive means with which to explain most of the completion effects and much about figural boundaries.

briefly activated by looking directly at any one of the features, and its activation comprises the perception of the whole triangle. But that is transient, and alternates with perception of the parts *rather than superceding them.* That is, *both global and local responses obtain.*

"Perceived objects" may therefore be viewed, in a different terminology, as "readinesses" to move fixation from one feature to one another, plus "anticipations" or primings of what stimulus patterns will then result (and have their cell assemblies facilitated).

The ideas behind phase sequences as such have received very little attention in their original form, but significant components are reappearing (see Carpenter & Grossberg, 1992; Grossberg, 1994); Zeki and Shipp (1988) report that while backward connections from the cortex do not excite cells in lower areas, they do affect how they respond to stimuli.

The fact is that present views of the eye and brain have changed so drastically in the last couple of decades that the original versions of cell assembly and phase sequence are thoroughly outmoded. Their function, however—the formation of local units and their integration over successive glances—is very much of current concern.

4. Figure, Shape, and Outline Revisited

In the context of the 1950s and early 1960s, the Gestalt phenomena invited a different approach, and the piecemeal nature of the looking process soon demanded it. Figure–ground attributes might plausibly derive from the behaviors that objects' surfaces and edges offer the eye, related to each other not by a unified self-organizing process (e.g., Figure 2B) but by the fact that they all arise from what the eye must do in exploring its environment. As in Figure 13A, changes in accommodation, convergence, and immunity to occlusion differ for the near surface and its further ground; as a separate fact, the movements by which eye can meet the edge normally is different from each side, *defining two different shapes* for the same edge (see Figure 17D) (Hochberg, 1962, 1972).

The fact that outlines provide recognizable objects (requiring no formal or informal training with pictures, Figure 13B), and manifest figure–ground segregation as well (Figure 4A), certainly needs explanation by any theory. Outlines are probably most frequently encountered at the Mach contrast markers (Mach, 1896/1959), or "zero crossings" (Marr, 1982), encountered at luminance-difference boundaries but (perhaps more importantly, given the limits on extrafoveal resolution) are also given directly to the eye in somewhat fuzzy form by curving corners and surfaces (the rightmost shape in Figure 13C; Hochberg, 1997). Finally, the microelectrodes and DC amplifiers, widely available since the 1950s, revealed receptive fields early in the visual system (Figure 13D) that respond to lines at some retinotopic slant (and in some direction of motion). Configurations no longer must start with a point-by-point modular analysis, as they did in Figure 1, but neither are they up to the experimental doodler to define. The questions of what is analyzed within each glance, and by the sequence of intended glances, and of how the glances are remembered and their objects mentally represented, now become the rich subject matter to which the Gestaltists led, and for that we must rejoin the mainstream cognitive enterprise. It itself has changed drastically.

B. Present Views of Eye and Brain: All Has Changed

1. Integrative Early Analyzers and the Separation of Specialized Pathways and Processing Centers

Since 1956 (Hartline, Wagner, & Ratliff, 1956), research with single-cell recording shows the early visual system to contain local networks sensitive to patterns in space and time, and not just to points of light. (For discussion, see Dosher & Sperling, chap. 8; Nakayama, chap. 9; and Proffitt & Kaiser, chap. 7, this volume.)

a. Early Pattern Analyzers

Cortical neurons receiving input from entire *receptive fields* of retinal sensitivity respond selectively to different aspects of spatial and temporal patterning in the retinal image—to stripes and edges of differing orientations (Hubel & Wiesel, 1960); to different spatial frequencies and different temporal periodicities (Blakemore & Campbell, 1969; Campbell & Robson, 1968; Graham, 1989). Such analyzers decompose each stimulus configuration before at least some routes of further processing occur (Graham, 1994), and still higher-order analyzers may respond mostly to edges and end-points—the bases of amodal contours (Peterhans & von der Heydt, 1994)—thereby contributing parts from which objects are in some sense formed (e.g., Attneave, 1982; Grossberg, 1994; Hochberg, 1974a; Palmer, 1982), or by which they may be evoked. The cortex is not in fact homogeneously interconnected, and the columnar structure of the visual cortex that serves these analytic functions is found even in cats deprived of visual sensory experience, although deterioration does follow continued deprivation (Crair, Gillespie & Stryker, 1998; see also Riesen, 1961). We therefore come already equipped with some portion of what Hebb's cell assemblies and Brunsik's probablistic learning were meant to provide. But the dissection of the stimulus input into these geometric components makes it harder to imagine a configuration-determined Gestalt process, and this fractionation continues when we ask what happens further upstream.

b. Separate Brain Processing of Stimulus Attributes

Modern brain-imaging techniques, increasingly available since the 1980s, show that activity in different regions differs with the brain owner's perceptual and cognitive tasks, and differs also in patients with various cognitive deficits. The brain is highly specialized, and not the equipotential "bowl of porridge" it was taken to be in the first half of the century (Hochberg, chap. 1, this volume; see Lashley, 1942). The brain appears to process elements of color and motion, slant, and shape (even patterns we recognize as faces; Desimone, 1991; Gross, 1992; Young & Yamane, 1992) through different routes to different regions of the central nervous system. In what is probably the most arresting view, these different channels, *modular* (or noninteractive; cf. section I.A.1) go from the striate cortex at different rates to different regions of the brain (Figure 14A, discussed by Lennie, in press). This raises a serious problem—the *binding problem*—of how all of these attributes, transmitted through different pathways and supposedly processed at different places in the nervous system, get together to form a perceived object.[19]

One answer may be the retinal reference preserved at each of the relevant cortical regions, as noted next, but the more general question remains as perhaps the most pressing one in visual organization, as discussed later.

2. What and Where in Eye and Brain: The Foveal Axis in a Retinotopic Visual System

The problem of combining information, gained through different visual channels, into a single perceived object is not a new one. See the problem of combining color and place, in section I.A.1, and the much more recent distinction between *focal* and *ambient* visual systems that separately process the "what" and the "where," respectively, of the perceived world. In both cases, it was argued that local signs (v, in Figure 1) tag the components within a spatial frmework.[20] The same solution may apply to the fragmentation of processing by the separation of processes in brain pathways and processing areas.

Based on single-cell recording, Lennie (in press) offers a view of brain organization very different from that of Figure 14A. All brain regions (V1–V4, in Figure 14B), except for MT (which receives primarily motion information) are *retinotopically mapped*. That is, *within each glance, everything is placed in relation to where the eye is pointing.* Each region above the lateral geniculate nucleus (LGN) feeds neural activity backwards as well as forwards; and each level furnishes *decisions* to the higher regions—for example, that a curved edge has been extracted in region (i), without

---

[19] For a tiny selection of the enormous body of recent readings and papers on this highly specialized brain, see Desimone & Schein, 1987; Desimone, Schein, Moran, & Ungerleider, 1985; Kandel, Schwartz, & Jessell, 1990; Livingstone & Hubel, 1987; Posner & Raichle, 1995; Ungerleider, 1995; Zeki, 1993. For criticisms of such modular dissociations, see Lennie (1994, in press) and Schiller (1994).

[20] Classically, local signs were proposed as serving to tag the information from independent rods and cones (Figure 1,v). That problem arose again with the distinction between the *focal* and *ambient systems,* based on the findings that object recognition (the "what") and spatial orientation and location (the "where") are not impaired in the same ways by lesions of cortex and superior colliculus. First framed by Schneider (1969), the idea rapidly received support from Held (1968) and Trevarthen (1968). But what about the object itself? An object (or an environmental structure) depends on *what* parts are *where,* presumably analyzed by separate systems, but which in the end must be referred to the same loci (Attneave, 1974).

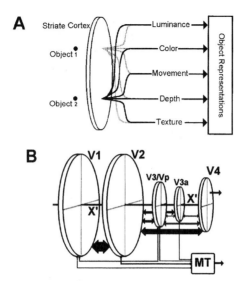

FIGURE 14   Two differing views of the visual brain as currently discussed by P. Lennie (in press). (A) The prototypical functional divisions as revealed by patient's losses and by brain imaging during some perceptual task. (B) Microelectrode recording reveals all regions but MT (largely, motion information) to be retinotopically mapped, to be heavily connected both up- and downstream, with the number of connections approximated by the thickness of the lines joining them, and strongly suggests that successively more abstract decisions are made at each level. X′ marks a common foveal referent.

the full information on which that extraction was based (cf. Figure 7D; cf. Grossberg, 1993), or that a 3D object is present in some orientation without details about the features of which it is composed (see Figure 16). Higher regions can therefore access each of the lower regions when the task requires attention to information left behind (e.g., the colors that form the edge) by accessing the relevant retinally tagged locus.

This elegant proposal is one way to solve the binding problem that was introduced by the independent analyzers and divided cortical processing of attributes, it makes sense evolutionarily, and it suggests research that might be done involving different comparisons between stimuli. But it exposes another binding problem: how we add something of the content of one glance to that of the next, which happens three or four times each second in normal perceptual behavior. In a sense, the problem of Figure 12 is repeated through most of Figure 14.

The next section, like Hebb's phase sequence, looks beyond the retinal image of the present glance and turns to perception as an ongoing behavior of search and inquiry: how and where we look, how much and in what form we store what each glance brings, and how such encoded information about the world affects our further inquiry.

IV. PERCEPTION AS PURPOSIVE BEHAVIOR

A. The Behavior of Visual Inquiry

1. Attention Determines Where We Look within the Stimulus Array:
The Interplay of Fovea and Periphery

Visual perception proceeds through successive directed acts of inquiry. This behavior is most overt in *ballistic saccades,* long studied as they serve in reading text and viewing pictures.[21] Such saccades are purposive, each with the attentional goal (Hoffman & Subramaniam, 1995; Kowler, Anderson, Dosher, & Blaser, 1995) of shifting fixation to some preselected feature in peripheral vision (usually a contour). Attention also shifts without overt change in fixation (Posner et al., 1980; Reeves & Sperling, 1986; Sperling, 1960), as it must if the next target is to be selected for fixation by the fovea and for the fine detail that only the fovea can provide. Loss of such local detail can change how an entire global configuration is perceived (compare the organizations obtained in Figure 15 when the *x* vs. the *y* is fixated).

Although the small high-resolution fovea (ca. 2°) dominates both in our introspections and in its cortical projection, *the low-resolution periphery contains most of the spatial layout of the world we see within each glance.* For a single eye, the fovea is only about 2% of the spatial layout that one's behavior must be prepared to address. Figure 12A and 15C show very rough visualizations (somewhat exaggerated[22]) of the joint field of view. Only *global* information survives outside the central region. There is ample evidence, however, that in even the very first glance at a normal (pictured) setting, the predominantly extrafoveal and undetailed view is often enough to reveal areas of inconsistency or potential informativeness (Biederman, 1972, 1981; Loftus, 1976; Mackworth & Morandi, 1967; Pollock & Spence, 1968). Pickup of such information seems to be faster for the low-spatial-frequency information channels than for higher frequencies (Hughes, Nozowa, & Kitterle, 1996): When both a global shape and its local components can each be readily identified and named, as in Figures 15A, the *global* pattern is recognized faster than those of the *local* patterns

---

[21] Ballistic saccades, in which fixations are abruptly shifted from one point in the visual field to another, have been studied for many years in a wide variety of tasks, but mainly in the context of reading. Reading movements, I believed, serve to test speech plans by which narrative is retrieved (Hochberg & Brooks, 1970), but in any case it does seem that fixations in reading are individually directed (see McConkie & Rayner, 1976; Prinz, Nattkemper, & Ullman, 1992), and not emitted in autonomous groups (Bouma & DeVoogd, 1974). For broad reviews, see Kowler (1990) and Rayner (1992). Fixations may also serve as "pointers" when needed (Ballard, Hayhoe, Pook, & Rao, & Rajesh, in press), and as the anchors for working memory, as may be introspectively evident when parsing complex patterns like Figure 11F.

[22] Peripheral resolution is usually measured while the viewer's attention is directed at the degree of retinal eccentricity being tested; the peripheral information loss must be substantially greater in normal vision, since attention is then usually directed at the foveal region. The loss in resolution can of course be expressed in terms of a filtering of the spatial frequency spectrum, but there are probably several quite different causes in addition to undersampling, including differential astigmatism (Leibowitz, Johnson & Isabelle, 1972) and poor calibration (Hess & Field, 1993).

FIGURE 15   Global, local, and extrafoveal. (A) Even when foveally viewed, the local Hs and Es at *i, ii,* are slower to detect, under a wide range of conditions, than the global Hs formed by each set (Navon, 1977). (B) With fixation and attention at *x, i* is clearly the nearer by interposition; with fixation and attention firmly at *y,* the reverse is true, and *iii* is then an "L" and not a square. (C) At right, a pair of rough simulations of what extrafoveal vision might offer during fixation at the lower left corner of each array of dots, at left. (See Ginsburg, 1980, for demonstrations of low-spatial frequency bases for Gestalt phenomena, but I know of no actual research to the point.) (B) and (C) are from Hochberg, 1997.

(Navon, 1977; Navon & Norman, 1983).[23] In any case, the extrafoveal context provides a region of low-spatial-frequency filtering, which Ginsburg (1980, 1986) has long argued underlies many of the Gestalt phenomena as in Figure 15C). Higher-level factors also produce grouping, like the objects' specified reflectances or lightnesses, as shown by Enns & Rensink (1990), Palmer, Neff, & Beck (1997), and Rock, Nijahawan, Palmer, & Tudor (1997), but these must depend on higher resolution. If blurring helps pick the object from the clutter more often than not, and provides global summaries most economically, these may in sum compensate for the loss of detail.[24]

Moreover, because successive peripheral views usually overlap a great deal, their contents are more stable across views, providing successive views with a shared context, with *landmarks* (Hochberg & Gelman, 1977; Lynch, 1960) that are needed in any but the simplest configurations or layouts. That context should afford the viewer cues as to where fixation would reveal informative detail, and cues as to which features in the field view are likely to move together (i.e., to turn out to be an object: cf. Kellman, 1993; Hochberg, 1972; Spelke, 1985, 1990). Such cues might then be learned when confirmed by subsequent fixations.[25]

[23] Such global dominance requires that the global pattern be regular (Hoffman, 1980), at least for some perceptual tasks (Lovegrove & Pepper, 1994). And for at least some tasks, the phenomenon reverses above middle-size degrees in size (Kinchla & Wolfe, 1979; but see Navon & Norman, 1983; Luna, Marcos-Ruiz, & Merino, 1995). Careful analyses of the reaction times in such phenomena by Hughes et al. (1996) supports the suggestion, as noted above, that the phenomenon occurs at least in part because low-frequency channels are processed faster than higher ones.

[24] We know little about the visual ecology defined by visual behaviors. In normal environments, most photic energy is carried by the lower spatial frequencies (Field, 1987). Most objects for our attention are in the lower half of the visual field (Previc, 1990), where illusory contours are more strongly obtained (Rubin, Nakayama, & Shapley, 1996), and most probably loom larger in the field of view than the attentional fovea.

[25] With no external teacher needed: see section III.A.3. If there is merit to this proposal, we would expect a varied and opportunistic set of organizational phenomena to develop (or evolve), united not

Perhaps most important to an understanding of cognition more generally, the shared context may allow the viewer to relate the successive glances to each other. This problem is most often ignored, or confronted by seeking some way to compensate for the eye movements (for review, see Matin, 1986), but alternatively one can argue that what is stored between glances is not visual, but much more sparse and abstract (Hochberg, 1968; Irwin, 1996; Irwin, Yantis, & Jonides, 1991; MacKay, 1973): perhaps no more detailed than the representation we have when we close our eyes (Irwin, 1992, p. 162). It is interesting in this regard that a pictured scene is robustly remembered as larger than it was, a *boundary extension* effect which may reflect expected contexts that glances normally provide for their potential successors (Intraub, 1962; Intraub, Gottesman, Willey, & Zuk, 1996).

That limited nature of visual integration was brought to the fore by the effects of attention on what is encoded from a single glance, considered next.

2. What Is Retained of What Meets the Eye: Attention and Encoding

In his watershed *partial report* experiments, using postexposure probes to direct attention to one or another part of a briefly flashed array of independent items (e.g., alphanumerics), Sperling (1960) showed that what amounted to a visual memory of the display—an *iconic memory* (Coltheart, Lea, & Thompson, 1974; Neisser, 1967), persisted briefly, decayed quickly, and gave the viewer about 500 msec to *encode*[26] the contents into short-term memory.

After that, the visual information is largely lost, and with it whatever else was potentially encodable. Similarly, directing attention to one attribute (like form, color, etc.) may lose the other attribute (color, form, etc.), by changing the order of encoding (Harris & Haber, 1963; see also Hochberg, chap. 1, section III.B.3, this volume).

B. Attention, Organization, and Consciousness: Perception as Schema Testing

To treat the stimulus configuration as a direct determinant or explanation of the perceptual experience or response should now seem frivolous. The viewer's inquiry is an integral part of the perceptual behavior, and not only in the avertible gaze. Subjects instructed to listen to one of two simultaneous speakers cannot report (or shadow) what the second speaker is saying (Treisman & Geffen, 1967). Instructed attention to one of two superimposed movies obscured the other (Neisser & Becklen, 1975); similarly, for superimposed figures (Mack, Tang,

---

by a single physiological organizing principle but as an approximate fit to visual ecology that predicts the outcome of visual actions (see section III.A).

[26] It has long been known that each single glance has a functionally limited *span of apprehension* (see Woodworth, 1938). That is, only a few independent or disconnected items, or *chunks* (Miller, 1956; Simon, 1974), can then be *encoded,* that is, retained for report, recognition, or further cognitive effect.

Tuma, Kahn, & Rock, 1992; Rock & Gutman, 1981); similarly for the unnoticed inconsistancies in 3D objects (Figure 11) and in cinematic editing (Hochberg & Brooks, 1996a,b).

One might invoke an attentional filter that passes only the sounds from the attended speaker (e.g., Treisman & Geffen, 1967), an explanation that need not posit mental representations. Passive models of listening to speech and of perceiving form remain defensible (cf. Broadbent & Broadbent, 1990; Morton & Broadbent, 1967). The Neisser and Becklen (1975) finding, however, and the ways in which a simple form, and short-cuts across it, are recognized when viewed only in a sequence of partial fovea-like segments (Figure 12B), virtually defines what one might mean by the intentional testing of a mental visual representation—in short, of an *image* in the sense in which Helmholtz described his idea of a table (see section I).

In his extremely influential book of 1967, *Cognitive Psychology,* Neisser sets prechunked, directed encoding at center stage. Perceptual attention thus consists of the active generation and sensory testing of *schemas* about what successive glances will find, providing a structure in which those findings are encoded.

This was and remains only a bare framework, of course. The two biggest steps needed to make it more concrete for the problems of form perception and perceptual organiztion are to spell out how the stimulus is encoded and the nature of the mental representation.

1. What Is Encoded and in What Form?

Most research here has relied on measuring the reaction times (RTs) needed to detect the presence of a target among other competitive items (or *distractors*). When the target and its distractors are too similar, detection times increase with the number of distractors, as though the separate elements are being searched serially, thereby allowing the search time per item to be estimated (if all of the assumptions are valid, as they almost certainly are not: see Nakayama & Joseph, 1998). But with a salient difference between target and distractors, search time does not so increase, as though the targets are detected by *parallel search* (Neisser, 1964).

This fact was suggested by Treisman and her colleagues as providing a tool to study the fundamental nature of perceptual components and their integration, arguing that targets *pop out* from arrays of distractors only if they share no *fundamental* attributes. The latter are supposedly independent channels of sensory analysis (e.g., colors, sizes, orientations), arrayed in independent, modular, retinotopic *feature maps.* A target defined by some conjunction of attributes (like color *and* orientation) should pop out only if none of its attributes appear among the distractors and if an act of attention is performed, and indeed attention may act to provide *illusory conjunctions* between such attributes where none were present.[27]

---

[27] Attention then supposedly operates by achieving *feature integration* (e.g., by linking attributes that are independent or *modular*—self-contained; Fodor, 1983), and that in fact can provide *illusory conjunctions* (e.g., reporting targets to have some color that in fact is only present in a distractor, Treisman, 1993; Treisman & Schmidt, 1982). We would probably take different visual attributes as preattentively inde-

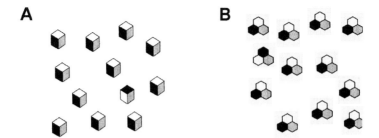

FIGURE 16   Objects of preattentive search. The presence of the target is rapidly found amidst the set of distractors at left (A), but not at right (B). [Redrawn with permission from Enns, J. T., & Rensink, R. A. (1990). Influence of scene-based properties on visual search. *Science, 247,* 721–723. Copyright 1990 American Association for the Advancement of Science.]

Since we now have no well-defined set of psychophysical units to replace those of the rods and cones in Figure 1, a procedure for identifying their successors would be very valuable indeed. Treisman's proposal has generated a great amount of research and debate. It does not seem, however, that this procedure actually captures only low-level attributes that are fundamental to the perception of forms and objects: Popout occurs with Figure 16A but not with Figure 16B (Enns, 1990; Enns & Rensink, 1990), even though both are composed of what are presumably the same fundamental features (orientation and color): the 3D forms and shading would have to be available to the searching eye at least as early as the fundamental features of which they are presumably composed. Similar findings point in the same direction (Found & Müller, 1997; Suzuki & Cavanagh, 1995). Moreover, Shiffrin, & Lightfoot (1997) report that arbitrary patterns can be "unitized" as measured by directed search methods.

It is implausible that our visual systems are organized into as many independent feature maps, with features of such complexity, as we would now have to postulate (see Nakayama & Joseph, 1998). Nor will illusory conjunctions (cf. footnote 27) serve to identify the building blocks we seek, since illusory conjunctions occur as well with larger units, like objects, in the course of rapidly presented successive scenes (Intraub, 1989).

It seems plausible that in normal search of the field of view for where to look next, what matters most is not the things' sensory attributes, but their habitual, chunked or unitized structures—that is, a fit to some mental representation or image.

2. Images Return to Perception, but with Reservations

At the opening of this chapter (section I.A.1), images (or mental representations) comprised most of what was meant by a percept. Vehemently opposed by both

---

pendent in this way, from the perspectives of Figure 14B versus that of 14A. From the former, we might well assume that these attributes depend on what is ecologically informative and robust, and may be objects or their familiar parts.

Behaviorists and by Gestalt theorists (and by Gibson and other Ecological Realists), this approach was revived vigorously with Neisser's (1967) proposal that perception is mental representation as confirmed by sensory information, and, moreover, that *imagery and perception draw on the same stored representations* (see Farah, 1988; Kosslyn, 1980; Kosslyn et al., 1993). Note that these are two completely separable proposals: A schema-testing approach to perceptual inquiry depends on mental representation, but it need not be the same as is drawn on in imagery tasks.

a. Images as Internalized Objects

The idea that images are introspectively observable mental events collapsed early in the century (see Hochberg, chap. 1, this volume). Objective tests of imagery ("if you really can visualize Low Library, count the steps"; see footnote 12) continued sporadically.[28] Research increased enormously with demonstrations in the 1970s that subjects who were asked to compare two objects at different orientations by rotating one of them in imagination, took times that were linearly proportional to the orientation differences (Cooper, 1976; Shepard & Metzler, 1971), and that the time to traverse an imagined (memorized) object varied linearly with the distance implied (Kosslyn, 1975). These results have been taken as supporting the view that the subject's mental representation is isomorphic to the physics of real events. There has since been an enormous amount of research supporting and opposing this view (see Cooper & Lang, 1996, for a recent review of both).[29]

Not surprisingly, image properties are not in fact simply an internalized physics of the object, either in performance[30] or in cortical activities,[31] and their attributes

---

[28] In the classical approach, an imagined object is like a perceived real object, but dimmer. (There have even been studies of images as sources of afterimages; e.g., Downey, 1901). If the image is enough like the perception of a real object to be confused with it, instructions to imagine an object should and do raise recognition thresholds for the object when the latter is surreptitiously presented (Perky, 1910; Segal & Gordon, 1969), but the effect does not seem to depend on stimulus configuration (Craver-Lemley & Reeves, 1992; Reeves, 1981), leaving the question in doubt.

[29] The opposition's generic and logically unassailable argument was that purely abstract, propositional processing of memory information can explain such findings, with no hints of analog (continuous) motion in the mind (Anderson, 1978; Pylyshyn, 1981).

[30] There are tasks in which subjects cannot retrieve similar information from past and imagined objects (see Hinton & Parsons, 1981); there is research showing that subjects cannot reconstrue imagined ambiguous objects (Chambers & Reisberg, 1985; Reisberg & Chambers, 1992), and research showing that they can under other conditions (Brandimonte & Gerbino, 1993; Finke et al., 1989; Peterson, Kihlstrom, Rose, & Glisky, 1992; Rouw, Kosslyn, & Hamel, 1997). There is much to be straightened out here, but in any case, it is clearly wrong to equate imagery with perception. As Reisberg (in press) notes, perception includes a stimulus; consulting that stimulus defines its perceptual reality (cf. J. S. Mill, 1865/1965, Ftn. 33), since we know that in its absence only a sparse encoding is available in memory.

[31] Although brain imaging techniques have shown the same regions to be involved in some perceptual tasks and in their imaging counterparts (Kosslyn et al., 1993), and brain damage that affects perception in specific regions of the visual field has been reported as affecting imagination in the same ways (Bisiach & Luzzatti (1978), patients with intact object recognition may have defective imagery (Farah, 1988; Riddoch, 1990) and vice versa (Behrman, Moscovitch, & Winocur, 1994). Memory for faces, which is

vary with the subject's task. In fact, there is most probably not one, single underlying system of mental representation composed either of objects' proximal or distal properties: different systems may serve different tasks (see Cooper, & Lang, 1996; Enns & Shore, 1997; Farah, 1988).

The task of storing objects or forms in working memory is the present concern.

b. Memory for Form: Not Internalized Objects, nor Autochthonously Configured Responses, but Schemas with Corrections

In a Gestalt-oriented assault on the mainstream view that mental representations are strictly aggregates of tagged sensory associations (section I), Wulf (1922) studied successive reproductions of nonsense shapes and concluded that over time the memory trace tends progressively toward the "better figure," which includes "object assimilation" toward some familiar object or form. Subsequent research however found that evidence for progressive change was scarce (as summarized by Woodworth, 1938), whereas evidence for forgetting was abundant.[32]

Most research on memory for form used unfamiliar nonsense shapes. As Bartlett noted (1932), subjects always strive after meaning, when asked to remember these, forming what Woodworth (1938) called a *schema with correction*.[33] Most dramatically, with the Street figures, which are unrememberable and remain so unless the viewer works at providing a meaningful organization, Leeper (1935) found that 97% of 930 such patterns which the viewer had organized meaningfully were recognized in a 500-ms exposure, weeks afterward!

We need to know what schemas the viewer can be assumed to have acquired from the world, and how they are acquired.

c. The Categorization and Encoding of Objects in the Visual World

i. A background of computational approaches   In this and the next section, the task considered is not to retrieve physical information from an image's structure, but to recognize the object—to name it or to judge correctly whether it had been in a previous set.

Inflection points, the high-information points in an object's outline (Attneave, 1954: see Figure 10A, p. 266), allow it to be distinguished from other objects and

---

impaired with certain brain damage (prosopagnosia), seems to involve a different system, neurophysiologically and functionally, than other objects (Farah, 1996).

[32] Gibson (1929) found familiarity rather than laws of configuration. Allport (1930) did find a tendency toward symmetry, whereas Carmichael, Hogan, and Walter (1932) reported that giving names to ambiguous figures biased how they were perceived and reproduced.

[33] Schemas (or schemata), as used by Head (1920), were postural models constructed from muscle movements and proprioceptive input. To Bartlett (1932), they were active attempts to fit sensory input into a mental representation adequate to the perceiver's task (see Oatley, 1978, for an extended discussion). See also J. S. Mill's introspection (1865/1965) that one's perception that something is real, and not imagined, rests on the permanent possibility of obtaining further sensations from it; also, the TOTE (Miller, Galanter, & Pribram, 1960), in which perception, action, and imagery intertwine.

afford information about where it can be grasped by a human or robot; D. Hoff-man and Richards (1984) offered a terminology for discussing shape in terms of the minima of curvature separating the protrusions, or *codons*. Such descriptions (which are not explanations—see Figure 17D) are viewpoint-specific and may therefore be considered as uneconomical and inelegant, so most recent theories entail encodings within long-term memory that are *object-centered*, needing only a single entry for each object (Marr, 1982; Winston, 1975; for a judicious review, see Bruce & Green, 1990).

There are many computational schemes for getting the information from the raw received retinal image to long-term memory.[34] The encoding methods most relevant to a psychology of object recognition include *feature analysis* (Neisser, 1967; Selfridge & Neisser, 1960) and *structural descriptions* (e.g., Oldfield, 1954; Winston, 1975), which list the parts and such relationships between them as are *mandatory* as opposed to optional (the opening at the bottom of an *R* is mandatory in distin-guishing it from a *B*, but serifs are optional). To get from retina-centered to object-centered description, Marr and Nishihara (1978) call on analyis into *generalized cones* (see also Lowe, 1987) whose axes are then translated into object-centered coordi-nates (using depth cues and preliminary consultation with stored 3D object descrip-tions). Finally, the axis-based object-centered descriptions are compared with 3D object descriptions in memory to achieve recognition.

All of the foregoing are influential but entirely speculative and highly incom-plete schemes by which machines or humans might recognize or perceive an object. A check on what people actually do is needed when contemplating models of how they might do it.

ii. Components in human category recognition   In 1975, Potter found that subjects could identify a target almost perfectly even when it was part of a rapid sequential visual presentation (RSVP) of 6 per sec, if the subject was given the target's *class name* before the sequence started. Rosch, Mervis, Gray, Johnson, and Boues-Braem (1976) found that viewers could recognize outline drawings, each produced by superimposing randomly selected members of the same *basic-level category* (e.g., table, dog, car) but could not do so with drawings made from superimposed mem-bers of the same *superordinate category* (e.g., furniture, animal, vehicles). These two experiments suggest that features shared by objects at the same basic level, and coarse enough to survive across averaged drawings, serve as the robust bases of encoding objects in brief glances.

In a bold step toward achieving both a visual lexicon of familiar objects, and an

---

[34] For a recent review of computational schemes on object recognition, see Ullman (1996). For extract-ing contours at steep changes in luminance gradients, see Mach (1896/1959), Marr and Hildreth (1980), Watt and Morgan (1985); for a hierarchy of increasingly abstract features, see Barlow (1972). To take the next step, Marr sought to segregate parts according to proximity and similarity of direction (see Marr, 1976, and for the ecological validity of doing so, see Brunswik & Kamiya, 1953; described here in sec-tion III.B), and from these to form a "raw primal sketch" (Marr, 1982) and then a retinotopic "2-½ D sketch," Marr, 1982), which is viewpoint-dependent and has only ordinal distance. The next step, achiev-ing a 3D object-centered representation, is noted in the text.

explanation of how they are recognized, Biederman (1985) proposed that such basic-level objects depend on *recognition by components* (RBC), where 36 components (called "geons") are *themselves* recognizable from most viewpoints.[35] A given class of objects would be defined by from 5–7 nonaccidental component shapes, each relatively independent of viewpoint and size constraints, and usually redundant so that some subset will serve.

The general idea here certainly seems a major step toward what we need to study and explain mental representation and object perception, but there are strong questions about its present adequacy for its proposed purpose,[36] and its purpose is too narrow in the kind of objects and components it can address. It has no components, for example, by which to address something like face perception and recognition, a field of great interest in its own right. The study of faces is also a corrective for the tendency to restrict perceptual studies to physical objects and to events for which scientific measures, which may be irrelevant to the perceptual processes, are already available.

iii. Facial recognition, exemplars, and the inversion effect   Faces are surely among the earliest learned and best attended objects, and face recognition is a remarkably powerful ability. A number of explanatory models intended to predict facial recognition have been offered in recent years, some being heavily influenced by the strikingly specific impairment of face recognition in certain cases of brain damage (prosopagnosia) and others by the need for achieving computer-based identification.[37] In research, they are generally studied by exemplar recognition—not "what category of object is this?", but "who is this?", and also "has this specific face appeared in a previous trials?"

Faces are certainly not assembled from nonaccidental components, they are not viewpoint independent, and they are better recognized when upright than when inverted (Goldstein & Chance, 1964; Hochberg & Galper, 1967; Yin, 1969). This inversion effect for recognition is reported to be much stronger for faces than for

---

[35] That is, they are are "nonaccidental" (see Binford, 1971; Lowe, 1985; Kanade, 1981, for contributory approaches). Although Biederman writes that the objects are 3D and viewer-independent, his scheme does not actually need the perception of 3D: Because the geons are largely nonaccidental, the objects' structural descriptions should be just as susceptible to a 2D (or 2-$\frac{1}{2}$D) representation as to a 3D representation. More generally, Todd, Chen, and Norman (1997) have data suggesting that the relative salience of object properties varies with their structural stability under change, which should apply to more than recognizing object categories (see footnote 27).

[36] There is as yet no evidence that viewers use or need proposed geons as elementary components in object recognition, rather than inflection points *per se* (cf. Figure 10A) or distinguishable strings of features that might be learned as chunks (Peterson, 1996) or *unitized* (Shiffrin & Lightfoot, 1997). Furthermore, it has been plausibly argued that geons could not account for object categorization (Tarr & Bulthoff, 1995), and that experimental data supports the case that objects are encoded as a set of multiple view-specific representations, with normalization into a familiar viewpoint being needed to recognize unfamiliar viewpoints (Tarr, 1995; Tarr & Pinker, 1990).

[37] For the former, see Bruce and Young (1986), Bruce (1994); for the latter, see Beymer and Poggio (1996) and Ullman (1996).

other objects (Diamond & Carey, 1986; Yin, 1969), perhaps because expertise depends more on processing the whole configuration and less on specific features than does basic-level or category recognition,[38] but in the next section we will see that in any case a general inversion effect holds in the perception of objects having a predominant or canonical orientation.

The inversion effect is a retinotopic phenomenon (as Köhler [1940] noted, faces and text in an upright newspaper are not rendered recognizable by having the viewer's head held upside down). Importantly, it allows us to vary nonautochtonous factors like familiarity while holding configuration constant, and brings us back to the relationship between figure–ground segregation and shape or object recognition that was set aside when starting section IV.

V. THE GESTALT PHENOMENA AND MENTAL REPRESENTATION

A. Must Autochthonous Factors Precede "Cognitive" Factors?

1. Figure–Ground Segregation: Not Really Independent of Familiarity and Meaning

Well-organized configurations can hide or embed familiar or recently practiced shapes (Figures 6A,B; Gottschaldt, 1926, 1929). It is commonly concluded from such findings that figure–ground segregation is subject only to autochtonous factors. Those findings have been strongly criticized (Woodworth, 1938), however, and it seems safe to discount any failures of familiarity or meaning where nonsense shapes were used, and where the familiarity rested only on experimental practice trials (e.g., Gottschaldt, 1926, 1929; Mens & Leeuwenberg, 1993).[39] It also seems safe to discount demonstrations in which mandatory structural features (see p. 286) are obliterated, like the 4's endpoints in Figure 6A.

In fact, what is perceived as figure segregation does *not* depend only on autochtonous factors. In demonstrations of an inversion effect like Figure 17A, the white regions (seen joined at *iii*) are more strongly seen as figures in *ii* than in *i*. More importantly, Peterson and her colleagues showed in a number of studies that highly meaningful or *denotative* shapes (as independently rated by judges) were more likely to be perceived as figures when shown in a classical figure–ground pattern in the upright orientation (Figure 17B), than when inverted (Peterson, 1994; Peterson & Gibson, 1993, 1994).

---

[38] In fact, Farah, Tanaka, and their associates have shown that the inversion effect is modified when subjects are led to attend to individual features (Farah, Tanaka, & Drain, 1995), and that recognition of facial parts is more impaired when the parts are viewed out of context than as parts of other objects (Tanaka & Farah, 1993; also, Diamond & Carey, 1986). Moreover, Enns & Shore (1997) found that the interactive effects of varying both the overall inversion of faces and of their direction of illumination depended on the viewers' task, stressing the contingent nature of such mental representations.

[39] Practice trials have indeed been effective with some figure–ground patterns: thus, Leeper (1935) had found that prior experience with an unambiguous figure strongly affected what viewers reported an ambiguous version to be.

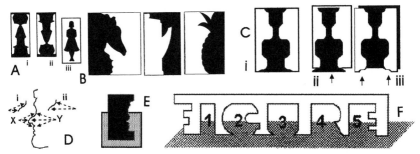

FIGURE 17   Shape, meaning, and the diversity of figural properties. (A) All three displays show versions of the same two shapes: *i* is an inverted version of *ii*, and both are split versions of *iii*. (B) Three highly denotative shapes shown by Peterson and her colleagues (see text) to be more dominant as figures when upright than when inverted, questioning the belief that figure segregation must precede recognition. (First and third patterns are redrawn from Peterson & Gibson, 1993, with permission; the second is from Gibson & Peterson, 1994, *Journal of Experimental Psychology: Human Perception and Performance, 20,* 299–316. Copyright © 1994 by the American Psychological Association. Reprinted with permission.) (C) In a display like *i,* subjects saw most rapidly the shape with contours whose color they had been asked to attend (*ii* or *iii*), even though both alternatives had of course been equally exposed (Driver & Baylis, 1995). This and similar research was offered to support the view that figure segregation must precede recognition. (D) Two different sets of eye movements would be needed to sample the line or edge from sides X and Y, which remain much the same and which define the same two chunks of shape (*i, ii*), regardless of which side is surface. These shape-realizing potential behaviors are (I think) what gives codons their perceptual meaning, and are dissociable from the other characteristics that surfaces' edges afford the eye (see Figure 13A). (E) The woman's face is clearly perceived although the autochtonous factors should make the black region figure and give its edges shape. (Was the face lost in Figure 7F when the darker film came forward?) (F) If you could not perceive the word in Figure 4G, you probably can do so here, although its letter's bases seem ground and not figure. My point is that surface quality is one property that figures often appear to possess, and so is the shape that a view of the edge from one side or the other affords the eye, but that the former is not the cause of the latter (from Hochberg, 1997, with permission).

The conguration is the same, whether upright or inverted; only the recognizable meaning varies.

The phenomenon is important in that it adds meaning and familiarity to the list of determinants of figural organization; without them, a schema-testing theory could not apply at that level. It also raises basic questions about the nature of figure–ground segregation and shape perception.

2. A Perceived Shape Is Not Only a Perceived Surface's Perceived Edge, and a Figure Is Not a Unified Thing

Within the Gestalt legacy, figure–ground segregation provides only one area with a shape, on something like a winner-take-all basis,[40] and shape recognition could "therefore" occur only *after* figure–ground segregation has occurred.

[40] For the argument that we must at some level perceive an object before its meaning can be a causal factor, see Köhler (1920), Metzger (1953), and Wallach (1949). Logic has been taken to suggest that one must perceive some object before recognizing it (e.g., Höffding, 1887, cited in Köhler, 1920; Kanizsa & Luccio, 1995), and that perception is protected from top-down influences (Kanizsa & Luccio, 1995), but I have not seen the premises fully spelled out and defended for figure versus ground.

It is true that the notion of shape as surface edge fits well with Rubin's familiar phenomena (Figure 3A). It is also true true that considered topologically (D. Hoffman & Richards, 1984), by crossing the edge maxima of curvature become minima and thereby define a different shape. Finally, in recent ingenious research designed to provide a quantitative approach to figure–ground study (using same–difference RTs), priming appeared only for the edges of that surface, like Cii versus Ciii, that viewers had previously been instructed to attend by color (Baylis & Driver, 1995; Driver & Baylis, 1995). Using RTs and error rates, such methods showed quantitatively that only the surface's edge had recognizable, rememberable shape. However, those methods were used only with nonsense shapes, so the issue remains open until they can be used to measure the effects of denotivity as well.

It is surely true, as Wever noted in 1927, that a figure need not be the nearest surface (see Figures 7E,F). In any case, it is easy to show show that shape is not inseparable from surface edge, in any defined sense: Figure 17F is easily read as a word (cf. Figure 4G); the transparent sheet in Figure 7F shows a recognizable face, although the surface edge is in the wrong direction for it to be a figure, and the same thing is seen in 17E. (Keyholes do, after all, have recognizable shapes.) Figure 5H showed us that contours are indifferent to direction of contrast, as noted earlier. Peterson and Gibson (1994a) found the same inversion effects when the denotative objects (as in Figure 17B) were presented as outline shapes and by subjective contours.

I see no paradox here: the question of whether figure–ground segregation must precede form or object recognition is in fact not a logical issue. One can easily imagine (or even model) how nonautochtonous factors might affect the figure–ground segregation.[41] In any case, we have seen evidence that figure assignment and shape recognition may be separable, and that organized forms may be active "preattentively" (e.g., Figure 16) and thereby determine what alternatives are encoded in the first fractions of a second. The effects of denotivity are certainly compatible with the schema-testing approach discussed above, and with a Hebbian phase sequence (pp. 276f).

It would be theoretically important, however, to determine the relative time scales of the various autochtonous and nonautochtonous factors in object organization, and whether one is a precondition for the other. At one extreme, *all* organization might be assumption-controlled, as in likelihood approaches; at the other, autochthonous factors must run their course before there is anything for more "cognitive" factors to work with. Neither of these is the way apparent motion has worked out (section II.A.1.c; see Dosher & Sperling, chap. 8, this volume): diverse mechanisms, sometimes quite insulated from each other, provide what seems to unaided introspection to be a unified experience.

Similarly, the aspects of experience lumped together as figural properties may

---

[41] See Hochberg (1997), Peterson (1994), Stadler & Kruse, (1995), and chapter 6 in Ullman (1996). Perhaps alternatives are extracted successively or simultaneously (Peterson, 1994); perhaps figure–ground segregation proceeds piecemeal, and local familiarities weight the outcome of that process (see Hochberg, 1972, 1997; Zimmer, 1995).

reflect not one but numerous expectations developed in the course of searching out and looking at objects in the world, related only by the fact that the eye normally encounters them under the same circumstances, and not by some single underlying process. For example, the viewer should come to expect that distinguishable points to one side of the contour in Figures 13A preserve their *relative* locations after a saccade, though points to the other side do not. Also to be expected when electing to cross the edge are the need for different accommodation and convergence, the expectation that differential occlusion will occur, and that shape-testing eye movements will have different outcomes (Figure 17D).

This should be true of perceptual organization more generally.

B. Diversity in Unity

If the Gestalt phenomena serve mainly to help the eye (and not primarily the hand) grasp objects, and if objects are important guides to visual inquiry, we should not be surprised to find multiple bases for each such phenomenon we can detect, whether because of a phylogenetic evolution that tolerates them even though they are sometimes wrong (as they are in virtually all of the demonstrations discussed in this chapter) or because of usefulness to the individual glances that supervise their acquisition.

I suggest, therefore, that the *laws of organization* are opportunistic guides to the viewer as to what will afford desired visual information, and that they probably vary widely in level, speed, and power. *Figure–ground* is a term referring to diverse mechanisms for the schematic anticipation and storage of the features (local and global) that will move together, the chunked loci and landmarks that we mean by shape, and the expectations about surface and occlusion that serve to guide further visual behavior. The *minimum principles* may indeed include some hill-climbing soap-bubble components, but predominantly reflect the varied resource limitations involved in vision, attention, encoding, and storage. (They are not exclusive to visual cognition: Narrative structures available in the working memory of the listener or reader without special efforts are sketchy and local, just like the visual configurations of objects and layouts).[42] Only an understanding of the nature and purpose of the behaviors of perceptual inquiry, and their ecological and physiological contexts, will serve as an explanation of the diverse processes of organization: not any unified isomorphic theory or mathematical model.

The organizational phenomena therefore offer windows into what otherwise seems a seamless process of perceptual inquiry in a unified physical world. Given the increasing dominance of our cognitive ecology by artificial visual displays I think that those phenomena will increasingly be used for diagnosis and prescription as the next half-century opens.

[42] For verbal narrative, see Dosher and Corbett (1982), Glanzer, Fischer, and Dorfman (1984), McKoon and Ratliff (1992); for visual narrative, see Hochberg and Brooks, 1996b.

References

Allport, G. (1930). Change and decay in the visual memory image. *British Journal of Psychology, 21*, 138–148.

Amit, D. J. (1989). *Modelling brain function: The world of attractor neural networks.* Cambridge, MA: Cambridge University Press.

Anderson, J. R. (1978). Arguments concerning representations for mental imagery. *Psychological Review, 85*, 249–277.

Anstis, S. M. (1980). The perception of apparent movement. In H. C. Longuet-Higgens & N. S. Sutherland (Eds.), *The psychology of vision* (pp. 153–167). London: The Royal Society.

Asch, M. G. (1995). *Gestalt psychology in German culture, 1890–1967: holism and the quest for objectivity.* New York: Cambridge University Press.

Attneave, F. (1954). Some informational aspects of visual perception. *Psychological Review, 61*, 183–193.

Attneave, F. (1957). Transfer of experience with a class-schema to identification-learning of patterns and shapes. *Journal of Experimental Psychology, 55*, 81–88.

Attneave, F. (1959). *Applications of information theory to psychology.* New York: Holt, Rinehart, & Winston.

Attneave, F. (1971). Multistability in perception. *Scientific American 225*, 63–71.

Attneave, F. (1974). Apparent movement and the what–where connection. *Psychologia, 17*, 108–120.

Attneave, F. (1981). Three approaches to perceptual organization: Comments on views of Hochberg, Shepard, and Shaw and Turvey. In M. Kubovy & J. Pomerantz (Eds.), *Perceptual organization* (pp. 417–421). Hillsdale, New Jersey: Erlbaum.

Attneave, F. (1982). Praegnanz and soap bubble systems: A theoretical exploration. In J. Beck (Ed.), *Organization and representation in perception* (pp. 11–29). Hillsdale, New Jersey: Erlbaum.

Attneave, F., & Arnoult, M. D. (1956). The quantitative study of shape and pattern perception. *Psychological Bulletin, 53*, 452–471.

Ballard, D. H., Hayhoe, M. M., Pook, P. C., & Rao, R. P. & Rajesh, P. N. (in press). Diectic codes for the embodiment of cognition. *Brain and Behavioral Science.*

Barclay, C. D., Cutting, J. E., & Kozlowski, L. T. (1978). Temporal and spatial factors in gait perception that influence gender recognition. *Perception & Psychophysics, 23*, 145–152.

Barlow, H. B. (1972). Single units and sensations: A neuron doctrine for perceptual psychology? *Perception, 1*, 371–394.

Bartlett, F. C. (1932). *Remembering.* Cambridge: Cambridge University Press.

Baylis, G. C., & Driver, J. (1995). One-sided edge assignment in vision: 1. Figure-ground segmentation and attention to objects. *Current Directions in Psychological Science, 4*, 140–146.

Beck, J. (1972). Similarity grouping and peripheral discriminability under uncertainty. *American Journal of Psychology, 85*, 1–20.

Beck, J., Prazdny, K., & Ivry, R. (1984). The perception of transparency with achromatic colors. *Perception & Psychophysics, 35*, 407–422.

Becker, S., & Hinton, G. E. (1992). A self-organizing neural network that discovers surfaces in random-dot stereograms. *Nature, 355*, 161–163.

Behrman, M., Moscovitch, M., & Winocur, G. (1994). Intact visual imagery and impaired visual perception in a patient with visual agnosia. *Journal of Experimental Psychology: Human Perception and Performance, 20*, 1068–1087.

Beymer, D., & Poggio, T. (1996). Image representations for visual learning. *Science, 272*, 1905–1909.

Biederman, I. (1972). Perceiving real-world scenes. *Science, 177*, 77–80.

Biederman, I. (1981). On the semantics of a glance at a scene. In M. Kubovy & J. Pomerantz (Eds.), *Perceptual organization* (pp. 213–253). Hillsdale, New Jersey: Erlbaum.

Biederman, I. (1985). Human image understanding: Recent research and a theory. *Computer Vision, Graphics, and Image Processing, 32*, 29–73.

Binford, T. (1971). Visual perception by computer. *Proceedings, IIEE Conference on Systems Science and Cybernetics.* Miami, FL.

Bisiach, E., & Luzzatti, C. (1978). Unilateral neglect of representational space. *Cortex, 17*, 129–133.

Blakemore, C., & Campbell, F. W. (1969). On the existence of neurones in the human visual system selectively sensitive to the orientation and size of retinal images. *Journal of Physiology, 201,* 237–260.

Boring, E. G. (1942). *Sensation and perception in the history of experimental psychology.* New York: Appleton-Century-Crofts.

Boselie, F., & Leeuwenberg, E. (1986). A test of the minimum principle rquires a perceptual coding system. *Perception, 15,* 331–354.

Bouma, H., & de Voogd, A. H. (1974). On the control of eye saccades in reading. *Vision Research, 14,* 273–284.

Braddick, O. J. (1980). Low-level and high-level processes in apparent motion. *Philosophical Transactions of the Royal Society of London, Series B, 209,* 137–151.

Bradley, D. R., Dumais, S. T., & Petry, H. M. (1976). Reply to Cavonius. *Nature, 261,* 77–78.

Brandimonte, M. A., & Gerbino, W. (1993). Mental image reversal and verbal recoding: When ducks become rabbits. *Memory & Cognition, 21,* 23–33.

Braunstein, M. L., & Andersen, G. J. (1986). Testing the rigidity assumption: A reply to Ullman. *Perception, 15,* 641–644.

Bridgeman, B., van der Heijden, A. H. C., & Velichkovsky, B. M. (1994). A theory of visual stability across saccadic eye movements. *Behavioral and Brain Sciences, 17,* 247–292.

Broadbent, D. E., & Broadbent, M. H. P. (1990). Human attention: the exclusion of distracting information as a function of real and apparent separation of relevant and irrelevant events. *Proceedings of the Royal Aociety, London, Series B, 242,* 11–16.

Brosgole, L., & Whalen, P. M. (1967). The effect of meaning on the allocation of visually induced movement. *Perception & Psychophysics, 2,* 275–277.

Brown, D. R., & Owen, D. H. (1967). Metrics of visual form: Methodological dyspepsia. *Psychological Bulletin, 68,* 243–259.

Brown, J. F., & Voth, A. C. (1937). The path of seen movement as a function of the vector field. *American Journal of Psychology, 49,* 543–563.

Bruce, V. (1994). Recognizing objects and faces. In V. Bruce & G. W. Humphreys (Eds.), *Object and face recognition.* (Special issue *Visual cognition, 1,* 141–180.

Bruce, V., & Green, P. (1990). *Visual perception: Physiology, psychology and ecology* (2nd ed.). Hove, UK: Erlbaum.

Bruce, V., & Young, A. (1986). Understanding face recognition. *British Journal of Psychology, 77,* 305–327.

Brunswik, E. (1947). *Systematic and representative design of psychological experiments: With results in physical and social perception.* Berkeley: University of California Press.

Brunswik, E. (1955). "Ratiomorphic" models of perception and thinking. *Acta Psychologia, 11,* 108–109.

Brunswik, E. (1956). *Perception and the representative design of psychological experiments* (2nd ed.). Berkeley, CA: University of California Press.

Brunswik, E., & Kamiya, J. (1953). Ecological cue-validity of "proximity" and other Gestalt factors. *American Journal of Psychology, 66,* 20–32.

Burtt, P., & Sperling, G. (1981). Time, distance and feature trade-offs in visual apparent motion. *Psychological Review, 88,* 171–195.

Burton, G. (1996). An ecological definition for psychology, or If Psychology's the study of behavior, what is behavior? *ISEP Newsletter, #22.*

Campbell, F. W., & Robson, J. G. (1968). Application of Fourier analysis to the visibility of gratings. *Journal of Phsyiology, 197,* 551–566.

Carmichael, L., Hogan, H. P., & Walter, A. A. (1932). An experimental study of the effect of language on the reproduction of visually perceived form. *Journal of Experimental Psychology, 15,* 73–86.

Carpenter, G. A., & Grossberg, S. (1987). A massively parallel architecture for a self-organizing neural pattern recognition machine. *Computer Vision, Graphics and Image Processing, 37,* 54–115.

Carpenter, G. A., & Grossberg, S. (1992). A self-organizing neural network for supervised learning, recognition and prediction. *IEEE Communications Magazine,* Sept., 38–49.

Cassirer, E. (1944). The concept of group and the theory of perception *Philosophy and Phenomenological Reserch. 5,* 1–35.

Cavanagh, P., & Mather, G. (1989). Motion: The long and short of it. *Spatial Vision, 4,* 103–129.

Chambers, D., & Reisberg, D. (1992). What an image depicts depends on what an image means. *Cognitive Psychology, 24,* 145–174.

Chapanis, A., & McCleary, R. A. (1953). Interposition as a cue for the perception of relative distance. *Journal of General Psychology, 48,* 113–132.

Coltheart, M., Lea, D. C., & Thompson, K. (1974). In defence of iconic memory. *Quarterly Journal of Experimental Psychology, 26,* 633–641.

Cooper, L. A. (1976). Demonstrations of a mental analog of an external rotation. *Perception & Psychophysics, 19,* 296–302.

Cooper, L. A., & Lang, J. M. (1996). Imagery and visual-spatial representations. In E. L. Bjork & R. A. Bjork (Eds.), *Memory: Handbook of perception and cognition* (2nd ed.) (pp. 129–164). San Diego: Academic Press.

Cooper, L. A., & Schacter, D. L. (1992). Dissociations between structural and episodic representations of visual objects. *Current Directions in Psychological Science, 1,* 141–146.

Coren, S. C. (1972). Subjective contours and apparent depth. *Psychological Review, 79,* 359–367.

Coren, S., & Girgus, J. S. (1978). *Seeing is deceiving: The psychology of visual illusions.* Hillsdale, NJ: Erlbaum.

Crair, M. C., Gillespie, D. C., Stryker, M. P. (1998). The role of visual experience in the development of columns in cat visual cortex. *Science, 279,* 566–570.

Craver-Lemley, C., & Reeves, A. (1992). How visual imagery interferes with vision. *Psychological Review, 99(4)* 633–649.

Cutting, J. E. (1982). Blowing in the wind: Perceiving structure in trees and bushes. *Cognition, 12,* 25–44.

Cutting, J. E. (1986). *Perception with an eye for motion.* Cambridge, MA: MIT Press.

Cutting, J. E., & Proffitt, D. R. (1981). Gait perception as an example of how we may perceive events. In R. D. Walk & H. L. Pick, Jr (Eds.), *Intersensory perception and sensory integration.* New York: Plenum.

Cutting, J. E., & Proffitt, D. R. (1982). The minimum principle and the perception of absolute, common, and relative motions. *Cognitive Psychology, 14,* 211–246.

Cutting, J. E., & Vishton, P. M. (1995). Perceiving layout and knowing distances: The interaction of relative potency, and contextual use of different information about depth. In W. Epstein & S. J. Rogers (Eds.), *Handbook of perception and cognition. Vol. 5. Perception of space and motion* (pp. 69–117). San Diego, CA: Academic Press.

Desimone, R. (1991). Face-selective cells in the temporal cortex of monkeys. *Journal of Cognitive Neuroscience, 3,* 1–24.

Desimone, R., & Schein, S. J. (1987). Visual properties of neurons in Area V4 of the macaque: Sensitivity to stimulus form. *Journal of Neurophysiology, 57,* 835–868.

Desimone, R., Schein, S. J., Moran, J., & Ungerleider, L. G. (1985). Contour, color and shape analysis beyond the striate cortex. *Vision Research, 25,* 441–452.

Diamond, R., & Carey, S. (1986). Why faces are and are not special: An effect of expertise. *Journal of Experimental Psychology: General, 115,* 107–117.

Ditzinger, T., & Haken, H. (1955). A synergetic model of multistability in perception. In P. Kruse & M. Stadler (Eds.), *Ambiguity in mind and nature.* Heidelberg: Springer-Verlag.

Dosher, B. A., & Corbett, A. T. (1982). Instrument inferences and verb schemata. *Memory & Cognition, 10,* 531–539.

Downey, J. E. (1901). An experiment on getting an after-image from a mental image. *Psychological Review, 8,* 12–55.

Driver, J., & Baylis, G. C. (1995). One-sided edge-assignment in vision: 2. Part decomposition and edge description. *Current Directions in Psychological Science, 4,* 201–206.

Duncker, K. (1929). Über induzierte Bewegung [On induced motion]. *Psychologische Forschung, 12,* 180–259.

Egeth, H., & Yantis, S. (1997). Visual attention: Control, representation, and time course. *Annual Review, 48,* 269–297.

Enns, J. T. (1990). Three dimensional fesatures that pop out in visual search. In D. Brogan (Ed.), *Visual search* (pp. 37–45). London: Taylor & Francis.

Enns, J. T., & Rensink, R. A. (1990). Influence of scene-based properties on visual search. *Science, 247,* 721–723.

Enns, J. T., & Shore, D. I. (1997). Separate influences of orientation and lighting in the inverted-face effect. *Perception & Psychophysics, 59,* 23–31.

Epstein, W. (Ed.) (1977). *Stability and constancy in visual perception.* New York: Wiley.

Farah, M. J. (1988). Is visual memory really visual? Overlooked evidence from neuropsychology. *Psychological Review, 95,* 307–317.

Farah, M. J. (1996). Is face recognition "special"? Evidence from neuropsychology. *Behavioral Brain Research, 76,* 181–189.

Farah, M. J., Hammond, K. M., Levine, D. N., & Calvanio, R. (1988). Visual and spatial mental imagery: Dissociable systems of representation. *Cognitive Psychology, 20,* 439–462.

Farah, M. J., Tanaka, J. W., Drain, H. M. (1995). What causes the face inversion effect? *Journal of Experimental Psychology: Human Perception & Performance, 21,* 628–634.

Field, D. J. (1987). Relations between the statistics of natural images and the response properties of cortical cells. *Journal of the Optical Society of America A, 4,* 2379–2394.

Finke, R. A., Pinker, S., & Farah, M. J. (1989). Reinterpreting visual patterns in mental imagery. *Cognitive Science, 13,* 51–78.

Fodor, J. A. (1983). *The modularity of mind.* Cambridge, MA: The MIT Press.

Found, A., & Müller, H. J. (1997). Local and global orientation in visual search. *Perception & Psychophysics, 59,* 941–963.

Fuchs, W. (1923). Experimentelle Untersuchungen über das simultane Hintereinander auf derselben Sehrichtung. *Zeitschrift für Psychologie, 91,* 145–235.

Garner, W. B. (1962). *Uncertainty and structure as psychological concepts.* New York: Wiley.

Garner, W. R. (1966). To perceive is to know. *American Psychologist, 21,* 11–19.

Garner, W. R., & Clement, D. E. (1963). Goodness of pattern and pattern uncertainty. *Journal of Verbal Learning and Verbal Behavior, 2,* 446–452.

Gerbino, W. (1988). Models of achromatic transparency: A theoretical analysis. *Gestalt Theory, 10,* 5–20.

Gerbino, W. B., Stultiens, C. I., Troost, J. M., & de Weert, C. (1990). Transparent layer constancy. *Journal of Experimental Psychology: Human Perception and Performance, 16,* 3–20.

Gibson, B. S. & Peterson, M. A. (1994). Does orientation-independent object recognition precede orientation-dependent recognition? Evidence from a cuing paradigm. *Journal of Experimental Psychology: Human Perception and Performance, 20,* 299–316.

Gibson, J. J. (1929). The reproduction of visually perceived forms. *Journal of Experimental Psychology, 12,* 1–39.

Gibson, J. J. (1950). *The perception of the visual world.* Boston: Houghton Mifflin.

Gibson, J. J. (1966). *The senses considered as perceptual systems.* Boston: Houghton Mifflin.

Gibson, J. J. (1979). *The ecological approach to visual perception.* Boston: Houghton Mifflin.

Gillam, B. (1979). Even a possible figure can look impossible. *Perception, 8,* 229–232.

Gillam, B. (1972). Perceived common rotary motion of ambiguous stimuli as a criterion for perceptual grouping. *Perception & Psychophysics, 11,* 99–101.

Ginsburg, A. (1980). Specifying relevant spatial information for image evaluation and display design: An explanation of how we see objects. *Perception & Psychophysics, 21,* 219–228.

Ginsburg, A. P. (1986). Spatial filtering and visual form perception. In K. Boff, J. Thomas, & L. Kaufman (Eds.), *Handbook of perception and human performance* (Vol. 1, pp. 34–1, 34–64). New York: Wiley.

Glanzer, M., Fischer, B., & Dorfman, D. (1984). Short-term storage in reading. *Journal of Verbal Learning and Verbal Behavior, 23,* 467–486.

Gluck, M. A., & Bower, G. H. (1988). From conditioning to category learning: An adaptive network model. *Journal of Experimental Psychology: General, 11,* 227–247.

Gogel, W. C., & Tietz, J. D. (1992). Absence of computation and reasoning-like processes in the perception of orientation in depth. *Perception & Psychophysics, 51,* 309–318.

Goldstein, A. G., & Chance, J. E. (1964). Recognition of children's faces. *Child Development, 35,* 129–136.

Gottschaldt, K. (1926). Über den Einfluss der Erfahrung auf die Wahrnehmung von Figuren. I. *Psychologische Forschung, 8,* 261–317.

Gottschaldt, K. (1929). Über den Einfluss der Erfahrung auf die Wahrnehmung von Figuren. II. *Psychologische Forschung, 12,* 1–87.

Graham, N. (1989). *Visual pattern analyzers.* New York: Oxford University Press.

Graham, N. (1994). Non-linearities in texture segregation. In G. R. Bock & J. A. Goode (Eds.), *Higher-order procssing in the visual system. Ciba Foundation Symposium 184.* (pp. 309–329). Chichester, England: John Wiley & Sons.

Gregory, R. (1972). *Eye and brain: The psychology of seeing* (2nd ed.). London: Weidenfeld & Nicolson.

Gregory, R. (1980). Perceptions as hypotheses. *Philosophical Transactions of the Royal Society of London, Series B, 290,* 181–197.

Gross, C. G. (1992). Representation of visual stimuli in inferior temporal cortex. In V. Bruce, A. Cower, A. W. Ellis, D. T. Perrett (Eds.), *Processing the facial image* (pp. 3–10). Oxford, England: Clarendon Press/Oxford University Press.

Grossberg, S. (1993). Boundary, brightness, and depth interactions during preattentive representation and attentive recognition of figure and ground. *Giornale Italiano di Psicologia,* 771–804.

Grossberg, S. (1994). 3D vision and figure-ground separation by visual cortex. *Perception & Psychophysics, 55,* 48–120.

Grossberg, S., & Mignolla, E. (1985). Neural dynamics of form perception: Boundary completion, illusory figures and neon color spreading. *Psychological Review, 92,* 173–211.

Haken, H. (1990). Synergetics as a tool for the conceptualization and mathematization of cognition and behavior—how far can we go? In H. Haken & M. Stadler (Eds.), *Synergetics of cognition* (pp. 2–31). Berlin: Springer.

Harris, C., & Haber, R. N. (1963). Selective attention and coding in visual perception. *Journal of Experimental Psychology, 65.*

Hartline, H. K., Wagner, H. G., & Ratliff, F. (1956). Inhibition in the eye of Limulus. *Journal of General Physiology, 39,* 651–673.

Hatfield, G. C., & Epstein, W. (1985). The status of the minimum principle in the theoretical analysis of visual perception. *Psychological Bulletin, 97,* 155–186.

He, Z. J., & Nakayama, K. (1994). Perceived surface shape not features determines correspondence strength in apparent motion. *Vision Research, 34,* 2125–2135.

Head, H. (1920). *Studies in neurology.* Oxford: Oxford University Press.

Hebb, D. O. (1949). *The organization of behavior: A neuropsychological approach.* New York: Wiley.

Heider, G. (1933). New studies in transparency, form and colour. *Psychologische Forschung, 17,* 13–56.

Held, R. (1968). Dissociation of functions by deprivation and rearrangement. *Psychologische Forschung, 31,* 338–348.

Helmholtz, H. von (1962). *Treatise on physiological optics, vol. III* (J. P. Southall, Trans.). New York: Dover. (Original work published 1866)

Helmholtz, H. von (1881). *Popular scientific lectures* (E. Atkinson, Trans.). New York: Appleton.

Helson, H. (1926). The psychology of *Gestalt. American Journal of Psychology, 37,* 25–62.

Hering, E. (1861). *Beiträge zur Physiologie. Heft. 1.* Leipzig: Englemann.

Hess, R. F., & Field, D. (1993). Is the increased spatial uncertainty in the normal periphery due to spatial undersampling or uncalibrated disarray? *Vision Research, 33,* 2663–2670.

Hinton, G. E., Dayan, P., Frey, B. J., & Meal, R. M. (1995). The wake-sleep algorithm for unsupervised neural networks. *Science, 268,* 1158–1161.

Hinton, G. E., & Parsons, L. M. (1981). Frames of reference and mental imagery. In A. D. Baddeley & J. Long (Eds.), *Attention and performance,* vol. IX (pp. 261–277). Hillsdale, NJ: Erlbaum.

Hochberg, J. (1950). Figure-ground reversal as a function of visual satiation. *Journal of Experimental Psychology, 40,* 682–686.

Hochberg, J. (1956). Perception: Toward the recovery of a definition. *Psychological Review, 63,* 400–405.

Hochberg, J. (1957). Psychophysics and stereotypy in social perception. In M. Sherif & M. Wilson

(Eds.), *Emergent problems in social psychology* (pp. 117–141). Norman, OK: University of Oklahoma Press.

Hochberg, J. (1962). The psychophysics of pictorial perception. *Audio-Visual Communication Review, 10,* 22–54.

Hochberg, J. (1968). In the mind's eye. In R. N. Haber (Ed.), *Contemporary theory and research in visual perception* (pp. 309–331). London: Holt, Rinehart & Winston.

Hochberg, J. (1970). Attention, organization, and consciousness. In D. I. Mostofsky (Ed.), *Attention: Contemporary theory and analysis* (pp. 99–124). New York: Appleton-Century-Crofts.

Hochberg, J. (1972). I. Perception, I. Color and shape. II. Space and movement. In J. W. Kling & L. A. Riggs (Eds.), *Woodworth & Schlosberg's Experimental Psychology* (pp. 395–550). New York: Holt, Rinehart & Winston.

Hochberg, J. (1974a). Higher-order stimuli and interresponse coupling in the perception of the visual world. In R. B. Macleod & H. L. Pick (Eds.), *Perception: essays in honor of James J. Gibson* (pp. 17–39). Ithaca, NY: Cornell University Press.

Hochberg, J. (1974b). Organization and the Gestalt tradition. In E. C. Carterette & M. Friedman (Eds.), *Handbook of perception. Vol. I* (pp. 179–210). New York: Academic Press.

Hochberg, J. (1978). *Perception.* (2nd ed.). Englewood Cliffs, NJ: Prentice-Hall.

Hochberg, J. (1980). Pictorial function and perceptual structures. In M. A. Hagen (Ed.), *The perception of pictures* (Vol. 2, pp. 47–93). New York: Academic Press.

Hochberg, J. (1981). Levels of perceptual organization. In M. Kubovy & J. Pomerantz (Eds.), *Perceptual organization* (pp. 255–278). Hillsdale, NJ: Erlbaum.

Hochberg, J. (1982). How big is a stimulus? In J. Beck (Ed.), *Organization and representation in perception* (pp. 191–216). Hillsdale, NJ: Erlbaum.

Hochberg, J. (1986). The representation of motion and space in video and cinematic displays. In K. Boff, J. Thomas, & L. Kaufman (Eds.), *Handbook of perception and human performance* (Vol. 1, pp. 1–64). New York: Wiley.

Hochberg, J. (1988). Visual perception. In R. Atkinson, R. Herrnstein, G. Lindzey, & D. Luce (Eds.), *Stevens' handbook of experimental psychology* (Vol. I, pp. 295–375). New York: Wiley.

Hochberg, J. (1996). The perception of pictures and pictorial art. In M. P. Friedman & E. C. Carterette (Eds.), *Cognitive ecology* (pp. 151–203). San Diego: Academic Press.

Hochberg, J. (1997). The affordances of perceptual inquiry: Pictures are learned from the world, and what that fact might mean about perception quite generally. In R. Goldstone, D. Medin, & P. G. Schyns (Eds.), *Perceptual learning* (pp. 15–44). San Diego: Academic Press.

Hochberg, J., & Beer, J. (1990). Alternative movement organizations: Findings and premises for modeling. [Abstract] *Proceedings of the Eastern Psychological Association,* p. 44.

Hochberg, J., & Brooks, V. (1960). The psychophysics of form: Reversible perspective drawings of spatial objects. *American Journal of Psychology, 73,* 337–354.

Hochberg, J., & Brooks, V. (1962). Pictorial recognition as an unlearned ability: A study of one child's performance. *American Journal of Psychology, 75,* 624–628.

Hochberg, J., & Brooks, V. (1970). Reading as intentional behavior. In H. Singer (Ed.), *Theoretical models and processes of reading.* Newark, DE: International Reading Association.

Hochberg, J., & Brooks, V. (1996a). The perception of motion pictures. In M. Friedman & E. Carterette (Eds.), *Handbook of perception & cognition: Cognitive ecology* (pp. 151–203). San Diego: Academic Press.

Hochberg, J., & Brooks, V. (1996b). Movies in the mind's eye. In D. Bordwell & N. Carroll (Eds.), *Post-theory: Reconstructing film studies* (pp. 368–387). Madison, WI: University of Wisconsin Press.

Hochberg, J., & Galper, R. E. (1967). Recognition of faces: I. An exploratory study. *Psychonomic Science, 9,* 619–620.

Hochberg, J., & Fallon, P. (1976). Perceptual analysis of moving patterns *Science, 194,* 1081–1083.

Hochberg, J., & Gellman, L. (1977). The effect of landmark features on mental rotation times. *Memory and Cognition, 5,* 23–26.

Hochberg, J., & McAlister, E. (1953). A quantitative approach to figural "goodness." *Journal of Experimental Psychology, 46*, 361–364.

Hochberg, J., & Peterson, M. A. (1987). Piecemeal organization and cognitive components in object perception: Perceptually coupled responses to moving objects. *Journal of Experimental Psychology: General, 116*, 370–380.

Hochberg, J., & Silverstein, A. (1956). A quantitative index of stimulus similarity: Proximity vs. differences in brightness, *American Journal of Psychology, 69*, 456–459.

Hock, H. S., Schoner, G., & Voss, A. (1997). The influence of adaptation and stochastic fluctuations on spontaneous perceptual changes of bistable stimuli. *Perception & Psychophysics, 59*, 509–522.

Höffding, H. (1889, 1890). Über Wiederkennen, Assoziation und psychische Aktivität. *Vierteljsschrift für wissenschaftliche Philosophie, 13*, 420–423; *14*, 27–28.

Hoffman, D. D., & Bennett, B. M. (1986). The computation of structure from fixed-axis motion: Rigid structures. *Biological Cybernetics, 54*, 71–83.

Hoffman, D. D., & Richards, W. A. (1984). Parts of recognition. *Cognition, 18*, 65–96.

Hoffman, J. E. (1980). Interaction between global and local levels of a form. *Journal of Experimental Psychology: Human Perception and Performance, 6*, 222–234.

Hoffman, J. E., & Subramaniam, B. (1995). Saccadic eye movements and visual selective attention. *Perception & Psychophysics, 57*, 787–795.

Hubel, D. H., & Wiesel, T. N. (1960). Receptive fields of optic nerve fibres in the spider monkey. *Journal of Physiology, London. 154*, 572–580.

Hughes, H. C., Nozowa, G., & Kitterle, F. (1996). Global precedence, spatial frequency channels, and the statistics of natural images. *Journal of Cognitive Neuroscience, 8*, 197–230.

Intraub, H. (1989). Illusory conjunction of forms, objects and scenes during rapid serial visual search. *Journal of Learning, Memory and Cognition, 18*, 98–109.

Intraub, H. (1992). Contextual factors in scene perception. In E. Chekaluk & K. R. Llewellyn (Eds.), *The role of eye movements in perceptual processes* (pp. 45–72). New York: Elsevier.

Intraub, H., Gottesman, C. V., Willey, E. V., & Zuk, I. J. (1996). Boundary extension for briefly glimpsed photographs: Do common perceptual processes result in unexpected memory distortions? *Journal of Memory and Language, 35*, 118–134.

Irwin, D. E. (1992). Visual memory within and across fixations. In K. Rayner (Ed.), *Eye movements and visual cognition: Scene perception and reading* (pp. 146–165). New York: Springer-Verlag.

Irwin, D. E. (1996). Integrating information across saccadic eye movements. *Current Directions in Psychological Science, 5*, 94–100.

Irwin, D. E., Yantis, S., & Jonides, J. (1991). Evidence against visual integration across saccadic eye movements. *Perception & Psychophysics, 34*, 49–57.

Ittelson, W. H. (1996). Visual perception of markings. *Psychonomic Bulletin & Review, 3*, 171–187.

Jastrow, J. (1900). *Fact and fable in psychology.* Boston: Houghton, Mifflin.

Johansson, G. (1950). *Configurations in event perception.* Uppsala: Almquist and Wiksells Boktryschker AB.

Johansson, G. (1973). Visual perception of biological motion and a model for its analysis. *Perception & Psychophysics, 14*, 201–211.

Johansson, G. (1982). Visual space perception through motion. In A. H. Wertheim, W. A. Wagenaar, & H. W. Leibowitz (Eds.), *Tutorials on motion perception* (pp. 19–39). New York: Plenum Press.

Julesz, B. (1971). *Foundations of cyclopean perception.* Chicago: University of Chicago Press.

Kanade, T. (1981). Recovery of the three-dimensional shape of an object from a single view. *Artificial Intelligence, 17*, 409–460.

Kandel, E. R., Schwartz, J. H., & Jesell, T. M. (Eds.) (1990). *Principles of neural science,* 3rd ed. New York: Elsevier.

Kanizsa, G. (1974). Contours without gradients or cognitive contours. *Italian Journal of Psychology, 1*, 93–113.

Kanizsa, G. (1979). *Organization in vision: Essays on Gestalt perception.* New York: Praeger.

Kanizsa, G., & Gerbino, W. (1982). Amodal completion: seeing or thinking? In J. Beck (Ed.), *Organization and representation in perception* (pp. 167–190). Hillsdale, NJ: Erlbaum.

Kanizsa, G., & Luccio, R. (1995). Multistability as a research tool in experimental phenomenology. In P. Kruse & M. Stadler (Eds.), *Ambiguity in mind and nature* (pp. 47–68). Heidelberg: Springer-Verlag.

Kellman, P. J. (in press). An update on Gestalt psychology. In B. Landau, J. Sabini, E. Newport, & J. Jonides (Eds.), *Essays in honor of Henry and Lila Gleitman*. Cambridge, MA: M.I.T. Press.

Kellman, P. (1993). Kinematic foundations of infant visual perception. In C. Granrud (Ed.), *Visual perception and cognition in infants* (pp. 121–173). Hillsdale, NJ: Erlbaum.

Kellman, P. J., & Shipley, T. F. (1991). A theory of visual interpolation in object perception. *Cognitive Psychology, 23,* 141–221.

Kellman, P. J., Yin, C., & Shipley, T. F. (in press). A common mechanism for illusory and occluded object comletion. *Journal of Experimental Psychology: Human Perception and Performance.*

Kienker, O. K., Sejnowski, T. J., Hinton, G. E., & Schumacher, L. E. (1986). Separating figure from ground with a parallel network. *Perception, 15,* 197–216.

Kinchla, R. A., & Wolfe, J. M. (1979). The order of visual processing: Top-down, bottom-up, or middle-out. *Perception & Psychophysics, 25,* 225–231.

Koenderink, J. J. (1994). Vector analysis. In G. Jansson, S. S. Bergstrom & W. Epstein (Eds.), *Perceiving events and objects. Resources for ecological psychology* (pp. 337–346). Hillsdale, NJ: Erlbaum.

Koenderink, J. J., & van Doorn, A. J. (1975). Invariant properties of the motion parallax field due to the movement of rigid bodies relative to an observer. *Optica Acta,* 773–791.

Koffka, K. (1935). *Principles of Gestalt Psychology.* New York: Harcourt.

Köhler, W. (1920). *Die physischen Gestalten in Ruhe und im stationären Zustand.* Braunscheig: Vieweg.

Köhler, W. (1929). *Gestalt psychology.* New York: Liveright.

Köhler, W. (1940). *Dynamics in psychology.* New York: Liveright.

Köhler, W. (1947). *Gestalt psychology: An introduction to new concepts in modern psychology.* New York: Liveright.

Köhler, W., & Wallach, H. (1944). Figural aftereffects: An investigation of visual processes. *Proceedings of the American Philosophhical Society, 88,* 269–357.

Kolers, P. A., & Pomerantz, J. R. (1971). Figural change in apparent motion. *Journal of Experimental Psychology, 87,* 99–108.

Kopfermann, H. (1930). Psychologische Untersuchungen über die Wirkung Zweidimensionaler Darstellunger körperlicher Gebilde. *Psychologische Forschung, 13,* 293–364.

Kosslyn, S. M. (1975). Information representation in visual images. *Cognitive Psychology, 7,* 341–370.

Kosslyn, S. M. (1980). *Image and mind.* Cambridge, MA: Harvard University Press.

Kosslyn, S. M., Alpert, N. M., Thompson, W. L., Maljkovic, V., Weise, S. B., Chabris, S. F., Hamilton, S. E., & Buonanno, F. S. (1993). Visual mental imagery activates the primary visual cortex. *Journal of Cognitive Neuroscience, 5,* 263–287.

Kowler, E. (1990). *Eye movements and their role in visual and cognitive processes.* New York: Elsevier.

Kowler, E., Anderson, E., Dosher, B., & Blaser, E. (1995). The role of attention in the programming of saccades. *Vision Research, 35,* 1897–1916.

Kubovy, M. (1994). The perceptual organization of dot lattices. *Psychonomic Bulletin & Review, 1,* 182–190.

Kubovy, M., & Wagemans, J. (1995). Grouping by proximity and multistability in dot lattices: A quantitative Gestalt theory. *Psychological Science, 6,* 225–234.

Lashley, K. S. (1942). The problem of cerebral organization in vision. In H. Klüver (Ed.), *Biological symposium. Vol. 7.* Lancaster, PA: J. Cattell.

Lee, D. N. (1980). The optic flow field: The foundation of vision. *Philosophical Transactions of the Royal Society of London, Series B, 290,* 169–179.

Leeper, R. (1935). A study of a neglected portion of the field of learning: The development of sensory organization. *Journal of Genetic Psychology, 46,* 41–75.

Leeuwenberg, E. (1971). A perceptual coding language for visual and auditory patterns. *American Journal of Psychology, 84,* 307–349.

Leibowitz, H. W. (1955). The relation between the rate threshold for the perception of movement and luminance for various durations of exposure. *Journal of Experimental Psychology, 49,* 209–214.

Leibowitz, H. W., Johnson, C. A., & Isabelle, E. (1972). Peripheral motion detection and refractive error. *Science, 177,* 1207–1208.

Lennie, P. (1994). Visual functions. *Science, 264,* 1011–1012.

Lennie, P. (in press). Single units and visual cortical organization. *Perception.*

Lettvin, J. Y., Maturana, H. R., McCulloch, W. S., & Pitts, W. H. (1959). What the frog's eye tells the frog's brain. *Proceedings of the Institute of Radio Engineers, 47,* 1940–1951.

Lippmann, R. P. (1987). An introduction to computing with neural nets. *IEEE ASSP Magazine,* April, 4–22.

Livingstone, M. S., & Hubel, D. H. (1987). Segregation of form, color, movement and depth: anatomy, physiology and perception. *Science, 240,* 740–749.

Longuet-Higgins, H. C., & Prazdny, K. (1980). The interpretation of a moving retinal image. *Proceedings of the Royal Society of London, Series B, 208,* 385–397.

Loftus, G. R. (1976). A framework for a theory of picture recognition. In R. A. Monty & J. W. Senders (Eds.), *Eye movements and psychological processes* (pp. 499–513). Hillsdale, NJ: Erlbaum.

Lotze, R. H. (1965). *Medicinische Psychologie, oder Physiologie der Seele.* Leipzig. Excerpt in R. H. Herrnstein & E. G. Boring (Eds.) *A source book in the history of psychology* (pp. 135–140), translated by D. Cantor. Cambridge, MA: Harvard University Press. (Original work published 1852)

Lovegrove, W., & Pepper, K. (1994). The influence of low-level processing in the global precedence effect. In S. Ballesteros (Ed.), *Cognitive approaches to human perception* (pp. 71–90). Hillsdale, NJ: Erlbaum.

Lowe, D. (1987). Three-dimensional object recognition from single two-dimensional images. *Artificial Intelligence, 31,* 355–395.

Luna, D., Marcos-Ruiz, R., & Merino, J. M. (1995). Selective attention to global and local information: Effects of visual angle, exposure duration, and eccentricity on processing dominance. *Visual Cognition, 2,* 183–200.

Lynch, K. (1960). *The image of the city.* Cambridge, MA: MIT Press.

McBeath, M., Morikawa, K., & Kaiser, M. K. (1992). Perceptual bias for forward-facing motion. *Psychological Science,* 363–367.

McConkie, G. W., & Rayner, K. (1976). The span of the effective stimulus during a fixation in reading. *Perception & Psychophysics, 17,* 578–586.

McCulloch, W. S., & Pitts, W. H. (1965). A logical calculus of the ideas imminent in nervous activity. In W. S. McCulloch (Ed.), *Embodiments of mind* (pp. 19–39). Cambridge, MA: The MIT Press. (Original work published 1943)

McKoon, G., & Ratcliff, R. (1992). Inference during reading. *Psychological Review, 99,* 440–466.

MacKay, D. (1973). Visual stability and eye movements. In R. Jung (Ed.), *Handbook of sensory physiology* (Vol. 7, No. 3, pp. 307–332). Berlin: Springer-Verlag.

Mach, E. (1959). *The analysis of sensations.* New York: Dover. (Original work published 1896)

Mack, A., Tang, B., Tuma, R., Kahn, S., & Rock, I. (1992). Perceptual organization and attention. *Cognitive Psychology, 24,* 475–501.

Mackworth, N. H., & Morandi, A. J. (1967). The gaze selects informative details within pictures. *Perception & Psychophysics, 2,* 547–552.

Markman, A. B. (1989). LMS rules and the inverse base-rate effect: Comment on Gluck & Bower (1988). *Journal of Experimental Psychology: General, 118,* 417–421.

Marr, D. (1976). Early processing of visual information. *Philosophical Transactions of the Royal Society of London, Series B, 275,* 483–524.

Marr, D. (1982). *Vision.* San Francisco: W. H. Freeman.

Marr, D., & Hildreth, E. (1980). Theory of edge detection. *Proceedings of the Royal Society of London, Series B, 297,* 187–216.

Marr, D., & Nishihara, H. K. (1978). Representation and recognition of the spatial organization of three-dimensional shapes. *Proceedings of the Royal Society of London, B, 200,* 269–291.

Matin, L. (1986). Visual localization and eye movements. In K. R. Boff, L. Kaufman, & J. P. Thomas (Eds.), *Handbook of perception and human performance: Vol. 1. Sensory processes and perception* (pp. 1–45). New York: Wiley.

Mens, L. H. M., & Leeuwenberg, E. L. J. (1993). Can perceived shape be primed? The autonomy of organization. *Giornale Italiano di Psicologia, xx,* 821–836.

Metelli, F. (1974). Achromatic color conditions in the perception of transparency. In R. B. MacLeod & H. Pick (Eds.), *Perception: Essays in honor of James J. Gibson* (pp. 92–116). Ithaca, New York: Cornell University Press.

Metelli, F. (1984). Some characteristics of Gestalt-oriented research in perception. In J. Beck (Ed.), *Organization and representation in perception* (pp. 219–234). Hillsdale, NJ: Erlbaum.

Metcalfe, J. (1994). A computational modeling approach to novelty monitoring, metacognition, and frontal lobe dysfunction. In J. Metcalfe & A. P. Shimamura (Eds.), *Metacognition: Knowing about knowing* (pp. 137–156). Cambridge, MA: MIT Press.

Metzger, W. (1934). Tiefenersheinungen in optischen Bewegungsfeldern. *Psychologische Forschung, 20,* 195–260.

Metzger, W. (1953). *Gezetse des Sehens.* Frankfurt-am-Main: Kramer, 1953.

Michaels, C. F., & Carello, C. (1981). *Direct perception.* Englewood Cliffs, NJ: Prentice Hall.

Michotte, A., Thines, G., & Crabbe, G. (1964). Les complements amodaux des structures perceptives. *Studia Psychologica.* Louvain: Publications Universitaires.

Mill, J. S. (1965). On the permanent possibilities of sensation. An examination of Sir William Hamilton's Philosophy. In R. J. Herrnstein & E. G. Boring (Eds.), *A source book in the history of psychology* (pp. 182–188). Cambridge, MA: Harvard University Press. (Original work published 1865)

Miller, G. A. (1956). The magic number seven, plus or minus two: Some limits on our capacity for processing information. *Psychological Review, 63,* 81–97.

Miller, G. A., Galanter, E., & Pribram, K. (1960). *Plans and the structure of behavior.* New York: Holt, Rinehart, and Winston.

Morton, J., & Broadbent, D. E. (1967). Passive versus active recognition models or is your homunculus really necessary? In W. Wathen-Dunn (Ed.), *Models for the perception of speech and visual form* (pp. 103–110). Cambridge, MA: The MIT Press.

Musatti, C. L. (1931). Forma e assimilazioni. *Archivio Italiano di Psicologia, 9,* 61–156.

Nakayama, K., & Joseph, J. S. (1998). Attention, pattern recognition, & popout in visual search. In R. Parasuraman (Ed.), *The attentive brain* (pp. 279–298). Cambridge, MA: MIT Press.

Nakayama, K., & Shimojo, S. (1990). Toward a neural understanding of visual surface representation. *Cold Spring Harbor Symposia on Quantitative Biology, 55,* 911–924.

Nakayama, K., & Shimojo, S. (1992). Experiencing and perceiving visual surfaces. *Science, 257,* 1357–1363.

Navon, D. (1976). Irrelevance of figural identity for resolving ambiguities in apparent motion. *Journal of Experimental Psychology: Human Perception and Performance, 2,* 130–138.

Navon, D. (1977). Forest before trees: The precedemce of global features in visual perception. *Cognitive Psychology, 9,* 353–383.

Navon, D., & Norman, J. (1983). Does global precedence really depend on visual angle? *Journal of Experimental Psychology: Human Perception and Performance, 9,* 955–965.

Necker, L. A. (1832). Observations on some remarkable phenomena seen in Switzerland; and an optical phenomenon which occurs on viewing of a crystal or geometrical solid. *Philosophical Magazine (Series 3), 1,* 329–33.

Neisser, U. (1964). Visual search. *Scientific American, 210,* 94–102.

Neisser, U. (1967). *Cognitive psychology.* New York: Appleton-Century-Crofts.

Neisser, U., & Becklen, R. (1975). Selective looking: Attending to visually specified events. *Cognitive Psychology, 7,* 480–494.

Oatley, K. (1978). *Perceptions and representations: The theoretical bases of brain research and psychology.* New York: The Free Press.

Oldfield, R. C. (1954). Memory mechanisms and the theory of schemata. *British Journal of Psychology, 45,* 14–23.

Orlansky, J. (1940). The effect of similarity and difference in form on apparent visual movement. *Archive of Psychology, 246,* 85.

Palmer, S. E., Neff, J., & Beck, D. (1997). Grouping and amodal completion. In I. Rock (Ed.), *Indirect perception* (pp. 63–74). Cambridge, Mass: MIT Press.

Palmer, S. E. (1982). Symmetry, transformation, and the structure of perceptual systems. In J. Beck (Ed.), *Organization and representation in perception* (pp. 95–144). Hillsdale, NJ: Erlbaum.

Parks, T. E., & Rock, I. (1990). Illusory contours from pictorially three-dimensional elements. *Perception, 19,* 119–121.

Penrose, L., & Penrose, R. (1958). Impossible objects: A special type of visual illusion. *British Journal of Psychology, 49,* 31–33.

Perky, C. (1910). An experimental study of imagination. *American Journal of Psychology, 23,* 422–452.

Peterhans, E., & von der Heydt, R. (1994). Subjective contours—Bridging the gap between psychophysics and physiology. In G. T. H. Gutfreund (Ed.), *Biology and computation: A physicist's choice. Advanced series in neuroscience, Vol. 3* (pp. 627–634). Singapore: World Scientific Publishing Co.

Petermann, B. (1932). *The Gestalt theory and the problem of configuration.* (M. Fortes, Trans.) New York: Harcourt, Brace.

Peterson, M. A. (1994). Object recognition processes can and do operate before figure–ground organization. *Current Directions in Psychology, 3,* 105–111.

Peterson, M. A. (1996). The relationship between depth, segregation and object recognition. Unpublished manuscript.

Peterson, M. A., & Gibson, B. S. (1993). Shape recognition inputs to figure-ground organization in three-dimensional displays. *Cognitive Psychology, 25,* 383–429.

Peterson, M. A., & Gibson, B. S. (1994). Must shape recognition follow figure–ground organization? An assumption in peril. *Psychological Science, 5,* 253–259.

Peterson, M. A., & Hochberg, J. (1983). The opposed-set measurement procedure: The role of local cues and intention in form perception. *Journal of Experimental Psychology: Human Perception and Performance, 9,* 183–193.

Peterson, M. A., & Hochberg, J. (1989). Necessary considerations for a theory of form perception: A theoretical and empirical reply to Boselie and Leeuwenberg. *Perception, 18,* 105–119.

Peterson, M. A., Kihlstrom, J. H., Rose, P. M., & Glisky, M. L. (1992). Mental images can be ambiguous: Reconstruals and reference-frame reversals. *Memory & Cognition, 20,* 107–123.

Pollack, I., & Spence, D. (1968). Subjective pictorial information and visual search. *Perception & Psychophysics, 3,* 41–44.

Pomerantz, J. R. (1983). The rubber pencil illusion. *Perception & Psychophysics, 33,* 365–368.

Pomerantz, J. R. (1981). Perceptual organization in information processing. In M. Kubovy & J. R. Pomerantz (Eds.), *Perceptual organization* (pp. 141–180). Hillsdale, NJ: Erlbaum.

Pomerantz, J. R., & Kubovy, M. (1986). Simplicity and likelihood principles. In K. Boff, L. Kaufman, & J. Thomas (Eds.), *Handbook of perception and human performance* (Vol. 2, Ch. 36, pp. 1–46). New York: Wiley.

Posner, M. I., Snyder, C. R. R., & Davidson, B. J. (1980). Attention and the detection of signals. *Journal of Experimental Psychology: General, 109,* 160–174.

Posner, M. I., & Raichle, M. E. (1995). Precis of Images of Mind. *Behavioral & Brain Sciences, 18,* 327–383.

Potter, M. C. (1975). Meaning in visual search. *Science, 187,* 565–566.

Prazdny, K. (1983). Illusory contours are not caused by simultaneous brightness contrast. *Perception & Psychophysics, 34,* 403–404.

Prazdny, K. (1986). Illusory contours from inducers defined solely by spatiotemporal correlation. *Perception & Psychophysics, 39,* 175–178.

Previc, F. H. (1990). Functional specialization in the lower and upper visual fields in humans: Its ecological origins and neurophysiological implications. *Behavioral and Brain Sciences, 13,* 519–575.

Prinz, W., Nattkemper, D., & Ullman, T. (1992). Moment-to-moment control of saccadic eye movements: Evidence from continuous search. In K. Rayner (Ed.), *Eye movements and visual cognition: Scene perception and reading* (pp. 108–129). New York: Springer-Verlag.

Proffitt, D. R., & Cutting, J. E. (1980). An invariant for wheel-generated motions and the logic of its determination. *Perception, 9,* 435–449.

Purghé, F. (1995). Illusory figures from stereoscopically three-dimensional inducers depicting no occlusion event. *Perception, 24,* 905–918.

Pylyshyn, Z. W. (1981). The imagery debate: Analog media *versus* tacit knowledge. *Psychological Review, 88,* 16–45.

Quinlan, P. (1991). *Connectionism and psychology: A psychological perspective on new connectionist research.* Chicago: The University of Chicago Press.

Ratoosh, P. (1949). On interposition as a cue for the perception of distance. *Proceedings of the National Academy of Science, 35,* 257–259.

Rayner, K. (Ed.). (1992). *Eye movements and visual cognition: Scene perception and reading.* New York: Springer Verlag.

Reed, E. S. (1988). *James J. Gibson and the psychology of perception.* New Haven, CT: Yale University Press.

Reeves, A. (1981). Visual imagery lowers sensitivity to hue-varying, but not to luminance-varying, visual stimuli. *Perception & Psychophysics, 29,* 247–250.

Reeves, A., & Sperling, G. (1986). Attention gating in short-term visual memory. *Psychological Review, 93,* 180–206.

Reisberg, D. (in press). Constraints on image-based discovery: A comment on Rouw et al. *Cognition.*

Reisberg, D., & Chambers, D. (1991). Neither pictures nor propositions: What can we learn from a mental image? *Canadian Journal of Psychology, 45,* 336–352.

Restle, F. (1979). Coding theory of the perception of motion configuration. *Psychological Review, 86,* 1–24.

Riddoch, M. J. (1990). Loss of visual imagery: A generation deficit. *Cognitive Neuropsychology, 7,* 249–273.

Riesen, A. H. (1961). Studying perceptual development using the technique of sensory deprivation. *Journal of Nervous and Mental Disease, 132,* 21–25.

Rock, I. (1977). In defense of unconscious inference. In W. Epstein (Ed.), *Stability and constancy in visual perception: mechanisms and processes* (pp. 321–373). New York: Wiley.

Rock, I. (1984). *The logic of perception.* Cambridge, MA: The MIT Press.

Rock, I. (1993). The logic of "The logic of perception". In *Giornale Italiano di Psicologia, 20,* 841–867.

Rock, I., & Gutman, D. (1981). The effect of inattention on form perception. *Journal of Experimental Psychology: Human Perception and Performance, 7,* 275–281.

Rock, I., Nijahawan, R., Palmer, S. E., & Tudor, L. (1997). Grouping and lightness. In I. Rock (Ed.), *Indirect perception* (pp. 47–61). Cambridge, Mass: MIT Press.

Rosenblatt, F. (1958). The perceptron: A probabilistic model for information storage and organization in the brain. *Psychological Review, 65,* 386–408.

Rosch, E., Mervis, C. B., Gray, W. D., Johnson, D. M., & Boues-Braem, P. (1976). Basic objects in natural categories. *Cognitive Psychology, 8,* 382–439.

Rouw, R., Kosslyn, S., & Hamel, R. (1997). Detecting high-level and low-level properties in visual images and visual percepts. *Cognition, 63,* 209–226.

Rubin, E. (1915). *Synoplovide Figurer.* Copenhagen: Glydendalske.

Rubin, E. (1921). *Visuell wahrgenommene Figuren.* Copenhagen: Glydendalske.

Rubin, N., Nakayama, K., & Shapley, R. (1996). Enhanced perception of illusory contours in the lower versus upper visual hemifields. *Science, 271,* 651–653.

Saucer, R. T. (1954). Processes of motion perception. *Science, 120,* 806–807.

Schiller, P. H. (1994). Area V4 of the primate visual cortex. *Current Directions in Psychological Science, 3,* 89–93.

Schneider, G. E. (1969). Two visual systems. *Science, 163,* 895–902.

Schumann, F. (1904). Einige Beobachtungen über die Zuammenfassung von Gesichtseindrucken zu Einheiten. *Psychologische Studien, 1,* 1–32.

Schwartz, B. J., & Sperling, G. (1983). Non-rigid 3D percepts from 2D representations of rigid objects. *Investigative Opthalmology and Visual Science* (ARVO) suppl.) *24,* 239 (Abstract).

Segal, S. J., & Gordon, P. E. (1969). The Perky effect revisited: Blocking of visual signals by imagery. *Perceptual & Motor Skills, 28(3),* 791–797.

Seidenberg, M. S., & McClelland, J. L. (1989). A distributed, developmental model of word recognition and naming. *Psychological Review, 96,* 523–568.

Sekuler, A. B., Palmer, S. E., & Flynn, C. (1994). Local and global processes in visual completion. *Psychological Science, 5,* 260–267.

Selfridge, O. G., & Neisser, U. (1960). Pattern recognition by machine. *Scientific American, 203,* 60–68.

Shannon, C. E., & Weaver, W. (1949). *The mathematical theory of communication.* Urbana: University of Illinois Press.

Shepard, R. N. (1984). Ecological constraints on internal representation: Resonant kinematics of perceiving, imagining, thinking, and dreaming. *Psychological Review, 91.* 417–447.

Shepard, R. N., & Metzler, J. (1971). Mental rotation of three-dimensional objects. *Science,* 701–703.

Shiffrar, M., Lichtéy, L., & Chatterjee, S. H. (1997). The perception of biological motion across apertures. *Perception & Psychophysics, 59,* 51–59.

Shiffrin, R. M., & Lightfoot, N. (1997). Perceptual learning of alphanumeric-like characters. In R. Goldstone, D. Medin, & P. G. Schyns (Eds.), *Perceptual learning* (pp. 45–81). San Diego: Academic Press.

Simon, H. (1967). An information processing explanation of some perceptual phenomena. *British Journal of Psychology, 58,* 1–12.

Simon, H. (1974). What is a chunk? *Science, 183,* 482–488.

Spelke (1985). Preferential looking methods as tools for the study of cognition in infancy. In A. Yonas (Ed.), *Perceptual development in infacny: The Minnesota Symposia on Child Psychology* (Vol. 20, p. 19). Hillsdale, NJ: Erlbaum.

Spelke, E. S. (1990). Principles of object perception. *Cognitive Science, 14,* 29–56.

Sperling, G. (1960). The information available in brief visual presentations. *Psychological Monographs, 74,* Whole no. 498.

Stadler, M., & Kruse, P. (1995). The function of meaning in cognitive order formation. In P. Kruse & M. Stadler (Eds.), *Ambiguity in mind and nature* (pp. 5–21). New York: Springer.

Stins, J. F., & van Leeuwen, C. (1993). Context influence on the perception of figures as conditional upon perceptual organization strategies. *Perception & Psychophysics, 53,* 34–42.

Suzuki, S., & Cavanagh, P. (1995). Facial organization blocks access to low-level features: An object inferiority effect. *Journal of Experimental Psychology: Human Perception and Performance, 21,* 901–913.

Tanaka, J. W. & Farah, M. J. (1993). Parts and wholes in face recognition. *Quarterly Journal of Experimental Psychology. A, Human Experimental Psychology, 46A,* 225–245.

Tarr, M. J. (1995). Rotating objects to recognize them: A case study on the role of viewpoint dependence in the recognition of three-dimensional objects. *Psychonomic Bulletin & Review, 2,* 55–82.

Tarr, M. J., & Bulthoff, H. H. (1995). Is human object recognition better described by geon structural descriptions or by multiple views? Comment on Biederman and Gerhardsstein (1993). *Journal of Experimental Psychology: Human Perception & Performance, 21,* 1494–1505.

Tarr, M. J., & Pinker, S. (1990). When does human object recognition use a viewer-centered reference frame? *Psychological Science, 1,* 253–256.

Todd, J. T. (1982). Visual information about rigid and nonrigid motion: A geometric analysis. *Journal of Experimental Psychology: Human Perception and Performance, 8,* 238–252.

Todd, J. T., & Norman, J. F. (1995). The visual discrimination of relative surface orientation. *Perception, 24,* 855–866.

Todd, J. T., Chen, L., & Norman, J. F. (1997). *On the relative salience of Euclidean, affine and topological structure for 3D form discrimination.* Unpublished manuscript.

Tolman, E. C. (1932). *Purposive behavior in animals and men.* New York: D. Appleton-Century.

Tolman, E. C., & Brunswik, E. (1935). The organism and the causal texture of the environment. *Psychological Review, 42,* 43–77.

Treisman, A. (1993). The perception of features and objects. In A. D. Baddeley & L. Weiskrantz (Eds.), *Attention: Selection, awareness, and control: A tribute to Donald Broadbent.* (pp. 5–35). Oxford, England: Clarendon Press/Oxford University Press.

Treisman, A., & Geffen, G. (1967). Selective attention: Perception or response? *Quarterly Journal of Experimental Psychology, 19,* 1–17.

Treisman, A., & Gelade, G. (1980). A feature-integration theory of attention. *Cognitive Psychology, 12,* 97–136.

Treisman, A. M., & Schmidt, H. (1982). Illusory conjunctions in the perception of objects. *Cognitive Psychology, 14,* 107–141.

Trevarthen, C. (1968). Two mechanisms of vision in primates. *Psychologische Forschung, 31,* 229–337.

Ullman, S. (1979). *The interpretation of visual motion.* Cambridge, MA: MIT Press.

Ullman, S. (1984). Maximizing rigidity: The incremental recovery of 3D structure from rigid and non-rigid motion. *Perception, 13,* 255–274.

Ullman, S. (1996). *High-level vision: object recognition and visual cognition.* Cambridge, MA: MIT Press.

Ungerleider, L. G. (1995). Functional brain imaging studies of cortical mechanisms for memory. *Science, 270,* 769–775.

van Leeuwen, C. (1995). Task, intention, context, globality, ambiguity: More of the same. In P. Kruse & M. Stadler (Ed.), *Ambiguity in mind and nature.* Heidelberg: Springer-Verlag.

von Ehrenfels, C. (1890). *Vierteljarsch wiss Philos, 14,* 249–292.

Von Hornbostel, E. M. (1922). Über optische Inversion. *Psychologische Forschung, 1,* 130–156.

Wallach, H. (1949). The role of memory in visual perception. *Journal of Personality, 18,* 6–13.

Wallach, H., & O'Connell, D. N. (1953). The kinetic depth effect. *Journal of Experimental Psychology, 45,* 205–217.

Wallach, H., O'Connell, D. N., & Neisser, U. (1953). The memory effect of visual perception of three-dimensional form. *Journal of Experimental Psychology, 45,* 360–368.

Warren, W. H. (1984). Perceiving affordances: Visual guidance of stair climbing. *Journal of Experimental Psychology: Human Perception and Performance, 10,* 683–703.

Warren, W. H., & Wang, S. (1987). Visual guidance of walking through apertures: Body-scaled information for affordances. *Journal of Experimental Psychology: Human Perception and Performance, 13,* 371–383.

Watt, R. J., & Morgan, M. J. (1985). A theory of the primitive spatial code in human vision. *Vision Research, 25.* 1387–1397.

Welch, R. B. (1986). Adaptation of space perception. In K. Boff, L. Kaufman, & J. Thomas (Eds.), *Handbook of perception and human performance* (Vol. 1, Ch. 24, pp. 1–36). New York: Wiley.

Werner, H. (1935). Studies on contour. *American Journal of Psychology, 47,* 40–64.

Wertheimer, M. (1912). Experimentelle Studien über das Sehen von Bewegung [Experimental studies on seeing motion]. *Zeitschrift für Psychologie, 61,* 161–265.

Wertheimer, M. (1965). Untersuchungen zur Lehre von der Gestalt, II. [Laws of organization in perceptual forms] In W. D. Ellis (Trans.) *A source book of Gestalt Psychology.* London: Routledge and Kegan Paul. (Original work published 1923)

Wever, E. G. (1927). Figure and ground in the visual perception of form. *American Journal of Psychology, 38,* 194–226.

White, B., & Mueser, G. (1960). Accuracy of reconstructing the arrangement of elements generating kinetic depth displays. *Journal of Experimental Psychology, 60,* 1–11.

Winston, P. H. (1975). Learning structural desciptions from examples. In P. H. Winston (Ed.), *The psychology of computer vision* (pp. 157–209). New York: McGraw-Hill.

Wohlgemuth, A. (1911). On the aftereffect of seen movement. *British Journal of Psychological Monographs,* (suppl. 1), 1–117.

Woodworth, R. S. (1938). *Experimental psychology.* New York: Holt, Rinehart, & Winston.

Wulf, F. (1922). Über die Veränderung von Vorstellungen (Gedächtnis und Gestalt). *Psychologische Forschung, 1,* 333–389.

Yantis, S. (1995). Perceived continuity of occluded visual objects. *Psychological Science, 6,* 182–186.

Yin, R. K. (1969). Looking at upside-down faces. *Journal of Experimental Psychology, 81,* 141–145.

Young, M. P., & Yamane, S. (1992). Sparse population coding of faces in the inferotemporal cortex. *Science, 256,* 1327–1331.

Zeki, S. (1993). *A vision of the brain.* Cambridge, MA: Blackwell Scientific.

Zeki, S., & Shipp, S. (1988). The functional logic of cortical connections. *Nature, 335,* 311–317.

Zemel, R. S., & Hinton, G. E. (1991). Discovering viewpoint-invariant relationships that characterize objects. *Advances in Neural Information Processing Systems, 3,* 299–305.

Zimmer, A. C. (1995). Multistability—More than just a freak phenomenon. In P. Kruse & M. Stadler, (Eds.), *Ambiguity in mind and nature* (pp. 99–139). Heidelberg: Springer-Verlag.

Zusne, L. (1970). *Visual perception of form.* New York: Academic Press.

CHAPTER 10

Vision Fin de Siècle

A Reductionistic Explanation of Perception for the 21st Century?

Ken Nakayama

The 20th century has been one of triumph, at least for science. In its explosive growth, myriad fields have been created, others have been altered beyond recognition. At the very beginning of the century, classical physics was considered by some to be exhaustive and complete. Yet almost immediately these foundations were shaken and superseded by strange and jarring ideas, special and general relativity, quantum mechanics, and so on. In biology, residual vitalistic thinking gradually gave way to a mechanistic conception of life, a consequence, in part, from Darwin's influential theory. A century later, this view was vindicated with Watson and Crick's structure for DNA and the subsequent rise of molecular biology. This reductionistic achievement provided a simple model accessible even to the layperson, explaining how a molecule could replicate itself, how it could also code for specific proteins. Thus, the central dogma of molecular biology (DNA→RNA→protein) provided a key insight about life. Much of course had to be done and significant questions still remain. Yet almost overnight there was no longer a "secret of life." No longer could one stare at the cell's protoplasm and see it as the mysterious life substance. Now within each cell, one could imagine a mixture of specific molecules with particular shapes and affinities.

The explosion of new concepts and findings resulting from the growth of molecular biology has been phenomenal; its ideas have completely transformed most areas of biology and medicine. Yet none of these subsequent developments can even be remotely compared to the discovery of DNA and the delineation of the genetic code when considered against a yardstick measuring the deepest of mysteries solved.

Perception and Cognition at Century's End

To be challenged by comparable mysteries, an increasingly diverse number of scientists are drawn to the brain, the most complicated physical and biological object known. Here the gulf between what is taken to be the outward phenomena and the possible explanation is the very widest. How does the brain, a physical object, go about the process of mediating complex behavior and conscious experience? More to the point for this chapter, how does the nervous system allow us to experience the visual world as we do? With the most talented scientists and armed with the most advanced technical instruments, is there any chance that we can understand seeing in such dramatic reductionistic terms? Will we, say in a generation or two hence, marvel at the definitive advance in understanding of perception at a mechanistic level?

Of course, this is a premature question, given the present state of knowledge. Yet even framing such a question may have some value in providing a different context to imagine what kinds of information are needed to envision goals. To even consider an answer, one must start at least briefly with some history.

I. ANTECEDENTS

First, I should note that the experimental study of visual perception was already very well developed during the earlier part of the 19th century, certainly well before the proclaimed birth of experimental psychology by Wundt in 1879. Several achievements stand out. Thomas Young's (1802) surprising and correct promulgation of the trivariant nature of color vision, followed by Helmholtz's (1909/1962) codification provided secure foundations for the science of color. Wheatstone's (1838) invention of the stereoscope provided a dramatic example of how the presentation of two flat images could give rise to the perception of three dimensions. Methodologically, there were important advances as well; in particular, the psychophysical methods developed by Fechner (1860) were foundational.

Alongside these more tangible advances, there was a broad current of theoretical assumptions about perception inherited from an earlier period when perception was mainly the province of philosophy. Two broad perspectives are discernible. First is a strong empiricist tradition, related to British associationism, assuming that the contents of perception, and particularly vision, are the consequence of learned associations of elementary sensations, coupled with motor-action and tactile feedback (Berkeley, 1709). For example, Helmholtz comments that as a child his mother took him to the town square where he thought he saw miniature puppets on the church tower which were really fully grown persons. According to Helmholtz, he had yet to learn that small figures (in terms of visual angle) at great distance were really full-sized persons. Thus, he argued that our perceptions require unconscious inferences, linking the elementary sensations through locomotor experience to acquire the correct perception of size and distance. An opposing line of thinking in a more nativist tradition, exemplified by Hering (1868), was more sympathetic to the idea of inborn characteristics of the organism, developing more or less independent of experience. Depth for Hering (1868) was indicated by the stimulation of various retinal loci in the two eyes according to the geometry of binocular vision (see Turner, 1994).

A novel and later much vilified approach was the program of the structuralists, an attempt to discern the relation between elementary sensations and perception. Much depended on introspection, a procedure requiring trained observers who could isolate their sensations for later understanding of how they contributed to perception. Most treatments consider this to be a somewhat misguided chapter in the history of experimental psychology, one that provides an object lesson of failed goals and methods. Flawed as it was, the underlying motivation did not seem out of step with the times. The modern science of chemistry was in its infancy (John Dalton proposed his theory earlier in the century) and Mendeleyev was just proposing the periodic table. So, why shouldn't the new science of psychology make an attempt along a parallel track to delineate the basic constituents of sensation and to see how they formed perception? Reasonable as it may have seemed then, it failed the ultimate of scientific tests. It didn't work, and it didn't lead anywhere except to provoke reaction. The detractors were many—William James (1892) in America, the Gestalt psychologists in Germany, and later and most enduringly, the behaviorists.

The Gestalt revolution launched against such structuralist thinking began with Wertheimer's (1912) famous paper on apparent motion (see also Hochberg, chap. 9, this volume). Although apparent motion was noted much earlier by Exner, also forming the basis of cinema, Wertheimer's contribution was still memorable because he was able to show in addition to seeing two stationary flashes, there was something not present in the stimulus: "phi," the perception of motion. Particularly significant to Wertheimer, there was a restricted range of spatial and temporal relations between the flashes where the stationary flashes themselves were invisible, yet vivid motion was still seen. One could experience pure "phi" without seeing the constituents that evoked it. Thus, argued Wertheimer, one simply could not analyze perception into its elementary sensations. To explain these phenomenon, Wertheimer suggested that there was, related to the presentation of the two successive flashes, a "short circuit" in the brain that was related to the perception of motion. The existence of this supposed physical phenomenon was a brain correlate of perception.

Other important phenomenon were quickly identified by the Gestalt psychologists and their numerous contemporaries. Most important was the phenomenon of perceptual grouping as well as the figure–ground distinction, highlighted most dramatically in Rubin's (1915) classic face–vase demonstration. The Gestalt psychologists saw these new phenomena as reflecting autonomous laws of perception, not determined by learned associations acquired through experience. Rather, they saw the phenomenon as revealing some as yet unspecified holistic physical process taking part in the medium of the brain. Kohler in particular was taken with brain field theory very early on and continued this line of thinking for many decades (Kohler, 1924, 1947).

Such ideas, however, were not enthusiastically received by those in the newly emerging behavioristic tradition. Developing at about the same time in the United States, behaviorism eventually became the reigning approach to psychology, largely stimulated by animal learning experiments conducted decades earlier (by Morgan, Thorndike, etc.), also buttressed by Pavlov's studies on conditioned reflexes. The latter did not shrink from the task. "Now, gentleman, we shall pass from peaceful affairs if we may so so, to matters of war, to Mr. Kohler. We are at war with him" (Pavlov, 1935, 1957, p. 599). Based on his own work and the prevailing Zeitgeist, he stated,

> Are not Helmholtz's famous "unconscious conclusions in his *Physiological Optics*—in reality conditioned reflexes? We may take as an example the case of a drawing imitating the visual character of a relief. In actual experience, of course, the tactile and muscular stimuli proceeding from a relief represent the initial and fundamental stimuli . . . which only subsequently obtain a vital significance by being constantly reinforced by tactile and muscular stimuli. (Pavlov, 1957, p. 215)

In America, Hull's (1943) axiomatic behavioral theory linked stimuli in the animals environment to responses that could be selectively strengthened during drive reduction. Obviously in hindsight there were many shortcomings of Hull's connectionistic theory and its immediate successors. Interestingly, even Hull acknowledged his own theory's limitations. He postulated somewhat surreptitiously the concept of "afferent neural interaction" to account for the organism's tendency to respond to Gestalt-like relations, for example, to the brighter of two lights, rather than to absolute luminance.

Hebb (1949) in his seminal book articulated the complementary strengths of earlier Gestalt theory and the behavioristic approach. Noting the extremes of each, he writes,

> Two kinds of formula have been used, leading at two extremes to (1) switchboard theory, and sensori–motor connections (2) field theory. . . . In the first type of theory . . . cells in the sensory system acquire connections with cells in the motor system, the function of the cortex is that of a telephone exchange. Connections rigidly determine what animal or human does and their acquisition constitutes learning. . . . (2) theory at the opposite extreme denies that learning depends on connections at all, and attempts to utilize instead the field conception that physics has found so useful. The cortex can be treated as a statistically homogeneous medium. (p. xvii)

Gestalt theory and related formulations (Lashley's theory of mass action) were more suited to handle the organizational aspects of vision, providing at least the beginnings of an explanation of how the relations between individual stimuli could play a role. Yet, Gestalt theory was silent in dealing with how such relational factors could be causally related to behavior. There was no mechanism in Kohler's brain state theory of how the global electrical pattern would plausibly actuate the specific nerves that would cause motor behavior. Gestalt theory with its preoccupation with dynamic states ignored the possible role of specific neural connections. In Hebb's terminology, distributed systems (i.e., brain state theories) were able to handle the problems of stimulus equivalence (that a triangle remained a triangle under various size changes, viewpoints, positions, colors, etc.) but were not able to deal with behavior.

Hebb's, frankly, speculative theory was able to provide at least a plausible account of how very specific neural circuits (cell assemblies and phase sequences) might actually respond to stimulus relations, and by virtue of their embodiment in a neural circuit, they had the potential to influence motor behavior.

Even though the specifics of Hebb's formulations were based on some outdated concerns (he needed to postulate reverbatory circuits to deal with short-term memory phenomena), his monograph was a milestone. Although in hindsight it provided no specific research agenda, it provided something of perhaps greater significance. It suggested a plausible and respectful reconciliation of the seemingly contradictory posturing of the Gestalt tradition and the behaviorists, acknowledging the contributions of each by presenting a speculative brain theory that would overcome their respective weaknesses. As such, Hebb's theory at mid-century provided hope and inspiration to serious workers in the still undeveloped brain sciences, giving them the courage to pursue their own research agendas with the expectation of future progress, overcoming what seemed like the current stagnation and futile debate.

II. VISUAL RECEPTIVE FIELDS

Single-unit visual electrophysiology emerged against this background in the 1950s. Before reviewing its development, however, we need to consider, at least briefly, some key concepts about brain tissue as it developed over the past 150 years.

In the 19th century scientists began to understand brain structure, which reflected a general growth in biological knowledge. For example, Schwann's (1839) cell theory marked the beginning of the modern era of histology, indicating that the constituents of biological tissue were made up of tiny repeating elements. Because the nervous system was so much more complex and the variation and tortuosity of neurons was so much greater, cell theory did not seem immediately applicable. Many thought the nervous system was formed by a complex continuous reticulum: that there were no elementary units. It was only after Ramon y Cajal perfected Golgi's technique that Waldeyer-Hartz (1891) was able to argue with force that nerve cells (neurons) were separate entities, that they made contact at specific points (the word synapse was not coined as yet), and that neurons were likely to form the elementary constituents of the brain (see Finger, 1994). Later, Sherrington was able to hypothesize mainly from behavioral experiments that the points of contact (synapses) were likely to be both excitatory and inhibitory, an intellectual leap later confirmed by Eccles (Sherrington's student) recording from within single neurons themselves. Presynaptic neurons could excite or inhibit neighboring cells, and the net result could be an action potential, the all-or-none impulse that was specialized for long-distance communication. The action potential represented a neural decision as to the sum total of excitatory and inhibitory influences. Thus, neurons could be conceived as having an integrative role, not simply being passive connectives, but more flexibly combining influences from many other neurons.

At this point, we begin our description of the transformative role played by the visual neurophysiologist at midcentury. The development of a very simple technique, the recording of neural impulses using the microelectrode was crucial. Eventually it was possible to simply insert a tiny probe into the tissue with little apparent damage, allowing investigators to "eavesdrop" on individual neurons one at a time during normal visual stimulation. Kuffler (1953) and Barlow (1953) were the first to truly exploit the technique, showing clearly that "on" and "off" responses were actually caused by light falling on different areas of the retina. Although anticipated by Barlow (1953), Lettvin and colleagues (Lettvin, Maturana, McCulloch, & Pitts, 1959) went much further to capture the imagination of a new generation, outlining properties of cells in the frogs retina that began to look startlingly like what was most important for the frog: little bugs to eat, growing shadows indicating predators looming closer.

The investigations of Hubel and Wiesel (1959, 1962) were the most systematic, comprehensive, and had the most lasting impact. Confirming Kuffler, they found concentric receptive fields in the retina and lateral geniculate nucleus. In the primary visual cortex they found something entirely different. Each cell required that light or dark regions be oriented. With a genius both for observation and taxonomy, they classified the cells into discrete categories of ascending complexity. Simple cells summed the excitatory and inhibitory effects of light from differing portions of the receptive field. Complex cells preserved the properties of orientation selectivity yet allowed oriented stimulus to vary in its exact position. Even higher order cells were also noted. Hypercomplex cells were orientation selective and responded, but only if the line did not spill over into more distant retinal regions. Hypercomplex cells of higher order generalized this property of line length limitation by not firing for any line that exceeded a certain length independent of the retinal area stimulated. Along the way Hubel and Wiesel also noted that many cells were direction selective, giving vigorous response for movement of an oriented bar in one direction but little or no response for movements in the opposite directions. Later studies by Barlow and colleagues demonstrated how specific these selectivities would be. For example, motion-selective cells in the rabbit's retina were selective to the direction of motion independent of shape, contrast, or contrast polarity (Barlow & Hill, 1963).

The combination of specificity and abstractness of the receptive fields was astonishing. Rivaling the autonomous relational processes posited by Gestalt psychologists 50 years earlier, cortical neurons were sensitive to "relations," not absolutes. Each individual cell seemed to be triggered by its own preferred local Gestalt, a very specific relation of dark, light, and even movement. Most impressive was the order and succession of taxonomic categories. The remarkable properties of each successive stage in the cortex was seen as the result of simple neuronal convergence from the previous stages. Linearly aligned receptive fields of neurons in the lateral geniculate nucleus were hypothesized to converge on cortical cells with excitatory connections bestowing orientation selectivity to simple cells (Hubel & Wiesel, 1962). Consequent convergence of aligned simple cell receptive fields were thought to comprise the input to complex cells and so forth. So the most remarkable visual properties of single neurons could arise from the most simple and successive application of excitatory and inhibitory processes, mechanisms proposed decades earlier by Sherrington and Eccles. The result of such simple combinations was indeed grand—units that seemed to mimic some of the as yet poorly understood elements of visual intelligence. Lettvin, Maturana, Pitts and McCulloch (1961) noted that there "was an odd discrimination in these cells, which, though we would not be surprised to find it in the whole animal, is somewhat startling in single units so early behind the retina," (p. 774). This was a far cry from the simple type of "atomic" psychophysics developed by Fechner, Wundt, et al., clearly more similar to Gestalten than to little patches of light. Specific neuronal connections, so dismissively rejected by the Gestalt psychologists (with their interest in brain fields) were capable of mediating patterns as or even more holistic than the simple Gestalten postulated years earlier.

III. BARLOW'S NEURON DOCTRINE

That these remarkable findings were obtained from just one class of physical brain signals, action potentials, is significant. Many techniques have been developed to measure brain activity before and since. Electroencephalograms (EEGs) and evoked potentials emerged before the advent of single-unit recording; MEG, positron emission tomography (PET), and functional magnetic resonance imaging (fMRI), emerged later. Yet the identities, or worse the multiple identities, of the sources of these signals remain obscure. Extracellular recorded action potentials, with their very brief durations, unvarying size, and short propagation distances leave little uncertainty regarding their distinct identity. In addition, spikes are not simply epiphenomenal complexities but the very signals that are presumably read by the most understood elements of brains, (i.e., neurons). As Horace Barlow once put it to me "action potentials are the fire, all else is . . . smoke."

Provoked by the central dogma of molecular biology, Barlow (1972) suggested a set of principles to link the activities of single neurons to sensation:

1. To understand nervous function one needs to look at interactions at a cellular level, rather than either a more macroscopic or microscopic level, because behavior depends upon the organized pattern of these intercellular interactions.
2. The sensory system is organized to achieve as complete a representation of the sensory stimulus as possible with the minimum number of active neurons.
3. Trigger features of sensory neurons are matched to redundant patterns of stimulation by experience as well as developmental processes.

4. Perception corresponds to the activity of a small selection from the very numerous high-level neurons, each of which corresponds to a pattern of external events of the order of complexity of the events symbolized by a word.

5. High-impulse frequency in such neurons corresponds to high certainty that the trigger feature is present.

Yet despite Barlow's bold claims, this neuron doctrine for perception has not had the same finality of DNA→RNA→protein nor has there been a comparable achievement like the cracking of the genetic code. Yes, the legacy of single-unit recording is still very strong. The same approach of recording from one neuron at a time in ever more complex visual displays and in behaving animals continues.

But the conceptual momentum behind Barlow's idea did not increase nor was there a subsequent expansion or codification of Hubel and Wiesel's tightly linked hierarchy. In fact, there has been slippage rather than advance (Cleland, Dubin, & Levick, 1971; Lennie, 1980). The reasons perhaps are many. First and perhaps even a priori, it would be difficult to imagine how Hubel and Wiesel's already stunning achievements could be further extended to a description of successive stages in their hierarchy given the forbidding combinatorics of the visual stimulation required. Wisely, Hubel, and Wiesel sidestepped the issue and devoted subsequent studies to other topics, including a masterful description of how various simple attributes get partitioned in the cortical tissue (functional architecture). Second, the findings since Hubel and Wiesel have shown the existence of separate parallel streams of information processing and connectivity running from retina to cortex. The existence of a slow parvo and a separate more rapidly conducting magno pathway begins in the retina and is evident even beyond the striate cortex (Cleland et al., 1971; Shapley, 1990; Stone, 1972). Each stream shows some degree of differential sensitivity, with the parvo system more sensitive to chromatic differences, and the magno system to motion. Instead of a convergent succession of connections arranged hierarchically, these results argue for separate parallel streams, inherently differentiated in function as early as the retina, and maintaining separate identities up through the cortex.

Yet despite these obvious shortcomings regarding the details of Hubel and Wiesel's hierarchy and residual skepticism regarding the extremes of Barlow's neuron doctrine, nothing since has had the force to displace the status of the single neuron as the basic unit of vision. And as we shall see, the newly emerging field of visual psychophysics would only strengthen this outlook.

IV. PSYCHOPHYSICS OF RECEPTIVE FIELDS

For a generation, starting approximately in the 1930s, visual psychophysics, in keeping with its roots in the 19th century, was concerned with detecting small patches of light, with stimuli varying along the simplest physical dimensions, such as intensity or wavelength. In the right hands such simple stimuli were to reveal important properties of early vision; for example, that one quantum is sufficient to activate a single photoreceptor (Hecht, Shlaer, & Pirenne, 1942), and that the detailed spectral characteristics of chromatic mechanisms could be discerned (Stiles, 1959). That one could learn about the properties of the retina at such a microscopic level of detail simply by asking a subject whether he saw something or not, contributed in no small measure to the growing respect accorded to visual psychophysics.

Later, stimulated by the new discovery of visual receptive fields, there was greater interest in a more broadened practice of visual psychophysics. In keeping up with these new results from physiology, the stimuli were to become much richer and more complex. Striking progress was made using new methods and stimuli in the area of depth and motion processing. Julesz's random dot stereogram was perhaps the most dramatic example. Using the new power of the modern digital computer, Julesz's (1961) ingenious demonstration confirmed Wheatstone's observation, but more important, it raised the hope that the brain's representation of space (encoding the third dimension) could be isolated from higher-order cognitive processes and understood as a separate and tractable problem. This view was strongly reinforced by the subsequent discovery of neurons specifically tuned to binocular disparity in the visual cortex (Barlow, Blakemore, & Pettigrew, 1967; Pettigrew, Nikara, & Biship, 1968). Also evident was a set of findings connecting motion perception to the properties of motion-selective cells. For example, the motion aftereffect and other effects of prolonged stimulation (Barlow, 1963; Barlow & Brindley, 1963; Sekuler & Ganz, 1963) were conceived of as the selective adaptation of hypothesized motion-selective cells in the human visual system.

As a consequence of these and other findings, there developed at least implicitly the notion of the visual system as a set of filters or detectors tuned to very specific sets of features. In each part of the visual field, there were receptors or detectors tuned to orientation, motion, bar width, and even depth. Vision, instead of being a hierarchical process, was conceived of as a set of separate dimensions, mapped onto the topographic map of the visual cortex.

Heretofore, visual stimuli had been described in fairly conventional terms; spatial extent, intensity, movement, and so on. This was soon to be replaced or at least temporarily overshadowed by descriptions less familiar, borrowing heavily from ideas developed in optics and electrical engineering, and in the process the idea of parallel channels became reinforced even further.

Perhaps the best example was the appropriation of linear systems analysis (including Fourier analysis) to describe visual function both psychophysically at the level of the whole organism and through electrophysiological experiments measuring the sensitivity of neurons in response to sine wave gratings. F. W. Campbell and colleagues argued that the contrast sensitivity curve obtained from human observers was the envelope of sensitivities of an underlying set of "channels," each sensitive to different ranges of spatial frequencies (Blakemore & Campbell, 1969; Campbell & Robson, 1968). The detection of a complex pattern could be predicted not by the peak-to-trough variations in luminance, but only by whether a given narrowly tuned mechanism had received sufficient contrast above its contrast threshold (Graham & Nachmias, 1971). The acceptance of these otherwise novel findings was strongly reinforced by an analysis of receptive field characteristics using linear theory. Thus, spatial-frequency tuning could be explained via the Fourier transform as the simple consequence of the spatial layout of Hubel and Wiesel's receptive fields, with their elongated strips of excitatory and inhibitory regions. These neurons were the same channels that determined the overall contrast sensitivity function. As such, the consequences of systems theory were significant. First, it provided a common metric or method of stimulus description that enabled one to link the behavior of single cells to the behavior of the whole organism. Second, it provided a rather different alternative to Hubel and Wiesel's conception of the receptive field.

Yet to those of us who had gratefully accepted Hubel and Wiesel's hierarchical edifice and who at least implicitly acknowledged at least some of the tenets of Barlow's neuron doctrine, these results seemed alien. For what possible reason could the visual system require such a coding scheme? The most extreme interpretation rested its case on Fourier's fundamental theorem. All functions, including the visual image, can be regarded as sums of sines and cosines. Thus, visual neurons could be conceived of as re-representing the image in terms of Fourier coefficients. This interpretation could not be strictly true, however, because even the narrowest receptive fields were localized and not fully distributed across the whole visual field as required. Less extreme is the now current idea of the representation of images in terms of wavelets, essentially Gabor functions, a hybrid representation, partaking some aspects of frequency analysis but also more localized in space. Such an interpretation suggested the utility of such units as a recoding of the image at different spatial scales, to enable the visual system to process different levels of spatial detail in an image. For example, for motion and stereopsis, there was some evidence that processing for low spatial frequencies had special precedence, and it was even argued that some types of object recognition also had preferential access to restricted sets of spatial frequency mechanisms (Parish & Sperling, 1991). More recently, Field (1994) has suggested that this narrow band tuning is the predicted outcome of a set of engineering constraints, the need to most efficiently code natural scenes (with their particular statistics) using a sparse code (where the majority neurons are inactive at any given moment).

Whatever the interpretation of these results, it appears that early visual receptive fields are indeed relatively narrowly tuned to spatial frequency. As such they are very much less selective to wide-band stimuli such as lines, bars, or gratings (DeValois, Albrecht, & Thorell, 1978). No longer could one regard Hubel or Wiesel's now classical receptive fields as detectors of the obvious visual elements in a scene, which are so evident to observers. One could not therefore regard receptive fields as the building blocks of our ordinary conscious visual perception, say as an artist or cartoonist would use lines and edges.

Thus greater currency of the visual system as a set of parallel channels continued to gain ground, and the spatial frequency findings only reinforced this view. Again, according to this view, each portion of the visual field was populated by so-called feature detectors or channels, each coding a different attribute of the image. Now it also included spatial frequency. Given this assortment of elementary units or "atoms" of vision, it would seem reasonable to see if one could understand the many phenomenon of visual perception in terms of receptive fields. Given some simple ways in which such channels might interact (either showing independence or coupled via inhibition), a wide range of applications of the receptive field concept to perceptual and cognitive phenomenon were attempted. Most successful were accounts about the visibility of fairly simple stimuli (Graham, 1989). As mentioned earlier, if the stimulus amplitude of the components of all possible neurons or channels were below their own individual thresholds, the pattern would remain invisible. This reinforced the view that visual sensitivity as measured by detection could be accounted for by the envelope of best sensitivity of all of the underlying neuronal receptive fields (Barlow, 1972).

The existence of cells with spatial frequency-selective cells sensitive to varying degrees of binocular disparity appeared to provide the beginnings of an explanation for the perceptual phenomenon of stereopsis. It also explained how perceived differences in depth in random dot stereograms could occur. Also satisfying was Adelson's missing fundamental illusion (Adelson & Bergen, 1985), where observers see motion in the direction of the most salient Fourier component rather than the motion of the overall pattern, which argued persuasively for the perceptual role of receptive fields. This coupled with the well-known waterfall effect (motion aftereffect) provided some of the strongest relations between perception and underlying mechanisms. Other equally ambitious but perhaps more ambiguous successes have been attempts to explain fine pattern discrimination (hyperacuity as coined by Westheimer, 1979) in terms of populations of receptive fields (Wilson, 1991). Even more ambitious efforts were seen in attempts to explain the characteristics of visual illusions (Wenderoth, 1992) and visual search behavior (Julesz, 1991; Treisman & Gelade, 1980) in terms of presumed elementary units. Here, however, the attempt was far less successful. Interactions of presumed visual channels could not explain the specific characteristics of visual illusions (see Gillam, chap. 5, this volume), and such channels were also found to lack any explanatory power in understanding visual search (Nakayama & Joseph, 1997). Also there was obvious failures in understanding what some might consider the simplest of visual domains, the perception of brightness. Originally, lateral inhibition, so closely related to the idea of receptive field surrounds was invoked (echoing Mach) in explaining various brightness and lightness illusions, such as simultaneous contrast and Mach Bands (see Ratliff, 1965). This approach has been largely abandoned, as there have been numerous demonstrations of much more powerful and more global influences (Adelson, 1993; Gilchrist et al., 1997; Land & McCann, 1971).

V. A VISUAL TAKEOVER: REDRAWING THE BRAIN

In the late 1970s a quiet revolution suddenly expanded the anatomical domain of vision. For many years, primary or striate cortex was deemed the presumed receiving area for vision, after which it would send its projections to "association" cortex. This fit well with the then current ideas of vision, inherited from British associationism, that a "picture of the world" was formed in the visual cortex. This was associated with other kinds of mental events in the brain (touch, sound, words, etc.), thus establishing the need for a large association cortex for the various connections to higher portions of the brain. Hubel and Wiesel (1962, 1965) largely confined their studies to the striate cortex but did confirm the existence of retinotopic areas anterior to and outside of striate cortex reported 20 years earlier using evoked potential methods (Talbot & Marshall, 1941). As such, there was an awareness of the existence of parastriate visual areas, but the full force of this realization was yet to come. This was to change dramatically, thanks to the pioneering efforts of a number of anatomically oriented neurophysiologists (Allman & Kaas, 1975; Zeki, 1975) and later Felleman and van Essen (1991). Using a variety of mapping techniques and drawing on several species of primate, it became clear that instead of 1 or perhaps 2 additional visual areas, at least 20 distinct areas could be identified. Not only were there many more distinct areas but, more importantly, the total cortical area devoted to vision expanded dramatically. It now comprised half of the brain, at least for the macaque monkey. The full consequences of these new findings cannot be exaggerated.

Within a few years, the relative importance of vision had increased dramatically, particularly when stacked against all other conceivable brain functions. Vision, which earlier was considered to deliver a mere picture of the world to be interpreted by other higher parts of the brain, had in itself become something much more. The enormous size and complexity of even half of the brain hinted to a comparable enormity for vision. The inevitable consequence of this territorial expansion was a much wider definition of what constituted vision. With this new visual "conquest" came an altered awareness of what this takeover had secured. For example, there had been a long tradition of painstaking analysis of degraded performance on various cognitive tasks following selective cerebral ablations in primates (Mishkin, 1982). These were originally considered to be explorations as to the physiological substrates of memory. Now with an expansion of vision extending well into the temporal lobe, the meaning of these studies changed in subtle but significant ways. Thus, the temporal lobe became identified not just with memory but was now linked to something more specifically visual, to a role in mediating visual object recognition. This realization in turn then supported otherwise puzzling and initially discounted findings, for example, that neurons in the temporal lobe selectively fired for specific high-level objects, particularly to faces (Gross, Rocha-Miranda, & Bender, 1972).

So, instead of considering vision as the simple creation of a picture projected onto the visual cortex, the existence of a greatly enlarged visual brain suggested that vision was not a single function but a staggering conglomerate of functions. This in turn led to a more systematic attempt to categorize such functions more globally. As an example, Ungerleider and Mishkin (1982) suggested that the many visual areas could be conceptually grouped in terms of gross anatomy, into a dorsal and a ventral system. They suggested a dorsal system projecting to the parietal lobes mediated functions related to spatial localization and a ventral system projecting to the temporal lobes mediating object recognition. More recently, this dichotomy has been further confirmed, although in a revised manner (Goodale, 1995), suggesting for the dorsal system, functions more closely related to visuomotor behavior.

In addition to the enlarged scope for vision, there was also a growing awareness as to vision's greater autonomy. Although not denying the connections of vision to other important functions, vision was now conceived as operating by rather vision-specific processes not so closely tied to other functions, particularly language (see Fodor, 1983).

VI. MARR'S INCLUSIVE FRAMEWORK

An important synthetic commentary on vision came from yet another quarter, primarily from artificial intelligence. Before describing David Marr's distinctive contributions, we mention some antecedents arising partly as a consequence of the mobilization of scientists for the war effort. These were the new disciplines of operations research, cybernetics, and information theory that emerged in the late 1940s. Physical systems were now described at a higher level of mathematical abstraction. Thus the concepts of feedback, information, stability, and so on, provided a language that could describe such systems in ways that were not closely tied to the physics of the machinery. As such, it also became a natural language to describe physiological as well as psychological systems. Thus by the mid-1970s there was already a long history in treating the brain more formally, independent of its physical characteristics. In psychology, the mind was now considered as an information-processing device, analogous to a computer (Neisser, 1967; Simon, 1968).

Against this background, Marr's (1982) contributions were more specifically inspired by early advances in artificial vision. Most critical was the work of a small group of founding pioneers who solved a restricted yet significant problem—that of correctly identifying the surfaces of multiple polyhedral objects represented in line drawings (Guzman, 1969; Huffmann, 1977; Waltz, 1975). They noted that there was a limited number of line junctions (L, T, fork, arrow, etc.) in such drawings. The interpretation of each junction considered by itself was ambiguous because multiple sets of three-dimensional (3D) surface configurations could have given rise to them (see Cutting & Massivoni, chap. 6, this volume). Nevertheless, if one considered the possible interpretation of line junctions in relation to neighboring junctions, recognizing that there must be consistency in the 3-D interpretation of the line joining neighboring junctions, a general solution to the polyhedral line drawing could be found. Line drawings of such objects could be correctly interpreted as 3-D scenes.

Critical for this early success was the notion of constraints. Line drawings of polyhedral objects are not arbitrary assemblages of lines but are the consequence of a lawful process of image formation dictated by the projection of 3-D scene onto a 2-D drawing surface. The understanding of this inherent grammar of junctional relations provided a powerful new way to understand vision *independent of the visual apparatus itself*. Recognizing the novel power of this approach, Marr's motivation was to adapt this way of thinking more broadly.

In generalizing beyond this artificially restricted world, Marr and colleagues followed the path parallel to that traversed earlier by J. J. Gibson (1950, 1966). Attempting to understand natural scenes instead of artificial and contrived visual worlds, Gibson's ecological optics provided an imaginative and rigorous analysis of the properties of the optic array as a potential carrier of information about the terrestrial world. Gibson's contribution was to see a rich underlying mathematical order in the optic array (see Cutting, chap. 4, this volume; Proffitt & Kaiser, chap. 7, this volume). Thus for Gibson there was much to be learned about vision from a purely optical analysis of the rules of image formation because the regularities and invariances here provided the key information about scenes and the observers relation to them (see also Nakayama, 1994).

Marr adopted this style of thinking and incorporated it as a key idea in his comprehensive framework to understand all of vision. Explaining vision, however, for Marr was a more complex affair than suggested by his predecessors; understanding could not come from a single perspective. For Marr it was critical to recognize the full scope of the endeavor—that vision required an explanation at many levels. Marr argued that a distinction between three separate levels of explanation was necessary—the computational, the algorithmic, and the level of implementation. The computational level—the most neglected and yet the most fundamental—rested on the type of analysis advocated by Gibson. It required the rigorous analysis of information available in the optic array in relation to the specific visual task. For example, from a mathematical analysis, it can be proven that if one assumes rigid motion, the full 3-D structure of an object can be computed given the image positions of points in three views (Ullman, 1979).

Having understood the computational problem there arises the need for an algorithmic explanation. How is the computation to be realized in a formal sense? For example, if the task were to compute the local motion of an image region a variety of algorithms could be considered based on the elementary operations of multiplication (Reichardt, 1961), addition (Adelson & Bergen, 1985), or division (Horn & Schunk, 1981). Marr suggested that the highly developed discipline of visual psychophysics was well suited to evaluate various candidate algorithms because each might fail in characteristic ways when subjected to the widest range of stimulus conditions.

A final level of description is that of neural implementation. How are the algorithms that solve the computational problem to be realized in neuronal hardware? For example, if the detection of motion requires the formal operation of multiplication or division (as required by Reichardt's model or gradient models) is there evidence that shunting inhibition is present in the cortex, and could it then mediate such an operation?

Over 10 years later, there has been much to criticize regarding these distinctions. Some have suggested that it proposed an optimality or grand design that was simply a hope rather than a scientific theory. Vision, rather than being a supremely adapted system, might be a series of adventitious processes that simply work well enough (see Kitcher, 1988; Ramachandran, 1985). Others, considering scientific tactics, have noted that advances rarely proceed by such a programmatic approach. Rather, knowledge about vision might bubble up in many unforeseen ways not along the route prescribed by Marr. Yet, the overall effect of these distinctions was positive, helping to delineate the various types of endeavors that had already emerged in the study of vision and to more clearly highlight the complementary rather than the competitive nature of various efforts.

In addition to distinguishing three different levels of explanation, Marr made another triple distinction, this time between different levels of visual representation. Acknowledging a greatly expanded visual system, Marr outlined three broad levels of analysis that vision must comprise. First was the level of the image or the primal sketch. This was perhaps the most familiar to physiologists and psychophysical workers and could be understood as mediated by receptive fields. Second was a viewpoint-specific intermediate level, the 2.5-D sketch where for each point in the visual field a surface-normal vector was represented. Third was a viewpoint independent level of visual object representation, where a full 3-D representation of the object resided.

The distinctions with different levels of processing were not unique to vision. In linguistics for example, the delineation between phonology, syntactics, and semantics was a crucial and influential one, clarifying the efforts required by keeping processes and questions distinct. With the explicit postulation of different levels of processing, one could more clearly see how specific research agendas could fit into a larger whole, even if Marr's particular levels would require substantial redefinition. Thus, the endeavor to understand vision as a series of filters was a reasonable way to examine early vision, say at the level of the image or primal sketch but perhaps not appropriate for the analysis of later representations. For example, there may exist visual processes related to object recognition that have little to do with the filtering aspects of earlier stages (see Ullman, 1995). My colleagues and I have been encouraged by Marr's distinctions and have postulated a distinct intermediate level of surface representation interposed between early vision and higher-level vision (Nakayama, He, & Shimojo, 1995). We argue that the encoding of surfaces has its own properties, not readily understood as emerging from the simple combination of cells with particular receptive fields. Thanks in part to Marr's distinction of separate levels, many researchers with very different interests and talents have been able to coexist almost peaceably, now recognizing their own efforts as a distinct part of a much larger endeavor.

In addition to these important distinctions, Marr and colleagues are also known for their more specific theories of visual processing, for motion, for edges and for stereo (Marr & Hildreth, 1980; Marr & Poggio, 1976; Marr & Ullman, 1981). These studies, important as they were at the time, have not had the same obvious influence. Yet here too, there have been indirect consequences. These papers attracted, perhaps by style as much as by substance, the attention of a wide range of scientific onlookers from the "hard" sciences, eager to test their mettle in a new field. Thus Marr and colleagues, like Hubel and Wiesel a generation earlier, captured the imagination of new talent.

VII. VISION FIN DE SIÈCLE

So where do researchers now find themselves at century's end? The picture I have painted so far has brought us up to the mid-1980s, shortly after Marr's posthumous publication (Marr, 1982). Because it is harder to capture events in the moment, I must be more cursory and yet cover a range of new developments.

A. Attention

First, there has been little said so far about the role of attention in vision. In fact, until fairly recently, it could not be easily observed in the laboratory and was not regarded as a major factor in perception. At best attention was seen as modulating vision, decreasing reaction time by a few tens of milliseconds. Only very recently has there been evidence, and it is now very compelling, that attention is not just a minor biasing factor in visual perception but that it is absolutely critical (see also Dosher & Sperling, chap. 8, this volume; Hochberg, chap. 9, this volume). In fact, evidence indicates that without attention, conscious perception simply does not occur (Mack, Tang, Tuma, & Kahn, 1992; Nakayama, Chun, & Joseph, 1997; Rensink, O'Regan, & Clark, 1997) confirming recent theoretical views (Nakayama, 1990; O'Regan, 1992) (for additional discussion to this point, see Hochberg, chap. 9, this volume). This suggests that the process of vision is a far more active one, perhaps more like exploratory touch as advocated earlier (Gibson, 1950; MacKay, 1973). Also related are new ideas suggesting that attention has an indexing or pointing function, marking items that are to be acted on or singled out for action (Allport, 1993; Ballard, Hayhoe, & Pelz, 1995). Along these lines, Cavanagh (1992) has suggested that the perception of motion can be understood as the active tracking of objects by attention. Such new findings and ideas about the indispensable role of attention provide the beginnings of an alternative view of vision, against the notion that vision is simply a sophisticated "picture."

B. Neuroimaging

One of the most significant developments in the last decade has been the explosive growth of the science of brain imaging in human subjects. After the initial discovery of X-rays, the most exciting advance came long after with computerized-axial-tomography (CAT), resting on a remarkable mathematical technique to reconstruct 3-D density map from a series of successive scans. This technique revolutionized the practice of clinical neurology and neuropsychology, which heretofore had to be satisfied with indirect behavioral testing. Later, and with an almost reckless invasiveness, PET emerged, using the brain itself as the source of some of the highest energy radiation ever used in a medical or biological setting. The addition of radioactive isotopes to the blood would lead to different image intensities depending on the brain's local need for more or less oxygen. Thus, those areas having the highest neural activity would have the greatest concentrations of gamma rays emerging from them. PET's promise was truly revolutionary for psychology and the brain sciences because it also provided a way to capture brain activity, not just structure.

Just as the virtues (and the dangers) of PET were to become more fully appreciated, MRI and fMRI superseded it. Based on radiation inherently less dangerous, it has more virtues than PET (much higher spatial and temporal resolution) but without the obvious risks. Presently, there are indications that eventually the resolution will be on a millimeter scale, such that one will be able to see selective activation of the ocular dominance columns of the striate cortex. Thus far most of the results from such methods have been largely confirmatory, but the promise of new and exciting findings is palpable. Potentially far reaching are successful efforts to make a map of the human visual system comparable to that outlined in the primate (Tootell, Dale, Sereno, & Malach, 1996).

C. Neuropsychology

Related to advances in neuroimaging are new developments in the examination of brain-damaged patients. Much of the recent impetus comes from new efforts to apply methods and concepts derived from cognitive psychology and visual psychophysics to disordered function. This has attracted new investigators to complement existing neuropsychological efforts. Moreover, the new techniques of brain imaging allow independent assessment as to the site of brain damage, enabling a stronger cross-comparison of so many of the new and specific deficits. Over the past few years clinical cases have been reported that demonstrate the existence of extremely specialized deficits—the inability to recognize faces, colors, as well as deficits in seeing motion. Each has its likely brain locus as well. These dramatic findings add weight to the emerging view that the visual system is indeed a very separate set of brain functions, and that even within vision itself there might be countless more specialized modules.

D. A Possible Rebirth of Gestalt Psychology?

As mentioned earlier in regard to psychophysics of receptive fields, the attempt to link receptive field characteristics to perception was strongly tied to the idea of the visual system as a series of passive filters analyzing the image at all portions of the visual field. Thus, the study of vision became a problem of systems engineering, trying to adduce the identity and characteristics of the fundamental filters using rigorous/quantitative psychophysics and quantitative modeling (see Dosher & Sperling, chap. 8, this volume). Regrettably, this significant yet specialized approach greatly overshadowed a richer and once vigorous tradition of research initiated by the Gestalt psychologists and their followers in Germany and Europe (Ash, 1995).

Even though all three leaders of the Gestalt movement were able to migrate to America at the peak of their influence (Koffka came to Smith College in 1927, Wertheimer to the New School in 1934, Kohler to Swarthmore in 1935), their trans-Atlantic move was largely a failure, particularly considering the great strength of their movement in Germany. In part this was the result of America's succumbing to behaviorism and positivism. Perhaps as decisive was the problem of scientific lineage and renewal. Few graduate students were trained to take up positions of needed leadership (Swarthmore and Smith were undergraduate institutions). Also significant was the ideological corner that Kohler permitted himself to become painted into (he alone survived into the postwar years). Kohler was seen to be a defender of a defunct global brain field theory which treated the brain as a more or less homogeneous, self-organizing, physical media, ignoring the role of specific neuronal connections. As such, proper credit for the more solid achievements of the Gestalt tradition in fundamental perceptual research was lost amidst the distaste for Kohler's Gestalt theory. By midcentury, the Gestalt tradition of vision research in America was essentially extinct (cf. Hochberg, chap. 9, this volume).

It is fortunate that Gestalt psychology still had a few vigorous and active adherents in Europe, among them Metzger (1936) in Germany and Kanizsa in Italy. The work of Kanizsa represents perhaps the best example of a continuing Gestalt tradition in perception (see Kanizsa, 1979). In contrast to Kohler, who was preoccupied with philosophical issues relating brain states to perception, Kanizsa followed a more phenomenological approach, carefully crafting sets of demonstrations to make important theoretical points about perception. One of his greatest contributions was his work on perceptual completion, the automatic visual propensity to complete figures either in back of occluding figures (amodal completion) or in front of them (modal completion) forming the now well-known illusory contours. Kanizsa suggested that these processes were exclusively visual, distinct from higher-order thinking despite the fact that such processes also seemed to show "intelligence," enabling the visual system to encode the world from sparse information. As such, Kanizsa's approach was an advance over the preceding Gestalt tradition, which was more static, preoccupied with "laws" linked perhaps to internal states rather than towards the goal of picking up information (see also Hochberg, chap. 9, this volume, for additional discussion of Gestalt psychology). Kanizsa's demonstrations now grace textbooks and contemporary research papers and form the foundation of a growing emphasis on midlevel vision, roughly analogous to Marr's 2.5-D sketch but based on a richer empirical data base (see also Nakayama et al., 1995).

Along with the greater recognition of Kanizsa's work came the implicit acceptance of visual phenomenology. After years of generalized suspicion associated with the results of Gestalt psychology, even the most tough-minded temperaments could not fail to be moved by a compelling perceptual demonstration. It helped, of course, that one of the most dramatic demonstrations, the Julesz random dot stereogram, could be interpreted at a mechanistic level. Strong demonstrations by Ramachandran and Gregory (1978) were soon to follow, showing a curious disassociation of color and motion. So, phenomenology, one of the staples of Gestalt psychology, is again back, popular, and nearly respectable. It has worked mainly for studies of early and midlevel vision, but there are also hopeful indications that it may be useful for higher-order vision, say object recognition (Thompson, 1980; see also Nakayama et al., 1995 for some additional justifications for the phenomenological method).

E. Dissociation of Conscious Visual Perception and Behavior

The Gestalt psychologists insisted that the phenomenology of visual experience must be the starting point to understand vision. Behavioristically oriented psychologists on the other hand were happy to ignore the issue of conscious experience, asking human observers or animals to make differential responses. Already limited as these traditions were, each would be even further taxed when confronted by a new disassociation—between conscious phenomenal experience and visuomotor behavior. First are examples of patients with brain lesions who are deficient in the conscious perception of a visual stimulus but act appropriately when urged to perform a motor response. Thus patients with hemianopia (resulting from striate cortex damage on one side) can reach appropriately for targets in the blind hemifields showing the phenomenon of blind sight. Milner and Goodale (1995) report the case of an agnosic patient who cannot consciously report the orientation of a large bar but who can correctly orient their hand when asked to regard it as a mail slot and to post a letter.

Against the possibility that these clinical cases represent rare curiosities, analogous phenomenon can also be seen in healthy human subjects. These have taken a number of forms. First are situations where persons perceive a visual configuration erroneously, whereas their motor system acts otherwise. One of the early studies indicated that the pattern of eye movements to misperceived spatial positions (occasioned by induced movement) was normal (Wong & Mack, 1981). Other studies show that observers did not perceive shifts of simple visual scenes during eye movements, but their subsequent unnoticed fixations belied this (Bridgeman, Hendry & Stark, 1975). More convincing perhaps are extended behaviors that have little opportunity for correction after repeated errors. Loomis, da Silva, Fujita, and

Fukusima (1992) show that observers consistently misjudge the distances of objects along a ground plane when queried by various psychophysical methods yet show veridical representation, at least implicitly, by walking blindfolded to distant points with surprising accuracy and ease.

The issue of dissociation between conscious perception and behavior has had a long history in psychology, going back to early studies on subliminal perception (McGinnies, 1949). Reviving this seemingly discredited topic, Marcel (1983) reported that observers cannot "see" a very short-duration stimulus that is quickly followed by a mask. Yet such stimuli facilitate the recognition of semantically related words presented subsequently. Although this finding has not been replicated, more recent studies using a wide variety of different methods argue for some form of dissociation. These studies report repeatable instances where observers cannot report the presentation of a particular stimulus, but there is evidence that it has been encoded rather fully. An interesting example is the phenomenon of repetition blindness, where observer's cannot report the presence of a repeated stimuli in an overlapping succession of letters, words, or pictures (Kanwisher & Potter, 1990). The "attentional blink," another form of "blindness" occurs after observers identify a critical target in a stream of letters or words (Raymond, Shapiro, & Arnell, 1992), yet show (via event-related potentials) that semantic processing of the unreported word occurs nevertheless (Luck, Vogel, & Shapiro, 1996). These are surprising and as yet controversial findings. If replicated and more fully described, they would force us to rethink vision both methodologically and conceptually. First, it suggests that the traditional methods of visual perception and psychophysics are probably too restrictive and may conceal what may be some of the most important factors in determining what aspects of a scene we visually encode. Using an unusual paradigm where observers do not expect additional visual stimuli, Mack and Rock (in press) show a surprising degree of inattentional blindness to what would seem to be the most obvious stimuli, including large shapes and moving patterns in a relatively uncluttered field. What is of particular interest is the fact that highly significant patterns requiring visual coding at rather semantic levels (one's own name, a happy face) appear to break through this inattentional blindness. This implies that a high level of semantic analysis can determine what is seen. Continuing the point regarding vision's analogy with touch (as originally outlined by Gibson and MacKay and mentioned earlier) and regarding the deployment of attention as analogous to a motor response, we might profitably regard the direction of attention as another example of motor responses controlled without visual awareness.

Taken together, the foregoing results indicate the possibility of a very different conception of vision and action from that currently conceived (see also the discussion of Hochberg, chap. 9, this volume). Our commonsense view is that we see and then we act. If the foregoing results are more representative of our normal vision and motor behavior, we may require some rather drastic reworking of our basic metapsychological and philosophical assumptions to move forward.

VIII. A REDUCTIONISTIC EXPLANATION FOR PERCEPTION IN THE 21ST CENTURY?

In surveying the achievements of the past 100 years, one cannot help being impressed by the tremendous progress yet also be aware of how limited our fundamental understanding is. Part of the reason of course has been the "growth" of the visual system, now comprising so much more of the brain's territory and with it so many more functions. The sheer size of the visual system should be our constant reminder as to the enormity of vision. Marr suggested at least three levels of visual representation, yet there may be many more. Yet even this idea of levels, especially if conceived of as a simple serial process, is bound to be wrong or, perhaps even worse, misleading. With so much of the brain devoted to vision and with the growing appreciation of new and unforeseen specializations as well as the humbling recognition of our own conceptual shortcomings, it would seem short-sighted to demand or to seek exclusively for reductionistic explanations. Yet, we must not rule out the possibility of substantial progress even here. The "single-unit" receptive field notion, worn though it is, has survived because there has been no evident replacement. It has not been for a lack of effort and some specific proposals are fairly well known. If some other more compelling unit of analysis were to emerge, say at a larger scale than single neurons themselves (Abeles, 1991; Edelman, 1987) or even smaller ones, the field could be transformed. Thus, we should salute valiant attempts to understand vision reductionistically, but we should also be mindful that the most important insights about vision are likely to come from almost any quarter. Large integrative theories in sciences can have an equal or even greater impact than mechanistic ones. Darwin's theory of evolution and Wegener's theory of continental drift are diverse examples. If the present is any guide, the next century promises riches to those of many persuasions. In a generation hence, I have the hopeful confidence that many will marvel at the achievements of the recent past.

Acknowledgments

Supported in part from grants from the Air Force Office of Scientific Research, the McKnight Foundation, and the Human Frontier Science Project. Thanks to Charles F. Stromeyer for critical reading of an earlier version of this chapter.

References

Abeles, M. (1991). *Corticonics: Neural circuits of the cerebral cortex.* New York: Cambridge University Press.
Adelson, E. H., & Bergen, J. (1985). Spatiotemporal energy models for the perception of motion. *Journal of the Optical Society of America, 2,* 284–299.
Adelson, E. H. (1993). Perceptual organization and the judgment of brightness. *Science, 262,* 2042–2043.
Allman, J. M., & Kaas, J. H. (1975). The dorsomedial cortical visual area: A third tier area in the occipital lobe of the owl monkey (Aotus trivirgatus). *Brain Research, 100,* 473–487.

Allport, A. (1993). Attention and control: Have we been asking the wrong questions? A critical review of twenty-five years. In D. E. Meyer & S. Kornblum (Eds.), *Attention and performance XIV: Synergies in experimental psychology, artificial intelligence and cognitive neuroscience* (pp. 183–218). Cambridge, MA: MIT Press.

Ash, M. G. (1995). *Gestalt Psychology in German culture 1890–1967: Holism and the quest for objectivity.* New York: Cambridge University Press.

Ballard, D. H., Hayhoe, M. M., & Pelz, J. B. (1995). Memory representations in natural tasks. *Journal of Cognitive Neuroscience, 7,* 66–80.

Barlow, H. B. (1972). Single units and sensation: A neuron doctrine for perceptual psychology? *Perception, 1,* 371–394.

Barlow, H. B. (1963). Evidence for a physiological explanation of the waterfall phenomenon and figural after-effects. *Nature, 200*(4913), 1345–1346.

Barlow, H. B. (1953). Summation and inhibition in the frog's retina. *Journal of Physiology, 119*(1), 69–88.

Barlow, H. B., Blakemore, C., & Pettigrew, J. D. (1967). The neural mechanism of binocular depth discrimination. *Journal of Physiology, 193,* 327–342.

Barlow, H. B., & Brindley, G. S. (1963). Inter-ocular transfer of movement after effects during pressure blinding of the stimulated eye. *Nature, 200,* 1346–1347.

Barlow, H. B., & Hill, R. M. (1963). Selective sensitivity to direction of movement in ganglion cells of the rabbit retina. *Science, 139*(3443), 412–414.

Blakemore, C., & Campbell, F. W. (1969). On the existence of neurones in the human visual system selectively sensitive to the orientation and size of retinal images. *Journal of Physiology, 203,* 237–260.

Berkeley, G. (1709). *An essay towards a new theory of vision.* Dublin: Aaron Rhames.

Bridgeman, B., Hendry, D., & Stark, L. (1975). Failure to detect displacement of the visual world during saccadic eye movements. *Vision Research, 15,* 719–722.

Campbell, F. W., & Robson, J. G. (1968). Application of Fourier analysis to the visibility of gratings. *Journal of Physiology, 197,* 551–566.

Cavanagh, P. (1992). Attention-based motion perception. *Science, 257,* 1563–1565.

Cleland, B. G., Dubin, M. W., & Levick, W. R. (1971). Sustained and transient neurones in the cat's retina and lateral geniculate nucleus. *Journal of Physiology* (London), *217,* 473–496.

DeValois, R. L., Albrecht, D. G., & Thorell, L. G. (1978). Cortical cells: bar and edge detectors, or spatial frequency filters? In S. J. Cool & E. L. Smith (Eds.), *Frontiers of visual science* (pp. 544–556). New York: Springer-Verlag.

Edelman, G. M. (1987). *Neural Darwinism: The theory of neuronal group selection.* New York: Basic Books.

Fechner, G. T. (1860). *Elemente der Psychophysik.* Leipzig.

Felleman, D. J., & van Essen, D. C. (1991). Distributed hierarchical processing in the primate cerebral cortex. *Cerebral Cortex, 1,* 1–47.

Field, D. J. (1994). What is the goal of sensory coding? *Neural Computation, 6,* 559–601.

Finger, S. (1994). *Origins of neuroscience, a history of explorations into brain function.* New York: Oxford University Press.

Fodor, J. (1983). *Modularity of mind: An essay on faculty psychology.* Cambridge, MA: MIT Press.

Gibson, J. J. (1966). *The senses considered as perceptual systems.* Boston: Houghton-Mifflin.

Gibson, J. J. (1950). *The perception of the visual world.* Boston: Houghton-Mifflin.

Gilchrist, A., Kossyfidis, C., Bonato, F., Agostini, T., Cataliotti, J., Li, X., & Spehar, B. (1997). *A new theory of lightness perception.* Unpublished manuscript.

Goodale, M. A. (1995). The cortical organization of visual perception and visuomotor control. In S. M. Kosslyn & D. N. Osherson (Eds.), *Visual cognition.* Cambridge, MA: MIT Press.

Graham, N. (1989). *Visual pattern analyzers.* New York: Oxford University Press.

Graham, N., & Nachmias, J. (1971). Detection of grating patterns containing two spatial frequencies: A comparison of single-channel and multiple-channel models. *Vision Research, 11,* 251–259.

Gross, C. G., Rocha-Miranda, C. E., & Bender, D. B. (1972). Visual properties of neurons in inferotemporal cortex of the macaque. *Journal of Neurophysiology, 35,* 96–111.

Guzman, A. (1969). Decomposition of a visual scene into three-dimensional bodies. In A. Grasselli (Ed.), *Automatic interpretation and classification of images.* New York: Academic Press.

Hebb, D. O. (1949). *The organization of behavior: A neuropsychological theory.* New York: John Wiley and Sons.

Hecht, S., Shlaer, S., & Pirenne, M. H. (1942). Energy, quanta, and vision. *Journal of Genetics and Physiology, 25,* 819–840.

Helmholtz, H. von (1962). *Physiological optics.* (Trans.). New York: Dover. (Original work published 1909)

Hering, E. (1868). *Die Lehre vom Bihocularen Sehen.* Leipzig: Verlag von Wilhelm Engelmann.

Hull, C. L. (1943). *Principles of behavior.* New York: Appleton-Century.

Horn, B. K., & Schunk, B. G. (1980). Determining optical flow. *Artificial Intelligence, 17,* 185–203.

Hubel, D. H., & Wiesel, T. N. (1959). Receptive fields of single neurones in the cat's striate cortex. *Journal of Physiology, 148,* 574–591.

Hubel, D. H., & Wiesel, T. N. (1962). Receptive fields, binocular interaction and functional architecture in the cat's visual cortex. *Journal of Physiology,* London, *160,* 106–154.

Huffman, D. A. (1977). Realizible configurations of lines in pictures of polyhedra. *Machine Intelligence, 8,* 493–509.

James, W. (1961). *Psychology: The briefer course.* New York: Harper. (Original work published 1892)

Joseph, J. S., Chun, M. M., & Nakayama, K. (1997). Attentional requirements in a "pre-attentive" feature search task. *Nature, 387,* 805–807.

Julesz, B. (1960). Binocular depth perception of computer-generated patterns. *Bell Syst. Tech. J., 29,* 1125–1162.

Julesz, B. (1971). *The foundations of cyclopean perception.* Chicago: University of Chicago Press.

Julesz, B. (1991). Early vision and focal attention. *Review of Modern Physics, 63*(3), 735–772.

Kanizsa, G. (1979). *Organization in vision: Essays on gestalt perception.* New York: Praeger.

Kanwisher, N. G., & Potter, M. C. (1990). Repetition blindness: Levels of processing. *Journal of Experimental Psychology, 16,* 30–47.

Kitcher, P. (1988). Marr's computational theory of vision. *Philosophy of Science, 55,* 1–24.

Kohler, W. (1924). Die Physischen Gestalten in Ruhe und im stationaren Zustand. Erlangen: Verlag der Philosophischen Akademie.

Kohler, W. (1947). *Gestalt psychology, an introduction to new concepts in modern psychology.* New York: Liveright.

Kuffler, S. W. (1953). Discharge patterns and functional organization of the mammalian retina. *Journal of Neurophysiology, 16,* 37–68.

Land, E. H., & McCann, J. J. (1971). Lightness and retinex theory. *Journal of the Optical Society of America, 61,* 1–11.

Lennie, P. (1980). Parallel visual pathways: a review. *Vision Research, 20,* 561–594.

Lettvin, J. Y., Maturana, H. R., McCulloch, W. S., & Pitts, W. H. (1959). What the frog's eye tells the frog's brain. *Proceedings of the Institute of Radio Engineers, 47,* 1940–1951.

Lettvin, J. Y., Maturana, H. R., Pitts, W. H., & McCulloch, W. S. (1961). Two remarks on the visual system of the frog. In W. A. Rosenblith (Ed.), *Sensory communication.* New York: MIT Press and John Wiley and Sons.

Loomis, J. M., da Silva, J. A., Fujita, N., & Fukusima, S. S. (1992). Visual space perception and visually directed action. *Journal of Experimental Psychology,* HPP, *18,* 906–921.

Luck, S. J., Vogel, E. K., & Shapiro, K. L. (1996). Word meanings can be accessed but not reported during the attentional blink. *Nature, 383,* 616–618.

Mack, A., Tang, B., Tuma, R., & Kahn, S. (1992). Perceptual organization and attention. *Cognitive Psychology, 24,* 475–501.

Mack, A., & Rock, I. (in press). *Inattentional blindness: Perception without attention.* Cambridge, MA: MIT Press.

MacKay, D. M. (1973). Visual stability and voluntary eye movements. In R. Jung (Ed.), *Handbook of sensory physiology* (pp. 307–331). Berlin: Springer.

Marcel, A. J. (1983). Conscious and unconscious perception: Experiments on visual masking and word recognition. *Cognitive Psychology, 15,* 197–237.

Marr, D. (1982). *Vision.* San Francisco, CA: Freeman.

Marr, D., & Hildreth, E. (1980). Theory of edge detection. Proceedings of the Royal Society of London, *B 207,* 187–217.

Marr, D., & Poggio, T. (1976). Cooperative computation of stereo disparity. *Science, 194,* 283–287.

Marr, D., & Ullman, S. (1981). Directional selectivity and its use in early visual processing. *Proceedings of the Royal Society of London, B 211,* 151–180.

McGinnies, E. (1949). Emotionality and perceptual defense. *Psychological Review, 39,* 244–251.

Milner, A. D., & Goodale, M. A. (1995). *The visual brain in action.* New York: Oxford University Press.

Metzger, W. (1936). *Gesetze des Sehens.* Frankfurt am Main: W. Kramer.

Mishkin, M. (1982). A memory system in the monkey. Philos. Trans. *Royal Society of London* (Biol), *278,* 85–92.

Nakayama, K. (1990). The iconic bottleneck and the tenuous link between early visual processing and perception. In C. Blakemore (Ed.), *Vision: Coding and efficiency* (pp. 411–422). Cambridge, MA: Cambridge University Press.

Nakayama, K. (1994). *James J. Gibson—An Appreciation. Psychological Review, 101,* 329–335.

Nakayama, K., He, Z. J., & Shimojo, S. (1995). Visual surface representation: a critical link between lower-level and higher level vision. In S. M. Kosslyn & D. N. Osherson (Eds.), *Visual cognition* (pp. 1–70). Cambridge, MA: MIT Press.

Nakayama, K., Chun, M. M., & Joseph, J. (in press). Attention, pattern recognition and popout in visual search. In R. Parasuraman (Ed.), *The attentive brain.* Cambridge, MA: MIT Press.

Neisser, U. (1967). *Cognitive psychology.* New York: Appleton Century Crofts.

O'Regan, K. (1992). Solving the "Real" mysteries of visual perception: The world as an outside memory. *Canadian Journal of Psychology, 46,* 461–488.

Parish, D. H., & Sperling, G. (1991). Object spatial frequencies, retinal spatial frequencies, noise and the efficiency of letter discrimination. *Vision Research, 31,* 1399–1415.

Pettigrew, J. D., Nikara, T., & Biship, P. O. (1968). Binocular interaction on single units in cat striate cortex: Simultaneous stimulation by single moving slit with receptive fields in correspondence. *Experimental Brain Research, 6,* 391–410.

Pavlov, I. P. (1957). *Experimental psychology and other essays.* New York: Philosophical Library.

Ramachandran, V. S. (1985). The neurobiology of perception. Guest editorial. *Perception, 14,* 97–104.

Ramachandran, V. S., & Gregory, R. L. (1978). Does colour provide an input to human motion perception? *Nature* (London) *275,* 55–56.

Ratliff, F. (1965). *Mach bands: Quantitative studies on neural networks in the retina.* San Francisco: Holden-Day.

Raymond, J. E., Shapiro, K. L., & Arnell, K. M. (1992). Temporary suppression of visual processing in an RSVP task: An attentional blink? *Journal of Experimental Psychology: Human Perception and Performance, 18,* 849–860.

Reichardt, W. (1961). Autocorrelation, a principle for the evaluation of sensory information by the central nervous system. In R. W. A. (Ed.), *Sensory communication.* New York: Wiley.

Rensink, R. R., O'Regan, J. K., & Clark, J. J. (1995). Image flicker is as good as saccades in making large scene changes invisible. *Perception, 24*(suppl.), 26–27.

Rensink, R. A., O'Regan, J. K., & Clark, J. J. (1997). To see or not to see: The need for attention to perceive changes in scenes. *Psychological Science, 8,* 368–373.

Rubin, E. (1921). *Synsoplevede Figur* (Copenhagen, 1915) trans. *Visuell wahrgemonnene Figuren.* Copenhagen, 1921: Gyldendalske Boghandel.

Simon, H. A. (1968). *The sciences of the artificial.* Cambridge, MA: MIT Press.

Schwann, T. (1839). *Mikroscopische Untersuchungen uber die Uberreinstimmung in der Structure und dem Wachsthum der Thiere und Pflanzen.* Berlin: G. E. Reimer.

Sekuler, R. W., & Ganz, L. (1963). Aftereffect of seen motion with a stabilized retinal image. *Science, 139*(3553), 419–420.

Shapley, R. M. (1990). Visual sensitivity and parallel retinocortical channels. *Annual Review of Psychology, 41,* 635–658.

Stiles, W. S. (1959). Color vision: the approach through increment-threshold sensitivity. *Proceedings of National Academy of Science, 45,* 100–114.

Stone, J. (1972). Morphology and physiology of the geniculo-cortical synapse in the cat: the question of parallel input to the striate cortex. *Investigating Ophthalmology, 11,* 338–346.

Talbot, S. A., & Marshall, W. H. (1941). Physiological studies on neural mechanisms of visual localization and discrimination. *American Journal of Ophthalmology, 24,* 1255–1263.

Thompson, P. (1980). Margaret Thatcher: A new illusion. *Perception, 9,* 483–484.

Treisman, A., & Gelade, G. (1980). A feature-integration theory of attention. *Cognitive Psychology, 12,* 97–136.

Tootell, R. B. H., Dale, A. M., Sereno, M. I., & Malach, R. (1996). New images from the human visual cortex. *Trends in the Neurosciences, 19,* 481–489.

Turner, R. S. (1994). *In the eye's mind: Vision and the Helmholtz-Hering controversy.* Princeton: Princeton University Press.

Ullman, S. (1979). *The interpretation of visual motion.* Cambridge, MA: MIT Press.

Ullmann, S. (1996). *High level vision.* Cambridge, MA: MIT Press.

Ungerleider, L. G., & Mishkin, M. (1982). Two cortical visual systems. In D. J. Ingle, M. A. Goodale, & R. J. W. Mansfield (Eds.), *Analysis of visual behavior.* Cambridge, MA: MIT Press.

Waltz, D. (1975). Understanding line drawings of scenes with shadows. In P. H. Winston (Ed.), *The psychology of computer vision.* New York: McGraw-Hill.

Waldeyer-Hartz, W. V. (1891). Uber einige neuere Forschungen im Bebiete der Anatomie des Centralnervensystems. *Deutsche medizinische Wochenschrift, 17,* 1213–1218.

Wenderoth, P. (1992). Perceptual illusions. *Australian Journal of Psychology, 44,* 147–151.

Wertheimer, M. (1912). Experimentelle studien uber das sehen von bewegung. *Zeitschrift fur Psychologie, 61,* 161–265.

Westheimer, G. (1979). The spatial sense of the eye. *Invest. Ophthalmol. Vis. Sci., 18,* 893–912.

Wheatstone, C. (1838). On some remarkable, and hitherto unobserved, phenomena of binocular vision. *Philosophical Transactions of the Royal Society of London B128,* 371–394.

Wilson, H. R. (1991). Pattern discrimination, visual filters, and spatial sampling irregularity. In M. S. Landy & J. A. Movshon (Eds.), *Computational models of visual processing.* Cambridge, MA: MIT Press.

Wong, E., & Mack, A. (1981). Saccadic programming and perceived location. *Acta psychologia, 48,* 123–131.

Young, T. (1802). On the theory of light and colors. *Philosophical Transactions of the Royal Society, 92,* 20–71.

Zeki, S. (1975). The functional organization of projections from striate to pre-striate visual cortex in the rhesus monkey. *Cold Spring Harbor Symposium Quantum Biology, 40,* 591–600.

CHAPTER 11

Nature, Nurture, and Development

Elizabeth S. Spelke

I. INTRODUCTION

How can human knowledge both be adapted to human experience and go beyond the evidence that experience provides? How can knowledge show both diversity, and universal properties, across different societies and cultures? How different would human systems of knowledge be if humans were to grow up in a radically different environment? Why do humans develop some domains of knowledge rapidly and with ease, and yet persist in reasoning erroneously, and with great effort, in other domains? Finally, how do humans develop systems of knowledge that are unique in the living world, from mechanisms and processes that appear to be closely similar to those of other animals?

After a century of intense study, the answers to these questions are still elusive. Nevertheless, psychologists have made considerable progress in characterizing the development of basic systems of human knowledge, and their characterizations hint at answers to deeper questions. In this chapter, I sketch some of the empirical progress made in the study of cognitive development, focusing on research on one topic in perceptual development (space perception), one topic on the border between perception and cognition (object perception and representation), and one topic in cognitive development (number). Although the sketches will emphasize what has been learned in these domains, each sketch will end with a set of persisting questions. In closing, I will suggest tentative answers to some of these questions and a path for future research.

Perception and Cognition at Century's End

II. DEVELOPMENT OF PERCEPTION OF DEPTH AND DISTANCE

The ability to apprehend a stable, three-dimensional layout from changing, two-dimensional patterns of optical stimulation has long occupied a central place in the dialogue between nativist and empiricist theories of perception. On the former views, the human visual system is intrinsically built to interpret particular patterns of stimulation as specifying particular arrangements of objects; on the latter views, humans learn such interpretations by looking around the world and acting upon it. These contrasting possibilities continue to guide research on perceptual development.

At the start of this century, debates about the origins and development of visual depth perception focused primarily on the findings of studies of the modifiability of depth perception in adults, coupled with arguments of logic, parsimony, and plausibility about the probable origins of modifiable systems. Studies of adaptation to inverting or displacing prisms suggested that depth perception showed considerable flexibility in the face of changing optical conditions: On first looking through new lenses, the world appeared distorted and actions were perturbed; with prolonged viewing, the world began to look more predictable, and skilled actions resumed (e.g., Helmholtz, 1867/1962; Stratton, 1897). In addition, studies of the information specifying depth and layout revealed that depth perception depends on a number of parameters that change with postnatal growth, including the size of the eyes and the distance between them, suggesting that the processes for recalibrating space perception found in adults are needed in children as well (again, Helmholtz, 1867/1962). If children have mechanisms for learning new relations between optical stimulation and perceived depth, however, then parsimony considerations suggest that they are not endowed with innate systems for perceiving depth as well. A nativist theory of space perception would appear to be "an unnecessary hypothesis" (Helmholtz, 1867/1962, vol. 3, p. 17).

More recent studies of perceptual adaptation have undercut aspects of this argument. The extent of the adaptability of the mature visual system to changes in the relation between optical stimulation and perceived depth has been called into question (e.g., Harris, 1965), as has the relation between learning in infants and relearning in adults (Bedford, 1989; cf. Ghahramani, Wolpert, & Jordan, 1996). If adaptation in adults depended on local remappings between visual and haptic information, for example, then such remappings also might account for the initial development of depth perception. If adaptation in adults, and adaptation to growth-induced changes in childhood, instead depend on a global recalibration of visual information, then the adaptation process itself might require an initially structured system for perceiving depth.

These developments suggest that logical arguments, coupled with studies of the learning capabilities of mature perceivers, are no substitute for direct investigations of perceptual development in children. Fortunately, the present century has seen a flowering of developmental studies. I focus here on three lines of research from the disciplines of developmental neurobiology, psychophysics, and behavioral ecology.

A. Developmental Neurobiology of Spatial Vision

Mature perception of the spatial layout depends on elaborate and precise patterns of connectivity in the visual pathways. Major insights into the nature of these patterns have been achieved in the second half of this century, beginning with Hubel and Wiesel's studies of the response properties of individual neurons in the visual cortex (see also Nakayama, chap. 10, this volume, for discussion). The discovery of cortical neurons in the adult cat and monkey that respond to edges at particular orientations and in particular regions of the visual field, organized in an exquisite topographic arrangement, has begun to unravel the code by which the mammalian visual system represents the positions of surface features in the visual field. The discovery that neurons relaying signals from the retina of each eye (the retinal ganglion cells) project to cells in different layers of a subcortical nucleus (the lateral geniculate nucleus or LGN), which in turn project to alternating bands of cells in the input layer of the primary visual cortex (the "ocular dominance columns"), begins to clarify the neural basis of stereoscopic depth perception, a process for computing depth from the relative positions of the projections of surface features to the two eyes. Importantly, psychophysical studies and functional brain imaging studies of normal humans and of patients with brain damage suggest that the basic organization found in the visual system of cats, monkeys, and other mammals exists in humans (see Goodale, 1995; Sereno & Allman, 1991). To a first approximation, therefore, studies of the development of neural connectivity in the visual systems of other mammals should shed light on this development in humans as well.

From Hubel and Wiesel's earliest investigations, studies of developing animals and of animals reared in darkness or with altered vision have probed the development of this neural organization. Studies of the development of layers of monocularly driven cells in the LGN and of the ocular dominance columns reveal that cells in both structures initially receive input from both eyes, and that the layered and striped patterns form later in development. Because the layered pattern in the LGN emerges prior to birth both in cats and in monkeys, visual experience evidently is not necessary for its development (see Shatz, 1992). In monkeys, the pattern of ocular dominance columns also is discernible at birth (Rakic, 1977). In both cats and monkeys, however, the pattern of ocular dominance columns undergoes considerable postnatal development, and so experiments have investigated the influence of visual experience on this development.

The most direct studies have compared the development of the ocular dominance columns in cats or monkeys reared in darkness to those of animals reared with normal vision. Ocular dominance columns were found to develop normally in dark-reared animals of both species (LeVay, Wiesel, & Hubel, 1980; Sherk & Stryker, 1976), providing evidence that visual experience is not necessary for shaping or sharpening this pattern. In further studies, animals were raised with a single eye occluded, and then visual function was assessed and patterns of connectivity from each eye to the primary visual cortex were mapped. Such monocular deprivation was found to have a marked effect both on an animal's ability to see with the occluded eye and on the relative widths of the alternating bands of ocular dominance, with wider bands of cells receiving inputs from the nonoccluded eye (LeVay et al., 1980). Nevertheless, the banded pattern of organization was discernible even in animals who had only viewed the world through one eye. These findings suggest that the basic pattern of binocular connectivity to the cortex is innate but can be influenced by visual experience that is systematically biased (LeVay et al., 1980).

A concerted goal of developmental neurobiology, since the time of these discoveries, has been to investigate the mechanisms by which visual experience comes to influence the connectivity and the functioning of the brain. Although these mechanisms have not been conclusively isolated, a growing consensus suggests that they operate in accord with principles articulated fifty years ago by Hebb (1949), following centuries of empiricist proposals (see Hochberg, chapter 9, section III.A.3, this volume; Proffitt & Kaiser, chap. 7, this volume). Hebb suggested that the connection between a neuron and its target is strengthened when the firing of the former is immediately followed by the firing of the latter. Because the firing of a target is more likely when many of the neurons that impinge upon it fire in concert, Hebb's principle implies the selective strengthening of connections from synchronously firing neurons to their common targets. When only one eye receives visual stimulation, synchronous activity in the visual pathway from that eye to the cortex may outweigh any such activity in the pathway from the occluded eye, increasing the active eye's cortical territory.

In addition to these studies of experience effects, neurobiologists have probed the developmental mechanisms that give rise to organized patterns of connectivity in the absence of visual experience. Highly interesting studies have focused on frogs, whose retinal ganglion cells normally project to nonoverlapping regions in the optic tectum and therefore produce no alternating bands of cells like those found in the mammalian cortex. When frog embryos were implanted with a third eye, close to one of the two normal eyes, and then were allowed to develop, the tectum of the frog was found to have alternating bands like those of cats and monkeys in the regions where the projection fields of the two eyes overlapped (see Constantine-Paton, Cline, & Debski, 1990, for discussion). These findings suggest that the ocular dominance columns do not develop in accord with a genetically specified program, for such a program could hardly exist either to guide the development of an eye that frogs normally do not have or to form ocular dominance columns that never appear under natural conditions. Some mechanism other than genetic specification evidently leads to the development of the alternating band pattern.

How can the organization of the visual cortex develop in advance of visual experience if that organization is not genetically specified? Recent research by Shatz and her colleagues (see Shatz, 1992) suggests that the same Hebbian mechanisms thought to produce plasticity in response to postnatal visual experience play a role in structuring the visual system before birth. In the prenatal eye of the cat or ferret, retinal ganglion cells are spontaneously active even before the visual receptors develop, and their activity follows a particular spatiotemporal pattern. Activity travels across the retinal ganglion cells of a single eye in waves, such that activity in one retinal ganglion cell is followed by activity in neighboring cells (see Feller, Wellis, Stellwagen, Werblin, & Shatz, 1996). If connections between these ganglion cells, their targets in the LGN, and the targets of those cells in the visual cortex are strengthened and stabilized by Hebbian associative processes, then these waves of activity will tend to produce a retinotopic organization both in the LGN and in the visual cortex. Moreover, if the activity waves of ganglion cells in the two eyes are uncorrelated but the targets of these cells are topographically overlapping, computational modeling reveals that Hebbian learning processes will give rise to segregated bands of cells in the cortex that are sensitive to inputs from each eye (Miller, Keller, & Stryker, 1989).

Evidence that spontaneous activity in the fetal eye in fact contributes to the prenatal development of topographic maps and monocularly driven layers of cells in the LGN comes from experiments in which the activity waves are chemically blocked in fetal animals. Such animals failed to develop the normal layered organization of the LGN (Shatz & Stryker, 1988), and infant kittens whose postnatal visual activity was blocked failed to develop normal ocular dominance columns (Stryker & Harris, 1986). Nevertheless, such animals do develop topographic maps, providing evidence that spontaneous activity is not the only mechanism producing organization in the developing visual system.

This brief excursion through the neurobiology of visual development suggests a recasting of the traditional debate between nativists and empiricists over the origins and development of space perception. As empiricists have always emphasized, the plasticity found in mature visual systems exists as well in developing systems, and it provides a means by which early visual experience can shape the brain. In accord with nativist theories, however, the very processes of activity-dependent change that alter the brain in response to visual experience also shape the connectivity of the visual system prior to an animal's first contacts with the external visual environment. This initial structuring constrains and guides subsequent visual learning, and it allows the newborn visual system to respond adaptively and systematically to visual stimulation. Activity-dependent processes therefore may account, in part, both for the adaptability of visual perception in response to visual experience and for the existence of perceptual capacities in advance of experience. Innate perceptual capacities may not be an "unnecessary hypothesis" but a product of the same mechanisms of plasticity that attune an animal's perception to the environment it perceives.

B. Psychophysical Studies of Space Perception in Infants

The first systematic studies of the perceptual capacities of human infants date from the same, fertile period in the 1950s that initiated the modern study of the neurobiology of vision. Fantz (see Fantz, 1961, for review) developed the preferential looking method, in which an infant human or other animal is presented with two visual displays side by side, and the infant's relative looking times to the two displays is assessed. Systematically looking longer at one of the displays, over pairs of trials in which the lateral positions of the displays are reversed, indicates that the infant discriminates the displays on some basis. By varying the properties of the two displays, investigators can probe both the extent and the basis of these discriminations.

Fantz found that human infants of all ages look longer at a display of thick, black-and-white stripes than at a display that is homogeneously gray, a finding that led both him and later investigators to develop tests of the development of visual acuity and contrast sensitivity over the first year (see Banks & Salapatek, 1983). Fantz also demonstrated that infants prefer solid objects to flat surfaces, a finding that laid the foundation for later, highly productive studies of depth sensitivity (see Held, 1985). In further studies, Fantz showed that 2-month-old infants prefer faces to other displays of comparable complexity, a finding that has given rise to vigorous and productive studies of face perception and recognition (see Johnson & Morton, 1991). Finally, Fantz found that infants look preferentially at novel over familiar (i.e., repeatedly presented) displays, a tendency that underpins much subsequent research on infant perception (see Bornstein, 1985; Spelke, 1985, and below). Other investigators showed other reliable preferences, including a preference for moving displays over stationary ones, making possible a variety of studies of motion and depth perception (see Kellman, 1993).

When do human infants first become sensitive to information for depth and distance? The answer appears to depend on the nature of the information presented. When depth is specified pictorially, by relations such as interposition and linear perspective, sensitivity to this information appears to develop rather late in human infancy, between 5 and 7 months (Yonas & Granrud, 1984). Sensitivity to binocular disparity, the basis of stereopsis, emerges in the fourth or fifth month, and stereoacuity improves rapidly thereafter (Fox, Aslin, Shea, & Dumais, 1980; Held, Birch, & Gwiazda, 1980). Before these developments, however, infants evidently perceive depth on some basis, for they have been shown to use information for an object's distance in perceiving its size and motion.

Kellman, Condry, Van de Walle, O'Halloran, and Hofsten (discussed in Kellman, 1993) investigated whether 2- and 4-month-old infants could perceive the absolute distance of an object by probing their capacity for position constancy. Infants who moved back and forth in a lateral translation were presented with objects that either were stationary or moved conjointly with them. When an observer moves, the patterns of retinal displacements produced by other objects depend both on the objects' motion and on their distance: Moving babies therefore would perceive the displacement of a conjointly moving object only if they perceived the object's distance. The investigators found that at 4 months, and under some conditions at 2 months as well, infants looked longer at the conjointly moving object. This preference provides evidence both for position constancy and for distance perception at these ages.

Two further experiments have investigated perception of object distance in newborn infants by focusing on the infants' capacity for size constancy (Granrud, 1987; Slater, Mattock, & Brown, 1990a; see also Bower, 1966). Slater et al. (1990a) familiarized infants ranging in age from 13 hours to 5 days with either a large or a small cube, presented at different distances on different trials. Then the infants were tested with the small and large cubes side by side, presented at two new distances chosen so as to equate their projected sizes in the visual field. The infants showed a highly reliable preference for the cube with the novel real size. Because the cubes' retinal sizes were equated, this preference provides evidence for size constancy, and distance perception, in the first days of life.

To date, the information used by newborn infants to perceive the relative distances of objects has not been clarified, although the ocularmotor cue of convergence is a plausible candidate (see Kellman & Arterberry, in press). This suggestion brings the modern study of depth perception back to Descartes (1637/1971), who first suggested that humans perceive depth from convergence "as it were by natural geometry" (p. 250).

These last experiments provide evidence that newborn human infants have some initial capacity to perceive object distance. Nevertheless, this capacity expands greatly over postnatal development. Older infants perceive depth and distance from more sources of information, and they exhibit this perceptual ability under a wider range of circumstances. Infants' capacities for perceiving space must be modifiable, moreover, in order to account for the considerable changes that occur over postnatal development due to the migration of visual receptors, the growth of the eyes, and the increase in interocular distance (see Aslin, 1988; Banks, 1988). Both initial structure and later growth and experience contribute to perception of depth and distance in humans.

C. The Comparative Psychology and Ecology of Perceptual Development: The Visual Cliff

Although psychophysical studies can reveal whether infants are sensitive to depth information, they do not reveal whether infants use such information to guide their spatial actions. This limitation is serious, because some of the most basic functions of spatial vision are to guide actions such as reaching and walking by bringing information about the existence and location of objects, supporting surfaces, and barriers.

At about the same time as the earliest investigations of Fantz and of Hubel and Wiesel, landmark studies of the emergence and the nature of these visual capacities were performed by Gibson and Walk (1960; Walk & Gibson, 1961), who tested depth perception and visually guided locomotion on the "visual cliff." Infants of a variety of species were placed on a centerboard between two tangible but nonvisible Plexiglas surfaces, through which a near surface was visible on one side and a distant surface—the cliff—was visible on the other side. Young animals of all the terrestrial species tested were found to locomote onto the optically near side and to avoid the optically specified cliff.

Visual cliff avoidance typically was observed at the earliest age at which an animal could be tested, when independent locomotion began. In precocial walkers such as goats, avoidance of the cliff was observed at birth, providing evidence for innate visual perception of depth and innate use of this information to guide locomotion. In animals who begin walking at later ages, such as rats, cats, and human infants, avoidance of the cliff was first tested, and exhibited, at those ages. In general, findings indicated that mechanisms for perceiving visually specified depth and guiding locomotion onto visibly supporting surfaces were present and functional at the time they were first needed, when an animal began to locomote independently. This developmental pattern makes sense, Gibson and Walk suggested, because later development of these mechanisms could lead newly locomoting animals to make costly, even fatal, errors.

Further studies of rats and cats investigated the effects of visual experience on the development of cliff avoidance, revealing interesting variations on a common theme. Rats who were reared in darkness were found to avoid the cliff on their first exposure to the light (Walk, Gibson, & Tighe, 1957). Just as visual experience is not necessary for the development of the basic patterns of connectivity in the visual system, it is not necessary for the development of this functional, visually guided behavior. In contrast, cats reared in darkness or in a visual environment in which they were displaced only passively showed no consistent visually guided locomotion when first exposed to the light (Gibson, 1991; Held & Hein, 1963). As in the case of rats and goats, however, trial-and-error learning appears to play no role in cats' developing cliff avoidance. In experiments described in Gibson (1991), dark-reared cats were given visual experience locomoting on the visual cliff apparatus itself. Because both sides of the cliff were covered with Plexiglas that prevented an animal from falling, one might predict these subjects would learn that the deep side of the cliff was a safe place to locomote. Nevertheless, the cats began to avoid the cliff just as much as their normally reared counterparts after 6 days of visual and locomotor experience. Similar conclusions come from Held & Hein's (1963) studies, in which cats who moved actively developed normal cliff avoidance, even though all their movements occurred within a harness that permitted no falls and obscured their view of their own bodies. These findings suggest that cats require experience with active motion in a visible environment in order to attune their visual system but do not require experience locomoting and falling in order to learn to avoid visible drop-offs.

Human infants begin to crawl at about 7 months of age. Given the ample evidence from psychophysical experiments that much younger infants perceive depth and distance, and given the finding that the development of cliff avoidance does not depend on trial-and-error learning in any nonhuman species yet tested, one might expect human infants to avoid the visual cliff as soon as they began to crawl, irrespective of experiences such as falling. Consonant with this expectation, the original studies of Gibson and Walk (1960) and some later investigations (e.g., Adolph, Eppler, & Gibson, 1993; Rader, Bausano, & Richards, 1980) revealed that visual information for a supporting surface guides locomotion in crawling infants. Nevertheless, further studies of human infants suggest truly surprising developmental changes in cliff avoidance.

First, cliff avoidance has been found to be affected by locomotor experience in human infants. More consistent avoidance of visible drop-offs is shown by infants who have been crawling for a longer time and by infants who have been given locomotor experience in a "walker": a device that supports prelocomotor infants in an upright posture and allows them to propel themselves forward by striking the floor (Campos, Bertenthal, & Kermoian, 1992). Second, even infants who avoid the cliff when they crawl are apt to cross it if placed in a walker: a finding that may account in part for the numerous accidents that have been reported when walkers are used in the home (Rader et al., 1980). Third, precrawling infants who are lowered over the shallow and deep sides of a cliff apparatus show, by raising their arms in anticipation of contact on the near side, that they perceive the relative distances of the two sides (Walters, 1981). When placed directly on the Plexiglas over the cliff, however, these infants show interest but no fear. Older infants show progressively more fear on the cliff, and fear reactions have been connected, at least anecdotally, to experience with falls. Finally, infants who have begun to show wariness on the cliff typically will look to a parent before beginning to cross it, suggesting that locomotion over uncertain visible surfaces engages social and communicative processes in our species (Campos et al., 1992).

Over the past two decades, research on visually guided locomotion has extended beyond the visual cliff to studies of crawling and walking infants' perception of the affordances for locomotion of a variety of visible surfaces (e.g., Adolph et al., 1993; Gibson & Schmuckler, 1989). With development, infants' perception of inclined surfaces and nonrigid surfaces becomes progressively differentiated. Interestingly, perception appears to be tied to the mode of locomotion; infants who have come to master an inclined slope by crawling must learn to do so again once they begin walking. In humans, visual-haptic exploration and locomotor experience evidently modify and extend the basic perceptuomotor coordination found in so many young animals.

D. A Puzzle

Three elegant lines of research, each starting in the 1950s and culminating today in a rich array of findings, appear to support the same general conclusion: Visual perception of space shows both initial structure and adaptability to experience. Perception and its neural mechanisms develop in accord with a set of epigenetic processes that begin to operate long before birth. In consequence, many nonhuman animals can use visual information for supporting surfaces to guide their actions in space on their first exposure to light, and newborn humans can use information for object distance to arrive at veridical, though imprecise, perceptions of object size and motion. After birth, perceptual systems continue to grow, both in accord with intrinsic processes and in accord with the structured visual environment.

A puzzle nevertheless remains. The human visual system evidently follows the same basic plan as that of other vertebrates. Moreover, the evolution of human perceptuomotor systems likely was subject to very similar ecological constraints to those of other terrestrial mammals: For humans as for mountain goats, mistaken steps off a cliff can be fatal. Finally, human infants, like the young of other species, show initial sensitivity to depth information. Despite all these findings, every parent knows that a newly crawling infant must be protected from drop-offs. Humans are the only species whose avoidance of the visual cliff has been shown to depend in part on locomotor experience, perhaps even experience with falls.

Another possible difference between humans and other animals emerges once infants begin consistently to avoid visual drop-offs. Whereas other animals may respond to the cliff by freezing or withdrawing, humans come to respond by manifesting fear or checking with a parent to confirm that all is well. Both fear of drop-offs and "social referencing" to a parent suggest a developing understanding of the consequences of locomoting without support. Although other animals avoid drop-offs, it is far from clear that they do so because of any understanding that walking off a cliff would lead to injury.

Research on perceptual development has done little to elucidate these possibly unique characteristics of human depth perception, but it invites some speculations. First, given the many homologies in the neural structures subserving space perception in humans and other animals, and given the common ecological constraints on all mammalian perceptuomotor systems, it is likely that humans and other animals have similar systems for perceiving depth and for using depth information to guide spatial actions, and that these systems develop in common ways, without shaping by trial-and-error learning. Second, humans may modulate these systems in distinctive ways, connecting their basic systems for perceiving depth and guiding locomotion to other systems for negotiating and making sense of the world. A human infant who plays near a parent on a bed may perceive a drop-off at the bed's edge, relate this perceptual information specifying the drop-off to other perceptual information specifying the parent's location and emotional state, and decide she is safe at the parent's side. Conversely, a child who sits at the edge of a visually continuous but structurally unsound surface may use the alarmed expression of her caretaker, as much as the signals form her own perceptual systems, as information for how to proceed. If these suggestions are correct, then a full understanding of human perception and perceptually guided action will require that investigators go beyond the basic perceptual and perceptuomotor systems revealed by the last half-century of research. Study of the uniquely human processes that coordinate and modulate distinct perceptual systems will become an important task for the decades ahead.

III. DEVELOPMENT OF PERCEPTION AND CATEGORIZATION OF OBJECTS

The world humans perceive, act upon, and reason about is not just an extended surface layout but an arrangement of stable, solid bodies with enduring properties: chairs, trees, cats, and houses. Although most objects in any layout are at least partly occluded, adults perceive objects seemingly at a glance, detecting their boundaries and complete shapes and categorizing each object as a member of a familiar and meaningful kind. How do we accomplish this feat? To what extent, and in what respects, are human representations of objects shaped by contacts with those objects, on the one hand, and by the inherent structure of human perceptual and cognitive systems, on the other? (See also Medin & Coley, chap. 13, this volume.)

Early in this century, a comprehensive set of answers to these questions was attempted by the Gestalt psychologists (see Koffka, 1935; Köhler, 1947) (see also Hochberg, this volume). Object perception, they suggested, results from inherent propensities to confer the simplest organization on perceptual experience. In the absence of any sensorimotor learning, perceivers will group arrays into figure and ground, perceiving solid objects with definite boundaries standing in front of surfaces that extend indefinitely behind them. The borders between two such objects also will be perceived, in part, through processes that produce the simplest, most regular figures that are consistent with the scene, grouping together surfaces of a common color and texture, with aligned edges and a symmetrical shape, that undergo common motion. Because natural objects tend to exhibit all these Gestalt relations, perceivers' inherent organizational tendencies typically will give rise to accurate perceptions of object boundaries in the absence of any specific learning about visual scenes.

Like Helmholtz, the Gestalt psychologists supported their claims primarily through studies of experience effects in adult perception and arguments from parsimony and plausibility. They showed, for example, that repeated presentation of an array sometimes has little influence on adults' perceptual organization (Gottschaldt, 1967), that even very commonly viewed figures, such as alphabetic characters, will fail to be perceived if Gestalt organizational principles do not favor them (Wertheimer, 1923/1958), and that Gestalt relations within a scene can overpower specific knowledge about the kinds of objects that the scene contains (Kanizsa, 1979; Michotte, Thines, & Crabbe, 1964). Because knowledge and experience do not influence adults' organization of scenes in these cases, they reasoned, it is unlikely that knowledge and experience give rise to humans' original abilities to perceive objects.

As in the case of the empiricists' opposite but symmetrical arguments, this reasoning can be questioned (see Brunswik & Kamiya, 1953; Hochberg, 1974) and is no substitute for direct study of the development of object perception in humans and other animals. Such research has advanced considerably in this century, although some basic questions remain outstanding. Here I consider two lines of study of the development of object perception: studies of the development of perception and categorization of objects using preferential looking methods, and studies of the development of actions on objects, such as reaching and visual following.

A. Object Perception and Categorization in Infancy

The early development of object perception has been investigated most extensively through experiments that rely on infants' tendency to look longer at displays that are more novel. These experiments provide evidence that 4- to 6-month-old infants perceive figure–ground relations in natural, 3-D displays as the Gestalt psychologists predicted: presented repeatedly with an object in front of a background surface, infants' looking times to other displays, including parts of the object or background, provide evidence that they perceive the object as bounded and the background to extend behind it (Arteberry, Craton, & Yonas, 1993; Termine, Hrynick, Kestenbaum, Gleitman, & Spelke, 1987). Infants also perceive objects to continue behind occluders under conditions similar to those studied with adults by Michotte et al. (1964). After repeated presentation of a moving object whose ends were visible and whose center was hidden by a nearer object, 4-month-old infants subsequently showed little interest in a nonoccluded, complete object and greater interest in a nonoccluded display with a gap where the occluder had been (Johnson & Nanez, 1995; Kellman & Spelke, 1983). This preference provided evidence that they had perceived the original display as a complete object that was connected behind the occluder (see Kellman, 1993, for more evidence and discussion).

Further preferential looking experiments have investigated infants' perception of an object that progressively becomes fully occluded. Michotte et al. (1964) proposed that Gestalt principles of organization lead adults automatically to perceive such an object as persisting over occlusion. To investigate whether infants perceive a persisting object in this situation, Craton and Yonas familiarized 6-month-old infants with a disk moving in and out of view behind an occluder and presented, in alternation, a nonoccluded complete disk, which had been visible only briefly in the original display, and a nonoccluded half-disk, which had been visible for a longer time. Infants looked longer at the half-disk, suggesting that they had perceived a complete disk, not just its visible surfaces, during the occlusion event (Craton & Yonas, 1990; see also Van de Walle & Spelke, 1996). Other preferential looking experiments provide evidence that infants represent objects that are fully hidden at ages as young as 2–3 months (e.g., Baillargeon & DeVos, 1991; Rochat & Hespos, 1996; Simon, Hespos & Rochat, 1995; Spelke, Kestenbaum, Simons, & Wein, 1995; Wilcox, Rosser, & Nadel, 1994; Wynn, 1992a).

Finally, Michotte (1963) proposed that perceivers automatically apprehend causal relations between the motions of two objects, under appropriate spatiotemporal conditions: If a stationary object is contacted by a moving object and immediately begins to move, the moving object is perceived as the cause of its motion. Preferential looking experiments provide evidence that infants as young as 3 months perceive the same causal relation in such events (Kotovsky & Baillargeon, 1994; Leslie, 1988), even when the launching of one object by another is partly occluded (Ball, 1973; Van de Walle, Woodward, & Phillips, 1994).

This brief review suggests that abilities to perceive the boundaries, complete shapes, and causes of motion of visible objects, and abilities to represent the existence, motion, and causal interactions of occluded objects, begin to emerge quite early in human infancy, consistent with Gestalt theory. Nevertheless, further studies exploring both the limits and the origins of these abilities have appeared to cast doubt on aspects of that theory. First, a series of experiments suggested that 3–5-month-old infants perceive objects primarily by analyzing spatiotemporal properties of the surface layout, grouping together surfaces that are connected and that move together (see Spelke & Van de Walle, 1993, for review). For example, 4-month-old infants perceive a center-occluded object as connected behind its occluder by analyzing the motion of its visible surfaces. In contrast, infants are less apt to perceive the connectedness of a center-occluded object by analyzing the similarity and alignment of its surfaces (Kellman & Spelke, 1983; Needham, 1994; Smith, Johnson, Spelke, & Aslin, 1996), even though they use similarity and alignment relations to organize surface patterns (Quinn, Brown, & Streppa, 1997; Johnson & Aslin, 1996). These findings initially led some investigators to propose, following Brunswik & Kamiya (1953), that Gestalt relations such as good continuation and similarity are learned (Kellman & Spelke, 1983; Spelke, 1988).

Further suggestions that learning gives rise to object perception were prompted by studies of object perception in younger infants. Two-month-old infants, presented with a center-occluded rod similar to that used by Kellman and Spelke (1983), were found to have no determinate perception of a connected object behind the occluder (Johnson & Nañez, 1995), although infants of this age did perceive a connected object when the size of the occluded region was reduced (Johnson & Aslin, 1995). More striking, newborn infants presented with the same display appeared to perceive two separated objects rather than one connected object (Slater et al., 1990b). This last finding suggested that the initial visual world of the infant might be a mosaic of visible surfaces after all, and that abilities to perceive complete objects over partial occlusion might depend on visual experience, such as the experience of viewing repeated object coverings and uncoverings (Slater et al., 1990b; see also Munakata, McClelland, Johnson, & Siegler, 1997).

Studies of object perception in chicks cast some doubt on both of these suggestions (Regolin & Vallortigara, 1995). These studies used an interesting variant of the familiarization and novelty preference method, based on the phenomenon of experimentally induced imprinting. A chick who is reared in isolation from any other animal, but in the presence of an inanimate object, comes to show filial behavior toward that object. Placed in an elongated test cage with the object of imprinting and a discriminably different object at opposite ends, the chick spends most of its time in proximity to the imprinted object (Horn, 1985). This "familiarity" preference allows for the design of experiments exactly analogous to the novelty preference test method of Fantz, except that it is the preferred test object, not the nonpreferred object, that is inferred to be perceptually more similar to the object of familiarization.

Using this method, Regolin and Vallortigara (1995) familiarized newborn chicks with a fully visible triangle that dangled from the end of a string at the center of an empty cage. Because the cage was devoid of other objects, a chick never saw the object occluded or disoccluded. After two days' exposure, chicks were tested with a center-occluded triangle and with a broken triangle containing a gap where the other triangle was occluded (see Regolin & Vallortigara, 1995, for further conditions of the experiment). The chicks spent most of their time near the occluded triangle. Together with their appropriate control conditions, this finding suggests that chicks who view a partly occluded object for the first time perceive the object to continue behind its occluder, contrary to Slater's findings with newborn human infants.

In a further experiment, newborn chicks were imprinted to a center-occluded, stationary triangle and then were tested with stationary complete and broken triangles. In an experiment with human infants using essentially the same displays, 4-month-olds had shown no differential looking at the two test displays (Kellman & Spelke, 1983). In contrast, the inexperienced chicks showed a consistent preference for the complete test triangle, providing evidence that they had perceived the original, stationary triangle as connected behind its occluder. This finding suggests that inexperienced chicks are predisposed to perceive objects by organizing the visual layout into bodies with aligned edges, homogeneous surfaces, and simple shapes.

Both these experiments support the original Gestalt analysis over the empiricist suggestions of Brunswik and Kamiya (1953), Slater et al. (1990b), and Kellman and Spelke (1983). Because the visual system of chicks is similar to that of humans but is more mature at birth, the authors suggest that maturational changes account for much of the development of object perception in humans (Regolin & Vallortigara, 1995). Nevertheless, this suggestion remains to be tested directly in our species.

Thus far, we have considered the development of abilities to perceive objects as unitary, bounded, and enduring. Adults also categorize objects rapidly, perceiving each body as a member of a particular kind, and recognize specific individuals such as a neighbor, dog, or favorite chair. When and how do children develop these abilities?

When object categorization and face recognition are tested by preferential looking methods, both are found to emerge early in infancy. For example, 4-month-old infants have been familiarized with a series of photographs of different species of cats and then have been shown novel photographs portraying a cat of a new species paired with a bird, dog, or horse. Infants looked longer at the photograph of the animal that did not belong to the familiar category, suggesting that they had formed a category including cats and excluding these other animals (e.g., Quinn, Eimas, & Rosenkrantz, 1993). Studies using this method provide evidence that young infants can make quite subtle categorizations, such as discriminations within the feline family (cat vs. female lion) and discriminations among more global and heterogeneous categories of objects (animals vs. vehicles) (see Eimas, 1994, for review and discussion). Mature animals of a variety of species, including pigeons, show similarly subtle categorization abilities (see Herrnstein, 1990).

Preferential looking studies also provide evidence that infants come to recognize visually the face of a parent within the first few days of life (Bushnell, Sai, & Mellon, 1989). Like chicks in an imprinting test, human infants exhibit this recognition by looking at the face of the mother in preference to the face of another woman of similar age and coloring. Although infants fail to discriminate the face of their mother if only the internal features of the face are available to distinguish her face from that of another person of similar appearance (Pascalis, de Schonen, Morton, Deruelle, & Fabre-Grenet, 1995; see also Diamond & Carey, 1977), attention to internal features increases over the first few weeks of life (Haith, Bergman, & Moore, 1977).

All these findings suggest that infants rapidly become sensitive to the patterns of perceptual similarity and difference that mark both distinct natural categories and distinct individuals. Abilities to recognize and categorize objects begin to develop early in the first year of life, hand in hand with abilities to perceive object unity, boundaries, and persistence over occlusion.

Nevertheless, infants' representations of objects have a curious limitation: Abilities to perceive object boundaries and to categorize objects do not appear to be well coordinated. For adults and older children, objects have enduring properties and belong to enduring kinds: a cat does not radically change its texture, internal structure, or boundaries over time, and it does not cease to be a cat as it moves about. Adults therefore can use information about kind membership to perceive where one object ends and another begins (perceiving a sleeping cat or a sofa as a distinct object and not as part of the sofa) and to trace the paths of objects over occlusion (perceiving the mouse that scurries out of a closet as a distinct object from the cat that previously entered the closet).

Research suggests that these abilities develop surprisingly late in infancy, between 10 and 12 months of age (Xu & Carey, 1994, 1996; see also Simon et al., 1995). At 10 months, infants who view a toy animal sitting on a toy vehicle, or an animal and vehicle that appear in succession from behind a single occluder, appear to have no determinate perception that the two toys are distinct objects. At 12 months, these perceptions change and converge with those of adults. This developmental change suggests that initial abilities to perceive objects as unitary and bounded are quite separate from initial abilities to perceive similarity relations among a set of distinct members of a single category. I will return to this suggestion.

B. The Development of Object-Directed Actions

Although the Gestalt psychologists provided the most thorough analysis of object perception, the central 20th-century figure in the study of the development of object representation is Piaget (1952, 1954), whose studies of infants' changing abilities to act on objects continue to dominate contemporary research and debates. Piaget discovered dramatic changes in children's actions on objects, from simple, early-developing actions, such as grasping and sucking, to complex, coordinated actions, such as making an object approach by pulling on something to which it is attached, or obtaining a hidden object by removing its occluder. His most well-known findings—that infants do not search for occluded objects until about 8 months, and that they do not confine their search to physically possible locations until almost a year later—prompted the well-known thesis that object representations are constructed slowly over the first 18 months of life as children come progressively to coordinate their object-directed actions. Before this coordination, Piaget suggested, infants have no ability to represent objects as enduring bodies.

More recent studies of object-directed action serve to qualify Piaget's conclusions in some respects and extend them in others. First, babies who are presented with an object that then is obscured by darkness have been found to reach for and obtain the object well before infants who are presented with an object that is hidden by an occluder (Hood & Willats, 1986; see also Clifton, Rochat, Litovsky, & Perris, 1991). Second, babies who are presented with an object hiding game, but with no hidden object, have been found to make the same search errors as those given Piaget's search tasks (Smith & Thelen, 1995; cf. Munakata & McClelland, 1996). Both these findings suggest that search failures stem, at least in part, from factors other than immature representations of unseen objects. Nevertheless, research by Munakata et al. (1997) has extended Piaget's essential findings by showing that young infants fail to search for hidden objects even when a search task is made extremely easy and the infants are trained to perform it. This finding and others (Munakata, 1997; Spelke, Vishton, & Hofsten, 1994) suggest that the occlusion of an object genuinely poses problems for an infant who would act upon it.

Comparative studies of object-directed actions cast an interesting perspective on the search errors of human infants. Nonhuman primates such as rhesus and capuchin monkeys solve Piaget's object search tasks in the same developmental order as human infants, but on an accelerated timetable. For example, rhesus monkeys begin to search successfully for an occluded object by removing its occluder at about 3 to 4 months (Antinucci, 1989; see also Diamond, 1990). Most interestingly, a version of Piaget's object search task has been presented to domestic chicks in the second day of life, using a variant of the imprinting paradigm described above (Regolin, Vallortigara, & Zanforlin, 1995a). On their first day, chicks were presented with a fully visible, moving inanimate object (a ball), to which they became imprinted. On the next day, chicks watched as the ball was placed behind one of two identical occluders. With high reliability, the chicks searched for the ball by moving around the appropriate occluder. Over successive trials, moreover, the chicks searched only physically possible locations (i.e., they did not return to the place where the object was hidden on a previous trial). Similar findings were obtained when the occluded object was a desirable food (Regolin et al., 1995a) and when a different procedure was used (Regolin et al., 1995b), suggesting that the ability to search for hidden objects is robust in this species (although Etienne, 1973, and Regolin et al., 1994, 1995a, describe conditions in which chicks fail to exhibit this behavior). Thus, 2-day-old chicks and 4-month-old monkeys succeed at "object permanence" tasks that are strikingly like the tasks that 7-month-old human infants fail.

The findings of these comparative studies suggest that object permanence is attained by many animal species, but at quite different times in postnatal development. Because 2-day-old chicks, 3-month-old monkeys, and 8-month-old human infants differ greatly in the nature and extent of their experience with objects, such experience appears to play only a limited role in the development of object permanence. In particular, the chicks in Regolin et al.'s, studies had had just one day of visual experience, they had never seen one object occluded and disoccluded by another, and they had never had the opportunity to follow an object behind a barrier. (The chicks did, however, view the object and move around it throughout the day.) Chick's success at retrieving the hidden object casts doubt on the thesis that perceivers learn to represent hidden objects by repeatedly witnessing their occlusion and disocclusion (Munakata et al., 1997). More positively, comparisons across species suggest that the common predictor of the time of emergence of object search is the state of maturation of the young animal: Animals that are relatively mature at birth, such as chicks, develop abilities to search for hidden objects long before those that mature more slowly. Maturational changes may play a large role in the development of actions on hidden objects (Regolin et al., 1995a, 1995b; Diamond, 1990).

Although the preferential looking studies described in the last section focused primarily on object perception, and the Piagetian studies described in this section focused primarily on object representation and action, psychologists have become intrigued by an apparent conflict between the findings from these two lines of research. When tested by preferential looking methods, infants appear to represent occluded objects and to use knowledge of constraints on object motion to infer how such objects move (see Baillargeon, 1993, for review). When tested by search methods, infants under about 8 months act as if occluded objects do not exist, and those under about 18 months act as if the movements of such objects are not constrained by physical laws.

A study that directly compared infants' behavior toward occluded objects in search tasks and in preferential looking tasks reveals this discrepancy clearly (Ahmed & Ruffman, 1996). Eight-month-old infants first were given a search task in which they repeatedly found an object that was hidden at one of two hiding places, then observed the object hidden at the other hiding place, and after a delay were allowed to reach for the object. As in Piaget's original studies, the infants reached to the incorrect location where the object had been found before. Then the same infants were given a preferential looking task, in which they viewed the same object hidden and revealed in the same locations, on the same succession of trials with the same delay. As in previous preferential looking studies, the infants looked longer when the object was revealed at the original, incorrect location than when it was revealed at the more novel, correct location. The infants' preferential looking therefore appeared to be guided by a veridical representation of the hidden object's location, whereas their search appeared to be guided by a misrepresentation of that location (see also Spelke et al., 1994).

In summary, young infants can act an objects both when they are visible and when they are occluded by darkness. In preferential looking experiments, young infants also appear to represent objects that are occluded and to keep track of an occluded object's location. Young infants fail, however, to put these two abilities together so as to reach for an occluded object. To date, there is much speculation but no consensus concerning the meaning of this dissociation or the developmental processes that overcome it (see Baillargeon, 1993; Bertenthal, 1996; Diamond, 1990; Mandler, 1992; Munakata, in press; Munakata et al., 1997; Spelke, Breinlinger, Macomber, & Jacobson, 1992; Thelen & Smith, 1994). I sketch one possible account below.

C. Overview

Research on the development of object perception and representation suggests that central features of mature human abilities to perceive and represent objects trace back to the early months of life. Under certain conditions, young human infants can perceive the unity and boundaries of objects and the complete shapes of objects that are partly hidden. Young infants also can perceive the existence and location of fully hidden objects, and they can recognize specific individuals and categorize objects as members of specific kinds. Studies of other animals suggest that these abilities are widespread among vertebrates, at least, and that some of the abilities arise with minimal shaping by visual experience. Nevertheless, the role of experience in the development of object representation has been far less well studied than the role of experience in the development of perception of depth.

Despite all the abilities outlined above, young human infants' perception of objects shows some striking limitations. One limitation is revealed by tasks that require infants to conjoin information about the properties and category membership of an object with information about the object's boundaries (e.g., Xu & Carey, 1996): Such tasks are surprisingly difficult for infants under 12 months of age. Another limitation is revealed by tasks that require infants to act upon objects that are occluded (e.g., Piaget, 1954): Such abilities undergo lengthy and extensive developmental change over the first 18 months of life.

Both the strengths and the limitations of infants' object representations prompt a suggestion and further questions. I suggest that humans have multiple, early-developing systems for perceiving and representing objects, and that these systems are poorly coordinated early in the development (see also Bertenthal, 1996; Xu &

Carey, 1996). Although 5-month-old infants represent visible objects as targets for reaching and represent the unity and persistence of objects that are occluded, they may not be able to conjoin these representations so as to reach for an occluded object. And although infants perceive spatiotemporally specified object boundaries in visual scenes and detect perceptible differences between objects in different categories, they may not be able to conjoin these representations so as to use perceptible differences between objects in different categories as information for object boundaries.

Evidence for separate systems of object representation abounds in other areas of visual science and neuroscience. In particular, there is evidence for separate cortical visual pathways for perceiving and categorizing objects, on one hand, and for grasping and manipulating objects on the other (Goodale, 1995; Jeannerod, 1994; cf. Ungerleider & Mishkin, 1982). There also is evidence that the neural processes subserving figure–ground organization and perception of object unity are quite different from those subserving detection of object features or spatial properties guiding actions (e.g., Singer & Gray, 1995). The present suggestion accords with these findings.

If humans form multiple, independent representations of objects early in development, then how does the relationship between these representations change over development? Studies of developmental changes in human object representations are consistent with the possibility that the initially separate systems of representation become intercoordinated over the course of the first 2 years. Developmental changes in search for objects may depend in part on emerging abilities to relate the system for representing hidden objects to the system of representation that is linked to action. And developmental change in object categorization may result from mappings of the categorization system to the action and perception systems. Nevertheless, this possibility remains to be tested, for existing research has hardly begun to investigate the existence of such coordinations, the processes by which they arise, or the changing representations of objects that they make possible.

IV. DEVELOPMENT OF KNOWLEDGE OF NUMBER

Knowledge of number contrasts with perceptual knowledge of space and objects in several respects. At its higher reaches, it is indisputably a distinctly human ability that may have emerged late in human evolution, coincident with a host of other developments, such as symbolism, rapidly changing technology, art, ritual, and language (Mithen, 1996). Knowledge of number continues to grow into adulthood. Extending this knowledge requires effort, whether it is the efforts of preschool children learning to count and perform intuitive addition, elementary school children learning arithmetic facts, or of high school students learning algebra or calculus. Finally, knowledge of number appears to vary to some degree across individuals and cultures: Although every normal person probably represents space and objects in much the same ways, not everyone achieves the same mathematical knowledge and skills.

Despite the striking differences between this topic and the preceding ones, insights into the development of knowledge of number have come from some of the same approaches that have shed light on the development of perception of space and object. Studies of human infants using preferential looking methods (e.g., Wynn, 1995), studies of young children's counting and spontaneous numerical reasoning (e.g., Gelman & Gallistel, 1978), studies in comparative psychology and behavioral ecology (e.g., Gallistel, 1990), and studies in cognitive neuroscience (e.g., Dehaene & Cohen, 1991) all have shed light on the origins and nature of humans' unique "number sense" (Dehaene, 1997). My brief summary of research focuses on studies of perception and representation of number in human infants and studies of developmental changes in number knowledge as children learn to count.

A. Number Representations in Infants

Experiments using preferential looking methods provide evidence that young human infants represent the number of objects or events in a scene, provided that number is small (up to three or four). For example, infants who are familiarized with a succession of arrays containing three objects show a novelty preference for a new array containing two objects over a new array containing three objects; infants habituated to a succession of arrays containing two objects show the reverse preference. This finding has been obtained with arrays of simple geometrical figures in varying positions (Antell & Keating, 1983; Starkey & Cooper, 1980), drawings of common objects varying in size and position (Strauss & Curtis, 1981), photographs of arrays of heterogeneous objects in varying arrangements (Starkey, Spelke, & Gelman, 1990), and animated displays of moving objects that progressively occlude and disocclude one another (van Loosbroek & Smitsman, 1990). Infants also dishabituate to changes in the number of events in a sequence, such as the number of jumps performed by a puppet (Wynn, 1995) or the number of syllables in a word (Bertoncini & Mehler, 1981). Small number discrimination has been shown at a variety of ages throughout the first year, including newborn infants (Antell & Keating, 1983).

Infants' sensitivity to number also has been tested with a different visual preference method: an intermodal matching test. Infants view two visual arrays containing two versus three objects, arranged side by side, while listening to a sequence of two or three sounds. In other research, infants sometimes have been found to look longer at a visual display that matches an accompanying sound: on hearing speech, for example, infants tend to look longer at a face that appears to be its source (e.g., Kuhl & Meltzoff, 1982; see Spelke, 1989). Accordingly, experiments have investigated whether infants would show this preference when number provided the matching variable. In one series of experiments, 6-month-old infants indeed looked longer at the visual array with the matching number of objects (Starkey, Spelke, & Gelman, 1990). In other research, however, infants showed the opposite preference or no preference (Moore, Benenson, Reznick, Peterson, & Kagan, 1987; Mix, Levine, & Huttenlocher, 1994). These inconsistent findings may stem from a competing tendency for infants to look preferentially at nonmatching or unfamiliar visual arrays. Alternatively, abilities to represent an intermodal numerical correspondence may be fragile or absent in infants.

Finally, the most dramatic studies of number representation in infants have focused on infants' capacities for small number addition and subtraction, using arrays in which objects become fully occluded. Wynn (1992a) presented 5-month-old infants with an array containing one object, covered the object by a screen, and then introduced a second object and placed it behind the same screen. When the screen was lowered to reveal either the correct number of objects (two) or the number of objects presented at the outset (one), infants looked longer at the latter outcome. Similarly, infants presented with an event in which two objects were screened and one was removed looked longer at the superficially familiar but incorrect outcome array of two objects. These findings provide evidence that infants represented the number of occluded objects in the original array, represented the occluded addition or subtraction of an object, and inferred the number of objects in the outcome array.

Numerous experiments have replicated and extended these findings. First, infants were found to succeed at the 1 + 1 addition task when the two outcome displays contained two (correct) versus three (incorrect) objects, suggesting that infants computed the exactly correct outcome in this condition (Wynn, 1992a). Infants also succeeded at the addition task when the screened objects stood on a moving turntable, such that the number of objects could serve as a basis for recognition, but the objects' spatial positions could not (Koechlin, Dehaene, & Mehler, in press). Finally, infants succeeded at the addition and subtraction tasks when the objects used to produce the events changed behind the screen, such that specific object features could not be tracked over time (Simon et al., 1995). All these studies suggest that object number is a salient property of visual displays for infants, even when objects are occluded.

Studies of infants also have revealed some striking failures in number-discrimination tasks. First, infants often fail to discriminate arrays containing more than three or four objects. For example, 6-month-old infants showed no preference to four objects after habituation to six objects or the reverse (Starkey & Cooper, 1980) and no preference for eight objects after habituation to twelve objects or the reverse (Xu & Spelke, 1998). These failures are noteworthy, because the numerosity ratios used in these studies are as large as those used in the successful, small-number studies. Nevertheless, infants do show a novelty preference for eight objects after habituation to 16 objects or the reverse (Xu & Spelke, 1998), providing evidence for some sensitivity to large numerosities.

Second, infants fail to exhibit number discrimination when they are presented with nonsolid substances or collections instead of solid objects. For example, Huntley-Fenner (1995) presented 8-month-old infants with a Wynn addition task involving either sand piles or solid objects with the shapes and textures of sand piles. Infants were familiarized with sand or with a solid object before the study, and they watched the sand piles (or solid objects) undergo nonrigid (or rigid) transformations whenever they were introduced into the display. Infants succeeded at the task when the stimuli were solid objects, as in Wynn's original studies, but they failed when the stimuli were sand piles. This finding suggests that infants do not treat nonsolid substances as enumerable entities. In a further study (Chiang & Wynn, 1996), infants were presented with the Wynn addition task using two sets of five construction blocks arranged so as to form pyramids. In principle, this task could be performed either by adding pyramids (1 + 1 = 2) or by adding blocks (5 + 5 = 10 rather than 5). Contrary to either possibility, infants failed Wynn's addition task with the pyramids but succeeded in a parallel experiment involving two pyramidal-shaped, solid objects. This finding supports two conclusions. First, although solid objects and certain events appear to be countable entities for infants, aggregates and collections are not. Second, although infants can discriminate large numerosities in a 2:1 ratio, they do not add such numerosities.

Studies of other primates suggest that the representations of number found early in human development are not unique to humans. Both cottontop tamarins and rhesus monkeys succeed at Wynn's addition and subtraction tasks (Hauser, MacNeilage, & Ware, 1996; Uller, Carey, & Hauser, 1996): an especially significant finding, because the tasks involve no training. A variety of animals including parrots, raccoons, rats, and primates also have been trained to discriminate small numerosities (see Davis & Perusse, 1988; see Boysen & Capaldi, 1993, for review). Laboratory and field experiments suggest, moreover, that a wide range of species represent the approximate numbers of objects and events in scenes or situations containing large numerosities (see Gallistel, 1990, for review). For example, rats and pigeons who are trained that food will arrive after they make, for instance, 50 bar presses or key pecks come to make approximately that number of responses before anticipating food delivery (e.g., Mechner, 1958). As the number of responses increases in these tasks, so does the variability in the animal's responding, suggesting that the accuracy of number representations decreases with increasing set size. In addition, ducks and fish distribute their time between two food sources in rough proportion to the rate of food provisioning at those sources (e.g., Harper, 1982; see also Herrnstein & Loveland, 1975), suggesting that they form some approximate representation of the amount of food presented in a given interval of time (Gallistel, 1990). Finally, rats can be trained to discriminate four from eight sound bursts, responding to relative number over variations in other qualitative properties of the items, such as the duration of each burst (Church & Meck, 1984). These findings provide no evidence that the sources of uniquely human number abilities lie in the abilities exhibited by young infants in preferential looking experiments.

B. Developmental Changes in Number Representations in Young Children

The most striking changes in number abilities occur after children begin school, where they learn to perform new arithmetic calculations and develop new number concepts such as zero, fractions, and negative numbers (Gelman, 1991). Nevertheless, important changes in number representations also occur before formal schooling, coincident with the development of verbal counting. I focus on these earlier changes.

At about 2 years of age, children begin to count, and their counting shows interesting systematicity. As documented in the landmark studies of Gelman and Gallistel (1978), early counting tends to conform to the principles of one–one correspondence (children apply each number term to exactly one object), stable ordering (children tend to use a sequence of count terms in a constant order, although the orders of early count sequences, and even the terms themselves, sometimes are idiosyncratic), and cardinality (the last term in the count sequence has special significance for the child, possibly indicating the numerical value of the set). Although the extent and the meaning of this systematicity has been debated (e.g., Fuson & Hall, 1983, Gallistel & Gelman, 1992; Wynn, 1990), the existence of early developing, systematic counting is beyond dispute. Children appear to learn some form of counting spontaneously, in nearly all the cultures of the world (see Gordon, 1994, for a possible exception). Early counting is performed only on the entities that infants enumerate in preferential looking studies: solid objects or discrete events (Shipley & Shepperson, 1990). When children are asked to count the forks in an array containing three solid forks and one fork that has been broken into two pieces, for example, they typically count five bodies rather than four forks. All these findings suggest that young children are predisposed to develop procedures for counting the entities that their early developing perceptual systems pick out, and that these procedures yield representations of number (Gallistel & Gelman, 1992).

Despite these findings, young children may have marked gaps in their understanding of counting procedures and number words. First, 2- to 3-year-old children who are presented with a pile of objects and asked to give an experimenter, for example, "four" of the objects typically will give a handful of objects, without counting. Although such children reliably give just one object when asked for one and give more than one object when asked for a different number, the number that children give in the latter case is essentially random with respect to the number requested (Wynn, 1990). Only at about $3\frac{1}{2}$ years of age, more than a year after children begin counting objects, do children count when asked for a specific number of objects and then give the number requested.

Similar findings emerge when children are given a number word comprehension task. Children at the same ages were shown two pictures of multiple objects (e.g., a picture of three fish and a picture of four fish) and were asked to point to "the three fish." Children pointed successfully when one of the two alternatives depicted a single object, providing further evidence that they knew the meaning of "one" and knew that other number words refer to numerosities above one. In contrast, children pointed at random when each of the two alternatives depicted more than one object (Wynn, 1992b).

Further studies of children's changing performance on these tasks suggested an interesting developmental progression (Wynn 1992b). About 9 months after the onset of counting and after mastery of the meaning of "one," most children came to understand the meaning of "two," pointing to or giving exactly two objects on verbal requests. Months later, most children came to understand the meaning of "three." Still later, children came to understand the meanings of the rest of the number words in their vocabulary, and they began to use counting when asked to produce a given number of objects. Because no children could be found who understood "four" but not "five," Wynn suggested that understanding of counting and number words developed in a regular progression, with children first coming to understand the words "one," "two," and "three," in that order, and then coming all at once to understand the counting routine and the rest of the number words within it.

A variety of animal species other than humans also have shown changes, with training, in their abilities to represent exact numerosities and to use symbols to stand for these representations. In a typical training study (e.g., Matsuzawa, 1985; see also Boysen, 1993; Pepperberg, 1987), an animal first is introduced to symbols for a few small set sizes and is reinforced for correctly pairing each set size with its corresponding symbol. After the animal reliably chooses the appropriate symbol when shown a given set size (a test of number word production) and creates the appropriate set size in response to a given symbol (a test of number word comprehension), a new set size is introduced and further training is given. With such procedures, a chimpanzee has been taught symbols (plastic Arabic numerals) for the numbers one through six (Matsuzawa, 1985) and a parrot has been taught symbols (aural "words") for even higher numerosities (Pepperberg, 1987; see Davis & Perusse, 1988, for discussion of these and other studies).

Although these experiments reveal impressive number discrimination abilities, their findings suggest that the process by which animals learn to match tokens with specific numerosities is quite different from the process by which human children learn the meanings of number words. First and most obviously, the animals in these studies required extensive training, whereas young children appear to learn to count spontaneously, with little or no correction. Second, animals appear to be less constrained than human children with respect to the kinds of entities they enumerate. Monkeys, for example, have been trained to enumerate the sides of a polygon (Terrell & Thomas, 1990), which would be unlikely to qualify as countable entities for young children (Shipley & Shepperson, 1990).

Third, the developmental progression in learning number symbols is strikingly different in nonhuman primates from the progression observed with human children. For animals, the task of learning a symbol for a given numerosity becomes harder and harder as symbols for progressively higher numerosities are introduced. In Terrell and Thomas's (1990) study, for example, three of four monkeys met criterion on discriminating between six and seven elements within the 1000 trials allowed for each pairwise number discrimination, but only two of the three monkeys met criterion on discriminating between seven and eight elements, and no monkey met criterion on discriminating eight from nine elements. Human children, in contrast, appear to have great trouble learning words for sets of two or three entities. Once they have mastered this task, however, they come very rapidly to learn the meanings of words for higher numerosities.

Finally, animals appear to relate number symbols to exact numerosities only as a last resort, when task demands require this. For example, after Matsuzawa's chimpanzee had learned to apply different symbols to sets of one, two, three, and four items, sets of five items were introduced, with a new symbol. At this point, the chimpanzee applied the symbol "4" randomly to the sets of four vs. five items, suggesting that she had learned to apply "4" to any set size other than one, two, or three. Once she mastered the symbols "4" and "5," the symbol "6" was introduced with corresponding set of six items. Once again, the chimpanzee treated "5" as applying indiscriminately to sets of five and six. This pattern suggests that the chimpanzee never came to appreciate that each symbol would apply to exactly one numerosity (see also Davis & Perusse, 1988). In contrast, children who have learned the symbols for the first three set sizes come to infer, all at once, that each remaining symbol refers to exactly one set size.

C. Overview

Human infants can represent the exact numerosity of small sets of objects, and infants can represent the approximate numerosity of larger sets of objects. Both these abilities are found in a variety of other vertebrates, suggesting that they alone do not account for the uniquely human capacity for formal mathematical reasoning.

In early childhood, children begin quite spontaneously to learn the counting procedure of their culture, and their counting subsequently shows striking systematicity and universality. Studies of the development of understanding of the words in the counting routine show a systematic but surprisingly slow developmental progression: children first learn the meaning of "one," then "two," then "three," and then they come all at once to use counting to represent higher numbers and to produce and comprehend the remaining terms in their count sequence. This developmental progression contrasts with that found in other animals, who require extensive training to learn any number terms and never show the burst of understanding found in children.

The sources of this uniquely human development are not clear. Gallistel and Gelman (1992) have suggested that children come to understand counting by reflecting on the isomorphic relation between the principles underlying verbal counting (the domain to be learned) and the principles underlying nonverbal representations of approximate numerosity. Bloom (1994), following Chomsky (1988), has proposed that an understanding of counting rests on an implicit understanding of the iterativity of language. Tsivkin and I have recently suggested that children achieve this understanding by using language (particularly the counting routine and the number words) as a medium for combining two nonverbal systems of number representation that initially are quite separate: a system of exact representation of small numbers (revealed most clearly in Wynn's addition and subtraction studies) and a system of approximate representation of large numbers (revealed in the large-number discrimination studies). By mapping words such as "two" and "three" to representations constructed by both of these nonverbal systems, children may come to conjoin the systems together to arrive at a new system of representation, unique to humans, that allows the representation of the exact numerosity of sets that are indefinitely large (Spelke & Tsivkin, in press).

If any of these suggestions is correct, then the number estimation abilities found in other animals might well serve as the foundation of human knowledge of number. Understanding our uniquely human capacity for representing and reasoning about number then would require study of the distinctive processes by which humans alone come to elaborate these foundational systems, possibly with the aid of language.

V. LOOKING AHEAD

The primary task of this chapter has been to depict where the field of perceptual and cognitive development has arrived. In closing, I consider some of the new directions in which it may move. I begin by discussing some of the changing disciplines that promise to contribute to this field. Then I consider a particularly difficult and persistent question that may become amenable to study.

A. A Synthesis

Although major insights into perceptual and cognitive development have come from the fields of experimental psychology, perceptual and behavioral ecology, and developmental neurobiology, each of these disciplines has developed rather independently of the others. With some notable exceptions (e.g., Held, 1985), studies of the emergence of topographic maps and ocular dominance columns in the developing visual system have connected only indirectly with studies of the development of depth perception or spatially guided behavior in humans. Fortunately, these fields now are beginning to converge. In particular, studies probing the visual pathways subserving spatial representation (e.g., Andersen, 1994), object representation (e.g., Goodale, 1995), and memory (e.g., Desimone, Miller, Chelazzi, &

Lueschow, 1994) suggest new insights into the development of depth perception, object representation, and even representations of number (e.g., Bertenthal, 1996; Dehaene, 1997).

This synthesis has been fostered by the rise of computational studies of perceptual and cognitive development (see Elman et al., 1996, for extended discussion of the potential fruits of such studies, and Johnson, 1997, for discussion of a synthesis of computational studies with studies in developmental neurobiology and psychology). At its best, developmental computational modeling takes as starting points the findings of (a) perceptual ecologists, concerning the information available to young perceivers; (b) developmental neurobiologists, concerning the perceptual and cognitive mechanisms by which this information is detected and transformed; (c) developmental psychologists, concerning the objects and events infants perceive and represent, and (d) behavioral ecologists, concerning the action patterns that perceptual and cognitive processes support. From these ingredients, computational modelers attempt to construct systems whose internal architecture mirrors that of infants and that, when given the information available to infants, solve the perceptual, cognitive, and action problems that infants solve. Because developmental studies in perceptual and behavioral ecology, neurobiology, and experimental psychology are works in progress, insights from computational modeling in turn can suggest which of the provisional conclusions from those fields are most promising. All these disciplines therefore can interact to foster accounts of perceptual and cognitive development.

In a sense, this disciplinary synthesis is not new, for it is foreshadowed in the 19th century in the writings of Helmholtz (1866/1962) and by earlier thinkers as well. What may emerge in the 21st century, however, is the ability to apply this synthesis to specific and concrete problems in perceptual and cognitive development. To date, such applications have not gone far, for they tend to be restricted to artificially limited problems and to engage only distantly the findings of each of the five contributing disciplines. Moreover, such applications have sometimes been hampered by the impulse to use computational models as grist for polemical arguments rather than as tools for empirical study. Nevertheless, recent computational studies of the developing object representations subserving imprinting in chicks (O'Reilly & Johnson, 1994) and of the developing spatial representations subserving aspects of navigation in ants (Muller & Wehner, 1988) begin to suggest how this synthesis could proceed.

B. Comparative Cognition

Central to the study of cognitive development is the problem of understanding how people come to think and reason in distinctly human ways. Solving this problem, psychologists have long known, requires systematic comparisons of the development of cognition in human children and in other animal species. Equally central to the study of cognitive development is the task of teasing apart the perceptual and cognitive abilities that are inevitable for all humans and universal across cultures from those that are variable across people in different circumstances. Accomplishing this task requires systematic comparisons of the development of cognition in children in different physical and cultural environments. The study of perceptual and cognitive development therefore connects to two fields of comparative research.

Until quite recently, progress in these two fields has been somewhat disappointing. The fields of animal cognition and cognitive anthropology have had their full share of brilliant investigators, but the disciplines themselves have been hampered by divisive controversies and conflicting perspectives. I believe this situation has begun to change, and that each of these disciplines will contribute substantially to future understanding of nature, nurture, and development.

Throughout much of this century, the study of animal cognition has suffered from a radical divide. On one hand, ethologists have studied animal behavior in its natural context with sensitive attention to the ecology and the evolutionary history of behaving animals but with less regard for the perceptual and cognitive processes that allow animals to act adaptively within the environment. On the other hand, comparative psychologists have studied animal behavior through laboratory experiments that have aimed for a mechanistic understanding of the processes governing animals' behavior, but often with little regard for ecology and evolution (Gibson & Walk, 1960, are a notable exception). Comparative psychologists also were hampered by the behaviorist movement, which long discouraged many investigators from addressing questions of perception and cognition directly, and by Morgan's canon (1895), which was interpreted to favor the most complicated noncognitive explanations for animal behavior over the most simple, cognitive explanations (see Gallistel, 1990, for extensive examples). Those who escaped these temptations faced a third: the temptation to demonstrate the cognitive heights that animals could scale with sufficient and appropriate training, rather than to study the cognitive processes that underlie adaptive behavior in natural settings.

Fortunately, the empirical study of animal cognition flourished despite its divisions. Rich comparative data have been obtained from field and laboratory experiments, providing the terrain for a newly unified, comparative study of perception, cognition, and action across ontogeny and phylogeny. This unification is now being attempted in a number of quarters (e.g., Cheney & Seyfarth, 1990; Cosmides & Tooby, 1994; Gallistel, 1990; Hauser, 1996; Marler, 1991; Tomasello & Call, 1997; see Kohler, 1925/1959, and Premack, 1976, for earlier examples). The successful unification of this field, and its eventual integration with studies in brain and cognitive science, may be one of the most important achievements to come.

Studies of cultural variation in human perception and cognition also have suffered from conflicting goals and perspectives, in my view. Until the middle of this century, much of this research appeared to consist of poorly designed experiments purporting to show that people in primitive cultures lacked some of the fundamental perceptual abilities and conceptual distinctions that ground the cognitive life of the civilized. In an understandable reaction against this research, more recent contributions to the study of cultural variation often have been founded on a radical critique of the enterprise of comparing individuals across cultures: a critique that leaves little room for systematic inquiry into the universal and variable properties of human cognition.

Today, there are signs that this situation is changing, and that anthropologists and cognitive psychologists are beginning to work together productively on problems of perceptual and cognitive development. Although space limits preclude any substantive discussion, I cite three examples that are relevant to the topics discussed in this chapter. First, investigators are beginning to shed light on the development of natural object categories, through focused study of cultural variability and invariance in mature object categories and in patterns of category development (e.g., Atran, 1990; Lucy, 1992; Medin, Lynch, Coley & Atran, 1997). Second, investigators are beginning to shed light on universal and variable aspects of spatial orientation and spatial representation, through systematic comparisons of the spatial language and cognition of people who live in different physical, cultural, and linguistic environments (e.g., Choi & Bowerman, 1991; Levinson, 1996; see Bloom, Peterson, Nadel, & Garrett, 1996; Bowerman & Levinson, in press). Third, investigators are beginning to probe the universal and variable properties of humans' domain-specific systems of knowledge, such as knowledge of number, physical causality, and intentional action (see the contributions in Hirschfeld & Gelman, 1994, and Sperber, Premack, & Premack, 1995). Importantly, none of the investigators just cited attempts to measure the cognitive performance of children and adults in other cultures against a yardstick of Western industrial societies. Instead, they seek to understand the universal and culturally variable properties of human cognition through a combination of ethnographic, linguistic, and experimental studies of children and adults in particular settings. Testifying to the potential importance of their efforts is the occasional startling insight into our own, familiar cognitive processes and patterns of cognitive development that can come from studying the language, cognition, and development of people whose lives seem most different from ours.

C. Cognitive Change

Do human cognitive capacities grow with development, such that older children perceive entities and entertain thoughts that are beyond the perceptual and conceptual resources of younger children? Can such changes be fostered by learning and experience? These questions have been particularly problematic for students of cognitive development in recent decades. On one hand, studies in the history of science and in science education suggest that the answer to both questions must be yes. When scientists and mathematicians discovered non-Euclidean geometries, or invented classical physics, their thinking underwent radical expansion and change (see Hatfield, 1990; Kuhn, 1957, 1977). When students learn these and other mathematical systems and physical theories, their thinking in turn is changed by the educational process (see Carey, 1985, 1991; Kitcher, 1988; Piaget, 1975). On the other hand, powerful arguments suggest that radical perceptual and conceptual change cannot possibly occur through learning (Fodor, 1975; Köhler, 1947). The important arguments of Köhler and Fodor continue to challenge the field of perceptual and cognitive development and merit a brief exposition.

Köhler considered whether it is possible to learn to organize the perceptual world into objects through one's experience with objects: whether, for example, experience in a world of relatively smooth, symmetrical, homogeneous, and cohesive bodies could lead one to learn the Gestalt organizational principles. Such learning is impossible in principle, Köhler concluded, because a perceiver can only learn about the properties of surrounding bodies if he or she can perceive those bodies: learning about objects requires the very perceptual capacity that is at issue. Fodor considered whether it is possible to learn to organize perceived objects into concepts or categories: whether, for example, experience in a world containing birds could lead a child who lacked the concept *bird* to acquire it. True learning of such concepts is impossible, Fodor concluded, because one can only learn about birds if one already can single out birds as a category: again, the ability at issue.

Most students of cognitive development have responded to these apparent paradoxes either by rejecting the lessons from the history of science and science education and concluding that genuine perceptual and cognitive change is a myth, or by rejecting the arguments of Köhler and Fodor on the grounds that something is wrong with them (although it isn't clear what; see however Hochberg, chap. 9, this volume). Recent developments, nevertheless, suggest a way to preserve the insights of Helmholtz and Köhler, Kuhn, and Fodor alike, granting to humans both innate abilities to perceive and categorize objects and abilities to learn genuinely new perceptual and conceptual organizations. I have hinted at this resolution in the discussion of substantive topics and now sketch it directly.

Empiricist and nativist approaches to perception and cognition have long shared the assumption that the capacity to perceive and conceptualize the world is unitary. On this assumption, infants of a given age either do or do not perceive a given object's boundaries, categorize a given object as a cat, or represent the number of objects in a scene. The nativist arguments of Köhler and Fodor rest on this assumption, for they presuppose that a child either does or does not perceive a given set of objects or possess a given conceptual category.

Research suggests, nevertheless, that this assumption is false: Humans have multiple systems of representation that develop at different times and in accord with different constraints. For example, I have reviewed evidence for three distinct representations of objects: a spatiotemporal system for perceiving object unity and boundaries, a system for perceiving and categorizing objects by their properties, and a system for guiding object-directed actions. Further evidence has suggested that young children have more than one system for representing space and for representing number. Each of these systems differs with respect to the environmental properties it represents, and each system is surprisingly independent of the others.

A young infant therefore both can and cannot perceive and categorize cats, and she both has and fails to have the concept *three*.

If infants possess initial systems of representation, then these systems may allow them to perceive and conceptualize aspects of the environment prior to learning, as Kohler's and Fodor's arguments require. Because these systems initially are separate from one another, however, the youngest children cannot represent complex perceptions or concepts whose elements derive from different systems. Qualitative changes in perceptual and cognitive abilities could come from processes that coordinate children's distinct systems of representation.

Consider, for example, the domain of knowledge of number. I suggested that infants have two early developing, unlearned systems of representation of number: a small-number system for representing the exact number of bounded objects or events in a scene up to about three, and a large-number system for representing the approximate number of entities in sets of indefinitely large size. Each of these systems would allow infants to represent certain set sizes exactly, and all set sizes approximately, prior to learning. If these systems initially are independent, then infants would be unable to perceive or represent sets of, for example, exactly seven elements and would lack the concept *seven*. Perceiving and conceiving of exactly seven entities would be beyond infants' capacities, because *seven* lies outside the range of their small number system and beyond the limits of discriminability of their large number system. By learning to count, children might come to conjoin these two systems of number representation to form new representations that are (a) sensitive to the effects of adding or subtracting exactly one object (a contribution from the small-number system) and (b) applicable to sets of indefinitely high numerosity (a contribution of the large-number system) (see Tsivkin & Spelke, in press, for further exposition).

More generally, processes that conjoin the representations constructed by unlearned perceptual and conceptual systems may yield new representations beyond the expressive power of any of the original systems alone: new representations of exact, large numerosities, new representations of visible drop-offs as dangerous, new representations of objects as spatiotemporal bodies with enduring, category-specific properties, and more. Conceptual changes that occur during science education or in the history of science might depend on the same capacity for conjoining separate systems of knowledge (see Carey & Spelke, 1994; Duhem, 1949). This capacity may account in some measure for the distinctively human features of human intelligence (see Mithen, 1996). It also may begin to explain why human knowledge has developed so much further than that of other species, when the building blocks of this knowledge appear to be so similar to those of other animals.

These possibilities suggest a research agenda for students of perceptual and cognitive development. To understand cognitive development, on this view, one must study the nature of each of humans' initial systems of knowledge and the changes that each system undergoes with growth and experience. In addition, one must study the new systems of knowledge that emerge as initial cognitive systems are combined. Finally, one must study the processes by which distinct representational systems become linked together over human development. The search for these processes will take developmental cognitive scientists into nearly uncharted territory. We may hope, however, that the tools that have helped to elucidate the development of domain-specific perceptual and cognitive systems will begin to shed light on these processes as well.

References

Adolph, K. E., Eppler, M. A., & Gibson, E. J. (1993). Crawling versus walking: Infants' perception of affordances for locomotion on slopes. *Child Development, 64,* 1158–1174.

Ahmed, A., & Ruffman, T. (1996). Do infants know when they are searching incorrectly? Looking times in a non-search A not B task. *Infant Behavior and Development, 19,* 297 (abstract).

Andersen, R. A. (1994). Coordinate transformations and motor planning in posterior parietal cortex. In M. S. Gazzaniga (Ed.), *The cognitive neurosciences.* Cambridge, MA: MIT Press.

Antell, S. E., & Keating, D. (1983). Perception of numerical invariance by neonates. *Child Development, 54,* 695–701.

Antinucci, F. (1989). *Cognitive structure and development in nonhuman primates.* Hillsdale, NJ: Erlbaum.

Arterberry, M. E., Craton, L. G., & Yonas, A. (1993). Infants' sensitivity to motion-carried information for depth and object properties. In C. E. Granrud (Ed.), *Visual perception and cognition in infancy.* Hillsdale, NJ: Erlbaum.

Aslin, R. N. (1988). Anatomical constraints on oculomotor development: Implications for infant perception. In A. Yonas (Ed.), *Perceptual development in infancy: The Minnesota Symposia on Child Psychology, Vol. 20.* Hillsdale, NJ: Erlbaum.

Atran S. (1990). *Cognitive foundations of natural history: Towards an anthropology of science.* Cambridge, UK: Cambridge University Press.

Baillargeon, R. (1993). The object concept revisited: New directions in the investigation of infants' physical knowledge. In C. E. Granrud (Ed.), *Visual perception and cognition in infancy.* Hillsdale, NJ: Erlbaum.

Baillargeon, R., & DeVos, J. (1991). Object permanence in young infants: Further evidence. *Child Development, 62,* 1227–1246.

Ball, W. A. (1973, April). *The perception of causality in the infant.* Paper presented at the Society for Research in Child Development. Philadelphia, PA.

Banks, M. S. (1988). Visual recalibration and the development of contrast and optical flow perception. In A. Yonas (Ed.), *Perceptual development in infancy: The Minnesota Symposia on Child Psychology, Vol. 2.* Hillsdale, NJ: Erlbaum.

Banks, M. S., & Salapatek, P. (1983). Infant visual perception. In P. Mussen (Series Ed.) and M. M. Haith & J. J. Campos (Eds.), *Handbook of child psychology, Vol. 2.* New York: Wiley.

Bedford, F. (1989). Constraints on learning new mappings between perceptual dimensions. *Journal of Experimental Psychology: Human Perception and Performance, 15,* 232–248.

Bertenthal, B. I. (1996). Origins and early development of perception, action, and representation. *Annual Review of Psychology, 47,* 431–459.

Bertoncini, J., & Mehler, J. J. (1981). Syllables as units in infant speech perception. *Infant Behavior & Development, 4,* 247–260.

Bloom, P. (1994). Generativity within language and other cognitive domains. *Cognition, 51,* 177–189.

Bloom, P., Peterson, M., Nadel, L., & Garrett, M. (1996). *Language and space.* Cambridge, MA: MIT Press.

Bornstein, M. H. (1985). Habituation of attention as a measure of visual information processing in human infants: Summary, systematization, and synthesis. In G. Gottlieb & N. A. Krasnegor (Eds.), *Measurement of audition and vision in the first years of life.* Norwood, NJ: Ablex.

Bower, T. G. R. (1966). The visual world of infants. *Scientific American, 215,* 80–92.

Bowerman, M., & Levinson, S. (in press). *Language acquisition and conceptual development.* Cambridge: Cambridge University Press.

Boysen, S. T. (1993). Counting in chimpanzee: Nonhuman principles and emergent properties of number. In S. T. Boysen, & E. J. Capaldi (Eds.), *The development of numerical competence: Animal and human models.* Hillsdale, NJ: Erlbaum.

Boysen, S. T., & Capaldi, E. J. (1993). *The development of numerical competence: Animal and human models.* Hillsdale, NJ: Erlbaum.

Brunswik, E., & Kamiya, J. (1953). Ecological cue-validity of "proximity" and of other Gestalt factors. *American Journal of Psychology, 66,* 20–32.

Bushnell, I. W. R., Sai, F., & Fullin, J. T. (1989). Neonatal recognition of mother's face. *British Journal of Developmental Psychology, 7,* 3–15.

Campos, J. J., Bertenthal, B. I., & Kermoian, R. (1992). Early experience and emotional development: The emergence of wariness of heights. *Psychological Science, 3,* 61–64.

Carey, S. (1985). *Conceptual change in childhood.* Cambridge, MA: Bradford/MIT Press.

Carey, S. (1991). Knowledge acquisition: Enrichment or conceptual change? In S. Carey & R. Gelman (Eds.), *Epigenesis of mind: Essays on biology and cognition* (pp. 1257–291). Hillsdale, NJ: Erlbaum.

Carey, S., & Spelke, E. S. (1994). Domain-specific knowledge and conceptual change. In L. A. Hirschfeld & S. A. Gelman (Eds.), *Mapping the mind: Domain specificity in cognition and culture.* Cambridge: Cambridge University Press.

Cheney, D. L., & Seyfarth, R. M. (1990). *How monkeys see the world.* Chicago: University of Chicago Press.

Chiang, W.-C., & Wynn, K. (1996). Eight-month-old infants' reasoning about collections. *Infant Behavior and Development, 199,* 390 (abstract).

Choi, S., & Bowerman, M. (1991). Learning to express motion events in English and Korean: The influence of language-specific lexicalization patterns. *Cognition, 41,* 83–121.

Chomsky, N. (1988). *Language and problems of knowledge: The Managua lectures.* Cambridge, MA: MIT Press.

Church, R. M., & Meck, W. H. (1984). The numerical attributes of stimuli. In H. L. Roitblat, R. G. Bever, & H. S. Terrace (Eds.), *Animal cognition.* Hillsdale, NJ: Erlbaum.

Clifton, R. K., Rochat, P., Litovsky, R., & Perris, E. (1991). Object representation guides infants' reaching in the dark. *Journal of Experimental Psychology: Human Perception and Performance, 17*(2), 323–329.

Constantine-Paton, M., Cline, H. T., & Debski, E. (1990). Patterned activity, synaptic convergence, and the NMDA receptor in developing visual pathways. *Annual Review of Neuroscience, 13,* 129–154.

Cosmides, L., & Tooby, J. (1995). From function to structure: The role of evolutionary biology and computational theories in cognitive neuroscience. In M. S. Gazzaniga (Ed.), *The cognitive neurosciences.* Cambridge, MA: MIT Press.

Craton, L. G., & Yonas, A. (1990). The role of motion in infant perception of occlusion. In J. T. Enns (Ed.), *The development of attention: Research and theory.* New York: Elsevier Science Publishers B. V. (North-Holland).

Davis, H., & Perusse, R. (1988). Numerical competence in animals: Definitional issues, current evidence, and a new research agenda. *Behavioral and Brain Sciences, 11,* 561–579.

Dehaene, S. (1997). *The number sense.* New York: Oxford.

Dehaene, S., & Cohen, L. (1991). Two mental calculation systems: A case study of severe acalculia with preserved approximation. *Neuropsychologia, 29,* 1045–1074.

Descartes, R. (1971). Dioptrics. In E. Anscombe & P. T. Geach (Eds. and Trans.), *Philosophical writings.* Indianapolis: Bobbs-Merrill. (Originally published 1637.)

Desimone, R., Miller, E. K., Chelazzi, L., & Lueschow, A. (1994). Multiple memory systems in the visual cortex. In M. S. Gazzaniga (Ed.), *The cognitive neurosciences.* Cambridge, MA: MIT Press.

Diamond, A. (1990). The development and neural bases of memory functions as indexed by the AB and delayed response tasks in human infants and infant monkeys. In A. Diamond (Ed.), *The development and neural bases of higher cognitive Functions. Annals of the New York Academy of Sciences, 608,* 517–536.

Diamond, R., & Carey, S. (1977). Developmental changes in the representation of faces. *Journal of Experimental Child Psychology, 23,* 1–22.

Duhem, P. (1949). *The aim and structure of physical theory.* Princeton: Princeton University Press.

Eimas, P. (1994). Categorization in early infancy and the continuity of development. *Cognition, 50,* 83–93.

Elman, J., Bates, E., Johnson, M., Karmiloff-Smith, A., Parisi, D., & Plunkett, K. (1996). *Rethinking innateness: A connectionist perspective on development.* Cambridge, MA: MIT Press.

Etienne, A. S. (1973). Searching behavior towards a disappearing prey in the domestic chick as affected by preliminary experience. *Animal Behavior, 21,* 749–761.

Fantz, R. L. (1961). The origin of form perception. *Scientific American, 204,* 66–72.

Feller, M. B., Wellis, D. P., Stellwagen, D., Werblin, F. S., & Shatz, C. J. (1996). Requirement for cholinergic synaptic transmission in the propagation of spontaneous retinal waves. *Science, 272,* 1182–1187.

Fodor, J. A. (1975). *The language of thought.* Cambridge, MA: Harvard University Press.

Fox, R., Aslin, R., Shea, S., & Dumais, S. (1980). Stereopsis in human infants. *Science, 207,* 323–324.

Fuson, K. C., & Hall, J. W. (1983). The acquisition of early number word meanings: A conceptual analysis and review. In H. P. Ginsburg (Ed.), *The development of mathematical thinking.* New York: Academic Press.

Gallistel, C. R. (1990): *The organization of learning.* New York: Crowell.

Gallistel, C. R., & Gelman, R. (1992). Preverbal and verbal counting and computation. *Cognition, 44,* 43–74.

Gelman, R. (1991). Epigenetic foundations of knowledge structures: Initial and transcendent constructions. In S. Carey & R. Gelman (Eds.), *The epigenesis of mind: Essays on biology and cognition.* Hillsdale, NJ: Erlbaum.

Gelman, R., & Gallistel, C. R. (1978). *The child's understanding of number.* Cambridge, MA: Harvard University Press.

Ghahramani, Z., Wolpert, D. M., & Jordan, M. I. (1996). Generalization to local remappings of the visuomotor coordinate transformation. *J. Neuroscience, 16,* 7085–7096.

Gibson, E. J. (1991). *An odyssey in learning and perception.* Cambridge, MA: MIT Press.

Gibson, E. J., & Schmuckler, M. A. (1989). Going somewhere: An ecological and experimental approach to development of mobility. *Ecological Psychology, 1,* 3–25.

Gibson, E. J., & Walk, R. D. (1960). The "visual cliff." *Scientific American, 202,* 64–71.

Goodale, M. A. (1995). The cortical organization of visual perception and visuomotor control. In S. M. Kosslyn & D. N. Osherson (Eds.), *Visual cognition.* Cambridge, MA: MIT Press.

Gordon, P. (1994). *Innumerate Amazonians and Kronecker's Theism: One-two-many systems and the artificialism of number.* Poster presented at the European Society for Philosophy and Psychology, Paris.

Gottschaldt, K. (1967). Gestalt factors and repetition. In W. D. Ellis (Ed.), *A source book of Gestalt psychology* (pp. 109–135). New York: Humanities Press.

Granrud, C. E. (1987). Size constancy in newborn human infants. *Investigative Ophthalmology and Visual Science, 28,* 5.

Haith, M. M., Bergman, T., & Moore, M. J. (1977). Eye-contact and face-scanning in early infancy. *Science, 198,* 853–855.

Harper, D. G. C. (1982). Competitive foraging in mallards: "Ideal free" ducks. *Animal Behavior, 30,* 575–584.

Harris, C. (1965). Perceptual adaptation to inverted, reversed, and displaced vision. *Psychological Review, 72,* 419–444.

Hatfield, G. (1990). *The natural and the normative: Theories of spatial perception from Kant to Helmholtz.* Cambridge, MA: MIT Press.

Hauser, M. D. (1996). *The evolution of communication.* Cambridge, MA: MIT Press.

Hauser, M. D., MacNeilage, P., & Ware, M. (1996). Numerical representations in primates. *Proceedings of the National Academy of Sciences, 93,* 1514–1517.

Hebb, D. O. (1949). *The organization of behavior.* New York: Wiley.

Held, R. (1985). Binocular vision: Behavioral and neural development. In J. Mehler & R. Fox (Eds.), *Neonate cognition*. Hillsdale, NJ: Erlbaum.

Held, R., Birch, E. E., & Gwiazda, J. (1980). Stereoacuity of human infants. *Proceedings of the National Academy of Sciences (USA), 77,* 5572–5574.

Held, R., & Hein, A. (1963). Movement produced stimulation in the development of visually guided behavior. *Journal of Comparative and Physiological Psychology, 56,* 872–876.

Helmholtz, H. von (1962). *Treatise on physiological optics* (J. P. C. Southall, Trans.). New York: Dover. (Original work published 1867)

Herrnstein, R. J., & Loveland, D. H. (1975). Maximizing and matching on concurrent ratio schedules. *Journal of the Experimental Analysis of Behavior, 24,* 107–116.

Herrnstein, R. J. (1990). Levels of stimulus control: A functional approach. *Cognition, 37,* 133–166.

Hirschfeld, L. A., & Gelman, S. A. (1994). *Mapping the mind: Domain specificity in cognition and culture.* Cambridge, UK: Cambridge University Press.

Hochberg, J. (1974). Organization and the Gestalt tradition. In E. C. Carterette & M. P. Friedman, *Handbook of perception, Volume 1: Historical and philosophical roots of perception* (pp. 180–211). New York: Academic Press.

Honig, W. K. (1993). Numerosity a dimension of stimulus control. In S. T. Boysen & E. J. Capaldi (Eds.), *The development of numerical competence: Animal and human models.* Hillsdale, NJ: Erlbaum.

Hood, B., & Willats, P. (1986). Reaching in the dark to an object's remembered position: Evidence for object permanence in 5-month-old infants. *British Journal of Developmental Psychology, 4,* 57–65.

Horn, G. (1985). *Memory, imprinting and the brain.* Oxford: Clarendon Press.

Huntley-Fenner, G. (1995). *On the infants' understanding of the logical distinction between count nouns and mass nouns.* Unpublished manuscript.

Jeannerod, M. (1994). The hand and the object: The role of posterior parietal cortex in forming motor representations. *Canadian Journal of Physiology & Pharmacology, 72,* 535–541.

Johnson, M. H. (1997). *Cortical plasticity and cognitive development.* New York: Oxford University Press.

Johnson, M. H., & Morton, J. (1991). *Biology and cognitive development: The case of face recognition.* Oxford: Blackwell.

Johnson, S. P., & Aslin, R. N. (1996). Perception of object unity in young infants: The roles of motion, depth, and orientation. *Cognitive Development, 11,* 161–180.

Johnson, S. P., & Aslin, R. N. (1995). Perception of object unity in 2-month-old infants. *Developmental Psychology, 31,* 739–745.

Johnson, S. P., & Nanez, J. E. Sr. (1995). Young infants' perception of object unity in two-dimensional displays. *Infant Behavior and Development, 18,* 133–143.

Kanizsa, G. (1979). *Organization in vision.* New York: Praeger.

Kellman, P. J. (1993). Kinematic foundations of visual perception. In C. E. Granrud (Ed.), *Visual perception and cognition in infancy.* Hillsdale, NJ: Erlbaum.

Kellman, P. J., & Arterberry, M. (in press). *The cradle of knowledge: Development of perception in infancy.* Cambridge, MA: MIT Press.

Kellman, P. J., Hofsten, C. von, Condry, K., & O'Halloran, R. (1991a). *Motion and stability in the world of the (moving) infant.* Unpublished manuscript.

Kellman, P. J., Hofsten, C. von, Van de Walle, G. A., & Condry, K. (1991b). *Perception of motion and stability during observer motion by pre-stereoscopic infants.* Unpublished manuscript.

Kellman, P. J., & Spelke, E. S. (1983). Perception of partly occluded objects in infancy. *Cognitive Psychology, 15,* 483–524.

Kitcher, P. (1988). The child as parent of the scientist. *Mind and Language, 3,* 217–228.

Koechlin, E., Dehaene, S., & Mehler, J. (in press). Numerical transformations in five-month-old human infants. *Mathematical cognition.*

Koffka, K. (1935). *Principles of Gestalt psychology.* New York: Harcourt, Brace & World.

Kohler, W. (1959). *The mentality of apes.* New York: Viking. (Original work published 1925)

Kohler, W. (1947). *Gestalt psychology.* New York: Liveright.

Kotovsky, L., & Baillargeon, R. (1994). Calibration-based reasoning about collision events in 11-month-old infants. *Cognition, 51,* 107–129.

Kuhn, T. S. (1957). *The Copernican revolution.* New York: Vintage.

Kuhn, T. S. (1977). A function for thought experiments. In T. S. Kuhn, (Ed.), *The essential tension.* Chicago: University of Chicago Press.

Kuhl, P. K., & Meltzoff, A. N. (1982). The bimodal perception of speech in infancy. *Science, 218,* 1138–1141.

Leslie, A. M. (1984). Spatiotemporal continuity and the perception of causality in infants. *Perception, 13,* 287–305.

Leslie, A. M., & Keeble, S. (1987). Do six-month-old infants perceive causality? *Cognition, 25,* 265–288.

Leslie, A. M. (1988). The necessity of illusion: Perception and thought in infancy. In L. Weiskrantz (Ed.), *Thought without language.* Oxford: Clarendon Press.

LeVay, S. Wiesel, T. N., & Hubel, D. H. (1980). The development of ocular dominance columns in normal and visually deprived monkeys. *Journal of Comparative Neurology, 191,* 1–51.

Levinson, S. (1994). Vision, shape, and linguistic description: Tzeltal body-part terminology and object description. *Linguistics, 32,* 791–855.

Levinson, S. (1996). Frames of reference and Molyneux's question: Cross-linguistic evidence. In P. Bloom, M. Peterson, L. Nadel & M. Garrett (Eds.), *Language and space.* Cambridge, MA: MIT Press.

Lucy, J. (1992). *Language diversity and thought.* Cambridge, UK: Cambridge University Press.

Mandler, J. (1992). How to build a baby II: Conceptual primitives. *Psychological Review, 99,* 587–604.

Mandler, J. M., & McDonough, L. (1993). Concept formation in infancy. *Cognitive Development, 8,* 291–318.

Marler, P. (1991). The instinct to learn. In S. Carey & R. Gelman (Eds.), *The epigenesis of mind: Essays on biology and cognition.* Hillsdale, NJ: Erlbaum.

Matsuzawa, T. (1985). Use of numbers by a chimpanzee. *Nature, 315,* 57–59.

Mechner, F. (1958). Probability relations within response sequences under ratio reinforcement. *Journal of the Experimental Analysis of Behavior, 1,* 109–122.

Medin, D., Lynch, E., Coley, J., & Atran, S. (1997). Categorization and reasoning among tree experts: Do all roads lead to Rome? *Cognitive Psychology, 32,* 49–96.

Michotte, A. (1963). *The perception of causality.* New York: Basic Books.

Michotte, A., Thines, R., & Grabbe, G. (1964). *Les compléments amodaux des structures perspectives.* [The amodal complements of perceptual structures.] Louvain, Belgium: Publications Universitaires de Louvain.

Miller, K. D., Keller, J. B., & Stryker, M. P. (1989). Ocular dominance column development: Analysis and simulation. *Science, 245,* 605–615.

Mithen, S. (1996). *The prehistory of the mind.* London: Thames & Hudson.

Mix, K., Levine, S., & Huttenlocher, J. (1994). *Infants' detection of auditory-visual numerical correspondences: another look.* Paper presented at the annual meeting of the Midwestern Psychological Association, Chicago, IL.

Moore, D., Benenson, J., Reznick, J. S., Peterson, M., & Kagan, J. (1987). Effect of auditory numerical information on infants' looking behavior. *Developmental Psychology, 23,* 665–670.

Morgan, C. L. (1895). *An introduction to comparative psychology.* London: Walter Scott.

Muller, M., & Wehner, R. (1988). Path integration in desert ants. *Proceedings of the National Academy of Sciences (USA), 85,* 5287–5290.

Munakata, Y. (in press). Task-dependency in infant behavior: Toward an understanding of the processes underlying cognitive development. To appear in F. Lacerda, C. von Hofsten, & J. Heimann (Eds.), *Transitions in perception, cognition, and action in early infancy.*

Munakata, Y. (1997). Perseverative reaching in infancy: The roles of hidden toys and motor history in the A not B task. *Infant Behavior and Development, 20,* 405–415.

Munakata, Y., McClelland, J. L., Johnson, M. H., & Siegler, R. S. (1997). Rethinking infant knowledge: Toward an adaptive process account of successes and failures in object permanence tasks. *Psychological Review, 104,* 686–713.

Needham, A. (1994). Infants' use of perceptual similarity when segregating partly occluded objects during the fourth month of life. Paper presented at the International Conference on Infant Studies, Paris, June.

O'Reilly, R. C., & Johnson, M. H. (1994). Object recognition and sensitive periods: A computational analysis of visual imprinting. *Neural Computation, 6,* 357–389.

Pascalis, O. de Schonen, S., Morton, J., Deruelle, C., & Fabre-Grenet, M. (1995). Mothers' face recognition by neonates: A replication and an extension. *Infant Behavior and Development, 18,* 79–85.

Pepperberg, I. M. (1987). Evidence for conceptual quantitative abilities in the African grey parrot: Labeling of cardinal sets. *Ethology, 75,* 37–61.

Piaget, J. (1952). *The origins of intelligence in childhood.* New York: International Universities Press.

Piaget, J. (1954). *The construction of reality in the child.* New York: Basic Books.

Piaget, J. (1975). Discussion of Fodor on the impossibility of acquiring "more powerful" structures. In U. Piatelli-Palmarini (Ed.), *Language and Learning.* Cambridge: MA: Harvard University Press.

Premack, D. (1976). *Intelligence in ape and man.* Hillsdale, NJ: Erlbaum.

Quinn, P. C., Brown, C. R., & Streppa, M. L. (1997). Perceptual organization of complex visual configurations by young infants. *Infant Behavior and Development, 20,* 35–46.

Quinn, P. C., Eimas, P. D., & Rosenkrantz, S. L. (1993). Evidence for representations of perceptually similar natural categories by 3-month-old and 4-month-old infants. *Perception, 22,* 463–476.

Rader, N., Bausano, M., & Richards, J. E. (1980). On the nature of the visual-cliff avoidance response in human infants. *Child Development, 51,* 61–68.

Rakic, P. (1977). Prenatal development of the visual system in rhesus monkey. *Philosophical transactions of the Royal Society of London, Series B, 278,* 245–260.

Regolin, L., & Vallortigara, G. (1995). Perception of partly occluded objects by young chicks. *Perception & Psychophysics, 57,* 971–976.

Regolin, L., Vallortigara, G., & Zanforlin, M. (1994). Perceptual and motivational aspects of detour behavior in young chicks. *Animal Behavior, 47,* 123–131.

Regolin, L. Vallortigara, G., & Zanforlin, M. (1995). Detour behavior in the domestic chick: searching for a disappearing prey or a disappearing social partner. *Animal Behavior, 50,* 203–211 (a).

Regolin, L., Vallortigara, G., & Zanforlin, M. (1995). Object and spatial representations in detour problems by chicks. *Animal Behavior, 49,* 195–199 (b).

Rochat, P. & Hespos, S. J. (1996). Tracking and anticipation of invisible spatial formations by 4- to 8-month-old infants. *Cognitive Development, 11,* 3–17.

Sereno, M. I. & Allman, J. M. (1991). Cortical visual areas in mammals. In A. Leventhal (Ed.), *The neural basis of visual function* (pp. 160–172). New York: MacMillan.

Shatz, C. J. (1992). The developing brain. *Scientific American, XX,* 61–67.

Shatz, C. J., & Stryker, M. P. (1988). Prenatal tetrodotoxin blocks segregation of retinogeniculate afferents. *Science, 242,* 87–89.

Sherk, H., & Stryker, M. P. (1976). Quantitative study of cortical orientation selectivity in visually inexperienced kitten. *Journal of Neurophysiology, 39,* 63–70.

Shipley, E. F., & Shepperson, B. (1990). Countable entities: Developmental changes. *Cognition, 34,* 109–136.

Simon, T., Hespos, S., & Rochat, P. (1995). Do infants understand simple arithmetic? A replication of Wynn (1992). *Cognitive Development, 10,* 253–269.

Singer, W., & Gray, C. M. (1995). Visual feature integration and the temporal correlation hypothesis. *Annual Review of Neuroscience, 18,* 555–586.

Slater, A., Mattock, A., & Brown, E. (1990a). Size constancy at birth: Newborn infants' responses to retinal and real size. *Journal of Experimental Child Psychology, 49,* 314–322.

Slater, A., Morison, V., Somers, M., Mattock, A., Brown, E., & Taylor, D. (1990b). Newborn and older infants' perception of partly occluded objects. *Infant Behavior and Development, 13,* 33–49.

Smith, C., Johnson, S., Spelke, E. S., & Aslin, R. N. (1996). Edge sensitivity and temporal integration in young infants' perception of object unity. *Infant Behavior and Development, 19,* 749.

Smith, L. B., & Thelen, E. (1995). *Tests of a dynamic systems theory: The object concept.* Symposium presented at the meting of the Society for Research in Child Development, Indianapolis.

Spelke, E. S. (1989). The development of intermodal perception. In P. Salapatek & L. B. Cohen (Eds.), *Handbook of infant perception, Vol. 2*. New York: Academic Press.

Spelke, E. S. (1985). Preferential looking methods as tools for the study of cognition in infancy. In G. Gottlieb & N. Krasnegor (Eds.), *Measurement of audition and vision in the first year of postnatal life*. Norwood, NJ: Ablex.

Spelke, E. S. (1988). Where perceiving ends and thinking begins: The apprehension of objects in infancy. In A. Yonas (Ed.), *Perceptual development in infancy: The Minnesota Symposia on Child Psychology: Vol. 20*. Hillsdale, NJ: Erlbaum.

Spelke, E. S., Breinlinger, K., Jacobson, K., & Phillips, A. (1993). Gestalt relations and object perception: A developmental study. *Perception, 22*, 1483–1501.

Spelke, E. S., Breinlinger, K., Macomber, J., & Jacobson, K. (1992). Origins of knowledge. *Psychological Review, 99*, 605–632.

Spelke, E. S., Kestenbaum, R., Simons, D., & Wein, D. (1995). Spatio-temporal continuity, smoothness of motion, and object identity in infancy. *The British Journal of Developmental Psychology, 13*, 113–142.

Spelke, E. S., & Tsivkin, S. (in press). Initial knowledge and conceptual change: Space and number. In M. Bowerman & S. Levinson (Eds.), *Language acquisition and conceptual development*. Cambridge, UK: Cambridge University Press.

Spelke, E. S., & Van de Walle, G. A. (1993). Perceiving and reasoning about objects: Insights from infants. In N. Eilan, W. Brewer, & R. McCarthy (Eds.), *Spatial representation*. Oxford: Basil Blackwell.

Spelke, E. S., Vishton, P., & von Hofsten, C. (1994). Object perception, object-directed action, and physical knowledge in infancy. In M. S. Gazzaniga (Ed.), *The cognitive neuroscience*. Cambridge, MA: MIT Press.

Sperber, D., Premack, D., & Premack, A. J. (1995). *Causal cognition: A multidisciplinary debate*. Oxford: Clarendon Press.

Starkey, P., & Cooper, R. G. (1980). Perception of numbers by human infants. *Science, 210*, 133–135.

Starkey, P., Spelke, E. S., & Gelman, R. (1990). Numerical abstraction by human infants. *Cognition, 36*, 97–127.

Strauss, M. S., & Curtis, L. E. (1981). Infant perception of numerosity. *Child Development, 52*, 1146–1152.

Stratton, G. (1897). Vision without inversion of the retinal image. *Psychological Review, 4*, 341–360, 463–481.

Stryker, M. P., & Harris, W. A. (1986). Binocular impulse blockade prevents the formation of ocular dominance columns in cat visual cortex. *Journal of Neuroscience, 6*, 2117–2133.

Termine, N., Hrynick, T., Kestenbaum, R., Gleitman, H., & Spelke, E. S. (1987). Perceptual completion of surfaces in infancy. *Journal of Experimental Psychology: Human Perception and Performance, 13*, 524–532.

Terrell, D. R., & Thomas, R. K. (1990). Number-related discrimination and summation by squirrel monkeys (*Saimiri sciureus sciureus* and *S. boliviensis boliviensis*) on the basis of the number of sides of polygons. *Journal of Comparative Psychology, 104*, 238–247.

Thelen, E., & Smith, L. B. (1994). *A dynamical systems approach to the development of cognition and action*. Cambridge, MA: MIT Press.

Tomasello, M., & Call, J. (1997). *Primate cognition*. New York: Oxford.

Uller, C., Carey, S., & Hauser, M. (1996, April). *Addition in human infants and nonhuman primates*. Paper presented at the International Conference on Infant Studies, Providence, RI.

Ungerleider, L. G., & Mishkin, M. (1982). Two cortical visual systems. In D. J. Ingle, M. A. Goodale, & R. J. W. Mansfield (Eds.), *The analysis of visual behavior*. Cambridge: MIT Press.

Van de Walle, G., & Spelke, E. S. (in press). Spatiotemporal integration and object perception in infancy: Perceiving unity vs. form. *Child Development*.

Van de Walle, G., Woodward, A., & Phillips, A. T. (1994, June). *Infants' inferences about contact relations in a causal event*. Paper presented at the International Conference on Infant Studies, Paris.

Van Loosbroek, F., & Smitsman, A. W. (1990). Visual perception of numerosity in infancy. *Developmental Psychology, 26*, 916–922.

Walk, R. D., & Gibson, E. J. (1961). A comparative and analytical study of visual depth perception. *Psychological Monographs, 75,* Whole No. 5.

Walk, R. D., Gibson, E. J., & Tighe, T. J. (1957). Behavior of light- and dark-reared rats on the visual cliff. *Science, 126,* 80–81.

Walters, C. (1981). Development of the visual placing response in the human infant. *Journal of Experimental Child Psychology, 32,* 313–329.

Wertheimer, M. (1958). Principles of perceptual organization. In D. C. Beardslee & M. Wertheimer (Eds.), *Readings in perception.* New York: Van Nostrand. (Original work published 1923)

Wilcox, T., Rosser, R., & Nadel, L. (1994). Representation of object location in 6.5-month-old infants. *Cognitive Development, 9,* 193–210.

Wynn, K. (1990). Children's understanding of counting. *Cognition, 36,* 155–193.

Wynn, K. (1992a). Addition and subtraction in infants. *Nature, 358,* 749–750.

Wynn, K. (1992b). Children's acquisition of the number words and the counting system. *Cognitive Psychology, 24,* 220–251.

Wynn, K. (1995). Infants possess a system of numerical knowledge. *Current Directions in Psychological Science, 4,* 172–177.

Xu, F., & Carey, S. (1996). Infants' metaphysics: The case of numerical identity. *Cognitive Psychology, 30,* 111–153.

Xu, F., & Carey, S. (1994, June). *Infants' ability to individuate and trace identity of objects.* Paper presented at the International Conference on Infant Studies, Paris.

Yonas, A., & Granrud, C. (1984). The development of sensitivity to kinetic, binocular, and pictorial depth information in human infants. In D. Ingle, D. Lee, & M. Jeannerod (Eds.), *Brain mechanisms and spatial vision* (pp. 113–145). Dordrecht: Martines Nijoff Press.

CHAPTER 12

Language and Action[1]

Current Challenges

Charles E. Wright
Barbara Landau

> *Certainly language presents in a most striking form the integrative functions that are*
> *characteristic of the cerebral cortex and that reach their highest development in human thought*
> *processes. Temporal integration is not found exclusively in language; the coordination of leg*
> *movements in insects, the song of birds, the control of trotting and pacing in a gaited horse,*
> *the rat running the maze, the architect designing a house, and the carpenter sawing a board*
> *present a problem of sequences of action which cannot be explained in terms of successions*
> *of external stimuli.*
>
> —Lashley (1951, p. 113)

Lashley's observations set the stage for the cognitive revolution. By pointing to a number of cases that classical behaviorist theory could not explain, he created a turning point in psychologists' notions of what could constitute an adequate theory of complex behavior, most notably, talking and acting. Lashley noted several key problems of serial order that could not be explained by then-current theories of behavior, which posited chained sequences of responses as the basis for all learning. One of Lashley's examples concerned the problem of timing: For any rapidly ordered set of actions—such as playing the piano or typing—the time required for sensory control of one action by the preceding one exceeded the actual time between actions. Explaining this fact required organization at some higher level. Another example concerned handwriting and the problem of "response equivalence": Humans can readily transfer a known motoric pattern (such as producing one's signature) to novel effectors, writing one's name with the preferred hand, the non preferred hand, and even with the teeth (see Figure 1, from Lashley, 1942). Such generalization could not be accounted for by sets of chained motor habits, which are by definition effector-specific, and hence shows the need for some higher, more abstract level of organization.

[1] Preparation of this chapter was supported in part by grants NSF SBR-9601140 and NIH AG-13967 to Wright and NICHD R01 HD-28675 and NIMH R01 MH-55240 to Landau. We thank Colin Phillips for helpful comments on a previous draft of the paper.

Perception and Cognition at Century's End

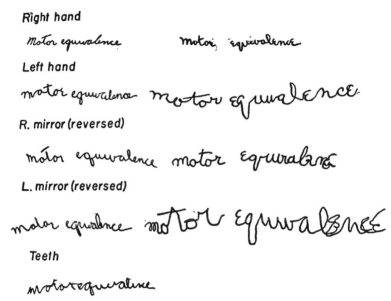

FIGURE 1   Lashley's examples of writing by two blindfolded subjects, using different effectors. (From Lashley, K. S. (1942). The problem of cerebral organization in vision. *Biological Symposia,* 7.)

But key to many of Lashley's arguments were examples from language, in which he argued that syntactic patterns, speech errors, even errors of typing, could not be explained by appeal to neighboring links between words. Lashley's comments on language highlighted these problems as part of the general failure of chained associationist theories in explaining sequenced behavior. But they also foreshadowed a complete revolution in thinking about the specific problem of language and language learning that was initiated by Chomsky's (1959) critique of Skinner. The critique and, more importantly, Chomsky's theoretical proposals about the nature of linguistic structure sealed the fate of behaviorist explanations of language and language learning. In particular, the assumptions underlying behaviorist theories—whether strict Skinnerian stimulus–response (S-R) theory or "mediational" theories due to Hull (1943) or Osgood (1963)—could not explain even simple facts of language, such as the need for recursive rules. Moreover, traditional "taxonomic" theories of linguistic structure, which many psychologists happily viewed as compatible with then-current learning theories, turned out to have problems of their own, including serious questions about internal consistency and doubtful methodological assumptions (see Fodor, Bever, & Garrett, 1974, for an excellent discussion).

More than 40 years later, cognitive theory would seem to have changed a great deal. Notions such as "symbolic representations," "plans," and "structures" are no longer radical notions; they are commonplace in the vocabulary of cognitive psychologists, and no one appears to doubt that explaining cognitive phenomena will require notions quite different from chained sets of responses. Still, most of the central problems of organized behavior are only partially understood: How are language and action represented? How are they learned? By now, both domains are acknowledged to involve highly structured systems, whose character requires multiple levels of representation that are mapped to each other. Furthermore, the nature of the computational problems within each domain strongly suggests that there must be unique, species-specific and domain-dependent representations (cf. Gallistel, 1990). Yet the specific character of these representations—how each level should be characterized, how they should be related, and how they are deployed in speaking, understanding, and learning—remain complex problems.

Aside from these issues, there is now afoot a set of issues that strongly echoes those that were prominent during the cognitive revolution inspired by Lashley and Chomsky. To some psychologists, this revolution convincingly spoke to the need to accept the existence of mental representations—in particular, symbolic representations. For many, this opened the door to understanding the exact nature of those representations. To others, however, the failures of symbolic representational systems in explaining the fine texture of mature behavior, learning, and development have led to discontent. Consequently, new theories of cognition—connectionist models and dynamical systems—have emerged and, to some, these apparently newer theories have created a second cognitive revolution.

There are many differences among these approaches (see Bechtel & Abrahamsen, 1991; Fodor & Pylyshyn, 1988; Pinker & Prince, 1988; Thelen & Smith, 1994, for contrasting reviews). For our purposes in this chapter, it is important to distinguish symbolic systems from connectionist and dynamical systems models as follows. First, theories embracing symbolic representations focus on the nature of representations and sometimes posit specialized computational mechanisms designed expressly for acquiring and using the representations characteristic of specific domains (see, e.g., Gallistel, 1990). In contrast, connectionist and dynamical systems models view the process of learning as quite general, and the resulting state as in some sense isomorphic to the learning process. Within these systems, what symbolic representations capture is actually just an emergent property of the functioning of the learning systems.

Second, whereas symbolic systems posit specific nodes or symbols as the locus of knowledge and its components, connectionist systems posit no role whatsoever for such nodes. Rather, the connectionist theorist argues that whatever can be accounted for by positing sets of symbols—to represent specific forms of knowledge, learning, and generalization—can be equally well accounted for by positing multiple patterns of activation over homogeneous sets of elements.

Third, whereas symbolic systems frequently posit specific nodes corresponding to different levels in a hierarchy, pure connectionist models invoke links that are more-or-less "horizontal"; that is, there are no specific levels of representation corresponding to, say, phonological or syntactic representations per se.

In this chapter, our purpose is not to assess the general success or failure of these classes of theories. Instead, we see our goal to be stepping back and reflecting on some of the key properties of language and action that need to be explained, and therefore still set the agenda for theories of complex structure in cognition. In our review, we focus on the specific nature of several central problems in each domain as they are currently understood, and we explore several examples within each domain that illustrate different approaches to these problems. We note in advance that the two domains of language and action have historically engaged somewhat different foci: Most (although certainly not all) of the study of language treats the domain as a structured symbolic system, largely ignoring the analog realization of language. The clearest exception here is speech production, wherein critical issues involve the realization of linguistic structure in real time. Indeed, it is for the latter set of problems that nonsymbolic models are currently being proposed and evaluated (e.g., Browman & Goldstein, 1995; Lapointe & Dell, 1989; see Levelt, 1989, for discussion).

In contrast, much (although, again, certainly not all) of the study of action has focused on modeling precisely these analog realizations and, especially, their neurophysiological underpinnings. This difference in emphasis across the two domains has led to different kinds of models, meant to explain different facets of these complex phenomena, and quite different ideas of what models should be explaining. We believe that these relative differences in focus are not problematic, however. Indeed, we believe that a balanced look at the variety of problems presented by language and action leads to the conclusion that a hybrid of theories may ultimately be needed in order to explain representation, acquisition, and use, even within a single domain.

In what follows, we attempt to set the problems for language and action in more detail. Although representations of action and language are clearly quite different in many ways, the nature of the central problems in the two domains is surprisingly similar. These problems include the nature of the multiple levels of representation and their relationship to each other, the rapidity with which these are deployed in production (and for speech, comprehension), and their acquisition in the absence of a proximal teacher and within a universal, relatively short time period.

I. ACTION

Action is, as Miller, Galanter, and Pribram (1960) so colorfully noted, what transforms the cognitive organism from a spectator to a participant in the drama of living. Skilled, fluent action is often a thing of beauty precisely because the incredible complexity of its mechanisms are largely hidden to the casual observer. The movements in skilled actions are typically rapid and smooth. The effort expended is minimized. Successive movements appear to flow from one to the next without pause or obvious juncture. Unexpected perturbations imposed by the environment are quickly assimilated and their continuing effects minimized.

Very little of what makes skilled movements fluent is innate. Repetitive practice and exploration are key components necessary for skill acquisition. The representations and mechanisms underlying action are, however, capable of impressive generalization. Having learned to make a movement one way—at one speed, one size, or with a particular set of body parts—we are usually much quicker to learn variations. Similarly, learning tends to be more effective if several variations are randomly intermixed during practice (Schmidt, 1988).

When considering the representations underlying action, at least two forms of structure need to be considered. The first concerns the multiple representations necessary to plan and carry out any single movement. The second concerns the organization of separate movements into coherent sequences of action.

A. Levels of Representation

Action brings about changes in the surrounding world. Before beginning the movements to carry out an action, that actor's abstract intention—for example, to pick up a pencil, shift gears, or scratch an itch—must be mapped onto locations in physical space. These locations may be known to us visually (One can see the pencil that he needs to pick up), from memory (sitting in the car's driver's seat, one does not need to look down to move a hand from the steering wheel to the handle of the stick shift), or from proprioception (the location of the spot that itches). Before starting to move, the specification of these goal locations must be transformed into a common form, the body-centered coordinate system used for planning by the motor system. This is but the first of a series of nontrivial coordinate transformations required in movement planning.[2]

Having determined the spatial target of the hand movement required to carry out our intended action, the central nervous system (CNS) must also, at least implicitly, select a trajectory to reach that target. In some cases this selection is critical—for example, reaching for the bottle in the middle of the table without knocking over the glass near your elbow—whereas in other cases this is more an issue of efficiency. Having selected a path to the target, the CNS must convert the coordinates of this path into the sequence of joint angles necessary to proceed along this chosen path to the target. This difficult problem, which has no unique solution, is known in robotics as the *inverse kinematics* problem. A second conversion is also required to determine the muscle activations that will drive the joints through the necessary series of angles determined by the desired path. This problem, often called *inverse dynamics,* is also computationally complex and has no unique solution (e.g., one might use the same movement path with different muscle activations to touch someone lightly on the nose or punch them in the nose). Thus planning even a simple movement involves transformations between several systems of representations,

---

[2] Actions are often much more complex in nature than those we will consider here. For example, they may be repetitive or they may involve simultaneous movements with separate, but related, goals, for example, the hand, leg, and head movements of a dancer. For simplicity of exposition, we have chosen to discuss actions here as if they involved only a single, discrete goal.

each of which requires solving a major problem: trajectory planning, inverse kinematics, and inverse dynamics (Hollerbach, 1982; Saltzman & Kelso, 1987).

These issues of multiple levels of representation and the transformations between them will play a central role in our discussion of language. Although we will discuss these issues more there, it is worth considering briefly the strategies that have been proposed to explain how the CNS solves the problems of inverse kinematics and inverse dynamics. These proposals fall on a continuum with structural, analytic models on one end and tabular, lookup or association models at the other (Hollerbach, 1982). Structural models (e.g., Schmidt, 1988) require an analytic description of the motor system for which the parameters must be estimated based on experience. Since these parameters may change substantially with growth, fatigue, or injury, the process of estimating is necessarily an ongoing one. An advantage of structural models is that they allow generalization of learned movements. Their primary disadvantages are their computational complexity and the difficulty of estimating the system parameters.

Tabular models can, in principle, solve the inverse-kinematic and/or inverse-dynamic transformations by constructing a table of associations that maps, for example, a desired hand position onto joint angles that can produce it. These models avoid the complications of a complex analytic model. In their simplest instantiations, however, such models are incapable of generalization. This limitation can, however, be relaxed by the inclusion of mechanisms for interpolation (Koh & Meyer, 1991; Rosenbaum, Loukopoulos, Meulenbroek, Vaughan, & Engelbrecht, 1995). Between these extremes are models using distributed (or connectionist) processing mechanisms to learn and approximate the analytic models in the structural approach. These formulations are capable of learning and generalization (e.g., Jordan, 1990; Kawato, Furukawa, & Suzuki, 1987). They may also avoid the pitfalls of a purely structural approach.

Multiple levels of movement representation and the necessary transformations between them raise problems for learning as well as production of movements. After an error during an action—an infant missing the hanging toy, a diner knocking over a glass when reaching for a bottle, a golfer slicing a drive—the available feedback contains little information directly relevant to correcting the error. The infant can see the discrepancy between her hand and the toy for which she is reaching but nothing in this visual image clearly indicates that, for example, it is the elbow angle that must be changed to eliminate the error. In essence, the infant's problem is how to use visual discrepancy information to update her inverse kinematics model. The diner can perceive his clumsiness, but how does he use that percept to update his rules for hand-path selection? The golfer may need an updated model of inverse dynamics to compensate for muscle fatigue, but only information about the flight of the ball is available.

Each of these examples illustrates the general problem of learning with a *distal teacher*. This problem is illustrative of the more general issue in research on action: Being able to describe a movement and its outcome accurately does not ensure that one can produce it or vice versa. Put another way, introspection about action is often misleading because of a seemingly great divide between the declarative knowledge of explanation and description and the procedural knowledge needed to produce skilled action.

B. Fluent Sequencing of Movements

We now turn our attention to the other main representational issue underlying action—fluent sequencing of the movements in an action sequence. This is the problem that Lashley (1951) addressed: the problem of serial order. Lashley's critique of the associative-chain account of skilled action sequences and his suggestion that these sequences are guided by central schema was the forerunner of a position that has become to be called the *motor program hypothesis* (e.g., Keele, Cohen, & Ivry, 1990; Schmidt, 1975).

Lashley's (1951) paper was important for later research in motor control both because it forcefully raised the question of serial order using action-sequence examples and because it provided a summary of the problem that was couched in theoretically neutral language and yet still is sufficiently incisive that it remains useful today. According to this summary, an account of serial order must include explanations of three events. The first of these events is the set, idea, or intention that provides the determining tendency of the action sequence. The second is the activation of the individual elements of the sequence that do not themselves contain temporal relations.

> Third, the syntax of the act, which can be described as an habitual order or mode of relating the expressive elements; a generalized pattern or schema of integration which may be imposed upon a wide range and variety of specific acts. This is the essential problem of serial order; the existence of generalized schemata of action which determine the sequence of specific acts, acts which themselves or in their associations have no temporal valence. (p. 122)

Given the role of Lashley (1951) in stimulating later workers in the motor control area to think about the nature of motor programs, it is ironic that the arguments and examples based on motor sequences (which Lashley used to motivate action schema, i.e., motor programs), have met with a more critical reception than did these and Lashley's other arguments in areas such as linguistics or learning and memory (Bruce, 1994). Lashley's motor-sequence arguments are seen, in hindsight, to be based on overly simplistic conceptions of the possible modes of control in the motor system. In addition, Lashley made an error, which is still common in much theorizing today, of conflating unpracticed performance and overlearned, highly practiced behavior.

However, Lashley raised many important issues by focusing on important questions. Thus an examination of Lashley's arguments, including the errors contained therein, provides a useful framework within which to consider some of the phenomena that motivate theorizing about cognitive representations. At the same time, these serve to illustrate some of the problems involved in inferring the nature of the representations from action sequences.

1. The Speed of Sequencing

Lashley (1951) argued that the timing of successive elements in the production of fast action sequences is inconsistent with the time required by the mechanisms postulated to be necessary according to the associative-chaining hypothesis: specifically, the time for the nervous system to transmit proprioceptive feedback to the brain, associate this feedback with the next action, and then to transmit the activation required for this action back to the periphery. Historically, this argument was important because it revealed flaws in the dominant explanation provided by associative chaining, and thereby created a theoretical vacuum in which new, more cognitive explanations developed. Although this argument was taken seriously when it was proposed, it is now considered weak for several reasons. First, new research has provided ever smaller estimates of the minimum time necessary to process feedback and initiate new motor actions. Each such reduction has the effect of decreasing the domain of action sequences to which this argument might be seen to apply. More generally, however, very fast action sequences are probably more the exception than the rule (MacKenzie & van Eerd, 1990), and a strong sensory role in sequencing is evident in the control of many action sequences, especially those that have not been overlearned.

A second problem with this argument is its implicit assumption that the feedback controlling associative sequencing must be generated by the parts of the body that are being moved. Lashley's thinking about this was, perhaps, strongly influenced by one of his other important early contributions. This was a case study of a patient with neurological damage due to a gunshot wound (Lashley, 1917). The resulting lesion did not interrupt control signals to the leg muscles but was thought to have eliminated completely the subject's ability to sense anything—position, motion, touch, heat/cold, etc.—from the legs. Despite this loss of sensory feedback, Lashley observed that the patient could control the speed and extent of flexion and extension movements of the knee as well as normal subjects, even if visual feedback from the leg was eliminated. Lashley offered this case study as evidence against the necessity of ongoing peripheral feedback in movement control.

Ignoring the always sticky issue of whether the nervous system damage did, in fact, completely eliminate all important proprioceptive feedback, this demonstration still fails to provide compelling evidence against the associative-chaining hypothesis. One problem is that it ignores the often important contribution of sensory modalities other than proprioception in motor control. More importantly, by focusing attention on peripheral feedback, this argument ignores the possibility that rapid chaining is based on efference copies (i.e., feedback produced at a central level from the motor commands themselves). Finally, recent research has shown that, although the gross character of unskilled movements is often preserved when peripheral feedback is absent, fined-grained coordination necessary for skilled movements suffers appreciably, especially in multijoint movements (e.g., Gordon, Ghilardi, & Ghez, 1995). However, if concurrent visual feedback is available, the degradation of coordination in movements made without proprioception can be largely overcome (Ghez, Gordon, & Ghilardi, 1995). From the perspective of hindsight, Lashley (1951) overgeneralized his 1917 data both because his conception of the motor system was too simple and because he conflated skilled and largely unskilled movements.

2. The Components of Sequencing

Another issue that is central to any discussion of the associative-chaining hypothesis is the identification of the units of action that are being sequenced by the chaining process. For example, Lashley (1951) suggests that a musician playing an arpeggio (which may involve up to 16 notes per second) cannot be using sensory information to initiate actions in the sequence. The force of this argument requires that the individual notes are the units of action being successively activated. If, however, performance at this level involves units consisting of more than a single note, much of the original force of the argument is lost.

Although the existence of multinote elements undermines the timing argument against the chaining hypothesis, the existence of such higher order elements itself provides a new piece of evidence for cognitive representations. Because individual notes contained in multinote elements were, presumably, themselves the elements of sequence production at some point during the learning process, the existence of multinote elements suggests that basic elements can be combined into higher level, centrally represented units that can then substitute for the original, single-note elements in the representation and production of action sequences. It is the theoretical necessity of hierarchical organization, such as that illustrated in this modest example, that forms the basis of the argument for cognitive representation. Lashley (1951) developed this line of reasoning somewhat, noting that "in rapid sight reading it is impossible to read the individual notes of an arpeggio. The notes must be seen in groups" (p. 123). Lashley certainly did not originate this notion that fluent action sequences are structured hierarchically and that skill learning involves the creation of higher level elements in these hierarchical structures. Discussions of this idea date back at least to the turn of the century (Book, 1908). However, Lashley's paper may have played an important role in generating new enthusiasm for this idea.

For this concern about the size of the elements in action sequences to be meaningful, there must be a method, other than intuition, to identify these elements. Many possible heuristics have been proposed (nine are discussed by Sternberg, Knoll, & Turock, 1990). These methods have met with more success in some domains than in others. One area in which several interesting approaches have been tried is typewriting. Typing behavior appeals to researchers studying these questions both because typing is a practically important communication skill and because skilled typists make keystrokes quite rapidly: a 60 words-per-minute typist produces a keystroke every 167 ms. on average and champion typists can type at rates of up to 100 words per minute. In addition, the timing of individual keystrokes can be accurately measured with a relatively modest investment in equipment.

Copy typing of passages consisting of words—either ordered as meaningful prose or with the words arranged as nonsense—is faster than typing passages of matched random-letter sequences (Shaffer, 1973). This result suggests that subjects can organize their performance more efficiently when they can use multi-keystroke or word-length elements. However, since copy typing is a perceptual-motor activity, it is not clear from this result that the advantage occurs in the organization of the action sequences rather than perception or memory.

There are also several types of evidence to suggest that the elements being sequenced by skilled typists are individual keystrokes. For example, it has been hypothesized that elements, once initiated, cannot be modified or terminated prematurely. But typists, if so instructed, can stop typing in response to a tone as well when the tone occurs within a word as when it occurs between words (Logan, 1982). In a more natural context, typists also often stop typing within words when they spontaneously detect having made an error. For example, Rabbitt (1978) observed that if he asked typists to stop typing as soon as possible after they noted an error, the erroneous keystroke was the last 95% of the time.

A second form of evidence that keystrokes function as units in typewriting comes from research of Sternberg and his colleagues (Sternberg, Knoll, & Turock, 1990; Sternberg, Monsell, Knoll, & Wright, 1978). These studies attempted to focus on the serial organization of action sequences, minimizing the perceptual component, by having skilled typists produce from memory nonsense strings of up to five consonants. When these materials were produced in response to a Go/No-Go signal, Sternberg et al. found that both the time to start typing the string and the average duration of each keystroke within the string increased with increasing string length.

Before considering how these data can be used to identify the units for action sequences, it is worth noting this result by itself provides strong support for Lashley's (1951) argument against the associative-chaining account for the production of serial order. Sternberg et al. (1978) observed that every keystroke-delimited interval in these sequences—the latency between the response tone and the first keystroke as well as the intervals between each successive pair of keystrokes—increased in duration with the length of the list. No matter what mechanism carries out the sequencing of these keystrokes, this lengthening can only have taken place if properties of the entire list, such as the overall length, have an influence on the processing at each point in the production of the list. These researchers have also reported similar results for subjects reciting memorized lists consisting of up to eight words or pronounceable nonwords (Sternberg et al., 1978; Sternberg, Wright, Knoll, & Monsell, 1982; see Wright, 1990a, for an introduction to this research).

Sternberg and his colleagues were able to determine the nature of the elements being sequenced by intermixing different types of materials in the lists being studied using this procedure. In speech, for example, the elements were found to be stress groups (Sternberg et al., 1982). Thus, adding a one-syllable word to a list slowed the production of the other elements just as much as adding a two-syllable word. And adding unstressed function words (such as, for example, *to*) between list elements did not slow the production of those elements at all. In typewriting, the elements were found to be nonrepeating keystrokes (Sternberg et al., 1978 and 1990).

To summarize briefly, both the interruptability of ongoing productions and changes in timing across sequence length may provide a way to identify the elements in the production of action sequences. For typewriting, both methods point to keystrokes as the elements of production. What then of the suggestion, discussed earlier, that there are word-level elements in typing because words are typed more quickly than matched pseudowords? One possibility is that the data or this inference from it are misleading. An alternative, which is certainly consistent with the cognitive perspective, is that typing behavior is guided by representations that may have a hierarchical structure. Under this supposition, there is nothing inconsistent with the existence of elements that influence typing speed and fluency at both the keystroke and the word level of organization.

Strong evidence for word-level elements in typewriting is provided by Viviani and Laissard (1996). Their extensive study of copy typing describes a number of previously documented effects of biomechanical and linguistic factors on interstroke intervals. In addition to these factors, however, they found that characteristic differences in the intervals required to produce specific keystrokes depend on the word in which the keystrokes are embedded. They also found that ratios between pairs of interstroke intervals remained unchanged across the variations of observed typing speed, which were often as large as 50% in their transcription paradigm. A similar argument, based on relative timing invariance, has been used (Benecke, Rothwell, Day, Dick, & Marsden, 1986) to make inferences about whether pairs of finger and arm movements can be incorporated into a single motor program. Schmidt has also used this approach to identify which segments in a complex arm movement sequence are aggregated into larger control elements and to track changes in this organization with training and instructions (Schneider & Schmidt, 1995; Young & Schmidt, 1990). These examples suggest that the principles of hierarchical organization do not depend on any special properties of action sequences for typing.

Thus, Lashley's (1951) arguments against associative chaining based on the timing of successive elements in the production of fast action sequences certainly provided the impetus for a variety of useful research, even if those arguments have proven to be overly simplistic. This research demonstrates that there is preplanning of rapid action sequences, it has provided techniques to identify the production elements (symbols) being sequenced, and it has shown that these elements exist within a hierarchical organization.

3. The Generalization of Sequences in Learning

Lashley (1951) took his argument against associative chaining further. He asserted that not only are the control mechanisms underlying the production of skilled action sequences central rather than peripheral, but they incorporate abstract representations of spatial patterns rather than specifications of particular sequences of muscle activation. Specifically, he asserted that "patterns of coordinated movement may often be transferred directly to other motor systems than the ones practiced" (p. 124). This idea is now usually referred to as *motor equivalence*. To support this claim, Lashley suggested that his readers try "upside-down mirror writing with the left hand and with the eyes closed" (p. 124).

As Bruce (1994) notes, this was one of Lashley's favorite arguments. His most extensive presentation of it (Lashley, 1942) includes a figure showing writing samples from two blindfolded subjects as they wrote with practiced and unpracticed effectors: their right hand and left hands, both normally and mirror reversed, and with the pen held in the teeth (see Figure 1). In this demonstration, the general features of shape in the writing appear to be preserved (with more or less accuracy) across the different response systems.[3]

What, however, should we infer from this demonstration? The quotation from Lashley in the previous paragraph suggests he understood this as an example of motor equivalence in which representations underlying skilled actions were transferred between the effectors. However, Wright (1990b) has shown that this description cannot be completely correct. Although unpracticed writing with the nondominant hand was found to share global shape characteristics with writing produced by the dominant hand, nondominant handwriting differed radically in speed, fluency, and details of local shape. This result suggested that although writing with the two hands shared similar goals—in the form of high-level shape specifications—the motor schema themselves were not shared as Lashley had suggested. For Lashley's purposes, this result is not all bad, however. This interpretation is consistent with the idea that writing with the unpracticed, nondominant hand and the skilled dominant hand share a central representation. The existence of such central representations was the main point of Lashley's argument. The shared central representation in this case, however, appears to be something closer to a spatially defined image of what the subject's handwriting should look like rather than specifications for patterns of coordinated movement as Lashley supposed. It appears that the unpracticed, nondominant hand uses this image as a guide in much the same way that an unskilled forger might use an example of someone else's handwriting, or that a beginning writer might use a template provided by the teacher.

Although Wright (1990b) showed that there is not immediate transfer of the patterns required for coordinated movement between the hands, it is still possible that such transfer could occur after a person has practiced writing with the nondomi-

---

[3] Similar, perhaps better known, demonstrations have been provided by Merton (1972) and Raibert (1977).

nant hand. Pushing this idea somewhat further, if we take seriously the suggestion that motor schema have a hierarchical organization, then we must consider the possibility there is transfer of abstract, hand-independent information contained in some levels of this representation, but that this can occur only after subjects have acquired the hand-dependent information represented in the lower level of such a hierarchy.

These are the issues addressed in a study by Lindemann and Wright (1998) in which subjects learned, over several months, to write fluently with their nondominant hand. This learning was structured, based on an analysis of each subject's dominant handwriting, to reveal which levels of the representation or control are common to the two hands. A prior analysis of dominant handwriting identified the strokes in different letters that were structurally similar. Between 25 and 30 such generic strokes were found in each subject's writing. In the initial training with the nondominant hand, subjects practiced a set of only eight or nine letters arranged in five or six words. The initial set of letters was chosen to include most of the generic strokes. When a degree of fluency had been achieved in writing these words with the nondominant hand, the subjects began to practice a new set of words composed of the same letters.

When subjects began writing this new, second set of words, Lindemann and Wright (1998) observed no loss in fluency of writing. Because the second word set differed from the first only by the ordering of letters that had already been practiced, not by the introduction of new letters, this result is, perhaps, not surprising. It does, however, confirm that the representation for writing at the word level is hand independent. Put another way, developing fluent writing with the nondominant hand apparently does not involve hand-specific fine-tuning or optimization at the word level. The word level may therefore be described as motorically abstract in this regard.

Later in practice, Lindemann and Wright (1998) introduced a third set of words. This set of words, however, included letters that the subject had not previously practiced with the nondominant hand. By the generic stroke analysis, these letters were, however, built up from the same set of generic strokes as in the original two word sets. Once again, they observed no measurable degradation of performance when the subjects switched to writing this third word set. This unexpected result suggests that the representation at the letter level is also effector independent and can be transferred between hands. The only change in materials that led to a decrement in fluency and performance was the introduction of generic strokes that the subject had not previously produced with the nondominant hand.

Taken together, these results are consistent with a hierarchical organization of the representation of writing. The levels of this hierarchy specify that the sequence of letters in a word or the sequence of strokes in letters are motorically abstract in the sense that they do not depend on information about the effector producing the writing. At the level of stroke production or below, however, the representation or control is effector specific. It is at this level that the learning required to write with a new effector occurs, at least for writing skills acquired to the degree of fluency studied here. Results such as these lead action theorists to posit cognitive representations that are hierarchical and, at least in part, symbolic. However, as our previous discussion of levels of representation in the control of actions suggested, symbolic, structural representations may not be the most appropriate way to model all of the motor system. For example, connectionist models may be a more useful way to understand the processing that underlies solutions to problems such as inverse kinematics and inverse dynamics.

II. LANGUAGE

The goal of mature speaking and understanding is obviously communication. Under normal conversational circumstances, this occurs with striking rapidity: Speakers routinely produce roughly 15 sounds per second, and individual speech articulators (tongue, lips, etc.) adjust within 200–300 msec (Levelt, 1989). The normal adult speaker produces about two to three words per second (Maclay & Osgood, 1959), making continuous lexical choices between two to five times per second from among the approximately 30,000 most commonly used words (Levelt, 1989). Yet error rates are extremely low, estimated at about one per thousand for slips of the tongue (Garnham, Shillcock, Brown, Mill, & Cutler, 1982); when they do occur, they are highly constrained by factors other than simple linear position (see Fromkin, 1973; Garrett, 1988). Thus, word exchanges are usually between members of the same form class, and the erroneous words occur in an appropriate syntactic position (e.g., "Seymour sliced the **knife** with a **salami**," Fromkin, 1973); in contrast, exchanges do not occur between adjacent items from different form classes ("Seymour sliced **salami the** with a knife").

Similarly, the language learner has the goal of communicating, and she must learn the formal means required by her native language to do so. Despite the formal complexity of the linguistic system and the impoverished database that the learner uses to construct this system, acquisition is normally accomplished within just a few years of life, before children are capable of tying their shoes. Explaining how speakers convert meanings into speech, how hearers convert speech into meaning, and how children learn the mappings among the multiple levels of representation constitutes one of the most formidable sets of problems confronting psychologists today.

A. Levels of Representation

As with action, the actual process of speaking and comprehending is quite complex, requiring steps at many levels of description. Without considering the exact ordering of these steps for the moment, and assuming that the steps are interleaved in production, the following components are minimally necessary for a speaker to produce a well-formed utterance (see Levelt, 1989, for a thorough review). These steps hold for adult speaker and child learner alike, except that the latter must also learn how the different levels map onto each other in his or her native language. Recent theoretical and empirical work has focused on the nature of each level of representation, as well as the nature of the mapping relationships between levels.

The speaker begins by formulating some message in a conceptual representation (see Levelt, 1989). Assume that the message concerns an event in which x transfers y to z. The nature of this conceptual representation may be a "language of thought" roughly equivalent to a natural language (Fodor, 1975), it may be a specialized format designed for mapping between nonlinguistic systems and syntax (e.g., conceptual structure; Jackendoff, 1983), or it may be something altogether different. The character of this level of representation is at the moment completely undecided.[4]

Once the message is formed, relevant lexical items can be selected. Let us assume that the message involves an action among three participants, encoded as the three noun arguments (John, Mary, the gift) and a predicate (give/receive), a verb that relates the three. Note that these elements need not be selected in any fixed order. Further, this encoding is by no means determinate with respect to the event: Language can encode an infinite set of messages with respect to any single scene or event, both the essence of flexible communication and the deepest challenge to our understanding.

At the point of word selection, certain classes of speech errors are presumed to occur because of simultaneous activation of alternative ways of expressing even a single part of any message. Two examples are "blends," in which two words closely related in meaning are fused into one (e.g., "Irvine is quite clear"—a blend of *close* and *near*; Fromkin, 1973), and *substitutions*, in which close semantic associates (often antonyms) are substituted (e.g., *speed* for *temperature, toes* for *fingers, last* for *first*; Levelt, 1989). Depending on the order of actual retrieval of an item, one may get "exchanges" between sentence fragments in which words of the same form class from adjacent phrases get switched (e.g., "This *spring* has a *seat* in it"), indicating that sequential phrases may be planned more or less simultaneously (Garrett, 1980). Speech errors have historically served as important evidence on the nature of language, both in terms of the individual units that are engaged in production and the possible interactions across levels of representation (Dell & Reich, 1981). Recent empirical investigations have brought this phenomenon into the lab for formal inquiry, and have served to spark controversy regarding the modular or nonmodular design of language production (see Dell, 1996, for an introductory overview).

---

[4] Characterizing the nature of concepts has never been easy, and although virtually all classical and modern theories espouse some form of feature combination (e.g., Rosch & Mervis, 1975; Smith & Medin, 1981; see also Medin & Coby, chap. 13, this volume), recent work in the domain of conceptual representation has tried to escape the many problems besetting featural theories in favor of either atomism (Fodor, 1981) or theories that stress the role of larger conceptual structures in interpreting featural representations (e.g., Murphy & Medin, 1985). Although the latter theories do help account for the large contextual effects on interpreting features, and it is generally agreed that features must be quite different from those envisioned by the classical empiricists, the prospects remain somewhat dim for adequately capturing the meanings of words via featural composition without begging significant questions (see Armstrong, Gleitman, & Gleitman, 1983, and Landau & Gleitman, 1985, for discussion).

As the sentence is composed, additional information is required about the semantic or thematic roles that each of the main participants will play with respect to the predicate and how these will be instantiated in the syntactic structure. In most current theories of linguistic structure, as well as language processing and acquisition, the choice of verb is a key factor in determining the structure of the sentence (Bock & Levelt, 1994; Gleitman, 1990; Grimshaw, 1990; Landau & Gleitman, 1985; Levin, 1993; Pinker, 1989). This is because different verbs select different numbers and types of noun-phrase arguments, and position them differently, depending on verb-specific meaning. In many cases, verbs that are quite closely related in meaning nevertheless appear in different syntactic contexts. For example, the verb *give* can occur in the sentence "John gave $1000 to the University" or "John gave the University $1000," but the closely related verb *donate* is only acceptable to most native speakers in the first of these ("John donated $1000 to the University" but not "John donated the University $1000"; see Jackendoff, 1990; Pinker, 1989, for discussion).

The verb *give* requires three arguments, one to express the agent (the "giver"), one the patient (the "recipient"), and one the theme (the thing that is given). The verb *receive* also selects these three arguments, but the agent and patient are assigned to different syntactic positions for the two verbs, rendering the difference between "John gave a gift to Mary" and "Mary received a gift from John." In the former, the agent is assigned to subject position, and the patient to indirect object position; in the latter, the patient is assigned to subject position and the agent is assigned to indirect object position.[5] Language is striking in its ability to utilize different structures to express slightly different meanings, such as *give* and *receive,* each of which encodes a different perspective on the same scene. A key question for studies of acquisition has been how learners determine which predicate meanings correspond to which syntactic structures—for example, how the learner comes to know that the "meaning" underlying the verbs *give* versus *receive* correspond to particular syntactic structures that position the three specific types of arguments (Gleitman, 1990; Landau & Gleitman, 1985; Pinker, 1994).

The lexical items are assigned to their position in a syntactic structure, along with other relevant information such as number (a gift/two gifts), tense (gives/gave), and person (John/I), again depending on information represented at some conceptual level. The independent existence of a syntactic level has been verified by studies of spontaneous speech errors, which show syntactic accommodation of misplaced items (e.g., Stemberger, 1985) and by experimental studies showing that sentence structures can be primed independent of particular content (Bock & Loebell, 1990). Further, the specific resulting structure will vary depending on additional rules of discourse in order to distinguish, for example, between a sentence that focuses on

---

[5] Whether Mary is indeed a "patient" in the second sentence is debatable, but we can safely assume that the subjects of the two sentences play somewhat different thematic roles. We thank Colin Phillips for raising this issue to us.

the giver or recipient versus the gift, as in the contrast between sentences (1), (2), vs. (3) below:

1. John gave a gift to Mary.
2. Mary received a gift from John.
3. It was a gift that Mary received from John/John gave to Mary.

Note that a word's syntactic position cannot be described in simple linear terms such as envisioned by the behaviorists. Rather, central facts about language such as subject–verb agreement and the licensed movement of elements within sentences show that speakers must possess representations that accommodate long-term dependencies and do so in a way that respects syntactic structure.

For example, both of the sentences below exhibit subject–verb agreement between *John* and *likes,* although the words clearly occupy very different linear positions in their respective strings. What conditions agreement is the status of the two words as subject and verb of a main clause.

4. John likes Mary.
5. My brother John, who the association has asked to join the other scientists, likes Mary.

Similarly, movement rules must respect an element's position defined within a structural context, rather than simple linear position. Thus the first three sentences below are well formed, but the fourth is not, even though it moves the "first" verb as does the second sentence in forming a question from the first sentence. The correct rule requires formulation with the structural notion of clause.

6. The man is here.
7. Is the man here?
8. The man who is tall is here.
9. *Is the man who tall is here?

A final set of mappings must be effected, in order to convert the syntactic representation into one including information about individual segments and their ordering—the "spelling out" of the sentence. This phonological representation can then be mapped into the actual output representation—a motoric representation in which the speaker speaks (or in the case of sign language, gestures), moving the articulators and other muscles (estimated at 100, see Levelt, 1989) through a highly complex orchestration in which the actual realization of individual segments is modulated by neighboring segments as well as syntactic context (e.g., clause boundaries) and pragmatic forces (e.g., topicalization; see, e.g., Mattingly & Studdert-Kennedy, 1991).

Comprehension presumably requires many of the same components: The hearer must decode an ongoing acoustic stream into a set of segments, group these into words and morphemes (which are not automatically unitized in the speech stream), recover their form class (noun, verb), syntactic position, and thematic role, and create a conceptual representation corresponding to the meaning of the utterance. Learning one's native language requires mapping together these different sets of elements over the different levels of representation; for example, learning to produce and decode linguistically relevant sounds (phonemes), ascertaining the form class of each word, assigning thematic relations to the principal arguments, assigning these to syntactic relations, and so forth.

B. Mapping between Levels

Each level of representation is highly structured according to different principles; for example, the rules and representations that assign noun arguments to syntactic positions engage a quite different vocabulary from the rules and representations that convert phonemes into articulation. But the processes of speaking, understanding, and learning require that there be mappings between adjacent levels. As an example, the lexicon is assumed to contain representations of individual words in the language, such as *dog, water, run, believe*. Each of these words must be represented in such a way that logical inferences can be made (a dog is a kind of animal), so that the word can be inserted into a syntactic structure, and so that it can be converted into a phonological representation suitable for later conversion into articulation. This means that a lexical item such as *dog* must contain the relevant conceptual representation (e.g., that it represents an animate object), syntactic information (e.g., that it is a count noun, capable of being expressed with quantifiers such as *a, one,* or *many*), morphological information (that the plural of dog is expressed by adding the plural morpheme /s/), and phonological information (i.e., that it is represented by the segments /d/ /ə/ /g/). Furthermore, this representation must somehow be connected to nonlinguistic systems such as vision, haptics, and audition, so that we can recognize instances of the category *dog* by seeing, feeling, or hearing (Jackendoff, 1996; Landau & Jackendoff, 1993). How are these correspondences achieved?

The mapping of objects at one level of representation onto another level presents special problems for the language learner because, as with action, the relationships between levels are not one-to-one: Rather, they are many-to-many. As one example, consider a conceptual category such as (physical) object. Objects in English (and many other languages) are typically expressed as count nouns, a subset of the syntactic category Noun. However, the obverse is not true: Count nouns can represent physical objects (a dog), abstract objects (an idea), places (the Eiffel Tower), actions (a leap), or even temporal objects (an afternoon). Similarly, a number of these conceptual categories can also be expressed by other form classes: Places are canonically expressed in English by prepositional phrases (in the park), as are temporal stretches (during the meeting, from 2 P.M. to 4 P.M.), and actions and states are typically expressed by verbs (sitting, rolling, playing, etc.). The issue of how conceptual categories are mapped onto syntactic categories has been especially important in studies of acquisition, where it is presumed that children begin with some conceptual categories (such as object, place) and use these to "bootstrap" into the linguistic system (Grimshaw, 1981; see Jackendoff, 1983, for proposed primitives, see also Medin & Caley, Chap. 13, this volume). The key problem here is that, if conceptual categories do not map simply onto syntactic categories, then how can the learner discover the true (complex) relationship between these levels?

As another example, there is a complex mapping between the semantic (or thematic) role that a noun argument will play, and its grammatical function (subject, object, indirect object). Although there is some tendency in mature production for animate agents to be preferentially mapped onto the grammatical function of subject (see, e.g., Bock, Loebell, & Morey, 1992), this relationship between the semantic and syntactic levels is by no means one-to-one. In the example considered above, John as "giver" is the agent and Mary as "recipient" is the patient; yet each thematic role can appear as either grammatical subject or indirect object, as in the sentences "John gave a gift to Mary" and "Mary received a gift from John." Agents can and do appear in subject position, and patients (the object affected) often appear as direct objects (as in "John kissed Mary"); however, patients can also appear as subjects ("Mary was kissed by John") as can experiencers ("Mary was frightened by John"). In reverse order, sentence subjects are not confined to the list of standard thematic relations; because the subject of a sentence is structurally defined (roughly, the noun phrase immediately dominated by the highest node in a clause), any noun phrase in the proper configurational location will be sentence subject, and hence will show appropriate reflexes of being subject (e.g., it will show agreement with the verb, it will hold nominative case-marking in case-marked languages, etc.) (see Pinker, 1984, for a relevant list of properties).

The same many-to-many relationships hold for mappings between other levels, for example, mapping between morphemes and phonemes, between phonemes and phonetic categories, between phonetic categories and articulatory commands (for production) or between the acoustic stream and the phonetic categories, etc. (for comprehension). Because there are only partial homomorphisms between levels, there is a need for mechanisms to map one to the other.

Quite different kinds of solutions have recently been proposed as mapping functions. Most work within linguistics and psycholinguistics has been conducted assuming symbolic representations and rules. As one example, a number of investigators have suggested "linking rules" or "correspondence rules" that function to coordinate representations of semantics and syntax (see, e.g., Jackendoff, 1990; Pinker, 1984). From a quite different perspective (and often, for different problems), others have rejected symbolic representations and rules, and have embraced either connectionist architectures (e.g., Rumelhart & McClelland, 1986) or dynamical systems (Browman & Goldstein, 1995), in which a unified nonsymbolic system is assumed to be capable of characterizing the relationships between morphology and phonology, or between phonology, phonetics, and articulation. These different solutions have strong implications for learning, because the mechanisms for learning are assumed by many to have implications for the nature of linguistic knowledge.

1. Symbols and Linking Rules for Mapping Semantics and Syntax

As discussed above, the mapping relationships between semantic roles and syntactic position are not simple one-to-one correspondences. Even for closely related pairs of verbs such as *give* and *receive* or *give* and *donate,* the same semantic role can appear in different surface syntactic positions, and the same syntactic position can be occupied by different semantic roles.[6] Such observations of complex mapping between semantic roles and syntactic position raise the question of how to characterize these relationships; in particular, whether they are systematic or wholly arbitrary (which would create enormous problems for learning), and if systematic, how the relationships should be represented.

There has long been an intuition that the relationship between semantic roles and their syntactic positions is constrained, such that certain kinds of roles (or positions in a conceptual structure, according to Jackendoff, 1990) will tend to occupy certain syntactic positions. The appeal of such constraints is in their potential for supporting learning (if they are part of some initial capacity), the rapid planning of speech (which requires assignment of elements of "meaning" to specific syntactic positions), and rapid comprehension (which requires determining which syntactic positions represent which semantic roles, as one converts the syntactic structure of a message into its meaning).

The relationship between semantic and syntactic levels has been actively debated (see, e.g., Foley & van Valin, 1984; Grimshaw, 1990; Jackendoff, 1990). However, one general framework posits *linking rules,* building on the fact that the semantic and syntactic levels of representation share a similar hierarchical structure: Those thematic roles highest in the thematic hierarchy will be assigned to those structural positions highest in the syntactic hierarchy. For example, in the thematic hierarchy, the role of agent is considered to be "higher" than either "patient" or "theme"; in the grammatical hierarchy, the syntactic function of subject is assumed to be higher than direct object, which is higher than indirect object (see, e.g., Baker, 1988; Grimshaw, 1990; Jackendoff, 1990). Aligning these two hierarchies will have the net result that, if there is an agent to be expressed in the sentence (e.g., using the verb *give*), that role will be assigned to subject position, with the patient or theme assigned to direct object. If there is no agent, then this frees the subject position for another semantic role. For example, the verb *open* optionally expresses an agent, and if the agent is expressed, it will occupy subject position, as in "Mary opened the door." But the same verb may occur without an expressed agent, and in this case the theme can move up to the position of surface subject, as in "The door opened." Despite these relatively simple examples, there is still considerable debate about exactly how to characterize these semantic roles, including questions such as how many inde-

---

[6] A currently active area of research concerns the question of whether these two sentence forms are actually part of the same underlying representation, and whether the process of production entails "direct" assignment of semantic roles to their surface positions or "mediated" assignment via the underlying representation (see, e.g., Bock & Levelt, 1994, for review).

pendent roles there are, what their proper level of description is, what their relationship is to the syntactic level, and even whether every noun phrase in a sentence can be assigned one and only one thematic role (the "Theta criterion," Chomsky, 1981; see, e.g., Jackendoff, 1990, for discussion).

Within psycholinguistic research, the nature and relationship between these two structural levels has also been a central issue, with additional questions building on formal linguistic theory. In the domain of speech planning, questions have arisen about the respective roles of semantics and syntax as separate mechanisms involved in the assembly of sentences. A model introduced by Garrett (1975) suggested separate levels of representation, one devoted to assigning lexical items to their functional roles (subject, object), and another devoted to assigning these items to "positional frames," syntactic planning frames carrying grammatical information such as tense markings (for a recent spelling out of some of the possible mechanisms involved, see LaPointe & Dell, 1989).

Building on this framework, some recent investigations have focused on the question of what semantic properties might predispose lexical items to be assigned to specific functional roles. There seems to be a tendency to assign animates to subject position, cross-linguistically and in both spontaneous and experimental settings (see Bock, Loebell, & Morey, 1992, for review); however, the structural characteristics of subject-hood (e.g., agreement with the verb) are completely impervious to the noun phrase's status as an animate (or, for that matter, to status as any specific conceptual category). This suggests two separate mechanisms, one in which conceptual entities (e.g., animates or possibly animate agents) are assigned to structural positions (e.g., surface subject), and another that controls characteristics such as subject–verb agreement (Bock et al., 1992). Such posited separation of levels is consistent with the evidence on speech errors, which shows that syntactic frames are planning units that may become accessible at a separate moment from the insertion of particular words into the frame (Garrett, 1975). It remains an open question, however, whether animates are preferentially assigned to subject position because of the hierarchy of linking rules (whereby agents, often animate, are assigned to subject position), or whether the preference is more a consequence of the relatively high degree of accessibility of animates during the course of speech planning (Bock et al., 1992).

Within acquisition, similar questions have arisen with respect to the status of linking rules. Some theorists have suggested that a bias to assume "agent → subject" might be innate and universal (Grimshaw, 1981; Pinker, 1984), providing a mechanism whereby children could identify which of the noun phrases in the speech stream is the subject of the sentence (and thereby supporting the acquisition of phrase structure). Because languages vary with respect to how syntactic relations are encoded (e.g., principally by word order in English, principally by case marking in Hungarian), the child must determine, based on input, whether his language relies strongly on word order to encode grammatical relations, and if so, what that ordering is (e.g., SVO in English). If the child can ascertain from observation of the event in which an utterance occurs that there is an *agent,* and if he possesses an innate bias specifying that the agent (if present) is encoded as subject, he will have a significant clue as to the word order of his native language.

Whether the preferential mapping between agent and subject should be characterized as a specific linking rule has been questioned, however. Although there is a tendency for animate (or animate-type) nouns to appear before verbs in English, even very young children do not restrict subject position exclusively to animates or agents. Fisher (1996) argues that the tendency for animates to appear as subjects might be due to a fundamental structural asymmetry between the conceptual roles played by various participants in an event structure, and a corresponding structural asymmetry between syntactic subject and object. The asymmetry inherent in events is due to an imbalance in the natural "salience" of certain participants, particularly the special salience of dynamic, mobile, and animate participants. The consequence of this imbalance for syntactic encoding of events has been noted by linguists such as Talmy (1983) and Fillmore (1977), and recent investigations have shown that both the character of the event participants and the syntactic frame itself have consequences both for adults' and children's judgments of sentence meanings (Fisher, 1996; Gleitman, Gleitman, & Ostrin, 1996). The strong effects of syntactic frames in biasing interpretation is consistent with a growing body of literature in acquisition showing that syntactic information itself can be an important guide to learning the meanings of words (Fisher, 1996; Gleitman, 1990; Landau & Gleitman, 1985).

2. Symbols and Rules versus Connectionist Architectures for Mapping Morphology and Phonology

Despite the dominance of symbolic representations in characterizing language and language learning, the past 10 years have witnessed a remarkable resurgence of interest in models of learning that would seem to be close relatives to those that Lashley forcefully rejected. However, it is of considerable interest that it has been difficult to design connectionist systems that adequately capture some of the basic facts discussed by Lashley—including agreement at a distance or speech errors that span phrases.

The current prominence of connectionist architectures in explaining language learning and language use can be traced to a treatment of the verbal past tense by Rumelhart and McClelland (1986). In that work, the authors proposed that, although linguistic rules might be able to capture many aspects of grammar, the actual mechanisms responsible for learning—and the resulting knowledge state—might contain no explicit representation of rules at all.

To explore this claim, Rumelhart and McClelland used the case of the verbal past tense. They chose this case in part because it has long been viewed as a very clear example of the need for symbolic representations and rules that govern the circumstances under which a verb should receive past tense, and the phonological form in which this tense should be realized. For example, regular verbs receive a past tense morpheme in accord with the rule, "add/ed." The phonetic realization of that morpheme will vary depending on the phonological nature of the verb stem, accounting for the phonetic difference between the past tenses of, for example, the verbs *walk (walked) vs. want (wanted)*.

Irregular past tense is not assigned using this rule (e.g., *ringed* is not the past tense of *ring,* as in ringing a bell), but rather, on the basis of partial analogies from the phonological properties of the verb stem (e.g., *ring* → rang, drink → drank; grow → grew, know → knew). (Note, however, that these analogies are not applied perfectly; e.g., *sting* → *stang, stow → *stew). The past tense rule for regulars has been proposed to account for the acquisition of the past tense by young children, who are known to freely generalize the regular past tense to both known and novel words (e.g., producing "comed" or "goed" instead of *came* or *went* or *riffed* as the past tense of the nonsense verb *rif*). Within the framework of symbolic representations, it is precisely the rule for regulars acquired by the child learning language. However, within the connectionist framework, the child is assumed to be learning—for all verbs—an association between some pattern of activation corresponding to the segmental phonological representation of the present tense verb and another pattern of activation corresponding to that of the past tense form. In these models, the learner is "tutored" (given feedback) until a given input pattern (a verb stem) results in a correct output pattern (past tense of that verb). In this framework, the (roughly specified) sound of a word serves as input, but there is no room for structural notions such as "root." However, the latter is required to account for the fact that novel verbs with noun roots (e.g., *grandstand*) receive the regular past tense ending (*grandstanded*) rather than the past tense ending that would be predicted from sound similarity (*stand* → stood, but not *grandstand* → grandstood; see Marcus et al., 1995).

Over the past 10 years, there has been a great deal of discussion between advocates of symbolic representations *versus* connectionist systems (see Fodor & Pylyshyn, 1988, for a penetrating critique; Bechtel & Abrahamsen, 1991, for overview). The criticisms of the connectionist model of the past tense acquisition have been numerous. They have included questions of whether the existing systems learn anything properly resembling a human language, whether the assumptions about learning input and course of acquisition are realistic, whether the characterization and modeling of children's overgeneralizations are accurate with respect to the empirical evidence from language learning, whether the kinds of similarities that the connectionist model is capable of using are indeed those that are used by human language learners; whether the connectionist system is improperly constrained at many levels, accounting for improper under- and overgeneralization; and many others (see Pinker & Prince, 1988, for an excellent and comprehensive critique). The response from connectionist modelers has been to alter aspects of the models and/or input (e.g., Plunkett & Marchman, 1993), and these modifications have also led to further critiques (see, e.g., Marcus et al., 1995).

Despite these quite profound problems, the connectionist framework has found sympathy among investigators eager to understand the details of learning mechanisms that might be capable of capturing learning across domains in a "biologically plausible" fashion. One can question whether the latter goal is, for now, scientifically feasible.

3. Symbols and Rules versus Dynamical Systems for Mapping Phonology and Articulation

Perhaps the most radical nonsymbolic mapping proposal has arisen in the context of inquiry into the relationship between phonology, phonetics, and articulation. The sound systems of languages have been well described within theoretical linguistics by symbolic representations and rules that operate upon them. However, these representations must be realized as coordinated movement of the articulators—continuous motion in real time. Hence understanding the nature of the relevant mapping relationships in this domain presents a significant challenge. How does one move from a static symbolic representation of the sound contrasts relevant for languages to a dynamical system capable of capturing the actual act of speaking? Historically, attempts to capture these relationships have ranged from assuming that there is no systematic or interesting relationship (Hockett, 1955) to proposing highly constrained featural representations of both phonological and phonetic levels (Chomsky & Halle, 1968) to "phonetic implementation" models wherein (symbolic) phonological representations are converted to physical parameterizations relevant for articulation (Liberman & Pierrehumbert, 1984).

Browman and Goldstein (1995)[7] proposed a quite different kind of system, called "articulatory phonology," to capture these relationships in a single unified manner. In essence, they propose a dynamical systems model of speech in which the putatively different levels of description are actually mutually constraining high- and low-dimensional descriptions of the same complex system. The low-dimensional description is meant to capture what formal phonology does (i.e., the equivalent of a symbolic representation including primitives [e.g., features] and their rules of combination). The high-dimensional description is meant to capture the dynamic biomechanical characteristics of articulation. The high-dimensional description can be collapsed onto the low-dimensional; as this property is characteristic of self-organizing systems in nature, it could be quite useful in understanding learning and development (see Thelen & Smith, 1994, for discussion of self-organizing systems in perceptual, action, and cognitive development).

The basic unit in articulatory phonology is the *articulatory gesture,* a dynamical system that begins with the goal (intention) of articulation and carries the articulators through the relevant motions; the trajectories of the articulators are specified by a characteristic set of parameter values. These gestures can be combined into gestural *constellations,* including information about phasing of the individual gestures relative to each other, which produces a *gestural score* specifying the temporal stream

---

[7] We thank Pim Levelt for guiding us towards this literature and pointing out its importance.

for larger units. At the highest level, then, one might have a gestural score for the word *ban,* which is essentially a plan for producing that word.

This plan captures information at both the macro- and microlevels. Articulatory phonology assumes that "macro" properties such as phonological contrast (e.g., the voicing contrast in English) can be captured as part of the same system that specifies the "micro" properties, the dynamics of articulation. Browman and Goldstein offer the example of lip closure, which would constitute the goal of the first articulatory gesture involved in saying the word *ban.* The parameter values that specify this gesture remain constant for the duration of the gesture, and contrast with a different constant for lip narrowing in the case of pronouncing /w/. Along with such constants relevant to phonology, however, the microscopic properties of change are also captured by the parameters in the articulatory gesture; furthermore, the changes that occur as the individual gesture or gestural score is realized over time naturally fall out of the dynamic nature of the system. The physical context dependence of phonological units, for example, emerges as a consequence of the system, rather that requiring an independent level of explanation.

Although the dynamical systems model of speech has the attractiveness of unifying levels that are otherwise captured by quite different kinds of formalisms, it remains an open question whether such systems will actually provide a true alternative to symbolic and rule-based systems.

C. Some Comments on Input and the Problem of Learning

Learning a complex system such as language presents further formidable problems. Unlike many cases of action, learning a particular language clearly *does* depend on input: Children who hear English spoken during their early years will learn English, whereas those who hear Farsi spoken will learn Farsi. This brute fact has often seduced psychologists into thinking that language learning must be a simple consequence of modeling the environment. Recent controversies about language learning have revolved around the extent to which innately specified principles of linguistic knowledge must be present, the nature of learning, and the degree to which it is involved.

Like the case of action, close inspection of the learner's problem reveals that regardless how rich the environmental input is, representational biases of the learner will play a critical role in representing and processing that input. For example, characteristics of the learner's input system do not always exactly duplicate those of their output (Gleitman & Newport, 1997; Goldin-Meadow & Mylander, 1990), making it difficult to argue for a learning system that straightforwardly, simply, and precisely models the environment. As another example, there is nothing obviously identifiable in the input that directly tells the learner which parts of the sound stream correspond to the formal categories (noun, verb, subject, direct object, etc.) that he will need to structure the system. To the extent that statistical properties of the input are correlated with these categories, patterns in the data may allow a properly predisposed learner a way to discover the relevant categories (see Kelly & Martin, 1994, for some examples). Recent evidence suggests that statistical learning is present early in life. Infants as young as eight months of age can learn to form word-like units based on the transitional probabilities among syllables presented continuously for only 2 min of exposure (Saffran, Aslin, & Newport, 1996). These results indicate that infants possess powerful learning mechanisms that might aid in decoding the linguistic environment. However, they do not provide evidence against the notion that some innate biases in and mechanisms will be necessary in order to perform such a statistical analysis, essentially searching for the correct units.

Finally, there is very little in the way of overt correction of the learner's production; even if there were, it is unclear, as with action, how the learner would actually map backwards from explicit correction of an error (e.g., "Say drove, not drived") to the correct level of representation and its rules, which will predict *drove,* not *drived,* but *derived,* not *derove.* In the case of verb morphology, these rules and representations appear to require the notion of a verb root rather than a string of phonetic segments (Marcus et al., 1995). To the extent that connectionist models of learning incorporate categories such as "verb root" in their architecture, they are essentially endorsing a learning theory that is constrained by built-in linguistic categories.

III. SUMMARY AND CONCLUSIONS

The conception that mental representations—specifically, symbolic cognitive representations—are valid objects of psychological theorizing has redirected the focus of much psychological research over the last 50 years. This shift, which we believe to have been crucially important, was motivated by the inadequacy of earlier conceptual paradigms to provide coherent explanations of behavior, such as the phenomena of serial ordering observed in action and language (i.e., hierarchical organization, generalization in learning, rapidity of acquisition and of performance). The value of this shift can best be seen in the richness and power of the research and theories that have arisen from it. Another indicator is the complexity of research topics that have begun to be tackled by cognitive scientists.

Despite, or perhaps because of this progress, several possible weaknesses associated with the use of symbolic representations as a theoretical cornerstone have lately come to the attention of some psychologists. Two problems we have discussed here are the difficulty in understanding the fine structure of learning and the computational difficulties associated with the computation of necessary but complex transformations such as that between phonology and articulation or, in action, inverse kinematics/dynamics.

More recently, cognitive theorists have begun exploring conceptual frameworks such as connectionism that reject traditional symbolic representations in favor of distributed, or what some have called, subsymbolic, representations. The connectionist approach has been compelling to some who seem convinced that it provides an account of learning and generalization. Connectionist models do seem to excel at being able to acquire, maintain, and compute good approximations for relatively smooth, if complex, transformations. Clear problems remain, however. For example, when well-developed symbolic theories (such as morphology and phonology) are compared to connectionist models of learning, the latter fall down on the ability to capture the same range of phenomena with the same degree of depth and generalization. Furthermore, the time scale for learning in connectionist models often seems unreasonable, they often generalize inappropriately in ways that rule-based models avoid, and there is still inadequate understanding of the formal properties of these models, which often makes their application seem more of a black art than a science.

Although there are some who might wish for connectionism to sweep away the symbolic approach to cognition (much as that approach previously eliminated behaviorism), the relative dominance of one over the other at the moment seems to us to depend as much on the sociology of science as the relative persuasiveness of each. This situation is not to be viewed as a disaster, however. The current tension between these views has provided an impetus to new research and probing questions in both camps. Among the problems that should remain central to much of this work are those that we have described here.

References

Armstrong, S., Gleitman, L., & Gleitman, H. (1983). What some concepts might not be. *Cognition, 13,* 263–308.

Baker, C. (1988). *Incorporation: A theory of grammatical function changing.* Chicago: University of Chicago Press.

Bechtel, W., & Abrahamsen, A. (1991). *Connectionism and the mind.* Oxford: Blackwell.

Benecke, R., Rothwell, J. C., Day, B. L., Dick, J. P., & Marsden, C. D. (1986). Motor strategies involved in the performance of sequential movements. *Experimental Brain Research, 63,* 585–595.

Bock, K., & Levelt, W. (1994). Grammatical encoding. In M. A. Gernsbacher (Ed.), *Handbook of psycholinguistics* (pp. 945–984). San Diego: Academic Press.

Bock, K., & Loebell, H. (1990). Framing sentences. *Cognition, 35,* 1–40.

Bock, K., Loebell, H., & Morey, R. (1992). Bridging the syntactic cleft. *Psychological Review, 99,* 150–171.

Book, W. F. (1908). The psychology of skill with special reference to its acquisition in typewriting. Missoula, MT: University of Montana.

Browman, C., & Goldstein, L. (1995). Dynamics and articulatory phonology. In R. Port & T. von Gelder (Eds.), *Mind as motion: Explorations in the dynamics of cognition* (pp. 175–193). Cambridge, MA: MIT Press.

Bruce, D. (1994). Lashley and the problem of serial order. *American Psychologist, 49,* 93–103.

Chomsky, N. (1959). Review of Skinner's *Verbal Behavior. Language, 35,* 26–58.

Chomsky, N. (1981). *Lectures on government and binding.* Foris: Dordrecht.

Chomsky, N., & Halle, M. (1968). *The sound pattern of English.* New York: Harper & Row.

Dell, G. (1996). Speaking and misspeaking. In L. Gleitman & M. Liberman (Eds.), *Invitation to cognitive science, Part I, Language.* Cambridge, MA: MIT Press.

Dell, G., & Reich, P. (1981). Stages in sentence production: An analysis of speech error data. *Journal of Verbal Learning and Verbal Behavior, 20,* 611–629.

Fillmore, C. J. (1977). The case for case reopened. In P. Cole & J. M. Sadock (Eds.), *Syntax and semantics, Volume 8: Grammatical relations* (pp. 59–81). New York: Academic Press.

Fisher, C. (1996). *Who's the subject? Sentence structures as analogs of verb meaning.* Unpublished manuscript, University of Illinois.

Fodor, J. A. (1975). *The language of thought.* New York: T. Y. Crowell.

Fodor, J. A. (1981). *Representations.* Cambridge, MA: MIT Press.

Fodor, J. A., Bever, T. G., & Garrett, M. (1974). *The psychology of language.* New York: McGraw-Hill.

Fodor, J. A., & Pylyshyn, Z. W. (Eds.). (1988). *Cognition, 28,* (special issue on Connectionism).

Foley, W., & van Valin, R. D. (1984). *Functional syntax and universal grammar.* Cambridge: Cambridge University Press.

Fromkin, V. (1973). *Speech errors as linguistic evidence.* The Hague: Mouton.

Gallistel, C. R. (1990). *The organization of learning.* Cambridge, MA: MIT Press.

Garnham, A., Shillcock, R., Brown, G., Mill, A., & Cutler, A. (1982). Slips of the tongue in the London-Lund corpus of spontaneous conversations. In A. Cutler (Ed.), *Slips of the tongue and language production,* (pp. 251–263). Berlin: Mouton.

Garrett, M. (1975). The analysis of sentence production. In G. Bower (Ed.), *Psychology of Learning and Motivation, 9.* New York: Academic Press.

Garrett, M. (1980). Levels of processing in sentence production. In B. Butterworth (Ed.), *Language production,* (pp. 177–220). San Diego: Academic Press.

Garrett, M. (1988). Processes in language production. In F. J. Newmeyer (Ed.), *Linguistics: The Cambridge survey, III: Language: Psychological and biological aspects* (pp. 69–96). Cambridge, UK: Cambridge University Press.

Ghez, C., Gordon, J., & Ghilardi, M. F. (1995). Impairments of reaching movements in patients without proprioception: II. Effects of visual information on accuracy. *Journal of Neurophysiology, 73,* 361–372.

Gleitman, L. R. (1990). The structural sources of verb meanings. *Language Acquisition, 1(1),* 3–55.

Gleitman, L. R., & Newport, E. L. (1996). The invention of language by children: Environmental and biological influences on the acquisition of language. In L. Gleitman and M. Liberman (Eds.), *Invitation to cognitive science, Part I, Language.* Cambridge, MA: MIT Press.

Gleitman, L. R., Gleitman, H., Miller, C., & Ostrin, R. (1996). "Similar" and similar concepts. *Cognition, 58,* 321–376.

Goldin-Meadow, S., & Mylander, C. (1984). Gestural communication in deaf children: The effects and non-effects of parental input on early language development. *Monographs of the Society for Research in Child Development, 49,* 1–121.

Gordon, J., Ghilardi, M. F., & Ghez, C. (1995). Impairments of reaching movements in patients without proprioception: I. Spatial errors. *Journal of Neurophysiology, 73,* 347–360.

Grimshaw, J. (1981). Form, function, and the language acquisition device. In C. L. Baker & J. J. McCarthey (Eds.), *The logical problem of language acquisition* (pp. 165–187). Cambridge, MA: MIT Press.

Grimshaw, J. (1990). *Argument structure.* Cambridge, MA: MIT Press.

Hockett, C. (1955). *A manual of phonology.* Chicago: University of Chicago Press.

Hollerbach, J. M. (1982). Computers, brains and the control of movement. *Trends In Neurosciences, 5,* 189–192.

Hull, C. L. (1943). *Principles of behavior.* New York: Appleton-Century-Crofts.

Jackendoff, R. (1983). *Semantics and cognition.* Cambridge, MA: MIT Press.

Jackendoff, R. (1990). *Semantic structures.* Cambridge, MA: MIT Press.

Jackendoff, R. (1996). The architecture of the linguistic-spatial interface. In P. Bloom, M. Peterson, M. Garrett, & L. Nadel (Eds.), *Language and space* (pp. 1–30). Cambridge, MA: MIT Press.

Jordan, M. I. (1990). Motor learning and the degrees of freedom problem. In M. Jeannerod (Ed.), *Attention and performance XIII: Motor representation and control* (pp. 796–836). Hillsdale, NJ: Erlbaum.

Kawato, M., Furukawa, K., & Suzuki, R. (1987). A hierarchical network model for motor control and learning of voluntary movement. *Biological Cybernetics, 57,* 169–185.

Keele, S. W., Cohen, A., & Ivry, R. (1990). Motor programs: Concepts and issues. In M. Jeannerod (Ed.), *Attention and Performance XIII* (pp. 77–110). Hillsdale, NJ: Erlbaum.

Kelly, M., & Martin, S. (1994). Domain-general abilities applied to domain-specific tasks: Sensitivity to probabilities in perception, cognition, and language. In L. R. Gleitman & B. Landau (Ed.), *The acquisition of the lexicon,* (pp. 105–142). Cambridge, MA: MIT Press.

Koh, K., & Meyer, D. E. (1991). Function learning: Induction of continuous stimulus-response relations. *Journal of Experimental Psychology: Learning, Memory, & Cognition, 17,* 811–836.

Landau, B., & Gleitman, L. R. (1985). *Language and experience.* Cambridge, MA: Harvard University Press.

Landau, B., & Jackendoff, R. (1993). "What" and "where" in spatial language and spatial cognition. *Behavioral and Brain Sciences, 16,* 217–266.

Lapointe, S., & Dell, G. (1989). A synthesis of some recent work in sentence production. In G. N. Carlson & M. K. Tannenhaus (Eds.), *Linguistic structure in language processing* (pp. 107–156). Dordrecht, The Netherlands: Kluwer.

Lashley, K. S. (1917). The accuracy of movement in the absence of excitation from the moving organ. *American Journal of Physiology, 43,* 169–194.

Lashley, K. S. (1942). The problem of cerebral organization in vision. *Biological Symposia, 7,* 301–322.

Lashley, K. S. (1951). The problem of serial order in behavior. In L. A. Jeffress (Ed.), *Cerebral mechanisms in behavior: The Hixon Symposium* (pp. 112–146). New York: Wiley.

Levelt, W. J. M. (1989). *Speaking: From intention to articulation.* Cambridge, MA: MIT Press.

Levin, B. (1993). *English verb classes and alterations.* Chicago: University of Chicago Press.

Lindemann, P. G., & Wright, C. E. (1998). Skill acquisition and plans for actions: Learning to write with your other hand. In S. Sternberg & D. Scarborough (Eds.), *Invitation to Cognitive Science,* vol. 4 (pp. 523–583). Cambridge, MA: MIT Press.

Logan, G. D. (1982). On the ability to inhibit complex movements: A stop-signal study of typewriting. *Journal of Experimental Psychology: Human Perception and Performance, 8,* 778–792.

Maclay, H., & Osgood, C. E. (1959). Hesitation phenomena in spontaneous English speech. *Word, 15,* 19–44.

MacKenzie, C. L., & van Eerd, D. L. (1990). Rhythmic precision in the performance of piano scales: Motor psychophysics and motor programming. In M. Jeannerod (Ed.), *Attention and Performance XIII* (pp. 375–408). Hillsdale, NJ: Erlbaum.

Marcus, G., Brinkmann, U., Clahsen, H., Wiese, R., Woest, A., & Pinker, S. (1995). German inflection: The exception that proves the rule. *Cognitive Psychology, 29,* 189–256.

Mattingly, I. G., & Studdert-Kennedy, M. (1991). *Modularity and the motor theory of speech perception: proceedings of a conference to honor Alvin M. Liberman.* Hillsdale, NJ: Erlbaum.

Merton, P. A. (1972). How we control the contraction of our muscles. *Scientific American, 226,* 30–37.

Miller, G. A., Galanter, E., & Pribram, K. H. (1960). *Plans and the structure of behavior.* New York: Holt, Rinehart, & Winston.

Monsell, S. (1986). Programming of complex sequences: Evidence from the timing of rapid speech and other productions. In H. Heuer & C. Fromm (Eds.), *Generation and modulation of action patterns* (pp. 72–86). Berlin: Springer-Verlag.

Murphy, G. L., & Medin, D. (1985). The role of theories in conceptual coherence. *Psychological Review, 92,* 289–316.

Newport, E., Gleitman, L., & Gleitman, H. (1977). Mother, I'd rather do it myself: Some effects and non-effects of maternal speech style. In C. E. Snoth & C. A. Ferguson (Eds.), *Talking to children: Language input and acquisition* (pp. 109–149). New York: Cambridge University Press.

Osgood, C. E. (1963). On understanding and creating sentences. *American Psychologist, 18,* 735–751.

Pinker, S. (1984). *Language learnability and language development.* Cambridge, MA: Harvard University Press.

Pinker, S. (1989). *Learnability and cognition: The acquisition of argument structure.* Cambridge, MA: MIT Press.

Pinker, S. (1994). How could a child use verb syntax to learn verb semantics? In L. R. Gleitman & B. Landau (Eds.), *The acquisition of the lexicon* (pp. 377–410). Cambridge, MA: MIT Press.

Pinker, S., & Prince, A. (1988). On language and connectionism: Analysis of a parallel distributed processing model of language acquisition. *Cognition, 28,* 73–193.

Plunkett, K., & Marchman, V. (1993). From rote learning to system building: acquiring verb morphology in children and connectionist nets. *Cognition, 48,* 21–69.

Rabbitt, P. M. A. (1978). Detection of errors by skilled typists. *Ergonomics, 21,* 945–958.

Raibert, M. H. (1977). Motor control and learning by the state space model. *Technical Report AI-M-351,* Massachusetts Institute of Technology. NTIS #AD-AO26-960.

Rosch, E., & Mervis, C. B. (1975). Family resemblances: Studies in the internal structure of categories. *Cognitive Psychology, 7,* 573–605.

Rosenbaum, D. A., Loukopoulos, L. D., Meulenbroek, R. G. J., Vaughan, J., & Engelbrecht, S. E. (1995). Planning reaches by evaluating stored postures. *Psychological Review, 102,* 28–67.

Rumelhart, D. & McClelland, J. (1986). On learning the past tenses of English verbs. Implicit rules or parallel distributed processing? In J. McClelland, D. Rumelhart, and the PDP Research Group (Eds.), *Parallel distributed processing: Explorations in the microstructure of cognition.* Cambridge, MA: MIT Press.

Saffran, J. R., Aslin, R. N., & Newport, E. L. (1996). Statistical learning by 8-month-old infants. *Science, 274,* 1926–1928.

Saltzman, E., & Kelso, J. A. S. (1987). Skilled actions: A task-dynamic approach. *Psychological Review, 94,* 84–106.

Schmidt, R. A. (1975). A schema theory of discrete motor skill learning. *Psychological Review, 82,* 225–260.

Schmidt, R. A. (1988). The process of learning. In R. A. Schmidt (Ed.), *Motor control and learning* (pp. 457–491). Champaign, IL: Human Kinetics Publishers.

Schneider, D. M., & Schmidt, R. A. (1995). Units of action in motor control: Role of response complexity and target speed. *Human Performance, 8,* 27–49.

Shaffer, L. H. (1973). Latency mechanisms in transcription. In S. Kornblum (Ed.), *Attention and performance IV* (pp. 435–446). New York: Academic Press.

Smith, E. E., & Medin, D. L. (1981). *Categories and concepts.* Cambridge, MA: MIT Press.

Stemberger, J. (1985). An interactive model of language production. In A. Ellis (Ed.), *Progress in the psychology of language, Vol. 1* (pp. 143–186). Hillsdale, NJ: Erlbaum.

Sternberg, S., Knoll, R. L., & Turock, D. L. (1990). Hierarchical control in the execution of action sequences: Tests of two invariance properties. In M. Jeannerod (Ed.), *Attention and performance XIII* (pp. 1–56). Hillsdale, NJ: Erlbaum.

Sternberg, S., Monsell, S., Knoll, R. L., & Wright, C. E. (1978). The latency and duration of rapid movement sequences: Comparisons of speech and typing. In G. E. Stelmach (Ed.), *Information processing in motor control and learning* (pp. 118–152). New York: Academic Press.

Sternberg, S., Wright, C. E., Knoll, R. L., & Monsell, S. (1982). Motor programs in rapid speech: Additional evidence. In R. A. Cole (Ed.), *Perception and production of fluent speech* (pp. 507–534). Hillsdale, NJ: Lawrence Erlbaum Associates.

Talmy, L. (1983). How language structures space. In H. Pick & L. Acredolo (Eds.), *Spatial orientation: Theory, research, and application* (pp. 225–282). New York: Plenum.

Thelen, E., & Smith, L. B. (1994). *A dynamic systems approach to the development of cognition and action.* Cambridge, MA: MIT Press.

Viviani, P., & Laissard, G. (1996). Motor templates in typing. *Journal of Experimental Psychology: Human perception and performance, 22,* 417–445.

Wright, C. E. (1990a). Controlling sequential motor activity. In D. Osherson, S. M. Kosslyn, & J. M. Hollerbach (Eds.), *Invitation to cognitive science: Visual cognition and action,* Volume 2 (pp. 285–316). Cambridge, MA; MIT Press.

Wright, C. E. (1990b). Generalized motor programs: Reevaluating claims of effector independence. In M. Jeannerod (Ed.), *Attention and performance XIII: Motor representation and control* (pp. 294–320). Hillsdale, NJ: Lawrence Erlbaum.

Young, D. E., & Schmidt, R. A. (1990). Units of motor behavior: Modifications with practice and feedback. In M. Jeannerod (Ed.), *Attention and performance XIII* (pp. 763–795). Hillsdale, NJ: Erlbaum.

CHAPTER 13

Concepts and Categorization

Douglas L. Medin
John D. Coley

I. INTRODUCTION

It has been said that psychology has a long past but a short history. Nowhere is this observation more apt than in the psychology of concepts. The study of concepts and categorization is directed at the most fundamental questions concerning the interaction of mind and world. What kinds of things are there in the world and how do people come to know them? What is the relationship between lexical terms and their referents? Do we simply *recognize* categories or do constructive processes operate to *create* categories and concepts? These are questions asked by early Greek philosophers, questions that persisted in monasteries through the dark ages, and questions that organized thought in biology from the emergence of systematics in the 17th century, through the development of evolutionary theory, and they continue to the present day.

Psychology and experimental studies of concepts and categorization, while burgeoning, are still in their infancy. As such, one might expect false steps, some falls, and uneven progress. As we shall see, the psychological study of concepts has lived up to this metaphor (to the occasional frustration of researchers). But learning to walk or even crawl promises new views and perspectives. In this chapter, we provide a selective review of research on concepts and categorization, focusing on the last 30 years or so. Even in this short span there have been a number of twists and turns, and it is not always easy to identify genuine progress. One should note, however, that progress also comes in the form of methodological and technical advances

Perception and Cognition at Century's End

that allow researches to ask sharper questions. From the latter perspective, the field has seen unambiguous advances.

An important characteristic of categorization research is a multiplicity of approaches. Although pluralism can be taken as an index of a lack of clear goals and means, we prefer to read it as a "divide and conquer" strategy appropriate for problems of the magnitude of the psychology of concepts. At the same time, however, there needs to be enough communication to recognize convergences and exploit progress in allied subareas. In that spirit our review will indicate points where greater interplay across approaches may be fruitful.

The remainder of this chapter is organized as follows. We first continue our somewhat belabored introduction by outlining the sometimes fitful progress in the psychological study of concepts and categories over the past 50 years or so. Next we turn to constraints and challenges that qualify key results, generate new findings, and (in our opinion) ultimately constrain what any theory of categorization must account for. This sets this stage for a discussion of current challenges and further opportunities for progress.

II. CONCEPTUAL FUNCTIONS

First, it will be useful to have a few definitions. By *concept* we mean a mental representation of a category serving multiple functions, one of which is to allow for the determination of whether or not something belongs to the class. A *category* refers to the set of entities picked out by the concept. As we shall see, concepts serve multiple functions and a focus on a single function comes at the risk of developing theories that are too narrow to do the work they will ultimately be asked to do (e.g., Matheus, Rendell, Medin, & Goldstone, 1989).

There are numerous possible taxonomies, but we will distinguish seven functions of concepts: categorization, understanding, inferences, explanation and reasoning, learning, communication, and combination. These are meant to be neither mutually exclusive nor exhaustive, but they illustrate the vast array of cognitive functions performed by concepts, and the enormous task facing any theory of concepts and categorization.

The categorization function of concepts refers to the fact that mental representations are used to determine the category membership of entities. Categorization allows us to bring relevant knowledge to bear in the service of *understanding* and *making predictions*. For example, after categorizing some novel object as a member of the category step ladders, people can understand its relevant parts and know how to interact with it. Categorization also allows one to make predictions or *inferences* concerning the affordances of some entity. For example, one might infer that this novel step ladder would support one's weight. Concepts are critically involved in *explanation* and reasoning. Having categorized some patient as an *anorexic* (a form of eating disorder) one might be able to explain why they insist on adding skim milk rather than half and half to their coffee.

Concepts also support *learning* in that new entities are not only understood in terms of old but also feed back to modify or update contexts. For example, learning that a penguin is a bird not only adds another instance to *bird* but also may cause the learner to rethink what is meant by *bird* to begin with. Just how this updating is done is an important theoretical question. For example, category modification needs to balance the need to be sensitive to particular contexts with the danger of discarding accumulated wisdom derived from a broader range of contexts.

Obviously we also use concepts for *communication*. The interpersonal aspect of concepts places constraints on virtually every other function. Communication is facilitated to the extent that conceptions of categories are shared across language users. Furthermore, communicative goals may determine whether some entity is referred to as a *cottontail,* a *rabbit,* or simply an *animal* (Grice, 1975).

Finally, *combining concepts* allows us to express and create an unlimited number of new concepts. People are able to understand novel combinations of concepts such as *green mouse* (presumably a mouse that is green) and *green uncle* (an uncle with lots of money, or perhaps a new and inexperienced uncle).

These functions place competing demands on conceptual structure. For example, one can *categorize* most easily by focusing attention solely on the presence or absence of a single salient feature (e.g., whether or not something is red). But the category *red things* fails to support other conceptual functions; knowing that something is a member of *red things* does little to support inferences about the object, increase understanding, or provide explanations. Thus, different conceptual functions might make different and even competing demands on conceptual structure.

III. THE EMPIRICAL STUDY OF CATEGORIZATION

We do not need to rehearse here the general merits of controlled experimental contrasts. Instead, our aim is to call attention to the ongoing interaction between laboratory studies of conceptual behavior and so-called real-world categories. The general form of this interaction has been as follows. On the basis of observation, intuition, or argument, ideas about the structural underpinnings of natural (real-world) categories are developed. Associated with these conjectures may be some ideas or theories concerning both the mental representations people develop of such categories and the processes that create and operate on these representations. To test these ideas, researchers often construct "artificial categories" in the laboratory where the "structure" is unambiguous or independently established. Participants in experiments then learn these categories and then may be given various tests of their knowledge. The resulting performances are used to test ideas and theories concerning representation and processing. Often these studies with artificial categories are run in parallel with studies of natural categories. If the experimental findings are also parallel, researchers have increased confidence that they have, in fact, successfully brought relevant structural properties into the laboratory. To the extent that this goal is realized, one also has more confidence that the laboratory findings with respect to representation and processing will generalize to real-world (natural) categories. Lack of corresponding findings suggests either that the relevant structure has not been captured or that conditions of category learning and use in the world differ from those in the laboratory. Under these circumstances, findings with natural and with artificial categories each may be useful in their own right, but questions about generalizing from artificial to natural categories loom large.

In short, analyses of natural categories and experiments with artificial categories are closely linked. To be sure, researchers will sometimes explicitly depart from realistic category structures in order to set up some contrast to theoretical interest. But even here the researcher does not lose sight of real-world categories. Explicit departure requires an awareness of "from what," and does not constitute a neglect of structure.

Why are we hammering away on this point about relationships between the natural and the artificial? One reason is that it's easy to get lost in the details of laboratory contrasts and to interpret differences in the trade-off between artificiality and generalizability as representing incompatible approaches to the study of categorization. We prefer to see the tension between laboratory control and worldly realism as admitting a variety of research strategies that may be variously successful depending on one's goals. But what is common to them all is that no one believes that artificial categories are an end in themselves, and everyone would like to make correct generalizations to and inferences about natural categories.

IV. SIMILARITY

Everyone agrees that category membership is not arbitrary, not simply a list where the only thing category members have in common is that they are on the list. For example, we put salmon in a category with trout rather with robins or pencils (and if the choices were restricted to the latter two, we would pick robins over pencils). The general claim is that the basis for this categorization goes beyond the simple knowledge that salmon and trout are *fish*. But precisely what *is* relevant to placing salmon and trout in the same category?

One very important idea is that *similarity* is the organizing principle for categories and categorization. That is, *salmon* fits into a category with *trout* because salmon are more similar to trout than they are to robins or pencils. Entities in the same category are generally more similar to each other than they are to examples from contrasting categories. Certainly this principle makes intuitive sense and it has been rarely contested (we'll consider an exception a bit later). Instead, the debate has concerned how to analyze the notion of similarity and, in turn, how to map this analysis onto principles of category membership.

The modal approach to analyzing similarity has been to assume that concepts are comprised of features. Two entities are similar to the extent that they share (underlying) features (e.g., Tversky, 1977). That is, the molar notion of similarity is to be understood in terms of molecular processes of feature matches and mismatches. For example, one's mental representation of *salmon* and *trout* may include the features of having scales, gills, and fins and being alive. For *robin* the corresponding features might be having feathers, lungs, wings, and being alive. We'll defer the question of what features of pencils correspond to gills or lungs and simply note that pencils are not alive. By this featural approach, salmon are very similar to trout because they share four features and more similar to robins than to pencils because of the shared feature of being alive.

One nice property of featural analyses is that they integrate perceptual and conceptual similarity. There is evidence that the nervous system has "feature detectors" sensitive to perceptual properties, and the idea is to generalize this approach to the conceptual level. On this view, even abstract concepts like *liberty* can be decomposed into features and compared with other concepts like *freedom* and *justice*. As we'll see, a critical question is just how to perform a decomposition of concepts into features. Strategies have ranged from formal semantic analysis to simply asking people to list things that are true of concepts.

With this abstract description as background we are ready to turn to the question of how this analysis of similarity into features has been linked to the empirical study of category structure. The next section will briefly describe the two main views of conceptual structure that have organized research on concepts (see Smith & Medin, 1981, for an extended review).

V. CATEGORY STRUCTURE

Much of the research on concept learning in the third quarter of this century had as its primary focus learning (e.g., Bourne, 1970; Levine, 1975; Trabasso & Bower, 1968). An important issue concerned whether learning was all-or-none or gradual, and the upshot of these studies was support for all-or-none learning. The corresponding theoretical analyses used hypothesis testing as a framework. The idea was that category learning consisted of testing hypotheses or rules for category membership—incorrect hypotheses would lead to chance performance, but as soon as the learner tried out the correct rule or hypothesis, categorization performance would be perfect.

A. The Classical View

Although, to our knowledge, no one was at that time drawing explicit connections between these rule-learning experiments and the structure of natural categories, the two orientations were compatible. Specifically, the prevailing idea was that natural categories were structured in terms of singly necessary and jointly sufficient features (Katz & Postal, 1964). This has come to be called the classical view of concepts. A set of necessary and sufficient features means that category membership is determined by a conjunctive rule. If some entity has the set of requisite features, its a member of the category; otherwise it is not. Consider, for example, the concept *triangle.* A triangle is a closed geometric form with three sides and interior angles that sum to 180 degrees. If any one of these properties is missing, one does not have a triangle.

It is easy to go from ideas about category structure to conjectures about learning. The classical view is consistent with the idea that learning is based on hypothesis testing where hypotheses concern which features are defining. When the set of defining features has been mastered one has a rule for determining category membership.

Note that the classical view falls within the general framework of similarity models. Every member of a category shares features (namely, the defining features) with every other member of the category, and nonmembers differ from members in at least one of these features. From this perspective one could predict that the more defining features a nonmember shares with category members the harder it should be to reject as a member. For example, people should take longer to say that a robin is not a trout than to say that a pencil is not a trout (see Smith, Shoben, & Rips, 1974).

The classical view seems to work for triangles, but is it correct for natural categories more generally? The consensus among psychologists who study concepts is that the classical view is inadequate as a theory of conceptual structure. This judgment is driven both by doubts about whether concepts necessarily have defining feature and by evidence that people's conceptual behavior is not restricted to defining features. The arguments and counter-arguments can become quite complex (see Smith & Medin, 1981, for details) but the most serious problems with the classical view can be readily summarized.

First, if concepts have defining features, we should be able to say what they are. Yet even seemingly simple concepts like *dog* or *game* defy analysis into defining features. People may believe that concepts have defining features, but the features given as candidates may not hold up to closer scrutiny (McNamara & Sternberg, 1983). For example, people may list "flies" as a necessary property of *bird* but clearly not all birds fly (ostriches, penguins, baby birds).

Of course, one might argue that defining features are not necessarily accessible to consciousness. Certain syntactic rules are inaccessible to laypeople who nonetheless follow them. Perhaps all the classical view requires is a procedure for determining category membership. But this raises a second problem—there are numerous cases in which it is not clear whether or not an example belongs to a category. Is a radio an instance of furniture? What about a rug? People not only disagree with each other concerning category membership but also show internal inconsistency when questions are asked on separate occasions (Barsalou, 1989; Bellezza, 1984; McCloskey & Glucksberg, 1978).

One might argue that uncertainty about category membership just reflects uncertainty about whether some necessary feature is present. Even when category membership is certain, however, some examples of a concept seem to be better than others. For example, people judge a robin to be a better example of *bird* than a turkey is and in a speeded categorization task are faster at verifying the category membership of good examples than for poor examples (e.g., Smith et al., 1974; Rosch & Mervis, 1975).

Again one might rescue the classical view by suggesting that some features help to determine that other (defining) features are present. Good examples may have more clues to the presence of defining features, and this may account for goodness of example judgments and category verification times. Although the above ways of salvaging the classical view are not wildly implausible, they have the effect of insulating it from psychological data. In effect, the classical view becomes less relevant and less useful in organizing work on categorization. Even this might not be fatal were it not for the fact that an alternative view of conceptual structure became prominent, a view capable of addressing the categorization phenomena we have just been discussing.

B. The Probabilistic View

The probabilistic view, true to its name, claims that concepts are organized in terms of properties or features that are only characteristic of category instances. For example, *flies* may be a feature of the concept *bird* because most (but not all) birds fly. An example belongs to a category if it has enough of these characteristic features. Whatever the characteristic features are of the category *bird,* birds have more of these features than nonbirds. Certain features may be necessary, and therefore weighted heavily, but probabilistic features (usually but not always present in category members) also influence categorization (see also Cutting, chap. 4, this volume; Proffitt & Kaiser, chap. 7, this volume).

The probabilistic view was motivated by a series of important studies by Eleanor Rosch. Consider, for example, the work reported in Rosch and Mervis (1975). In one condition participants were asked to list features of category examples. In another participants listed superordinates of category members and then listed features of members of contrasting categories. The measures were then correlated with goodness of example or typicality rating. Typical (or good) members of a category tended to share features with other category members and not to share features of members of contrasting categories. Atypical or poor category members showed the opposite patterns: They were less likely to share features with category members and more likely to share features with members of contrasting categories. In short, the feature-listing data predicted goodness-of-example ratings with considerable precision.

Of course, ratings and feature listings are both dependent variables, and so far the data are correlational. But Rosch and Mervis went beyond this by creating artificial categories patterned after the feature-listing data. Specifically, they created analogs of natural categories where the examples were strings of letters and numbers. Each letter or number was considered to be a feature, and each example had five such features. The distribution of features within and across categories paralleled the feature-listing data from the early experiments. Individual examples had high, medium, or low family resemblance scores based on feature distribution. That is, examples with high family resemblance scores shared feature with other members of their own category and tended not to share features with members of contrasting categories. Participants learned the categories to a criterion, then received speeded category verification tests and finally made typicality ratings. Rosch and Mervis found that examples with high family resemblance scores were easiest to learn, had the fastest category verification times, and were rated as highest in typicality. Overall then, the studies with both artificial and natural categories converged to support the probabilistic view.

The probabilistic view is consistent both with goodness-of-example effects and unclear cases. Robins may be better examples of the category *bird* than turkeys because they have more characteristic features of birds than turkeys (e.g., singing, eating worms, migrating). Unclear cases may arise because "having enough characteristic features" is a criterion that examples may come very close to. The criterion itself might vary somewhat across occasions and lead to individual variability in category membership decisions.

This view is a prototypical similarity-based approach to categorization. If an example has more characteristic features of category A than category B (more similar to A than B) then it is placed in category A. Of course, one is still left with issues such as how one determines characteristic features and a criterion for classification but investigators have employed a variety of converging techniques that support the probabilistic view (e.g., see Mervis & Rosch, 1981, for a review).

One consequence of the probabilistic view is the idea that category membership is determined by computing similarity to a prototype. If category membership is probabilistic, then rule-based classification procedures should be less effective. If category membership is based on features that are only generally true of a category then a hypothesis-testing strategy that abandons a rule in the face of negative evidence will not be likely to succeed in learning. As an alternative instantiation of the probabilistic view, people have suggested that, based on experience with exemplars, people form an impression of the central tendency (e.g., mean or modal values for features) and that category judgments come to be based on this central tendency or prototype.

Other work with artificial categories conducted around this time provided evidence consistent with prototype formation. In these studies one begins with some prototype pattern, such as a meaningless pattern of dots, and generates category examples to be used in training by distorting the prototype pattern to varying degrees (e.g., by shifting the locations of the dots; see Posner & Keele, 1968, 1970). After training old patterns, new distortions and the prototype are presented to be classified. One striking result is that participants are as good or better at classifying the prototype pattern that they have never seen before, as they are at categorizing old patterns (e.g., Homa & Chambliss, 1975; Peterson, Meagher, Chait, & Gillie, 1973). Transfer performance is well predicted by distance from the prototype, showing a typicality or goodness-of-example effect. Finally, when delays on the order of days are inserted between learning and transfer tests, significantly greater forgetting is observed for the old training stimuli than for the prototype or other new patterns (e.g., Homa, Cross, Cornell, Goldman, & Schwartz, 1973; Posner & Keele, 1970). This result is consistent with the idea that judgments are based on a mixture of specific items and category level (prototype) informance and that the specific item information is forgotten more rapidly. As the delay increases, by this account, it is increasingly likely that judgments will be based on the prototype. All together this seems to add up to strong parallels between natural and artificial categories and strong evidence in favor of prototype theory.

There has not been a great deal of discussion of the exact form of prototype representations (but see Farah & Kosslyn, 1982; Barsalou, 1993), but even at this abstract level of description, it has been straightforward to contrast prototype theory with alternative theories. But we are getting ahead of ourselves.

Another important consequence of the probabilistic view was a seminal series of studies by Rosch, Mervis, and their associates (Rosch, Mervis, Gray, Johnson, & Boyes-Braem, 1976) looking at the hierarchical structure of natural categories. Objects and events in the world can be categorized at a number of different levels, varying in their abstractness. For example, a *large mouth bass* is also a *bass,* a *fish,* a *vertebrate,* an *animal,* and a *living thing.* Rosch et al. singled out one such level in such hierarchies, which they called the *basic level,* as playing a central role in categorization. Let's take a closer look at what they did. In a feature-listing task participants are able to list many features in common for members of categories like *chair, car,* and *dog* and list many fewer common features for superordinate categories like *furniture, vehicle,* and *animal.* In addition, there is only a small increase in common features listed for subordinate categories, such as *recliner, convertible,* and *poodle.* Rosch et al. (1976) took these feature-listing data as suggesting that the level of *chair, car,* and *dog* was the most informative level of categorization; that is, the basic level. Furthermore, Rosch et al. used a variety of converging operations and they each converged on the same level as basic. For example, the basic level is preferred in naming, first learned by children, the most abstract level at which an averaged (prototype) shape can be recognized, and the level at which people can categorize most rapidly.

These observations (which we can only call stunning) were interpreted as indicating that entities in the world come in natural chunks or clusters of correlated features (e.g., animals with feathers are also likely to have wings and beaks), and that human cognition is sensitive to these chunks. The clusters maximize within-category similarity relative to between-category similarity at the basic level according to Rosch et al. (1976). They did suggest that experts might become sensitive to additional features and that subordinate categories might become basic, but the central message was that (basic level) categories are given by the structure of things in the world.

Again analogs to studies of the basic level have been conducted with artificial categories (see Lassaline, Wisniewski, & Medin, 1992, for a review), but here we must sound our first discordant note. Studies with artificial categories have almost exclusively used a single measure of basicness—the level in a hierarchy where categorization is fastest. More relevant for our purposes is that the artificial categories have been structured to have a defining feature or features at the basic level, a practice in line with the Classical rather than the probabilistic view. Consequently, the parallelism and generalizability of studies with artificial categories is in question (we hasten to add that these studies may be useful in developing and testing categorization models; however, their probative value for understanding basic-level categories is in doubt).

This has been a long brief history so let's pause a bit. So far our capsule history has taken us to the mid-1970s. There is little doubt that the most exciting and important development in the psychology of concepts in the 1970s was the shift from the classical to the probabilistic view, and the corresponding emergence of ideas about the basic level and prototype representations. A critical event in this shift was the strategy of directly analyzing the structure of natural categories and bringing conjectures about structure into controlled laboratory studies. We now turn to a more detailed review and analysis of research conducted either within the framework of the probabilistic view or in reaction to it.

VI. CONSTRAINTS AND CHALLENGES FOR THEORIES OF CATEGORIZATION

In this section we consider theoretical and empirical challenges to both prototype and exemplar versions of the probabilistic view, and more general constraints to any similarity-based approach to categorization.

A. Challenges for Prototype Approaches

Earlier, we argued that different conceptual functions require somewhat different kinds of information; it should not be surprising if conceptual representations contained more information than would be expected on the basis of any one function considered by itself. Indeed, virtually all theories of concept learning assume that some types of information are preserved and other types are lost or inaccessible; comparing these assumptions to data has motivated an important component of research on classification learning. As we shall see, human conceptual behavior displays conservatism with respect to category information (Medin & Ross, 1989), a conservatism that poses problems for prototype theory.

1. Discarding Information

Prototype theory implies that the only information abstracted from categories as their central tendency. A prototype representation discards information on category size, variability of examples, and correlations among attributes (e.g., large spoons are more likely to be made of wood than small spoons). Studies with both artificial and natural categories suggest, however, that people are sensitive to all three of these types of information (Billman & Knutson, 1996; Estes, 1986a; Flannagan, Fried, & Holyoak, 1986; Fried & Holyoak, 1984; Malt & Smith, 1983; Medin, Altom, Edelson, & Freko, 1982; Medin & Schaffer, 1978; Medin & Shoben, 1988). Even notions about typicality can be shown to be sensitive to context. When one reads about a bird on a Thanksgiving platter, one does not instantiate the concept *bird* with a robin or a sparrow (Roth & Shoben, 1983). In short, prototype representations appear to discard too much information that can be shown to be relevant to human categorization.

2. Constraints on Learning

Another problem for prototypes is that they make the wrong predictions about which category structures should be easy or difficult to learn. Classifying examples on the basis of their similarity to prototypes is equivalent to a summing of evidence against a criterion. Therefore, in order to succeed, prototype models require some weighted combination of properties that accepts all category members and rejects all noncategory members. The technical term for this constraint is that categories must be linearly separable (Sebestyn, 1962) if categorization by prototypes is to be successful.

Thus, prototypes require that categories are linearly separable. As such, a key question is whether linear separability facilitates human category learning. That is, with other factors controlled, people should find it easier to learn categories that are linearly separable than those that are not. If so, this would provide important support for prototype theory. This support has not, however, appeared. Studies employing a variety of instructions, stimulus materials, and subject populations have failed to find evidence that linear separability facilities human category learning (e.g., Kemler-Nelson, 1984; Medin & Schwanenflugel, 1981; see also Shepard, Hovland, & Jenkins, 1961, and Nosofsky, Gluck, Palmeri, McKinley, & Glauthier, 1994). Later on, we will take up an exception to this rule, but the failure of linear separability represents a serious problem for prototype theory.

3. Prototypes versus Exemplars

One response to the above limitations of prototype theory is to assume that people both form prototypes and store information about specific examples. The idea would be that prototypes are needed to account for the findings considered earlier where prototypes are classified more accurately than old exemplars and show less forgetting over a retention interval. Storage of old examples would be invoked to explain the problems for prototypes just mentioned. Attractive as this strategy might appear, it has not generated much support (Busemeyer, Dewey, & Medin, 1984; see also Homa, 1984; Homa, Sterling, & Trepel, 1981), and it is instructive to see why.

First of all, to posit exemplar storage is only part of the problem; one also needs a set of retrieval assumptions and an associated mapping onto performance. One could, for instance, assume that people store examples during learning but that new examples are classified by "computing" prototypes and comparing the similarity of the new example to these newly constructed prototypes. Indeed, it may be that the stored examples are so similar to each other that the *only* information people can successfully access is the central tendency or prototype. Such a model would have all the shortcomings of theories that assume that prototypes are formed during learning.

There are exemplar-based models of categorization that allow retrieval of more than the category central tendency (e.g., Hintzman, 1986; Medin & Schaffer, 1978), but they introduce a more serious problem for mixed models—they do not need prototypes to account for the data (e.g., Brooks, 1978, 1987). Exemplar models are perfectly capable of predicting that a newly presented prototype pattern may be classified more accurately than old examples (because it is highly similar to many same category members and has low similarity to members of contrasting categories) and that retention intervals will affect old patterns more than prototype patterns (e.g., Hintzman & Ludlum, 1980; Medin & Schaffer, 1978). Although these predictions may not be intuitively obvious, mathematical models based on these ideas provide both a qualitative and a quantitative account of these phenomena. This undercuts the initially strong underpinning for prototype theory. In head-to-head competition, exemplar models have been substantially more successful than prototype models (Busemeyer et al., 1984; Estes, 1986b, 1994; Medin & Smith, 1981; Nosofsky, 1988a,b, 1991, 1992; Shin & Nosofsky, 1992).

4. Summary

The initial flush of success of prototype theory proved to be a poor predictor of its future. One of the main functions of classification is that it allows us to make inferences and predictions on the basis of partial information. In general, the pairs of storage and retrieval assumptions associated with exemplar models preserve much more information than prototype models, information that people show sensitivity to. The context sensitivity of exemplar models is also consistent with much of the memory literature (e.g., Tulving, 1983).

The exemplar view of conceptual structure has a number of characteristics than distinguish it from other probabilistic view models. The prototype view claimed that categories were represented in terms of characteristic properties that worked together to create (linearly separable) categories where examples could be successfully classified on the basis of their similarity to prototypes. The exemplar view has no such requirement. The features used to categorize are the features of the category examples, and these need *not* be characteristic of the category overall. Some models with the Exemplar framework allow feature weighting to vary from example to example (e.g., Medin & Edelson, 1988). In short, the exemplar view appears to imply virtually no constraints on category membership. This is an issue we'll return to, but first we add a few more complications.

B. Challenges for Exemplar Approaches

We are nowhere near the end of our review. There's more to categorization than storing exemplars, and even if we restrict our attention to work with artificial categories, there have been developments that have served to motivate another basic shift in perspective. In this section we consider two of these developments.

1. Strategies and Rules

Neither prototype nor exemplar theories say anything about rules, but people who run as participants in laboratory studies of category learning often report that they are looking for and using rules. The structure of ill-defined categories is typically such that no simple rules are valid, but people may resort to more complex rules and strategies such as memorizing exceptions. There is also fairly good evidence that rules are not simply epiphenomena (e.g., Martin & Caramazza, 1980; Medin & Smith, 1981; Medin, Dewey, & Murphy, 1983; Medin, Wattenmaker, & Michalski, 1987; Nosofsky, Clark, & Shin, 1992) and models based on rules (e.g., Asby & Maddox, 1992; Nosofsky, Palmeri, & McKinley, 1994) may provide an excellent account of data involving artificial categories.

If people are using rules, why have exemplar models been so successful? There are three complementary possibilities that come to mind. One is that strategies do not eliminate exemplar coding, but they may bias it in a way that increases the parallels between rule-guided and exemplar-guided categorization (Medin, 1986; Medin & Wattenmaker, 1987). A second possibility is that the constraints associated with exemplar-based theories correspond to those of rule-based theories and the data reveal these common constraints (e.g., Wattenmaker, 1991, 1993). Third, rules and exemplar storage may be more or less independent, but performance may reflect a mixture of strategies (e.g., Brooks, 1987; Reagher & Brooks, 1993; Wattenmaker, 1993). Just how to model effects of these various strategies is a matter of considerable current concern (e.g., Estes, 1994; Kruschke, 1993; Nosofsky & Kruschke, 1992).

The influence of rules and strategies is reflected in other conceptual tasks as well. For example, Medin, Wattenmaker, and Hampson (1987) constructed artificial stimuli according to a family-resemblance principle and then asked participants to sort the stimuli into categories. The family-resemblance structure allowed people to create two categories, each organized around a prototype or best example (the resulting categories would be linearly separable). Over a range of stimuli and instructions Medin et al. failed to observe family-resemblance sorting. Instead, participants sorted on the basis of a single dimension. If the task structure prohibited unidimensional sorting, they would make an initial, partial sort on the basis of a single contrast and then employ a variety of strategies for dealing with the exceptions of leftovers. Sometimes these strategies will produce what appears to be family-resemblance sorting.

Follow-up studies showed that subjects could indeed be induced to produce family-resemblance sorting, and that a two-stage model embodying this general strategy (simple initial sort followed by dealing with leftovers) was able to predict when family-resemblance sorting would or would not be observed (Ahn & Medin, 1992; see also Spalding & Murphy, 1996; Reagher & Brooks, 1995). There are two implications of these observations. One is that participants do not simply assimilate probabilistic structures but rather organize them in terms of discrete structures plus noise. Second, a key characteristic of these discrete structures is that people prefer to create categories that are easy to describe. These observations underline the point that sorting is not simply driven by similarity computations. Whether or not this departure from similarity represents a bias associated with the communicative function of concepts, it represents a phenomenon not addressed by either prototype or exemplar models.

2. Feature Independence

The debate between prototype and exemplar theories has been about how featural information is integrated across examples and not about the nature of the features themselves. Indeed, predictions of category models depend crucially on being able to specify what the features are and having the research participants' analysis of stimuli agree with that of the experimenter. Researchers take care to ensure that agreement is realized either by using simple stimuli with salient dimensions (e.g., geometric shapes differing in size and color) or by employing multidimensional scaling techniques to identify (or confirm) dimensions (e.g., Nosofsky, 1987). Although this general strategy is absolutely necessary for proper theoretical contrasts, it does carry with it the implicit assumption that the specific realization of abstract category structure is not important. To be sure, researchers are vigilant about establishing the generality of their results by employing a variety of stimuli. Nevertheless, this variety may tend to be biased toward realizations where the features of examples are independent and unrelated to each other (e.g., a triangle can be any color).

Are the properties or features of concepts generally independent? Probably not. First of all, the components of concepts are unlikely to have the status of being primitive features. Consider, for example, the features people typically list for the category *bird:* living, laying eggs, flying, having wings and feathers, singing, building nests, and so on. Each of these "features" is itself a complex concept with both an internal structure and an external structure based on interproperty relationships. For example, laying eggs implies a living organism and building nests is, in part, in service of protecting eggs. Flying requires wings and affords building nests in trees. In short, rather than independent features one has a web of relationships. This fact not only raises questions about how to define similarity over entities with interrelated features but also calls attention to issues of how the phenomena that we have been discussing might change as a function of nonindependent feature structure.

And change they do. Consider again, linear separability, which we mentioned could be characterized in terms of a summing of evidence against a criterion. In a series of experiments, Wattenmaker, Dewey, Murphy, and Medin (1986) found that linearly separable categories were easier to learn than nonlinearly separable categories, if the stimuli or instructions facilitated interproperty coding that was compatible with a summing of evidence (features). An example from one of their studies involved a category whose modal properties were "made of metal," "medium-sized," "has a regular surface," and "easy to grasp." The contrasting category had differing modal values on each of these dimensions. Out of context, one can think of many interproperty relationships, and no one appears to be particularly salient. In category-learning conditions run without further instructional elaboration, no advantage for linearly separable categories was observed. In a second condition, however, participants were given the further hint that the objects in one category might serve as a substitute for a hammer. This hint improved performance overall to some extent, but most striking was the observation that the linearly separable category structure was now much easier than the nonlinearly separable structure. This result might appear to support prototype theory, but remember that prototype theory requires featural independence (nor can it explain when linear separability matters and when it does not).

This selective facilitation of linearly separable categories reflects something beyond making the stimulus materials more meaningful. In other studies Wattenmaker et al. showed that instructional hints could selectively improve performance on nonlinearly separable categories—the key factor was the relationship between the types of interproperty encoding induced and the category structure. A clear implication of these findings is that one cannot make generalizations in terms of abstract category structures and expect them to carry through across contexts, because different types of interproperty or relational coding may take place (see Medin et al., 1987, and Murphy & Spalding, 1996, for corresponding observations from sorting tasks. Family-resemblance sorting is readily observed under appropriate relational coding conditions). Equally significant is the point that interproperty relationships are outside the boundary conditions of almost all current categorization models (including prototype, exemplar, and rule-based models). Therefore, these models currently have limited generality, and this limitation is most evident where one might most want to generalize—meaningful stimuli.

In summary, although exemplar models show a lot of promise (see Smith & Zarate, 1992, for a recent informative extension of exemplar models to social categories), this section has revealed two important problems and limitations. One is that people employ rules and strategies, even for artificial, relatively meaningless stimuli. The other limitation (which also applies to all the other models that have been under discussion) is that exemplar models have only been developed for contexts where the features of category members are independent. That is, interproperty relationships are not addressed. The latter problem is quite serious, as one would like to move freely between natural and artificial stimuli in our analyses of concepts. To do this, we need to address meaningful stimuli and attendant issues of relational coding. In the next section this issue will be developed further, both with respect to ideas about similarity and with respect to the role of knowledge structures in category organization.

C. General Constraints: Similarity and Theories

A series of related concerns, none by itself perhaps too serious, has culminated in a fundamental shift away from feature-based similarity models. This has given rise to two major trends that appear to be contradictory but actually may serve to reinforce each other. One important position is that similarity is too unconstrained to perform a useful explanatory function and that, instead, the claim is that categories are organized in terms of theories about the world (e.g., Murphy & Medin, 1985). The alternative perspective argues that we need better theories of similarity (e.g., Goldstone, 1994a, 1995; Medin, Goldstone & Gentner, 1993).

1. Similarity

Why do we have the categories we have and not others? A major problem with using similarity to explain categories is that similarity is too flexible. For example, in Tversky's (1977) contrast model similarity is a weighted function of shared and distinctive features. Similarity will depend critically on the weights given to particular features or properties. To borrow an example from Medin (1989), a *zebra* and a *barber pole* would be more similar than a *zebra* and a *horse* if the feature "striped" is weighted sufficiently. To complicate the picture, Tversky and others (e.g., Gati & Tversky, 1984; Landau, Smith, & Jones, 1988; Medin, Goldstone, & Markman, 1995, for a review) have demonstrated that the weight given to a feature depends on the context instructions, experimental task, and even the concept under consideration (Ortony, Vondruska, Foss, & Jones, 1985).

What's wrong with flexibility? The key issue concerns explanatory power. To the extent that similarity is an outcome of a series of other processes, it is more a dependent variable than an independent variable. That is, the processes that determine feature weighting are doing the explanatory work, and the general appeal to similarity only serves to conceal that fact.

A related set of problems derives from determining what counts as a feature. Returning to the Rosch and Mervis (1975) studies, it would be a mistake to assume that people asked to list features of concepts were able to "read" and report their mental representations in an accurate manner. Indeed Keil (1979, 1981) noted that category examples (e.g., *robin, ostrich*) share many important properties that virtually never appear in feature listing (e.g., has a heart, has blood, sleeps, occupies space, can be thought about, etc.). Keil argued that knowledge about just these sorts of predicates serves to organize children's conceptual and semantic development. In short, to understand feature listings we need a process model for access to conceptual knowledge.

To take things a step further, one could argue that without constraints on what is to count as a feature, any two things can be arbitrarily similar or dissimilar. Thus as Murphy and Medin (1985) suggest, the number of features that *plums* and *lawnmowers* share could be unlimited: both are found on Earth, both are found in our solar system, both are touched by people, both do not see or hear well, both do not shave, both can be dropped, and so on (see also Goodman, 1972; Watanabe, 1969). The general point is that attempts to describe conceptual behavior in terms of similarity will prove useful only to the extent that one specifies what is to count as a relevant feature and which principles determine the importance of particular properties. And the explanatory work is being done by the principles that specify these constraints, not some amorphous notion of similarity.

Even when similarity can be nailed down, it may not explain conceptual behavior. Consider, for example, experiments by Gelman and Markman (1986), which pitted category membership against perceptual similarity in an inductive reasoning task. Children were first shown pictures of two animals and taught that different (novel) properties were true of them. They were then asked which property was true of a pictured new example where the example was perceptually similar to one of the first pictures but shared category memberships with the (less similar) other example. Children judged that the new example would have the property of the animal that was of the same category but perceptually different. It appears that similarity can be overridden by other forms of knowledge.

Studies with adults have identified conditions under which similarity is neither necessary nor sufficient to determine category membership (e.g. Rips, 1989; Rips & Collins, 1993). One could argue that the problem is that similarity is so dynamic that similarity in a similarity rating task is different from similarity in a categorization task. Although this argument could in principle have validity, in practice it tends to undermine using similarity to understand conceptual behavior. That is, the burden of proof shifts to similarity theorists to develop computational models that address these conjectured interactions of similarity with tasks.

2. Theories

Many philosophers of science have argued that observations are necessarily theory laden, and recently researchers have begun to adopt the framework that conceptual behavior may be knowledge-based and driven by theories (e.g. Carey, 1985; Keil, 1986; Lakoff, 1987; Markman, 1987; Massey & Gelman, 1988; Medin, 1989; Murphy & Medin, 1985; Oden, 1987; Rips, 1989; Schank, Collins, & Hunters, 1986; Wisniewski & Medin, 1991, 1994; and see Komatsu, 1992 and Medin & Heit, in press, for reviews, and Hirschfeld & Gelman, 1994; VanMechlen, Hampton, Michalski, & Theuns, 1993, and Nakamura, Taraban, & Medin, 1993 for relevant edited volumes). One difference in perspective is that according to the theory-based view, categorization is not simply based on a direct matching of properties of a concept with those of an example, but rather requires that the example have the right "explanatory relationship" to the theory organizing the concept. Informally one could say that the relationship between a concept and an example is like the relationship between theory and data. The general notion is that many concepts may be organized around features that are more abstract than the (perceptible) features of examples. Information from examples may be used to infer the presence of more abstract, possibly causal properties. For example, there is no simple checklist of properties that define a person as an introvert or extrovert; features that typically are linked to these concepts (staying home on a Friday night implies introversion) may be "blocked" or defeated by other information (i.e., the person may be recovering from a wild night of partying on Thursday).

Theories help determine which properties are relevant to a categorization task. One way of reconciling similarity and explanation is to argue that similarity operates on features selected by theories. The nice feature of this view is that laboratory studies with artificial knowledge-poor stimuli could be informative with respect to how conceptual behavior proceeds once the relevant set of features has been determined. Wisniewski and Medin (1994) argue, however, that more tightly coupled systems are needed. Theories may do more than act as filters determining feature relevance. Wisniewski and Medin gave participants categorization and rule induction tasks where the examples (children's drawings of people) were associated with different domain theories cued in by different category labels. For example, in one condition participants were told that the drawings were done by creative versus noncreative children but in another participants were told that these same drawings were done by mentally healthy versus emotionally disturbed children. The results show, first of all, that it is not reasonable to assume some *a priori* set of unambiguous features. The "features" comprising participant's category descriptions varied as a function of category labels and the same aspect of drawing was interpreted differently for different labels. In addition, participants sometimes reinterpret features when given feedback about category membership. For example, they might have classified a drawing as one by a creative child because it did not have the usual simple smile, but when told that the drawing was done by a noncreative child the participant might decide that how the mouth was drawn reveals that the child was unhappy about their lack of creativity. Finally, participants' rules often involved abstract features that are operationalized differently as a function of learning history (e.g., how detailed does a drawing have to be to qualify as "detailed?"). In the absence of meaningful category labels, the rules of participants involved fairly superficial features in the drawings (e.g., buttons visible on shirt); when the labels were meaningful, participants appeared to treat the labels as implying causes where properties of drawing were "effects." In the latter case learning consisted of establishing linkages between ideas about the categories and properties of the children's drawings. On the basis of these observations, Wisniewski and Medin argued that theories not only select features but also "create" features and determine how they will be instantiated. This is consistent with the general view that categorization is not simply a syntactic matching of features between concepts and examples.

A key aspect of the theory-based view is that it may address the question of why we have the categories we have. Coherence may even be achieved in the absence of any obvious source of similarity among category examples. The category composed of money, pets, photo albums, and children seems unusual to say the least. In the context of a goal-derived category of "things to take out of one's house in case of a fire," the category immediately becomes sensible (Barsalou, 1983; see also Barsalou, 1985) and could even be projected to predict further instances (valuable and personal papers, furniture passed down from relatives, etc.).

There is evidence that even very young children's category learning is constrained by domain-specific theoretical biases (e.g., Keil, 1989). Carey (1985) concurs and suggests that young children's biological reasoning is organized by a form of naive psychology. She has evidence that 5–7 year old's inferences are guided by similarity to humans, not an unbiased overall similarity. For instance, they are more sure that a *bug* has some novel property if they are told that *people* have it than if they are told *bees* have it. More recent work (Coley, 1995; Inagaki & Hatano, 1993) challenges Carey's claim about the psychological nature of children's early explanatory theory about living things. However, note that the debate is over the specific nature of the theory; it is agreed that explanatory theories play a crucial role in organizing the concepts of even preschool children.

It may be that people approach all categories with something of a theoretical stance in the sense of having generalized expectations concerning the basis for category membership. For example, people might believe that the key organizing principle for artifacts is function or the intentions of the builder but view biological kinds as depending on intrinsic underlying properties (e.g., Atran, 1990; Keil, 1989; Rips, 1989; Malt, 1990, 1994; Medin & Ortony, 1989; Gelman & Wellman, 1991). In the case of biological kinds, people appear to believe that a true underlying nature or essence that imparts category identity. This view has been dubbed *psychological essentialism* because it is concerned with people's assumptions about the world, not how the world truly is (with respect to the latter, see Mayr, 1988, for a review of how essentialist biases have slowed the development of modern biological thought).

What is the basis for these claims about psychological essentialism? Gelman, Coley, and Gottfried (1994) point to four types of evidence as relevant: (a) appeal to invisible causal mechanisms to explain appearance and changes associated with growth, (b) the assumption of innate dispositions or inborn capacities to explain capacities that emerge later, (c) belief in the maintenance of identity despite changes in superficial appearance, and (d) the assumption that members of a category share a large number of other properties (i.e., that these categories have rich induction potential). Gelman et al. (1994) review supportive evidence for each of these assumptions (see also Shipley, 1993).

Overall, then, there is considerable evidence that knowledge, theories, and belief systems affect categorization and reasoning in a manner unanticipated by the classical, probabilistic, or exemplar views of categorization. In some ways these views seem orthogonal to the theory-based perspective because they seem to be about structure, whereas theories seem to be more about content. We are not so sure such a glib distinction can or should be made because content may determine how structure is encoded and instantiated. What does seem clear is that the notion of independent features embodied in all three views may be off the mark for many (if not most) categories. The question we take up in the next section is whether the cumulative evidence suggests that the marriages between similarity models and theories of conceptual behavior and between studies with artificial categories and studies with natural categories should be broken up.

3. Implications

What do recent views on theory-based categories mean for research in artificial categories? Are findings from studies using random dot patterns or large, red triangles as stimuli relevant to the rich causal structure that links the observation that *robins* have hollow bones to the expectation that *eagles* have hollow bones? It is tempting to argue that stimuli associated with laboratory studies of artificial categories are simply too impoverished and that theories based on such studies will likewise be impoverished. Not only are the stimuli impoverished, but they have typically been constructed to have independent, unrelated features. Strike two.

But not strike three. We believe that progress is cumulative but difficult, and we should not abandon any tool without careful consideration. A shift in theoretical orientation does not nullify previous research or the potential insights growing out of it. Consider, for example, the shift from the classical to the probabilistic view. Laboratory studies of rule learning associated with well-defined categories seemed, on the surface, irrelevant to ill-defined categories where any rules would have numerous exceptions. Nonetheless, when researchers began to pay attention to the strategies learners employ for probabilistic categories, rules again received attention. Furthermore, even when a theoretical orientation does not survive intact, some of its insights may be passed on. For example, early work on hypothesis testing carried the key idea of selective attention, an assumption that now is taken for granted and embodied in virtually all current categorization theories.

A pragmatic reason to avoid a divorce between artificial and natural categories is that there is no simple line that can be drawn between them. Is a large red triangle artificial and a children's drawing of a person natural, or does the drawing become a natural stimulus only when it is associated with a meaningful category label? In addition, just as researchers found that research participants imported knowledge to render nonsense syllables meaningful, so also do learners bring knowledge and bias to organize random dot patterns (Hock, Webb, & Cavedo, 1987). It seems to us that there is a continuum of research strategies available that may trade theoretical precision and experimental control for richness and generalizability. In short, we would be very much surprised if laboratory studies with so-called artificial stimuli did not continue to inform the discussion of concepts and categories.

At the same time, however, we do believe that the fruitfulness of work with artificial categories (that is, work tending toward the artificial end of the artificial–natural continuum) is directly tied to our understanding of natural categories. What we've learned from research on natural categories could be usefully applied to research with artificial categories. Researchers are far more likely to use ill-defined than well-defined categories because they believe that the classical view is less viable than the probabilistic view. Likewise, researchers might profitably come to favor stimuli with nonindependent, structured constituents rather than restricting themselves to the narrow set of situations where the assumption of independent features may be viable. In a similar vein, the categorization function of concepts is but one of many, yet work with artificial categories has focused almost exclusively on it. Although it may take a bit of ingenuity, we see no principled reason why virtually every conceptual function could not be instantiated with (relatively) artificial stimuli. Finally, we think that laboratory studies favoring artificial categories and stimuli (again, employing some ingenuity) could create more effective parallels between conditions in the laboratory and outside of it. This form of scrutiny has been useful in the past, and we see no reason why it could not be effective. In short, we support a continuing dialogue and interaction between the artificial and the natural.

What about the implications of theory-based categories for models of similarity? To be honest, we see only a limited future for similarity-based models based on relatively unconstrained, independent features. For purposes of some analyses one only needs to be in the right ballpark, and feature-based models are easy to work with. More generally, however, objects and events of interest are composed of more than a list of properties—instead, they are structured in terms of a variety of inter-property and even hierarchical relationships. The evidence is mounting that we need more powerful models of similarity that address not only structure but also processing principles (e.g., Goldstone, Medin, & Gentner, 1991; Gentner & Markman, 1995; Goldstone, 1994b; Goldstone & Medin, 1994; Holyoak & Thagard, 1991; Markman & Gentner, 1993a,b; Gentner & Markman, 1994; Medin et al., 1993).

Will enriched models of similarity be able to address the phenomena associated with research on contextually rich theory-driven categorization considered earlier? Our opinion is that dynamic, structural models are at least necessary; whether they are also sufficient remains to be seen (for more positive readings see Goldstone, 1994a; Jones & Smith, 1993, but also Gelman & Medin, 1993). It also remains to be seen whether similarity-based models will constitute an important component of conceptual behavior or whether their key ideas will be so closely integrated with theory-based considerations that one will not be able to isolate any one module and label it as "similarity." In any event, far from abandoning models of similarity, we would argue that considerably more energy should be directed at their further development, including their more context-dependent creative aspects.

D. Summary

We have had to strain chronology quite a bit to force a number of uneven, parallel developments into the story as so far presented. And much has been left out (for reviews from a different perspective see Goldstone, 1994a,b; Homa, 1984; Komatsu, 1992; Medin & Heit, in press; Oden, 1987; Rips, 1990). Still, we do not think we have strayed too far in pointing to the shifts from the classical to the probabilistic view, and the ensuing tensions between prototype and exemplar models and between similarity-based and knowledge-driven categorization. Missing so far, however, has been an account of what we might call a form of "adaptive radiation" of work on conceptual behavior. Not only are a broader range of conceptual functions being studied, but researchers are also focusing on new and distinct domains of inquiry. This focus on domains represents less a lack of faith in general principles of categorization than a positive conviction that certain phenomena and principles may be more readily seen in some contexts than others. In any event, we see adaptive radiation as a positive development so long as there is a flow of ideas and information across psychological niches. The final main section of this chapter briefly samples some of this ongoing activity.

VII. CONCEPTUAL FUNCTIONS AND COGNITION IN CONTEXT

In this final section we have space to do little more than point to some current salutary trends. Questions about concepts and categorization are central to understanding the nature of mind. The burgeoning current activity may be distressing to those who think that a monolithic enterprise is a guarantor of coherence and quality, but we see the diversity as an unequivocal healthy sign.

A. Perception and Representation

Readers of the present volume may have been asking themselves the question of what the difference is between object recognition and categorization. It seems obvious that object recognition *is* a form of categorization and that, therefore, there should be an ongoing interchange of ideas between object recognition and categorization research. Although there has been far less interplay than one might imagine, there are some encouraging signs.

First of all, there is at least some convergence in terms of theoretical ideas. The influential geon theory of object recognition (Biederman, 1985; Hummel & Biederman, 1992) aims to recognize objects at the basic level and incorporates both components (geons) and relations between them. Template models, an alternative to the geon approach, incorporates structure implicitly (e.g., Tarr, 1995). Most recently, researchers have begun to apply ideas and models from object recognition to phenomena such as typicality judgments and categorization reaction times (Kurbat, 1995). There is even evidence that measures of shape similarity predict unique variance in situations where the names of objects rather than the objects themselves are presented (Kurbat, 1995). This suggests that perceptual representations may be activated and used for verbal categorization and reasoning (see also Barsalou, 1993; Barsalou, Solomon, & Wu, in press).

Ideas deriving from categorization are also relevant to object recognition. For example, there is increasing evidence that categorization is not a passive consumer of features or components but instead directly influences feature construction

(Goldstone, 1995c; Schyns & Murphy, 1994; Thibaut & Schyns, 1995; Wisniewski & Medin, 1994). That is, people may not come with a present vocabulary of features but rather features may be learned. If so, then theories of object recognition need to be sensitive to learning history and the possibility that the nature and importance of features might change across domains (cf. Hochberg, chap. 9, this volume).

Overall, there has been limited contact across areas but what there is, is very promising. We predict increasing interaction between mainstream perception and mainstream categorization (see also Harnad, 1987).

B. Conceptual Functions beyond Categorization

Another promising avenue of research is more in-depth exploration of conceptual functions beyond categorization. We will look at two such functions—conceptual combination and induction—in a little more detail. For work on other conceptual functions see Barsalou (1993); Markman, Yamauchi, and Makin (1997); Murphy and Wisniewski (1989); and Wisniewski, (1995).

1. Conceptual Combination

Conceptual combination is important because it allows a productive use of conception. From a vocabulary of simple concepts we can create and understand a potentially unlimited set of combined concepts. Although we are rarely faced with the task of understanding a single concept in isolation, most categorization models do not address combined concepts (Rips, 1995). Conceptual combination is also important because it requires an analysis of conceptual structure and of relations between concepts (e.g., Osherson & Smith, 1981; Smith & Osherson, 1984). For example, a *blackboard* is judged to be a member of the combined category *school furniture* but not a member of the simple category *furniture* (Hampton, 1982, 1987, 1988).

It is far from easy to develop process models for conceptual combination. Nonetheless, a clear, but limited model may point to where progress is needed. Consider the selective modification model of Smith, Osherson, Rips, and Keane (1988), which aims to address adjective noun combinations such as *green apple*. According to this model, to understand this combination a person would retrieve the prototype representation for *apple,* pay extra attention to the dimension of color, and replace the default value of red for applies with the value green. In brief, the person would be constructing a new prototype for *green apple* by modifying the apple prototype. The selective modification model then uses the *green apple* prototype and associated weightings to predict categorization judgments and typicality ratings of potential examples of the new concept.

Although the modification model has enjoyed some success, conceptual combination is more complex than the model allows. People use their general knowledge about relations among features so that dimensions other than the one named by the adjective may be affected. For example, a *brown apple* is not only of an atypical color, but people may infer that it is rotting (Medin & Shoben, 1988). Indeed, conceptual combination sometimes leads to inferences about emergent features that are not expected to be true of either constituent concept taken singly (Hampton, 1987; Hastie, Schroeder, & Weber, 1990; Kunda, Miller, & Claire, 1990; Murphy, 1988; Rips, 1995). For example, people expect neither a *carpenter* nor a *Harvard-educated person* to be a nonconformist, but they do expect a *Harvard-educated carpenter* to be a nonconformist (Kunda et al., 1990). These observations suggest that knowledge outside of the two constituent concepts is brought to bear in understanding combinations.

If understanding adjective–noun combinations is hard, noun–noun combinations are even harder. One interesting approach to noun–noun combinations is the idea that people align the nouns, then attribute a salient property of the modifying noun to the head noun (Wisniewski & Gentner, 1991). Thus a *skunk squirrel* may be a smelly squirrel and a *zebra horse* may be interpreted as a horse with stripes. Another strategy that Wisniewski (1996) calls "relation-linking" seems to emerge when the constituent concepts are less similar. For example, a *skunk box* may be interpreted as a box for containing skunks rather than as a smelly box. The idea of analyzing conceptual combination into constituent strategies is appealing, but the challenge is to then integrate these processes into a unitary model (see Wisniewski, 1997, for some ideas along these lines). Overall, conceptual combination is emerging as a challenging and important area of research.

2. Induction

Concepts are used in reasoning. The issue of how we infer novel properties of categories has been addressed by Osherson, Smith, and their associates in the form of a category-based induction model (CBIM). This model was inspired by earlier work on category-based induction by Rips (1975). For example, suppose that you are told that *cows* have some enzyme in their blood and you are asked to assess how likely it is that *bears* also have this property. According to the CBIM, two factors determine the soundness of such inductive inferences. The greater the similarity between the premise category (e.g., *cow*) and the conclusion category (e.g., *bears*) the more confident one should be that the inference carries over.

The second factor is the *coverage* of the premise that is defined as the similarity between the category (or categories) in the premise and members of the lowest level superordinate category that encompasses the categories in the premise and conclusion. The most specific category that includes cows and bears is *mammal*. The category *cow* is fairly similar to other members of the category *mammal* (cows are considered to be typical mammals). Thus if cows have some enzyme in their blood, it is plausible that all mammals might have this enzyme and bears are mammals. According to the CBIM, the overall confidence in this induction is a weighted average of the similarity and coverage components.

One might wonder why the coverage component of the model is even needed. Isn't similarity enough? The answer is that coverage accounts for some phenomena that the notion of similarity by itself may not. For example, inductive inferences are stronger when they go from a typical category member (e.g., for mammals, *cow*) to an atypical member (e.g., *anteater*) than in the reverse direction (Rips, 1975). The CBIM assumes that similarity is symmetrical (*b* is as similar to *a* as *a* is to *b*) but the coverage component accounts for the asymmetry in reasoning. The category *cow* is more similar to other members of *mammal* than is the category *anteater;* therefore, inferences from *cow* are stronger than inferences from *anteater.*

The CBIM accounts for a variety of phenomena involving how people use similarity and category information in making inferences (e.g., Smith, Shafir, & Osherson, 1993). So far, however, the model has focused on the role of categories and has not addressed the role of properties. Specifically, the model is tested using "blank predicates," (e.g., "requires biotin for hemoglobin synthesis"). These properties are chosen so that subjects are likely to have few prior beliefs about how the properties are linked to specific categories. It seems clear, however, that even at an abstract level, "kinds" of properties may influence induction. The "blank predicates" used by Osherson et al. were almost all physiological in nature. That may have been enough information to lead subjects to highlight certain relations at the expense of others. For example, Heit and Rubinstein (1994) found that different similarity relations guided inferences about unfamiliar behavioral properties versus information about unfamiliar anatomical properties. Thus, patterns of induction probably depend crucially on the content of the properties. "Blank" properties may not be truly blank, and an important challenge for models of induction is to incorporate the information embodied in meaningful properties (for some initial ideas along these lines, see Smith et al., 1993). Overall, the CBIM and associated studies have sparked a resurgence of interest in induction.

C. Language, Categories, and Induction

Another promising trend we would like to highlight is the careful examination of the impact of language on conceptual functions. Most of this research has been done with children, but results reveal that language has a powerful organizing effect on conceptual structure and function. Specifically, we will discuss research indicating an early impact of language on categorization and induction.

1. Categorization

One line of work bearing out this point has been done by Waxman and colleagues (Waxman, 1990; Waxman & Gelman, 1986; Waxman & Markow, 1995). Waxman and colleagues show that children use linguistic cues to establish conceptual hierarchies, and that the effects of language vary depending on the hierarchical level and the perceptual support for the category being learned. Specifically, providing a label for a category helps children to sort at the superordinate level. For instance, children asked to sort objects into superordinate classes (e.g., *food, animals*) did better when given a novel (Japanese) label for that class than when given no label at all (Waxman & Gelman, 1986). Moreover, Waxman (1990) found that while providing a novel label for a category (e.g., *dobu*) enhanced preschoolers' sorting at the superordinate level, it had little effect on sortings at the basic level, and actually interfered with sorting at the subordinate level. In contrast, labeling a category with a novel adjectival phrase (e.g., *dobish ones*) enhanced sorting at subordinate levels, but interfered with sorting at superordinate levels.

In summary, nouns organize higher-order categories, and appear to emphasize the commonalities among disparate objects; adjectives organize lower-order categories and emphasize differences between similar objects. Interestingly, performance for basic-level categories tested by Waxman and colleagues is consistently at ceiling; apparently, salient perceptual cues are sufficient to induce classification at the basic level without additional support. These results suggest that the conceptual organizing role played by language is specific as well as powerful.

D. Expertise and Culture

Another salutary trend is a growing focus on how knowledge impacts conceptual systems. This takes the form of examining both how expertise effects reasoning in a particular domain, and investigating conceptual similarities and differences among members of different cultures.

1. Expertise

Psychologists have become increasingly interested in studying expertise (see Bedard & Chi, 1992, for a review). One way that expertise is useful is in comparing novices to experts. Studies of expertise have revealed profound reorganizations of knowledge as a function of amount and type of expertise (e.g., Chi, 1992; Chi & Bjork, 1991; Medin, Lynch, Coley, & Atran, 1997; Tanaka & Taylor, 1991). Such studies potentially reveal both how knowledge is structured in a well-known domain, and what conceptual changes lead to that structure. We feel this is an important and understudied aspect of conceptual functioning. Most of our contact with the world may involve domains with which we are relatively familiar. Indeed, we find it conceivable that further investigations of expertise will reveal that some if not many of the findings of cognitive psychology are more accurately seen as novice heuristics than as general characterizations of conceptual functioning.

Another way in which expert subjects can inform theories of conceptual organization is by allowing the interplay of mind and world in shaping conceptual structure to be examined. By comparing experts from different subfields within the same domain, the subject matter ("world") can be held constant, but the knowledge, goals, and naive theories of the experts ("mind") may well vary. In this way the contributions of mind and world may be assessed. Along these lines, we are currently undertaking a large-scale study of tree expertise (Medin et al., 1997). We examine how landscapers, maintenance workers, and taxonomists categorize and reason about the same set of trees. Therefore, any differences we find cannot be attributed to difference in the content domain and must instead be attributed to differences in the conceptual structure of our experts. Care must still be exercised; similarities between kinds of experts are not necessarily due to common perceptions of structure in the world. For instance, our experts agree on clusters for a subset of the tree species we used as stimuli, but differ systematically on their justifications for these clusters. Almost all experts grouped black walnut with shagbark hickory, but based on justifications, landscapers did so because both are large, attractive trees useful as a centerpiece in a landscape layout, maintenance workers did so because both are nut trees, and taxonomists did so because both belong to the scientific family *Juglandaceae*. True, these facts about black walnut and shagbark hickory are not unrelated, but apparently different components of the correlational structure of the world was salient to different kinds of tree experts. Our studies also show a role of language in reasoning, at least among one of the subgroups. Landscapers and taxonomists privilege the genus level in reasoning but maintenance workers do so only when the common term marks the shared genus (e.g., white oak and burr oak are both oaks, belonging to the genus, *Quercus* versus pairs like eastern cottonwood and white popular, which are not marked but belong to the genus *Populus*).

2. Role of Culture

Older cross-cultural research on categorization documented apparent deficits in "primitive thinking" along members of traditional societies. For instance, free sorting tasks performed in traditional societies often revealed a preference to sort on the basis of perceptual or functional characteristics, rather than "more advanced" toxonomic classification (e.g., Greenfield, Reich, & Olver, 1966; Price-Williams, 1962; Suchman, 1966). However, more recently, such interpretations have been seriously questioned; performance of members of traditional cultures more likely reflect different interpretations of the task or of the experimenter's expectations. An anecdote reported by Ciborowski (1980) is particularly enlightening: Conducting an experiment among the Kpelle of Liberia, J. A. Glick found that the Kpelle almost always based free-sorts of objects on perceptual or functional similarities, rather than taxonomic kind. He was told that in the traditional Kpelle sense, this was the "clever" way to do the task. In response to this, Glick asked his subjects to perform that task as a "stupid" Kpelle might do it, and the result was perfect taxonomic sorting. Clearly, the fact that the Kpelle were not originally disposed to taxonomic sorting cannot be taken as evidence of primitive thought.

More recent work in cognitive anthropology documents rich systems of knowledge in a variety of domains. For example, ethnobiologists have documented the folk-biological classification systems of members of traditional cultures (e.g., Atran,

1990; Berlin, 1992). Closer examination of conceptual structures in different cultures reveals deep commonalities. Patterns of nomenclature, hierarchical levels of classification, and correspondence of various folk categories to scientific classes show remarkable commonalities across cultures and geographical regions.

One important task remaining for research is to carefully document similarities and differences among conceptual systems of members of different cultures, and among traditional cultures and members of modern, industrialized states. Commonalities may signal deep cognitive universals or a standard interpretation of information in the physical environment (see Coley, Medin, & Atran, 1997). Differences may simply reflect expertise, or different explanatory frameworks, akin to those that Carey (1985) argues characterize adults' and children's conceptions of biology. Either way, careful interdisciplinary research on cultural influences on conceptual systems promises to be interesting, valuable, and extremely difficult.

E. Domain Specificity

Another important trend in recent research on concepts and categorization is the notion of domain specificity. Although there are many ways to characterize the specifics of this proposal, or what counts as a domain (e.g., Hirschfeld & Gelman, 1994; Wellman & Gelman, 1992), what this position boils down to is that all concepts are not necessarily created equal. Understanding concepts necessitates understanding the content of those concepts, and the theoretical framework in which they occur.

1. Biology versus Psychology

One current debate in the study of conceptual development is whether children's understanding of living kinds is embedded in an autonomous biological explanatory theory (Coley, 1995; Inagaki & Hatano, 1993; Keil, 1992, 1994; Springer & Keil, 1989, 1991) or whether concepts of living things are instead imbedded in a protheory that conflates adult notions of biology and psychology (Carey, 1985, 1988, 1995; Solomon, Johnson, Zaitchik, & Carey, 1996). Although the details of the evidence on either side of the issue are beyond the scope of this chapter, the important point is that the meaning of a concept such as *living thing* depends on what framework theory that concept plays a part in.

2. Social Categories

Many of the issues we have been discussing carry over into the social domain (e.g., Smith & Zarote, 1992). With respect to domain specificity, one question is whether people naturalize social categories (Rothbart & Taylor, 1993) or whether social categorization is an autonomous domain with its own constraints and organizing principles (Hirschfeld, 1993, 1994, 1995). Hirschfeld has evidence that the category of race is socially constructed and develops differentially as a function of the ethnic diversity of children's social environments. For example, consider children's reasoning about the skin color of a child born to mixed race, European-American, African-American parents. Young children give the normatively correct answer of intermediate skin color, but by the sixth grade children living in relatively nonintegrated environments shift to the normatively incorrect view that the child will be have skin color matching that of the African-American parent (Hirschfeld, 1993, 1994). The implications of these sorts of studies remain to be worked out, but their relevance to theories of categorization in general and social cognition in particular can hardly be doubted.

F. Summary

In this section, we have outlined some promising avenues for future research in concepts and categorization. For one, studies of object perception and category representation appear to have much to learn from each other. In general, increasing interaction across subareas would be salutary. Another tend we'd like to see continue is the examination of other conceptual functions beyond categorization; we mentioned conceptual combination and induction to name just two, but many more await more detailed exploration. Studies of the impact of language, culture, and expertise, all promise to enrich and challenge our current notions of conceptual structure and function. And finally, examination of concepts in different domains promises to add even more complexity to the picture. Indeed, none of these avenues of research promises to simplify our portrait of human categorization. However, we feel that they will all help bring it into sharper focus.

VIII. CONCLUSIONS

The field of categories and concepts is very much a work in progress. We anticipate that the twists and turns mentioned at the beginning of this chapter will continue. However, when the field is viewed from a larger time scale, it is easy to see that advances are being made on empirical, methodological, and theoretical fronts. We hope and expect that the present trends will continue: a mutually beneficial interplay between work with natural and with artificial categories, attention to multiple conceptual functions, and greater diversity and interaction with respect to subject populations, kinds of categories, and theoretical perspectives. We hope that reviewers at the end of the next century will be able to refer not to a short history but a *rich* history.

Acknowledgments

This work was partially supported by NIH Grant MH 55079 to Douglas Medin. Sandra Waxman and Edward Wisniewski provided helpful comments on this paper.

References

Ahn, W., & Medin, D. L. (1992). A two-stage model of category construction. *Cognitive Science, 16*, 81–121.

Ashby, F. G., & Maddox, W. T. (1992). Complex decision rules in categorization: Contrasting novice and experienced performance. *Journal of Experimental Psychology: Human Perception and Performance, 18*, 50–71.

Atran, S. (1990). *Cognitive foundations of natural history: Towards an anthropology of science.* Cambridge, UK: Cambridge University Press.

Barsalou, L. W. (1983). Ad hoc categories. *Memory & Cognition, 11*, 211–227.

Barsalou, L. W. (1985). Ideals, central tendency, and frequency of instantiation as determinants of graded structure of categories. *Journal of Experimental Psychology: Learning, Memory, and Cognition, 11*, 629–654.

Barsalou, L. W. (1989). Intra-concept similarity and its implications for inter-concept similarity. In S. Vosniadou & A. Ortony (Eds.), *Similarity and analogical reasoning* (pp. 76–121). Cambridge, UK: Cambridge University Press.

Barsalou, L. W. (1993). Flexibility, structure, and linguistic vagary in concepts: Manifestations of a compositional system of perceptual symbols. In A. C. Collins, S. E. Gathercole, M. A. Conway, & P. E. M. Morris (Eds.), *Theories of memories* (pp. 29–101). Hillsdale, NJ: Lawrence Erlbaum Associates.

Barsalou, L. W., Solomon, K., & Wu, L.-L. (in press). Perceptual simulation in conceptual tasks. In M. K. Hiraga, C. Sinha, & S. Wilcox (Eds.), *Cultural, typological and psychological perspectives in cognitive linguistics: The proceedings of the 4th conference of the International Cognitive Linguistics Association, Vol. 3.* Amsterdam: John Benjamins.

Bedard, J., & Chi, M. T. H. (1992). Expertise. *Current Directions in Psychological Science, 1*, 135–139.

Bellezza, F. S. (1984). Reliability of retrieval from semantic memory: Noun meanings. *Bulletin of the Psychonomic Society, 22*, 377–380.

Berlin, B. (1992). *Ethnobiological classification: Principles of categorization of plants and animals in traditional societies.* Princeton, NJ: Princeton University Press.

Biederman, I. (1985). Recognition-by-components: A human image understanding. *Psychological Review, 94*, 115–147.

Billman, D., & Knutson, J. F. (1996). Unsupervised concept learning and value systematicity: A complex whole aids learning the parts. *Journal of Experimental Psychology: Learning, Memory, and Cognition, 22*, 458–475.

Bourne, L. E., Jr. (1970). Knowing and using concepts. *Psychological Review, 77*, 546–556.

Brooks, L. R. (1978). Nonanalytic concept formation and memory for instances. In E. Rosch & B. B. Lloyd (Eds.), *Cognition and categorization* (pp. 169–211). Hillsdale, NJ: Erlbaum.

Brooks, L. R. (1987). Decentralized control of categorization: The role of prior processing episodes. In U. Neisser (Ed.), *Concepts and conceptual development: The ecological and intellectual factors in categorization* (pp. 141–174). Cambridge, UK: Cambridge University Press.

Busemeyer, J. R., Dewey, G. I., & Medin, D. L. (1984). Evaluation of exemplar-based generalization and the abstraction of categorical information. *Journal of Experimental Psychology: Learning, Memory, and Cognition, 10*, 638–648.

Carey, S. (1985). *Conceptual change in childhood.* Cambridge, MA: Bradford Books.

Carey, S. (1988). Conceptual differences between children and adults. *Mind and Language, 3*, 167–183.

Carey, S. (1995). On the origins of causal understanding. In A. Premack (Ed.), *Causal understanding in cognition and culture* (pp. 268–308). New York: Oxford University Press.

Coley, J. D. (1995). Emerging differentiation of folkbiology and folkpsychology: Attributions of biological and psychological properties to living things. *Child Development, 66*, 1856–1874.

Coley, J. D., Medin, D. L., and Atran, S. (1997). Does rank have its privilege? Inductive inferences within folkbiological taxonomics. *Cognition, 64*, 73–112.

Chi, M. T. H. (1992). Conceptual change within and across ontological categories: Examples from learning and discovery in science. In R. Giere (Ed.), *Cognitive models of science: Minnesota studies in the philosophy of science* (pp. 129–186). Minneapolis, MN: University of Minnesota Press.

Chi, M. T. H., & Bjork, R. (1991). Modeling expertise. In D. Druckman & R. A. Bjork (Eds.), *In the mind's eye: Enhancing human performance.* Washington, DC: National Academy Press.

Ciborowski, T. (1980). The role of context, skill and transfer in cross-cultural experimentation. In H. C. Triandis & J. W. Berry (Eds.), *Handbook of cross-cultural psychology: Vol. 2. Methodology* (pp. 279–296). Boston: Allyn & Bacon.

Estes, W. K. (1986a). Memory storage and retrieval processes in category learning. *Journal of Experimental Psychology: General, 115,* 155–175.

Estes, W. K. (1986b). Array models for category learning. *Cognitive Psychology, 18,* 500–549.

Estes, W. K. (1994). *Classification and cognition.* Oxford: Oxford University Press.

Farah, M. J., & Kosslyn, S. M. (1982). Concept development. In H. W. Reese & L. Lipsett (Eds.), *Advances in child development and behavior, Vol. 16.* New York: Academic Press.

Flannagan, M. J., Fried, L. S., & Holyoak, J. K. (1986). Distributional expectations and the induction of category structure. *Journal of Experimental Psychology: Learning, Memory, and Cognition, 12,* 241–256.

Fried, L. S. & Holyoak, K. J. (1984). Induction of category distributions: A framework for classification learning. *Journal of Experimental Psychology: Learning, Memory, and Cognition, 10,* 234–257.

Gati, I., & Tversky, A. (1984). Weighting common and distinctive features in perceptual and conceptual judgments. *Cognitive Psychology, 16,* 341–370.

Gelman, S. A., & Markman, E. M. (1986). Categories and induction in young children. *Cognition, 23,* 183–209.

Gelman, S. A., & Medin, D. L., (1993). What's so essential about essentialism? A different perspective on the interaction of perception, language, and conceptual knowledge. *Cognitive Development, 8,* 157–167.

Gelman, S. A., & Wellman, H. M. (1991). Insides and essences: Early understandings of the nonobvious. *Cognition, 38,* 213–244.

Gelman, S. A., Coley, J. D., & Gottfried, G. M. (1994). Essentialist beliefs in children: The acquisition of concepts and theories. In L. A. Hirschfeld & S. A. Gelman (Eds.), *Mapping the Mind.* pp. 341–367. Cambridge, England: Cambridge University Press.

Gentner, D., & Markman, A. B. (1994) Structural alignment in comparison: No difference without similarity. *Psychology Science, 5,* 152–158.

Goldstone, R. L. (1994a). The role of similarity in categorization: Providing a groundwork. *Cognition, 52,* 125–157.

Goldstone, R. L. (1994b). Similarity, interactive activation, and mapping. *Journal of Experimental Psychology: Learning, Memory, & Cognition, 20,* 3–28.

Goldstone, R. L. (1994c). Influences of categorization on perceptual discrimination. *Journal of Experimental Psychology: General, 123,* 178–200.

Goldstone, R. L. (1995). Mainstream and avant-garde similarity. *Psychological Belgica, 32,* 145–165.

Goldstone, R. L., Medin, D. L., & Gentner, D. (1991). Relations attributes and the non-independence of features in similarity judgments. *Cognitive Psychology, 23,* 222–262.

Goldstone, R. L., & Medin, D. L. (1994). Time course of comparison. *Journal of Experimental Psychology: Learning, Memory, and Cognition, 20,* 29–50.

Goodman, N. (1972). Seven strictures on similarity. In N. Goodman (Ed.), *Problems and projects* (pp. 437–447). New York: Bobbs-Merrill.

Greenfield, P. M., Reich, L. C., & Olver, R. R. (1966). On culture and equivalence. In J. S. Bruner, R. R. Olver, & P. M. Greenfield (Eds.), *Studies in Cognitive Growth* (pp. 270–318). New York: Wiley.

Grice, H. P. (1975). Logic and conversation. In P. Cole and J. L. Morgan (Eds.), *Syntax and semantics III: Speech Acts.* New York: Seminar Press.

Hampton, J. A. (1982). A demonstration of intransitivity in natural concepts. *Cognition, 12,* 151–164.

Hampton, J. A. (1987). Inheritance of attributes in natural concept conjunctions. *Memory & Cognition, 15,* 55–71.

Hampton, J. A. (1988). Over extension of conjunctive concepts: Evidence for a unitary model of concept typicality and class inclusion. *Journal of Experimental Psychology: Learning, Memory, & Cognition, 14,* 12–32.

Harvard, S. (Ed.) (1987). *Categorical perception.* Cambridge, England: Cambridge University Press.

Hastie, R., Schroeder, C., & Weber, R. (1990). Creating complex social conjunction categories from simple categories. *Bulletin of the Psychonomic Society, 28,* 242–247.

Heit, E., & Rubinstein, J. (1994). Similarity and property effects in inductive reasoning. *Journal of Experimental Psychology: Learning, Memory, and Cognition, 20,* 411–422.

Hintzman, D. L. (1986). "Schema abstraction" in a multiple-trace memory model. *Psychological Review, 93,* 411–428.

Hintzman, D. L., & Ludlum, G. (1980). Differential forgetting of prototypes and old instances: Simulation by an exemplar-based classification model. *Memory & Cognition, 8,* 378–382.

Hirschfeld, L. A. (1993). Discovering social difference: The role of appearance in the development of racial awareness. *Cognitive Psychology, 25,* 317–350.

Hirschfeld, L. A. (1994). Is the acquisition of social categories based on domain-specific competence or on knowledge transfer? In L. A. Hirschfeld & S. A. Gelman (Eds.), *Mapping the Mind: Domain Specificity in Cognition and Culture* (pp. 201–233). Cambridge, England: Cambridge University Press.

Hirschfeld, L. A. (1995). Anthropology, psychology and the meanings of social causality. In A. Premack (Ed.), *Causal understandings in cognition and culture* (pp. 313–350). New York: Oxford University Press.

Hirschfeld, L. A., & Gelman, S. A. (Eds.) (1994). *Mapping the Mind: Domain specificity in cognition and culture.* New York: Cambridge University Press.

Hock, H. S., Webb, E., & Cavedo, L. C. (1987). Perceptual learning in visual category acquisition. *Memory & Cognition, 15,* 544–556.

Holyoak, K. J., & Thagard, P. (1989). Analogical mapping by constraint satisfaction. *Cognitive Science, 13,* 295–355.

Homa, D. (1984). On the nature of categories. In G. Bower (Ed.), *The Psychology of Learning and Motivation, 18,* 49–94.

Homa, D., & Chambliss, D. (1975). The relative contributions of common and distinctive information on the abstraction from ill-defined categories. *Journal of Experimental Psychology: Human Learning and Memory, 1,* 351–359.

Homa, D., Cross, J., Cornell, D., Goldman, D., & Schwartz, S. (1973). Prototype abstraction and classification of new instances as a function of number of instances defining the prototype. *Journal of Experimental Psychology, 101,* 116–122.

Homa, D., Sterling, S., & Trepel, L. (1981). Limitations of exemplar based generalization and the abstraction of categorical information. *Journal of Experimental Psychology: Human Learning and Memory, 7,* 418–439.

Hummel, J. E., & Biederman, I. (1992). Dynamic binding in a neural network for shape recognition. *Psychological Review, 99,* 480–517.

Inagaki, K., & Hatano, G. (1993). Young children's understanding of the mind-body distinction. *Child Development, 64,* 1534–1549.

Jones, S. S., & Smith, L. B. (1993). The place of perception in children's concepts. *Cognitive Development, 8,* 113–139.

Katz, J. J., & Postal, P. M. (1964). *An integrated theory of linguistic descriptions.* Cambridge, MA: MIT Press.

Keil, F. C. (1979). *Semantic and conceptual development: An ontological perspective.* Cambridge, MA: Harvard University Press.

Keil, F. C. (1981). Constraints on knowledge and cognitive development. *Psychological Review, 88,* 197–227.

Keil, F. C. (1986). The acquisition of natural kind and artifact terms. In W. Demopoulos & A. Marras (Eds.), *Language Learning and Concept Acquisition* (pp. 133–153).

Keil, F. C. (1989). *Concepts, kinds, and cognitive development.* Cambridge, MA: MIT Press.

Keil, F. C. (1992). The origins of an autonomous biology. In M. A. Gunnar & M. Maratsos (Eds.) *Minnesota Symposium on Child Psychology, Vol. 25,* (pp. 103–138). Hillsdale, NJ: Erlbaum.

Keil, F. C. (1994). The birth and nurturance of concepts by domains: The origins of concepts of living things. In L. A. Hirschfeld & S. A. Gelman (Eds.), *Mapping the mind* (pp. 234–254). Cambridge: Cambridge University Press.

Kemler-Nelson, D. G. (1984). The effect of intention on what concepts are acquired. *Journal of Verbal Learning and Verbal Behavior, 23,* 734–759.

Komatsu, L. K. (1992). Recent views of conceptual structure. *Psychological Bulletin, 112,* 500–526.

Kruschke, J. K. (1993). Three principles for models of category learning. In G. V. Nakamura, R. Taraban, & D. L. Medin (Eds.), *The Psychology of Learning and Motivation: Categorization by humans and machines,* vol. 29. pp. 57–90. San Diego: Academic Press, Inc.

Kunda, Z., Miller, D. T., & Claire, T. (1990). Combining social concepts: the role of causal reasoning. *Cognitive Science, 14,* 551–577.

Kurbat, M. (1995). Part-based models of visual similarity, typicality, and categorization. Doctoral dissertation, Department of Psychology, University of Michigan.

Kurbat, M., Smith, E. E., & Medin, D. L. (1994). Shape similarity, typicality and categorization. In *Proceedings of the Sixteenth Annual Conference of the Cognitive Science Society.* Hillsdale, NJ: Erlbaum.

Lakoff, G. (1987). *Women, fire, and dangerous things: What categories reveal about the mind.* Chicago: University of Chicago Press.

Landau, B., Smith, L. B., & Jones, S. S. (1988). The importance of shape in early lexical learning. *Cognitive Development, 3,* 299–321.

Lassaline, M. E., Wisniewski, E. J., & Medin, D. L. (1992). Basic levels in artificial and natural categories: Are all basic levels created equal? In B. Burns (Ed.), *Percepts, concepts, and categories: The representation and processing of information* (pp. 323–378). New York: Elsevier.

Levine, M. (1975). *A cognitive theory of learning: Research on hypothesis testing.* Hillsdale, NJ: Erlbaum.

Malt, B. C. (1990). Features and beliefs in the mental representations of categories. *Journal of Memory and Language, 29,* 289–315.

Malt, B. C. (1994). Water is not H_2O. *Cognitive Psychology, 27,* 41–70.

Malt, B. C., & Smith, E. E. (1983). Correlated properties in natural categories. *Journal of Verbal Learning and Verbal Behavior, 23,* 250–269.

Markman, A. B., & Gentner, D. (1993a). Splitting the differences: A structural alignment view of similarity. *Journal of Memory and Language, 32,* 517–535.

Markman, A. B., & Gentner, D. (1993b). Structural alignment during similarity comparisons. *Cognitive Psychology, 25,* 431–467.

Markman, A. B., Yamauchi, T., & Makin, V. S. (1997). The creation of new concepts: A multifaceted approach to category learning. To appear in T. B. Ward, S. M. Smith, & J. Vaid (Eds.), *Conceptual Structures: Emergence, Discovery, and Change* (pp. 179–208). Washington, DC: American Psychological Association.

Markman, E. M. (1987). How children constrain the possible meanings of words. In U. Neisser (Ed.), *Concepts and conceptual development: The ecological and intellectual factors in categorization,* pp. 256–287.

Martin, R. C. & Caramazza, A. (1980). Classification of well-defined and ill-defined categories: Evidence for common processing strategies. *Journal of Experimental Psychology: General, 109,* 320–353.

Massey, C. M., & Gelman, R. (1988). Preschoolers' ability to decide whether a photographed unfamiliar object can move itself. *Developmental Psychology, 24,* 307–317.

Matheus, C. J., Rendell, L. R., Medin, D. L., & Goldstone, R. C. (1989). Purpose and conceptual functions: A framework for concept representation and learning in humans and machines. In *Proceedings of the Seventh Annual Conference of the Society for the Study of Artificial Intelligence and Simulation of Behavior.*

Mayr, E. (1988). *Toward a New Philosophy of Biology.* Cambridge, MA: Belknap Press of Harvard University Press.

McCloskey, M., & Glucksberg, S. (1978). Natural categories: Well-defined or fuzzy sets? *Memory and Cognition, 6,* 462–472.

McNamara, T. P., & Sternberg, R. J. (1983). Mental models of word meaning. *Journal of Verbal Learning and Verbal Behavior, 22,* 449–474.

Medin, D. L. (1986). Comment on "Memory storage and retrieval processes in category learning." *Journal of Experimental Psychology: General, 115,* 373–381.

Medin, D. L. (1989). Concepts and conceptual structure. *American Psychologist, 44,* 1469–1481.

Medin, D. L., & Edelson, S. M. (1988). Problem structure and the use of base-rate information from experience, *Journal of Experimental Psychology: General, 117,* 68–85.

Medin, D. L., & Heit, E. J. (in press). Categorization. In D. Rumelhart & B. Martin (Eds.), *Handbook of cognition and perception.* Hillsdale, NJ: Erlbaum.

Medin, D. L., & Ortony, A. (1989). Psychological essentialism. In S. Vosniadou & A. Ortony (Eds.), *Similarity and Analogical Reasoning,* 189–223.

Medin, D. L., & Ross, B. H. (1989). The specific character of abstract thought: Categorization, problem-solving and induction. In R. J. Sterberg (Ed.), *Advances in the Psychology of Human Intelligence, 5,* 189–223.

Medin, D. L. & Schaffer, M. M. (1978). Context theory of classification learning. *Psychological Review, 85,* 207–238.

Medin, D. L. & Schwanenflugel, P. J. (1981). Linear separability in classification learning. *Journal of Experimental Psychology: Human Learning and Memory, 7,* 355–368.

Medin, D. L., & Shoben, E. J. (1988). Context and structure in conceptual combination. *Cognitive Psychology, 20,* 158–190.

Medin, D. L., & Smith, E. E. (1981). Strategies and classification learning. *Journal of Experimental Psychology: Human learning and Memory, 7,* 241–253.

Medin, D. L., & Wattenmaker, W. D. (1987). Category cohesiveness, theories, and cognitive archeology. In U. Neisser (Ed.), *Concepts and Conceptual Development: The Ecological and Intellectual Factors in Categories* (pp. 25–62). Cambridge, England: Cambridge University Press.

Medin, D. L., Altom, M. W., Edelson, S. M., & Freko, D. (1982). Correlated symptoms and simulated medical classification. *Journal of Experimental Psychology: Learning, Memory, and Cognition, 8,* 37–50.

Medin, D. L., Dewey, G. I., & Murphy, T. D. (1983). Relationships between item and category learning: Evidence that abstraction is not automatic. *Journal of Experimental Psychology: Learning, Memory, and Cognition, 9,* 607–625.

Medin, D. L., Goldstone, R. L., & Gentner, D. (1993). Respects for similarity. *Psychological Review, 100,* 254–278.

Medin, D. L., Goldstone, R. L., & Markman, A. B. (1995). Comparison and choice: Relations between similarity processes and decision processes. *Psychonomic Bulletin & Review, 2,* 1–19.

Medin, D. L., Lynch, E. B., Coley, J. D., Atran, S. (1997). Categorization and reasoning among tree experts: Do all roads lead to Rome? *Cognitive Psychology, 32,* 49–96.

Medin, D. L., Wattenmaker, W. D., & Hampson, S. E. (1987). Family resemblance, concept cohesiveness, and category construction. *Cognitive Psychology, 19,* 242–279.

Medin, D. L., Wattenmaker, W. D., & Michalski, R. S. (1987). Constraints and preferences in inductive learning: An experimental study of human and machine performance. *Cognitive Science, 11,* 299–339.

Mervis, C. B., & Rosch, E. (1981). Categorization of natural objects. In M. R. Rosenzweig & L. W. Porter (Eds.), *Annual Review of Psychology, 32,* 89–115.

Murphy, G. L. (1988). Comprehending complex concepts. *Cognitive Science, 12,* 529–562.

Murphy, G. L., & Medin, D. L. (1985). The role of theories in conceptual coherence. *Psychological Review, 92,* 289–316.

Murphy, G. L., & Wisniewski, E. J. (1989). Categorizing objects in isolation and in sciences: What a superordinate is good for. *Journal of Experimental Psychology: Learning, Memory, and Cognition, 15,* 572–586.

Nakamura, G. V., Taraban, R., & Medin, D. L. (Eds.). (1993). *The Psychology of Learning and Motivation: Categorization by humans and machines,* vol. 29. San Diego: Academic Press, Inc.

Nosofsky, R. M. (1987). Attention and learning processes in the identification and categorization of integral stimuli. *Journal of Experimental Psychology: Learning, Memory, and Cognition, 13,* 87–108.

Nosofsky, R. M. (1988a). Exemplar-based accounts of relations between classification, recognition, and typicality. *Journal of Experimental Psychology: Learning, Memory, and Cognition, 14,* 700–708.

Nosofsky, R. M. (1988b). Similarity, frequency, and category representations. *Journal of Experimental Psychology: Learning, Memory, and Cognition, 14,* 54–65.

Nosofsky, R. M. (1991). Tests of an exemplar model for relating perceptual classification and recognition in memory. *Journal of Experimental Psychology: Human Perception and Performance, 17,* 3–27.

Nosofsky, R. M. (1992). Exemplar-based approach to relating categorization, identification, and recognition. In F. G. Ashby (Ed.), *Multidimensional models of perception and cognition* (pp. 363–393). Hillsdale, NJ: Erlbaum.

Nosofsky, R. M. & Kruschke, J. K. (1992). Investigations of an exemplar-based connectionist model of category learning. In D. L. Medin (Ed.) *The Psychology of Learning and Motivation* (Vol. 28) (pp. 207–250). New York: Academic Press.

Nosofsky, R. M., Clark, S. E., & Shin, H. J. (1989). Rules and exemplars in categorization, identification, and recognition. *Journal of Experimental Psychology: Learning, Memory, and Cognition, 15,* 282–304.

Nosofsky, R. M., Bluck, M. A., Palmeri, T. S., McKinley, S. C., & Glauthier, P. (1994). Comparing models of rule-based classification learning: A replication and extension of Shepard, Hovland, and Jenkins (1961). *Memory & Cognition, 22,* 352–369.

Nosofsky, R. M., Palmeri, T. J., & McKinely, S. C. (1994). Rule-plus-exception model of classification learning. *Psychological Review, 101,* 53–79.

Oden, G. C. (1987). Concept, knowledge, and thought. *Annual Review of Psychology, 38,* 203–227.

Ortony, A., Vondruska, R. J., Foss, M. A., & Jones, L. E. (1985). Salience, similes, and the asymmetry of similarity. *Journal of Memory and Language, 24,* 569–594.

Osherson, D. N., & Smith, E. E. (1981). On the adequacy of prototype theory as a theory of concepts. *Cognition, 11,* 35–58.

Peterson, M. J., Meagher, R. B., Jr., Chait, H., & Gillie, S. (1973). The abstraction and generalization of dot patterns. *Cognitive Psychology, 4,* 378–398.

Posner, M. I., & Keele, S. W. (1968). On the genesis of abstract ideas. *Journal of Experimental Psychology, 77,* 353–363.

Posner, M. I., & Keele, S. W. (1970). Retention of abstract ideas. *Journal of Experimental Psychology, 83,* 304–308.

Price-Williams, D. R. (1962). Abstract and concrete models of classification in a primitive society. *British Journal of Educational Psychology, 32,* 50–61.

Reagher, G., & Brooks, L. R. (1993). Perceptual manifestations of an analytic structure: The priority of holistic individuation. *Journal of Experimental Psychology: General, 122,* 92–114.

Reagher, G., & Brooks, L. R. (1995). Category organization in free classification: The organizing effect of an array of stimuli. *Journal of Experimental Psychology: Learning, Memory, and Cognition, 21,* 347–363.

Rips, L. (1995). The current status of research on conceptual combination. *Mind and Language. 10,* 72–104.

Rips, L. J. (1975). Inductive judgements about natural categories. *Journal of Verbal Learning and Verbal Behavior, 14,* 665–681.

Rips, L. J. (1989). Similarity, typicality and categorization. In S. Vosniadou & A. Ortony (Eds.), *Similarity and analogical reasoning.* Cambridge: Cambridge University Press.

Rips, L. J., & Collins, A. (1993). Categories and resemblance. *Journal of Experimental Psychology: General, 122,* 468–486.

Rosch, E., & Mervis, C. B. (1975). Family resemblances: Studies in the internal structure of categories. *Cognitive Psychology, 7,* 573–605.

Rosch, E., Mervis, C. B., Gray, W., Johnson, D., & Boyes-Braem, P. (1976). Basic objects in natural categories. *Cognitive Psychology, 8,* 382–439.

Roth, E. M., & Shoben, E. J. (1983). The effect of context on the structure of categories. *Cognitive Psychology, 15,*346–378.

Rothbart, M., & Taylor, M. (1992). Category labels and social reality: Do we view social categories as natural kinds? In G. Semin and K. Fiedler (Eds.), *Language, Interaction, and Social Cognition* (pp. 11–36). London: Sage Publications.

Schank, R. C., Collins, G. C., & Hunter, L. E. (1986). Transcending inductive category formation in learning. *Behavioral and Brain Sciences, 9,* 639–651.

Schyns, P. G., & Murphy, G. L. (1994). The ontogeny of part representation in object concepts. In D. L. Medin (Ed.) *The Psychology of Learning and Motivation, 31,* 305–354. San Diego, CA: Academic Press.

Sebestyn, G. S. (1962). *Decision-making processes in pattern recognition.* New York: Macmillan.

Shepard, R. N., Hovland, C. I., & Jenkins, H. M. (1961). Learning and memorization of classifications. *Psychological Monographs, 75.*

Shin, H. J., & Nosofsky, R. M. (1992). Similarity-scaling studies of dot-pattern classification and recognition. *Journal of Experimental Psychology: General, 121,* 278–304.

Shipley, E. F. (1993). Categories, hierarchies, and induction. In D. L. Medin (Ed.). *The Psychology of Learning and Motivation, Vol. 30.* (pp. 265–301). New York: Academic Press.

Smith E. E., & Medin, D. L. (1981). Categories and concepts. Cambridge, MA: Harvard University Press.

Smith, E. E., & Osherson, D. N. (1984). Conceptual combination with prototype concepts. *Cognitive Science, 8,* 337–361.

Smith, E. E., Osherson, D. N., Rips, L. J., & Keane M. (1988). Combining prototypes: A selective modification model. *Cognitive Science, 12,* 485–527.

Smith, E. E., Shafir, E., & Osherson, D. N. (1993). Similarity, plausibility, and judgments of probability. *Cognition, 49,* 67–96.

Smith, E. E., Shoben, E. J., & Rips, L. J. (1974). Structure and process in semantic memory: A featural model for semantic decisions. *Psychological Review, 81,* 214–241.

Smith, E. R., & Zarate, M. A. (1992). Exemplar-based models of social judgment. *Psychological Review, 99,* 3–21.

Solomon, G. E. A., Johnson, S. C., Zaitchik, D., & Carey, S. (1996). Like father, like son: Young children's understanding of how and why offspring resemble their parents. *Child Development, 67,* 151–171.

Spalding, T. L. & Murphy, G. L. (1996). Effects of background knowledge on category construction. *Journal of Experimental Psychology: Learning, Memory & Cognition, 22,* 525–538.

Springer, K., & Keil, F. C. (1989). On the development of biologically specific beliefs: The case of inheritance. *Child Development, 60,* 637–648.

Springer, K., & Keil, F. C. (1991). Early differentiation of causal mecanisms appropriate to biological and nonbiological kinds. *Child Development, 62,* 767–781.

Suchman, R. G. (1966). Cultural differences in children's color and form perception. *Journal of Social Psychology, 70,* 3–10.

Tanaka, J. W., & Taylor, M. (1991). Object categories and expertise: Is the basic level in the eye of the beholder? *Cognitive Psychology, 23,* 457–482.

Tarr, M. J. (1995). Rotating objects to recognize them: A case study of the role of mental transformations in the recognition of three-dimensional objects. *Psychonomic Bulletin & Review, 2,* 55–82.

Thibaut, J.-P., & Schyns, P. G. (1995). The development of feature spaces for similarity and categorization. *Psychological Belgica, 35,* 167–185.

Trabasso, T., & Bower, G. H. (1968). *Attention in learning.* New York: Wiley.

Tulving, E. (1983). *Elements of episodic memory.* New York: Oxford University Press.

Tversky, A. (1977). Features of similarity. *Psychological Review, 84,* 327–352.

VanMechlen, I., Hampton, J., Michalski, R., & Theuns, P. (Eds.). (1993). *Categories and Concepts: Theoretical Views and Inductive Data Analysis.* London: Academic Press.

Watanabe, S. (1969). *Knowing and guessing: A formal and quantitative study.* New York: Wiley.

Wattenmaker, W. D. (1991). Learning modes, feature correlations, and memory-based categorization. *Journal of Experimental Psychology: Learning, Memory, and Cognition, 17,* 908–923.

Wattenmaker, W. D. (1993). Incidental concept learning, feature frequency and correlated properties. *Journal of Experimental Psychology: Human learning and memory, 19,* 203–222.

Wattenmaker, W. D., Dewey, G. I., Murphy, T. D., Medin, D. L. (1986). Linear separability and concept learning: Context, relational properties, and concept naturalness. *Cognitive Psychology, 18,* 158–194.

Waxman, S. R. (1990). Linguistic biases and the establishment of conceptual hierarchies: Evidence from preschool children. *Cognitive Development, 5*(2), 123–150.

Waxman, S. R., & Gelman, R. (1986). Preschoolers' use of superordinate relations in classification and language. *Cognitive Development, 1,* 139–156.

Waxman, S. R., & Markow, D. B. (1995). Words as invitations to form categories: Evidence form 12-month-old infants. *Cognitive Psychology, 29,* 257–302.

Wellman, H. M., & Gelman, S. A. (1992). Cognitive development: Foundational theories and core domains. *Annual Review of Psychology, 43,* 337–375.

Wisniewski, E. J. (1995). Prior Knowledge and functionally relevant features in concept learning. *Journal of Experimental Psychology: Learning, Memory, and Cognition, 21,* 449–468.

Wisniewski, E. J. (1996). Construal and similarity in conceptual combination. *Journal of Memory & Language, 35,* 1–20.

Wisniewski, E. J. (1997). When concepts combine, *Psychonomic Bulletin & Review, 4,* 167–183.

Wisniewski, E. J., & Gentner, D. (1991). On the combinatorial semantics of noun pairs: Minor and major adjustments to meaning. In G. B. Simpson (Ed.), *Understanding word and sentence* (pp. 241–284). Amsterdam: North Holland.

Wisniewski, E. J., & Medin, D. L. (1991). Harpoons and long sticks: The interaction of theory and similarity in rule induction. In D. H. Fisher, M. J. Pazzani, & P. Langley (Eds.), *Concept formation: Knowledge and experience in unsupervised learning.* pp. 237–278. San Mateo, CA: Morgan Kaufman.

Wisniewski, E. J., & Medin, D. L. (1994). On the interaction of theory and data in concept learning. *Cognitive Science, 18,* 221–281.

CHAPTER 14

Imagery, Visualization, and Thinking

P. N. Johnson-Laird

All our ideas and concepts are only internal pictures.
—Ludwig Boltzmann (1899)

I. INTRODUCTION

What is the relation between the ability to see the world and to think? For the Renaissance humanist, Leonardo da Vinci, the two processes were almost one and the same: to visualize *was* to think. The eye was the instrument of thought, and the artist's ability to make pictures provided a special medium in which to carry out "thought experiments." This view, however, has been supplanted by the development of quantum mechanics and other abstract disciplines in which the objects of thought are all but impossible to visualize. The manipulation of abstract representations—if it occurs—does indeed seem to be a mode of thinking that is not visual. The emphasis on abstraction and mathematics can be found in many intellectual disciplines—from logic to mechanical engineering—in which practitioners concomitantly play down the role of visualization. These pedagogical trends, however, may have little basis in fact. The aim of the present chapter is accordingly to reconsider the nature of mental representations and thinking, that is, of how the mind's eye may help the mind's mind. It will use the results of psychological experiments to reach some new conclusions about the relations between visualizing and thinking.

Section II of the chapter begins with the traditional account of visual imagery—the introspective reports of individuals claiming to use images, and the commentators' claims—according to which visualization is central to the creation of novel ideas. One source of renewed interest in the topic was the rediscovery of imagery by psychologists. After years of deliberate neglect during the Behavioristic era, cognitive

Perception and Cognition at Century's End

psychologists took up the topic again. The chapter describes some of their key findings. No sooner had images been rediscovered than certain skeptics, notably the Canadian cognitive scientist, Zenon Pylyshyn, argued that they are epiphenomenal, that is, they play no causal role in mental life. If these skeptics are right, the emphasis on visualization in thinking is misplaced. The real work is done by so-called "propositional representations," that is, representations of propositions in a mental language. Hence, we need to establish whether images, propositional representations, or some other sort of mental representations underlie thought.

With this aim, Section III of the chapter turns to a test case: reasoning. Its mechanisms are not accessible to introspection, but they can be characterized theoretically. The chapter describes the orthodox theory that reasoning depends on propositional representations and formal rules of inference like those of a logical calculus—a view advanced by most cognitive scientists. It then outlines an alternative theory that reasoning is not a formal process at all, but a semantic process that depends on the manipulation of "mental models" of states of affairs according to the fundamental principle of validity, an argument is valid if its conclusion must be true given that its premises are true. The theory yields a surprising prediction: certain inferences should be like illusions (i.e., they will have conclusions that are compelling, yet that are completely wrong). A recent discovery is that these illusory inferences do exist.

What is the relation between mental models and mental images? Section IV of the chapter argues that models underlie the experience of imagery, but models themselves may contain elements that cannot be visualized, such as an annotation representing negation. Experiments confirm the existence of such annotations, and they show that reasoning is unaffected by the "imageability" of the materials. The operations that can be directly carried out on images correspond to visual transformations rather than to deep conceptual processes. Even mental rotations of images representing objects are likely to depend on an underlying three-dimensional model. Images, however, may have a symbolic function, and thus diagrams can help people to reason about entities that cannot be readily visualized.

Finally, the chapter draws some morals about visualization (in Section V). The result is a rehabilitation of imagery in the face of the skeptics, but a limitation on imagery in the face of its more ardent adherents.

II. VISUALIZATION

A. Introspections about Visualization

The aim of this section is to review visual imagery. According to many commentators, it is fundamental to scientific and technological invention (e.g., Ferguson, 1977; Miller, 1984; Shepard, 1988; Valéry, 1894). The claim is based in part on the traditional views of scientists themselves, particularly 19th century physicists (see, e.g., Boltzmann, 1899). It is also bolstered by a number of celebrated anecdotes.

Friedrich August von Kekulé, for example, described how in 1865 the ring-like structure of benzene came to him in a dream:

> I turned my chair to the fire and dozed. Again the atoms were gamboling before my eyes. This time the smaller groups kept modestly in the background. My mental eye, rendered more acute by repeated visions of this kind, could now distinguish larger structures, of manifold conformation; long rows, sometimes more closely fitted together; all twining and twisting in snakelike motion. But look! What was that? One of the snakes had seized hold of its own tail, and the form whirled mockingly before my eyes. As if by a flash of lightning I awoke. (Findlay, 1937, p. 43)

The snake biting its tail had given him the clue to the puzzle.

Other scientists are said to have thought in terms of images. Gruber (1974, p. 237) reports that Darwin's notebooks are full of images, though Darwin himself wrote that he found it just as easy to think about abstract ideas as concrete ones. It is worth noting that Darwin's "thought experiments" in *The Origin of Species* do not hinge specifically on visualizable events, for example:

> It is good thus to try in our imagination to give any form [of plant or animal] some advantage over another. Probably in no single instance should we know what to do, so as to succeed. It will convince us of our ignorance on the mutual relations of all organic beings; a conviction as necessary, as it seems to be difficult to acquire. All that we can do, is to keep steadily in mind that each organic being is striving to increase at a geometrical ratio; that each at some period of its life, during some season of the year, during each generation or at intervals, has to struggle for life, and to suffer great destruction. (Darwin, 1859/1968, p. 129)

Darwin was a subject of Galton's well-known questionnaire study of imagery among Fellows of the Royal Society (Galton, 1880/1928), which revealed—somewhat to Galton's consternation—that many of them claimed to think without using images. Yet most scientists who have written on their own thought processes have emphasized the role of imagery. Perhaps the best known testimonial occurs in Einstein's letter to Hadamard (1996):

> The words of the language, as they are written or spoken, do not seem to play any role in my mechanism of thought. The psychical entities which seem to serve as elements in thought are certain signs and more or less clear images which can be "voluntarily" reproduced and combined.
>
> There is, of course, a certain connection between those elements and relevant logical concepts. It is also clear that the desire to arrive finally at logically connected concepts is the emotional basis of this rather vague play with the above mentioned elements. But taken from a psychological viewpoint, this combinatory play seems to be the essential feature in productive thought—before there is any connection with logical construction in words or other kinds of signs which can be communicated to others. (p. 142)

Max Wertheimer, one of the founders of Gestalt psychology, had occasion to interview Einstein, and corroborated the role of visualization (Wertheimer, 1961, p. 228;

for corrections to other aspects of his account, which are historically inaccurate, see e.g., Miller, 1984, Ch. 5). Gleick (1992, p. 131) has similarly emphasized the role of imagery in the late Richard Feynman's thinking. And even one psychologist, Feldman (1988), claims that an image played a significant part in his own thinking.

B. The Rediscovery of Images

Mentalistic psychologists studied visual imagery in the last century and the early years of this century (e.g., Binet, 1894; Perky, 1910). But the topic fell into disrepute as a result of a dispute, the so-called "imageless thought" controversy. A group of psychologists at Würzburg led by Karl Marbe and Oswald Külpe claimed that their subjects often reported a kind of conscious but unanalyzable experience that was neither an image nor an awareness of an intention or act of will. These *Bewusstseinslagen,* or "imageless thoughts," ran contrary to the Aristotelian view of thinking as an association between ideas. They were taken to imply the existence of unconscious processes leading to their appearance in consciousness. To base a theoretical argument solely on introspections, however, was an egregious error. It is impossible to establish their authenticity—even Kekulé's dream, for example, may turn out to have been a fraud (see Wotiz & Rudofsky, 1984, cited by Gruber, 1994). Wundt, the leading psychologist of the day, challenged the Würzburg school, as did his student, Titchener, one of the founders of American psychology, who declared that his thinking was always accompanied by imagery (see Humphrey, 1951, for an authoritative history). The controversy was never settled; rival theorists traded rival introspections, but it was swept away, along with the study of imagery, by the rise of Behaviorism.

With the revival of mentalism and the cognitive revolution in psychology, psychologists rediscovered imagery (Holt, 1964). They were soon to distinguish between what they termed verbal and visual representations (Bower, 1970; Paivio, 1971). With Shepard's studies of the mental rotation of visual images (e.g., Shepard & Metzler, 1971), the topic appeared to have been rehabilitated within psychology. Shepard and his colleagues demonstrated that individuals can transform objects mentally in a variety of ways. In the first of their experiments, which itself was suggested by a spontaneous kinetic image in one of Shepard's dreams, the subjects saw two drawings of a "nonsense" figure assembled out of ten blocks glued together to form a rigid object with right-angled joints. Their task was to decide whether the pictures depicted one and the same object from different points of view. The time they took to make their decision increased linearly with the angular difference between the orientations of the two objects. This result held both for rotations in the picture plane and for rotations in depth. It implied that subjects could mentally rotate their representation of such objects at a rate of about 60° per second.

Kosslyn and his colleagues obtained similar results when they asked their subjects to scan from one landmark to another in their image of a map that they had committed to memory (see, e.g., Kosslyn, Ball, & Reiser, 1978). Kosslyn (1980) also estimated the size of the mental "screen" on which images are projected: subjects had to form an image of, say, an elephant and then imagine walking toward it until the image began to overflow their minds' eye. They stopped further from their image of an elephant than from their image of a smaller animal, such as a dog. The size of the mental screen is about the same for an image as it is for a visual perception. Many other investigations of imagery, from its mnemonic value (Luria, 1969) to its special storage in short-term memory (Baddeley & Hitch, 1974), seem to imply that visual images are a distinct medium of mental representation.

This view was challenged by Pylyshyn (1973). He argued that a distinct medium of representation would be part of the functional architecture of the mind and so its properties could not be affected by an individual's beliefs or attitudes. The case is comparable, he claimed, to the architecture of a digital computer: the design of its hardware cannot be modified by a program that the computer is running. Mental architecture is thus "cognitively impenetrable," whereas imagery is easily influenced by an individuals' beliefs. Indeed, Pylyshyn argued, the results of the rotation and scanning experiments might merely reflect the ability of subjects to simulate how long it would take to rotate an actual object, or to scan across an actual map. Such simulations would reveal nothing about the real nature of mental representations. In Pylyshyn's view, the mind depends on formal computations carried out on a single sort of representation: syntactically structured "propositional representations" expressed in a mental language. Images undoubtedly occur as subjective experiences, but they are epiphenomenal (i.e., they do not play any causal role in mental processes).

There are two ways to resolve the argument between imagists and propositionalists—the "thoughtless imagery" controversy, as it might be dubbed (Johnson-Laird, 1983, Ch. 7). In one sense of "propositional representation," the propositionalists must be right. All mental life depends on the brain's "machine code," and so everything must be reduced to nerve impulses and synaptic events, just as all computations no matter how complex can be reduced to the shifting of bits from one computer register to another. In another sense of "propositional representation," the imagists may be right, and there is a real distinction between images and propositional representations. In this sense, they are both high-level representations within the same computational medium, just as lists of symbols and arrays of symbols are distinct representations within a high-level programming language, such as LISP. If we draw the distinction in this way, we are left with an empirical question: What sorts of high-level mental representation does human thinking depend on? The aim of Section III is to answer this question by considering the psychology of reasoning.

III. THE PSYCHOLOGY OF REASONING

A. The Theory of Formal Rules and Propositional Representations

Consider the following problem about a particular hand of cards:

1. There is a king in the hand, or there is an ace in the hand, or both.
2. There is not a king in the hand.
3. What follows?

Most people respond rapidly with the correct conclusion:

There is an ace in the hand.

How did you carry out this inference? Introspection alone cannot tell you. Psychologists have studied reasoning since the turn of the century, and Störring (1908) found that his subjects reported using either images or verbal methods to reason. But the dominant view these days is that the mind is equipped with formal rules of inference, which it uses in order to reason, either deductively or inductively—a view that implies that visualization plays no role in reasoning.

In general, *formal rule* theories, as I shall henceforth refer to them, postulate that reasoners construct propositional representations of premises, identify their logical structure, apply formal rules of inference one at a time in a chain of steps that leads from the premises to the conclusion, and express this conclusion with its appropriate linguistic content (see, e.g., Braine, Reiser, & Rumain, 1984, Rips, 1994). Thus, the logical structure of the example above matches the formal rule of inference:

> p or q, or both
>
> not-p
>
> ∴   q,

which yields the conclusion. Formal rule theories postulate separate rules of inference for each of the main logical connectives: "if", "and", and "or". Table 1 summarizes the main rules. The theories predict that the greater the number of steps in a derivation, the harder the deduction should be, but they allow that certain rules may be harder to use than others.

One disquieting phenomenon for formal rule theories is that the content of the premises can have a striking effect on deductive performance (Wason & Johnson-Laird, 1972). Twenty years ago, however, there appeared to be no alternative to for-

TABLE 1   Some Typical Formal Rules of Inference Postulated as Part of Mental Logic by Many Psychologists

Rules that eliminate connectives	Rules that introduce connectives
p & q ∴ p	p q ∴ p & q
p or q not-p ∴ q	p ∴ p or q
if p then q p ∴ q	p ⊢ q ∴ if p then q (where "⊢" signifies that q can be derived from hypothesizing p)

mal rule theories, and most investigators took for granted the existence of a mental logic. Yet an alternative did exist: reasoning could be based on a semantic method rather than the syntactic method of formal rules. In logic, a comparable distinction is drawn between "proof-theoretic" methods based on formal rules and "model-theoretic" methods based on semantic principles. The next section outlines a psychological theory based on a semantic method.

B. The Theory of Mental Models

The physicist Ludwig Boltzmann (1890) wrote of scientific thinking in the following terms:

> The task of theory consists in constructing an image of the external world that exists purely internally and must be our guiding star in thought and experiment; that is in completing, as it were, the thinking process and carrying out globally what on a small scale occurs within us whenever we form an idea. (p. 33)

The Scottish psychologist and physiologist, Kenneth Craik, similarly conceived of thinking in terms of the following programmatic idea:

> If the organism carries a "small-scale model" of external reality and of its own possible actions within its head, it is able to try out various alternatives, conclude which is the best of them, react to future situations before they arise, utilize the knowledge of past events in dealing with the present and the future, and in every way to react in a much fuller, safer, and more competent manner to the emergencies which face it. (Craik, 1943, Ch. 5)

Mental models can be constructed on the basis of visual perception (Marr, 1982) or verbal comprehension (Johnson-Laird, 1983). Their essential characteristic is that their structure corresponds to the structure of what they represent. Like a diagram (Maxwell, 1911) or an architect's model, the parts of the model correspond to the relevant parts of what it represents, and the structural relations between the parts of the model are analogous to the structural relations in the world. Hence, a model represents a set of individuals by a set of mental tokens, it represents the properties of the individuals by the properties of the tokens, and it represents the relations among the individuals by the relations among the tokens. And like a diagram, the model is partial because it represents only certain aspects of the situation. There is therefore a many-to-one mapping from possible states of affairs to the model. Images have these properties, too, but as we shall see, models and images differ from one another. Models need not be visualizable and, unlike images, they may represent several distinct sets of possibilities.

The theory of mental models postulates that human reasoners who have no logical training represent states of affairs using mental models. Psychologists cannot directly inspect mental models, and so the evidence for their existence and format is indirect. In the case of reasoning—deductive and inductive—the model theory postulates that reasoners construct a model, or set of models, based on the meaning of premises, perception, and any relevant general knowledge. They formulate a conclusion by describing a relation in the models that was not explicitly asserted by any single premise. Finally, they attempt to assess the strength of the inference. Its strength depends on the believability of its premises and on the proportion of models of the premises in which the conclusion is true (Johnson-Laird, 1994). The theory accordingly provides a single psychological mechanism for reasoning about necessary, probable, and possible conclusions:

1. A conclusion that holds in all possible models of the premises is *necessary* given the premises (i.e., it is deductively valid).
2. A conclusion that holds in most of the models of the premises is *probable*.
3. A conclusion that holds in at least one model of the premises is *possible*.

To illustrate reasoning by model, reconsider the earlier example:

1. There is a king in the hand, or there is an ace in the hand, or both.
2. There is not a king in the hand.
3. What follows?

The first premise calls for a set of models that represent the three possibilities, shown here on separate lines:

k

    a

k   a

where "k" denotes a king in the hand, and "a" denotes an ace in the hand.

A crucial assumption of the model theory is that individuals normally minimize the load on working memory by representing explicitly only those contingencies that are true (Johnson-Laird & Byrne, 1991). The models above, for example, do not make explicit what is false (i.e., an ace does *not* occur in the first model and a king does *not* occur in the second model). Reasoners should make a mental "footnote" to this effect, which can be used to make the models wholly explicit if necessary, but the theory assumes that footnotes are rapidly forgotten. For many deductions in daily life, there is no need to make models completely explicit. The premise,

The king is not in the hand,

rules out two of the models in the initial set, and all that is left is a single model:

a

which supports the conclusion,

There is an ace in the hand.

No other model of the premises refutes this conclusion, and so it is valid.

The theory postulates that a conditional, such as:

If there is a king in the hand then there is an ace in the hand is initially represented by the following two models:

k   a

. . .

In this case, people realize both cards may be in the hand, which they represent in an explicit model, but they defer a detailed representation of the case where the antecedent is false (i.e., where there is *not* a king in the hand), which they represent in a wholly implicit model denoted here by an ellipsis. Reasoners need to make a mental footnotes that a king cannot occur in the hands represented by the ellipsis, whereas an ace may, or may not, occur in these hands. Once again, the theory assumes that footnote are rapidly forgotten. Table 2 summarizes the models for the major connectives, and it also shows the fully explicit models, which do represent the false contingencies. There are occasions where reasoners do represent them.

The theory may seem to be no more than a notational variant of formal rule theories, but in fact it makes predictions that cannot be made by them. First, given the mind's limited processing capacity, the theory predicts that the greater the number of models that have to be constructed to make a deduction, the harder the task should be. More models mean more work. Second, the theory predicts that erroneous conclusions should occur because reasoners sometimes overlook possible models of the premises. Third, the theory predicts that certain inferences will be illusory (i.e., they will have conclusions that are compelling but completely wrong). In the following sections, we will review the experimental evidence for these predictions.

TABLE 2   The Sets of Models for the Main Sentential Connectives[a]

Connective	Initial Models		Fully Explicit Models	
A and B:	A	B	A	B
A or else B:	A		A	¬B
		B	¬A	B
A or B, or both:	A		A	¬B
		B	¬A	B
	A	B	A	B
If A then B:	A	B	A	B
	. . .		¬A	B
			¬A	¬B
If, and only if, A then B	A	B	A	B
	. . .		¬A	¬B

[a]The central column shows the initial models that the theory postulates for human reasoners, and the right-hand column shows the fully explicit sets of models. The symbol "¬" denotes negation, and the symbol " . . . " denotes a wholly implicit model. Each line represents a separate model.

C. The Evidence for Mental Models

1. Mental Models and Spatial Reasoning

The ability to reason about spatial relations is likely to depend on the construction of mental models. Byrne and Johnson-Laird (1989) investigated the following sort of problems, which describe the layout of objects on a table top:

   1. The cup is on the right of the spoon.
   2. The plate is on the left of the spoon.
   3. The knife is in front of the cup.
   4. The fork is in front of the plate.
   5. What's the relation between the fork and the knife?

The premises call for the model:

plate	spoon	cup
fork		knife

where the left-to-right axis represents the left-to-right axis in the world, and the vertical axis represents the front-to-back axis in the world. Reasoners may well visualize the shapes of the various utensils. The model yields the answer to the question:

The fork is on the left of the knife.

No model of the premises refutes this conclusion, and so it is valid.

Now consider the following problem in which one word in the second premise has been changed:

   1. The cup is on the right of the spoon.
   2. The plate is on the left of the cup.
   3. The knife is in front of the cup.
   4. The fork is in front of the plate.
   5. What's the relation between the fork and the knife?

The premises are spatially indeterminate because they are consistent with at least two distinct layouts:

plate	spoon	cup
fork		knife

or:

spoon	plate	cup
	fork	knife

In either case, however, the same conclusion follows as before:

The fork is on the left of the knife.

The model theory predicts that the first problem, which calls for one model, should be easier than the second problem, which calls for at least two models. The process of constructing such models from verbal assertions has itself been modeled in a computer program (see Johnson-Laird & Byrne, 1991).

Formal rule theories of spatial reasoning, such as those proposed by Ohlsson (1984) and Hagert (1984), make exactly the opposite prediction. The first problem requires a formal derivation to establish the relation between the plate and the cup, which is then used to derive the relation between the fork and the knife. The second problem does not require a formal derivation of the relation between the plate and the cup, because the second premise directly asserts it. The second problem has a derivation that is just part of the derivation of the first problem, and so according to the formal rule theories it should be easier than the first problem.

Byrne and Johnson-Laird (1989) presented their subjects with sets of one-model and multiple-model spatial inferences, and a further set that did not support a valid answer. The subjects did all three sorts of problem, which were presented in a random order. They made 70% correct responses to the one-model problems, but only 46% correct responses to the multiple-model problems. Their correct conclusions were also reliably faster to the one-model problems (a mean of 3.1 sec) than to the multiple-model problems with valid answers (3.6 sec). In the example above, however, the multiple-model problem has an irrelevant first premise, and so a second experiment examined one-model problems with an irrelevant first premise. The results were the same: one-model problems were reliably easier than multiple-model problems.

One adherent of formal rules has argued that the trouble with these experiments is that the subjects were asked to imagine the objects on a table top, and that this instruction "obviously biased the subjects to use an imaginal strategy that favored the mental-model predictions (or placed a strong task demand on them to respond as if they were trying to image the arrays)" (see Rips, 1994, p. 415). This argument is unlikely to be correct, because the results have been replicated for problems based on temporal relations, such as,

a before b.
b before c.
d while a.
e while c.
What's the relation between d and e?,

where "a," "b," etc., stand for everyday events, such as "John shaves," "he drinks his coffee," and so on (see Schaeken, Johnson-Laird, & d'Ydewalle, 1996). In these studies, the subjects were obviously *not* told to imagine a table top; and, as in the spatial studies, they were given no instructions about how to do the task. The evidence accordingly corroborates the model theory and runs counter to the formal rule theories.

Inferences cannot be based on models alone. When the deductive procedure searches for an alternative model of the premises to refute a putative conclusion, it needs access to an independent representation of the premises. Consider, for example, the following model:

$$|\bigcirc|\triangle|\star|$$

and the putative conclusion:

The circle is on the left of the star.

The following model refutes the conclusion:

$$|\star|\triangle|\bigcirc|$$

but it will be relevant only if it is also a model of the previous premises, and the model itself does not allow these premises to be reconstructed in a unique way. It follows that deduction calls for an independent record of the premises, and such a record is provided by their propositional representations, which capture the propositions expressed by the premises. Some experimental evidence bears out the existence of such representations (see Mani & Johnson-Laird, 1982).

The model-building system, as the computer program shows, must be based on a set of underlying concepts. These *subconcepts* are built into the lexical semantics and the procedures for manipulating arrays, and they are based on increments to Cartesian coordinates, where the first coordinate is left–right, the second is front–back, and the third is up–down:

on the right of	1	0	0
on the left of	-1	0	0
in front of	0	1	0
behind	0	-1	0
above	0	0	1
below	0	0	-1

How the mind represents the meanings of spatial relations is not yet known, but it must deploy some set of underlying subconcepts that are used by the procedures for constructing models. These subconcepts are ineffable; they are not available to introspection, and they are probably innate and universal. They and the procedures that use them govern the mapping from linguistic expressions to models, and the mapping from models back to linguistic expressions again. Hence, the operations for reasoning by building mental models are essentially conceptual: reasoners use their understanding of descriptions to envisage situations, and this understanding ultimately depends on tacit conceptual knowledge. Readers should now be able to understand the essential characteristics of mental models. The key feature of a spatial model, for example, is not that it represents spatial relations, because a propositional representation can also do that, but its structure. In particular, the model is functionally organized in terms of axes so that information in it can be accessed by values on these axes. Such an organization in a mental model does not necessarily imply that information is laid out physically in a spatial way in the brain. It could be laid out in this way, but it need not be. The spatial reasoning program relies on arrays, which are a standard form of data structure in the programming language LISP, but these data structures are only functionally arrays and no corresponding physical arrays of data are likely to be found in the computer's memory. The same functional principle is likely to apply to high-level spatial models in human cognition.

2. Errors in Reasoning from Double Disjunctions

If the model theory is correct, then it should be possible to test human deductive competence to the point of breakdown merely by increasing the number of models. Johnson-Laird, Byrne, and Schaeken (1992) have confirmed this prediction using so-called "double disjunctions," such as:

1. Jane is in Seattle or Raphael is in Tacoma, but not both.
2. Jane is in Seattle or Paul is in Philadelphia, but not both.
3. What follows?

Each premise calls for two models, but their combination yields the following two models:

s

    t   p

where "s" denotes Jane in Seattle, "t" denotes Raphael in Tacoma, and "p" denotes Paul in Philadelphia. The two models support the conclusion:

Jane is in Seattle, or Raphael is in Tacoma and Paul is in Philadelphia.

If, instead of exclusive disjunctions, the premises are based on inclusive disjunctions:

1. Jane is in Seattle or Raphael is in Tacoma, or both.
2. Jane is in Seattle or Paul is in Philadelphia, or both.
3. What follows?

then they yield five alternative models:

s   t   p
s   t
s   p
s
    t   p

These models support the conclusion:

Jane is in Seattle, or Raphael is in Tacoma and Paul is in Philadelphia, or both.

As the theory predicts, the problems based on exclusive disjunctions (21% correct conclusions) were reliably easier than the problems based on inclusive disjunctions (8% correct conclusions). The problems were so difficult for the subjects, who were paid adult volunteers from all sorts of backgrounds, that they generally drew erroneous conclusions. The vast majority of these conclusions were based on only some of the models of the premises, typically just a single model. The results thus corroborated the second prediction of the model theory.

Other studies have shown that if reasoners reach a believable or congenial conclusion they tend not to search for alternative models (e.g., Oakhill, Johnson-Laird, & Garnham, 1989). This tendency is a frequent cause of everyday disasters, both minor and major. For example, the engineers in charge at Three-Mile Island inferred that a leak was the cause of the overheating of a relief valve, and overlooked the possibility that the valve was stuck open. The master of an English channel ferry, *The Herald of Free Enterprise,* inferred that the bow doors had been closed, and overlooked the possibility that they had been left open—an oversight that led to the drowning of several hundred passengers when the ferry capsized. The engineers at Chernobyl inferred that an explosion had damaged the reactor, and overlooked the possibility that there had been a meltdown of the reactor itself. The tendency to overlook possibilities seems an obvious danger. Yet strangely it cannot be predicted by formal rule theories, which have no elements within them corresponding to models of situations.

3. Illusory Inferences

Consider the following problem about a specific hand of cards:

One of the following assertions is true about the hand of cards, and the other assertion is false:

1. There is a king in the hand or there is an ace in the hand, or both.
2. There is a queen in the hand or there is an ace in the hand, or both.
3. Which is more likely to be in the hand: the king or the ace?

Recent studies carried out in collaboration with the author's colleagues, Fabien Savary and Patrizia Tabossi, have shown that almost all subjects tend to conclude:

The ace is more likely to be in the hand than the king.

The models of the first premise are:

k

        a

k   a

and the models of the second premise are:

    q

        a

    q   a

The assertion that one of the two disjunctions is true and one is false calls for an exclusive disjunction of them, and the models for an exclusive disjunction, X or else Y, are according to Table 2:

X

    Y

and so the disjunction calls for a list of all the models in the two alternatives. Hence, the problem as a whole calls for the following models:

k

        a

k   a

    q

        a

   q a

If subjects judge the probabilities of two events by assessing which event occurs in more models, they will indeed infer that the ace is more probable than the king.

This conclusion is compelling, but it is wrong. If only one of the two assertions is true, then the other assertion is false: the two premises are in an exclusive disjunction, and so when one is true, the other is false. The models, however, represent only the true cases. When the false cases are taken into account, the correct answer emerges. When the first disjunction is false there is *neither a king nor an ace,* and when the second disjunction is false there is *neither a queen nor an ace.* Either way, there is no ace—it cannot occur in the hand. Hence, the king, which can occur in the hand, is more probable than the ace, which cannot occur in the hand.

My colleagues and I have established that there are a number of different illusory inferences, which depend on a variety of sentential connectives. All that they appear to have in common is that their initial models, which fail to represent false contingencies, support conclusions that are quite wrong (i.e., that are contravened by fully explicit models of the premises). Thus, the third main prediction of the model theory is confirmed. Moreover, the existence of illusory inferences is contrary to all current theories based on formal rules of inference. They are based solely on valid rules of inference, and are accordingly unable to explain any phenomenon in which reasoners systematically draw invalid conclusions.

In general, experiments have confirmed all the main predictions of the model theory. These experiments cover the main domains of deduction, including syllogisms and inferences based on multiple quantifiers (see Johnson-Laird & Byrne, 1991).

IV. MODELS AND IMAGES

The mental model theory postulates that individuals represent verbal descriptions in the form of mental models, which are constructed from propositional representations of the descriptions. Our task in Section IV is to elucidate the relations between models and images. We will show that a principled theoretical distinction should be drawn between them: models can contain elements that are not visualizable, and empirical evidence supports the existence of such elements in models. We then consider the sorts of mental operation that can be carried out on images, and how in many cases the transformation of an image may depend on an underlying model. This idea leads us to reconsider Kekulé's dream and to argue that problems cannot be solved by visual imagery alone.

A. How Models Differ from Images

Could the models that underlie reasoning be visual images? Some individuals report using imagery, but many do not—and their performance is equally predictable by the model theory. Indeed, we can go further: if reasoning depends on forming an image of the situation described in the premises, then an explicit manipulation of the "imageability" of the situation should affect inferential performance. A study carried out in collaboration with Ruth Byrne and Patrizia Tabossi examined this prediction (Johnson-Laird, Byrne, & Tabossi, 1989). The experiments used doubly quantified assertions, such as,

1. None of the artists is in the same place as any of the beekeepers.
2. All the beekeepers are in the same place as all the chemists.
3. What follows?

which can be represented in a model, such as:

| [a] [a] | [b] [b] [c] [c] |

where a's denote artists, b's denote beekeepers, c's denote chemists, and the vertical bars demarcate separate places. This model supports the valid conclusion:

None of the artists is in the same place as any of the chemists.

We manipulated the "imageability" of the premises by using three sorts of relation: "taller than," "in the same place as," and "related to" (in the sense of kinship). An independent panel of judges rated how easy it was to visualize premises based on these relations, and their ratings differed significantly over the three relations. The experiment confirmed that one-model problems were easier than multiple-model problems, but there was no hint of an effect of imageability. Other experimenters have likewise failed to detect any influence of imageability on reasoning (see, e.g., Newstead, Manktelow, & Evans, 1982; Richardson, 1987). One can indeed reason from verbal descriptions that refer to abstract relations just as well as from those that refer to visualizable relations.

A major crisis occurred in the development of quantum mechanics, when the theory ceased to concern visualizable objects. Oddly, many mundane concepts are not visualizable either, but they are not in the least problematical in daily life. A good example is the ownership of property. One cannot perceive the relation between owner and owned, only *evidence* for ownership. The concept of ownership can be glossed in the following terms (see Miller & Johnson-Laird, 1976, p. 558 et seq.):

> If an individual, x, owns an entity, y, then:
> i. it is permissible for x to use y, and it is not permissible for others to prevent this use.
> ii. it is permissible for someone else to use y if x gives permission to this individual to do so; and it is permissible for x to give such permission.
> iii. x can act to transfer ownership of y to someone else, and such an action is permissible.

The details of this analysis are not so important as the general point: ownership hinges on deontic matters concerning what is permissible, and permissibility is not a visual property. One may visualize a permitted action; one may visualize a conventional symbol denoting permissibility (e.g., a check mark), but one cannot visualize the fact that an action is permissible.

An inferential system based on models can represent abstract elements. Earlier in the chapter, for example, we introduced the idea of negated elements in models, which are in essence "annotations" that serve a semantic function (Newell, 1990). Several studies have provided empirical evidence for such elements in models (Johnson-Laird & Byrne, 1991). Reasoners may of course use a visual image to represent negation (e.g., a large red cross that they superimpose on the model to be negated), but the image itself does not do the work of negation (as Wittgenstein, 1953, pointed out). The real work is done by the knowledge that the cross denotes negation, and by the system that uses this knowledge both to construct images and to interpret them. Reasoners do sometimes report using such images, but most people make no such reports and remain sublimely unaware of how they represent negation.

B. The Creative Manipulation of Images

The operations that are carried out in reasoning with models, as we argued earlier, are conceptual and semantic. But what about the operations that are carried out on images? What is their function? The question is complicated, but its answer will help to clarify the distinction between images and models. Images represent how something looks from a particular point of view—they may well be Marr's (1982) two-and-a-half-dimensional sketches, and operations on images are visual or spatial. Underlying an image of an object or scene is a three-dimensional (3-D) model, and operations on such models correspond to physical or spatial operations on the entities or scenes represented in the models. Hence, one way to explain the mental rotation experiments, which we described in Section II, is that visual system constructs a 3-D model from the first picture of the object, computes its major axis, and rotates the model via this axis to bring it into alignment with a model constructed from the second picture. It is not the image that is rotated by an underlying model constructed from it. The evidence for this claim, and for the relative unimportance of the features of the 2-D pictures, is that rotations in depth produced the same pattern of results as rotations in the picture plane. As Metzler and Shepard (1982) remark:

> These results seem to be consistent with the notion that . . . subjects were performing their mental operations upon internal representations that were more analogous to three-dimensional objects portrayed in the two-dimensional pictures than to the two-dimensional pictures actually presented. (p. 45)

Operations on images per se correspond to visual rearrangements. They can lead to the construction of new objects out of existing elements or shapes. Here, for example, is a task that the reader can carry out:

> Imagine the letter "B". Rotate it 90 degrees counter-clockwise. Put a triangle below it having the same width and pointing downwards. Remove the horizontal line. What have you got?

As Finke, Pinker, and Farah (1989) have shown, individuals can carry out such tasks with reasonable success, and they are unable to predict the outcome—they have to carry out the operations on their images in order to "see" the result. The answer in the present case is a heart shape.

Finke and his colleagues have also shown how the manipulation of images can yield a creative result. They used an array of the following 15 simple shapes: circle, square, triangle, rectangle, horizontal line, D, I, L, T, C, J, 8, X, V, P, (see Finke & Slayton, 1988). On each trial, the experimenter named three of the shapes, and the subjects had to close their eyes and to imagine assembling these shapes into a recognizable figure. The subjects were free to combine the parts in any way: rotating, translating, superimposing, or juxtaposing them. They could change their sizes, but they were not allowed to distort the shapes. They were surprisingly successful at this task, and about 15% of their efforts were rated by an independent panel of judges as creative. The task seems to depend on a creative "play" with images, and again the subjects were wholly unable to predict in advance what its outcome would be.

In an unpublished study, Jung-Min Lee has observed that a constraint on the required outcome can speed up the process. The subjects had to use any three shapes from Finke's array to synthesize an image. They were reliably faster to synthesize a so-called basic-level object (Rosch, 1977), such as a house, an apple, or a chair, than an instance of a superordinate category, such as a building, a fruit, or a piece of furniture. Instances of a basic-level object, as Rosch showed, have more uniform shapes than instances of their superordinates (e.g., two chairs are likely to be more similar in shape than two pieces of furniture). Hence, the subjects could proceed by imagining the canonical shape of, say, a chair, search the array for appropriate elements, such as the "L" shape and the square, and then assemble them. With superordinates, this strategy can be used only after the subject has called to mind an object with a canonical shape, and this step presumably takes the extra amount of time. In another unpublished study, Richard Feit has implemented a computer program that will find an optimal match of three given shapes to a canonical representation. The algorithm is, technically speaking, intractable; that is, as the number of shapes to be matched increases so it takes exponentially longer to find a match. Human imagers are also likely to be defeated by a large number of component shapes, and so it is an open question whether they, too, rely on an intractable procedure.

The "visual play" with images that occurs in these studies is reminiscent of scientists' reports of their own use of imagery in solving problems. Visualization alone, however, cannot solve problems. Just as models need to be backed up by propositional representations if they are to be used to reason, so too images need to be backed up by an independent representation of the problem if they are to be used to solve it. As an illustrative example, I return to Kekulé's problem, which I described at the start of the chapter, and reanalyze it in the light of Findlay's (1937) account.

Kekulé's goal was to formulate the molecular structure of benzene in terms of the theory of valencies—of which he was one of the founders. He knew that each benzene molecule contained six carbon atoms and six hydrogen atoms, and that the valency of carbon was four (i.e., each carbon atom should combine with four other atoms). The only known molecular structures at that time were in the form of strings, but a string of six carbon atoms required three hydrogen atoms to combine with each of the two atoms at its ends, and two hydrogen atoms to combine with each of the four atoms in the middle of the string. Hence, there did not seem to be enough hydrogen atoms to do the job. The puzzle stumped him until in mental play with a string-like structure, he formed an image of a circle. A merely circular arrangement of the atoms still does not solve the problem, because it calls for 12 hydrogen atoms. Kekulé had to make the further assumption that alternate links between the carbon atoms had a double valency, and so each carbon atom had a single link to one carbon atom and a double link to another. There remained only a single valency left unaccounted for, and it was the bond to a hydrogen atom. Because carbon atoms are identical, the single and double bonds oscillated from moment to moment. As Findlay (1937, p. 149) suggests, this oscillation may have been suggested by the atoms in his image "all twisting and twining in snake-like motion," but we do not know whether the solution really came to him in this way.

The manipulation of images is preeminently a method for solving visuospatial problems. Indeed, some theorists argue that the major function of visual imagery is to aid the process of object recognition: some perceptual cues trigger the synthesis of an image of an object from long-term knowledge, and the visual system tries to project this image onto the visual input (cf. Lowe, 1987; Marr, 1982). The manipulation of images accordingly yields spatial or physical rearrangements of entities. In solving problems, such as the structure of benzene, forming an image is only part of the process. The image must relate to an independent representation of the problem—just as the use of models in reasoning must relate to an independent representation of the premises. Visualization can yield deep conceptual innovations only within a system that can represent more abstract information.

C. Images and Diagrams

The moral of the previous section may lead skeptics to dismiss imagery as epiphenomenal: the real work in conceptual innovation is done, they may say, by underlying propositional representations. In this section, I intend to rebut this argument on the basis of experimental evidence, and to show that images cannot be reduced to propositional representations; both are high-level representations necessary to explain thinking. The argument will hinge on the role of diagrams in reasoning.

Diagrams are often said to be helpful aids to thinking. They can make it easier to find relevant information—one can scan from one element to another element nearby much more rapidly than one might be able to find the equivalent information in a list of numbers or verbal assertions (see also Cutting & Massivoni, chap. 6, this volume). Diagrams can make it easier to identify instances of a concept—an iconic representation can be recognized faster than a verbal description. Their symmetries can cut down on the number of cases that need to be examined. But can diagrams help the process of thought itself? Larkin and Simon (1987) allow that diagrams help reasoners to find information and to recognize it, but doubt whether they help the process of inference itself. Barwise and Etchemendy (1992), who have developed a computer program, Hyperproof, for learning logic, write:

> Diagrams and pictures are extremely good at presenting a wealth of specific, conjunctive information. It is much harder to use them to present indefinite information, negative information, or disjunctive information. For these, sentences are often better. (p. 82)

Hyperproof accordingly captures conjunctions in diagrams, but expresses disjunctions in verbal statements. The model theory, however, makes a different prediction. The problem in reasoning is to keep track of the possible models of premises. Hence, a diagram that helps to make them explicit should also help people to reason.

Malcolm Bauer and the author tested this prediction in two experiments based on double disjunctions (Bauer & Johnson-Laird, 1993). In the first experiment, the premises were either in a verbal form, such as:

1. Julia is in Atlanta or Raphael is in Tacoma, or both.
2. Julia is in Seattle or Paul is in Philadelphia, or both.
3. What follows?

or else in the form of a diagram, such as Figure 1. To represent, say, Julia in Atlanta, the diagram has a lozenge labeled "Julia" lying within the ellipse labeled "Atlanta." Inclusive disjunction, as the figure shows, is represented by a box connected by lines to the two component diagrams making up the premise as a whole. The experi-

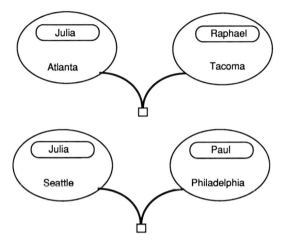

What follows?

FIGURE 1   The diagram representing a double disjunction (a negative inclusive one) in the first diagram experiment.

ment confirmed that exclusive disjunctions were easier than inclusive disjunctions (for both the percentages of correct responses and their latencies); it also confirmed that problems in which the individual common to both premises was in the *same* place in both of them ("affirmative" problems) were easier than problems in which the individual common to both premises was in different places in them ("negative" problems, such as the one above). But the experiment failed to detect any effect of diagrams: They yielded 28% correct conclusions in comparison to the 30% correct for the verbal problems. Double disjunctions remained difficult and diagrams were no help at all.

With hindsight, the problem with the diagrams was that they used arbitrary symbols to represent disjunction and thus failed to make the alternative possibilities explicit. In a second experiment, we used a new sort of diagram, as shown in Figure 2, analogous to an electrical circuit. The idea, which we explained to the subjects, was to complete a path from one side of the diagram to the other by moving the shapes corresponding to people into the slots corresponding to cities. We tested four separate groups of subjects with logically equivalent problems: one group received diagrams of people and places (as in Figure 2); one group received problems in the form of circuit diagrams of electrical switches; one group received problems in the form of verbal premises about people and places, and one group received problems in the form of verbal premises about electrical switches. There was no effect of the content of the problems—whether they were about people or switches—and so we have pooled the results. The percentages of correct responses are presented in Figure 3. As the figure shows, there was a striking effect of mode

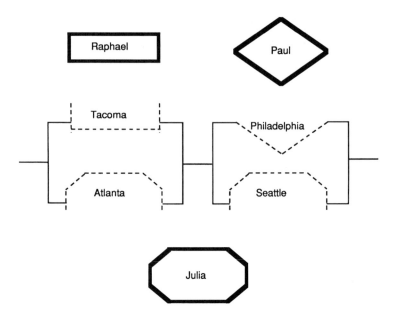

**The event is occurring.
What follows?**

FIGURE 2   The diagram representing a double disjunction (a negative inclusive one) in the second diagram experiment.

of presentation: 74% correct responses to the diagrammatic problems in comparison to only 46% correct responses to the verbal problems. The results also corroborated the model theory's predictions that exclusive disjunctions should be easier than inclusive disjunctions, and that affirmative problems should be easier than negative problems. The latencies of the subjects' correct responses had exactly the same pattern, and they were reliably faster to respond to the diagrammatic problems (mean of 99 sec) than to the verbal problems (mean of 135 sec).

People evidently reason by trying to construct models of the alternative possibilities, and diagrams that enable these alternatives to be made explicit can be very helpful. In a series of unpublished studies, Victoria Bell and the author have found that merely teaching people to maintain lists of the separate possibilities, either in diagrams or in the mind's eyes, improves their reasoning. Likewise, with a diagram of the sort shown in Figure 2, individuals perceive the layout and in their mind's eye they can move people into places and out again. By manipulating a visual image that has the external support of a corresponding diagram, they can construct the alternative possibilities more readily than they can do so from verbal descriptions. It follows that diagrams are not merely encoded in propositional representations equivalent to those constructed from descriptions.

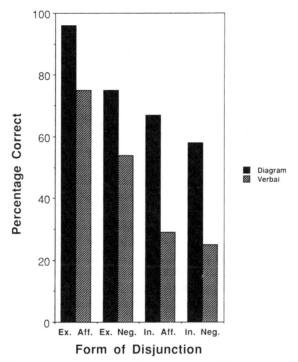

FIGURE 3   The percentages of correct conclusions in the second diagram experiment. There are four sorts of problem: Ex. Aff., affirmative problems based on exclusive disjunctions; Ex. Neg., negative problems based on exclusive disjunctions; In. Aff., affirmative problems based on inclusive disjunctions; In. Neg., negative problems based on inclusive disjunctions.

V. CONCLUSIONS

This chapter has focused on thinking with a propositional content. Other sorts of thinking lack such content, such as the mental processes controlling the improvisations of a musician, the gestures of a painter, or the movements of a dancer. The aim of the chapter was to understand the role of visualization in thinking about propositions, and it has reached three main conclusions.

First, thinking depends on propositional representations and mental models. Propositional representations capture the meaning of premises, and they are used to construct mental models representing the situation under discussion. Reasoners test the strength of an inference (or argument) by searching for alternative models of the propositional representations in which a putative conclusion is false. The experimental evidence corroborates the theory's predictions: more models mean more work, erroneous conclusions are a result of overlooking possible models, and illusory inferences arise from a failure to represent false contingencies.

Second, models and images differ. Models can be 3-D, and can embody abstract predicates that are not visualizable. Hence, they can represent any situation, and operations on them can be purely conceptual. In contrast, images represent how something looks from a particular point of view. They are projected from the visualizable aspects of underlying models. Images and diagrams, however, can be used in a symbolic way. If one wishes to convey what is going on in a complex domain with many varying numerical quantities, such as the flow of air around an airplane, then the translation of the data into a visual display can capitalize on the power of the visual system to extract high-level patterns from low-level data. To make sense of an array of 100 million numbers (the intensities of light falling on the cells in the retina) the brain has "software" that uses these data to construct a high-level model of the world suitable for the limited powers of consciousness. The visual display is symbolic; that is, it does not correspond directly to the external world. Our experimental study with diagrams showed that most individuals are able to imagine moving a shape from one position to another and in this way to envisage a proposition with a wholly different content (people in places). Some logicians claim that diagrammatic methods of reasoning are in some way improper (cf. Tennant, 1986), but Barwise and his colleagues have shown that they are valid, and indeed can be complete systems, which capture all valid inferences (Barwise & Etchemendy, 1991; Shin, 1992).

Third, people can construct novel images out of given components. They can retrieve the canonical shape of an object and then in their mind's eye assemble that shape out of the preexisting components—a process that calls for moving one shape in relation to another, juxtaposing or superimposing them, and so on. Humans can simulate phenomena dynamically, and some individuals spontaneously carry out such simulations (e.g., Nicola Tesla, the inventor, was said to be able to imagine the wear in his machines by simulating running them in his mind's eye; Shepard, 1978).

Could visualization lead to profound innovations and novel scientific concepts? Could it, for example, lead from an Aristotelian concept of velocity to the Newtonian concept of instantaneous velocity, or from an absolute concept of simultaneity to a relativistic concept? The answer in our view is that it could play a part in such transitions, but that lying behind a scientist's "picture" of the world is likely to be a mental model representing more abstract relations, and its associated subconceptual apparatus. Visualization can help thinkers to envisage possibilities, and it may help them to imagine certain spatial and physical properties and operations. They cannot, however, directly visualize abstract concepts or conceptual relations. Manipulations of an image can be reinterpreted in terms of the model and can lead to conceptual innovations. Kekulé's visual manipulations of snake-like images is one such example. Thinking also depends on more than models or images. They can be exploited only within a system that carries out conceptual operations. The underlying machinery depends on a set of subconceptual elements, which are tacit, primitive, and probably innate. The interplay between models and subconcepts is the most likely locus of conceptual innovation. It depends on a new sort of model, which typically embodies concepts that are neither observable nor visualizable, and in turn rest on the construction of new concepts from the subconceptual repertoire. Such models may generate fresh problems and, as Wise (1979) points out, their solution may call for a reorganization of the models themselves.

References

Baddeley, A. E., & Hitch, G. (1974). Working memory. In G. H. Bower (Ed.), *The psychology of learning and motivation: Vol. 8* (pp. 278–301). London: Academic Press.

Barwise, J., & Etchemendy, J. (1991). Visual information and valid reasoning. In W. Zimmermann & S. Cunningham (Eds.), *Visualization in teaching and learning mathematics* (pp. 120–132). Mathematical Association of America.

Barwise, J., & Etchemendy, J. (1992). Hyperproof: Logical reasoning with diagrams. In N. H. Narayanan (Ed.), *AAAI Symposium on reasoning with diagrammatic representations* (pp. 80–84). Stanford, CA: AAAI.

Bauer, M. I., & Johnson-Laird, P. N. (1993). How diagrams can improve reasoning. *Psychological Science, 4,* 372–378.

Binet, A. (1894). *Psychologie des grands calculateurs et joueurs d'echecs.* Paris: Hachette.

Boltzmann, L. (1974). On the significance of physical theories. In. B. McGuiness (Ed.), *Ludwig Boltzmann: Theoretical physics and philosophical problems* (pp. 33–36). Boston: Reidel. (Original work published 1890)

Boltzmann, L. (1974). On the fundamental principles and equations of mechanics. In B. McGuiness (Ed.), *Ludwig Boltzmann: Theoretical physics and philosophical problems* (pp. 101–128). Boston: Reidel. (Original work published 1899)

Bower, G. H. (1970). Analysis of the mnemonic device. *American Scientist, 58,* 496–501.

Braine, M. D. S., Reiser, B. J., & Rumain, B. (1984). Some empirical justification for a theory of natural propositional logic. In G. H. Bower (Ed.), *The Psychology of Learning and Motivation, Vol. 18.,* (pp. 313–371). New York: Academic Press.

Byrne, R. M. J., & Johnson-Laird, P. N. (1989). Spatial reasoning. *Journal of Memory and Language, 28,* 564–575.

Craik, K. (1943). *The nature of explanation.* Cambridge: Cambridge University Press.

Darwin, C. (1859/1968). *The origin of species by means of natural selection or the preservation of favoured races in the struggle for life.* J. W. Burrow (Ed.). New York: Viking Penguin.

Feldman, D. H. (1988). Dreams, insights, and transformations. In R. J. Sternberg (Ed.), *The nature of creativity* (pp. 271–297). Cambridge, UK: Cambridge University Press.

Ferguson, E. S. (1977). The mind's eye: Nonverbal thought in technology. *Science, 197,* 827–836.

Findlay, A. (1937). *A hundred years of chemistry.* London: Duckworth.

Finke, R. A., Pinker, S., & Farah, M. (1989). Reinterpreting visual patterns in mental imagery. *Cognitive Science, 13,* 51–78.

Finke, R. A., & Slayton, K. (1988). Explorations of creative visual synthesis in mental imagery. *Memory and Cognition, 16,* 252–257.

Galton, F. (1928). *Inquiries into human faculty and its development.* London: Dent. (Original work published 1880)

Gleick, J. (1992). *Genius: The life and science of Richard Feynman.* New York: Pantheon Books.

Gruber, H. E. (1974). *Darwin on man: A psychological study of scientific creativity.* (2nd ed.). Chicago: University of Chicago Press.

Gruber, H. E. (1994). Insight and affect in the history of science. In R. J. Sternberg and J. Davidson (Eds.), *The nature of insight* (pp. 397–431). Cambridge, MA: MIT Press.

Hadamard, J. (1996). *The Mathematician's Mind: The psychology of invention in the mathematical field.* Princeton: Princeton University Press. (Original work published 1945).

Hagert, G. (1984). Modeling mental models: experiments in cognitive modeling of spatial reasoning. In T. O'Shea (Ed.), *Advances in artificial intelligence.* (pp. 121–134). Amsterdam: North-Holland.

Holt, R. R. (1964). Imagery: The return of the ostracized. *American Psychologist, 19,* 254–264.

Humphrey, G. (1951). *Thinking.* London: Methuen.

Johnson-Laird, P. N. (1983). *Mental models: Towards a cognitive science of language, inference, and consciousness.* Cambridge, MA: Harvard University Press.

Johnson-Laird, P. N. (1994). Mental models and probabilistic thinking. *Cognition, 50,* 189–209.

Johnson-Laird, P. N., & Byrne, R. M. J. (1991). *Deduction.* Hillsdale, NJ: Lawrence Erlbaum Associates.

Johnson-Laird, P. N., Byrne, R. M. J., & Schaeken, W. (1992). Propositional reasoning by model. *Psychological Review, 99,* 418–439.

Johnson-Laird, P. N., Byrne, R. M. J., & Tabossi, P. (1989). Reasoning by model: The case of multiple quantification. *Psychological Review, 96,* 658–673.

Kosslyn, S. M. (1980). *Image and mind.* Cambridge, MA: Harvard University Press.

Kosslyn, S. M., Ball, T. M., & Reiser, B. J. (1978). Visual images preserve metric spatial information: Evidence from studies of image scanning. *Journal of Experimental Psychology: Human Perception and Performance, 4,* 47–60.

Larkin, J., & Simon, H. (1987). Why a diagram is (sometimes) worth 10,000 words. *Cognitive Science, 11,* 65–99.

Lowe, D. G. (1987). Three-dimensional object recognition from single two-dimensional images. *Artificial Intelligence, 31,* 355–395.

Luria, A. R. (1969). *The mind of a mnemonist.* London: Cape.

Mani, K., & Johnson-Laird, P. N. (1982). The mental representation of spatial descriptions. *Memory and Cognition, 10,* 181–187.

Marr, D. (1982). *Vision: A computational investigation into the human representation and processing of visual information.* San Francisco: W. H. Freeman.

Maxwell, J. Clerk (1911). Diagram. In *The Encyclopaedia Britannica. Vol. XVIII.* New York: The Encyclopaedia Britannica Company.

Metzler, J., & Shepard, R. N. (1982). Transformational studies of the internal representations of three-dimensional objects. In R. N. Shepard & L. A. Cooper, *Mental images and their transformations* (pp. 25–71). Cambridge, MA: MIT Press. (Original work published in Solso, R. L. (Ed.) *Theories in Cognitive Psychology: The Loyola Symposium.* Hillsdale, NJ: Lawrence Erlbaum Associates, 1974.)

Miller, A. (1984). *Imagery in scientific thought: Creating 20th-century physics.* Boston, MA: Birkhauser.

Miller, G. A., & Johnson-Laird, P. N. (1976). *Language and perception.* Cambridge, MA: Harvard University Press.

Newell, A. (1990). *Unified theories of cognition.* Cambridge, MA: Harvard University Press.

Newstead, S. E., Manktelow, K. I., & Evans, J. St. B. T. (1982). The role of imagery in the representation of linear orderings. *Current Psychological Research, 2,* 21–32.

Oakhill, J. V., Johnson-Laird, P. N., & Garnham, A. (1989). Believability and syllogistic reasoning. *Cognition, 31,* 117–140.

Ohlsson, S. (1984). Induced strategy shifts in spatial reasoning. *Acta Psychologica, 57,* 46–67.

Paivio, A. (1971). *Imagery and verbal processes.* New York: Holt, Rinehart, and Winston.

Perky, C. W. (1910). An experimental study of imagination. *American Journal of Psychology, 21,* 422–452.

Pylyshyn, Z. W. (1973). What the mind's eye tells the mind's brain: A critique of mental imagery. *Psychological Bulletin, 80,* 1–24.

Richardson, J. T. E. (1987). The role of mental imagery in models of transitive inference. *British Journal of Psychology, 78,* 189–203.

Rips, L. J. (1994). *The psychology of proof.* Cambridge, MA: MIT Press.

Rosch, E. (1977). Classification of real-world objects: Origins and representations in cognition. In P. N. Johnson-Laird & P. C. Wason (Eds.), *Thinking: Readings in cognitive science* (pp. 212–222). Cambridge: Cambridge University Press.

Schaeken, W., Johnson-Laird, P. N., & d'Ydewalle, G. (1996). Mental models and temporal reasoning. *Cognition, 60,* 205–234.

Shepard, R. N. (1978). Externalization of mental images and the act of creation. In B. S. Randhawas & W. E. Coffman (Eds.), *Visual learning, thinking, and communication* (pp. 133–189). New York: Academic Press.

Shepard, R. N. (1988). The imagination of the scientist. In K. Egan and D. Nadaner (Eds.), *Imagination and Education.* New York: Teachers College Press.

Shepard, R. N., & Metzler, J. (1971). Mental rotation of three-dimensional objects. *Science, 171,* 701–703.

Shin, Sun-Joo (1992). A semantic analysis of inference involving Venn diagrams. In N. H. Narayanan (Ed.), *AAAI Symposium on reasoning with diagrammatic representations* (pp. 85–90). Stanford, CA: AAAI.

Störring, G. (1908). Experimentelle Untersuchungen über einfache Schlussprozesse. *Archiv für die gesamte Psychologie, 11,* 1–27.

Tennant, N. (1986). The withering away of formal semantics. *Mind and Language, 1,* 302–318.

Valéry, P. (1894/1972). Introduction to the method of Leonardo da Vinci. In *Leonardo Poe Mallarmé. Vol. 8 of the Collected Works of Paul Valéry* (pp. 3–63). Princeton, NJ: Princeton University Press.

Wason, P. C., & Johnson-Laird, P. N. (1972). *Psychology of reasoning: Structure and content.* Cambridge, MA: Harvard University Press.

Wertheimer, M. (1961). *Productive thinking.* M. Wertheimer (Ed.). London: Tavistock.

Wise, M. N. (1979). The mutual embrace of electricity and magnetism. *Science, 203,* 1310–1318.

Wittgenstein, L. (1953). *Philosophical investigations.* New York: Macmillan.

Wotiz, J. H., & Rodofsky, S. (1984). Kekulé's dreams: Fact or fiction? *Chemistry in Britain,* 720–723.

Index

469